RESEARCHES INTO THE HISTORY AND CIVILIZATION OF THE KIRATAS

RESEARCHES INTO THE HISTORY AND CIVILIZATION OF THE KIRĀTAS

G.P. Singh
With a Foreword
by
Prof. R.S. Sharma

GYAN PUBLISHING HOUSE
NEW DELHI-110002

Researches into the History and Civilization of the Kirātas

Rs. 750

ISBN: 81-212-0281-7

Published in 2008 in India by
Gian Publications House
New Delhi-110002
E-mail: gian@hotmail.com
Phone : 9212729499

Lasser Type Setting by: Quick Media, Delhi
Printed at : Salasar Imaging System, Delhi

Dedicated

WITH PROFOUND RESPECT AND ADMIRATION

TO

THE SACRED MEMORY

OF

DR. B.C. LAW, M.A., B.L., Ph. D.,

D. Litt. FRASB; FRGS (LONDON)

WHOSE CONTRIBUTION

TO THE DISCVOERY OF ANCIENT INDIAN TRIBAL

HISTORY & CULTURE

ALWAYS PROVED TO BE A SOURCE OF INSPIRATION

FOR ME

गिरयस्ते पर्वता हिमवन्तोऽरण्यं ते पृथिवि स्योनमस्तु

अथर्ववेद, १२.१.१.११

O Earth ! Let thy mountains, the Himalayas and Forests be Enchanting for us. *Atharva Veda, 12.1.1.11*

Preface

The author feels great pleasure in placing this volume before scholars. Some newly discovered facts relating to the subject have been incorporated in it. All necessary corrections, modifications and additions have been made. No pains have been spared to make it more accurate and up-to-date. All possible attempts havebeen mde to make it useful to the historians, anthropologists, and others, interested in the study of historical ethnography of ancient India.

The work is divided into six books further sub-divided into parts.

The author craves the indulgence of the readers for any errors that may have crept into the volume.

G.P. Singh

Foreword

Dr. G.P. Singh has collected a good deal of material relating to the origin, society, economy, political organisation and cultural aspects of the Kirātas in earlier times. He has also tried to reconstruct their history from the beginning to medieval times and assessed their contribution to the making of the history and culture of India. I hope that this book will provide a wealth of data to scholars and prepare the ground for further studies of this type.

Patna **R.S. Sharma**

Acknowledgements

At the outset, I consider it my pleasant duty to express my profound sense of gratitude to those whose writings on ethnography of ancient India in general and different Āryan and non-Āryan social groups including the ancient Indian tribes in particular inspired me again and again to make a historical enquiry into the life and culture of the Kirātas and their contribution to the Indian civilization. In this connection. I would like to mention the names of B.C. Law (a pioneer in the field of historical study of ethnography of ancient India), F.E. Pargiter, D.R. Bhandarkar (whose contribution to ethnological studies as Indologist for more than two decades, 1901-21 is well known), B.A. Saletore, R. Shafer, N.L. Dey, Gustav Oppert, V.S. Agrawala, R.P. Chanda, H.C. Chakladar, D.D. Kosambi; Romila Thapar (Image of the Barbarian in Early India cf. *Comparative Studies in Society and History,* Cambridge, 1971, *Ancient Indian Social History,* Delhi, 1984), R.S. Sharma (*Sūdras in Ancient India*), Radha Krishna Choudhary (*Vratyas in Ancient India*), Upendra Thakur (*The Hunas in India*), P. Kauffman (An Historical Account of the Bhils , a Ph.D., Thesis completed in 1982 at Australian National University, Canberra, Department of Asian Civilizations), D.C. Sircar, K.K. Dasgupta, S. Chattopadhyaya, Suniti Kumar Chatterji, R.C. Jain and others. Their works, which I have utilized for my purpose, appear in the general bibliography appended at the end of the work.

I am extremely grateful to R.S. Sharma, one of the noted authorities on ancient Indian history, for his foreword to the book. In spite of being slightly indisposed, he was kind enough to write the same for which I shall ever remain obliged to him. The author and the publisher deeply regret the omission of acknowledging their gratitude to him in the first edition of the book.

I shall be failing in my duty, if I do not express my sincere thanks to all other scholars, whose works I have consulted and referred to in the book.

I gratefully acknowledge the debt of gratitude which I owe to Dr. H.K. Barpujari (formerly Head, Department of History Gauhati University) who as the General President of the first session of North-East India History Association held at Shillong in 1980 not only strongly supported my view-points which I had put forth (in my paper, the North-East Indian Tribal Races as described in Literary and Classical Sources presented in this session) to question the validity of the Mongoloid theory of the origin of the Kirātas as propounded by Suniti Kumar Chatterji but also encouraged me to pursue further research on this aspect of the subject and to discover more new evidences to establish a new theory.

I gratefully record my deep sense of gratitude to B.P. Mazumdar (former Profesor and Head, Department of History, Patna University) who was kind enough to spare some of his valuable moments at Visva-Bharati University, Santiniketan (where he had come to deliver the presidential address at Silver Jubilee Session of Institute of Historical Studies held during 25-27 October, 1986 and I had gone to attend the session as a delegate), so as to enable me to have a discussion with him on the contribution of the Kirātas to Hindu religion and culture.

I am extremely grateful to Prof. K.J. Mahale, the then Vice-Chancellor, Manipur University, who always evinced his keen interest in my research works and helped in identifying the French sources which I have utilized in my work.

I extend my grateful thanks to Dr. Talgeri (Prof. of German), Prof. (Retd.) Mr. Paranjape (French) and Mrs. S.Y. Rahman (Fellow in Chinese, Centre for East Asian Languages), School of Languages, J.N.U., Delhi, who during their stay at our University in 1986 afforded me an opportunity to discuss about these three foreign sources which I have mentioned in the present work.

I am very much indebted to Dr. P.K. Agrawala, Department of Ancient Indian History, Culture and Archaeology, Banaras Hindu University, who not only supplied at my request some of the very rare books written by Prof. Vasudeva Sharana Agrawala but also kindly permitted me to utiliser them for the purpose concerned.

My special thanks go to the Librarian and staff of the Asiatic Society Library Calcutta form where I collected maximum source-material during my several visits to the Library over past three decades. I am highly obliged to my friend A. Warjari (ex-member, Rajya Sabha) with whose help I could be able to have access to quite a good number of valuable books on the histories of Tibet, Burma, China and South-East Asia in the Parliament Library, Delhi.

I also express my gratefulness to Mr. Bhagwati, former Librarian, Research Section, Arunachal Secretariat, Shillong, Mr. Pandey, Librarian, C.I.F.L. Regional Centre, Shillong, Librarian and Staff, NEHU Library, Shillong, St. Anthony s College library, Shillong (where I was formerly lecturer, 1973-84) and Manipur University library for giving me free access to all the books and journals, etc.

I am indeed very much thankful to Dr. K.N.P. Magadha (former Prof., Dcpartment of IIindi, Manipur University) and Dr. L. Jha (former Associate Prof. Department of Hindi, in the same University) for not only providing me with many ancient literary texts and other important sources but also for offering valuable suggestions and removing some of my genuine doubts from my mind in the course of my frequent discussion with them on various aspects of the present subject.

Dr. S.C. Saha, formerly Associate Professor, Department of English Manipur also deserves my sincere thanks for all the help he university, extended to me in completion of my work.

I acknowledge with thanks all the support and co-operation that I received from my former departmental colleagues, Prof. S.N. Pandey, Prof. G. Kabui and Prof. L.B. Verma during my research work.

I am really grateful to R.K. Somorjit Singh, then Cartographer, Department of Earth Science, Manipur University, for giving final shape to a map illustrating the location and expansion of the Kirātas in ancient times originally prepared and designed by me.

I cannot but thank two of my former Ph.D. Students Dr. L. Kunjeswori Devi (now Associate Professor, Department of History, Manipur University) and Dr. Prabhabati Devi who assistd me in getting the press work done in time.

My thanks are also due to Smt. Th. Ibechaobi Devi, then Junior Stenographer and Shri L. Bikram Singh, then Steno-typist, Department of History, Md. A Rashid Khan, then Stenographer Grade-I, attached to the Dean, School of Humanities and Shri A. Somorendro Sharma, then Junior Assistant, Department of Hindi (all from Manipur University) for taking maximum pains in connection with typing of my thesis.

Once again I wish to thank all those whose kind help and co-operation enabled me to accomplish this assiduous task.

Abbreviations

AA	Academica Asiatica, Delhi.
AAQ	*The Āryan Marriage with Special Reference to the Age Questions.*
ABORI	*Annals of the Bhandarkar Oriental Research Institute,* Pune.
ACAI	*The Astronomical Method and its Application to the Chronology of Ancient India.*
ACR	*Assam Census Report.*
ADG	*Assam District Gazetters.*
AGI	*The Ancient Geography of India.*
Agn	*Agni Purāna.*
AHNE	*The Ancient History of the Near East.*
AI	*Ancient India.*
AI (AHCAH)	*Antiquities of India: An Account of the History and Culture of Ancient Hindustan.*
AICL	*Ancient India as Described in Classical Literature* (being a collection of Greek and Latin Texts Relating to India).
AIHA	*Aspects of Indian History and Archaeology* (A Collection of Research Papers of H.D. Sankalia).
AIHT	*Ancient Indian Historical Tradition.*
AIIC	*Ancient India and Indian Civilization.*
AIK	*Ancient India as Described by Ktesias the Knidian.*
AIMA	*Ancient India as Described by Megasthenese and Arrian.*
AIP	*Ancient India as Described by Ptolemy.*
AISH	*Ancient Indian Social History.*

AIT	*Ancient Indian Tribes.*
Ait. Br.	*Aitareya Brāhmaṇa.*
AJF	*American Journal of Folklore.*
AJPh	*American Journal of Philology.*
AKN	*An Account of the Kingdom of Nepal.*
ALb. Ind	*Alberuni's India.*
Alt. Leb	*Altindisches Leben* by H. Zimmer.
AMM	*Arya-Manjusri-Mulakalpa.*
AN	*Ancient Nepal.*
AO	*Anecdota Oxoniensia.*
AOEI	*The Āryan Occupation of Eastern India* (Indian Studies, Past & Present, Calcutta).
Ar. Ant.	*Ariana Antiqua: A descriptive Account of the Antiquities and Coins of Afghanistan.*
ASB	The Asiatic Society of Bengal, Calcutta.
ASIAR	*Archaeological Survey of India, Annual Reports.*
As. Res.	*Asiatic Researches* (Comprising History and Antiquities, the Arts, Sciences, Ethnology and Literature of Asia).
AV	*Atharva Veda.*
AV. Sam.	*Atharva Veda Saṁhitā.*
BABO	*Bengal and Assam, Bihar and Orissa.*
BAC	*The Background of Assamese Culture.*
BASI	*Bulletin of the Archaeological Survey of India,* New Delhi.
Bau. Dh. Sū.	*Baudhāyana Dharma-Sūtra.*
Bhag	*Bhāgavata Purāṇa.*
Bhav	*Bhaviṣya Purāṇa.*
BHI	*Bihar-the Heart of India.*
BHS	Bibliotheca Himalayica Series.
BI	*Buddhist India.*
BIS	Bibliotheca Indica Series (a collection of oriental works), Asiatic Society, Calcutta.

Bmd	*Brahmānda Purāṇa.*
BORI	Bhandarkar Oriental Research Institute.
BOS	Bhandarkar Oriental Series.
BPP (JCHS)	*Bengal Past and Present* (Journal of the Calcutta Historical Society).
Br. Sam.	*Bṛhat Saṁhitā.*
Brah.	*Brahma Purāṇa.*
BRWW	*Buddhist Records of the Western World.*
BSL	*Bulletin of Socio-Linguistics.*
BSOAS	*Bulletin of the School of Oriental and African Studies,* London.
CAI	*Classical Accounts of India* (Compiled and edited by R.C. Majumdar).
CBM	Catalogue of Buddhist Manuscripts.
CCAI	*Culture and Civilisation of Ancient India in Historical Outline.*
CCIM	*Catalogue of Coins in the Indian Museum,* Calcutta.
CHI	*Cambridge History of India* (Vol. I, *Ancient India*).
CHIP	*Concise History of the Indian People.*
CHN	*Chronology and History of Nepal* (c. 600. B.C. 300 A.D.).
CHVP	*Cultural History from the Vayu Purana.*
CII	Corpus Inscriptionum Indicarum.
Civ. An. Ind.	*Civilization in Ancient India.*
CNES	*Commerce and Navigation of the Erythraean Sea.*
CNH	*Cambridge Natural History.*
Co. A. I	*Coins of Ancient India.*
CPAIM	*Catalogue of Prehistoric Antiquities in the Indian Museum,* Calcutta.
CPI	*Commercial Products of India.*

CPMDN	*Catalogue of Palm-Leaf and Selected Paper Manuscripts belonging to the Durbar Library,* Nepal.
CR	*Calcutta Review,* Calcutta.
CSARM	*Classical Studies in Ancient Races and Myths.*
CSSH	*Comparative Studies in Society and History.* Cambridge University Press.
CTSI	*Castes and Tribes of Southern India.*
Cul. Her. Ind.	*Cultural Heritage of India, Calcutta.*
CUP	Cambridge University Press.
DAA	*Descriptive Account of Assam.*
DAG	*Dwivedi Abhinandan Granth, Kāśi.*
DCSM	Descriptive Catalogue of Sanskrit Manuscripts in the Govt. Collection of the Asiatic Society of Bengal, Calcutta.
DEB	*Descriptive Ethnology of Bengal.*
DGAI	*Development of Geographic Knowledge in Ancient India.*
Dh. It.	*Dharmśastra Kā Itihāsa.*
DHNI	*Dynastic History of Northern India.*
Dh-Sū.	*Dharma Sūtras: A Study in their Origin and Development.*
DPPN	*Dictionary of Pāli Proper Names.*
EAB	*Ethnology of Ancient Bhārata.*
EAI	*Ethnography of Ancient India.*
EB	*Encyclopaedia Britannica.*
EC	*Epigraphia Carnatica,* ed. by. Rice, Bangalore.
EFRL	*Elementary Forms of Religious Life.*
EGI	*Economic Geology of India.*
EHD	*Early History of the Dekkan.*
EHI	*Early History of India.*
EHID	*Early Hindu India: A Dynastic Study.*
EHK	*Early History of Kāmarūpa.*

EHNI	*Early History of North India.*
EI. Or. Ep. Ind.	*Epigraphia Indica,* Delhi.
EIC	*Encyclopaedia of Indian Culture.*
EIP	*Early India and Pakistan.*
EISE	*Light on Early Indian Society and Economy.*
ELLRNT	*Essays on the Language, Literature and Religion of Nepal and Tibet,* London.
ERE	*Encyclopaedia of Religion and Ethics,* ed. by J. Hastings (Edinburgh, 1908-26).
ERWT	*Eastern Religions and Western Thoughts.*
ESAI	*Ethnic Settlements in Ancient India.*
Etude.	*Etude Sur La Geographie Grecque et Latine de L'Inde* (Geography of India as derived from the Greek and Latin Sources) by P.V. de St. Martin.
GAKW	*Geographical Aspect of Kalidasa's Works.*
GARSI	Graphic Arts Research Society of India.
Gau. Dh. Su	*Gautama Dharma-Sūtra.*
GBNEI	*Gazetteer of Bengal and North-East India.*
GCPI	*Gazetteer of the Central Provinces of India.*
GDAMI	*Geographical Dictionary of Ancient and Medieval India.*
GDEP	*Geographical Data in the Early Purāṇas.*
GDOM	*Geschichteder Ost-Mongolen* (a Mongolian Treatise by Senangsatsen, tr. by I.J. Schmidt)
GEB	*Geography of Early Buddhism.*
GESM	*Geographical and Economic Studies in the Mahabharata.*
GJ	*Geographical Journals,* London.
GK	*Geography of Kālidāsa.*
GNAII	*Geographical Names in Ancient Indian Inscriptions.*
Gop. Br.	*Gopatha Brāhmana.*

GOS	Gaekwad Oriental Series, Baroda.
GP	*Geography of the Puranas.*
Grd.	*Garuda Purana.*
GSH	*Geographical System of Herodotus.*
GTCPNW	*Glossary of the Tribes and Castes of the Punjab and North-West Frontier Province.*
HAG	*History of Ancient Geography.*
HAI	*History of Ancient Indian.*
HABL	*History of Ancient Sanskrit Literature.*
HATSEI	*History, Antiquities, Topography and Statistics of Eastern India (Studies in Indian History).*
HAV	*Hymns of the Atharva Veda.*
HCDBP	*Historical and Cultural Data from the Bhavisya Purana.*
HCIP	*History and Culture of the Indian People.* (Bharatiya Vidya Bhavan, Bombay).
HCSL	*History of Classical Sanskrit Literature.*
HG	*Himalayan Gazetteer.*
HGAI	*Historical Geography of Ancient India.*
HIIA	*History of Indian and Indonesian Art.*
HIL	*History of Indian Literature.*
HISI	*Historical Inscriptions of Southern India.*
HJ	*Himalayan Journals.*
HLI	*Historical and Literary Inscriptions.*
HMSAC	*History of Merchant Shipping and Ancient Commerce.*
HN	*History of Nepal* (tr. from the *Parbatiya Vaṁśāvali* by Munshi Shiva Shankar Singh and Pt. Gunananda).
HNEI	*History of North-Eastern India Extending from the Foundation of the Gupta Empire to the rise of the Pala Dynastry of Bengal* (c. A.D. 320-760).
HNSK	*History of Nepal and Surrounding Kingdoms.*
HOS	Harvard Oriental Series, Cambridge, Mass USA.

HRIAS	*Historicity of Ramayana and the Indo-Aryan Society in India and Ceylon.*
HRPNA	*Historical Researches into the Politics, Intercourse and Trade of the Principal Nations of Antiquity: Asiatic Nations.*
HSL	*History of Sanskrit Literature.*
HTC	*Hindu Tribes and Castes.*
HV	*Harivamsa.*
IA or *Ind. Ant.*	*Indian Antiquary* (a journal of Oriental Research), Bombay.
IAA	*Inscriptions of Ancient Assam.*
IAC	*Indo-Asian Culture.*
IAH	*Indo-Aryan and Hindi.*
IAN	*Inscriptions of Ancient Nepal.*
IAR	*The Indo-Aryan Races* (a Study of the Origin of Indo-Aryan an People and Institutions).
IBV	*India as Seen in the Brhat-Samhita of Varahamihira.*
IC	*Indian Culture,* Calcutta.
ICHR	Indian Council of Historical Research, Delhi.
ICS	Indian Civilisation Series, Varanasi.
IDM	*India as Described by Manu.*
IEGW	*India as Described by Early Greek Writers.*
IETBJ	*India as Described in Early Texts of Buddhism and Jainism.*
IGER	*Idea of God in Early Religions.*
IGI	*Imperial Gazetteer of India,* Oxford, 1907-09.
IGJ	*Indian Geographical Journal.*
IHC	*Indian History Congress.*
IHQ	*Indian Historical Quarterly,* Calcutta.
IHR	*Indian Historical Review,* Delhi.
IIH	*An Introduction to Indian Historiography.*
IK	*India in Kalidasa.*

IKP	*India as Known to Panini:* A Study of the Cultural material in the Astadhyahi.
IN	*Inscriptions From Nepal.*
In. As.	*The Inhabitants of Asia: the History of Existing and Extinct Nations their Ethnology, Manners and Customs.*
Ind. Alt.	*Indische Alterthumskunde (A German work on the History and Antiquities of India).*
Ind. Pal.	*Indische Palaeographie.*
Ind. Stu.	*Indische Studien,* by A. Weber.
IP	*Itihăsa Prakăśa.*
IRGL	*International Review of General Linguistics.*
ISIH	*An Introduction to the Study of Indian History.*
ITP	*India in the Time of Patañjali.*
JA	*Journal Asiatique,* Paris.
JAAAS	*Journal of the American Academy of Arts and Science,* Boston, Massachusetts, U.S.A.
JAOS	*Journal of the American Oriental Society.*
JARS	*Journal of the American Oriental Society* (Kamarupa Anusandhan Samiti), Gauhati.
JAS	*Journal of the Asiatic Society,* Calcutta.
JASB	*Journal of the Asiatic Society of Bengal,* Calcutta.
JASL	*Journal of the Asiatic Society Letters,* Calcutta.
JBBRAS	*Journal of the Bombay Branch of the Royal Asiatic Society,* Bombay.
JBORS	*Journal of the Bihar and Orissa Research Society,* Patna.
JBRS	*Journals of the Bihar Research Society,* Patna.
JGIS	*Journal of the Greater India Society,* Calcutta.
JGRI	*Journal of the Ganganath Jha Research Institute,* Allahabad.
JIH	*Journal of Indian History,* Trivandrum.
JISR	*Journal of Institute of Social Research,* Shillong.

JLAR	*A Journey of Literary and Archaeological Research in Nepal and Northern India.*
JNEICSSR	*Journal of the North-East India Council for Social Science Research,* Shillong.
JNV	*Jaiminiyanyamalavistara* (Gold Stucker s Edition).
JPASB	*Jsournal and Proceedings of the Asiatic Society of Bengal.*
JRAI	*Journal of the Royal Anthropological Institute of Great Britain and Ireland,* London.
JRAS	Journal of the Royal Asiatic Society of Great Britain and Ireland, London.
JRASB(L)	*Journal of the Royal Asiatic Society of Bengal, Letters,* Calcutta.
JRGS	*Journal of the Royal Geographical Society,* Lucknow.
JSA	*Journal of the Royal Society of Arts,* London.
JUPHS	*Journal of the U.P. Historical Society,* Lucknow.
Kal.	*Kalika Purana.*
KHR	*Karnatak Historical Review,* Dharwar.
KRS	Kannada Research Society.
KS	*Kamarupa Sasanavali.*
KTAI	*Some Ksatriya Tribes of Ancient India.*
Kur.	*Kurma Purana.*
LAIJC	*Life in Ancient India as depicted in Jaina Canons.*
LAIM	*Life in Ancient India in the Age of the Manrtas.*
LE Nepal	*Le Nepal Etude Historique d'un Royaume Hindou* by Sylvain Levi.
List.	*List of Brahmi Inscriptions from the Earliest times to A.D. 400.*
LKA	*Licchavi Kal Ka Abhilekha.*
LLRBNB	*Language, Literature and Religion of the Buddhas of Nepal and Bhot.*
LMO	*Le Monde Oriental.*
LRS	Law s Research Series.

LSI	*Linguistic Survey of India.*
MAI	*Magadhas in Ancient India.*
Manu.	*Manu Smrti.*
MARIBL	*Memories des L'Academie Royale des Inscriptions et Belles Lettres.*
Mark.	*Markandeya Purana.*
MASB	*Memoirs of the Asiatic Society of Bengal,* Calcutta.
MASI	*Memoirs of the Archaeological Survey of India.*
Mass.	Massachusetts, U.S.A.
Mat.	*Matsya Purǎna.*
Mhb.	*Mahǎbhǎrata.*
Mbh. Ko.	*Mahǎbhǎrata Kośa* (A Descriptive Index to the Names and Subjects in the Mahabharata).
MI	*Magasthenese's Indika.*
MI (QAJ)	*Man in India* (A Quarterly Anthropological Journal), Ranchi.
MIC	*Mohenjo-Daro and the Indus Civilisation.*
MR	*Modern Review,* Calcutta.
MRAI	*Man: Journal of the Royal Anthropological Institute,* London.
MSR	*Manual of the Science of Religion.*
Mys. Arch. Repo.	*Mysore Archaeological Report.*
NEB	*New Encyclopaedia Britannica.*
NHH	*Notes on the History of the Himalaya of the N.W.P. India.*
NHIP	New History of the Indian People.
NIGC	*Nepalese Inscriptions in Gupta Characters.*
NLAE	*New Light on the Most Ancient East.*
NO	*Numismata Orientalie.*
NRTCA	*Notes on the Races, Tribes and Castes inhabiting the Province of Avadh.*

ODBL	*Origin and Development of the Bengali Language.*
OGCI	*Origin and Growth of Caste in India.*
OHI	*Oxford History of India.*
OIB	*Original Inhabitants of Bharatavarsa.*
OM	*Ordinances of Manu* (tr. of *Manava Dharmasastra).*
ORLI	*An Outline of the Religious Literature of India.*
OSAA	*Outlines of a Systematic Anthropology of Asia.* *Original Sanskrit Texts* (on the Origin and History of the people of India, their Religion and Institutions).
OUP	*Oxford University Press*, London.
Pad.	*Padma Purana.*
PAHCI	*Place of Assam in the History and Civilisation of India.*
PAHI	*Prehistoric Ancient and Hindu India.*
PAPD	*Pre-Aryan and Pre-Dravidian in India.*
PASB	*Proceedings of the Asiatic Society of Bengal,* Calcutta.
PE	*Puranic Encyclopaedia:* A Comprehensive Dictionary with Special Reference to the Epic and the Puranic Literature.
Periplus.	*The Periplus of the Erythraean Sea.*
PG	*Panini's Grammatik.*
PHAI	*Political History of Ancient India.*
PIHC	*Proceedings of the Indian History Congress.*
PK	*Pauranic Kosa.*
PNEIHA	*Proceedings of the North-East India History Association.*
PPHEI	*Prehistory and Protohistory of Eastern India.*
PPIP	*Prehistory and Protohistory of India and Pakistan.*
PRIA	*Proceedings of the Royal Irish Academy.*

PSEHEI	*Perspectives in Social and Economic History of Early India.*
PSHG	*Political and Statistical History of Gujarat.*
PTDKA	*The Purana Text of the Dynasties of the Kali Age.*
PTIOC	*Proceedings and Transactions of the All-India Oriental Conference.*
PTS	Pali Text Society, London.
QRHS	*Quarterly Review of Historical Studies* (Institute of Historical Studies), Calcutta.
QSTE	*Quarterly Study of Trends and Events,* Shillong.
RASB	*Royal Asiatic Society of Bengal.*
RATA	*Report of the Archaeological Tour in Assam.*
RBK	*A Rcord of Buddhistic Kingdoms.*
RCI	*Races and Cultures of India.*
ReNIT	*Racial Affinities of Early North Indian, Tribes.*
RGHSA	*'Recherches Geographiques et Historiques Sur L'a Serique des ancients.'*
RGS	Royal Geographical Society, London.
RI	*Rigvedic India.*
RJTTC	*Recollections of a Journey Through Tartary Tibet and China.*
RNI	*Races of Northern India.*
RPGEA	*Researches on Ptolemy's Geography of Eastern Asia.*
RPVU	*Religion and Philosophy of the Veda and Upanishads.*
RRV	*Religion of the Rgveda.*
RSTF	*Report on a visit to Sikkim and the Tibetan Frontier.*
RV	*Rgveda.*
SAA	Statistical Account of Assam.
SAB	*Statistical Account of Bengal.*
SAI	*Sudras in Ancient India.*
SAII	*Study of Ancient Indian Inscriptions.*

SAK	*Statistical Account of Kumaon.*
SANSM	*Statistical Account of the Native State of Manipur and the Hill-Terrirory under its Rule.*
Sat. Br.	*Śatapatha Brāhmana.*
SBA	*Sacred Books of the Aryan Series,* Delhi.
SBE	*Sacred Books of the East,* Oxford.
SBLN	*Sanskrit Buddhist Literature in Nepal.*
SCEMI	*Social Changes in Early Medieval India* (c. A.D. 500-1200).
SDSM	*Studies in the Dharmaśāstra of Manu.*
SED	*Sanskrit English Dictionary.*
SGAMI	*Studies in the Geography of Ancient and Medieval India.*
SHB	*Studies in 'Honour' of Bloomfield.*
SHK	*Social History of Kāmarūpa.*
SHMT	*A System of Hindu Mythology and Tradition.*
SHN	*A Short History of Nepal.*
SIA	*Studies in Indian Antiquities.*
SIIHC	*Select Inscriptions bearing on Indian History and Civilisation.*
SIPI	*Sources of Indian Philosophical Ideas.*
Skd.	*Skanda Purana.*
SLAI	*Social Life in Ancient India.*
SLPM	*Social Life of Primitive Man.*
SO(R)	Serie Orientale, Roma.
SPHI	*Studies in the Proto-History of India.*
SPIMC	*Studies in Proto-Indo-Mediterranean. Culture* (Heras Institute of Indian History and Culture, Bombay).
SPRHRC	*Studies in the Puranic Records on Hindu Rites and Customs.*
SRAMI	*Studies in the Religious Life of Ancient and Medieval India.*

SSAAMI	*Studies in the Society and Administration of Ancient and Medieval India.*
Sv.	*Śiva Purāna.*
TAI	*Tribes in Ancient India.*
Tai. Br.	*Taittiriya Brāhmaṇa.*
Tai. Sam.	*Taittiriya Saṁhitā.*
Tand. Br.	*Taṇdya-Mahā-Brāhmaṇa (Pañcaviṁśa Brāhmaṇa).*
TCAAS	Transactions of the Connecticut Academy of Arts and Sciences.
TCAI	*Trade and Commerce in Ancient India.*
TCB	*Tribes and Castes of Bengal.*
TCH	*Travels in the Central Himalayas.*
THAI	*Tribal History of Ancient India:* A Numismatic Approach.
THDAT	*Trans-Himalayan Discoveries and Adventures in Tibet.*
THEI	*Tribal History of Eastern India.*
TICO	*Transactions of the International Congress of Orientalists.*
TM	*Travels of Marco-Polo.*
TR	*Tribes and Races: A Descriptive Ethnology of Asia, Africa and Europe.*
TRCIN	*Tribes, Races and Cultures of India and Neighbouring Countries.*
TRIA	*Transactions of the Royal Irish Academy.*
TSS	Trivandrum Sanskrit Series, Trivandrum.
TWYV	*The Texts of the White Yajurveda.*
Vaj. Sam.	*Vājasaneyi Saṁhitā.*
Val. Ram.	*Vālmiki-Rāmāyana.*
Vas. Dh. Su.	*Vasiṣṭha Dharma-Sūtra.*
Ved. Stu.	*Vedische Studsen, by R. Pischel and K.F. Geidner.*
VE	*Vikram Era.*
VI	*Vedic Index of Names and Subjects.*

Vis. Dh. Mah.	*Visnu-Dharmottara Mahă-Purăna.*
Vmn.	*Vamăna Purăna.*
Vrh.	*Văraha Purăna.*
VRK	*Vălmiki Rămayana Kośa (Descriptive Index. to the Names and Subjects of Ramayana).*
VS	*Vikram Samvat.*
VSMRS	*Vaisnavism, Saivism and Minor Religious Systems.*
Vṣṇ.	*Viṣṇu Purăṇa.*
Vy.	*Văyu Purăṇa.*
WTI	*The Wild Tribes of India.*
WTIH	*The Wild Tribes in Indian History.*
YCTI	*Yuan Chwang's Travels in India* (A.D. 629-45).
YV	*Yajur Veda.*
ZDMG	*Zeitschrift der Deutschen Morganlandischen Gesellschaft, Leipzig.*
ZFKDM	*Zeitschrift Furd' Kunde d'es Morgenlandische*

Contents

BOOK FOUR

THE EMERGENCE AND FALL OF JANAPADAS, KINGDOMS, PRINCIPALITIES AND TOWNS

(From the Epic Age down to the times of the Hoysalas)

BOOK ONE
INTRODUCTORY

I

PURPOSE, SCOPE, METHOD AND UTILITY OF THE WORK

The Kirâtas pre-eminently figure among the tribes described in ancient Indian and classical (Greek and Latin) literature. The ancient Indian writers as well as classical geographers and historians, while dealing with the primitive races of India, have accorded prominence to the Kirâtas. They constitute one of the major segments of the tribal communities living in the Himalayan and sub-Himalayan regions, forest tracts, mountainous areas and the Gangetic plains, valleys and delta of India.

The Kirâtas were widely diffused tribe. Broadly speaking, the areas inhabited by them covered some parts of eastern, north-eastern, central, western, northern, southern and so-called Greater or Farther India. Their habitation even beyond the confines of India can also be proved.

The primary objective of undertaking this research work is to provide a comprehensive historical account of the life and culture of the Kirâtas from the pre-historic age down to the end of the twelfth century A.D. dealing with their origin, antiquity, identification, expansion within and beyond the geographical limits of ancient Bhâratavarsa, colonization of different parts of the country, primitive life and culture, settlement patterns, social life, economic condition, polity and administration, religion and philosophy, art, language and literature, cultural contacts with different Âryan and non-Âryan social groups, janapadas in the epic and Paurânic traditions, the kingdoms, principalities, urban culture, subjugation by the contemporary rulers, dynastic rule in Nepal, role in the early annals of India and contribution to the Indian culture and civilization.

No serious attempt has yet been made to provide a trustworthy account of the subject concerned in a correct historical perspective. The picture emerging out of the researches carried out so far into their history and culture is neither very graphic nor fully dependable. The sources available on their history and culture have not yet been properly and thoroughly investigated. It is true that the anthropologists have taken the lead in the field of the study of ethnography of India and made proportionately greater contribution than others to the discovery of primitive culture, but the data furnished by them particularly about the origin and antiquity of ancient Indian tribes are, professedly, not of sufficiently reliable character from the historical point of view. Until and unless, the primitive races of India receive the proper attention of historians, it will not be possible for us to acquire a perfect and accurate knowledge of the history and culture of dim past. The historical treatment of the subject under discussion will help us, to a considerable extent, in dispelling many of our erroneous conceptions about the racial elements in the primitive population of India. Such kind of treatment is also helpful in dissipating the haziness enveloping the early phases of Indian civilization.

Remarkably, the history and culture of the Âryans have been extensively dealt with by different scholars, but the non-Âryanas (with particular reference to the aboriginal tribes) have not been assigned the place they deserve in our ancient history. We very often acknowledge the contribution of the Âryanas to ancient Indian history and culture, but do not give much recognition to the non-Âryan primitive races. Only the partial assessment of the subject concerned will not help us overcome the related problems. Such approach will be considered as tantamount to an attempt at glorification of one group of people and the neglect of other. Many interesting mysteries with regard to the history of the non-Âryan races are yet to be unravelled. While dealing with early history of India, particularly, the proto-historic and historic periods, it is the primary task of a classical historian to strike a balance between divergent arguments concerning both group of races. The fact remains that both the Âryanas and non-Âryans, par-excellence, are the joint makers of history and culture of the Indian sub-continent. In fact, the whole superstructure of early history of India has been erected on the foundation collectively laid by the primitive inhabitants belonging to different categories of races.

The non-Âryan tribes have a distinct place in the ethnographic history of ancient India. They have left behind some distinct marks on the pages of ancient history of India.

The careful and dispassionate study of the ancient Indian historical tradition and the classical records reveals that there are quite a good number of valuable data about them, which are very useful for the purpose of making a historical study of the subject dwelt upon here. J. Talboys Wheeler has correctly stated that "The races who occupied India prior to the Vedic Aryans have been excluded from the division of the ancient history into Vedic and Brahmanic times. Indeed they have no history apart from Vedic and Brahmanic traditions. The remains of so-called aboriginal races may be treasured up as memorials of primitive man but they furnish few data which are available for the purpose of history. For ages their relics have been turning to dust in caves or cromlechs, or lying buried beneath the shapeless mounds. A few dry bones, a few weapons of stone and rusted metal, a scattering of nameless implements and ornaments, are occasionally discovered amongst the debris of ancient settlements and forgotten battle fields, which for ages have passed into oblivion. But such vestiges of the past can only interest the antiquarian, and throw no light upon religious or political culture. In the course of ages many of the primitive races may have been incorporated in the general population, and form in the present day the lower strata of the Hindu social system...Living representatives of primitive races are still, however, lingering in secluded and difficult regions, but they have long ceased to play any important part in the annals of humanity. They represent the human race in its earliest childhood......In the later annals of India some of the tribes occasionally rise to the surface, and then drop back into their old obscurity and it will accordingly suffice to describe them as they individually appear."[1]

Schlegel also observes: "in the background of old, mighty, and civilized nations we can almost always trace the primeval inhabitants of the country, who, dispossessed of their territory have been reduced to servitude by their conquerors or have gradually been incorporated with them. These primitive inhabitants, when compared with their later or more civilized conquerors, appear in general rule as barbarous; though we find among them a certain number of ancient customs and arts, which by no means tend to confirm the notion of an original and universal savage state of nature."[2]

The Kirâtas, one of the living representatives of the primitive non-Âryan race, offer a wide scope for making a historical study of their culture and civilization. They stand in sharp contrast to the Âryans race. Their existence in India since time immemorial can be established with the help of contemporary literature. For some time they influenced early history of India quite independently, but after the advent of the Vedic Âryans many significant changes took place. After having been conquered and driven by the Aryan race, they took refuge in dense forests, mountains and hills. Many of them were absorbed in the Âryan race. But, by and large, they continued to maintain their separate existence. Their dispersion, on a large scale, over rugged mountains, their seclusion, their extreme ignorance and prejudices, their repugnance to frequent intercourse with both the Âryan and other non-Âryan tribes did not render it possible for the early writers to obtain full or correct knowledge of their history. The so-called aboriginal tribes including the Kirâtas are now widely scattered and divided. In ancient times the North-Eastern, North-Western, Central and Deccan regions were the cradles of the Kirâta culture. Their history underwent metamorphosis at different periods. In order to get an accurate picture of their history and culture' whatsoever it may be, an objective study of the past is very essential.

A thorough investigation of the past in this particular context and a more sympathetic treatment of the tribal people of ancient India will definitely widen the horizon of history. We should not be guided by what some historians have opined about the past. They have adopted very unhealthy attitude towards the past ages. They have always regarded the past ages with contempt and disgust. They have treated the gone-by ages as unenlightened and barbaric. We should rather try to find in them the expression of genuine and valuable human achievements and reflection of the primitive civilization. The principle, on which Rousseau has presented his explanation can be applied not only to recent history but to the history of all ages and all races. He is perfectly justified in holding that "primitive savagery is superior to civilized life". Many scholars can question the historical validity of his statement. But we uphold it only because of the fact that the primitive races mistaken by the Indian and British anthropologists as barbarous or savages also had to contribute their shares to the making of history. The so-called civilized races imbibed many things particularly in the field of religion and culture from them. Their place in the history should be judged in the contemporary situation, not strictly in the present context; and henceforth any degree of comparison between the civilised and savage race in the primitive situation will not eject any clear picture of the subject. While determining the extent of savagery or civilized state of any particular race in ancient times, the possibility of adoption of relative judgment theory by a scholar can't be precluded. The historians of Romantic school have reasonably maintained that the primitive tribes represent a form of society with diverse elements of culture and civilization. Such a Romantic sympathy with the past positively extended the scope of historical thought and "historians began to think of the entire history of mankind as a single process of development from a beginning in savagery to an end in a perfectly rational and civilized society."[3]

In the light of the above discussion one can get a very clear picture of the importance attached to the study of the primitive society and culture. Thus, in order to have a perfect understanding of the various phases of the growth of Indian culture and civilisation the scientific study of the tribal history of ancient India is very much needed. D.D. Kosambi, who has strongly advocated the need of making a historical study of the tribal people of ancient India, has rightly observed that "The entire course of Indian history shows tribal elements being fused into a general society."[4]

The remnants of the ancient Kirâtas are still visible in different tribal belts of India. For a better understanding of their past and present we shall have to depend on the available semi-historical and historical records. These records bear an eloquent testimony to the truth that the Kirâtas, as one of the very popular ancient Indian tribes, appeared on the scene in an intermittent fashion and left behind an indelible imprint on the contemporary civilization. The post-Vedic age, the classical age, the Mauryan age and the period extending from the 7th century to the 12th century A.D. are also characterised, to a considerable degree, by the participation of the Kirâtas in the various events that took place on various occasions. It can be proved beyond doubt, that for a certain period of time they rose to prominence and by virtue of their exalted position in the society brought large number of Âryans closer to them, which eventually resulted in the interaction and cultural fellowship of the two. Such a popular tribe, generally known and singularly used as the Kirâtas, has been pushed into the background. Hence for the purpose of bringing all the Kirata people living today in different regions of India to limelight a correct historical approach has been made to the problems involved in the present study.

The subject undertaken for fresh study has, of course, been examined by few oriental and occidental scholars in the past. But, none of them has made painstaking effort to carry out intensive research in the subject concerned. There are still wide gaps in our existing knowledge about the subject, which can be further filled in. Here an attempt has been made to test the credibility of all the accounts presented so far to ascertain as to what extent there may be a further scope for re-examining the subject. While doing so, all possible care has been taken to discover both the merits of and deficiencies in the works.

G.A. Grierson's statement that "the name Kirâtas recalls fabulous Kirâtas of Sanskrit literature"[5] exposes his complete ignorance of the subject. To call Kirâtas a fabulous or a mythical race will be a distortion of historical truth. They have been distinguished from the fabulous races in all the writings. Their historicity has already been well ascertained by different scholars. Hence, his view can be outrightly rejected.

As a matter of fact, the subject began to attract the attention of scholars since the first decade of the present century. F.E. Pargiter, a well known oriental scholar in his translation of the *Mârkandeya Parâna*[6] published in 1904 (BIS) from Calcutta, has discussed in detail some aspects of the subject. He has mainly referred to the Kirâtas as described in the few *purânas* and the few Parvas of the *Mahabharata.* His conclusion about their origin is not based on sound logic. He has not covered all the relevant points in the treatment of the subject.

Sylvain Levi, the most competent authority on the history of Nepal has also discussed the subject to some extent. In his *magnum opus,*[7] which came out in the year 1905, (Paris), he has incidentally referred to the Kirâtas. He has critically examined the views of the ancient Hindu writers about the Kirâtas by quoting few passages from the *Mahabhârata* and other literary texts. He was the first scholar to examine the racial affinities of the Kirâtas. He, no doubt, took up this question very seriously and concluded that they belong to the Mongoloid stock. He has associated them with foreign people i.e. the Sakas, the Yavanas, the Pahlavas, the Cinas or the 'Chinese', etc. It appears that he has drawn some of his conclusions very abruptly without having deeper insight into all the relevant sources. The Mongoloid racial affinities of the Kirâtas were first of all proposed by him and ever since this term has been in use. No scholar has taken any pain to examine the validity of use of the term in historical perspective. The term Mongoloid has given rise to many misconceptions about their origin. However, he has provided a very valuable description of the Kirâtas of Nepal".

Nagendra Nath Vasu in his famous work[8] published in 1922 has touched on few points about the Kirâtas of north-east India on the basis of few literary sources. His account is very sketchy, but it contains some relevant information about the early life of the Kirâtas.

The account given by N.L. Dey in his book[9] (published in 1927) is too meagre to project any clear picture of the subject concerned. He has described the Kirâtas only in few lines. His geographical dictionary has not been found very useful for our purpose.

B.C. Law in his different research articles and other monumental works[10] has dwelt upon the subject collecting the data from very relevant sources. But, a thorough examination of all his works creates an impression that he has not made a deep study of the subject. Moreover, the same account has, more or less, been reproduced in all the works. No attempt was made on his part to make further additions to the subject in his later works. All aspects of the subject have not been prolixly narrated. However, as a pioneer in the field of historical ethnology, he has made a significant contribution to the racial history of India. One of the important features of his writings is that he has discovered few important sources, which are not much known. At the same time we can't deny the usefulness of the data highlighted by him. The learned exposition of the subject deserves appreciation.

B.A. Saletore, in his work[11] (published from Lahore in 1935) has focussed on some relevant aspects of the Kirâtas basically relying on some important literary sources, but, he has not discussed all the points in a systematic manner. Before drawing any positive conclusion about a particular point he seems to have proceeded to explain the other point. Large number of valuable sources of great historical importance are conspicuous by their absence in his work.

Some of the data have not been critically examined. The analysis of the subject presented by him is not purely historical. However, we cannot deny that he has successfully attempted to present a faithful account of the subject before us. While dealing with some wild tribes, he has devoted his full attention to the Kirâtas, which is obvious from the description of the subject given in his work. The chief merit of the work lies in the details of epigraphic evidence, which are very helpful for confirming the settlement, expansion and kingdoms of the Kirâtas in the south.

Kasten Ronnow in his long article entitled *Kirâta—A study on some Ancient Indian Tribe* published in 1936[12] has provided a detailed account of the subject concerned. The background of the subject is very impressive. He has examined many pertinent questions directly related to the subject without any bias or prejudice. He was bold enough to cast his doubt on the Mongoloid affinities of all the Kirata people. He has reasonably suggested that a scientific enquiry should be made about their origin. He has explored the possibility of discovering a new theory about this particular aspect. Some of his views have strengthened my arguments and fortified my belief about non-Mongoloid origin of some section of the Kirâtas. Despite certain amount of speculation as discernible from the extracts, he has tried his best to go as deep into the subject as possible. Some explanations as given by him about the meaning of the word

Kirata are not very convincing. Further, this article does not throw full light on the subject concerned. Only certain aspects of the subject have been discussed.

The Kirâtas also figure in the *Encyclopaedia* prepared by R.N. Saletore.[13] Though the account is very scanty yet it abounds in some useful information, particularly, about the later Kirâtas of the south. The information supplied by him about the expansion of the Kirâtas in the south, is of considerable importance.

E.T. Atkinson's[14] account of the Kirâtas is important only from the point of view of their geographical distribution, expansion and settlements in Nepal, Bhutan, Sikkim, Kumaon and other parts of the Central, Northern and Eastern Himalayas. He has not made an exhaustive study of the subject. He has elaborated only few points in his work. He has made only passing reference to some of the literary sources.

Robert Shafer[15] has slightly touched on the subject without giving any details. However, few points highlighted by him are worthy of credence. It may be of some value from the standpoint of general study of the subject.

After going through the contents of the research monograph of Suniti Kumar Chatterji[16] very minutely (which appeared first in *J.A.S.B.* Calcutta, 1950 and then released in the book form in 1951), we find that it is not the study of the Kirâtas as such. The table of contents does not justify the selection of the title of the book. Because, by and large, its contents are at variance with the subject-matter concerning the Kirâtas. He has unnecessarily incorporated the Nordic Âryans, Dravidians, the Licchavi dynasty of Bihar and Nepal, the history of the Meitheis or Manipuris, Kuki-Chins, Ahoms, several dynasties of Assam like Salastambha, Pralambha and Pala, Muslim invasions of Assam and Bengal, Koch empire of the 16th and 17th centuries, Bhaskarvarman of Kâmarüpa, Nepal-Tibet relationship, the Thakuri dynasty, Karnâtaka dynasty, the Malla kings and Gorkhas of Nepal, the Newari literature, etc. in his work. Quite a good number of pages of the book have been filled in with the description which do not form part of the Kirâtas. All Indo-Mongoloids of north-eastern and other parts of India have been misunderstood by him as the Kirâtas. He has associated the Kirâtas with the Tibeto-Burman family and Sino-Tibetan speaking tribes, who are supposed to have come from northwestern China and spread in different parts of the Himalayan and sub-Himalayan regions in the early centuries of the Christian era without distinguishing them from those, who had been living in India as autochthones, since time immemorial. The term "Sino-Tibetan Mongoloid" has been repeatedly and frequently used without giving any satisfactory explanation thereof. We do not find any justification for using the term for all the Kirâtas indiscriminately. His logic is not very convincing. Some of his findings are inconclusive. In confirmation of his hypothesis he has propounded some theories which are yet to be tested. His arguments about the term Indo-Mongoloid advanced in his monograph are heavily weighted with fantastic description, which deplorably lack an appreciable degree of distinctness. His "Indo-Mongoloid" theory has been blindly supported and quoted by a large number of scholars, particularly in north-east India without examining the credibility of the views expressed in this regard.

Secondly, he has not consulted all the relevant sources on the subject concerned. Only few original sources like the Vedic literature, the *Râmâyaṇa,* the three Parvas of the *Mahâbhârata,* three *Purâṇas,* one Pâli source, one Greek text, one Tantric text and few modern works have been used in the said work. All the literary texts, the classical accounts, epigraphic records and other valuable sources available on the subject do not figure in the work. Therefore, it is not possible to accept any view or the conclusion, which is based only on few sources. Further, those books on ancient China, Tibet and Burma, which are of immense value for determining the racial affinities of the so-called Tibeto-Burman Mongoloids, have not been properly consulted. For the rectification of some mistakes generally committed in respect of the identification of these people, the study of all contemporary sources are indispensable. Thirdly, as a distinguished philologist he has adduced the linguistic evidence in support of his contention. He has not made any historical approach to the study of the Kirâtas. The absence of coherence, continuity and chronological sequence in his account confirm our belief. The norms generally applied in historical researches are missing. Lastly, on the whole his work appears to be periscopical, peripheral and perfunctory, so far as, the scientific study of the subject is concerned.

Prof. Chatterji in his other works[17] has made passing references to the Kirâtas using the term "Mongoloid-Sino-Tibetan speaking tribes" again and again as equivalent for them. In spite of some inaccuracies and discrepancies which have been found in his all works, we get some valuable information about the Kirâtas. However, the greatest merit of his works lies in the strenuous endeavour which he has made to highlight their contribution to the history and culture of India. This is the quintessence of his work. Apart from it, he is the first scholar, who correctly used the term Kirâtas for some of their remnants in the North-East India. It is undeniable that all the tribes discussed in his works are not the Kirâtas but some of them are definitely affiliated to them. On the whole we find his works very valuable for our limited purposes.[⊕]

D.R. Regmi, a popular authority on the history of Nepal, in some of his valuable works[18] has elucidated the dynastic rule of the Kirâtas in Nepal deriving his authority from Sylvain Levi. He has not presented some of his arguments with as much confidence as he ought to have done. Some of his ideas are contradictory. Sometimes he has failed to draw any definite conclusion on certain points. Besides the Kirâtas of Nepal, he has also attempted to sketch the details of the Kirâtas of North-East India but he has failed in accomplishing his task. Because, the details concerned are full of ambiguity and appear to be fragmentary and disjointed. However, his effort for bringing to light the Kirâtas of Nepal has resulted in a success. It is altogether a different thing that there

---

⊕The comments I have made on Suniti Kumar Chatterji's famous work, *Kirâta-Jana-Kṛti,* and his other writings relating to the Kirâtas, while critically estimating their value, do not cast any aspersion on his scholarship. Difference of opinion is a part of research process. And, hence, my comments on his aforesaid work should not be misconstued as an attempt to denigrate him.

is a fair scope for filling in some vacuum in his account of the Kirâtas of Nepal.

Prof. Sudhakar Chattopadhyaya had devoted only few pages to the Kirâtas in his very important work.[19] His study of the subject is not based on original sources. He has made only passing references to the subject touching on only few points. He has discussed the subject in a disjointed manner. It appears to be scrappy. He has quoted B.S. Guha,[20] an eminent anthropologist in support of his identification of the Kirâtas with the so-called "Proto-Mongoloids" or "Palaeo-Mongoloids" without justifying the use of the term.

R.P. Chanda, a celebrated Indian anthropologist and a highly accomplished scholar of indology has also thrown some light on the Kirâtas in his famous work.[21] He has treated his subject combining in himself the qualities of both an anthropologist and a historian. He has provided a very useful data about their origin. Though mentioned incidentaly, a new vista of research regarding Kirâtas has been opened by him.

H.C. Chakiadar[22], a competent scholar of both anthropology and history, has described the subject only in few lines. He has not provided sufficient data for our purpose.

Since the Kirâtas do not distinctly figure in any numismatic record, it was beyond the purview of the treatment for K.K. Das Gupta who has made a historical study of few ancient tribes in his thesis[23] by making a numismatic approach to the problem concerned.

From the foregoing discussion it is quite evident that the present subject has not yet engaged the serious attention of any historian or ethnologist or anthropologist. Honestly speaking, no scholar has yet presented a comprehensive-account of the subject embracing all the aspects by using all the available Sanskrit texts, Tantra literature, Buddhist and Jaina canonical texts, Greek, Roman, French, German and Persian sources, epigraphic evidence, travellers' accounts, royat chronicles, genealogical records, standard historical texts and other contemporary sources. All these relevant sources have not been handled as yet together by any particular scholar properly and meticulously. There are still various scattered threads, which can be woven together in the texture of the present history. Most of the researches conducted earlier are based on meagre data available in few sources. Some valuable accounts recorded in both Indian and non-Indian sources, hitherto, unused by the scholars concerned have been incorporated for the first time in the present work. Their origin, antiquity, expansion, kingdoms, dynasty, society, trade and commerce, religion and culture, language and literature, role, contribution and place in ancient Indian history are some of those very very important aspects, which are still wrapped in mystery. Only few questions relating to these aspects have, hitherto, been examined or answered, but not all. Many hidden truths are yet to be explored. Thus, there is an ample scope for recasting the subject in a historical perspective. Since many valuable data are lying unused, the subject offers a fair scope for producing an original, meaningful and productive work.

The application of methodology in research largely depends on the nature of the subject. The study of the tribal people of ancient India definitely calls for an inter-disciplinary approach. And therefore, reliance has been placed on the combined testimony of historical, ethnological, anthropological and philological data. But, treatment of the subject is purely historical. It has been experienced that the methods applied by anthropologists, ethnologists and linguists do not always fit in with the historical method of enquiry, which is to examine the relevance of the data strictly on the basis of positive or concrete evidence. However, the importance of their findings cannot be denied, because they provide clues, which sometimes constitute an addition to other collected evidence.

History is such a positive science which can very easily detect the blunders of various researches. Some anthropological and linguistic data have been tested on the touchstone of history and found absolutely wrong. All the data collected from different sources have been critically examined, properly analysed and scientifically interpreted. All possible attempt has been made to examine the historical authenticity of conventional explanations given and the views expressed in stray accounts and interspersed sources. There are some areas, where we do not find reliable evidence. In such cases the only appropriate techniques generally applied in historical methodology are the imaginative interpretations and presumptions.

While dealing with primitive population or races, generally two methods are applied; one is analytical and scientific and the other selective and aesthetic. Actually, they do not conflict with rather complement and illuminate each other. The duality of vision sometimes helps us to discover the secrets of history.

Our dependence on the so-called "auxiliary sciences", which encompass the archaeology, epigraphy, chronology, etc. has also helped us to a considerable degree to confirm some of the views, which have not yet been given assent to. For the purpose of identification of place-names, tribes and janapadas geographical data have been found of great use. The historical description of the tribal people of ancient India demands the clear understanding of contemporary geographical situation.

Keeping in view the geographical extent of ancient India, the Kirâtas of Nepal, which formed the part of northern India in ancient times and was limited to the undulating plain, twenty miles long and fifteen broad between the Gandak and Kosi rivers, have also been made subject of our historical enquiry. They very much fall within the parameter of the subject. The reason for their inclusion in the list of other Kirâtas of ancient India is not far to discover. Geographically, politically and culturally Nepal remained an *integral* part of ancient India for a considerable period of time. Râjasekhara in his *Kâvyamimamsa* has placed Nepal in northern India, as well as, in eastern India along with Videha as a janapada of Âryâvarta (chs. 8 & 17 respectively). During the time of Mauryan emperor Asoka, Nepal was a part of the Magadh empire. During the times of the Guptas and Pusyabhutis also it formed part of India.[24] The Allahabad pillar Inscription[25] of Samudragupta bears witness to the fact that Kamarupa, Nepal, Krtrpura, etc., were the vassal frontier states during his time. Significantly enough, the greater part of Nepal formed the part of Videha or Mithila region in ancient times, which is amply substantiated by the fact that the two ancient capitals of Mithila, popularly known as Janakapura Simaramapura (modern Simraon) are still lying within the frontiers of Nepal.[26]

In ancient times, a large territory lying between Mithila and Nepal was the seat of the seven principalities of the Kirâtas as referred to in the *Mahâbhârata*. They possibly might have set up a large kingdom, with its boundaries extending up to Nepal or even including some part of Nepal. Before coming within the pale of Aryandom both Nepal and Mithila were the political and cultural centres of the Kiritâs. Because of geographical proximity of Nepal and Mithila, the Kirâtas were ruling over a large territory in both the regions, which had no clear-cut demarcation line in ancient time. Actually, Mithila, Nepal and Bengal constituted one cultural zone in ancient times both historically and geographically. The extension and contraction of the geographical boundary of both Nepal and Mithila were conditioned by the contemporary historical development up to the 14th century A.D. Further, the Kirâtas had a dynastic rule in ancient Nepal from the epic age down to the 7th century A.D. Thus, bringing the Kirâtas of Nepal within the purview of our treatment of subject stands justified.

The subject under our notice is of paramount importance from the point of view of a historical study of one of the most popular races of ancient India. This is the first humble attempt to make a micro-study of history and culture of the Kirata people. Our findings will open a new avenue of historical research in the ethnology of ancient India. It will be useful for historians, indologists, antiquarians, linguists, the ethnologists, anthropologists and other social scientists. The present study, we hope, will throw new light on many an obscure aspect of our history, contribute to the enrichment of our knowledge about very little known Himalayan communities and finally constitute an important chapter in the history and culture of ancient India.

Notes and References

1. *India From the Earliest Ages*, Vol. III *(History of India)*, pp. 10-11.
2. Quoted in Mrs. C. Speir, *Phases of Indian Civilization (A Historical and Cultural Outline)*, p. 17.

3. For a detailed discussion on this point see R.G. Collingwood, *The Idea of History,* pp. 87-88.
4. ISIH., p. 27.
5. LSI., Vol. I, Pt. I, p. 58.
6. Vol. II. Pt. II, pp. 322, 369-70, 382-83 ; see also JASB. 1897 Vol. LXVI, Pt. I, pp. 85, 105, 108-10.
7. *Le Nepal,* Vol. II. pp. 72-79.
8. SHK. Vol. I. pp. 38-44, 92-95.
9. GDAMI, pp. 32, 100.
10. (*a*) *Countries and Peoples of India (Epic and Pauranic Sources)* cf ABORI, April 1936, Vol. XVII, Pt. Ill, pp. 217-42 ; July 1936 Vol. XVII, Pt. IV. pp. 319-39.
    (*b*) ABORI, 1939-40, Vol-XXI, pp. 203-12.
    (*c*) *Some Ancient Indian Tribes* cf. 1C. Vol. I. N. 3. pp. 381-82.
    (*d*) TAI. (BOS.), pp. 282-83.
    (*e*) AIT. (LRS.), Vol. 2, pp. 20-22.
    (*f*) HGAI., PP. 10, 83-84, 98-99, 228-253.
    (*g*) IETBJ. pp. 72, 80-86, 271.
    (*h*) GEB. p. 33.
11. WTIH., Ch. II. pp. 13-37.
12. cf. LMO. (Uppsala), Vol. XXX, pp. 90-169.
13. EIC., Vol. II. pp. 750-52.
14. HG. Vol. II. Pt. 1, pp. 363 ff.
15. EAI. pp. 124-25, 140.
16. *Kirata-Jana Krti,* pp. 26-38, 39-58, 66-130, 142-66.
17. (*a*) IAH. pp. 49-50.
    (*b*) PAHCI. pp. 15-18, 31, 83.
    (*c*) HCIP. *The Vedic Age,* pp. 169-70.
    (*d*) *Cul. Herit. Ind.* Vol. V. Preface, XIX, 659-60, 952.
18. (*a*) AN. pp. 13-33, 48-50, 54-58, 61-63, 74, 78, 81, 136-37, 169.
    (*b*) IAN, Vol. I. pp. 85 ff ; Vol. 3. pp. 17-18, 155-58, 291-92.
19. RENIT. pp. 2, 10, 32, 38, 70, 102, 104.
20. *Racial Elements in the Population.* N. 22 of the Oxford pamphlets on Indian affairs, 1944, p. 16.
21. IAR. pp. 5-6.

22. AOEI., p. 40.
23. THAI.
24. See J.A. Hammerton (ed.) ; TRCIN, p. 317 ; R.S. Tripathi HAI, pp. 331-32; Rajabali Pandey, *Bhartiya Itihasa Ka Parichaya,* p 113; R.C. Majumdar, AI. p. 351. Thomas Watters (YCTI Vol. II no. 84) has placed Nepal (Ni-Po-Lo) in "Mid India". See also R.G. Basak, NHEI., pp. 389-90.
25. Fleet, CII. Vol. III. Line-22, p. 14.
26. B. Hodgson, JASB. 1835, Vol. IV; JBRS., March-June, 1957, Vol XLIII, pts. I & II, pp. 1-5; Luciano Pateeh, *Mithila and Nepal,* JBRS 1962, Vol. XLVIII. Pts. 1 to 4, pp. 16-17. Ganganath Jha (cf. Pt. Udayavira Sastri, *Sankhya Dorsan Ka Itihasa,* Delhi, VS. 2006, pp. 341-42) has expressed the view that between the 9th century (the time of Vachaspati) and the 14th century A.D. the rulers of Nepal and Mithila were extending their political hegemony over each other's territory.

II

SOURCES AND THEIR VALUE : A CRITICAL ESTIMATE

In the arena of research the presentation or delineation of subject matter concerned presupposes a critical evaluation of all sources at our disposal. An investigation should not be confined only to those sources, which have been adequately churned and copiously used, rather repeated attempts should be made for discovering some new sources in the hope of bringing some new ideas, facts and data into sharp-focus. In order to get better result, we have to depend on various sources containing variegated mosaic of information, rather on isolated or fragmentary source-material. The sources highlighted below are broadly divided into diiferent categories and placed under different headings :

Literary Sources

The ancient Indian literary texts constitute very valuable source of the history and culture of different races and tribes, who settled in India during the pre-historic and proto-historic periods. The literary source is very helpful for throwing light on the origin, ethnology, migrations, movements, settlements, expansion, identification, antiquity, Janapadas, etc. of various primitive Aryan and non-Aryan races. But this source needs to be handled carefully and objectively because facts and fictions have jumbled and myths and history have coalesced together in this category of source in such a manner that sometimes it becomes really difficult to use the data with certain amount of confidence. However, we can not wholly dismiss the historical importance of literary source. There are some literary texts, which contain both historical and quasi-historical material. It all depends on how and in what context we use them in our writings. While dealing with any aspect of ancient Indian history and culture, these texts can't be ignored. History can be safely extracted out of various details narrated in these. Some scholars still suffer from illusion about the historical value of the data contained in these sources. It has been found that in some of the writings concerning the racial history of ancient India, the importance of these sources have been completely neglected. It is undeniable that there are various discrepancies, interpolations, contradictions, inaccuracies, etc. in these sources, which have apparently crept in because of various additions and alterations in the texts. But it must be kept in mind that the style of presentation in a particular literary text is governed by the compulsion of the age. In any way, it will not be fair to cast doubt on the historicity of all the literary texts. Some of them are definitely worthy of credence.

J.A. Baines,[1] Census Commissioner for India, while dealing with the origin of races of India, remarked that the materials for the early history of India are singularly defective. His statement that "attempt to reconstruct the ancient history of India from the literature that has come down to us, judging from the want of harmony amongst the experts, who have made them, are remarkable only for their brilliant failure" runs contrary to the truth.

D.D. Kosambi, while stressing the need for making a scientific study of the primitive people and reconstructing history of the culture that existed before any written record, observed, that most of the surviving ancient Indian documents are overwhelmingly religious and ritualistic. The writers were not concerned with history or with reality. Trying to extract history from them without some previous knowledge of the actual structure of Indian society at the time of writing gives either no results or the ludicrous conclusion that may be read in most histories of India."[2] We don't find ourselves in perfect agreement with Mr. Kosambi. Because his statement is not absolutely correct. Further, his view,[3] that the literary sources can be considered trustworthy only to the extent that they can be substantiated by an archaeological evidence does not appear to be based on sound logic.

Such erroneous views have been expressed by other scholars too. They hold that only archaeology can supply reliable data for the study and reconstruction of ancient Indian history and culture. Some distinguished archaeologists like D.H. Gordon (*The Pre-historic Background of Indian Culture,* Bombay, 1958), Stuart Piggott *(Pre-historic India,* Penguin Books, 1950), R.E.M. Wheeler *(Early India and Pakistan,* London, 1959), Woolley and others have treated the literary evidence with distrust and diffidence. They are too much obsessed with their archaeological data. Gordon, while condemning the literary evidence went to the extent of'saying that major portions of the *Mahabharata* and the *Puranas* "provide little except fuel for the blaze of controversy." Sometimes, the archaeological discovery also furnishes 'dry bones' of history. The. interpretation of archaeological material sometimes appears to be highly speculative A true historian has to take cognizance of both literary and archaeological data which are supplementary to each other. It is not always necessary that the literary evidence shall have to be corroborated by the archaeological evidence. Otherwise, we find that the large number of literary data have been supported by the archaeological findings. We should believe in the relative value of both the sources. The broken chains of ancient Indian history can't be restored by only one kind of data. There is need to collect data from as many sources as possible. The absolute dependence on one particular method will not help us much. Thus the views current among some scholars, that the reliability of the literary data should be determined by the extent to which it is corroborated by the archaeological evidence, does not hold good.

H.D. Sankalia, an archaeologist of international repute, has made a balanced approach to the problems concerned. He has correctly stated that an analytical and synthetic study of various details scattered throughout the vast literature of India includmg the Vedic and the Paurānic literature and the epics—the *Rāmāyana* and the *Māhabhārata–,* however, they may be contaminated by later interpolations or inflated, may help us in the reconstruction of the history of various Āryan and non-Āryan tribes or peoples. He finds that the traditions preserved in ancient literature of India are of great value for an archaeologist.

The most popular race known as the Kirātas have been described in various literary sources but unfortunately no satisfactory explanation thereof has been provided as yet. The earliest recorded references alluding to the appellation Kirāta occur in the Vedic literature including the Samhitas and the Brahmanas, which were compiled roughly between 4,500-1,000 B.C. The hymns of the two later Vedic texts the Sukla-*Yajurveda*[4] and the *Atharva Veda*[5] throw light on their dwellings in the caves and mountains of the Eastern Himalayan region, their contacts with the Vedic Āryans, antiquity, etc. The *Vajasaneyi Saṁhitā* (XXX. 16), the *Taittrinya Brāhmaṇa* (iii. 4.12:1.), the *Satapatha Brāhmaṇa* (1.1.4.14.), the *Aitreya Brahmana* (Xiii, 1.2.5), the *Satyayanaka Brahmana* (apud-Sāyana on Rv. X. 57.1; 60.1) and the *Jaiminiya Brāhmana* (iii. 1, 6.7) also contain some vague references to the Kiratas. While assessing the historical value of the available contents, we get an impression that nothing is explicitly expounded in the above mentioned Samhitas and the Brahmanas except for the primitive style of their living, and their contacts with the Vedic Aryans and priests.

In the post-Vedic times we come across large corpus of literature. The epics—the *Rāmāyaṇa* and the *Mahābhārata*—are very useful for our purpose. The *Balākanda*[6] and the *Kiskindhaā Kānda* (a faithful record[7]) of Valmiki's *Rāmāyana* deal with their origins, movements, physical characteristics, dwellings in the marshy region near the sea-coast, etc. (Tulāsidsa also refers to the Kirāta and Khasa together in the Uttarkanda of his *Rāmacaritamānasa).* However, no clear picture of the subject emerges from the twilight of early history, till we come to the period of the *Mahābhārata.*

The *Mahābhārata*—a semi historical work—is an encyclopaedia of Indian culture and civilization. The kernel of truth embodied in this epic is generally accepted by the history. This epic provides a very faithful account of different aspects of ancient Indian history and culture. Despite, the flight of fancy, allegories, embellishments, exaggerations, etc. in the details provided in the epic, its historical value, to a considerable extent, can't be doubted. From the point of view of a historical study of ancient Indian tribes, this source is immensely useful for us. In this epic a very clear and reliable account of the Kiratas is available. Out of the eighteen Parvas of the *Mahābhārata,* ten[8] are valuable for our purpose. After analysing the data collected from all these Parvas we find that this particular source is. very helpful for throwing light on their origins, antiquity, expansion and settlements in different parts of India, socio-economic conditions, political life, religion and culture, janapadas, kingdoms, principalities, forts, and Nagaras, participation in the Mahabharata war during the time of Bhagadatta of Pragjyotia and their conquest by the epic heroes.

The puranic records comprising both the *Mahāpurāṇas* and the *Up-purāṇas* are the repository of historical information about ancient Indian tribes and races. The composition of some of the original puranas began concurrently with the *Vedic Saṁhitās,* which received their final form later on. Most of the *Purāṇas* in their present recension were finaly compiled like those of the *Rāmāyana* and the *Mahābhārata* in the 5th century A.D. Some of them were completed between 5th and the 11th century A.D. Some old *Purāṇas* can be placed earlier than the Gupta period. The two important phases of the compilation of the Puranic texts are B.C. 600-200 A.D. and 300-600 A.D. Many genuine historical traditions of remote antiquity have been recorded in the Puranic texts. The Puranic accounts, which is the traditional history, contain many useful contemporary historical data. It is true that the traditional accounts, contained in the *Purāṇas* have been vitiated by mythological details, interpolations, exaggerations, the religious bias and other anomalies. However, in spite of many obvious defects, the Puranic texts cannot be regarded as wholly untrustworthy. The Kirātas have been described in different Puranas.[9] The-Purāṇas supply very positive information about different aspects of the life and culture of the Kirātas. They have been described as the peoples, the countries and Janapadas of the eastern, northern or Uttarapatha, southern, western and mountainous regions of India. We also get glimpse of their association with other contemporary cognate tribes. The sources concerned are also helpful for highlighting their settlement" patterns, identification, expansion, manners and practices, kingdoms, principalities, religions and cultures, the impact of the Bhagavat cult on them in the Puranic age and subjugation by contemporary rulers. One of the popular Up-purāṇas known as the *Kālikā Purāṇa* provides us with valuable information abcut the war of the Kirātas with mytho-historical king, Naraka in Prāgjyotiṣa situated on the eastern fringe of Bharatavarṣa and the subsequent changes which took place in their history and culture.

The Buddhist texts written in the Pāli language and finally compiled in the second century B.C. and the Jaina canonical texts written in Prākṛit and finally compiled in the sixth century A.D. also contain some references to the Kirātas. The Buddhist Pāli texts, *Sasanavanisa Himavantapadesa, Apadāna* (11. 358-9), two Pali commentaries-*Sumangala-Vilāsini* on *Digha Nikāya* (1.176) and *Sāmmoha-Vinodani* on *Abhidhamma Pitaka* (388)[10]—and *Milinda-Panha* (IV.8.94)[11] composed by Buddhist scholar Nagasena before C. 400 A.D. in a more or less dialectical Sanskrit preserved in a Pali recension refer to Cinas and Kirātas as Sub-joined. Malalasekera[12] refers to the language of the Kirātas. The *Lalita-Vistara* proves the Kiratās' knowledge of writing. This text deals with some aspects of Palaeography. The Kirātas find mention in the Pali commentaries as a tribe and people living in the forests. The Pali texts on the whole are very useful for throwing some light on the identification, settlements, expansion in the north-east and north-west, dialect, language, etc. of the Kirāta. The reference to the Barbaras and the Kirāta in the *Mahābhārata* (XII. 207.43) can be corroborated by the Buddhist text *Apadāna.* Because, this text also speaks of Cinas and Barbaras. The Barbaras associated with the Kirātas have been placed in the *Mahābhārata* in the Uttarapatha along with the Yavanas, Kambojas and Gandhara.

The Jaina canonical texts mention the 'Ciratas' (which fairly corresponds to the Sanskrit and Pāli Kirātas) as a people without furnishing any details about them. The text, *"Jambud-vipa-Prajñapatih"* (also known as *"Jambudiva-Pannātti"*), one of the twelve sub-canonical texts (Upānga Granth) of Svetā-mbara sect, composed by Āchārya Amitgati in the first half of the llth century A.D. in the Puranic fashion is also helpful for our purpose, to a considerable extent. It supports the epic and the Puranic statements about the subject concerned.

The secular literature comprising the Dharma-Sūtras and Smrtis popularly known as Dharmaśāstras also deal with the subjėct-matter. The *Manu Smrti* or *Mānava-dharmaśāstra* (B.C. 200-100 A.D.)[13] refers to the Kṣatriya origin of the Kirātas, which has sparked off a lot of controversy among the scholars concerned. This text, no doubt contains some interpolated verses which creates sometimes unavoidable confusion. The Aryan and non-Aryan foreign races have been inextricably mixed-up in this text which creates scope for misinterpretation of the subject. However, it can't be denied that the statements recorded by Manu contain some substratum of historical truth. In order to extract the truth from the verses of this text the logical interpretation is very essential. Further, there are some other literary sources, which confirm the statements of Manu. T.W. Rhys Davids has aptly remarked that "The puzzles of Indian history have been solved by respectable men in Manu and the Great Bharata, which have the advantage of being equally true for five centuries before Christ and five centuries after".[14]

The *Vedavyāsa Smṛti* (100 A.D.-300 A.D.)[15] provides a brief description of the Kirātas with particular reference to their position in the society. They have besn described along with other groups of people as the Śūdras, Thus we find that the Kirātas did not escape the notices of the Smṛtikāras.

The *Ashtādhyāyi* of Pānini (500-400 B.C.) and the *Mahābhāsya* of Patañjali (184 – 148 B.C.-100 A.D.) are also of considerable importance particularly for the purpose of confirming some of the literary and classical data. The Vasāti tribe of Pāṇini (IV. 2.53) and Patañjali (IV. 2.52) can be identified with the Basatai of *Periplus* which include the Kirātas too. Pāṇini had some knowledge of the ethnic distribution of the population in the North-western India. Like the classical scholars he has also described the tribes and other people of North-western region. He also refers to the Barbaras (IV. 3.93) who are generally associated with the Kirātas. The Barbara-

Kirātas are supposed to have settled in the North-westein region in remote antiquity.[16] Thus for the purpose of identification, confirmation, etymological meaning and transliteration of some appellations occurring in the literary and classical records the aforesaid sources can be profitably used. The value of geographical and historical information supplied by both Panini and Patanjali cannot be underestimated.

Kautilya's *Arthaśāstra,*[17] which was compiled in the fourth century B.C., provides reliable information about the physiognomical features, settlements, the military qualities, and the status of the Kirātas during the age of the Mauryas.

The *Nātyaśāstra* of Bharata Muni[18] (200 B.C.-200 A.D.) one of the rare sources, specifically deals with the Prakrt language of the Kirāta. He has focussed on the Prākrt Group of language spoken by various tribes like Bāhlikas, Khasas, Shabaras, Abhiras, the tribes of north-western zone and other forest tribes. This text has also used the Barbara-Kirāta together. This source provides some clues about the languages poken by the Barbara-Kirātas inhabiting north-western region.

The information contained in the Sanskrit literature of the post-Christian era are not only copious but also very valuable from the historical point of view. The works of especially Kālidāsa, Viśākhadatta, Dandin, Varāhamihira, Bharavi, Amarasiṁha and Banabhatta are worthy of our attention so far as the treatment of the subject in historical perspective is concerned.

Kālidāsa (c. 380–413 A.D.), who was the most brilliant luminary in the literary firmament of the Gupta Age and adorned the court of Chandragupta II Vikramaditya of Ujjain, combined in himself the qualities of a poet, a geographer and a historian. He has presented a very authentic account of various peoples and the tribes living in different parts of India. In his three famous works known as the *Kumārasaṁbhava*[19] *Raghuvaṁśa*[20] and *Vikramorvasiyam*[21], he has dealt with some of the significant aspects of the history of the Kirātas. In the *Kumārasaṁbhava,* the Kirātas have been described as wild tribe living in the hills, mountains and forests. They have been classed as the mlecchas. Their characteristic physical feature, dress, manners, habits, etc. also find reflection in this work. The *Raghuvaṁśa* furnishes very interesting details about the subject. The dealings of king Raghu, the great conqueror, with the ferocious and barbarous Kirāta tribes in the northern Himalayas, the battle between the former and the mountain tribes and other episodes have been elucidated by Kilidasa. The Kirātas have been associated with Sabaras, Pulindas and other mountain tribes as Mlecchas. The Kirātas have been incidentally refered to also in the *Vikramorvasiyam*. But details are lacking. Historically speaking, this work suffers from lack of clarity. Hence, its contents are not of much use for us.

The *Mudrārākṣasa* of Visākhadatta (placed between 5th and 6th century A.D.), a historical play, is very important source of information about the Kirātas of the Maurya age. Scholars difer widely about the data of composition of this play and the place which its author belonged to. Some are of the opinion that this play was composed during the time of Pallava King Dantivarman (779-830 A.D.) and some hold that it was written during the time of Maukhari king, Avanti-Varman (580 A.D. to 600 A.D.). It is not possible to suggest a definite date about its composition because of absence of any positive evidence and lack of unanimity among the scholars concerned. However, this play may tentatively be placed between 6th and 7th century A.D. It will be out of place to discuss whether Visakhadatta belonged to Gauda country or he was contemporary of Chandragupta Vikramāditya and Kālidāsa. Any way, this is the only source which has highlighted the role of the Kirātas in the early annals of India during the Maurya period. The part, which they played as a warrior and political ally of Chandragupta Maurya in overthrowing the Nanda dynasty and the ascendancy of the former as a ruler of Magadha, has been illustrated in this play.[22]

Dandin (500 – 650 A.D.), who flourished as Court poet of the Pallava King of Kanchi, in his historical work *Daśakumāracarita* has trasmitted very valuable information about the Kirātas. He is credited with having presented an intelligible account of the subject matter. The Brahmanhood of the Kirātas living in the heart of Vindhya forest and the impact of the Brahmanical culture on them, their Āryan origin, which vindicates the theory of Manu, religion, culture, social system, etc. have been trophicilly described in this source.[23] This information of exceptional importance has not attracted the attention of any scholar so far, who has, particularly, dealt with the subject concerned.

Varāhamihira, ascribed to the 5th century A.D., has frequently referred to the Kirātas in his famous astronomical work *Bṛhatsaṁhitā*[24] devoid of any explanation. Kern in his translation of this work[25] has placed them in both north-east and north-west.

Bhāravi (who is ascribed to Śaka 556 or 634 A.D. as testified to by the Aihole Inscription of a Chalukya Prince Pulakes in II of South, found in one Jaina temple of Aihole village mentioning his name along with Kālidāsa)[26], in his *Kirātārjunīyam*[27] supported by Mallinatha (14th century A.D.) mentions the Kiratas as low born mountaineers and foresters of the Himalayas with particular reference to the combat of Arjuna with the God Śiva in the disguise of wild mountaineers, who were no other than the Kiratas.

Amarasiṁha, who flourished in the 6th century A.D,[28] in his very popular work *Amarakośa*[29] has given a very satisfactory explanation of the racial characteristics and ethnological features of the Kirātas. This source helps us to examine the correctness of the statement relating to their identification with the mlecchas and non-Āryan races like other ethnic groups and cognate tribes.

Bānabhatta, who fluorished as a Court poet of Harṣavardhana (606–647 A.D.) and belonged to the School of Dandin and Subandhu, in his work *Kādambarī*[30] has dwelt upon some important aspects of the subject concerned. In this source a reliable historical account of the battle between the Kirātas of the northern Himalayas and the Prince named Candrapida of the celebrated city of Ujjain during the course of his expedition, the subjugation of the former, the urban life of the Kirātas, their expansion up to the northern boundary of the Bhāratavarsa, settlements in the vast forest extending up to the mountain Kailāśa in Tibet, etc. have been illuminated.

The early medieval literature also deals with the subject to some extent. *Rājataraṅgini*[31] of Kalhana, the chronicler of Kashmir and the first celebrated historian of ancient India between A.D. 1140 and 1150, mentions Kirātas as associated with some other aboriginal tribes living in the Vindhya hills and Rajputana. Their settlements and expansion in the Himalayan region can be proved by this source.

The *Subhāsitavali* of Vallabhadeva of Kashmir (not earlier than the 15th century A.D.) describes the Kirātas as degraded mountain tribe, who lived mostly by hunting. The *Vijyāditīkā* of Sumati and Hemacandra's *Abhidādnacintāmanipariśiṣṭa* (1088–1172 A.D.) have also slightly touched the subject.

The Tantra literature of early and late Medieval period is also very useful for our purpose. In the list of fifty-six countries enumerated in the *Sammoha Tantra* (composed before 1450 A.D. according to Gode) the Kirātas figure along with the Bāhlikas, Kambojas, Videhas, Kosalas, Kuntalas, Surasenas,. etc. The settlements of the Kirātas in the Madhya-desa and north-west can also be confirmed by this source.[32] The same list of fiftysix countries has also been incorporated in the *Śaktisaṅgama Tantra,*[33] which fairly describes the Kirātas. country extending from Tapta-Kunda and Rama-Ksetra as far as the Vindhyas.

The *Yogini Tantra,* composed sometime between the late sixteenth century and the middle of seventeeth century, is another important Tantric text, which depicts the Kirātas' war with Naraka in Prāgjyotisapur, their faith in the cult of Mother Goddess or Śāktism, and other religious practices at Kāmākhyā or Yoginipitha, etc. The socio-religious life of the Kirātas inhabiting the Kāmākhyā region (situated in the modern Gauhati) in the ancient times can be described to some extent with the help of this source.[34]

The *Hevajra Tantra* of the Buddhist (composed shortly before 693 A.D.), *Bṛhannilatantra, Rudrayamala Tantra* (composed earlier than 1052 A.D.), *Kularnava Tantra, Kubjika Tantra* (composed sometime between the 7th and the 9th century A.D.), *Prānatosini Tantra, Jnānārnava Tantra* (similar in contents to *Tantracudāmani and Brahmānanda's Saktānandatarangini)* and the *Tantrasāra* (a Tantric encyclopaedia composed little earlier than circa 1600 A.D. or in the first half of the seventeenth century A.D.) by Krishnananda Āgamavāgtśa are important for dealing with the Sakti cult of the Kirātas of eastern India and the Vindhyan region.

The *Jyotiṣtatvam,* an astronomical literature, is not less important than the similar category of works. This source describes the Kirāta as a part of Tibet, which needs further classification and elaboration.

In addition to the above-mentioned Sanskrit, Pāli and Prākṛt literature we have some Kannada literature, which deal with the subject matter to a considerable extent. The class of literature ranging between the tenth century and the sixteenth century A.D. supplies miscellaneous information about the life of the Kirātas in Karnataka and outside during the Medieval Age.

A well known Kannada writer Abhinava Pampā iṇ his work called *Vikramārjunavijaya* or *Pampā Bhāratā*[35] (Śaka 863–A.D. 941) shows the activities of the Kirātas as the messengers or duta of Yudhiṣṭhira during the epic period.

In an equally celebrated work called *Pampā Rāmāyana*[36] by a later writer named Abhinava Pampa (12th century A.D.), the Kirātas' location in the Vindhyas, their role as a warrior class during the time of Raudrabhuti, a Mleccha king of the Vindhya forest etc. have been clearly described. The said Mleccha king of the Vindhya forest with the help of the countless army of the Kirātas won laurels of victories in several battles fought against his political adversaries.

Nijaguṇāvogi, a Kannada Lexicographer of the later times, in his work *Viveka-Cintāmaṇi*[37] mentions a Kirāta kingdom. Also a noted Kannada poet Virabhadraraja (circa-A.D. 1530) describes briefly the Kirāta women.[38] The incidental notices of the Kirātas can also be found in some other works like *Linganna Kelādinṛpavijaya,* etc.

The conspectus of the literature belonging to different categories and ages, as discussed above, give us the impression that for the purpose of restoring several missing links in our knowledge about the tribal history of ancient India, we can safely depend on them to a considerable degree. The judgment, which is pronounced about the historical authenticity of the data contained therein without thoroughly examining them, proves to be misleading and sometimes results in great academic loss. Therefore, only an objective historical study of the sources concerned prove their utility.

Archaeological Evidence

The importance of an archaeology as one of the reliable sources of history of ancient India need not be overemphasized. The epigraphic, numismatic and monumental evidences help us a lot in corroborating the literary account, determining the chronology of kings and rulers and episodes and events and throwing light on various obscure aspects of ancient Indian history. The reconstruction of history in the true sense of the term largely depends on archaeological data. So far as the study of present subject is concerned, we don't have any archaeological evidence other than the epigraphic records, which directly or indirectly deal with the subject.

Epigraphical records or inscriptions constitute very important part of archaeology. Their value as contemporary documents of unimpeachable character can't be denied. They form the firm foundation on which the edifice of history of ancient India can be further built-up. Inscriptions engraved on rocks, stone pillars, copper-plates, temple walls, etc. are of various types and forms. The Kiratas figure in various kinds of inscriptions, which fall under the different headings, notably, religious and didactic, votive or dedicative, donative, commemorative, eulogistic and copper-plate grants, charters, records, etc. They were written in different languages such as Prakrit, Sanskrit and various other regional languages. The earliest inscriptions were recorded in the Prakrit language in the 3rd century B.C The adoption of Sanskrit as a popular medium of epigraphy commenced in the second century A.D. and became widespread in the fourth and fifth centuries. Nevertheless, the use of Prakrit was not totally discarded, and hence it flourished simultaneously with the Sanskrit and retained its value as an epigraphic medium during the period concerned. The eighth and ninth centuries virtually marked the beginning of regional variations, so far as the composition of inscriptions from the linguistic point of view is concerned. Inscriptions in its early phase were carved on rocks and stones, but in the early centuries of the Christian era copper-plates, by and large, took the place of the former. However, the well-established practice of engraving inscriptions on stone continued, even in post-Christian era, particularly in South India.

The oldest epigraphic record, though dealing indirectly with the subject-matter, belongs to Aśoka and is ascribed to the third century B.C. From the Rock-Edicts found at Girnar in Kathiawar in the west, Kalsi near Dehra Dun, Yerragudi in the Kurnool district, Shahbazgarhi near Peshawar, etc. it appears that the forest tribes living within the conquered territories of Asoka were treated very sympathetically. Asoka tried to bring them within the pale of Buddhism through his missionary zeal. We do not find any valuable information in Asoka's inscriptions about the subject dealt with here. However, depending on the authority of B.M. Barua;[39] we can't afford to neglect the historical value of Asoka's inscriptions in context of an historical study of the tribal people of ancient India. He states that the said inscriptions provide some clues about the nature, manners and habits of the Kirātas living in the Uttarapatha or Northern India. Their expansion towards north-western India can, of course, be substantiated by this epigraphic evidence. Here we also find some glimpse of their affinity with other Himalayan tribes, particularly the Pulindas living in the Vindhya forest. Some specimen of Asokan inscriptions were discovered in the valley of Nepal,[40] which hint at the impact of Buddhism on the Kirātas of Nepal. Aśoka is believed to have visited the valley of Nepal during the time of Sthunka, the fourteenth Kirātas king of Nepal, and contemporary of the former. The details of the said inscription are not available. However, the visit of Asoka to Nepal has been supported by some authorities[41] on the subject. The inscriptions of the post-Asoka period are the principal source of our information regarding the socio-religious and cultural history of the Kirātas.

We have two inscriptions of the Suṅga period, which supply some positive information bearing on the history and culture of the Kirātas. The Hathigumpha cave inscription of King Kharvela of Kalinga (a contemporary of the Suṅgas) dated first century B.C., which was obtained from Udayagiri on the Kumari Hill located in Bhuvaneswar (Orissa) refers to the Cinas and Kirātas.[42] This inscription was composed in Sanskrit language with Brahmi script. The line of the said inscription, which is useful for our purpose, does not convcy thc complete sense because of the effacement of some words sub-joined with the Kirāta. A considerable portion of this inscription has not been properly deciphered. Notwithstanding, it reflects the truth that the Kirātas were living peacefully during the time of Kharvela enjoying his patronage.

One of the stone railings enclosing the Great Stupa of Sanchi bears the following inscription : "Chirātiya-bhicchu-nodanam,"[43] which cammemorates the visit of Kirāta Monks or Bhiksus to this place. Their faith in Buddhism finds expression in it. It was also donative in nature. According to established practice, sometimes pieces of land were given and sometimes cash endowments were made to the Bhiksus for their maintenance.

The aforesaid two inscriptions of the Suṅga period (185-73 B.C.) present a picture, however gloomy and imperfect it may be of the socio-religious life of the Kirātas. They supply very valuable material on the whole, for the centuries preceding the Christian era.

In one of the Nāgārjunakonda inscriptions of the Iksvāku king, Virapurusadatta (successor of the Satavahanas), ascribed to the 3rd century A.D., which was found on the right bank of the Krishna river in Andhra Pradesh, the Cilātas, fairly corresponding to the Kiratas, have been associated with the Cinas, Yavanas and other tribes.[44] This inscription records that the Kiratas along with other tribes came within the pale of Buddhism. They embraced the doctrine of Buddhism after being profoundly influenced by the Buddhist teachers. This fact can be substantiated by the regular visits of the Kiratas to Nagarjunakonda, important seat of Buddhist culture, to attend the religious discourses of the Arhats.[45] Perhaps this is the inscription which H.D. Sankalia has also referred to in his two important works.[46] Because, we find that he has candidly stated that the Kirātas and the Nisadas occur in an inscription, ascribed to the 2nd century A.D. However, he has not provided any details of it.

The above inscription is of great historical value for us. Because, it helps us not only in confirming the literary description of the Cinas-Kirātas, but also understanding their religious faith and approving their expansion in the south during the Sātāvahana and Post-Sātāvahana periods.

Apart from the early inscriptions dealing with the subject, we have some other inscriptions too, which can reasonably be considered very important source of our information regarding the political and cultural history of the Kirātas.

In one of the old Cham Inscriptions of Champa in Indo-China the Kirātas have been associated with Vrlah race of Champa ("Vṛlah-Kirāta-Vita")."[47] The information derived from this inscription is of considerable importance. It shows the expansion of the Kirātas from Central India, as far as, Cochin China.

Some Sanskrit inscriptions of Arakan supply valuable evidence as to the milieu for Brahmanisation and Indianisation of the Kiruta people of north Arakan and Chittagong before the dawn of the eighth century as stated by E.H, Johnston.[48] A number of Sanskrit inscriptions going back to the middle of the 1st Millennium A.D. gives the impression that north Arakan, the abode of the Kiratas, was the eastern most outpost of India.

The Pandukesvar Copper-plate inscription or the charters and Grants of Lalitasura (middle of the 9th century) and the Grants of Padmata (middle of the 10th century), both of the Kumaon-Garhwal region have been addressed to the Kirata people, the Khasas, the Dravidas and others.[49] These two inscriptions also testify to the settlements of the Kiratas in v Garhwal-Kumaun region.

In an old city of Kiradu, now in dilapidated condition with its twenty-seven temples, situated within the Jodhpur State in western Rajasthan (near the Railway station of Khadin on the Jodhpur-Barmer line) an inscription of Sarhvatera-1235 found in the Siva temple, refers to Kirādu which stands for the Kirātakupa (wells of Kirāta) of Kirāta Kuta (Kirāta hillock). The city of Kirādu is hallowed by its association with the Kiratas in the past. It is commonly believed that the name Kirādu itself stands for the Kirātas. This inscription reveals the truth that they had expanded towards Rajasthan also.

One of the Pandukesvar inscriptions[50] provides a glimpse of the kingdom of princely Kirātas (Raji-Kirātas) or the Kirātas of 'Rajya' *(i.e.* Kumaon and Karttikeyapur). This inscription proves the existence of the Kirāta kingdom as well their settlements in Garhwal and the Kumaon region.

Line-21 of the Allahabad Pillar Inscription of Samudragupta (c. 335-380 A.D.)[51] gives us some idea of the subjugation of the chiefs of the atavika-rajyas or forest states by him.

Balaghata plate of Prithvisena II *(c.* 470-490 A.D.)'[52] a ruler of the Vakataka dynasty of the Deccan and two other inscriptions of Pratihara rulers of Northern India : the Gwalior inscription of Nagabhatta—II (c. 805-833 A.D.) or Sagar Tal inscription of Mihira Bhoja (c. 836-885 A.D.)[53] and Bhaturya inscription of Rajyapala (c. 991-1018 A.D.)[54] bear witness to the victories of the rulers concerned over the Kiratas and their subjugation by them.

The stone inscription of Yaśovarman (c. "25-752 A.D.)[55] of Kanauj shows the extension of his political sway over the Kirātas of the Vindhya region as well as the nature of their habitations.

Some of the Kannada inscriptions falling in between the 8th and 17th century A.D. are also very important for the study of the later Kirātas in ancient India. Actually, they are the trustworthy contemporary records of the south, The Kirātas distinctly figure in the annals of the ancient Karnataka kingdoms, the Pallava records, etc. of the south. The details of inscriptions concerned are highlighted below.

A Grant of Ganga king Sivamara-I dated A.D. 713 records the praise bestowed on the Kirāta women in the palaces of kings.[56] This is of eulogistic nature.

An inscription dated A.D, 973 ascribed to king Satyavakya Konguni Varma Dharmamaharaja of the Ganga dynasty, records the dwellings of the Kiratas on the outskirts of the Vindhya forest in the tenth century and their destruction by the said Ganea King. This also reveals that inspite of being vanquished and subjugated by the Ganga king they continued to survive there till the 12th century.[57]

A record dated A.D. 943 of the Pallava king Diliparasa of Kanchi shows that Nolambadhiraja or Nolambavadi rulers conquered some of the Kirata kings.[58]

From the record dated A.D. 1007 it appears that the great Chola king Rajaraja Deva destroyed the race of hill-chiefs.[59] This document makes a vague reference to the episode concerned.

An inscription dated A.D. 1117 records how Punisa, the most famous general of the greatest of the Hoysala kings, Visnuvardhana Bitti Deva, ousted the Kirāta chiefs and gave protection to some of them who were left with no power.[60]

The Grant of Virabhadra Nayaka dated A.D. 1641 reveals how his grandfather (A.D. 1582-1629) came into conflict with the Kirātas and thereafter, how the latter penetrated into the kingdom of Keladi. The Keladi rulers and Mysore rulers are believed to have vanquished the Kirātas.[61]

Venkatapa Nayaka, Keladi ruler and his grandson Virabhadra Nayaka inflicted a crushing defeat on the Kirātas. Then the celebrated monarch of Mysore named Cika Deva, grandson of Campa Raja, won over the Kirātas after having defeated them in several battles as described in an epigraphic record dated A.D. 1680.[62]

On the testimony of the above epigraphic records it can be pointed out that during the period extending from the eighth century to the 16th century the Gaṅga kings, the Pallava, the Chola and the Hoysala rulers the Keladi and Mysore rulers were very much hostile to the Kirātas. Over and above, these records also confirm the settlements of the Kirātas in the Vindhyas, their existence in the different parts of the south during the period concerned, establishment of kingdom, their repulsion, expulsion and destruction by the southern rulers, etc. They received blows after blows from the soutern rulers which caused their annihilation in the south and proved to be the chief reason for their disappearance from the pages of south Indian history.

The inscriptions from Nepal are important for the study of the Kirātas living in Nepal of hoary antiquity. The five line inscription engraved on a long slab of stone forming a part of the platform of Degutale temple in the Hanumandhaka palace complex contains very valuable information about the Kiratas concerned. It was composed in late Brahmi script of northern variety belonging to 7th century A.D. The translated passage of the inscription reads as follows : "Kirāta Varṣadhara and Chirantanam Licchavirāja Karitam Purātanabritti bhuja rupeksam".[63] This belongs to the age of Ansuvarma, (placed between the latter half of the 6th century and 1st half of the 7th century), the most prominent ruler of the Licchavi dynasty. This particular inscription constitutes a monumental evidence to the dynastic rule of the Kiratas in pre and post Licchavi period.

There are some inscriptions of the Licchavi period which help us to fix the chronology of the Licchavi rulers with regard to their relations with the Kirata kings. Apart from it there are some additional information which can be derived from other documents bearing on our subject.[64] However information suppplied by this category of inscriptions seems to be meagre.

An over all assessment of aforesaid inscriptions give us an impression that a large section of the Kirāta people living in northern, central and southern India had maintained an indigenous culture, which can be fairly attested to by their socio-religious and political conditions. The theories propounded by anthropologists and historians relating to the general identification of the Kirātas of India with so-called "Tibeto-Burman Mongoloids" can be disapproved of with the help of some epigraphic evidence. Further, the data obtained from the literary sources can also be supplemented by inscriptions. The high degree of historical importance of epigraphy has been widely acknowledged. Its utility can best be explained by the fact that the validity of the literary evidence after being supported by an archaeological data becomes unquestionable.

Foreign Accounts

(a) Classical (Greek & Roman) Accounts : The contribution made by classical geographers and historians to the discovery of ancient Indian history and culture can't be underestimated. They have bequeathed to posterity the most comprehensive and

faithful records of history, geography, ethnography, archaeology, etc. of ancient India. These texts throw a good deal of light on the obscurity of early Indian history. Significantly enough, several voids in the recorded history of ancient India can be filled in with the materials contained in the classical sources. For better result, a comparative study of both the literary and classical sources and harmonization of the contents of both in respect of identification of place names, tribal people etc. seem to be indispensable.

The classical tradition about India dates back to the sixth century B.C.

The first Greek historian as well as geographer to speak clearly of the races of north-western India was Hecateus (Hekataios) of Miletus (B.C. 549-486). In his geographical work, "*The Periodos Ges*" he mentions Kalatiai or Kallatiai[65] along with other tribal people, who were living on the frontier hills. The Kalatiai can etymologically be identified with the Kiratas living on the upper Indus. The picture presented by him appears to be very faintish. His knowledge did not advance beyond the region extending from the frontier of the Persian empire to the Indus and Gandhar. However, his attempt proved to be a milestone for the classical scholars immediately posterior to him. His findings influenced the writings of his successors for more than a century.

The writings of Herodotus (B.C. 484-431) heralded the dawn of a new age in the classical history of India. He refers to Kallatiai or Kalantiai[66] who were perhaps no other than the Kiratas. They were living along with other hill-tribes in the Kabul valley. He also refers to their social life, nomadic habits, etc. The Marsh-dwellers beyond the Persian frontier mentioned by him, in all probability were the Kiratas living in large numbers in a vast territory stretching from Bactria and its adjoining countries to the Indus. A considerable portion of his account seems to have been drawn from Hecateus, who was his source of information. His knowledge, as it appears was most vague and meagre and did not go beyond the remotest povinces of the Persian empire towards the east. However, the accounts of both Hecateus and Herodotus confirm the settlement of the Kiratas in north-western region.

The writings of the classical scholars of post-Herodotus, period, go to widen the horizon of our knowledge of the subject concerned. Ktēsias the Knidian was the first classical writer to present a treatise on India in the true sense of the term. In his *Indika*[67] (compiled in 398 B.C.) the distinctive physical features, the life-style, pattern of settlement, socio-political life, manners, habits, the actua) position of habitation, etc. of the Kiratas find reflection.[68]

Scholars have cast doubt on the historical authenticity of Ktesias' narratives concerning India for several reasons. He has been stigmatized as a fabulist and a liar. He is believed to be a writer of unscrupulous mendacity. His account is so abridged and incomplete that it is not possible to make full use of it. He had acquired a second hand knowledge about India during the course of his stay for seventeen years (B.C. 415-397) in Persia as private physician to king Artaxerxes. He has in most cases repeated those statements which he heard from the Persians, who themselves had received from the Indians, who sojourned in their country. Thus, he received the information about the aboriginal tribes of India not directly from the Indians themselves but from the Persians. That is why,, most of his statements have turned into palpable exaggeration. Some of the fictions of his own invention have got intermixed with what he borrowed from others. The special significance of his narrative does not lie in the isolated elucidation of Indian antiquity but in the fact that he communicated to his. countrymen the mass of knowledge about India and presented a first written account on the geographical science relating to India before the time of Alexander. It was left to the geographers and historians who followed Alexander to give to the world a fairly accurate account of the country and its inhabitants.

After having gone through the contents of Ttesian's *Indika* very minutely and analysed the data obtained therefrom, we find that some useful information about the Kirata can be derived from this source. This writer, however, is not, at all, untruthful, when he says in the conclusion of his *Indika* (33) that "he omits many of these stories and others still more marvellous, that he may not appear to, such as, have not seen these to be telling what is incredible, for he could have described many other fabulous races."[69] Anyway, in spite of some contribution, whatsoever it may be which he has made to the subject discussed here, he can't be acquitted of accusations of mendacity, which have already been heaped on him both by classical and non-classical authors. But in any case it is not possible to subscribe to the view of E.R. Bevan, who has observed that the contribution made by him is the "most worthless of all those which went to make up the classical tradition."[70]

The name of Megasthenes stands the foremost in the galaxy of later Greek writers, who made substantial discovery about ancient India. The account of India, presented by him from his personal knowledge of the country which he visited for about five years sometimes between B.C. 305-298 as a Greek ambassador, sent by Seleucus to Chandragupta Maurya, is justly held as invaluable and trustworthy. Unfortunately, it is not exteant in its original form. It has been partially preserved by means of epitomes and quotations scattered in the Greek and Roman writings. Dr. Schwanbeck of Bonn was the first scholar to collect and arrange in the proper order the detached fragments of his original work *"Indika"* and to present them in the form of historical literature by publishing his book *"Megasthenese's Indica."* This source throws light on manifold aspects of the subject.

Megasthenese's Scyritae or Skiratai[71] has been identified with the Kirātas of Sanskrit literature. His account is helpful for making investigation into their origin, physical features, manners, food habits, expansion in India and beyond, etc.

The historical value of Megasthenese's account of India has not been properly judged. He has also been branded as a liar. The foremost amongst those classical authorities who generally discredit his narratives and disparage him are Eratosthenes, Strabo, Pliny and Diodorus. No doubt, his writings bear the stamp of Ktesias style of presentation and conception of India. However, it will not be perfectly justified to rank him almost at par with Ktesias. He can't be considered totally unworthy of credit. He wrote his account on the basis of a first hand knowledge of India, which can be commended for accuracy. The account handed down to posterity by him is in perfect agreement with what we have discovered from

some reliable Indian sources. The fables, which appear in his work were, actually, not deliberately invented by the author, but they originated in fictions current among the Indians, which was taken by him perfectly in good faith. He was misled by some fabricators, as well as, by his own imperfect knowledge of Indian languages. Actually, he synthesized the matters,, which were communicated to him by those Brāhmans, who were the rulers of the State and whose learning and wisdom were held in the utmost veneration. The whole thing came directly, under his observation. Thus, his relative veracity can't be questioned, for he related truthfully both what he actually saw and what was told to him by others. Anyway, it can't be denied that he has greatly mythologized his account of fabulous races.

The work of Megasthenes marked the culmination of the knowledge, which the ancients ever acquired of India. His. work is not only a part of Greek literature and of Greek and Roman learning, but also a rich mine of authentic information about India. The geographical science of the Greek attained afterwards perfect form. The merit of his work lies in the fact that those, who wrote after him on India, borrowed a greater part from his *Indika.* He exercised a powerful influence on the whole sphere of Latin and Greek scientific knowledge.[72]

The geographical work of Strabo (c. 64 B.C.—19 A.D.) of Amasia in Asia minor contains incidental notices of India relating to its geography, ethnology, manners and customs."[73] He has largely drawn the material from the works of the companions of Alexander and from the *Indika* of Megasthenes. So far as the description of races of India including the Kiratas are concerned, he has not added anything to what was already explained by Megasthenes. He entirely depended on the work of Megasthenes for providing a sketch of Kirātas.

The encyclopaedic work called the *Naturalis Historia* by Pliny the Elder (Gaius Plinius Secundus), ascribed to A.D. 23-70 contains numerous references to India, particularly its geography.[74]

This work, which he dedicated to Titus, was given to the world in the year 77 A.D. His "Scyrites" or "Syrictes," no doubt, can be identified with the Kirātas. His description of the Kirātas is mainly based on the *Indika* of Megasthenes. This source is helpful for the study of their physical features, location in eastern side of India near the source of the Ganges in the 4th century B.C. economic activities, etc. Some of the points mentioned by him were not touched by Megasthenes.[75]

The first part of the *Indika*[76] (Chs. I-Xvii) of Arrian. (Flavius Arrianus, a Greek or Hellenised native of Bithynia and official of the Roman Empire during the period, *c.* 130 –172 A.D.) based chiefly on the accounts of Megasthenes, Eratasthenes (B.C. 240) and Nearchos (companion of Alexander and famous for his journal of his voyage) also contain some references to the geography, the races, etc. of India. He has made mistake in determining the position of the "Kirrhadae" (Kirāta).[77] This source is of little use for our purpose.

While making a comparative estimate of Strabo, Pliny and Arrian in terms of reference to the subject-matter concerned, we find that Strabo in his eagerness to make his account entertaining and picturesque and to delight his readers has omitted those part, which would have greatly helped our knowledge of ancient Indian history, Pliny has no doubt written the account of the ancient tribes of India with his usual wonderful diligence, but most frequently he writes with too little care and without any judgment. He gives in his boldest language an ill-digested enumeration of names. He frequently commends Megasthenes but more frequently transcribes him without an acknowledgment. Arrian wrote his account in an agreeable style and with strict regard to accuracy abridging the description of Megasthenes. However, he seems to have given a much less carefully considered account of India.

The Periplus of the Erythraean Sea (first century A.D.)[78] by an anonymous writer is a trustworthy document like the journals of Marco-Polo, Columbus and Vespucci in the field of geographical discovery. This source is of immense value for our present concern. The appellation 'Cirrhadae' and 'Besatae' as referred to in this source have been fairly identified with the Kiratas. For the purpose of determining their location and position in different Himalayan and sub-Himalayan regions,

identifying them with several hill-tribes of north-east India and describing their trade and commerce, origin, settlement, expansion, etc., the careful study of this document is very essential.

Another text, *The Commerce and Navigation of the Erythraean Sea* (Being a translation of the Periplus *Maris Erythraei* and partly from Arian's Account of the voyage of Nearkhos and the *Indika* of Ktesias the Knidian)[79], is singularly important for trade and commerce of the Kirradai (Sanskrit Kirāta).

The treatise on Geography written by Klaudios Ptolemaios, popularly known as Ptolemy (first half of the second century A.D.).[80] is of unique value for our purpose. He has presented an exhaustive account of the tribal people of ancient India including the Kirātas. He has invariably used the term 'Kirradia, 'Kirrhadia' and 'Airrhadoi' for the Kirātas. He has fairly described their expansion and settlements in trans-Gangetic India, Arakan in Burma, north-east India and north-west India extending upto Sogdiana and their trade and commerce, origin, etc. This work is very important particularly, for their identification.

This treatise is of unique value. It may be reckoned as a masterpiece of classical literature. It differs essentially from all the earlier works. Like Megasthenes (who presented a list of 118 tribes) Ptolemy has also presented a long list of tribes, but the treatment of the subject by the latter is far better than that of the former. By applying his encyclopaedic knowledge he has recast the notions of all his predecessors and contemporaries, who were always on the look out for first hand information from the navigators, travellers and traders returning from India and Far-East. He has handed down to us a complete record of the tribes, nations, towns, trade and commerce, ethnology, geographical data, etc. of Eastern Asia.

A great epic poem in hexameter verse called *Dionysiaka* or *Bassarika* composed by Nonnos,[81] who flourished about the beginning of the fifth century A.D. or a century earlier, is the last classical text on the Kiratas. The information supplied by the author of this work is of exceptional value. The expansion of the 'Cirradioi' (used in the text, equivalent to the Kiratas) in the Ariana (the land between north-western India and Persia), Kashmir and some parts of the Sapta-Sindhu region can be irrefutably proved by the evidence furnished in this text. Further the names of their chiefs and their practice of naval warfare in the form of a peculiar system have also been slightly touched. The information is of course, very scanty but its quality is very high.

A critical evaluation of the classical treatises in general reveals certain striking facts. They are, no doubt, of vital importance, so far as the study of the tribal people of ancient India is concerned. We can safely rely on them for making a historical enquiry into the origin, migrations, settlements, expansion, social life, economic institutions and political conditions of the Kirātas in both pre and post Christian era, as well as, their contacts with the Āryans and other ethnic groups of non-Āryan tribes, etc. The importance of their accounts can't be dismissed simply under the pretext that they are the figments of classical imagination. Nor can we accept everything blindly. As a matter of fact, the classical account of India in a broader term is a compendium of both facts and fictions. Actually, it is based on both classical and Indian traditions. However, sweeping generalization will not be the correct medium of their judgment. The classical writers of pre-Alexanderian period, in general, and Megasthenes, in particular, were greatly influenced by the fables, which were communicated to them by the learned Brāhmaṅs with figurative description and some glow of poetic fervour and by the traditions which were not only orally current among them, but also embedded in their imaginative piece of literature. The traditions current among the Indo-Aryans were, in point of fact the means by which they gave a very pointed expression to their proud sense of superiority over tie barbarous indigenous tribes by which they were surrounded. The Indian fables and traditions were absorbed by the early Greek writers which is evident from their own writings. The tradition of presenting the facts with fables continued upto the time of Pliny. In this respect the early classical literature can hardly be

distinguished from the historical literature of the contemporary period. The later Greek writers adopted scientific approach to the problems concerned. Such writers as Periplus and Ptolemy have presented a reliable historical account of the subject. Their writings are marked by accuracy, precision and minuteness. On the whole, the classical source is the storehouse of information on the current subject. The oriental scholarship can be enriched by the classical tradition of writings. In view of the above facts it is not possible to accept the verdict of Strabo that all his predecessors are set of liars, and deserve impeachment. As a matter of fact, he levelled this charge against them out of his apparent bias.

(b) French, German and Chinese Accounts : The subject under notice has also attracted the attention of the French, German and Chinese Scholars. The sources discovered are separately described below.

The accounts provided by the French savants are of great historical value for the purpose concerned. St. Martin[82] in his study of the Greek and Latin geography on India has specifically dealt with the ethnology, antiquity, expansion and identification of the Kiratas as described in classical literature. While referring to different ethnic groups of the Kirātas of upper Gangetic basin, he has focussed his attention on the causes of their shifting towards the Himalayan region. This source is very important for explaining the reason why the Brāhmin Āryans, while pushing their conquest to the east of the Ganges and Jamuna, drove the Kirātas back towards the Himalayas and Vindhyas. For the confirmation of various statements made by Megasthenes in his *Indika,* the study of this particular source has been found useful. He has also commented on the views of Manu about the Āryan origin of the Kirātas. The rare and curious narratives of Foucher[83] are also worthy of our attention. He has supplied very important geographical and historical information in his work on ancient trade routes of India. The settlement of the Kirātas in north-western frontier areas stretching from the Hindukush mountain and Balkh to Afghanistan, their contacts with Āryans in course of the advancement of the latter towards India through north-west, their aggressive nature, etc. can very well be ascertained with the help of this work.

Ronnow Kasten's article *"Kirāta-A study on some Ancient Indian tribe'"*[84] also merits our attention for the graphic description of the origin, migration, settlement, expansion, etc. of the Kiratas inhabiting different regions of India. He deserves the credit for presenting the detailed account of the subject, as well as for critically examining the views of different scholars regarding the "Indo-Mongoloid" theory of the origin of the Kirata. The details appear to be satisfactory. His attempt at presentation of the subject-matter along the scientific lines seems to be crowned with success. His rational and critical approach to the problems is not only worth-appreciating but inspiring too.

Sylvain Levi's work,[85] marked by all its intelligibility, can definitely be taken as reliable treatise on the origin of Indo-Mongoloid tribes of the Himalayan region of north-east India, their migration to Nepal in the post-Bharata war period, invasion of Nepal by the Kirātas of Assam of primeval antiquity, their political and cultural triumphs over Austro-Asiatic and other indigenous tribes and Indo-Aryans of Nepal in ancient times anterior to the 8th century B.C. the outline of the history of their dynastic rule, etc.

In another dependable source[86] Sylvain Levi has provided little data about the Kiratas, which can be used together with the data provided by the *Mahabharata* and Manu. He has categorically mentioned the Kirata in conjunction with Cina, the mlecchas and other races who had fallen to the ranks of the Sudras.

Equally important are the German sources, Lassen in one of his monumental works,[87] which is no less than an antiquarian record, deals with manifold aspects of history of the Kirātas. He has portrayed a vivid picture of their socio-economic life, political condition, religious system, expansion in Bengal, Bhutan, Tibet and other Himalayan belts, dynastic rule in Nepal, contacts with the Aryans in the contemporary age, etc. within a reasonable compass. His review of the classical accounts of India is also remarkable. For his comments on and further explanations and interpretations of the various statements made by the classical authors, notably, Ktēsias the Kinidian and Ptolemy in their respective works, the study of this source either in original or in the form of the extracts extent in the Greek literature is beneficial. His analysis of the data furnished in the Periplus also deserves our notice.

He has made valuable observations on the subject in some of his other works too.[88] While critically examining the validity of literary tradition recorded in the *Mānavadharmasāstra* relating to the Ksatriya origin of the Kiratas, he has reserved his own judgment, as it transpires from his expression. In order to make a deep study of this aspect of the subject the examination of the views expressed by different scholars is absolutely necessary. He has also quoted and supported one passage from the *Rāmāyana* concerning the Kirātas. He also provides a glimpse into the Kiratas of Tipperah (Tripura), Nepal and north-western India. Weber, a popular authority on ancient Indian literature has also dilated on the ancient races as depicted in the *Rāmāyana* and the *Mahābhārata.* His work[89] is no doubt, very important for analysing the data contained in the literary texts about the origin of the Kiratas, as well as, those tribes, who have affinity with them. The races of both the Indian and foreign origins have been discussed by him.

The work of Zimmer,[90] which may fairly be considered authentic one on ancient Indian life, also contains some kernel of historical truth about the Ksatriya origin of the Kiratas. However, the utilization of this source is confined to the discussion on the views of Manu in this regard.

Dr. Buhler's[91] observations and the information contained in other source[92] of general character are important for shedding some side light on the subject in connection with the history of Nepal and the archaic language spoken by some section of the Kirātas.

A treatise on the history of Mongols bearing the title *Gesichte der Ost-Mongolen* translated and edited by I.J. Schmidt, which was origingally written by Senangsatsen, is important only for understanding the general background of the Mongoloid origin of the Kirata concerned.

Few classical Chinese texts are also worthy of mention. The most ancient text *Po-ou-yeo-Jing* translated in 308 A.D. refers to an appellation "Yi-ti-Sai", which is from the Chinese point of view an exact equivalent to the Kiratas. This is an act of transposition. The expression means the barbarous tribes bordering on the north. The other works entitled *Fo-Pen-Hing-tri-Jing* translated in 587 A.D. and *Fang-Guang-ta-Zhao (ta-tchoang) Yen-Jing* translated in 683 A.D. simply give the transcription. *Ki-Lo-to,* which definitely stands for the Kiratas. However, these sources are not much profitable for us because of the lack of details as well as the unintelligibility of the Chinese versions.[93]

(c) *Travellers' Accounts :* The accounts left behind by the Chinese, Ārabian and Venetian travellers are also important for our purpose. They have both direct and indirect bearings on the current subject.

The travels of Chinese pilgrims give some clues about the non-Aryan origin of the so-called 'Mongoloid' Kirātas. Fahien (A.D. 399-414),[94] who visited India during the Gupta period, has made a passing reference to the antiquity of Mongoloid people, generally identified with the Kirātas.

Hiuen-Tsang (A.D. 629-645)[95] who visited India during the time of Harsa, has left behind an elaborate account of India. His account is important only for the purpose of identification of the Kirata people of the hill-areas of north-east India. He has compared the people of hill areas to the east of Kamarupa (Ka-Mo-Lu-Po) with Man and the Lao on the basis of his findings, that these areas touched the south-west of barbarians of China. This is indirect indication about the hill people of Assam, who are known as "Mongoloid" Kiratas. Further, he refers to the people of small stature with dark yellow complexion.[96]

The accounts of both the Chinese travellers are of limited value. However, in context of the identification of the Kiratas of the hill-areas of north-east India with the Mongoloids of China, they have proved to be of some use. In order to ascertain as to how far they area Tribeto-Burman tribes, the examination of the correctness of their statements is necessary.

Alberuni,[97] a celebrated Arabian Scholar, who extensively travelled in India during the time of his patron, Sultan Mahmud of Ghazni (997-1030 A.D.), has referred to the Kirātas along with various countries of eastern India namely, Pragjyotisa, Lohitya, Paundra, Udayagiri and Manipur, as well as, China, Suvaranabhumi etc. in his scholarly work, *Tahqiq-i-Hind* of *Kitab-ul-Hind* primarily based on Indian literature. This particular source is of special significance for determining the actual position of Cīnas-Kiratas, usually referred to in Sanskrit literature conjointly and location of China. With the help of this source as well as other corroborative evidence we can falsify the views of those scholars who have identified the 'Cinas' with the modern China and linked the Kirātas with this part of the world. Actually, the 'Cina' stands for the Chin-Hills bordering Manipur, which can be amply substantiated by the statement made in the translated text. The scholar concerned has used Kirata in conjunction with China and Manipur, Suvarnabhumi and China together in context of using the names of countries of eastern India. This is clear reflection of truth that Cīnas-Kiratas were the Kiratas of contemporary India not the modern China. Hence the evidence furnished in this text constitutes an addition to that of collected from other sources and discussed in the subsequent part in an attempt to lift the curtain of mystery befalling the subject concerned.

The travels of Marcopolo (a Venetian traveller, who visited India in the 13th century) is another valuable source of information about the trading activities of the Kirātas in the frontier eastern Himalayas. This source deals with the Malbathrum, which was the principal article of trade of the Kiratas in the Himalayan region. The graphic description of the subject as provided by Sir Henry Yule,[98] a popular authority on the subject, can profitably be used.

Ibn Battuta,[99] another famous Arabian traveller who visited India in the fourteenth century during the time of Muhammad-bin-Tughlaq has left behind an interesting account about the subject concerned based on his personal experience. While dealing with Indian Archipelago, Bengal, China and 'Thubbat' (Tibet) he has incidentally referred to the origin of the

Indo-Chinese population with Mongolian characteristics. He has used the word 'Kamru', which, no doubt, corresponds to Kāmarūpa.

Some of the above sources have been used merely to show that what are the views of foreign travellers about the origin of the Kiratas, who are sometimes believed to be of Indo-Chinese stock, sometimes Tibeto-Burman and sometime of Mongolian extraction. Actually all these different appellations are used for those tribes, who are the remnants of the Kirāta population. While repudiating the theories relating to the Mongoloid origin of the Kiratas, in general, an attempt has been made to examine the relevance of statements made in such sources. Apart from this the sources concerned are not of much use.

Cecil Bendall's account[100] based on his journey undertaken in Nepal and northern India during the winter of 1884-85 is also of considerable importance from the historical point of view. While dealing with literary and archaeological research in the areas concerned in a broader framework, he has casually mentioned the ancient people of Nepal described in contemporary literature. The literary account, which forms the part of his work, has an indirect bearing on our subject.

Native Chronicles, Genealogical Records and Other Contemporary Accounts

The Buddhist chronicle entitled *Manjuśri-Mulākalpa* (Tibetan-text)[101] ascribed to the 9th century A.D. is very helpful for filling the vacuum in our existing knowledge about the later Kirata rulers of contemporary Nepal.

Another Buddhist text known as *Svayaṁbhū Purāṇa,* apparently composed in its present form in the 15th century describes the Kirātas' settlement in the Himalayan mountain especially Nepal. This local purana or chronicle of Nepal is as informative as the *Nilamata Purāna* of Kashmir, so far as the details of local events are concerned. Another Chronicle named *"Itihāsa Prakāsa"*[102] lying in Mrgastbali (Nepal) is very important for the study of the dynastic rule of the Kiratas in Nepal.

The genealogical records or *Vamśāvali* texts, two in Sanskrit probably composed in c. 1350 and other popularly known as

Gopālarājā Vaṁśāvalī[103] a composite work in three parts, partly in Sanskrit and partly in old Newari apparently put together and supplemented in c. 1390 are very authentic records on the Kirātas of Nepal. Both the Vaṁśāvali and *Svayambhū Purāna*[104] tradition trace the rule of the Kirātas in the valley of Nepal to the Kaliyuga era. The Vaṁsāvali tradition records the names of twentynine Kirāta kings. The name of their capital in the early medieval period, the visit of Mauryan emperor Asoka to the valley of Nepal during the time of the fourteenth Kirata king, Licchavi conquest of the Kirātas in the early centuries of Christian era and other interesting episodes directly connected with the history of the Kiratas distinctly figure in the said records.

The *Parbatiy a Vaṁśāvalī*[105] or genealogical history of Nepal is another valuable source of information about the dynastic rule of Kirātas. This text provides both mythological and historical accounts of their rule in Nepal tracing its antiquity from the pre-Bharata war period. The list of the Kirāta kings with little variations from other texts also appear in this source.

There are several discrepancies in the chronicles of Nepal. Such kind of sources are to be used with little bit of caution. They do not tally with each other. In fact, the compilers of the chronicles and Vaṁśāvalis lacked the perfect historical sense. That is why, the reliability of their accounts are always of dubious nature, and, hence, becomes subject of controversy. However, despite being influenced by the ancient Indian historical tradition they did not deviate from the main line of truth. Only the method of the treatment of subject was something different.

The royal chronicle of Tripura known as *Rājamālā*[106] provides a detailed account of the Kirātas, who ruled over Tripura in north-eastern region, known as Kirātadeśa in ancient times, from pre-Yudhiṣṭhira period to the advent of Muslim rule.

In the genealogical chart supplied by this chronicle the names of the Kirāta rulers of Tripura are given. Besides, the text also gives the graphic description of their ancient kingdom, social, political and religious life, etc.

Some scholars have doubted the historicity of this chronicle which docs not strike any wonder. It will suffice to say that every chronicle contains some myths, as well as, some elements of truth. Some Kirata kings as appearing in the genealogical list are taken as fictitious or legendary figures. It is true that some mythical figures appear in the earlier part of the list but on the whole we find it very dependable source. Some Kirāta kings bearing both Mongoloid and Āryanised or Sanskritized names also figure in the list, which definitely points to the fusion of two different cultures, which they represent.

One of the laudable features of this chronicle is that it bears all the marks of antiquity. The description is charming, style of recording the facts is fascinating and materials contained in it are far more trustworthy than that of many contemporary chronicles. Rev. James Long reasonably described it as a "genuine record of the Tippcroh family."[107] D.C. Sircar[108] also observes that the historical basis of its accounts can not be doubted. Its earlier period based on tradition, recorded or unrecorded requires verification from other sources. But the accounts of the period witnessed by the compilers are reliable. Suniti Kumar Chatterji's[109] view that "the historical value of this chronicle is not much for the period prior to the 15th century" is not absolutely incorrect.

After making a general survey of all the sources belonging to different categories as mentioned above we find that the Kirātas have been copiously used in both the Indian and non-Indian sources. In order to get a satisfactory result of our enquiry into the subject under discussion, we shall have to place our reliance on the combined testimony of all these sources. The history of the Kirātas can be reconstructed on the basis of these sources.

Notes and References

1. General Report on the Census of India, India Office, London, 10th July, 1893, p. 122.
2. CCAI., p. 16.
3. *Ibid.,* p. 13.
4. XXX. 16.
5. X. 4. 14.

6. 55.3.
7. 40, 27-28.
8. Ādi Parva, 1, 109; 2, 107; 165. 35-36; Sabha Parva, 4, 21-22; 13, 19 ; 23,17-20; 27, 13; 29, 15 (in some versions 32, 17); 47, 12 ; 48, 8-11; Aranyaka Parva, 40, 2-26, 39-47; 141, 25, 26 & 29; 177, 11-12; Udyoga Parva, 19, 14-15; Bhisma Parva, 10, 49, 55 & 67; 20, 13; Drona Parva, 4, 6 ; also chs. 112 & 119 ; Karoa Parva, 65, 20 ; (in some versions 73, 20); Santi Parva, 65, 13-23; 207, 43; Anusasana Parva, 35, 17-18; Āsvamedha (or Aivamedhika) Parva, 72, 24; 84, 4.
9. Agn: 1, 118, 6; Bhag; II, 4, 18; IX, 20, 30; Bmd; 2, 16, 60; 2, 16, 68; 3, 48-49; 4, 7, 19; 49, 53-55; Brah; 19, 8 & 16; 27, 17, 49, 50 53, 62-64 ; Grd; 55, 5 i HV; II, III, 7-11; 22, 53-54, 58-59; 59, 32-34 ; Kāl: 38 100-47; Kur; 1, 45, 25, & 39; Mark; 54, 8, 40, 44 & 57; 55, 31, 44-45, 49-52; Mat; 114, 11, 34-36, 44, 56-57; 121, 49-54; Pad; II, 27 42-43; 6, 46 & 52; 6, 64; Ch. 19; 218, 8; Skd; 39 127-28; Sv; Chs. 38-41; Vmn; 13, 11, 41-42, 44-46 & 57; Vrh ; 28, 34: Vsn; 2, 3, 8 & 15; Vy; 45, 82, 109-11, 119-20, 123. 135-36; 47, 48-53; 58, 78-83; 98, 106-9 ; Vis. Dh. Mah; 1, 207, 1-4.
10. *cf.* B.C. Law, IEFBJ , pp. 85-86.
11. V. Trenckner (ed.), pp. 331, 337. See also R.D. Vadekar's edition of this text, (Bombay, 1940), pp. 320-21.
12. DPPN., l,p. 607.
13. X. 43-44.
14. *Buddhist India,* Preface, iii-iv.
15. 1. 10-11.
16. V.S. Agrawala, IKP. pp. 63, 455 ; See also his article Geographical Data in Panini's Ashadhyāyl, JUPHS., 1943, Vol. XVI, Pt. 1 and B.N. Puri, ITP., p. 62, F.N. 3.
17. Vāchaspati Gairola (Ed. & Trans.), BK. 1, Prakarana 7. Ch. 11, Vs. 3, p. 33 ; Prakarana 16, Ch. 20, Vs. 1, p. 69.
18. Extract quoted in Vararuchi's *Prakrta Pāakāsa* (5th Cen. A.D.) p. 1 (facing page, 6).
19. Canto—1, VS. 6, 10, 15.
20. Canto-IV. VS. 76-77 ; Canto-16, VS. 19, 57.
21. Act-V, VS. 5, 20-21.
22. Act-ii.
23. UCCHAVASA. 11, pp. 22-24.

24. Ch. V. VS 37, 80 ; Ch. IX, VS. 17, Ch. XI, VS. 60 ; Ch. XIV, VS. 18–30.

25. XIV, 17, 18, 30, pp. 90-92.

26. The *Kirātār juniyam* also finds mention in the copper plates discovered at Gummareddipura, Kolar dated 40th year of King Durvinita, assigned to early part of the 6th century A.D. see Mys. Arch. Repo., 1912, 65-9 ; IA. XLII, 204 ; JRAS., 1913, 389.

27. Canto-XII, VS-39, 82-86 ; Canto-XIII, VS-36 ; Canto; XIV. VS-33-34 45, 63-64.

28. Some scholars suggest that he was one of the nine jewels of Chandragupta Vikramaditya and hence may be considered contemporary of Dhanvantri, Kalidāsa and Varāhamihira. But the date suggested above has been widely accepted by scholars. This can be further proved by the fact Gunaraja. a noted scholar translated the *Amarakosa* in the Chinese language, as stated by Max Muller and supported by a great astronomer, Pt. Girija Prasad Dwivedi in his Essay entitled "Bhattachhir-Swami".

29. ii, 10, 20 ; ii, 4, 143 ; ii, 2, 20.

30. *Purvabhāga,* Ch. III.

31. (a) M.A. Stein (trans.), pp. 71, 417.

    (b) R.S Pandit (trans.), pp. 71, 417.

32. List. 1, V. 5 ; List ii, V. 5 ; ABOR1, Vol. XIX, pp. 184 f.

33. BK. III, Patala-VII *(Satpańcāsddesavibhaga),* VS. 29. This Tantric text is generally assigned to the first quarter of the 18th century A.D. Shree B. Bhattacharyya, the then Director of the Oriental Institute, Baroda assigned this work to a period between 1555 and 1607 or roughly to c. 1581 A.D. But according to other evidences this work was composed sometime between 1581 and 1744 A.D. A copy of the Manuscript of this text Satpańcasaddesavibhaga) was supplied by him for the library of the Asiatic Society (N. 9660). The earliest work containing a list of 56 countries is believed to be the *Chandragarbhasutra* or *Chandragarbhavaipulya,* which was trans. into Chinese by Narendrayasa in 566 A.D. For further details see D.C. Sircar, SGAMI. pp. 75-78, 84, 102. See also 1C. 1941, Vol. III, No. 1.

34. Purvakhanda, Patala—12, v. 6 ; Patala—14, v. 65 ; Uttarakhanda, Patala-IX, v. 13.

35. VII. p. 157 (Rice, Bangalore, 1898).
36. VII, VS.—109-115, pp, 193-95 (Rice, Bangalore, 1892).
37. pp. 423-4 (Bangaloae, 1893).
38. Vide *Narasimacarya Kavicarite,* 11. p. 219.
39. *Asoka and His Inscriptions,* pp. 100-1.
40. Pt. Baldeva Pd.-Mishra, *Nepal Kā Itihasa,* p. 45.
41. See A.K. Warder, IIH. pp. 89-90.
42. El., Vol. XX, p. 72 ; Vasudeva Upadhaya, SAII *(Prachin Bharatiya Abhilekhon Ka Adhyayana),* Vol. II, pp. 271-72, Line—14 ; S.B. Choudhary, ESAI., p. 170. This inscription was edited by K.P. Jayaswal (JBORS., 1917-18, Vol. Ill, pp. 425 f; Vol. VI, pp. 364 f; Vol. XIII, pp. 221 f) and R.D. Banerjee (JBORS., 1917-18, Vol. III. pp. 486 f). For the revised text of the inscription by B.M. Barua, See IHQ., 1938, pp. 461 ff. See also Bhagwanlal Indraji, TICO (Leiden, 1883) Pt. II, Sec. Ill, pp. 152 f. ; IA. Vol. XLVII, pp. 223 f ; XLVIII, pp. 187 f; XLIX, pp. 43 f. The authenticity of its date is not a subject of controversy. D.C. Sircar (SIIHC. Vol. I, p. 209) also confirms its data. According to him the inscription belongs to c. 2nd-1st century B.C.
43. R.D. Banerji, *Lekhamālnnukramanī,* Pt. I. No. No. 210, p. 99.
44. J. Ph. Vogel, Ep. Ind. Vol. XX, Pt. 1, pp. 22 f; D.C. Sircar, SIIHC (1965), Vol. I, Line-1, pp. 234-35 ; also B.C. Law, IETBJ ; pp. 85-86 ; HGAI ; pp. 98-99.
45. El, Vol. XX. Pt. I. pp. 22 ff.
46. (a) PPIP., p. 556.
    (b) *Pre-History of India,* 175.
47. G.E. Gerini, RPGEA., p. 257, No .1.
48. BSOAS., 1943-46, Vol. XI, pp. 357-85.
49. (a) EL, Vol. XXX, pp. 282-83, Vol. XXXI, p. 289. -
    (b) D.C. Sircar, *Indian Epigraphy,* pp. 368-69 ; SIIHC ; Vol. II, pp. 268-70.
50. Atkinson, HG, Vol. II, Pt. I, p. 365.

    Four copper-plate grants were preserved in the temple of Pandukesvar near Badrinath through the kindness of Sir Henry Ramsay. The facsimile of one of the plates was obtained by photozincography from the original.

For the full text of the original one and transliterated passages prepared under the supervision of Shree Rajendralal Mitra. See, *Ibid.,* pp. 473-81.

51. Fleet, CII; III. pp. 13 f.
52. EL, IV. p. 270.
53. El., XVIII, pp. 108, 112 ; D.C. Sircar, SIIHC ; Vol. II, Line-8, pp. 242 and 244.
54. EI., XXXIII, p. 150.
55. EL, 1, p. 131.
56. EC. III, 13, 113, p. 51.
57. EC. II. p 119.
58. EC. XII. SL. 28. p. 92 ; See also Rice, Mysore—A Gazetteer (Revised) I, p. 307.
59. EC. III. TN. 44. p. 76.
60. EC. IV. Ch. 83, p. 10.
61. (a) EC. VII. SI. 2. p. 3.
    (b) R.N. Saletore, EIC. pp. 750-52.
    (c) *Karnataka (Kannada) Historical Review,* 1937, Jan., July, Nos. 1 & 2, Vol. IV., p. 98.
62. Mysore inscriptions, p. 310 ; Rice, *Mysore and Coorg from the inscriptions,* pp. 129-30; See also *Madras Epigraphical Report for the year 1901 and South Indian Inscriptions,* VII. No. 328, pp. 168 ff for general idea.
63. (a) D.R. Regmi, IAN., Vol. I, p. 85, LXXXV.
    (b) ——*Ibid,* Vol. 3, p. 155.
    (c) Dhanavajra Vajrāchārya, LKA., (Kathmandu, V.S. 20 30), No. 91.
64. For Details See Bhagwanlal, Indraji and G. Bhluer, *Inscriptions from Nepal* (Bombay 1885) ; IA ; (JOR.), 1880, (Bombay, 1885), Vol. IX, pp. 163 ff ; R. Gnoli, NIGC. (Rome, 1956), SOR. X. 2 ; Bend all, JLAR. 1984-85, (CUP., 1886), pp. 71-79 ; I.A. 1884 pp. 413, 427 ; Dr. Fleet, CIL, Vol. III, pp. 177 ff.. Dr. Hoernic. JASB., 1889 Pt. I, Synchronistic table. Dr. Buhler's Gundriss, (Ind. Pal.) Table-IV ; Bendall, CBM. Cambridge, Introd. VI and ZDMG., 1882, p. 651.
65. (a) AIM A., p 3.
    (b) AICL. p. XIV.

(c) E.R. Sevan, *India in Early Greek and Latin Literature,* cf. CHI ; Ch. XVI, p. 354. See also C. Muller (ed.), *Fragments of Hecataeus work,* F.H.G.I, 1-31.

66. (a) BK. III. 38 cf. CHI. p. 355.
    (b) AIMA. p. 3.
    (c) Rennell, GSH., Vol. I. pp. 303-426 ;
    See also Bunbury, HAG. I pp. 229 ff and Herodatus' *History* ed., by O. Hude and trans. by G. Rawlinson and Cary.

67. The translation of the abridgement of his *Indika* was made by Photoios and the Fragments of that work were preserved in other writings.

68. AIK. pp. 88-90 ; Fragments 1-2 and iii are also important for his observation. For further details and comments see Lassen's Review of the Reports of Ktesias concerning India translated from his famous work Ind. Ait. (2nd edn. 1874), Vol. II, pp. 641 ff cf. *Ibid,* pp. 66-90 ; C. Muller (ed.), *Fragments of Ctesias's Indica.* pp. 16, 18 ; Wilford. As. Res. Vol. VIII, pp. 331 ff ; IA. Vol. VIII, pp. 150 ff ; For an account of the various fabulous Indian races mentioned by the classical writers and for their identification with races mentioned in Sanskrit See IA. Vol. VI, pp. 133-35 ; AICL. p. 61 ; Dr. V. Ball's views, cf. PRIA., 1883, April, 21, N. 572, p. 277 ; AIMA., (Fragm. XXIX, Strabo XV. I.—57, p. 711) pp. 73-75 (For J.W. McCrindle's Note on Ttēsias the Kinidian's view-points) and Schwanbeck, ML, pp. 8, 68,70.

69. (a) AIMA. p. 25.
    (b) JAS. Burgess (ed.) ; IA. (JOR), (Bombay 1877), Vol. VI, pp. 117, 18.

70. *Op. cit.* p. 356. ; See also H.H. Wilson's *Notes on the India of Ctesias* (Oxford 1836).

71. Fragms. Ms. XXIX, XXX, XV. B. cf. AIMA., pp. 73-75, 80, 173-74, 177-78. The translated and annotated text by J.W. McCrindle is also helpful for examining the credibility of the theory propounded by Ktēsias the Knidian, views expressed by Manu, the information supplied by Pliny and other related matter in this regard. The notes of E. A. Schwanbeck, MI. (Bonn 1846), pp. 16-18, 57-60, 66-70 are also very useful: See also R.C. Jain (ed.), AIMA., pp. XLV, 80, 173, Appendix, 4, pp. 230, 233 ; A collection of the Fragments of Megasthenes contained in C. Muller's *Fragmenta Historicorum Graecorum,* Vol. II, pp. 397-439 is another valuable source.

72. Cf. Schwanbeck, MI, 64-74, 76-77 and IA. 1877, Vol. VI, pp. 118-19.

73. Book XV, Ch. I is devoted to India ; His *Geographica* edited by A. Meineke (Leipzig, 1852-53) and published in 1866-67 and translated into English by H.C. Hamilton and W. Falconer (London, 1854-57 is very authentic text; see also AICL. p. 61, fn. 1 and AIMA., pp. 74, 75 Note.

74. Book-IV, C. 17 (217—C. 21 (23), 21-8-23-11. VII. I. 14-22. The original text ed. by C. Mayhoff (Leipzig, 1892-1909) is also useful.

75. For additional information See AICL. p. 61. F.N.I. ; AIMA, p. 74, 80 ; Schwanbeck, MI. pp. 16 f ; 57 f ; For explanation of positive information supplied by him (VII. 7). See Periplus, pp. 266-67.

76. Book, IV, 1.7.15 is a very important part of the work. The text edtd. byR. Hercher (2nd edn. Leipzig 1885) pp, 1-55 and trans. in English by E.J. Chinnock (London, I893j and J.W. Mccrindle-(AIMA) are important sources.

77. JASB., 1847, Vol XVI, Pt. I, p. 11 ; See also Wilford, *Essay on the Sacred Isles in the West.* cf. As. Res., 1805, Vol. VIII, p. 338 and Vol. IX, pp. 68 ff for comment on Arrian's mistake.

78. pp. 47, 63-65, 253-54, 256, 266-67. 278-79, 281 from the translated and annotated text by W.H. Schoff are of great value. As subsidiary source and for further comments and analysis see James Taylor, Cf. JASB., 1847, Vol. XVI, Pt. I. pp. 4, 10-11 ; Vincent's *Periplus of Erythracan Sea,* Vol. II, pp. 523-28 ; Murray's, *Ency. Geograh.* Pt. I, B.K.I. Ch. II, Sec. XII ; Wilford, As. Res, Vol. VIII, p. 338, Vol. XIV, pp. 391-405 ; *Anonymi (ARRIANINT-FERTUR) Periplus Maris Erythraei* trans. from the text as given in the Latin work *Geographi Groeci Minores* edtd. by C. Muller (Paris 1855) by J.W. Mccrindle cf. JAS. Burgess (ed.), IA. (JOR.) 1879 Vol. VIII, p. 150 ; Bunbury, HAG., 1, 565, II. 166, 658 ; AICL p. 199, fn. 8 ; R.C. Majumdar, CAL, p. 307 and Ammianus Marcellinus, Resgestae (3 Vols. London 1935-39) XXIII. VI.

79. Cf. J.W. McCrindle (translated and annotated), pp. 145, 148-49.

80. AIP. pp. 191-94, 210-11, 221-23, 235 ; See also notes by J. Burgess, cf. *Ibid,* p. 391 ; G.E. Gerini, RPGEA., pp. 28-29, 51-53, 256-57, Table VIII. X. ; R.C. Jain (ed.) ; AIP-192-94, 219, 235, App. 7. pp. 449-50, App. 8 p. 452; JASB., 1847, Vol. XVI, Pt. I, pp. 11-12, 16, 30-33 ; Wilford, *On the Ancient Geography*

of India, cf. AS. Res., 1822, Vol. XIV, pp. 373-470 ; AICL ; (Both complete and abridged text), p. 61 also fn. I ; See also G.P. Singh, *The north-east India tribal races as described in Literary and Classiial Sources,* PNEIHA., First Session, Shillong, 1980, p. 16.

81. Ref. to AICL., p. 199.
82. *Etude Sur La Geographic Grecque et Latine de L' Inde,* pp. 195-97, 327-28, 410-14.
83. *L'ancienne Route de L' Inde,* Pt. II. pp. 184-85.
84. Cf. *Le-Monde Oriental,* 1936, Vol. XXX, pp. 90-170.
85. *Le Nepal Etude Historique d'un Royaume Hindou* (3 Vols., 1905-9), Vol. II, pp. 72-78 is important for us ; See also G.P. Singh." *some newly discovered sources on the History and Culture of north-east India"* PNEIHA, Fourth Session, 1983, pp. 26-27.
86. Sylvain Levi, Jean Przyluski and Jules Bloch : *Pre-Aryan and Pre-Dravidian in India* (translated from French by P.C. Bagchi), Pt. Ill, p. 89.
87. Ind. Alt. Vol. I, pp. 279-85, 441-50, 530-34 ; Vol. II. pp. 555-61, 641 ff ; Vol. III, pp. 38, 235-37.
88. ZFKDM., 11, 40-45, III, 245, See also IA. 1876-77, Vol. VI, pp. 127f; 133f, (249f for Lassen's views) ZG ; p. 128.
89. Ind, Stu. (trans. by Rev. D.C. Boyd), IA. Vol. II ; IA. Vol. IV, pp, 244ff : Vol. VI, pp. 301f.
90. Ait. Leb, 32.
91. *Grundriss,* Ind. Pal., Table IV.
92. ZDMG. pp. 77, 651.
93. The Chinese texts have appeared in Sylvain Levi's work already mentioned in the preceding French Section, but he seems to have not taken proper care of those sources. Because, some of the words have been used incorrectly. For instance he has used the word king instead of Jing. I regret my failure to make the literal meanings of the sources concerned clear, in spite of my best efforts. The Chinese teacher concerned helped me only in correcting the use of some words, which are archaic in nature. Further attempts will be made to enquire about the authenticity of the texts.
94. James Legge (trans.) RBK., pp. 14, 34.
95. Thomas Walters, YCTL, Vol. II, p. 186.

96. BRWW. Vol. II. p. 196.

97. E.C. Sachau (trans.): *Alaberum's India,* Vol. I., pp. 201. 299-303.

98. *Travels of Marco Polo* (trans.) II, XIVI. *Cathay and the way Thither* Vol. IV edited by H. Cordier, Hakluyt Society, (London 1916) is also informative.

99. H.A.R. Gibb (trans.), Ibn-Battuta's *Travel in Asia and Africa,* 1325-1354 (London 1929).

100. JLAR (Oup. 1886); See also HNSK (JASB, LXXII, 1903. pp. 1.32), reprinted as historical introduction in CPMDN (2 Vols. Calcutta 1905-6.).

101. K.P. Jayaswal (tians.), cf. JBORS, Sept. 1936, Vol. XXIII, Pt. III, pp. 211if. The text ed. by Ganapati Sastri (Trivandrum Sanskrit series, 1920), VS. 553-559 is also useful. It mainly deals with the countries of the east.

102. Vol. I, (1955-56) Pts. I & II, pp. 133ff.

103. The three parts of this *Vimsāvali* in the Darbar library Kathmandu was discovered by C. Bendall.

104. Ref. to A.K. Warder, IIH. pp. 89-90.

105. According to the Buddhist recension it was translated by Munshi Shiva Shankar Singh (attached to British Residency, who lived in Nepal for almost thirty years) and Pt. Shri Gunananda (a native of Nepal residing at Patan, whose ancestors have been the compilers of Vaśavali history for many generations). The Original Mānuscript written in Parbatiya with an admixture of Sanskrit and Newari was first in the possession of Prof. Cowell of Cambridge. He as well as Prof. Eggeling (an authority on *Satapatha Brāhmana)* of Edinburg found the history based on Vamsavali very important. Daniel Wright translated this text (Cambridge 1877 and Reptd, Kathmandu, 1972) into English with the introductory sketch of the country and its people with the help of above two oriental scholars as well as his own brother Prof. W. Wright of Cambridge, Pt. Baldeva Pd. Mishra *Nepal Kā Itihāsa.* p. 45) has also maintained that *Parbatiya Vamsnvali* with its Buddhist recension is important document. Pt. Bhagawanlal Indraji (IA, Vol. XIII, pp. 41Iff.) is another authority on the Vamśāvalis of Nepal. His *Some Considerations on the History of Nepal* and James Prinsep's table are also of some use.

106. It is generally believed that the first part of the Chronicle (originally, written in Sanskrit) was compiled during the reign of Dharma Manikya in the 15th century by Durlabhendra, a royal priest and two other Brahmins, Pandits Śukreswara and Baneswara. The second part was compiled during the reign of Amar-Manikya in the 16th century, the third part was compiled during the reign of Govinda Mānikya in the 17th century and the fourth part during the reign of Krsna Manikya in the Second half of the 18th century A.D. in Bengali. This is the oldest specimen of the Bengali composition extant in the fifteenth century. The text was edited by Shree Kaliprasana Sen Vidyabhushana and published in different volumes in different years (Vol. I, 1336 — A.D. 1926; Vol. II, 1337 — A.D. 1927 and Vol. III, 1341 — A.D. 1931, Agartala). This is the text which the present author consulted in the Asiatic Society Library Calcutta. See also Kailas Chandra Sinha, *Rajamala.* Pts. I & II, pp. I ff, 6f.

107. *Analysis of Rājamāla,* JASB., 1850, Vol. XIX, pp. 536ff

108. JASL. 1951, Vol. XVII, Nos. 1.3, pp. 76-80.

109. *Kirāta-Jana-Krti,* p. 131.

BOOK TWO

ORIGINS, ANTIQUITY, IDENTIFICATION, EXPANSION AND COLONIZATION

I

PRELIMINARY REMARKS

An accurate and graphic picture of the origin, migration, settlement and antiquity of any ancient Indian tribe can be obtained only by placing our reliance on the historical, indological, archaeological, anthropological and philological data available to us adopting multi-disciplinary approach to the study of such subject. In our historical investigation into the subject under notice, the *vamsâvali* records and oral tradition of some of the tribal communities are also of great help to us.

The origins and antiquity of the Kirâtas are still veiled in mystery. The rationale of Conventional Classification and explanation of the races of ancient India based mainly on ethnological and philological considerations have not yet been strictly and critically examined by the historians. No correct judgement can be formed in this regard without a deep study of ancient Indian and Classical literature. The careful analysis and logical interpretations of literary data help us to a great extent in delineating the correct picture of the subject.

It is very unfortunate that the Kirâtas like other ancient Indian tribes generally described as aborigines originally having their settlements in the Gangetic plains in Madhya-desa, in the wild tracts on the banks of different rivers and their tributaries, at the base of the Kailasa mountaing near the lake Manasorovara and its adjoining regions, in the Gangetic provinces, in the hills and valleys, in the mountainous regions, in the forests, along the Northern and Eastern Himalayan border land, in the Vindhya region and in other different parts of North-Western, Central and Western India and the Deccan from the remote antiquity as highlighted in literary texts have been misunderstood as immigrants. But the fact remains that they were by and large autochthones.

"India", as observed by Pittard "was never an uninhabited land, over which a flood of comparatively late civilizations was to flow with the first races to occupy it...From the Quaternary onwards the soil of India has been trodden by the foot of man"[1]. There was no migration of the tribal population to India from outside at least in the pre-Christian era. Both ancient history and geography bear witness to the fact that the door of India for coming from ouside during the period concerned was closed because of the persence of the Seas and the Himalayan mountains.

In ancient Indian literary texts, there is no reflection at all of the foreign origin of the Kirâtas and other primitive tribes. But later in the nineteenth and twentieth centuries different Indian and British anthropologists and linguists, their followers and other scholars placed all ancient Indian tribes of indigenous origin under different racial groups and tried to prove them of foreign origin.

In order to get an accurate picture of the subject so far as the Kirâtas' origin is concerned, every possible attempt has been made to strike a reasonable balance between these two extreme propositions. Their origins, antiquity, expansion in different parts of ancient Bhâratavarsa and the areas colonized by them have been discussed in the following pages in detail.

II

ORIGINS : INDIGENOUS–MONGOLOID DICHOTOMY

The racial and cultural identifies of the Kirâtas appears to have changed from age to age and from region to region. Their indigenous origin in general as well as in particular, can be proved mainly by the evidences furnished in ancient Sanskrit literature, which can be further supplemented and confirmed by other authentic sources.

The description provided in the Vedic literature[2] gives us an impression that they were basically the cave-dwellers and mountaineers. Their place of habitation was determined by the Vedic Âryans themselves. The position assigned to them as explained in the text (*Yajur Veda*) is indicative of the fact that they were the tribes of low status and living outside the Âryan fold during the Vedic age.

The allusions to the separate family of the Kirâtas (Kirâta Kula) in some of the *Brâhmaṇas*[3] also indicate that they were the original inhabitants of India. Relying on the information supplied in the Vedic *Saṁhitas* and *Brâhmanas* herein referred to it has been correctly stated that the name Kirâta was applied to the aboriginal hill folk. They were the class of people, who inhabited the woods and the caves of mountains and supported themselves by hunting. They were barbarous-non-Aryan tribes representing the degraded race.[4]

The Pulindas, Úabaras and Mutibas (the cognates of the Kirâtas living together in the extensive forest tracts of the Vindhya region, who later merged with each other) are said to be the offspring of the cursed elder sons of the Vedic seer Visvamitra. They were outside the Brâhmanic community. They were called Dasyus *i.e.* outcast (dasyunâm bhûyistâḥ)[5] who were living on the border of the Âryan settlements. This may appear as legendary, but its importance in ancient Indian context cannot be totally dismissed. The relevance of the statement is proved by the support it has received from number of scholars.[6] We do not have any systematic account of their lineages. However, there are similar instances recorded in the Brahmanic and Puranic traditions, which go to prove that several non-Âryan tribes were originally the descendants of the Âryans. After being subjugated by their counterparts they fled away from the plains towards the hills and forests and took up their abode. Because of leading a savage life of the foresters many of them were included in the catalogue of non-Âryan races.

In former times there was also a kind of socio-religious convention among the Brâhmaṇs to declare those as outcaste, who were not observing the established customs and practices. Those, who were excluded from their community, were admitted into the non-Âryan fold.

In the *Sûtra* period the Indo-Âryan nationalities were divided into two groups—the inner or Vedic group and outer or non-Vedic group. The racial and cultural admixture had mostly taken place among the latter group because of their mutual contacts. The inhabitants of the outer countries *i.e.* western and eastern frontiers were of mixed origin (Sankîrna-Jâti).[7] The admixture of Âryan with the earlier non-Âryan ethnic strata represented by the aborigines became a regular phenomena. The Kirâtas of the Vedic age were very much akin to the people of the outer countries.

In the epic age also there was no racial purity. The Kirâtas too were of mixed origin. They were both of Âryan and non-Âryan extraction. They along with the mlecchas and Harita are said to have originated from 'Romakûpa,'[8] which has not been identified as yet. This information therefore, can be passed over in silence. However, from another faithful literary record which deals with the people of different parts of India, we find that one section of the Kirâtas of the eastern region were of golden complexion and extraordinary strength and nomadic, cannibals, and fair looking with sharp pointed hair knots or conical heads, whereas, the another section were island dwellers, raw fish eaters and fierce by nature, etc.[9] From the details provided in the text it appears that they were no other than the tribes of ancient Assam, who were originally living in the forests, caves of the mountains and in the marshy region near the sea-coast which extended up to the eastern Bengal. They were living on both sides of the 'Lohita' (Lauhitya=Brahmaputra) river from the remotest antiquity.

The Kirâtas in the east are included among the aborigines of the Râmâyaṇa age. They were the Tipperahs and the tribes of Assam.[10] In the twilight of the early literary description it can be affirmed that there were two classes of. the Kiratas, one of these lived in the mountain caves and were charming in appearance, while the other lived on the marshy sandbanks or on the island and were aquatic in character. They had different appearance, character, manners, customs and modes of living due to different circumstances. This shows that they originally, sprang from two different ethnic stocks.

The racial composition of India in ancient times was completely different from that of the modern times. Apart from the Âryans, non-Âryans, mlecchas or barbarians and several small mountain tribes possessing rude culture, and other races of mixed origin were living originally in different geographical settings.[11]

Further, in the *Mahâbhârata,* the Kirâtas evidently appear as a degraded race, as the descendants of Brâhmaṇs and

Kṣatriyas and as Daisyus, Vaiysas and Úūdras. The Paundras, Dravidas, Simhalas, Barbaras, Daradas, mlecchas, Pahlavas, Úabaras, Úakas, Yavanas along with the Kirâtas represent an impure race.[12] Their origin has been described in such a peculiar manner that sometimes our confidence gets shaken in the authenticity of the statement concerned. However, it symbolizes the impurity of the races of non-Âryan group and reflects the contemptuous outlook of the Âryans towards them.

The Kirâtas were also known as Dasyus.[13] In all likelihood, this status might have been conferred on them by the Aryans by whom they were conquered. Vasudeva Sarana Agrawala, while giving the historical interpretations of the *Mahâbhârata* in his monumental work[14] has remarked that the eighteen kinds of Dasyus comprising both indigenous and foreign races, *i.e.* the Kiratas, Yavanas, Gândhâras, Cmas, Úabaras, Barbaras, Úakas etc. had settled in different parts of India before the dawn of the Gupta age and they were leading the life of the Dasyus. They were not reconciled to the contemporary situation. They had not joined the mainstream of Indian culture. They had not fully accepted the prevailing Indian social and religious system. Therefore, the contemporary rulers were confronted with the problem of bringing them within the Aryan fold. Ultimately, a considerable section of them were Aryanised.

There are some other evidences to show that as the aborigines of India they belonged to the stock of the Dasyus. They are also joined with the Sabaras Sakas, etc. as Dasyus.[15] Further, the Kirâtas (non-Âryans of Magadha), Candalas, Parnakas, Simyus etc. were known as Dasa tribes, who mostly inhabited the Gangetic valley and fought the Bharatas in their advance towards the east and south-east.[16]

The epithet Dasyu or Dâsa was actually applied to a wild indigenous race, who were opposed to the Âryans, to the conquered or enslaved tribes of aborigines, to the non-Aryans, who stood outside the Brâhmanical pale and knew no gods, no laws and no sacrifice and later to all those people, who did not follow the Vedic ritual and observe the essential Brâhmanical ceremonies. The expression continued to be used disdainfully even by one group of Âryans against another. The fair skinned Âryans sometimes used to call dark or black skinned Âryans as

Dasyus. The colour or varna was the main basis of distinguishing one branch of Âryans against another. Thus it may not be having any ethnic significance. The composers of the Vedic hymns in order to distinguish their own stock from that of their enemies who were the earlier inhabitants of India applied this term for them. Even those Aryans, who were semi-civilized, nomads, robbers, and hunters in a savage condition and were inhabiting the mountains and forests were also called Dasyus or Dasas. They became dark-skinned because of their nomadic habits and leading the life of foresters. The Âryan dissenters from the orthodox Vedic faith also received the same name. Some of them were absorbed in the Âryan communities, who had settled both in the rural and urban areas. Some of them were designated as the Úudras and some of them merged with non-Âryans. A considerable section of then went outside the Sapta-Sindhu region, which is proved by the fact that the hostile population living side by side with the Hindus of the north-west in the early age were stigmatized as the Dark Dasyus. The Dasyus were distinguished from theVedic Âryans mainly on the religious ground. They were rite-less (a-Karman), non-sacrificing (a-Yajvânah), without devotion (a-brâhman), having no religious observances (a-vratah). etc.[17]

Those tribes, who were outcastes among the Brâhmanas, Ksatriyas and Vaiúyas because of neglect'ng religious rites and rituals and were speakers of either mleccha or Ârya language were also called Dasyus.[18]

The above description, which is of general nature, explains why and on what grounds the Âryans, as well as non-Âryans were called Dasyus or Dâsas. This provides us some clues to surmise that those Kiratas, who were dark-skinned, foresters, and mountaineers, hostile to Âryans and conquered by them and not following the established laws, were addressed by their counterparts as Dasyus. However, it will not be correct to say that only non-Âryan tribes were called Dasyus. It was also on the grounds of physical, religious and cultural differences within the same Aryan grours that a particular designation was applied by one against the other. In fact, the ethnic character of the tribals had undergone some changes between the *Rgvedic* and the epic age. In the age, of the *Mahâbhârata* the aboriginal

Kiratas because of living outside the Aryan fold have figured as Dasyus in the text.

The Kirâtas along with Yavanas, Gandharas, Cinas, Úabaras, Birbaras, Úakas, Tusaras, Pahlavas, Madrâkas, Odras, Pulindas, Ramathas *(Ramana between Ghazni and Wakhan,* Levi, J.A., 1980, p. 126), mlecchas, etc. are described on the one hand, as descendants of Brâhmaṇas and Kṣatriyas, and as Vaiúyas and Úûdras, on the other.[19]

In another context, the Mekalas, Dravidas, Paundras, Saundikas, Daradas, Darvas, Cauras, Sabaras, Barbaras, Kirâtas, Yavanas and other tribes are mentioned as Kṣatriyas,. who were degraded to the status of Vrsalas (Sudra or the low born caste) owing to the wrath of the Brâhmaṇas.[20] They were known as Ksatriyas because of living on the borders of Âryâvarta. This is further supported by others.[21]

The *Mahâbhârata* is further corroborated by the evidences of *Smṛtikâras.* The ethnology of ancient India as illustrated in the *Smṛtis* is of considerable historical value. Some interpolated verses are of course inserted in their works, however, they contain some truth which can be extracted after getting them thoroughly examined. The ancient view of ethnology, which has got some rationality, was not exclusively based on racial theory, rather it was partly based on the theory of birth and partly on the theory of Karma. The ancient writers lacked the modern concept of ethnology, they were, nevertheless, aware of the fusion of Âryan and non-Âryan elements into the Indian society.

We get more clear picture of their Ksatriya origin in the *Mânava Dharmaúâstra.* The Paundrakas, Odras, Dravidas, Kambojas, Yavanas, Úakas. Paradas, Pahlavas, Cinas. Kirâtas, Daradas and Khasas are said to have been degenerated to the rank of Úūdras from their original position as Kṣatriyas because of the omission of the Sacred rites, neglect of the prescribed religious duties and ordinances of the Vedas, transgressing the religious injunctions and laws and not consulting the council of Brâhmanas.[22]

The fusion and admixture of non-Âryan elements with the body of Âryan population presented a formidable problem in the epic age as well as in the time of Manu. This particular point needs some explanations. Actually, the style of presentation of facts in the *Mahâbhârata* and the *Manu Smṛti* are such that smethme their credibilitiesare doubted. There are, of course, some on biguities and aracies but, these can be reconciled. The Âryans and non-Âryans have been mixed together. The Kirâtas have also been mixed with such races, whose Kstriya igin is sometimes questioned, but after having deeper insight into all the details their Ksatriya origin can be proved beyond all doubts. In ancient times, extending from Brâhmâna period to the age of puranas, among the Âryans there had been an established tradition of expelling a person from his society on the charge of violating the established norms and secular laws. Many castes were also created by persons driven from their own group through the infraction or non-performance of the caste rules. Even sons of Brahmanas failing to perform the asigned ceremonies on being invested with the Brâhmanaical code or in any other way breaking the rules of their order were declared as outcastes and debarred from enjoying other religious socilities. They were called *Vrâtyas.* No fewer than twelve castes, as stated by Manu, owe their origin to persons ejected from the Ksatriya tribe alone for the reasons given above. Initially the outcastes were known only as *Vratyas,* but this practice of expulsion further, continued and later they were also known as Dasyus, mlecchas, Úūdras, etc.

In *Aitareya Brâhmaṇa,* we find that fifty sons of Visvâmitra after having been expelled by their father were assimilated among the mlecchas of the frontier region. Some of them were pushed towards the South, where their decendants appeared as Pulindas, Úabaras, Mutibas, etc. The Puranic records are also littered with such instances. Yayâti had also expelled his sons including Turvasu, who later got mixed with the Yavanas and mlecchas. Rajâ Sagara also instead of exterminating the Úakas, Yavanas and Kâmbojas declared them anti-Vedic and expelled them in different directions. Several declared outcastes of Âryan tradition spread upto different parts of Asia, Europe, Africa, Australia and Medagascar. In *Brahma purana* also the Yavanas, Kambojas, Pâradas and Pahlavas are mentioned as degraded Ksatriyas. Moreover, the Yavanas, Kâmbojas and Cinas were not the foreign races as erroneously inferred by many. The Yavanas do not necessarily mean the Greeks. Many degraded Ksatriyas were also called the Yavanas who can be distinguished from the

Greeks. The Kâmbojas were also regarded as Kṣatriyas during the times of Pânini, Kâtâyana and Patañjali, Pâṇini (2.4.10) has also described the Sakas and Yavanas as Sûdras. The *Gau. Dh. Sû.* (Ch. IV. *21*) speaks of the Úakas, Yavanas, etc. as a Pratiloma caste of the Âryans. Grierson[23] has also considered the Khasas of extreme north-west, Nepal and Kashmir as Ksatriyas of Âryan origin. Actually, the Kiratas, Khasas, Kâmbojas, Pâradas, Pahlavas, Yavanas, Cinas, Dradas and Sakas, who were well-organised in north-western region, were originally of Ksatriya stock but later, after having lost their contrast with Brâhmanas and abondoned the established religious practices sank to the ranks of Vrsalas or Sudras and mlecchas.

Some of the early Purâṇas[24] lend strong support to the testimonies provided in the *Mâhâbhâraıa* and *Manu Smṛti* regarding the Kṣatriya and Úûdra origins of the Kirâtas. In the said Puranic texts it is clearly stated that the Kṣatirya colonies (Kṣatriyōpaniveúaúca) were inhabited by the Gandharas, Yavanas, Sindhu-Sauvîras, Úakas, Âbhiras, Bahlikas, pahlavas, Madrakas, Pulindas, Ramathas, Vaiúyas and Úûdras.

Depending on the combined testimony of the *Mahâbhârata,* the *Manu Smṛti* and the *Purânas* mentioned above, it can be postulated with certainty that a few section of the Kirâtas like some other tribes of both indigenous and foreign origins were originally of the Ksatriya Varna but later became degraded members of the Âryan stock because of the reasons already stated and were designated as the Úûdras, exactly like those Âryanised group, who became Dasyus and the mlecchas for the same reason. After having been expelled from the Kṣatriya caste because of failure to make their way into Vedic Âryandom they might have taken shelter in the forest tracts and mountain regions of the frontier countries, where they formed the part of non-Âryan communities, mixed with other foreign races and set-up their own kingdoms. Most of the Kirâtas of north-west were known as the Úûdras.

The view expressed by Manu regarding the indigenous origin of the Kirâtas in particular has sparked off great controversy among the Indian and foreign scholars who can be broadly divided into these groups. One group of scholars have strongly supported his view. A group among these has strongly supported his view. The second group comprises those whose statements are by and large paradoxical which may, however, be amicably resolved. The third group consists of those, who are not inclined, at all, to give their assents to his view by advancing counter arguments. The majority of them[25] have supported the Katriya origin of the Kirâtas later degraded to the rank of Úûdra. Manu has not classed the Kiratas with the mlecchas as it has been misquoted by E. Gait.[26]

James Taylor's interpretation, that the Cinas and Kiratas mentioned by Manu as degraded Ksatriyas should be regarded not as ancestors of the aboriginal tribes but as foreigners of Hindu descent to whom the names of the tribes they conquered were given by the nation from whose society they had beea exiled,[27] is not absolutely correct. The Kirâtas in this particular context are not described as foreigners but as indigenous tribes.

While referring to the Epic, Purânic and Smrti traditions, H.H. Wilson considers the northern tribes including the Kirâtas of Ksatriya stock. He has further pointed out that Bengal, Orissa, whole of Dekkan and the borders in the heart of the country were inhabited by degraded outcastes known as barbarous tribes. While quoting the traditional evidence in support of his contention he adds that king Sagara, son of Bahu, decided to exterminate also the Úakas, Yavanas, Kâmbojas, Paradas, Kirâtas and other Ksatriya race. But they appealed to Vasistha, his family priest for protection. Thus in compliance with the injunction of his spiritual guru the king spared their lives and pushed them by imposing peculiar distinguished marks on them. These Ksatriya race were degraded and reduced by him to the rank of mlecchas. He also deprived them of the established usages of oblation of fire and the right of study of the *Vedas* and separated them from religious rites. These different tribes reigned over the seven zoned earth. The Kirâtas and others since they became degraded were known as Mongoloid or mlecchas, Asuras or non-Âryans, etc.[28]

Manu's theory of Ksatriya origin of the Kirâtas, and their affinity with so-called Indo-Âryan race and Indo-Mongoloids have also been advocated together by Pargiter[29] without drawing any plausible conclusion. His argument in favour of Mongolian extraction of the Kiratas, that the view of Manu of comparativelylate age and the term debased Ksatriya betrays the sentiment of the races of later age, is not valid. He seems to have fallen in the grip of confusion.

Suniti Kumar Chatterji, who has strongly pleaded in favour of Mongolian origin of the Kirâtas, has also made incidental notices of the Ksatriyas as mentioned in the *Mânava Dharma-Úâstra*. However, his view that "When a non-Aryan or foreign people is described in an old Indian text as being of degraded Kṣatriya origin there is always an implication that they were to some extent at least advanced in civilisation or military organisation and as such could not be dismissed as utter barbarians"[30] only indicates that degraded Ksatriyas belong to only non-Aryan stock or are of foreign origin and so were the Kiratas. But in the real sense of the term the Kirâtas of Manu's time were originally living in north-west and were of indigenous origin.

P.C. Choudhury also appears to have supported the Ksatriya origin of the Kiratas as propounded by Manu, but at the same time, in an attempt to contradict it, suggests that some sections of them, who settled in south-east Bengal and western Assam before the Bodos, represent an early wave of Mongolians, and they possibly like most of the Tibeto-Burmans got mixed up with the Alpines of eastern India and Assam.[31]

The Kirâtas of the Vedic, Epic, Smṛti and Purâṇic periods have been mistakenly confounded with the Mongoloids by a number of scholars. The question relating to their Mongolian origin has been examined at length separately. Here it will suffice to say that the Kirâtas of early period had no connection with the Mongoloids, who penetrated into the Indian subcontinent comparatively at later age. Therefore, both, one bearing the stamp of Indian origin and the other of the foreign cannot be mixed up with each other, as it has been done in most of the cases. As a matter of fact, some of the early Kirâtas were absorbed in the later immigrant tribal groups, and they are generally called Mongoloids.

The Kṣatriya origin of the Kirâtas has caused embarrassment to some scholars because the inclusion of the so-called wild and hostile tribes like the Kirâtas and some other races of non-Indian origins like the Yavanas, Cînas and Úakas into Ksatriya community appears to them improbable. It is true that the Âryans and non-Âryans have been mixed together in some of the early literary texts, but the allegations levelled against the ancient Indian writers that there was a common tendency amongst them to show that the whole mankind have descended from the Ksatriya stock of high antiquity[32] is not perfectly justified. At the same time this is also not tenable that Manu's theory of degraded Ksatriya origin of the Kirâta is highly fanciful and absurd.[33]

The probable explanation that can be given to justify the admission of the Kirâtas into Ksatriya community and their degradation from this original position to the status of the Úûdras is that they were originally living in north-western India as a class of warriors, and were following the Vedic rites and the Brâhmanical code, but after coming under the foreign influence during the settlements of the Graeco-Bactrians, Parthians, Pahlavas and the Úakas (with whom they later mixed) before the time of Manu (placed between c. 200 B.C. and c. 200 A.D.) lost the contact with the Brahmans and abandoned the *Vedism,* which resulted in the change of their social status. And, consequently, the Âryans out of their contempt for them reduced them to the status of the Sûdra, which was sometimes used for the degraded people too. The same was the case with the Yavanas, who were not necessarily the Greeks, but the outcaste people. Later they were identified with the Greeks. The Cinas were not the Chinese but the tribes of Indian origin. In this connection the fact should not be lost sight of that formation of many social groups in those days were taking place through the inter-marriages among the four original Varnas which had been going on from the time of composition of the *Dharma Sûtras* to the time of Manu. Many castes and ethnic groups emerged out of 50 racial groups, which Manu speaks of. Moreover, many aboriginal tribes originally formed the part of Indo-Aryan community but after being pushed towards the hills and forests by the Âryans for manifold reasons they lost the identity, switched over to a new life and finally got the tribal designation. There might have been probably a transitional stage in the life of the, Kirâtas, so far as the change of status from caste to tribe is concerned. Some of them might have assumed the tribal character after quitting the fold of the caste.

The view expressed by Atkinson, a great authority on the Himalayan tribes, goes to strengthen the arguments advanced above. He has candidly admitted that "the Hills and forests of Northern India were occupied by the tribes regarded more as degraded members of the Âryan stock than aliens in race... In the northern Himalayas were the Daradas, Chînas, Sakas, Nagas, Khasas and Kirâtas. These tribes became Vrsalas or outcastes in consequence of the extinction of sacred rites and from having no intercourse with Brâhmanas All the tribes, because of the loss of sacred rites, became outcaste from the pale of four castes as Âryas are called Dasyus and speak mleccha language. He has established the link between the earlier and the later record and made natural exploration of the entire phenomena". He further observes that "as in Africa at the present day the tribes coverted to Islam leaving behind them their heathen practice looked with contempt and hatred on their brethren in race, who adhere to paganism, so the Âryas despised those of their race, who remained content with the primitive beliefs which was once their common property and refused to accept the sacerdotal innovations or who belong to non-Aryan descent declined to accept the Brâhmaṇical creed. The term of abuses used towards these tribes by the priestly writers prove nothing more than the existence of the *Odium theologicum,* which has burned fiercely in all countries from the earliest dawn of history to the present day... out of all the names the only names that are justified by the tradition and the fact in connecting them with the hills are the Khasas, Kirâtas, Úakas, the Nâgas and Hunas... The Hills and forests of northern India were occupied by tribes who are regarded more as degraded members of the Âryan stock than as aliens in race. They attained a considerable degree of civilisation and lived in forts and walled towns. The Daradas, Úakas, Cînas, Nagas, Kirâtas and others in northern Himalayas were of degraded stock. This difference is further intended to distinguish between the degraded Âryans and the autochthonous tribes or rather those of early immigrants... The Bhotiyâs of Tibet also are little inclined to admit that they are of Tibetan origin or Mongoloid tribes. In the traditional account of the colonisation of Bhotiyas they declare themselves as offspring of the Rajput immigrants. The Tibetan annals undoubtedly mention the existence of trans-Himalayan Ksâtriya kingdom and the Hindu origin of their rulers. On the boundary line between the Khasiyas and the Bhotiyâs we find a mixed population. Hindu immigrants from the plains monopolised all the countries that contributed to what we call upper grade of hill society....".[34]

Both the Varṇa and Karma were the determining factors in awarding the ranks to the tribes and castes in the social hierarchy in the *Smṛti* age. There is an evidence to show that the Vaṇikas, Kirâtas, Kâyasthas, etc. became Úûdras in consequence of their Karma or actions.[35]

It is believed that the Kirâta, Nisâda, Parnaka, Paulkasa and Bainda (*Vaj. Saṁ.* XXX. 6-21; *Tai. Br.* 111. 4.2-17) of the *Samhitâ* and *Brâhmaṇa* periods were included in the broad term of the Sûdra.[36] Those who were reduced to the position of Úudra by the Âryan conquerors later formed the non-Âryan population. It appears that large section of the Âryan and non-Âryan tribes, who were defeated and dispossessed through both internal and external conflicts, were reduced to this position.[37]

The term Úûdra covers numerous inferior races and tribes defeated by the Âryan invaders, but originally it denotes one special tribe. It has been reasonably supposed that Sudra was the name given by the Vedic Indians to the non-Vedic tribes opposing them and that these were ranked as slaves besides the three castes, just as in *Anglo-Saxon* and early German constitution besides the priests, Nobles and ordinary freeman there was a distinct class of slaves in terms of the use of generic expression.[38]

The tribes and castes who were barbarians or proportionately less civilized or speakers of mleccha language or of mixed origin were classed as mlecchas. A considerable section of the non-Âryan Kirâta tribes were also of mleccha origin or mleccha race. The image of the Kiratas as barbarians or mlecchas emerged mainly in the post-Gupta period, though we have some vague references to this effect in the literary texts composed anterior to this period also.

The Kirâtas, Úabaras and Pulindas have been associated together with the mleccha race (mlecchajatayah).[39] On the basis of the incorporation of the above three mleccha tribes in the 'Úûdravarga' of the text it has been presumed that large masses of tribal population were absorbed in the Úûdra community.[40] There are some evidences to support this presuption. Actually, various castes and tribes of mixed origin *(Samkîrna Jâti),* coming as a result of the process of *anuloma* (where the mother is of inferior caste than the father) and *pratiloma* (where mother is of a superior caste than the father) marriages, were given the rank of Úudras, mlecchas, Cândâlas, etc. Many such instances are located in the *Smrtis* and Sutras. Here, the Kirâtas, Pulindas, Khasas, Andhras and other, mlecchas are ranked among the *anuloma.*[41] It is also said that the mlecchas were born through Úûdra women and Kṣatriya father.[42] The indigenous origin of the Kiratas, Pulindas and Úabaras as mentioned in the said text, as well as their inclusion in the list of mleccha tribes inhabiting the mountain region of the Vindhyas can also be supported by other evidences.'[43] The text speaks of Pratyanta (frontier) countries,[44] generally identified as mleccha-desa' where the non-Âryan tribes did not abide by the orthodox rules regarding the Varnas and the Âsramas, as testified to by the *Dharma Sûtras.*[45] In the *Mahâbhârata,* Bhagadatta king of Pragjyotisa has been called the lord of the mlecchas,[46] which is a positive indication towards the Kiratas, who were directly governed by him.[47] The tribes of *mlecchajâti* were, no doubt dwelling in the frontier regions of India.[48] Some of them were born outcaste or barbarous races and as black as collyrium. The Kiratas and Barbarous fall in this category.[49] The Kirâtas, the Yavanas, Úakas, Hûnas, Khasas, Ândhrakas, etc. as mlecchas, were well known for their hostile attitudes towards the class of Brahmanas.[50] The performance of purification ceremony (Sraddha) was not permissible in the Kirâta countries.[51]

It was not only the racial concept that was kept in view, but the nature and character, manners and customs and linguistic and cultural factors were also taken into consideration, while applying the epithet mleccha to a particular group of people in ancient times. It was basically on these factors that the Araya-desa was distinguished from the mleccha-deúa.

The Kirâtas, and Pulindas and other tribes who were the speakers of non-Indo-Âryan language, were frequently given a a low rank and called mlecchas.[52] The Pulindas, Úabaras, Yavanas, Úakas, etc. are also included among the tribes of mleccha origins.[53] The speakers of the mleccha language were called Milakkhas. The term mlekha[54] was used for the first time by the Brahmanas in the sense of a barbarous language spoken by all those (including degraded Âryans and non-Âryan tribes) who were out side the pale of Âryan culture.

From the Buddhist and Jaina texts it is evident that the Kirâtas, Pulindas. Ândhrakas, Yonakas, Barbaras, Úabaras and others were speakers of this language *(Milakkhânâmbhâṣâ)* which was by and large unintelligible to the Ârayans. This language had some thirteen to eighteen forms.[55] In the post-Christian era this term was also applied to those foreigners, who had settled on the northern frontiers and were beyond the pale of Indian culture, but Rapson's statement that it was particularly applied to them[56], is not absolutely correct. Even the Âryan offshoots, who were ruling in the Vahya (external) deúa without following the caste rules of Âryans were reduced to the status of the mlecchas, and they were denounced as Arya-mlecchas, i.e. denationalised Aryans. It was on this ground that the countries of Sindhu-Sauviras, Dravidas, Bengal, Kamarupa, Orissa, etc. have been included in the mleccha deúa.[57] Kautilya also makes distinction between forest tribes (atvikah) and the mleccha (aranyacarah),[58] which shows that those, who were other than the forest tribes, were also designated as the mlecchas.

The Kirâtas, Bhillas, Niṣâdas, Nahalakas, Bhramaras, Pulindas, Úabaras and other mleccha tribes, who settled in the hills and forests are also said to be the descendants of Nisida or Niṣâda.[59] In this connection greater weight should be attached to the view of R.P. Chanda, who relying on the Epic and Puranic traditions relating to aboriginal tribes of Nisada race, has admitted that the "Kirâtas, Pulindas and Úabaras"— "the barbarians of the Vindhya hills belonged to the Nisada stock."[60] The Nisâdas have affinities with the so-called pre-Dravidian forest tribes of India. The Niṣâdas were having the "complexion of a charred stake with flattened feature and dwarfish stature."[61] They were "black like crow, very low statured, short armed, having high check bones, low-topped nose, red eyes and copper-coloured hair."[62]

"The Niṣâdas, Dâsas, Dasyus, Pulindas and the Kirâtas were mostly aboriginal, rude, savage tribes in a very primitive stage of civilization. All these tribes lived in hilly tracts and some of them were cannibals. The Nisâdas, known as Mlecchhas, were according to ancient traditional views a mixed race of Âryan origin born from a Brahmana male and a Úûdra female. They are associated with the hills of Central India and the Vindhyan tracts. They had also settlements in the Vatsabhûmi and further east near Allahabad.... The Kirâtas had settlements in Assam and Nepal."[63]

The Kirâtas of Gangâ-Yamuna Doab in Madhya-deúa or Central region of the country lying between the Himalaya and the Vindhya (which constitute the nucleus of Âryavarta) were of Aryan origin. They along with the Pulindas, Kuru-Pâncalas, Ânga, Vañga, Magadha, Tâmralipti, etc. have been placed in the Arya-deúa, watered by sacred Ganges, which striking against the Vindhya Hills falls in the Southern Sea.[64] It is exactly on this ground that F. Wilford was also led to believe that "the tribes of Kirâtas ...... as pronounced in the spoken dialect are native of India or signifies a native of India. The Hladini (one of the streams of the Ganges) goes through the countries of Nisâdas—Kirâtas".[65] The oriental scholars on the basis of the Puranic evidence concerned have also professed that some of them were degraded Âryan tribes living on the frontiers of Bharatavarsa and some degraded mountain tribes.[66]

The Kirâtas consisting of both civilized and uncivilized Brahmanas and non-Brâhmanas, living together in the extensive forest tract of Vindhya region, were of indigenous origin. They did not come from outside. Their Brâhmanahood was ascertained from the sacred thread lying across the shoulder of one of them, named Matanga, who himself claimed to be the son of a Brahmana Kirata in course of his discourse with a prince, named Rajavahâna, whom he met in the heart of Vindhya forest. Actually, the said prince was sent there by Râjahamsa, the king of Magadha (with its capital at Pusapâpura) who, after being defeated by Manasara, the king of Malwa, took refuge in the forest of the Vindhya mountain. After having been received, hospitably by the Kirâta, a son of Brâhmana, the prince asked him why he resided in that dreadly Vindhya forest, destitute of human habitation. The sacred thread pronounces him to be a Brahmana while the scars of wounds inflicted by weapons on his body gave indication of his being the Kirata. The Kirâta, in his reply to all such questions, revealed that there in that forest resided many who were Brâhmans only by name (Brâhmana renegades), because they did not follow their caste rules and lead the savage life of the foresters (Vanacarâh). They consisted of barbarians, who went in quest of sinful acts foregoing the study of the Vedas, and others, who ignored the observances of their socio-religious duties. Still more were very civilized and stood in defence of Brahmanas. Many of them learnt about Úastras and Tantras from their fellow Brâhmanas.

Praharavarman, the king of Mithila and a close associate of the king of Magadha, while going back to his native capital after being defeated by Malawa's king passed by a perilous forest path, where he saw with his own eyes the dedication of the Kiratas and Úavaras (both identical as aboriginal tribes of the Vindhyas) to the goddess Candika, or Durga, which constitutes a proof of their being the descendants of Brâhmanas. The authenticity of this eye-witness account as provided by Dandin[67] is beyond question. It is really of a paramount historical importance. Such a unique combination of barbarism and Brahmanism among the same tribal community is hardly to be found anywhere. This also, indirectly, goes to vindicate the view of Manu.

The indigenous origin of the Kirâtas of Nepal can better be qualified in the words of James Taylor: " . . . one of the ancient dynasties of Râjâ that governed Nepal belonged to the Kirât tribe of Eastern mountaineers . . . The founders of this dynasty were probably Hindus, viz. the Kirâtas classed by Manu among the tribes, who are expelled from the caste of the Kshatriyas".[68] The original Kṣatriyas have been called pre-Âryan non-Âryan Bhâratîya people.[69]

All the chiefs of the Kirâtas called Rais are believed to be "hill Rajputs" or Kṣatriyas. They belonged to noble caste. But on the other hand it is said that they are clearly marked by their features as being a tribe of "Chinese or Tartars"[70]. We do not have any supporting evidence to uphold this contention. Further, the statements, that they were foreigners not Hindus; they are not of Mongolian, but of pure Turanian descent[71], can be dismissed as utterly baseless.

Actually, the Alpine basin of the Sapta-Kausika or the country of the seven Kosis was the original homeland or the seat of the Kirâtas of Nepal, who were once very powerful and dominant race, though they have long since succumbed to the political supremacy of other races.[72]

The Kiratas living in Morung (presently in Nepal) west of Sikkim are said to be the descendants of Bhota (ancient Tribistapa=Tibet) tribe. They are also said to be of Turanian race but with marked Mongolian features[73], which appears to be very inconsistent. Actually, the Kirâtas, who had formerly provided a dynasty of considerable duration in Nepal, were living originally in the valleys of the Himalayas since time immemorial. The name of the Bhota race, who were allied to the Tibetans survives more in the modern Bhutan than in Nepal. They inhabited much of Bengal at the time of the Âryan migration It cannot be denied that the Tibetans are a fragment of a great primitive population that occupied both the northen and southern slopes of the Himalayas at some very remote prehistoric time. But, they did not have any connection with those Kiratas, who were ruling in the valleys of Nepal.

Lassen, while describing fully the Bhota race, names ten different tribes one being the Kirâta, whose native capital was at Mokwanpuf in Eastern Nepal.[74] He nowhere establishes the link either between the Kirâta of Nepal and the Tibetans or between them and the Mongolians.

The racial mixture of the Kirâta tribes of Nepal on the northern frontier of the Himalayas is a fact to be reckoned with because of the existence of several castes and ethnic groups there.[75] This is the factor by which their real origin has been obscured. However, half of them are said to have been "Brahmanic" and half "Buddhist".[76]

It is note worthy that the Kirâtas wee known to the Âryans as a group of tribe whose original home was on or near the slopes of the Himalayas. Some of them had their original settlementsonthe mountain Kailâúa and in the territisy aroundthe Mânasarovar (Tibet) inthe northern Himalayas and were worshippers of Lord Úiva-their supreme God. Their descendants are still found in Nepal and Sikkim.

Most of the ancient Kirâta tribes of northern and eastern Himalayas were of indigenous origin. Those who had been dwelling from a very remote period in the valleys and mountain regions until the migration of the tribes of Mongolian origin were, no doubt, the original inhabitants of the country. A numbers of Kirâta tribe of Mongolian origin had, of course, settled in Nepal, and Sikkim (called Indrakil in the epic age and later Sukhima) in the second half of the first millennium A.D.

The Kirâtas of ancient Nepal were of mixed origin. They were originally living between the Sapta-Kaushaki and Sapta-Gandaki. The seven tributaries of the river Koshi-Arun, Dudhkoshi, Tamrakoshi, Linkhu, Tambor, Sunkoshi and Milanchi or Indrani-combined together is called Sapta-Kaushaki, which is eastern Nepal. Likewise, the seven tributaries of the river Gandak-Bharigar, Narayani, Shveta gandaki, Matsyandhri, Trisul, Dharmadi and Gandi (all originating from the mountain ranges of Dhavalagiri and Gosainthan)—combined together is called Sapta-Gandaki (*i.e.* Central Nepal). Eastern Nepal because of being the cradle or original seat of the Kirâtas was called Kirâtadeúa (the land of Kirâtas) in ancient times. The Kirâtas in he valley of Nepal, including those who established the dynastic rule, were no doubt of indigenous origin. The Kulung, Thulung, Yellung and others were the most popular among the ancient Kirâtas of Nepal.

The Khambu (Rai), Limbu, Yakha, Magar, Sunuwar, Gurung and Bhujel of Nepal and Sikkim constitute very important section of the Kirât communities. They are of Mongolian or Tibetan origin. After having migrated from their native home they settled down in the mountain regions lying between the rivers of eastern Nepal and in its neighbourhood and in the mountain regions of Sikkim.

It may be noted here that those who migrated from Tibet (called Bhotadesh for the first time in the 7th century A.D..) towards eastern frontiers, sub-Himalayan tract of Nepal or eastern Himalayan State of Sikkim before the seventh century were of purely Tibetan origin. The tribes of so-called Mongolian race migrated from there from the seventh century onwards. They are identified with Mongoloids generally on the basis of their physical features.

Because of the geographical contiguity of Nepal and Sikkim the frequent migration of the above mentioned Kirâta communities from one place to another at different periods of history seems quite probable. Shiva Kumar Rai has correctly stated that "some parts of Nepal were under Sikkim once and likewise some parts of Sikkim were under Nepal....Therefore, it is natural that the various communities living in Sikkim and Nepal.... freely moved and settled in various parts of Sikkim and Nepal."[77]

The Kirât Mundhum (Kirât-Ko Ved) is a collection of oral, mythological and historical traditions (all inextricably interwoven) of the Kiranti people. These traditions were collected in the Kiranti language and published in the Nagari character with a Nepali translation form Patna in 1971 by Iman Singh Chemjong. Some clues about the origins and migrations of the Kirâta tribes of Sikkim are to be found in *Mundhum*.

The Khambus also called Khambas were one of the races of Bhotadesha or Tibet (north of Nepal and Sikkim). They moved from their original home in Tibet towards the south and first penetrated within the eastern frontier of Nepal some time in the early period. The racial movement from Tibet in both pre-and-post seventh century is historically a proven fact.

The first entry of the Khambus into eastern Nepal can fairly be attested to by the local traditions as well as by the evidence recorded in some reliable sources. "Rai tradition relates that the first of the ancestral Kiranti entered Nepal's eastern hills through the Barakshetra (Varahakshetra) gorge of Koshi valley, the natural gateway into the region through the Mahabharata range which separates the hilly interland from the plains"[78] According to Kulunge Rai version, there were three brothers, Khambuho, Menho and Meratup. Once through the gorge the brothers separated, each taking his respective followers and set out independently as they penetrated up the different river valleys such as Sun-Koshi, Dudh-Koshi and Arun-Koshi.[79] Turning to the myths and traditions of the Rais and Limbus themselves, it is asserted that they arrived as immigrants from elsewhere, and that there are none who claim to always have been where they are now. Physically, linguistically and to some extent culturally, the Rais and Limbus are related to the larger

Mongoloid tribal people spread eastward through the sub-Himalayan region and hills of Assam. It is said that their movement into Nepal hills must be understood in relation to the spread of Mongoloid. Tibeto-Burman speaking people throughout the eastern Himalayan region as a whole which was probably gradual and effected by a series of displacements.[80]

After having migrated from Tibet, the Khambus occupied the middle part of eastern Nepal (ancient Kirâtadesh) and settled in the mountain region between the two rivers, Likhu and Arun. The place of their settlement became known as "Khambuan"[81] (the mainland of the Khambus and their descendants). Various sub-groups of the Khambu like Bontawa, Rodong, Dungmali, Khaling, Bahing, Thulung, Kulung, Dums and Sangpang were located by Hodson[82] in this part of Nepal. One section of the Khambus selected the slopes of the Himalayas or the mountainous region lying between the Dudh-Koshi and Karki rivers and the other the mountain tract between the Sun-Koshi and Likhu river for their habitation. They (the mountain tribe Khambus of Kirata Stock) must be distinguished from those Kiratas who had been in occupation of the valley of eastern Nepal since the epic age. Different groups of the Khambu tribe moved from their habitat in eastern Nepal at different periods of history, particularly in ancient and early medieval period, towards the east. Sikkim, which became a new home for them from the perspective of a new settlement or commencing a new life.

According to Eden Vansittart, the Khambus or Khambas (Rais) are one of those aboriginal tribe who have descended from Tibetan or Mongolian Stock. This fact, he says is inscribed in very plain characters in their faces, forms and language. He further adds that physically speaking, there is a very strong resemblance between the Rais, Limbus, Gurungs, Mangars and Sunwars. The Khambus or Rais, Limbus or Yakthumbas and Yakhas have been distinctly placed by him under the Kiranti (Kirati) group.[83] The physical characteristics of the Kirât Khambu Rais -diminutive stature, broad heads and cheeks, flat nose, oblique eyes, yellowish or golden colours, etc - bear the stamp of their Mongoloid features. Martin Gaenszle also describes them as a Mongolian race. But his statements that they are descendants of the Kiratas described in ancient Sanskrit texts, particularly the epicsy[84] is controvertible. They are generally described as "Barbarians" or uncivilized people, hunters and gatherers of fruits and roots. It has become almost a convention to describe the primitive or ancient tribes as savages and barbarous. But this fact should not be lost sight of that they had their own tribal way of living and distinct culture different from those of the Aryans. Both the Âryan and non-Âryan elements form the part of Indian culture.

M. Martin's statement, that the Rais (Chiefs of the Kirâtas) are clearly marked by their features as being a tribe of "Chinese or tartars",[85] is absurd. E.T. Dalton's statement, that they are not of Mongolian but of pure Turanian descent[86] is also bunkum. They were neither of Chinese nor of Tartar nor of Turanian origin. Hence both these statements can be dismissed as utterly baseless. However, the remark of the latter that they were of foreign origin and not Hindus[87] is based on truth. According to an archaeological evidence, the use of the word Rai can be traced back to the fourteenth century. But it was exclusively used for ruling class (including the Kirâta's chief). The word Rai distinctly figures in the copper plate inscription dated Shaka era 1259=A.D. 1337 of Punya Malla, the king of Jumla (Nepal), but the fact remains that the word did not get wide currency in Nepal or Sikkim before 1773. As a matter of fact, the famous Gurkha king Prithvi Narayan Shah after having conquered the Kathmandu valley in 1768 and established his rule there and extended his political influence eastward as far as Sikkim made up his mind to bring the Kirâtas of Nepal under his political hegemony as he saw a potential threat to the shah rule in Nepal from them because of their large population and unity. In 1773, he issued a proclamation to the Kirâtas of eastern Nepal asking them to acknowledge him as their overlord and as the ruler of Makwanpur principality and transfer their allegiance to him in return for which he promised them the security of their lives and allowed them to maintain their autonomy. Since the rapidly extended Gurkha kingdom lacked the administrative machinery to directly rule the newly conquered territories, he appointed the Kirati headmen or chiefs from different ethnic groups as local rulers to act as intermediaries between them and the. state. The ruling class belonging to the Khambu community became known as Rai, the Limbu community as Subedar or Subba, the Yakha community as Dewan and the Sunuwar community as Mukhia. In some districts, the local rulers particularly from the Khambu community, were called Jimdars (corrupt form of Zamindars). These honorific titles came into use among the communities concerned both in Nepal and Sikkim.

It is significant to note that the ruling class of the Khambus called Rai continued to maintain their tribal identity even after 1773. Those of the Khambus who did not belong to this class continued to retain their identity as the Khambu. That is the reason why the Rai, Jimdar and others (with total population of 2,020)and the Khambu (with total population of 1,963) have been shown separately in the distribution of population of various communities of Sikkim in a Census conducted in February 1891.[88] However, the fact remains that they all belong to the Khambu community. The ethnic name Khambu is often used to refer collectively to the Rais. The word Rai has become over the years the popular generic term of reference for the entire ethnic group. That is why the term Khambu Rai is used in combination with each other. The Rai includes Chamling, Bakhim, Kandongwa, Mangthang, Mangdenwa, Lohorung and other sub-groups. Charles McDougal, while dealing with the origin of the word Rai, observed that Rais are not a single tribe rather a collection of tribes exhibiting among themselves difference in language (dialects) culture, manners and customs and social organization although they do share a common cultural base and have similar social structure.[89] The Kirata chiefs represented by Rai are still found in association with Limbus in the hilly areas of present Nepal, West Bengal and Sikkim.

The Kirat Khambu Rai, one of the tribal communities of eastern Himalayan state of Sikkim and Nepal, should not be equated with the Hindus bearing the surname Rai, Roy or Ray, particularly in Bihar and Bengal.

The history of the origin and migration of the Gurungs, one of the ethnic tribes of Sikkim, is preserved in their folktales or folklore which have been passed down from generation to generation by their priest called *Pachyu* in *Mundhum* which speaks of their ancestors and their homeland. There is a reflection of some historical truth in their folktales about their past life. Moreover, some of the facts are worthy of corroboration.

According to the folklore tradition of the Gurungs, particularly of those who are followers of Bonism (pre-Buddhist religion or the advanced form of animism), the original homeland of their ancestors was *Cho-Nasa* in western Mongolia that lies to the south of Sinkiang in western China and north of China in the Tur-fan Depression. From there they spread out to various places. One of the groups migrated to Tibet falling within the northern Himalayan range. *Mhina Kugi* people of the nine clans of the Gurung came to Chamdo in eastern Tibet. At that time Chamdo was the gateway to Tibet for the immigrants. From Chamdo the *Mhina Kugi* further moved to the western part of Yarlung valley of the Lhoka region from where they came to be known as *Tamu-Gurung* in "1000 B.C.". As recorded in ancient history of Central Asia, the Gurungs, originally known as "Gyarungs", were one of the nomadic tribes of western China. One group of this tribe moved to central Asia. Those who migrated to Tibet remained there for a considerable period of time. According to our findings, the Gurungs moving southward from Tibet came to Nepal and Sikkim after the dawn of the Christian era. The successive waves of their migration from Tibet to both the Himalayan states took place between the first and seventh century A.D. The migration southward into the eastern Himalayan belt took place not earlier than the first century A.D. The Mongoloid tribes had established themselves on the southern slopes of the Himalayas in the early centuries of the Christian era.

According to the Rai and Limbu tradition also, the mountain tribes of Sikkim are basically of Tibetan origin. Munaimua is said to have been the first person to come from Tibet. He had two sons and the name of one of them was Gurupa who is regarded as the ancestor of Gurungs. Accoridng to the Kirati legend, the name Gurung is derived from 'Gu' means nine and 'Rong' means chief. In the chronicles of the Gurungs, they are described as the descendants of the "Mongoloid Kirat" tribe.

"Sheep rearing being their main occupation, the Gurung tribe had earlier lived a nomadic life, looking for forests and sustainable green pastures along the Himalayas, which bear trails of the migration of the Gurungs from Central Tibet to Sikkim".

There is a substantial historical evidence to prove the Tibetan origin of the Gurungs. Gurung is a Tibetan word meaning personal bodyguards. The Gurungs, like the Tamangs (meaning cavalry force in Tibetan), were in the armed force of king Srong-btsan Gampo of Tibet (A.D. 629-50). Both Gurungs and Tamangs were used as forces by the said Tibetan king in his war with Amshuvarman, the king of Nepal. The Gurungs migrated from Tibet to both Nepal and Sikkim in the latter half of the seventh century too. This might have been probably the later phase of their migration from Tibet.

The linguistic evidence also goes in support of their Tibetan origin. Their dialects are more allied to Tibetan than any other language. They are the speakers of Tibeto-Burman group of language (of Sini-Tibetan family) locally known as Tamu.

E. Vansittart has placed the Gurungs in the list of aboriginal tribes of Mongolian or Tibetan stock.[90] The French scholar Bernard Pignede (the author of *Less Gurung,* 1966), Northey and Morris (authors of *The Gurkhas,* 1928) and Hodgson (a noted authority on the aborigines of the Sub-Himalayan and Himalayan regions) are of the same view that the Gurung tribe originated from the "Mongolian race of Tibet". This view is supported by anthropological, historical and philological evidence available to us. Their physical appearance resemble with that of the ethnic tribals of Mongoloid origin.

The Gurungs have a characteristic tribal culture and a lifestyle of their own. They have their own customs, traditions, and religion which is basically animistic. They have not yet abandoned their age-old tribal beliefs and practices. The primitive traits are still discernible in their socio-religious life. Their indigenous tribal religion coexists side by side with Hinduism and Buddhism. Ethnologically linguistically and culturally they belong to a tribal group. In ancient times, they were also known as Kirâta.

As regards the settlement pattern of the Gurungs, a cluster of small villages have been set up over the centuries on mountains of high altitude for their habitation. They are settled in all parts of Sikkim but mainly concentrated in the West and South Sikkim.

The history of origin, migration and settlement of the Sunwar tribe of Sikkim can be dealt with on the combined testimony of their *Vaṁshavâli* records based on their traditions, their oral tradition *(Mukdhum* or *Mundhum)* handed down from one generation to another by their priests called *Poibo* and *Natso,* and some authoritative works on the subject.

The name Sunwar has been derived from those who were residing to the east of the Sunkoshi river in eastern Nepal in ancient times. The lineage of the Sunwar (Mukhia) Koinch can be traced back to the progeny of Rama Simha having settlements on the Sunkoshi river and in the mountains north of valley. Being in the valley and mountains of the eastern Nepal (the land of the Kirâtas) the Sunwars became popularly known as Kirata. They still call themselves Kirâtavaṁshi.

The Sunwar are undoubtedly of Mongolian descent. They are closely allied to Rais, Gurungs and Magars, with a touch of the Tibetans.[91] It has been categorically stated that the Rais, Limbus, Gurungs, Tamangs, Magars and Sunwars are tribes of Mongoloid origin.[92]

Sunuwars' traditions relate that they originally migrated from Tibet until they reached the basin of the Ganges in India, from where they worked their way via Simanggarh (Simraungarh, situated about six miles east of present Birganj) into Nepal. On reaching the Sunkoshi river, they settled on its both banks, but more especially in the Dumja or Duluka (Dolkha) district on the western side of the river. One of their traditions relates that they left Tibet and reached India via Kashmir and the Punjab, and further moved to Simraungarh (after crossing over the border of north Bihar) from where they entered Nepal. Their another tradition states that they came from Tibet via Assam across the Brahmaputra and so on. They appear to have migrated from Tibet to Nepal in different groups[93] at different periods in ancient times.

Of the four *Vaṁshâvalis* of the Sunwars: *Sunuwar Jat Ko Vaṁshâvali* (in 10 pages), by Bikram Bahadur Sunuwar (Samvat – 2004 = A.D. 1947), *Kirat Jat Ko Vaṁshâvali* (revd. 2nd edition of the 1st one under the changed title by the same author, Samvat, 2007 = A.D. 1950), *Sunuwar Rai Kirâta Ko Vaṁshâvali* (in 26 pages) by Tika Ram Sunuwar, ed by Pt. Ganga Prasad Chavahilale (Sanvat, 2010 - A.D. 1953), and *Sunuwar Jat Ko Vaṁshâvali,* also called *Sunuwar Jat Ko Itihasa* (in 72 pages), by Ram Bahadur Sunuwar (Samvat, 2013 = A.D. 1956), the fourth one is comparatively of greater historical value, though it, like the other three, is also not free from the myths and legends and facts and fictions all jumbled up.

On the basis of the first three *Vaṁshâvalis* and the *Mundhum* in general and the fourth *Vaṁshâvali* (by Ram Vahadur Sunuwar) in particular it can be established that Sundarvira, the progenitor of the Sunwar tribe, belonged to Mongolian race. He had five sons, Lal Simha, Sur Simha, Rama Simha, Maṇa Simha and Dhana Simha. It is very difficult to establish their identity, find their original names and affirm as to how and where they got these names. However, these names are not fictitious. In all probability, their original names might have been changed after reaching India, particularly in the Punjab. From the details available in the sources mentioned above it appears that the descendants of Lal Simha settled in Lhasa in Tibet. The descendants of other four brothers migrated from Tibet to India (called Muktikshetra). All entered eastern Nepal through Simanggarh or Simraungarh. The descendants of Sur Simha settled down on the northern side of the Sunkoshi river i.e. in Jiri Khola and Siri Khola. They were, therefore, called Jirel and Sirel Sunwars. The so-called ten *Thars* (denoting the subdivision of the tribe on the basis of clan kinship, etc.) comprised Jirel, Surel, Krelu, Mohira, Pahari, Suinu, Suname, Thanu and Wangdi. The lineal descendants of Rama Simha having settled on the eastern side of the Sunkoshi became popularly known as Sunwar. They are regarded as ancestor of the Sunwar (Mukhia) Koinch who fall in their line. In larger sense, their territories were located between the Sunkoshi and Likhu rivers and between the Sunkoshi and Tamrakoshi rivers. They were divided into twelve *Thars* or clans - Bujuwar, Chiaba, Jujukha Mekephite, Nakasojphite, Jenti, Jobo, Linhochha, etc. A number of Sunuwar tribe settled in the mountain region north of valley. The offspring of Mana Simha set -off to the southeast and settled in the land of Khambus or Rais between the Likhu and Arun rivers and assimilated themselves with them to such a degree that they were practically absorbed into them. They were confined to the mountain region between these two rivers. Some of the descendants of Dhana Simha settled on the southern slopes of the Himalayas. Their territory was located near the Dudhkoshi river. They gradually spread out in the fertile area lying within the Sapta-Kaushaki region. Dhanakuta, Tapalejung, Sainglung, ham and Mewakhola were the main centres of their settlement.[94] It has been rightly pointed out that the Sunwars (Mukhia) were settled in the mountain regions of eastern Nepal. According to the Sunuwar tradition, they had entered the mountain regions from Simraungarh through Varahkshetra (also called Barakshetra).[95] One branch of the Sunwar tribe dwelling in the mountain regions of eastern Nepal migrated to Sikkim in ancient times. In Nepal, the habitat of the Sunwars is one both banks of the Sunkoshi river, but more especially to the west and north, and they might roughly be described as inhabiting that portion of Nepal which lies to the North of the Nepal valley between the Gurungs on the west and the Rais in the east, with Tibet as the northern boundary. They are still known as one of the mountain tribes of Nepal. According to an account of the Sunwars published by Namgyal Institute of Tibetology, Gangtok, they have "settled in the north-east, from the district of the Rai to that of the Newar. Kisi and Busi, two places rather centrally situated are said to be the most important settlements. Djoi and Kimti were near the Tibetan frontier".[96] Tradition relates that they Sunwar tribe came to Nepal from the very distant land of Churdji-bangchi after the Newars but before the Brahmins[97] which shows their primaeval antiquity. Their script called *"Koincha Brehs"* is as old as the Newari. And their language called *"Koinchlo"* belongs to the Tibeto-Burman group (of Sino-Tibetan family).

The Sunwars in Sikkim live in distant and difficult hilly terrain. They are found in few villages in the West District and are sparsely scattered in other districts (East, North and South) of Sikkim. They have, no doubt, a distinct ethnic identity.

The Magaras or Mangars, one of the aborigines of Sikkim and Nepal, belong to the Kirâta community of the eastern

Himalayas. They are one of the oldest tribes of Sikkim. Rajesh Verma has Reasonably stated that the Kiratis include Rai, Limbu, Gurung, Mangar and Tamang tribes of Sikkim.[98] The Mangars, Limbus and Lepchas are the earliest settlers of ancient Sikkim.[99]

Placing his reliance on the *Kirata Mundhum,* Iman Singh Chemjong states that a place called Shin in the northern part of the Himalayas was the original home of the Mangars. From there a group of people under the leadership of Shing Mangar and Chitu Mangar came to the south. The southern people called them Tangsang Thapa which means the people who came from the far away north. Later on, these Mangar tribes multiplied and were divided into twelve groups and called themselves "Barah Mangars" (twelve Mangars). The name of the twelve Mangars were Shinjali Thapa, Honjali Thapa, Hungchun Thapa, Chhodey Thapa, Pudkey Thapa, Mundey Thapa, Udhro Thapa, Bairong Thapa, Ishar Thapa, Barahi Thapa, Hangyung Thapa and Hangshe Thapa. When they came to Sikkim they settled there permanently.[100] The history of origin and migration of the Mangar tribe preserved in the *Kirata Mundhum* has, no doubt, some reliability. However, the author (Iman Singh Chemjong) has not left any clue regarding the identification of the place of their origin mentioned by him. Shin is generally identified with Chin but here it apparently stands for Tibet.

Iman Singh Chamjong further writes that "In the East Nepal and Sikkim the Mangars are so called because they were the children of Mang, Mong or Mongol people. The Chinese and Burmese people call Mang or Mong for Mongolians and ar or arui means children. So Mangar means the children of Mongols .... their complexion proves that they are no other than scattered Mongolians".[101] He is himself not sure about what he says as it appears from his own statement. He takes it as a mere postulation. However, he has not denied their Mongolian origin. On the authority of *Madhya Asia Kâ Itihâsa (History of Central Asia),* by Rahula Sânkrityâyan, the learned author has identified the ancient Mangar Kirat tribe of Sikkim and Nepal with "Kirait", one of the nomadic tribes of Central Asia. He says that long before the adoption of the name Mongol or Mongolians (in the 12th or 13th century A.D.) in Central Asia, one branch of the tribe Kirait and Mongku tribe of Central Asia spread towards Suchuwang, Yunan, Burma, Eastern India and Nepal. They did neitherhear the name Mongol nor they claim to be of their origin. The Mangar tribe of Nepal, he says, must be from the composite group of Kirait and Mongku who came to Sikkim and became Mangar.[102] The identification of Kirat Mangar of Sikkim or Nepal with the composite group of Kirait and Mongku of Central Asia is not worthy of our acceptance. There are certain Lepcha tribe called Mongormu. It appears that some of the Mangar tribe of Sikkim mixed with the Lepcha tribe and became a Lepcha Kirat people. The close affinity of language of Mangar with that of the Lepcha and Limbu is another proof that these tribes were contemporary settlers in ancient Sikkim.

Harsha Bahadur Buda Magar places the Mangars in Central Asia. They, according to him, were of Mongolian origin. They later occupied Bhotadesha or Tibet and Central Nepal. He further states that the place of their origin was Kham province east of Lhasa and west of China.[103]

The Mangars have been described in their *Vamshavali* as a Himalayan tribe and the descendants of Lord Shiva (the God of the Kiratas on the Kailash Mountain). There is an indication about their location near the Tsangpo river of Tibet.[104], B.K. Rana Magar has rightly pointed out that it will be wrong to consider India as the original homeland of the mountain tribes like Rais, Limbus and Magars. The Magars, according to him, were of Tibetan or Mongolian origin.[105] E. Vansittart has also unambiguously stated that the Magars are of Mongolian or Tibetan stock.[106] Their Mongoloid appearance and their language of Tibeto-Burman family support this view.

The Mangars or Magars after having settled in Sikkim in ancient times roughly before the fifth century A.D. ruled in its various parts independently like the Lepchas and Limbus. One of the groups of the Mangar tribe migrated from Sikkim to central Nepal sometime after the seventh century A.D. and settled in the mountain region between the rivers Bheri (Bharigar) and the Matsyandhri - the two of the seven tributaries of the Gandaka or Gandaki.

John Dalton Hooker, who conducted a scientific exploration in Sikkim in 1848-49, has mentioned that the "Mangars, a tribe now confined to Nepal west of Arun, are aborigines of Sikkim, whence they were driven by the Lepchas westward into the country of the Limboos and by these latter further west (Nepal) still. They are said to have been savages and not of Tibetan origin and are now converted to Hindooism".[107] It is significant to note that wherever the Mangars settled, they built *Jongs* (forts or castles in Mangar language). Their places of settlement were well fortified. The tradition of building *Jongs* or forts began in ancient times and continued till late medieval period. The Mangal kings built *Jongs* and established their rule forming small independent principalities in various parts of Sikkim. H. Risley, while dealing with the "History of Sikkim and its Rules" also mentioned about the rule of the Magar kings or chiefs in Sikkim.[108] The ruins of palaces and forts of the Mangars can still be seen at various places in Sikkim. Mangsari Mangarjong, Berthang-Berfok Mangarjong, Kamrang Mangarjong and Kateng Mangarjong are of historical and archaeological significance. Besides Sikkim, the *Jongs* or forts of Mangar tribe can be seen also in Nepal and Darjeeling.

The ruins of ancient villages, towns and forts of the Mangars in the valley of Kangpachena in East Nepal testify to their rule there. The Mangars established their rule also in West Nepal with the seat of their government at Bhirkot. There they called themselves Magar instead of the original name Mangar.[109] The migration of the Mangars from Sikkim to Nepal had taken place not only in ancient period but also in medieval period.

The Mangars are divided into twelve sub-groups called Thapa, Rana, Allay, Pun, Burhatoki, Gharti, Bohra, Roka, Chaohan, Konwar, Uchai and Jhakri and each tribe is sub-divided into many clans.

In Sikkim, the Mangars are mostly settled in the hilly terrain and near the forests. A very few reside in urban areas. They are thickly populated particularly in East and West Sikkim.

The Dewans, originally called Yakhas and commonly known as the Kirat, are one of the aboriginal tribes of Sikkim and Nepal. They are traditionally believed to be the descendants of Yaksha Raj of the Vedic age, but historically it cannot be authenticated. In fact, Tibet was their original home from where they first migrated to eastern Nepal and settled in its valleys and hills from where some moved to Sikkim in ancient times. Their Tibetan origin can be supported by the statement of E. Vansittart.[110] Some of the Yakhas dwelling in the mountain regions between the Sunkoshi and Likhu rivers and between the Dukhkoshi and Karki rivers in Nepal migrated to Sikkim and settled there. L.S.S.O' Malley has rightly pointed out that they "come from the same tract of country as the Khambas (Khambus) and Limbus".[111] The Yakhas were not known as Dewans before 1773 the reason for which has already been spelt out while dealing with the origin of the Rai. They are divided into thirty-three clans and six sub-clans. They have their own dialect like their closet Kiratis kins Rai and Limbu.

Bhujels, the ethnic hill tribe of Mongoloid origin, belong to the Kirâta domain. As evident from the history, the Mongols in the northern part of Central Asia were leading a nomadic life until the fifth century A.D. They were hunters who also reared cattle. The rivulets and streams of the Himalayas were used as tracking trails while hunting. Due to constant movement in search of newer pastures they lacked permanent settlement and mostly lived in natural shelters like caves. These people kept moving southwards over a period of time in the early centuries of the Christian era. Towards the end of the fifth century they settled in groups on the southern slopes of the Himalayas. The petty kingdoms were established over the period of time comprising few small villages. These petty kingdoms under various kings known as *Bhure Rajya* were established around the sixth century. The hilly regions of Nepal were ruled by different kings of the Khambu Rai, Magar, Limbu and other communities belonging to the Mongoloid group during the early medieval period.

In A.D. 885, the tribal kingdom of the Bhujel king (of Mongoloid origin) with its capital at Bhujikot was established in the Nisi-Bhuji region situated in the south-western side of the mountain Dhavalagiri (now called Dhaulagiri in Nepal) in the Himalayan range. The name Bhujel is derived from Bhujikot. The Bhuji kingdom comprised seventeen hundred small villages. Twenty-two kings of the Bhuji dynasty ruled over the kingdom between A.D. 885-1315. The Bhujels were displaced when the last king was defeated, dethroned and ruthlessly killed by the Khasa-Mallas (of the Karnali region of Nepalin A.D. 1315. The conqueror ordered all Bhujel male members above twelve years of age to be slaughtered. Few escaped and fled to safer and isolated places of Nepal, Sikkim, Darjeeling and Uttaranchal. The Bhujels of the present day Sikkim are the offspring of those who came here from the Nisi-Bhuji region of Nepal after A.D. 1315. They adopted the Bhuji Kura language which can be placed under the eastern Himalayan branch of Tibeto-Burmese family. Their Mongoloid features bear witness to the fact that they are not autochthones.

The Bhujel have been living in Sikkim since the fourteenth century A.D. They are settled in Daramdin, Salangdang and Soreng in West Sikkim, Gomkitam, Turuk and Tokal Barmiok in South Sikkim; and Jitlang, Pakyong, Rhenock and Tadong in East Sikkim. Like other ethnic tribes of Sikkim, they have their own culture, tradition and language.

The Kirâtas of Uttarâkhanda, extending from Kali on the east to Tons river on the west comprising Garhwal and Kumaon region or Kumanchal (present Almora, Nainital and Pithauragadh) were of indigenous origin. This part of India was one of the noted centres of human habitation in ancient tunes. The Kirâta tribes had been living in different forest tracts since prehistoric Age. In the Râmâyan age Uttarakhanda formed the part of North Koúala. Inspite of being surrounded by the Khasa, Úaka, Gujara, Bhotiya and allied races of the north and speakers of Âryan language on all sides they maintained their racial and cultural identities for a considerable period of time. But subsequently, because of inroads of Tibetans in succession in their territories the racial fusion had started resulting in admixture of blood.

Originally they belonged to Nisida stock, but after coming into contacts with the Tibetans, they got mixed with them. They are of both black and yellowish complexion, and on this basis they are believed to be of mixed origin, representing both Misâda and Mongoloid race.[112] Later many of them became Âryanised.

The origin of one of the very important section of the Kirâta tribes of Uttarakhanda, popularly known as the Rajis (royal men of the jungle) or Rajya Kirâta dates back to the prehistoric period. They represent descendants of one of aboriginal princes of Askot in Kumaon, who with his family fled to jungle to escape the destruction threatened by an usurper. The Uttarakhanda tradition also confirms it. According to another traditional belief handed down from generation to generation, they are supposed to be the descendants of a 'Candravamúî' king, named Wahin, which vindicates their claim of royal descent. Some of the caste Hindus consider the Rajis of dwarf stature and black complexion to be the descendants of Nisada. Their belief, that their forefathers dwelt on Nanda Devi, provides us a clue to their memories of the past, which have, unfortunately, taken the form of a legend. It is also suggested that the Kirâtas represented by the Limbus of eastern Nepal and Sikkim and the Rajis of Askot are of common origin. The Raji-Kirâtas were driven into the jungles by the dominating force of the Âryans. Some of them are also the descendants of the Ksatriyas. They still claim their descent from the Hindus on the basis of their Hindu names like Nandâ, Pârvatî, etc. Many of them fell into the category of tribes because of their settlements in the forests of Askot. They possibly, represent a living link between the Kiratas of somewhat Tibetan physique and the Khasas of equally pronounced Âryan form and habits. From the point of view of their physical appearance, language and religion they form the path of tribes of indigenous origin. It will be wrong to assume that they have Mongoloid feature with little intercourse with Âryans or Âryanised tribes.[113] The Kirâtas as described in *Kâlikâ Purana* appear to be aboriginal inhabitants of Kâmarûpa.[114]

It is noteworthy that the Kirâtas were known to the Âryans as a group of tribe whose original home was on or near the slopes of the Himalayas. Some of them had their original settlements on the mountain Kailaúa and in the territory around the Manasarovar (Tibet) in the northern Himalayas and were worshippers of Lord Siva their supreme God. Their descendants are still found in Nepal and Sikkim.

Most of the Kirâti tribes of northern and eastern Himalayas were of indigenous region. Those, dwelling from a very remote period on the banks of different rivers and in the mountain regions till the migration of the tribes of Mongolian origin, which started at later period, were, no doubt the origional inhabitants of the country. The dwellers of the mountain Kailasa in Tibet adjacent to Manasarovara, the marshy region near the sea-coast in the east, the hills and forests of Assam, south-east Bengal, Orissa, Magadh region in south Bihar, Nepal, north of Videha, Punjab, Himachal Pradesh, Kasmir and north-western region and of trans-Himalayan region extending upon the Oxus or Vamksu river can not be included among the tribes of Mongolian origin.

In the history of Kashmir the Kirâtas figure as one of the low caste groups along with Kaivartas and Candalas. Kalhana (1148-50 A.D.), chronicler of Kashmir speaks of them as one of the primitive forest tribes of Indian origin[115].

Some of the Kirâtas of south India like Boyas and Bedas were of Hindu castes. They were formerly Hindu cotton-cleaners. Some of them call themselves *Nishadulu* meaning legitimate descendants of 'Nishâdu'. They have also been classed as forest tribes, who used to employ Brâhmanas as. their priest.[116]

The description provided by the classical writers of the aboriginal Indian tribes of the Himalayas including the Kiratas also leads us to warrant the belief that a major section of them had their original home in India. On the basis of the accounts provided in the Fragments of Ktçsias and other supporting evidence it has been stated that the Kiratas and other tribes of the black aborigines dwelling in the upper Gangetic region or in the Himalayas bear the stamp of their Indian origin.[117]

Megasthenes' remark that "India being of enormous size when taken as a whole is peopled by races both numerous and diverse of which not even one was originally of foreign descent,. but all were evidently indigenous..."[118] It is a clear indication of the truth that till the fourth century B.C. no one came from outside to settle here.

It has also been correctly stated that "the wild hill-tribeson the frontier dwelling in recesses of jungles and hills as the relics of first inhabitant are the proper representative of the people in their pristine condition. Large number of them might have been humanised by amalgamation with more civilised emigrants. Foreign colonists had perhaps poured in by the land route from the teeming plains of Hindustan proper."[119] V.N. Reu, depending on various Indian and foreign sources concluded that all the non-Âryans conquered by the Âryans and driven to the forest and mountains to take shelter were the original people.[120]

On the basis of the evidences adduced so far it can be established without any hesitation that the Kirata tribes were by and large, of Indian origin.

In contrast to the above some attempts have been made in the past to prove the Mongolian origin of the Kirâtas both, in general and in particular, on the philological ground and on the similarities of customs and traditions without making any distinction between them and the indigenous one, which amounts to sweeping generalisation. However, the theories propounded by various scholars relating to their Mongolian origin are not to be put aside as wholly unworthy of attention nor are they to be summarily explained by *prima facie'* comments. Here we will examine thoroughly the relevance of various statements made in this regard keeping in view the few basic questions: what is the justification of the use of the term "Indo-Mongoloid" for them ? ; when did their migration begin from China? ; when did they settle in Tibet and Burma and mix with them?: are all the Tibeto-Burmese, with whom the affiliation of the Kiratas has been established, Mongoloids?; when did they move from their original home towards north-eastern frontiers and how did they merge with the Kiratas? where lies the demarcation line between the Indigenous Kirâtas and the Mongoloid Kiratas ? ; did the Kiratas not maintain their separate existence before the migration of Tibeto-Burman's or 'Sino-Tibetrans' or Mongoloids?, etc.

Before we proceed to find out the answers to all the questions and examine the different views of different scholars, here it will be profitable to make it clear at the very outset that the migrations of tribes of Ãhinese and Tibeto-Burman origins, so-called-Mongoloids and identified with the Kirâtas towards the northern and eastern frontiers of India had not taken place earlier than the first or second century A.D. After their settlements they got mixed with the Kirâtas living originally in the forest tracts and hilly areas right from the prehistoric age and absorbed many of them within their fold. Here lies the root cause of the whole confusion so far as the distinction between the Kiratas of indigenous origin and Mongolian origin is concerned. However in any case it will be a fundamental mistake to call all the Kiratas as Mongoloids.

The origin of the Mongols themselves is still veiled in mystery. It will be quite befitting to mention that the tribes of Mongolian or Tartar origin representing barbarous speech were first driven out by Hûnas in circa B.C. 180, who conquered Punjab, 'Cashmere' (Kashmir) and greater part of India during the time of Kaniska, as it distinctly appears from the Travels of Fa-hien (C.A.D. 399-414).[121] This proves that they entered India through north-west not before the first century A.D. Their migration towards Tibet and Burma, their mutual contacts and further the migrations of all three towards different directions will be discussed later so as to reach at any definite conclusion.

Yuan Chwang (Hiuen-Tsang), who visited Kâmarûpa (*Ka-Mo-Lu-Po)* in C.A.D. 640 had further observed that to the east of Kâmarûpa the country was a series of hills and hillocks ... and it reached to the south-west barbarians (of Chinese Province of Shu), hence the inhabitants were akin to the Man and the Lao. He further said that the people of Kâmarûpa were of small stature and they had a dark and yellow complexion.[122] There is no doubt that before the seventh century A.D. the racial admixture of the north eastern frontier tribes of Chinese and Burmese origins had already started. Ibn Battuta, an Arabian traveller, who visited India in the 14th century also referred to the Indo-Chinese population of Mongoloid origin, who had settled in north-eastern frontier.[123]

B.H. Hodgson, while dealing with the aborigines of the sub-Himalayas and of the eastern frontier in the late 40's of the19th century tried to create an impression that the Kirâta tribes of ancient Assam, Tripura and Nepal were all of Tibeto-Chinese or Mongoloid origin.[124] But he could not give any satisfactory explanation thereof. Nor did he produce any concrete evidence to make us believe that they were so.

J.W. McCrindle in the late 70's of the 19th century identified the Kiratas as described in the Indian and classical (Greek and Roman) literature with the Mongoloid race[125].

Sylvain Levi was another scholar to fall in order. In complete disregard of the evidences recorded in the Indian . literature some of which he has himself quoted, he proposed the racial affinities of the Kiratas with the Mongoloid people in 1905.[126] Ever since then it became almost a convention to connect the Kirâtas in all parts of the Himalayas with the Mongoloids merely on the basis of their physical characteristics yellowish complexion, dwarfish stature, round face, projecting chin, broad head, flat nose, oblique eyes, etc. whose descendants are believed to be mountaineers and foresters.

We find some contradictions in the statements of Rahula Sânkrtyâyana. On the one hand, he has admitted that the Kirâtas dwelling in the valleys of the Himalayas, Punjab and Kashmir were the oldest tribe, who had moved up to Kamboja through Burma and Assam in the east. On the other hand he has placed them under Mon-Khmer race of 'Sino-Mongoloid' group, whose branches are found from Champa to Nepal and from Burma to Kamboja ; and further he has opined that in spite of belonging to Mongoloid race the Kirâtas were not closely allied with the races of Chinese origin. The several branches of the Kiratas—Lahula, Milana (Kullu), Kanaur, Marcha (Garhwa), Rai-limbu, Yakha (Nepal) and Lepcha (Sikkim) living in the mountain regions were the speakers of their own language.[127]

From the above statements it appears that the migration of the Kirâta tribes started from India, but not from China. Even if we connect them with the Mon-khmer race of Kamboja which was within the geographical limits of Bhâratavarsa and where Sanskrit was the main language of communication, they cannot be taken as foreign as immigrants. It is not very clear is to how they have been connected with the Mongolian race. Anyway the most striking point in his proposition is that he has not directly linked them with the Chinese race. Nor has he attempted to prove them as the speakers of Sino-Tibetan or Tibeto-Burman group of language, as it has been done by others.

Suniti Kumar Chatterji, one of the chief exponents of Mongolian origin of the Kirâtas, has placed his arguments in support of his contention in different sources but in almost similar fashion. He has repeatedly called the Kirâtas of Sanskrit literature as '"Mongoloids" or Sino-Tibetan speaking tribes or speakers of Tibeto Burman branch of the Sino-Tibetan speech family. They, according to him, were connected with the Cinas or the Chinese, the Bhotas or the Tibetans, the Burmese and other Mongoloid peoples. He further states that the Kiratas or Indo-Mongoloids speaking languages of the Sino-Tibetan family, were present in India as early in the tenth century B.C., when the Vedic texts were composed. They were known to the Âryans as Kirâtas from Vedic times onwards in the Himalayan and Eastern Indian tracts. The Mongoloid Kirâtas came to India from China and Tibet before the advent of Âryans or when the foundation of a composite civilisation jointly formed by the Negritos Austrics or Nisadas, Dravidians and Âryans was already laid. It has been further presumed that the Âryans called the Dravidians as Dasas, Austrics as Kols, Bhils and Nisadas and Mongoloids as the Kirâtas. His statement, that "the Kirata, Indo-Aryan word, is Sanskritisation of some Sino-Tibetan tribal name" is no longer tenable in historical perspective. According to him, "the Sanskrit term Kirâta indicated the wild non-Âryan tribes living in the mountains, particularly the Himalayas and in the North-Eastern areas of India, who were Mongoloid in origin. These Kirâtas were connected with the Cinas or the Chinese, the Bhotas or the Tibetans and other Mongoloid peoples". He further states that the original home of the Kirâtas the Sino-Tibetan speaking Mongoloid tribes was western or north-western China. They spread from the upper reaches of the Yang-tse-Kiang and the Hwang-Ho rivers in different directions. They entered India partly from Tibet down the valley of Brahmaputra and partly from China through Burma before c. 1000 B.C. Their movements, according to him, began at large scale in the early part of the first millennium B.C. Their migration, as stated by him, covers the period extending from the prehistoric age down to the beginning of the Christian era. The said Mongoloid tribes gradually spread into different parts of the north-east and northern and eastern Himalayas. Then again, the Tibeto-Burman groups of Sino-Tibetan speaking tribes penetrated within the frontiers of India and established themselves in the sub-Himalayan barrier, they moved to Garhwal-Kumaon, Nepal and Sikkim. Some groups of the Tibetans in particular entered Bhutan and Sikkim. Most of the Kirata tribes of Nepal and

Sikkim, notably Magar, Gurung, Sunwar, Limbu, Yakha and Khambu (Rai) are speakers of language of Tibeto-Burman group or branch of Sino-Tibetan family.[128] The wild non-Âryan tribes living in the Himalaya mountains and in the north-eastern India called Kiratas are said to be Mongoloid in origin.

There are some fallacies in the above propositions. The Kiratas tribes having the pre-Âryan settlements were the original inhabitants of India. They were dwelling in caves, mountains and forests from very remote antiquity. Those tribes. who were called the Kiratas by the Vedic Aryans were neither the Mongoloids nor did they come from China, or Tibet or Burma during the Vedic period. Moreover, the Vedic texts were composed much earlier than the 10th century B.C. The successive waves of migrations of the Mongoloids started comparatively at later age, which has been discussed in detail little later. This is the common blunder on the part of scholars to identify the Kirâtas of the pre and post-Vedic periods with the Mongoloids or the Chinese, Tibetans and the Burmese. It is striking to note that neither all the Kirâtas were Mongoloids nor all the Mongoloids Kirât. That is why, Kasten Ronnow aptly remarked that "Suniti Kumar Chatterji's extension of the term Kirâta .to be an equivalent for Indo-Mongoloid was unfortunate.[129] Further, he also divides the Kirâtas into two sections viz. those who have affinities with Mongoloids and those, who are of mixed origin. Most of the Kirâta tribes of northern and eastern India according to him are of Indian origin.[130]

Robert Shafer (a noted ethnographer) has also quoted the above view of Ronnow but not supported it. Instead, he has classed the Kirâtas under Mongoloid race on the basis of their golden complexion as. described in the *Râmâyana* and the *Mahâbhârata.* He also holds that they were speakers of Tibeto-Burmic language.[131] It is very strange that without taking into consideration both the darkish and yellowish complexion as described in ancient Sanskrit literature he hastily put them under the category of the Mongoloids. The dark complexion is not an indication of the Mongolian origin of the Kiratas.

By no stretch of imagination the Kirâtas can be considered of Chinese origin. Some sections of them were, of coruse, Tibeto-Burman people. Most of the ancient Kirâta tribes in India were autochthones and not immigrants. The migration of tribes of Mongolian or Tibeto-Burman origin, called Mongoloids and identified with the Kirâtas, towards the north-eastern frontiers of India has taken place both anterior and posterior to the first century A.D. After their settlements they got mixed with the Kirâtas living originally in the forest tracts, hilly areas or mountain regions right from the prehistoric age and absorbed many of them within theirfold.

The Kiratas bearing the golden complexion and dwelling on the far slopes of the Himalaya in the mountain regions of the east and of the rising Sun in the Karusa by the shores of the Sea and on the banks of the Lauhitya as described in the scared writings of the Hindus have also been called Mongols and are identified with the Bodos of Assam, the Tibeto-Burmese race on the ethnological ground.[132] We do not have any evidence to support this hypothesis.

Depending fully on an anthropological explanation,[133] an attempt has been made by a historian to prove the Kiratas, as depicted in Indian literature, the 'Proto-Mongoloids'" or 'Palaeo-Mongoloids' (Brachycephals or long-headed and the broad-headed types), who formed a dominant element in the tribal population of sub-Himalayan region and Assam.[134] But this is not a valid analogy. Further, it is maintained that since the Kirâtas are condemned in the epic as 'low and barbarian' they can be undoubtedly called non-Âryan people of Tibeto Chinese or Tibeto-Mongoloid origin. They can be associated with the Cinas too.[135] The nature of explanation renders the theories hardly tenable.

R.P. Chanda combining in himself the qualities of an indologist, an anthropologist and a historian has made a very valuable comment. Criticising the approach made by Risley relating to the Mongolian origin of the people of Eastern India he stated that "his theory involves the assumption of that Mongoloid invaders preceded in large numbers the carriers of Aryan speech and culture in Bengal and Orissa. Further Kâmaûpa or Assam bounded on the west by the Karatoya was inhabited by powerful and cruel Kiratas. The Puranas relating to the origin of the people of Eastern India "know nothing of Chinese and Kirâta immigrants or aborigines." The people of Assam and Nepal have racial affinities with the Mongoloid people. But the Head form alone, unless accompanied by other Mongoloid characteristics, cannot be accepted as a sign of considerable Mongolian strain."[136]

The view that "in the later Vedic age the inroads of Kiratas or Mongoloid tribes from the east drove many of the Âryan settlements out of the district to the north of the Himalayas and entirely cut off the Uttarakuru country from all connexion with the plains to the south,"[137] is based on mere assumption.

The tradition is completely silent about the Mongolian invasions of north and east Bengal, held by the Prâgjyotisa kingdom, from the north-east.[138] Nevertheless, repeated attempts have been made by a number of scholars to connect the Kiratas of northern and eastern Himalayas including Assam, Bengal, Nepal and Sikkim linguistically with the Tibeto-Burmans or Sino-Tibetans and ethnologically with the tribes of Mongolian origin[139] without giving any justification or advancing any convincing arguments in support of their claims or suggesting any acceptable date of their migration from their original home—so-called China. Kirata was definitely not the general name of the Mongoloid people. In absence of any positive evidence the views concerned appear to be highly speculative. The supposition, that they were of Mongolian origin, is evidently wrong.

Further, the Kiratas, Cinas and mlecchas associated with Pragjyotisa in the *Mahâbhârata* and living on the extreme eastern fringe in the sea-coast region are also said to be of Mongolian extraction, who were known as aliens by the Brâhmanical Âryans of the Âryâvarta.[140] There is no reason to believe that the Kirâtas of the epic age were of the Mongolian family. R.N. Saletore has also remarked that the assertions that the Kiratas were an ancient Mongolian tribe...are merely imaginary and baseless."[141]

H.H. Wilson states that the Kirâtas like the Nisadas, Bhilas Bharamaras, Pulindas and other mlecchas living in the mountain side on the eastern extremity of Bharatavarsa were also the outcastes having the dwarfish stature with short arms broad head, flat nose, etc. They were living in the centre of the country of Kâmarupa.[142]

It is true that successive hordes of immigrants from the great hive of the Mongolian race in western China had poured into the plains of india through the gate of Assam and many are believed to have formed a considerable element in the tribal population of eastern Bengal and Assam,[143] but all are not pure Mongoloids or the Kiratas. The people of Mongoloid race are characterised by broad face, brownish-yellow complexion, small stature, high cheekbones, Chinese eyes, etc. This type is plentiful in Tibet and the high valleys of Bhutan, Kashmir and Nepal. Across the Himalaya and Burmese valley a continuous infiltration of Mongols had taken place and their further expansion took place all along the Ganges valley,[144] but all these outlying developments took place much later.

The Tibeto-Burman groups of the entire eastern Himalayas are generally called Kirâta by the historians, indologists, philologists and anthropologists. The eastern Himalayan tracts including Sikkim and Bhutan and adjacent tracts were the lands of the Kirâtas.

Some of the ancient most Kirâtas tribes of north-east India, popularly known as the Nagas (of 'Negroid' or 'Negrito' stock), Khasi-Jaintias (of Austric group and speakers of Monkhmer language), the Garos, Kacharis, Chutiyas and Hill-Tipperahs (of 'Bodo' group) and the Âkas and Mishmis (north Assam group) have been frequently called'Indo-Mongoloids.'[145] All of them have difierent racial background. All of them are of mixed origins. Some of the Nagas are believed to have come from Africa. The vast majority of them are said to have come from South-East Asia (Indonesia, Malaysia and Philippines). Some sections of them were also living originally in the plains and hills of Assam. The Nagas cannot be placed under the Mongoloids of Tibeto-Burman group either linguistically or ethnologically. The 'Proto-Australoid' or Austric Khâsis—the speakers of the Austro-Asiatic group of language—Mon or Talaing of South Burma and South Slam and Khmer of Cambodia are supposed to have migrated from south-east Asian countries. They are said to have "descended from some of the earliest Mongoloid immigrants, who changed their language through contact with Austric speakers either in Burma or on the soil of India in pre-historic times." The Khâsi-Jaintias are called Indo-Mongoloid by race and

Austric by speech. But these are all hypothetical views. Some of them have of course racial affinities with the Khmer family of Indonesia and Cambodia. But, it does not mean that they were Mongoloids. Traditionally, the Garos are believed to have migrated from Tibet.

Actually, the large section of the Khâsis.-Jaintias, Garos and Kacharis were living originally in the peains and hills of Assam in ancient times. But they were pushed towards hills by the Âryan conquerors from the Brahmaputra valley. The Tipperahs or the ancient Kirâtas of Tripura living originally in the hills belonged to both Ksatriya and Mongoloid stock. The Âkas and the Mishmis were inhabiting the extreme northeast frontier tract from very remote antiquity. They were the original inhabitants of the country. The Mishmis are connected with the sacred place of Brahmakunda—the easternmost place of Hindu pilgrimage in India, which was visited by Parasuram. The Chutiyas were also the original inhabitants of the Sadiya region in Assam. Many of the Kirâta tribes of present north-east India like the Jaintias, Kacharis and Tripperahs claim descent from both Âryan and non-Âryan stocks.

The Kiratas of ancient Nepal in the sub-Himalayan region are also of mixed origin. According to the *Vamsavalis* of Nepal they are of Ksâtriya origin of Âryan stock.[146] The "Kirâtas were the earlier inhabitants of the Nepal valley.[147] They did not come after the Australoids and Dravidians as supposed by others. But on the other hand, on ethnological ground they are called the descendants of the Mongoloids of Tibeto-Burmans and are believed to have migrated across north Burma and come into contact with original inhabitants of the valley. It is said that they formed a section of the migrants population of the valley."[148] From the nature of explanation it appears that they followed other races, who had settled in the valley. But as a matter of fact, they had their original home in Nepal.

D.R. Regmi's statement is self-contradictory. On the one .and, he calls them Indo-Mongoloid people, but on the other on the basis of the description provided by Kautilya[149] he observes that "we might also not hastily try to identify the ancient Kirata with any section of the Indo-Mongoloid tribes of the Himalayan region"[150].

Robert Shafer on the linguistic basis includes the Kiratas of Eastern Himalayan section among the Sino-Tribetans. The Kiratas of Assam and Nepal, according to him, were Mongoloid by race. On the basis of the nomenclature of a few Kirâta kings of Nepal such as Ya-Lam-ba, Ba-lam-ba, etc. he considers them as Mongoloid by race and Tibeto-Burmans by speech.[151] We find that their rulers belong to both Ksatriya and Mongoloid traditions. From their genealogical chart (as discussed in the chapter on dynastic rule) it appears that rulers belonged to both Aryan and non-Aryan stocks. Thus it will not be fair to call them only by the name of Mongoloid.

It will be wrong to say that bulk of population of Nepal are Tibetans or Mongoloids, and only the Khasa tribes descended from Hindu Rajputs and had Âryan characteristics.[152] Ancient Nepal also represents the mixture of races. The Tibetans penetrated in the most part of Nepal at much later age.

The testimonies, which are usually placed in confirmation of the hypothesis of the Monoglian origin of the Kiratas, as a whole, of the early period, particularly, of northern and eastern frontiers of India, run as follows :

The original home of the Sino-Tibetan speaking tribes or the people of Mongolian race was north-western China. They spread from the upper reaches of the Yang-tse-Kiang and the Hwang-Ho or Yellow rivers in diferent directions. They infiltrated into India partly from Tibet down the valley of Brahmaputra and partly from China through Burma by the Mekong, the Chindwin, Salween and Irrawady. Gradually they spread into different parts of Assam, Bengal, sub-Himalayan tract of Nepal and down to the Ganges valley. The Tibeto-Burman groups of Sino-Tibetan speaking tribes dispersed in some tract to the west and north of Tibet (the present day Chinese province of Si-Kiang) from where they began to spread east and south. Some of these early Tibeto-Burmans had penetrated within the frontiers of India either along the southern slopes of the Himalayas through Assam or by way of Tibet and further crossing the Himalayas barrier they established themselves into Nepal and Garhwal-Kumaon.[153] It is only on this ground that the Kirata tribes are not recognised as autochthones in India, but immigrants.

There may be some truth in the statements regarding the movements of the tribes of Mongolian origin towards Burma, Assam and Bengal, but so far as prehistoric race movement is concerned there is "no real evidence to show why the Mongolian invasion was diverted eastward".[154]

Robert Shafer has gone to the extent of presuming that ""Sino-Tibetan" and "Tibeto Burmic peoples" had pushed west and had occupied the Gangetic valley the richest part of Madhyadeúa, before the time of the *Mahâbhârata*"[155] In fact, the question of occupation of the Ganges valley by these .group of peoples before the epic age does not arise at all.

Different dates have been suggested about the migrations of the Kiratas or so-called "Indo-Mongoloids' from their original home already spoken of. According to S.K. Chatterji the original Sino-Tibetan speech, which was the ultimate source of ancient Chinese and its variant form Tibetan and Burmese had taken its form at least 3,000 years before the Christ.[156] The speakers of this group of language started pushing south and west probably from 2000 B.C. onwards.[157] Further, their movements towards the east might have been as old as that of the Aryans in the west at some period before 1,000 B.C.[158] The migration of the people of "Mongolian race called the Kiratas in Sanskrit literature from Isana (north-east) direction sometime before Buddha is also recorded.[159]

It is obvious that these dates are all conjectural. The dates and course of their migrations and meeting points of Sino-Tibetans and Tibeto-Burmese and their dispersion towards the north and east need further verifications in the light of the evidences furnished by the authorities on the histories of China, Tibet, Burma and South-East Asia in order to get a clear picture of the subject with special reference to the drawing of demarcation line between the Kirâta tribes of in digenous origin and Mongoloid origin.

Migration was professedly a law of ancient civilization. It is true that succesive hordes of immigrants from the great hive of the Mongolian race in Westrn China had poured into the vlaleys and hills of north-eastern India and many of them formed a considerable elements in the tribal population there, but they were not all Kirâtas. The migration of Mongoloid tribes of China has, of course, been admitted by some authorities on the history if China.

There were several branches of the Mongols in ancient China and their migrations from their original home took place at different periods. Actually, the history of the origins of the Mongoloid tribes of China are very obscure. The prehistoric, record of the Chinese bears testimony to the fact that the area around the great bend of the Hwang-Ho river and the wilderness of the mountain and sub-tropical jungle near Yang-tse-Kiang were penetrated by the aboriginal tribes. Then eventually Chinese spread all the way to the edges of the Mongolian and Central Asian desert, the Tibetan highlands and the frontiers of Burma and Indo-China. The Mongolians were the barbarous people of the outlying regions of Ãhina. In the west of north-western provinces (Mongolia, Chinese Turkestan and Tibet) the people were largely of Mongolian race "but their history is not strictly Mongol".[160] The original home of the Mongols is also believed to be the region on the south-east of Lake Baikal. They are called the descendants of Hunas. Another wave of Mongolian immigration started from Hukong valley and south-western China.[161]

As a matter of fact, from the sixth century B.C. onwards the Chinese Records make frequent references to the developments, which took place on the south of the Yang-tse-Kiang. It was in the early centuries of the Christian era that racial movements started from China.[162] A.C. Bouquet (Penguin Lecturer, comparative study of Religions in the University of Cambridge, 1932-1955) has clearly stated that out of the three groups of Mongol-Northern, Southern and Oceanic, the southern group includes the Chinese proper, the Burmese, the people of Indo-China and the various tribes inhabiting north-east Tibet and the Slopes of the Himalayas. Incursions ol Mongols took place in the 'early middle age'.[163] This statement is nearer enough to the truth.

The region, which is now known as Tibet (ancient Indian name Tribistap and Chinese Tu-fan) is said to have come into direct contact with China during the Seventh Century A.D..[164] The Tibetan tradition also confirms it. There was no influence of the Mongolian race or of the Chinese on Tibetans up to this period. Therefore, the use of the word Sino-Tibetan[165] for those of Kirata tribes, who had maintained their existence in the hill regions of north-east India and in the Sub-Himalayan tract of Nepal before the seventh century, will not be historically fair.

Tsepon W.D. Shakabpa, on the basis of 57 original Tibetan sources established that traditionally the Tibetans are of "Indian ancestry". He further reveals the truth that "Modern anthropologists call them Mongoloid race but up to now no comparison of the skulls of the Tibetans and the Mongols has been made."[166] This can also be confirmed by other evidence according to which the Tibetans are racially believed to be of the Chinese and Indian origins.[167]

The Burmese like the Tibetans are also of mixed origin. In fact, the Mongoloid stock, slant eyed and yellow skinned, left the principal home (in China), reached the Indo-Chinese Peninsula and blended with earlier stock in the early historical period. Though, the Burmese are believed to be a Mongolian race, yet their tradition instead of harping back to China refers to India. It has been clearly spelt out that there is no evidence to show that they came only from China. There is no trace of Chinese influence on vernacular alphabet of Burma. About thousand of vernacular inscription in Burma admittedly prove their Indian origin. Their chronicles also prove that they descended from Buddha's clans who lived in upper India. The Indian immigrants came to upper Burma through Assam and formed a large proportion of the population. Indian settlers no doubt in few generations became merged in the mass of Mongoloid tribes, who were also found in the country. The union of Mongolian tribes and Âryan immigrants or Ksatriyas from Gangetic India was gradually accomplished. The assimilation of smaller groups including the Indian and Chinese immigrants was actually progressing so steadily and imperceptibly through the centuries that the history of the origin of the various races became blurred. In ancient times the assimilation of three sub-families—Mon khmer, Tibeto-Burmans and Shans also took place. The Mongoloid in Burma mixed with many other races of darker stock from India by the first century A.D. The hill-tribes of Burma are considered to be the remnants of earlier races whom the present inhabitants of the plains pushed up into the hills. The Mons called Talaing by Burmese, whose language was akin to Khmer of Cambodia, are called Mongoloid, who inhabited Irrawady Delta and absorbed Indian culture and Hsnayana Buddhism.[168]

According to the reliable records the Burmese entered Burma sometime between the ninth and the eleventh century A.D. Their original home seems to have been somewhere in the north west of China, probably, Kansu between the Gobi-desert and north east Tibet.[169]

However, it will be a mistake to suppose that all Tibeto-Barmans migrated from north west or south-west of China. A number of authorities have racially classified them as Mongoloids. But they have failed to trace out their real origins as well as the processes of racial and cultural fusions going on in whole Indo-Chinese Peninsula comprising Burma, Siam and French Indo-China in the post Christian era. As a matter of fact, the Indo-Chinese Peninsula became a battle ground between the people of Indian and Mongolian origins. There was, of course, some blending, but Indian elements triumphed everywhere. Both ethnic and linguistic features of Tibeto-Burmans show that they were of mixed origin. They represent a strange mixture of the overflowing from the two great neighbouring countries. They belong to both Âryan and non-Aryan stocks including the Mongoloids of Chinese stock. It is very difficult to say as to what percentage of Âryan and non-Âryan bloods were flowing through the veins of ancient Indian tribes . and that of people of Tibet and Burma. In this respect we are actually handicapped because of lack of sufficient reliable evidence.

The comparative study of the data, as a whole, analysed and explained above gives us the result that the ancient Kirata tribes do not belong to any particular race, rather they are of mixed origin. Collectively speaking, they are of both Indian and Mongolian origins.

III

ANTIQUITY

While determining their antiquity it should be made clear at the very outset, that they were, by and large, pre-Aryan and pre-Dravidian tribes of India. We don't have much recorded evidence of their pre-Aryan settlements; nor do we have sufficient archaeological data to prove their pre-historic antiquity. However, only with the help of meagre evidence we can overcome the problem.

The Kirâtas of north-east India, no doubt, have primeval antiquity. The earliest centre of their habitation was the Brahmaputra valley. The references to the Kirâtas and their king Ghatak, who were defeated in a war with Naraka[170] and to their participation in the Great Bhârata war (c. 3102 B.C.) along with the Cînas and other mleccha as troops of king Bhagadatta,[171] the successor of Naraka and contemporary of Yudhiṣṭhira, irrefutably testify to their settlements long before c. 3102 B.C. and disprove c. 2000 B.C. or c. 1000 B.C. as erroneously supposed by many.

Further, the settlements of the Nagas in the upper Palaeolithic age as well as in the Neolithic age have already been proved by the discovery of several caves, rock shelters, stone tools and memorial stones in the hilly areas of present Manipur and Nagaland. The Khasis, Jaintias and the Garos had also settled in the Neolithic age, which is abundantly proved by the archaeological discovery of stone celts, as well as by the remains of different kinds of Megaliths. The Kacharis were the settlers of late Neolithic period. The Kirâtas of present Tripura had settled at later age, probably in the protohistoric period, as we have some indications to that effect. According to traditional evidence as recorded in their native chronicle, *Râjamâta* they can be associated with the Yayâti period (c. 3000—2750 B.C.), because they are believed to be descendants of Druhyu of Lunar dynasty. The Akas are connected with Banasura as their progenitor. The Mishmis were found during Parasurama period (c. 2550—2350 B.C.). The Chutiyas history begins with the early medieval period. They had settled in the region which was known as Sâdhyapuri in ancient times.

The Kirâtas of Nepal and Garhwal—Kumaon region are believed to be the settlers of prehistoric age. The systematic history of the Kirâtas of particularly Nepal begins with the epic age. The Vindhyan Kirâtas have not left any reliable record of prehistoric period. However, on the basis of literary evidences their antiquity can be traced back roughly to the pre-Christian era. During the Puranic period they were known by the names of Pulindas and Úabaras. They came into lime-light during the times of Dandin and Bânabhatta. The Kirâtas of Madhyadeúa were also one of the oldest inhabitants of the country. Their Âryan Janapadas have been mentioned along with that of Kuru-Pâñcala, Kâúi, Kosala, Anga, Variga, Magadha, etc. The Kirâtas of extreme north-west are as old as the Âryans. In the northern Himalayas and other parts of northern, central and eastern India they had settled at different periods of history. It is not possible to determine their exact antiquity. Their settlements in the Deccan in the second-third century A.D. during the time of trie Iksvakus, the successsors of the Satavahanas is proved by the epigraphic evidence. Those, who had settled in the far south in the twelfth century and during the period beyond it were no other than the Kiratas, who were dispossesed of their original seats located in the hills and forests of the Vindhyan regions.

The antiquity of Kirâtas of indigenous origin in Nepal goes back to the pre-epic age. The Kiratas of Mongolian or Tibetan origin in Nepal and Sikkim belong to both pre-and post-seventh century.

IV

IDENTIFICATION

The Kiratas mentioned in Indian and classical literature, epigraphic records and other interspersed sources under different denominations have not yet been properly identified. This will not be improper if some light is thrown on the origin and meanings of the word Kirâta. It has been said that the name Kiratas is a "Sanskritisation of some Sino-Tibetan tribal name...."[172] But historically we find it incorrect. It is more or less a misinterpretation of the fact. Actually, the Kirâta was a well known tribal name in ancient India. This name has been used in ancient Sanskrit literature for the tribes of Indian origin, but not the Sino-Tibetan origin. There is no evidence in our ancient historical records to prove the penetration of any tribe of either Sino-Tibetan or Tibeto-Burman family bearing the name 'Kirata' into the Indian territory before the dawn of the Christian era. In fact, the migrations of the tribes of Sino-Tibetan and Tibeto-Burman families towards India commenced from the early centuries of the Christian era onwards. Some of them, of course, mixed with those tribes of the Kirâtas stock, who had been originally living in India since pre-Vedic times. The 'Kirata' became a general designation of the tribes of the said families at much later stage. Therefore, the question of the Kirâta' being the Sanskritised name does not arise at all.

It is not correct to state that the term Kirâtas was loosely applied to any hill folk, no doubt, aborigines or used only for the primitive cave dwellers of the Himalayas, foresters and uncivilized or barbarous mountain tribes.[173] It is also not a correct explanation that in Sanskrit literature the term seems to have been used indiscriminately to designate only the border tribe of the northern and eastern frontier.[174] Nor is it quite proper to call the Kirâias as a mere Himalayan mountaineers and to identify them only with the Kirantis, who once reigned over a large portion of eastern Nepal.[175] They were a distinct class of tribe having their settlements in the Gangetic plain, the valley of Nepal, the hills and mountains of northern, central, and eastern Himalayas, including Sikkim, Vindhya region, etc.[176] As a matter of fact, not only the non-Aryan mountain tribes possessing the rude culture but also the degraded members of the Aryan stock leading the savage life of the foresters were known as the Kirâtas in ancient times.

In fact, the entire Himalayan belt has been regarded as the land of the Kirâtas. It seems probable that the Kiratas were once specifically the Himalayan people but the term was later expanded to embrace any hill tribe.

In the different literary texts of the pre and post-Gupta period we find that mostly those who were in the habit of wandering along the forests and mountains of the frontier regions or who living on the borders of hills or mountains named themselves as the Kirâtas. Their actions and mode of behaviour justified their nomenclature. Many of them were also known as wild tribe or degraded mountain tribe or a class of barbarian hunters, robbers, etc. and living upon fruits and roots.[177]

The word 'Kirâta' has also been possibly derived from Cirâta or Cireta or Cirayita. also known as Kirâta-tikta Prâkṛt = Cilaa-ittâ or Ciraa-ittâ) or Anârya-tikta—a very bitter plant of the non-Âryans,[178] grown in the lower regions of the Himalayas, which form the country of the modern Kirântis or Kirâtas. This is the name of a drug which was obtained from the Kirâtas by the Âryans and used for medicinal purposes. It is also possible that the Kirâtas themselves might have given the name to this drug, which was as bitter in taste as they were.[179]

The most popular Pali and Prakrit form of an appellation 'Kiratas', used in Sanskrit and common parlance, is 'Cilata'. In one of the Nâgârjunakonda inscriptions[180] and in the Hathigumpha cave inscription of king Khâravela[181] they appear as Cilata (Cina-Cilata) and Criata (Cina-Cirata) respectively. Actually the word has variant readings. The stone railings of Sanchi Stupa refers to them as 'Chirâtiya, (Cirata).[182]

The epigraphic evidence is also corroborated by the description provided in the Buddhist and Jaina texts. The Kirâtas were familiar to the compiler of the questions of Milindâ as the 'Cilatas'. In the Pâli '*Milinda-Pañha*' (IV, 8,94) there occurs the expression Cîna-Vilâta',[183] which has been identified with Cina-Cilâta, i.e. Cina-Kirâta.[184] T.W. Rhys Davids takes Vilata as Milâta and means 'Tartary' by it,[185] which is not a correct identification. The word is certainly identical with Cilâta= Kirâta. The letters for C and V are frequently interchanged in old script as they are in Devanagari. It is also believed that the reason for the use of the word Kiratas as Cilata in different texts and incriptions is the replacement of the letter 'r' by 'l', which was probably introduced by the people of the Kirata race themselves. This linguistic transformation seems to have taken place first in the east during the Brâhmana period as we find the use of the word 'Kirata' (which is the form of the name Kirata) in some of the *Brâhmanas,* already described in the preceding pages. Subsequently, between the sixth and fifth century B.C. they became popular by this name both in the north and in the east as we find them in the classical, Pali and Prakrit texts. Further, the transmission of this word followed in different other parts of India from the centuries immediately preceding the Christian era onwards. This also indirectly shows the impact of non-Âryan culture of the Kirâtas on the Indo-Âryan.

The Jaina canonical texts mention them as the 'Cirâtas'. The 'Cinarattha' as referred to in the Pali *Sâsanavamsa Himavantâpadeúa* and in the *Apadâna* (11. pp. 358-359)[186] may be an equivalent to Cina-Cirâta. The Kirâtas find mention in the Pali commentaries *(Sumaṅgalavilâsini,* 1. p. 176 and *Sammohavinodani,* 1. p. 388) as a wild tribe.

It is significent to note that in the different literary texts as well as, in ancient Indian inscriptions the Cilâtas or Cirâtas or Kirâtas are associated with the Cinas,[187] which have been mistaken for the Chinese by a number of scholars for lack of extensive search. And it is because of this misunderstanding that sometimes the Kirâtas are connected with the Chinese and described as Mongoloids in origin. As for instance, B.A. Saletore was led to believe that the "Cinas and the Kirâtas were associated together because of their Mongolian origin."[188] But the truth runs far from it.

The classical geographers and historians of pre and post-Christian era have applied different designations to the Kiratas and supplied both reliable and fabulous accounts thereof.

The 'Kallatiai' of Hecataeus[189] and Herodotus[190] (very much identical with the Kiratas of the *Brâhmaṇas* and the Ki-Lo-to of the Chinese texts) can be identified with the Kirata tribes of north-western India. While describing the nomadic, barbarous and settled tribes on the Indo-Persian frontier and farthest towards the east of the fertile lands of the Indus, they casually refer to the Kallatiai (also known as Calatians), who were the hill-tribes of the Kabul valley. Some of them inhabited the marshes of the rivers and were eaters of the raw fish, which they used to take going out in boats made of reeds.[191] The said tribe as mentioned by Herodotus has been connected with the Kirrhadia or Kirâtas represented by the aboriging tribes of low country beyond the Ganges or the ancient inhabitants of the marshes of Mymensing and Sylhet. The existence of canni-bal in the hilly countries on the eastern frontiers of Bengal was known to Herodotus.[192]

The Kiratas, because of their being of small stature in comparison with the 'Arian Indians' (Âryans) have consequently been confounded with the pygmies, as it appears from Ktçsias the Knidian's account furnished in his *Indika*. They are described at some length in his work. "They dwelt in the interior of India, were black and deformed, had snub noses, long hair and extraordinarily enormous beards, etc. They were excellent archers and three thousand of them were in the retinue of the king. Their sheep, oxen and asses and mules were unusually small... They were very brave and hunters of wild animals. They followed the Indian laws and were just men."[193] The Indians themselves considered this dwarfish people as belonging to the

'Kiratas' race they were barbarous people and degraded mountain tribe inhabiting woods and mountains and living by hunting. They were so diminutive that their name became a synonym of dwarf and through their neglect of all prescribed religious ritcs were reduced to rank of Ǘûdras.[194]

Ktçsias also refers to the battle of the Indian pygmles with the Cranes (as Homer mentions it in his *Iliad;* III, 3ff). According to Indian myhology "the Garuda the bird of Viúnu, had enmity towards the people of the Kirâta, which for this reason is called Kirâtasin i.e. the devourers of the Kirta and the name of this people has also then meaning of a dwarf". Megasthenes[195] designates the dwarfish race of the Kirâtas as 'Trispithamoi' *i.e.* men three spans long.[196] "If in mythology a simple bird of this kind usually occurs, it is to be remarked that it passes at the same time for the father and king of the divine birds, and there is nothing to hinder us from believing that according to the ideas of the people a battle of this bird with the Kirâta was thought to have occurred. The pygmies with their battle against the Cranes have also been transferred to Ethopia from their original home in India. Whether the legend concerning them had already reached the Greeks at the time, when the poems of Homer were composed, may be left undecided."[197]

Some portions of the above account may, however, appear fabulous and mendacious. Moreover, the style of writing is not distinguished by any conspicuous merit.

If the remark that they lived in the interior of India does not agree with their actual position which is assigned to the east of Bengal, in the Himalaya and further to the north, it must be understood that foreigners had attributed a wider extension to the name, so that it designated even a people in Orissa.[198] From the further application of the name several characteristics attributed to the pygmies explain themselves, which partly suit the true Kirâtas, who were beardless, but, on the other hand, wore long hair. Among them occur the flat noses,[199] but not the black complexion by which the Gonda and other Vindhya tribes are on the contrary, distinguished. Here also, a commingling of characteristics may be assumed. Both these peoples, however, are distinguished by their shortness of stature. It has been rightly said "the pygmies were a race of small stature, covered with long hair and lived by hunting. They dwelt in the upper valley of Irrawady between Momein and Manipur."[200]

Megasthenes (the Greek historian of the 4th century B.C.) mentions them under two different names *i.e.* 'Scyritae' and 'Skiratai'. The former is placed among the nomadic race of India, who instead of, nostrils had merelye orifices and whose legs were contorted like snakes.[201] It is believed that the tribes of this group were living on the very confines of India on the east near the source of the Ganges.[202] They were also identified with a Naga clan.[203] The latter group is placed beyond India, which is not perfectly correct. And it is further said that "they are snub-nosed either because in the tender years of infancy their nostrils are pressed down, and continue to be so throughout their later life or because such is the natural shape of the organ."[204] Whatever may be the truth, the tribes of both these groups are identified with the Kirâtas: And it is further described that some of them dwelt in Mount Mandara and others used their ears as a covering. They were horrible, black-faced and cannibals. Those, who were brave, could not be exterminated.[205] Such figurative description are usually in the *Indika* of Ttesias and Megasthenes. None of them can, however, be an exception to the classical practice of very often presenting the accounts of the subject concerned in the similar fashion.

J.W. McCrindle (an authority on classical writings on ancient India) describes them as a "barbarous people" who inhabited the mountains and lived by hunting and were of diminutive stature. He further says that the distinctive feature of that race are indicative of their "Mongolian origin". (AIMA, pp. 74-75, note.)

They were also living beyond Kaukason.[206] Lassen places one branch of them on the south bank of the Kosi in Nipal (Nepal) and another in Tippera (Tripura).[207] The identity of Chirotsosagi of Magasthenes (Chisiotosagi of Pliny) has been established with the Kiratas,[208] but this identification is of a dubious value.

Pliny (the Roman geographer and historian of the Ist century A.D.) in his *Natural History* (BK. VII. 2, 14-22) refers to them as Scyrites or Syrictes.[209] It has been pointed out that the appellation 'Scyritae' represents a curious mixture of Seres (applied to the peoples through whose hand the Silk product came) and 'Cirrhadae' (generally identified with the Kiratas). He describes them as having "merely holes in their faces instead of nostrils," which denotes the face of flat-nosed people. He connects them with an allied race, the' Astomi' a people who were living on the eastern side of India near the source of the Ganges; their bodies were rough and hairy and they covered themselves with leaves of trees.[210] The expression is Partly believed to be a reflection of his possession of knowledge of the silk trade, which was carried on through Assam. The word Scyritae appears to have been originally referred to the dealers in silk,[211] which was produced both in Assam and China. It is suggested that in ancient times traders from different parts of Tibet, Central Asia and China flocked to Assam through various routes, and as they traded mostly in silk, they were called Seres, Scyritae or Cirrahadoi or Kirrhadoi or Kirata.[212]

Aelian's (middle of the Second Century A.D.) 'Schiratae' also seems to be identical with the Kiratas.[213] Arrian has made mistake in placing the 'Kirrhadae' on the coast and on the western side of the Ganges. He also refers to some of the fabulous tribes, which are not only a fiction, but also an absurdity. He, like other Greek writers, might have borrowed it from the natives of the country.[214]

In the classical accounts of India we frequently come across one section of the Kirâtas, who were mountaineers, eaters of raw fish and nomadic, and spread practically over whole of the northern part of the Indian sub-continent. Pliny also describes them as a wild tribe, allied to the 'Ichthyophagi Oritae', who were subsisting on raw fish. He describes them to be mountaineers and places them after the Gedrusi (Baluchistan) and the Pasires.[215] They also lived on the coast near the mouth of the river Thomeros (modern Hingol), and were a wild race, ignorant of the use of iron and covering themselves with the skins of wild beasts.[216]

The author (anonymous) of the *Periplus* who was the Greek merchant and traveller of the first century A.D. mentions the Kirâtas under the names of 'Cirrhadae' and 'Besatae'. The author himself states that "beyond the region of Dosarene, the course trending towards the north, there are many barbarous tribes, among whom are the Cirrhadae, a race of men with flattened noses, very savage; another tribe, the Bargysi...who are said to be cannibals."[217] This statement has given rise to a lot of speculation about the location and identification of the place inhabited by the Kirata race.

The Greeks in the first century A.D. heard of them during their visits to Western India and South India as a tribal people living in the regions to the north-east of Dosarene (Sanskrit Dasarna) or Orissa by the sea possibly in the delta of the Ganges. They may be the Kiratas of West Bengal to the West of the Ganges in the regions to the north-east of Orissa. The Bargysoi identified with the Bhargas of the *Visnu Purana* are mentioned as neighbours of the Kirâta race.

Schoff identifies the Dasarna as mentioned in the *Râmâyaṇa,* the *Mahâbhârata* and the *Viṣṇu Purâṇa* with modern Orissa ('the holy land of India') and opines that it was a populous and powerful country. He, on the other hand, identifies Ptolemy's Dosaron with modern Mahanadi.[218]

There is also an another evidence to show that the cirrhadae, identified with the Kirata, has been regarded as a tribe of the mountain and jungle tracts of Orissa.[219] The Dosarene as mentioned in the text denotes Orissa or extreme tract of jungle on the Southern parts of Bengal viz. *Sunderbuns* bordering the sea, Arrian mentions Dosarne as situated not in the vicinity of the Ganges, but at a considerable distance from it. It is quite probable that he refers to an inland country or that tract of a jungle lying on the south-west side of Bengal, which was called in ancient times 'Dasaranya' or Dasarna, because of, constituting ten forests cantons. It seems to have comprised "Sumbhulpore, Sirgoojia, Ramghur (Ramgadh) and Chotanagpur." Dasârna signifying ten forests or strongholds contained ten chiefs. The tribes of this region were like the savage tribes of Rajmahal. These forests in general were also called 'Jhati-Chanda' or Jhari Khanda which signifies a country abounding with Jhari or place overgrown with thickets. The extensive forest tracts of both Bengal and Orissa were inhabited by the Kirâtas.[220] In the *Periplus* the Dosarene is placed at much greater distance from the Ganges. The tribal people styled as Cirrhadae and placed in the intermediate space has been relegated by Ptolemy on the eastern side near the source of the Ganges. Lassen supposes it to be Brahmini.[221] The Dosaron of

Ptolemy is also said to be the river of Orissa region inhabited by the Daúâinas, a people mentioned in the *Visnu Purana* (tr. Wilson, pp. 186-192) as belonging to the Southeast of Madhya-desa (the Midlands) in juxtaposition to the Sabaras or Suars. It was one of the four rivers, which entered the Gulf of Bengal between Kannagara and the Western mouth of the Ganges. Yule has located the Sabarai (Sabaras) in Dosarene near Sambhalpur. They were a wild race living in the jungles without any fixed habitation.[222]

Lassen has observed that the "account in the Periplus shows that ship sailing northward from Dosarene or the country on both sides of the *Vaitarani* arrived at the land of the wild, flat-nosed Kirrhadai, who like other savage tribes were the men eaters. Since the author of that work did not proceed beyond *Cape Comorin* and applied the name of the Kirâta to a people ; who lived on the coast to the South-west of the Ganges it is certain that he had erroneously used the name to denote the wild and fabulous races."[223] The position assigned to them may not be correct, but the credibility of the statement of the author of a classical document, which is based on an eye-witness account cannot be doubted, so far as the existence of the Kirata is concerned. Moreover, there is no logic behind placing them under the fabulous races. In this regard the statement made by J.W. McCrindle is, no doubt, worthy of credence. He says: "by the Cirradioi are meant the Kirata, a race spread along the shores of Bengal to eastward of the mouths of the Ganges as far as Arracan. They are described by the author of the Periplus of the 'Erythraean Sea', who calls them the Kirrhadai as savages with flat noses. He places them on the coast to the west of the Ganges, but erroneously. They are the Airrhadoi of Ptolemy."[224]

Taylor, on the basis of their Indo-Chinese feature as generally ascribed to them, identifies them with the tribal people of Eastern India. He does not agree with Vincent, who considers them as the 'Mughs of Arracan'. He equates them with the Kiratas of the *Puranas*. Like the Dosaren their country is erroneously described by Arrian as bordering the sea. They are called the inhabitants of the mountains of eastern India, north-east Bengal, and identical with the Kirâtas of Morung to the west of Sikkim.[225] This is supported by other evidence also.

Schoff, while identifying the Cirrhadae of the *Periplus* with a Bhota tribe, says that their descendants known as the Kiratas lived in the Morung and in the valley of Nepal. Their location, according to him, is not on the sea as indicated by the text, but in the valleys of the Himalayas. They are also located on the Brahmaputra.[226] Lassen identifies them with the Bhota race of modern Bhotan; who were allied to the Tibetans and inhabited much of Bengal at the time of Aryan settlements. The Kiratas, one of the ten different tribes have been reckoned as poweful and placed in Eastern Nepal.[227]

The Âryan professed the greatest contempt for the Kiratas (so-called 'the Tibeto-Burman races') at their eastern frontier. Some of the references to this effect, full of exaggeration and fable, were later transmitted to the Greeks. The contemptuous description of their faces as 'noseless' finds reflection both in the accounts of Megasthenes and Pliny (VII. 2). Being under-sized they were called 'pygmies'. The *Varaha-Samhita Purâna* mentions a race "in the mountains east of India, that is, in the hills on the Assam-Burma frontier as Aúvavadanah, horse-faced." The 'horse-faces' and 'long-faces' as used by an author of the Greek text[228] for the peoples living to the north of the Kirrhadai and known as cannibals are almost equivalent to the term 'Hayamukha' mentioned in early Jaina literature for the mleccha and barbarian people. It is quite apparent that such kind of expression is not only an invention of classical mind but, to some extent, it was also borrowed from Sanskrit writings. Their description as cannibals is not at variance with that of Herodotus. The ancient Tibeto-Burman tribes in the 'Chin Hills between Assam and Burma' are also placed in this category.

The Besatae as mentioned in the Greek text were allied to the Cirrhadae or Kiratas. They have been called Tibeto-Burman tribes and identified with the Kuki-Chins, Nâgâs, and Garos.[229] Lassen identifies them with a tribe of Sikkim.[230] But the author of the text himself locates them on the borders of the land of 'This'.[231] which is difficult to determine. However, there some supporting evidence to prove that this was the border of Assam and China, where the Khasi tribes traded in *malabathrum* (tezpat) with the Chinese through the Tibetan intermediaries, the details of which are provided in connection with their are external trade system in this work. In the text it is clearly stated that on the borders "there comes together a tribe of men with short bodies and broad flat faces and by nature peaceable: they are called Besatae and are almost entirely uncivilized... They meet in a place between their own country and the land of 'This' and bring *malabathrum,* which is produced in the country of the Cirrhadae in the Eastern Himalayas. This is native in this part of the Himalayas being one of the principal trees." They are further referred to as people of the Himalaya mountains exporting this product to China.[232]

The above description shows that they were the tribes of present north-eastern India. It is true that *malabathrum* was also produced in Tibet in abundance,[233] but it will not be correct to state that the borders of the land of 'This' indicates that Tibet was then subject to China.[234] It may be the border of Tibet, where the Kirâta tribes of north-east and the Chinese might have entered into commercial intercourse. The Besatae also known as Bisadae were of very diminutive stature and living m caves among the rocks in ancient times.[235]

The Besatae or Basati are also identified with the Tibeto-Burman tribes living about the modern Gangtok near the eastern border of Tibet.[236] McCrindle on the authority of Hemachandra's *Abhidhânacintâmani* places them between the Indus and the Jhelum.[237]

From the *Mahâbharata* it appears that they were the people of the mountain regions. The Parvatiyas and Basatidesa figure together. They also joined the army of Duryodhana.[238]

They were known to Pâṇini *(Aṻṭâdhyâyi,* IV. 2. 53) and Patañjali *(Mahâbhâṣya,* IV. 2. 52) as the Vasati tribe. They have been identified with the Greek Ossadioi, who had settled if somewhere in the region of the confluence of Chenab and Sutlej with the Indus.[239] Pânini had knowledge of many tribes and janapadas of north-west, which the Greeks have described. It appears that one branch of them had also settled in the north-west, where they were known by different names.

Ptolemy is one of those classical authors, who mentioned them under various names in the first half of the second century A.D. in his geography, which is, undoubtedly, a faithful historical record. While elucidating the geographical position of India beyond the Ganges *(India extra Gangem),* he uses the term 'Airrhadoi' by which are generally meant the "Kirrhadia or Kiratas". He had, of course, very hazy ideas about the geography of the countries to the north of the Ganges delta, particularly, of the north-eastern corner of India, which also comprised Pragjyotisa. Notwithstanding the fact, it must be admitted that he had a sound knowledge of the ancient tribes inhabiting different parts of India including north and the east.

By the name Kirrhadia (also Kirradia) he designates a country on the coast of further India extending from the city of Pentapolis in the north (perhaps the present Mirkan Serai) to the mouth of the Tokosanna or Arakan river. The name of this land however, indicates that it was inhabited by those Kirâta people, who are placed in the great Indian epic in the neighbourhood of the Lauhitya or Brahmaputra, somewhat further to the north than Ptolemy locates them.[240] Hence, arises the question whether the Kiratas, as we know them, and, who also belong to the 'Bhota' and are still found in Nepal, had spread themselves to such a distance in earlier times or whether their name has been erroneously applied to a different people? He has given to the name Kirata a signification, which did not originate with himself. Although, the Kirâta long before the time in which he lived, had wandered from their northern Fatherland to the Himalaya and thence spread themselves to the regions on the Brahmaputra still it is not to be believed that they should have possessed themselves of territory so far South as Chaturgrama (Chittagong) and a part of Arakan. We can, therefore scarcely be mistaken if we consider the inhabitants of this territory at that time as a people belonging to further India and, in fact, as tribal relatives of the Tamerai, the members of the same Kirata family, who possessed the mountain regions that lay back in the interior. Betwteen the name of the city Pentapolis *i.e.* five cities and the name of the most northern part of Kirradia, Chaturgrâma *i.e.* four cities, there is a connexion that can scarcely be mistaken. Since Chaturgrama could not originally have denoted a country, but only a place, which later on became the capital of four village communities over which a common headship was possessed and while pentapolis was the seat of a headship over five towns or rather villages, it can scarcely be believed that the rude tribes of Kirradia were civilized enough to possess towns. A confirmation of this view is offered by the circumstances that the Bunzu, who must have been descendants of a branch of the Tamerai, lived m villages under the headships.[241]

The Airrhadoi or Kirrhadia of Ptolemy (the Greek geographer of the second century A.D.) is identical with Kirâta (AIP, pp. 191-92 and 219) which, according to G.E. Gerini (who carried out an extensive research on Ptolemy's Geography), is a generic team for the mountain trihebs with Mongoloid featurs. They inhabited hill and mountain tracts. He has placed them in the hills of the north-east, Burma (ancient Brahmadesa, now Myanmar), upto the borders of Tibet, and in Assam, Bengal and Orissa. (RPGEA, pp. 28 ff and 829-30).

Wilford was misled by a corrupt reading and consequently took the name of the Airrhadoi to be another form of Antibole, and described it as the eastern most branch of the Ganges. He identified Airrhadon with Hardana as the name of the Brahmaputra. He has identified Chaturgrama and Pentapolis of Ptolemy with Chataon or Chittagong and Pattanphulli respectively,[242] which were flourishing seats of politico-cultural activities in ancient times. But he has not indicated the position of the Kirrhadia.

The view expressed by St. Martin (a French Sholar, who derived his authority from the ancient Indian, Greek and Roman writers) is worth quoting here: "the Kirrhadia of Ptolemy, a country mentioned also in the *Periplus* as lying west from the mouths of the Ganges and the Skyritai of Megasthenes are cantons of Kirata, one of the branches of the aboriginal race, the widest spread in Gangetic India and the most anciently known. In different passages of the *Puranas* and of the epics their name is applied in a general manner to the barbarous tribes of the eastern frontiers Âryav-arta and it has preserved itself in several quarters, notably, in the eastern districts of Nepal. There is a still surviving tradition in Tripuri (among the Tipperahs), precisely, where Ptolemy places his Kirrhadia and the first name of the country was Kirat (Long, *Chronicles of Tripura,* JASB VoL. XIX, p. 536). The Tamerai were a tribe of the same family".[243]

The Airrhadoi, whose country embraced in Ptolemy s time the eastern coast of the Gulf of Bengal from the mouth of the Brahmaputra down to the mouth of the Arakan river, have been clearly identified with the Kirrhadia-(Kirâtas). In support or this identification, the evidence recorded in *Vâlmiki. Râmâyaṇa* (*Kis. Kâṇ.* already quoted) alluding to the Kirâtas has been fairly attested to by Gerini. According to him, at an earn period the tribes of rude mountaineers such as one generically termed as the Kiratas occupied the region to the east of the lower Brahmaputra even down to the sea coast and the islands of the Gulf of Bengal. This is further strengthened by his arguments that the Kirâtas with stiff hair tufts were dwelling in islands and subsisting on raw fish in the regions to the east of India. These fish eating tribes occupied at an early period the littoral, the adjoining islands of the Indo-Chinese coast and they racially belonged to the same stock of the hill men or Kirâtas as evidenced by the passage of the *Râmâyaṇa.*[244]

It appears that, on the basis of the testimony of Ptolemy Gerini with greater accuracy has assigned to them an island position eastward of the river Ganges, which denotes their settlement in the eastern region of India *(intra-Gangem)* corresponding to present Assam. But, on the other hand, we find that while identifying Ptolemy's Airrhadoi with the "Kirâtas, he has made certain mistakes.

He has inferred that in subsequent times they were driven back towards the hill-tracts by invasions of Dravidians chiefly Ândhras and Kalingas, from the opposite coast of the Gulf, who forced their way along the littoral as far as the limits of Arakan and, probably, even to the Gulf of Martaban, establishing colonies, as they proceeded. These Dravidian invasions are said to have occurred before c. 295 B.C..[245] The fact remains that those, who were pushed back towards the hills and forests by the Dravidians, were the Kirâta tribes of the Deccan and southern Peninsula, but not of the east. In fact, there is no corroborative evidence to prove that the Kiratas of the hill regions of north-east migrated from the land of the Dravidians. He has gone too far in the realm of imagination.

Depending on Pliny, the Elder's references to the Kalinga and Ândhra as being situated near the sea and on both sides of the Ganges in the last part of its course, and the position, assigned to *Andra-Indi* in *Peutingerian Tables* a century later corresponding to the Coast between the left bank of the Ganges and the present Arakan river and taking the term 'Indra-dvipa' of *Viúnu Parâna,* called in the middle of the 12th century A.D. by Bhaskara-Carya as Aindra for the eastern position of Bharatavarsa, he has mistakenly identified the Airrhadoi of Ptolemy with the people called Andhras or Aindras of Dravidian extraction.[246] This seems hardly plausible for various reasons.

Ptolemy's Kirrhadia also denotes the land of the Kirâtas.[247] His statement (VII.II. 16), that their country was famous for the best quality of *malabathrum*[248] is a positive indication towards the land of the Khasi-Jaintia tribes of ancient Assam (or present Meghalaya), where to this very day tezpat is largely produced. This identification is also supported by other statements. James Taylor also holds that since *malabathrum* is a indigenous product of eastern part of Bengal and is grown in abundance in the valleys of the mountain range of Assam, Kachar and Jaintia and in Sylhet and Rangpur, the Kirrhadia of Ptolemy can be no other than the people inhabiting them.[249] J.W. McCrindle has also asserted that in Sylhet, which is not very remote from Chaturagrama, *malabathrum* is produced in abundance.[250] Lassen calls it the principal product of the eastern Himalaya mountain.[251] Sir George Watt, a recognised authority on the commercial products of India also affirms that this product was obtained from the tribes of eastern Bengal, Khâsi-Jaintia hills and from Jaintia Pargana in Sylhet.[252] We do not see any reason to doubt the correctness of this identification.

Gerini with firm conviction identifies Ptolemy's Kirrhadia with the ancient Kirata tribes of Sylhet, Tipperah (Tripura) and Kachar.[253] He has further added that "the Garo tribes of the hills not far away to the north call themselves Achikranghill people *i.e.* Kirata". On the basis of the position assigned to the Kirrahadia of Ptolemy in Nicholas De Doni's map (west of Anina=Yung Ning No. 67 and far away to the north of Arisabion=Shenbo, No. 54 *i.e.* in No. Lat 28) he locates them at the headwaters of the Iravati and Chindwin in the present Khampti country and Hukong valley north of Burma and up to the borders of the Tibetan Kham district. He also employs the term Kirâtas for Kiutsz, Kachins, Kadus and Chins of the hills in the South-West.[254] We do not have any basis to support the view that the Kirrhadia from the relative situation given to it % Ptolemy may be regarded as the country of the Kirâtas in the Morung. Vincent, on the supposition, that their country was well known for *malabathrum,* wrongly locates them in Arakan about the mouth of Megna.[255].

The Kirâtas have also been used by Ptolemy albeit under their alternative appellations of Tiladai and Beseidai or Besadae.[256] All were of the same family. The Tiladai are placed by him to the north of Maiandros i.e. a range of mountains about Garo Hills to the east of Sylhet and Mymensing. The same position has been assigned to them by D'Anville in his *Geography.* They are said to be subsequent invaders of Tibeto-Burman race.[257] Regarding Tiladai McCrindle says that "We here leave the regions adjoining the Ganges and enter the valleys of the Brahmaputra".[258] The upper part of the Maiandros was also called tilas or hillocks and Tiladai were naturally the inhabitants of Tiladri hills or Tila mountains (Cachar Hills').[259] More or less the same interpretation is given in *Kshetra Samasa.* The same people is mentioned in the *Periplus,* but under the corrupt form of Sesatai. The picture drawn of them by the author of that work corresponds so clearly with Ptolemy's that both authors may be supposed to have drawn their information from the same source. Ptolemy places the Basadai above the Maiandros, and from this, as well as, other indications we can take them to be the hill-people in the vicinity of Sylhet. One of the reasons for applying this name to them is said to be their physical features. He mentions that they were short in stature, shaggy, broad faced and flat-nosed, but of a fair complexion, which are characteristic features of most of the hill tribes on the eastern frontier of Bengal.[260] The tribes in the eastward of Kachar ("Heramba-deúa or Tipperah") were also called ' Basadae. On the one side of the mount Maiandros the 'Nangalogai' ("Nanga-loga=the Nagna-deúa or the country of the naked Nâgâs") is-also placed by Ptolemy. The 'Bhasada' tribe as mentioned in the *Vamana Parana* are identified with those 'Bsadae' who were living in the eastern most part of India.[261]

The Beseidai are located in the map of De Donis south west of Kirrhadia and north of Alosanga (Shillong No. 37) *by* which

Gerini means the population of Bisa and Sadiya in modern Lakhimpur (N.E. Assam), who are evidently the Mishmis of the adjoining hills. By Tiladai he presumably means the tribes of Sylhet, Kachar, Chin Hills etc. He clearly identifies the Tiladai and Beseidai people to the north of Maiandros (Garo Hills) with the Kirrhadia or Kirata people of Sylhet, Kachar, eastern Assam, Sheila, Shillong, Sadiya and Bisa.[262]

The ramification of the tribes of Kirâta family figures under the names of Zamirai and Tamarai in the great geographical catalogue of Ptolemy. The Zamirai, a race of cannibals are located near mount Maiandros. They are also placed in the midst of the "Savage districts extending to the south and south-east of Magadha and to the west of the Sone". They bear resemblance to the inhabitants of the so-called Silver Country corresponding to Arakan and the gold country, the golden frontier land of Burma being fair complexioned, shaggy, squat figure and flatnosed. The Tamarai, as well as Zamirai inhabited the Garo Hills located near Kirrhadia's land.[263]

The people called Sesatae,[264] who inhabited the country on the confines of Thinae, are identical with the Besadae of Ptolemy and placed on the range of mountains, called Maiandros, as uncivilized tribe. The tribes exhibiting so-called Indo-Chinese features are also called Sesatae. They are identified with northern Garos, Khâsis, Kacharis, Nâgâ tribes (Nangalogae) etc.[265] In Vincent's translation rendered by Heeren's *Asiatic Nations*. They are described as aboriginal tribes of the region bordering Assam.

It is quite evident that the Greeks and Romans have applied not only the racial but also occupational designations to them. As for example, those who dealing in silk were called Scyritae and those who were trading in *malabathrum* the Basadae or Sasatea.

The presence of the Kirâtas proper (not Mongoloids in origin) in Assam, Nepal, Sikkim, Tibet and Burma in pre and post-Christian era can fairly be attested to by the evidence furnished in the classical literature. They may be distinguished from those Kirâtas who are of Mongolian or Tibetan origin.

The accounts of the early Greek and Roman geographers have been strongly supported by B.C. Law,[266] N.L. Dey[267] and E.T. Atkinson.[268] They have expressed their agreements with the author of *Periplus,* as well as, with Megasthenes, Pliny and Ptolemy, so far as the use of Scyritae and Kirrhadia for the Kirata tribes of north-eastern India is concerned.

The classical writers from the fourth century B.C. ownwards place them near the marshy regions in south-east Bengal and hills of Assam. Depending exclusively on the classical testimony, the Kiratas of Pragjyotisa as mentioned in the epics, the *Pur-âanas,* the *Tantras,* etc. can undoubtedly, be identified with the Khasis, the Jaintias, the Garos, the Kacharis. the Akas, the Nagas (Nangalogoi), the Tipperahs, the Mishmis, the Chutiyas and those tribes who were living during the times of Naraka and his successor, Bhagadatta and further settled in the neighbourhood of Lauhitya or Brahmaputra.[269] This finding will further carry some weight, if we are allowed to put forth the views of some local authorities on the history of Assam. K.L. Barua identifies the Kirâtas with the country inhabited by the tribes from the foot of the Garo and Khasi Hills to hill-tracts of Tipperah along the eastern coast of Brahmaputra.[270] In the words of R.M. Nath: "The Austrics (the Khasis and the Jaintias), and the Bodos (the Garos, the Kacharis. the Chutiyas and the Hill-Tipperahs) were termed as the Nisâdas, Kiratas and Dasyus in the same way as the Dravidians were termed as the Danavas and Daityas and Negroids as the Vanaras. They were at feuds with each other for establishing their position".[271]

According to P.C. Bhattacharya, "the people known in the present day Assam, Nagaland, NEFA (present Arunachal), Manipur and Tripura as Boro, Rabha, Garo, Lalung, Miri (Mishing), Monpa, Aka, Dafla, Adi (Abor), Mikir, Khâsi Synteng, Dimasa, Meithei, Tipra, Hajong, Mizo (Lushai), Nâgâ Mishmi, Singphou, Apatani, Nokte, Wancho, Kuki-Chin, Khamti and a large number of so-called tribes residing in the hills and plains belong essentially to the Mongoloid or Kirata race."[272] He has blindly identified the Kiratas even with all those tribes, who had no existence in ancient times in North East India. The Mizo, Hajong, Dafla, Adi Singphos, Âpatanis,. Nokte, Wancho, Kuki and Khampti were the settlers of the later period, and, moreover, they were not racially connected with the Kiratas. Only those tribes of north-east can be Identified with the Kiratas, who had settled in the early period extending from the Pre-Vedic age down to the tenth century A.D. Moreover, all the Kiratas, as stated earlier did not belong to the Mongoloid race. Therefore, it is very difficult to endorse his view in toto.

Here it will be quite befitting to the context to mention that the Meithei (the people of Manipur Valley) are not included among the Kiratas as erroneously supposed by some writers. Only the Nâgâ tribes of the hill areas form the part of the Kirata population of Manipur. L. Iboongohal Singh has correctly stated that "The original inhabitants of Manipur were the Kiratas—some tribes of Nagas. But that time Manipur Valley was full of water... The bulk of population in the eastern India are of Kirata origin."[273] Atombapu Sharma has simply referred to the 'Kirata of Manipur'[274] without providing any further details thereof. J. Roy's statement that "Hindu Purâna locates Manipur within Kirâtadesa"[275] can very easily be falsified, because, we have not come across any such reference so far in the Puranic records. Further, in the *Kriatakalpadruma* of Lakshmidharna (placed between 1100–1150 A.D.) also, Manipur has been located in eastern India beyond the Kirata region :

"Purve Kirâtaḥ jasyante Manipurastatâḥ Param..."

Ptolemy's 'Kirrodes' or 'Kirrhodoeis' (Kirrhadai) located on the northern extremity of India (Uttarapatha) under the Oxus (Vamksu river) adjacent to Sogdian mountains" have been clearly identified with the "Kirâtas as foresters and mountainers" and have been included in the list of Indian tribes.[276] We can scarcely doubt the validity of the identification and their location.

The last classical writer to mention them was Nonnos, who flourished sometimes between the fourth and the fifth century of the Christian era. In his work called *Dionysiaka* or *Bassarika* he mentions them under the name of 'Cirradioi', who are evidently the people of the Kirâta race. He places them near Ariana (Airya or Âiryana or Arya-deúa or Airyanem-Vaejo *Zend Avesta,* west of the Indus or south of the Hindukush forming part of ancient Bharatavarsa or the country between Persia and India with eastern boundary at the Indus comprising the Bactrians of Bâhlikas of the Hindus, eastern Persians, Sogdians and Âryans), Kashmir (Kaspeiria) and the region immediately to the west of the Indus and adjacent to a territory lying between the Indus and the Bidaspes (Hydespes or Jhelum).[277]

The Kirâtas, on the whole, as described in the classical literature, can be identified with those tribes of north-western India, north-eastern India including Assam, Bengal, Tripura, Orissa, Nepal and Sikkim and of Tibet and Burma who had settled in the plains, valleys and hills between the epic age and the fifth century A.D.

In some of the *Purâṇas* the Kirâtas and Pulindas inhabiting the Vindhya region appear to be very much similar.[278] Actually, the name Pulinda was applied to Vindhyan mountaineers in general and in some cases to any aboriginal tribe. The meaning of the Kirâta, originally a Himalayan tribe wasalso similarly modified.[279] There were three branches of the Pulindas. viz. (*i*) a Western branch, (*ii*) a Southern branch and (iii) a Himalayan branch. The Himalayan branch was closely related to the Kiratas and Tanganas.[280] In the *Mûhabhârata* also the Kiratas, Pulindas and Tanganas appear to be identical tribes dwelling in the mountain regions of the Himalayas under the kingship of Suvâhu.[281] These three hill tribes appear to have mixed with each other and lived amicably together. They, along with their common king were residing in the region around Mansarovara lake, which comprised the ranges of Kailâsa, Mandara and Haima.[282]

The lexicographer, Amara Simha has rightly described the Kirâtas, Sabaras and Pulindas as three different branches of the mlecchas. He does not find much difference between these kindred wild tribes.[283] The confusion relating to the similarities among the different classes of the wild tnbes was not only confined to him, but to many other ancient writers. We find that even Kautilya mentions some of them in more or less same style He also refers to the Sabaras, Pulindas, Cândalas and other wild tribes (aranyacarân) together.[284]

The Kirâtas are spoken of in a seventh century text as identical with the Bhilla and Lubdhaka tribes and Matanga of the Vindhyas. The Kirâtas and Sabaras have been mentioned by Dandin again and again as the same people.[285] All of them were, of course, mountaineers and foresters, but those, who were archers and fighters, became popularly known as the Sabaras and the hunters as the Pulindas.

The identification of the Kirâtas with some sections of the Bhills and aboriginal Indian tribe rof Vindhya Hills and

Rajputana is also corroborated by Kalhan's account.[286] He has also described the Kirâtas and Sabaras in an identical manner.[287]

It is generally held that the name Kirâta was applied to the numerous fair complexioned or yellow coloured hil! tribes of Mongolian race that lived in all parts of the Himalayas. But, on the basis of the description of their physical features available in the epics and the *Purâṇas,* we find that they were of both yellowish and darkish complexion. Therefore, only on the basis of their yellow colour it will not be reasonable to place them in a Mongolian family. Their general physical characteristics show that they were a race of dwarfish stature with short arms, round face, projecting chin, broad head, flat nose, oblique eyes, etc., whose descendants are mountaineers and foresters (girikânana gocara). H.H. Wilson[288] has rightly suggested that those, who constitute the posterity of the race with black complexion and other general features, also include the Kirâtas, Nisadas, Bhillas, Bahanakas, Pulindas, Bhramaras and other barbarians living along the mountain side.

The ancient Kirâtas have not at all disappeared from the history of India. One section of them is geographically, racially and linguistically represented by the modern Kirantis in the easternmost province of Nepal.[289] The identification of the name Kirant with the Kirata of Sanskrit litereture has also been supported by Gait.[290] But the statement, that "It is not however, of any importance to speculate on the history of the word" made by Grierson[291] amounts to falsification of the truth. His further observation that the dialects of so-called Kiranti group are closely related to dialects spoken by tribes, who have never claimed to be Kirânts[292] also runs contrary to the truth. It is true that the term is used in different sense by different authorities, but the fact remains that the speakers of this group of dialect are still known as the Kiranti, which is corruption of the word Kirati.

The Kirântis or Kiratis are, no doubt, those who were dwelling on the slopes of the Himalayas especially in the Kirant-deúa or the mountainous country lying between the Dudh-Kosi and Karki rivers in Nepal. They are generally identified with the Khambu, Limbu and Yakha or Yakthumba tribes. They are believed to be the descendants of the ancient Kirâtas of Nepal. Formerly their name was used in comprehensive ways.[293]

The ancient name Kirâta still survives as the designation of a sub-Himalayan tract extending from Dudh-Kosi to Arun river on the east. This region, which has been famous as the Kirâta-deúa from very ancient times, was the habitat of the tribes collectively known as the Kirâtis or Kirântis.[294]

The Kirata tribes even at present occupy the portion of the eastern territories of Nepal between the rivers Sunkosi and Arun. The Nepalese tradition and chronicles or *Vamúavalis* also prove that they were an offshoot of the tribes now living in that part of the country called Kirâta-desa.[295] It has been rightly pointed out that there was a "Ciratas country to the east of Nepal."[296] The Kirântis living between the Sapta-Kauúaki and Sapta-Gandaki (representing ancient Nepal) have been correctly identified by Hodgson with classical 'Cirrhadae' (Kirâtas).[297] They are now numbered mostly amongst the Limbu tribes of the central region of the eastern Nepal and on the frontier between Sikkim and Nepal the Kiratas are regarded generally identical with the Limbus. According to him the Sub-division of the tracts inhabited by the Limbus are two in numbers—Kiranta-deúa extending from Dudh Kosi to the Arun river and the Limbudesa from the Arun to the Konki. He considers the word Limbu a corruption of *Ekthumba* (Yaka-thumba), the correct denomination of the people and generally used to designate the whole population of the country between the Dudh-Kosi and Meeni or Mechi except such as belong to the well-marked tribes of the Murmis, Lepchas and Bhotiyas, who are Buddhist and the Parbatiyas, who are Brahmanical.[298] With regard to the affinity of the tribes, thus conjoined, he observed, that they are closely allied race having essential community of customs and manners and they all intermarry. In the generic term also the Kirâtas include the Limbus, the Ekas (Hodgson's Yakhas) and Rais and that in appearance and habits they are all very much akin to each other. They are placed under two great divisions called Hung and Rai. These are sub-divided into various tribes. Some sections of them are believed to have come from the province of Chung in Tibet. Campbell thinks Limbus, of Mongolian family but as they are much mixed up with the Lepchas, he evidently considers them a less Mongolian than that tribe. A vast majority of the Rai-Limbus now found in Sikkim, Nepal and Darjeeling still call themselves as the Kirâtis.

The identification of the Kirântis of Nepal with the Limbus,. an important segment of the population of Sikkim, is also supported by T. Dalton. The Kirântis, according to him were also found in Dinajpur, which formed the part of ancient Matsya-desa.[299] He calls the Kiratis, Kharwars and Kols a cognate race.

The ancient Kirantis of Nepal, a very powerful people in the neighbourhood of the tribes on the northern frontier of the Himalayas are said to have held dominion down to the delta of the Ganges.[300] They were both short and tall in stature having well-formed face, fair camplexion, small, as well as, large oval eyes, scanty beards, short nose, etc.

Eastern Nepal and its neighbourhood have been appropriately named as Kirânt country. The Kirântis or Kirâtis inhabiting this country in the larger sense are sub-divided into three different parts, viz: (*a*) Wallo Kirânt or Hither Kirânt from the Sunkosi to the Likhu including the Limbus, Yakhas and Lohorongs, (*b*) Majh or middle Kirant from Likhu to Arun comprising Bontawa, Rodong, Dungmali, Khaling, Dums, Sangpang. Bahing, Thulung, Kulung, etc. and (*c*) Pallor further Kirant from Arun to the Mechi and the Singilela inhabited by the Chourasyas. An old name of the Kirât a country in Eastern Nepal was "No-Lakh Kirât." The Khambus live to the north-east of Jimdars and Yakhas on the southern spurs of the Himalayas. The country of the Khambus of Nepal is also known as Mahakulung. Their name is also associated with the fighting tribes of Nepal, who are placed under the head of Kiranti.[301] Gait's statement, that the Khambus are not Kirantis,[302] can be outrightly rejected.

Hodgson has placed the complex pronominalized language of Nepal under the head of Kirânti, which is connected with Tibeto-Burman group. He has carefully analysed and described them. He further connects the Kirânti language with that of the Kolarian group. He also notes analogies of formation between the Kirânti and Dravidian language.[303] They have no written characters of their own. Their language, because of being labial and palatal rather than nasal and guttural is pleasing to the ear. Linguistically too the Limbus are connected with the Kiranti.[304]

The most powerful section of the Kirântis who settled down in the Valley of Nepal in ancient times, probably in the pre-Christian era, are identified with the present day Kirâtas *i.e.* Kulung, Thulung and Yellung.[305] The Newaris, who happen to be one of the oldest inhabitants of Nepal Valley are also identified with the Kiratas. They are supposed to have lived between Gandaki and Sunkosi. In support of this identification it has been noted Newari name of Patan Yellai is a changed form of Yellung and nence, most probably, they were the Yellung Kirâtas.[306] A.K. Warder, while referring to the Kiratas, who are familiar in Sanskrit literature as the inhabitants of the Himalaya mountains, also identifies them with ancient Kirata people, entertaining some doubts in his mind.[307] We don't have any reliable evidence to approve such identification. By no stretch of imagination, the Newaris, Gurungs, Magars and Lepchas can be identified with the Kirâtas.

It is believed that in Nepal, the Kirata people lived in the Karnali, Koshi and Gandaki regions in ancient times before the arrivals of the Aryans and Tibeto-Burmese there from the south-west and north-east directions respectively. It is said that "the Kiratas of North (Rais) and the Limbus of the south were known to the ancients by name of Kirata on account of their living by hunting and carrying on trade with natives of the plains with yak tails, shellac, cardamom, etc. from the earliest period. (S.C. Das, *A Journey to Lhasa and Central Tibet, 1904, p. 3, note.)*

The Kiranti people of eastern Nepal, more commonly known as Rai and Limbu, form together one of the largest single ethnic groups in Nepal. W. Brook, Northey and C.J. Morris (*The Gurkha*, London, 1928) speak of tripartite division of the Kiranti, Khambus, Limbus and Yakhas. The Magar, one of the aborigines, were in the valley of the Arun to the west of Sikkim. They inhabited the eastern and western parts of Nepal. The Sunuwars were originally settled in central and eastern Nepal. One branch of this tribe migrated from eastern Nepal to Sikkim. We are informed by B.P. Mishra that the Magars are the dwellers of the mountain regon between the two rivers, Bheri and Matsyandhri. And the Gurungs occupy the large mountain tracts extending from the land of the Magars upto the Pall region of the Himalayas. (*Nepal Kâ Itihâsa*, pp. 19-20). The hilly regions of Nepal were ruled by the chiefs of the Magar, Khambu and Limbu tribes of so-called Mongoloid group during the early medieval period.

W.H. Schoff notesthat the cirrhadae mentioned inthe *periplus* was a Bhot tribe whose descendantsstill known as Kirata live in Morung (Nepal), west of Sikkim, with marked Mongolian features, fromelly independent and powerful, having provided a dynasty of considerable duration in a Nepal. Their location in the valleys of the Himalayas is beyond dispute (*Periplus*, p. 253, note.)

It has been rightly pointed out that there was a "ciratâs country" (Kirâtadeúa) to the east of Nepal, *i.e.,* sikkim ("An Account of the kindgom of Nepal", by Giusepee, communicated by John Shore, *As. Res.,* Vol. II, Delhi, 1979, p. 253) Ancient Nepal and Sikkim were, in fact, thetwo famous heartlands of the Kirâtas.

The "Danaur, Hayu and Thami tribes also claim to be Kirântis",[308] but their claim is disputed by other Kiranti tribes of Nepal.' They have also no connection either in appearance or language or religion with any important section of the people now inhabitants of the tract between Tons and the Sardâ It has also been attempted to connect them with the Katyurs but the arguments advanced in this regard have no worth.[309]

The ancient Kirâta tribes of Uttarâkhanda are identified with Ban Râji or Râjis (Râjya Kirâtas of the *Purânas*) or Ban Rawats or Ban Manusa dwelling chiefly in the forests and reveral other villages of Pargana Askot on the bank of Kali (Sarada) in the eastern part of Kumaon (also known as Kali-Kumaon) and in the Darukavana near Jageswar (Yagisvara), ancient Amaravana, in the Chaugarkha Pargana and the forests of Bhavara in Almora and in the Chipalakot jungles between the Gori Ganga and the Dharam Ganga. Besides, the raji Kiratas are numerous along the foot of the hills below the province of Doti, the most Westerly district of Nepal, and it is on this basis that they are considered an equipvalent to the tribes inhabiting the localtiy assigned to the Chepang viz. the forests of Nepal, west of the great valley, and, therefore, between the Kirantis and the Khasiyas. From their language also it appears that they are of ordinary aboriginal stock like the Kirântis of Nepal. One of their brnaches, the Limbus of Nepal and Sikkim, and the Râjis of Askot are, without any doubt, identical with the Kiratas. The identification established here is primarily based on the historical researches of some prominent authorities on the subject concerned.[310] It has been conjectured that the Rajis resemble the other numerous aboriginal tribes found along the Himalayan border all possessing the physical features of the Bhotiyas in general.[311]

The Thadus or Tharus occupying the Tarai region from Nepal and eastern Rohilkhanda along the frontiers of Oudh to Gorakhpur are also supposed to be identical with the Kirâtas. The great bulk of them are now subjects of Nepal Government.[312]

The Kichak occupying the mountainous country between Nepal proper and Bhotan have been identified by M. Martin with the Kirâtas. This identity was disclosed to him by some of the mountain chiefs with whom he had some conversation before 1838.[313] Their identification, particularly, with the Kiratas of Nepal has also been confirmed by R.G. Latham.[314] The people of Matiyare district have also confused traces of invasions and conquests of the "Kichak or Kirâtas" and mention several old princes of Morung—a country of the Kiratas, to whom they still offer worship, and whose usual priests were the Pariyal, who are said to have been their Soldiers. In his account of 'Rangapoor' (Bengal) Martin has mentioned that he was informed by some Pandits of Puraniya that the Kichak were known as the Kirata, an infidel or Asura tribe. The ruins of one of their large buildings in 'Rangapoor' called Asuragarh or the house of infidel to whom the neighbouring Hindus used to offer worship, constituted the mute evidence of their existence in the past in Bengal. The dynasty of Prithu Raja, which preceded that of Dharmapala, one of the kings of Kamarupa is said to have been destroyed by a vile tribe called Kichak.[315]

One of the principal sub-divisions of aboriginal hill-tribes in Central Provinces of India, known as Kirârs, who were emigrants from Bundelkhanda and Oudh[316] can of course, be identified with the Kirâtas.

There are certain words current in new Indo-Âryan language, which are said to be connected with the racial name Kirâta. In Bengali the word name Kirât/Kiret is applied disparagingly to money-lenders extorting money from poor debtors, to an exceeding miserly person and to those, who are noted for their cruelty. This shows "a pejorative employment of the tribal name (Kirâta = Vṛtta=those who behave like Kirâtas, cruel and stingy people>Kirâvatta>Kirâvata>Kirât >Kiret)". 'Kirad', a common caste name in Uttar Pradesh, Rajasthan, Madhya Pradesh and Berar in Maharashtra is used in the sense of a (Hindu) merchant. It also means 'a corn-chandler and a robber'. It is also used for 'a dalesman, a forester' in the Punjab. In the Western Punjab, the Hindus, who were in a minority, were scornfully called by their Muhammadan neighbours as Kirâd, The form of the word Kirâd as opposed to the Bengali Kirât/Kiret appears to have come from a "contemptuous expression Kirâta-ta (Kirâ-a-da>Kirâd) an originally implied to a person, who was like a bad Kirata, a bad man, a robber or Swindler". The name Kirâta employed for an uncouth non-Âryan tribe is believed to have acquired some sort of stigma among Âryan speakers. It is suggested that "This stigma came to be applied partially at least to the name Kirâta as early as the age of the Brahmanas c. 8th—7th centuries B.C."[317]

In a separate list, showing identification of ancient places, as well as, tribes appended at the end of R.C. Majumdar's work, only this much information has been supplied that "The Kirâtas formed a series of allied yet distinct tribes or clans inhabiting the Himalayan range and its southern slopes from the Punjab to Assam and Chittagong".[318]

The identification of the 'Kirâta' with "an urban region in ancient India"[319] does not help us to establish anything with certainty. Perhaps this refers to a region in the north which fell under their occupation before the seventh century.

The Kirâtas of South are mainly identified with Bedars or Boyas inhabiting mostly the hilly regions, forest tracts and outside areas in Mysore and Andhra Pradesh. They are found in Bellary and Kurnool Districts. They are believed to be the descendants of the old Kirâtas, classed as forest tribe, hunters and mercenaries or fighters. According to Mysore Census Reports of 1891 and 1901, the Bedars had tow divisions—the Kannada and Telugu, twenty Sub-divisions of which one was called "Kiratâka". The founder of the Bedas family was a Boya Taliari, who on subversion of the Vijayanagar dynasty seized various other districts. The name Kirâta was also assumed by *Ekaris,* who according to the Madras Census Reports of 1891 and 1901, were found in northern Taluks of North Arcot and in the adjoining districts of Cuddapah.[320]

The description of the Kirâta women given by the Kannada poet Virabhadrarâja (c. A.D. 1530)[321] has been taken as that of the Bedar women.[322]

The Bedars also figure in the early epigraphic records of Mysore. Between the seventh and the twelfth century A.D. they were in the habit of plundering the neighbouring villages of Brahmanas, as well as, non-Brahmanas. It was Ganga king Kongunivarman who in order to pacify them gave a land grant to some of their chiefs in A.D. 887.[323] But till the thirteenth century the Deccan greatly suffered from their depredations.

In ancient times the Bedars were a mleccha tribe or a class of barbarians but, in course of time, they felt the deep impact of Sanskritization, and, consequently, attained a higher grade of culture. As a result of their gradual cultural transformation, most of them joined the fold of Hindus and assumed the Hindu names. That is why, at present they mostly represent the Hindu caste.

V

EXPANSION AND COLONIZATION

The Kirâtas were a widely diffused race in ancient India. There were different phases of their expansion in northwestern, northern, central (Madhya-deúa), eastern, western, southern and greater India. Nothing definite can be postulated about the period which marked the beginning of their expansion in any particular region. However, on the basis of certain available indications it can be established that this process, completely different from that of the Âryans, began sometime in the Vedic period in the north and the Gangetic Doab, in the epic age in greater part of north-eastern India and further went on intermittently there as well as in different other parts of India, and ended with their expansion in the South towards the close of the twelfth century A.D. In the early phase of their expansion as evidenced by the contemporary sources, they were confined to northern and eastern India only. But with the passage of time they gradually spread over other parts of India also, because of socio-economic and political compulsions and several other historical factors. However, they could not colonize as many places as they desired, owing to various reasons. In absence of sufficient authentic historical and archeological data and systematic writings, it is not possible here to present the account of the subject coherently and chronologically.

Their settlements in different parts of north-western and northern India in remote antiquity is provided by their constant association with the Gandharas, Yavanas, Sakas, Barbaras, Cinas, Daradas, Ramathas, etc., as reflected in the *Mahâbhârata*[324] as peoples of Uttarapatha (Uttarâpathajan-milnah) and with Lampakas and Jâgudâ (in Afghanistan), Culikas or Sulikas (Sughdha as known to the Avestic writers, Suguda in inscription of the kings of Achaemanian dynasty and Greeks' Sogdians, Hellenised after Alexander, and living to the north of the river Oxus, called Vamksu or Caksu in Sanskrit and Vakku in Prâkrit), Aurasa (Urasa of Panini, IV. 3. 93—the people of modern Hazara District in northern Afghanistan), Kambojas, Hamsamargas, Kasmira, etc., as depicted in the *Purâṇas.*[325]

The evidence furnished above may be taken to suggest that they had not only settled down and found their territory near Gandhâra (modern Kandhar) to the west of the Indus, but also spread in the Upper Kabul Valley (Paropanisadae of the Greeks), Hazara District and other parts of Afghanistan (Arachosia of the Greeks, the then part of India), the mountain region of the Oxus Basin (Ketumala of ancient times) and later in Punjab (Vahika) and Kashmir. The epic and Purânic location of the Kiratas in north-western extremities and other parts of northern region is not only supported by foreign (Greek and French) accounts, but also by a number of other reliable evidences.

Ptolemy has rightly placed them (as one of the mountain tribes) in Sogdiana (Ramanaka varsa of the Purânas, Parakanda of Strabo and Samarkanda of modern times in Central Asia) along the river Oxus,[326] which rises near the Pamirs and winding its course through Central Asia... reaches to Aral Sea. Actually, the Sogdiana region occupied by the Kiratas was divided from Bactriana by the river Oxus in ancient times. The Kirâtas of this region were later identified with Central Asiatic tribes.

Ptolemy's statement is not only attested to, but, also supplemented by H.H. Wilson. He locates them (as foresters and mountaineers) near the Oxus and in a country between the Caucasus (the whole of northern chain, also known as Hindukush or Paropamisus, identified with modern Charikar or Opian near Kabul) and Imaus (the eastern chain and South-Eastern portion of the chain, the Himalaya), called Vandabanda[327], in which perhaps some imperfect indications of Badakhshan may be conjectured. The position assigned to them in the north-west, particularly, by Ptolemy, has also been accepted by B.C. Law[328] and B.A. Saletore.[329] The *Sammoha Tantra* (List-1, v. 5) also associates the Kiratas with the Bahlikas.

We may not be wrong in assuming that they might have crossed the Hindukush mountain (which constituted the last north-western boundary of India) and occupied the banks of the Oxus. The Oxus basin might have been their home in some remote period of history. They might have formed the part of ancient tribal population, who had settled in Suguda or Sogdiana at the sources of the Oxus sometime between the fourth and third millennium B.C. This region was one of the most ancient sites of human settlement. The ancient Indian tradition concur with those of the Persian in considering the tribes immediately west of the Indus and even those towards the Oxus as their countrymen.

They seem to have spread themselves practically over whole of the northern part of the Indian Sub-Continent. They occupied the whole mountain range west of the Indus and north of Kabul river as far as the vicinity of Herat. The regions lying on both sids of the Hindukush mountain, forming part of Afghanistan, were very much within the geographical limits of ancient Bhâratavarṣa. They had spread widely upto the ancient Bâhlika country (known to the Persians as Balkh and to the Greeks as Bactria) on the Oxus in the northern part of Afghanistan beyond Hindukush. The region contiguous to the Hindukush mountain and western Gandhar was known in ancient times as Kapisa-deúa, in the north and west of which the modern Balkh and Badakhshan were known in ancient times, respectively, as the Bahlika country and Kâmboja. It has been reasonably assumed that "the Kirâta tribes had at one time spread to the border of Dardistan and Balkh".

The extent of the Kirâta settlements in north-west cannot be satisfactorily determined. However, we have some reasons to believe that a great part of the modern kingdom of Afghanistan and its dependencies from Kabul to Sea was under the occupation of the Kirâtas and olher tribal population of Indian origin for many centuries before, as well as, after the invansion of Alexander in the fourth century B.C. That is why, we find some reflections of their settlements in this region in the *Mahâbhârata* and the *Purâṇas*.

Without extending the limits of India, however, too far to the north there is no reason to doubt that the valleys of the Indian Caucasus were properly included within them and their inhabitants as far to the Pamir mountains and those of the whole of mountainous region above Kashmir, Badakhshan and Bokhara were Indians.[330] There is every possibility that some sections of them like that of Âryans might have moved from this region in hoary past towards Punjab from where they might have further expanded over those parts of the country, which were covered by the Gaṅgâ-Yamunâ Doab.

It is also significant to note that because of several ups and downs in the topography, geography and history of north-west in the wake of frequent incursions and invasions of the Persians, the Greeks and the Scythians, ranging, as a whole, from the sixth to the second century B.C. their position also might have undergone some change. Some Sections of them also might have been, presumably, either absorbed or destroyed by the foreign invaders. During the period concerned, a sizable section of their population, in all probability might have moved from one region to another in Northern India. The possibility of their mixing with other local population cannot be excluded. Curiously enough, Ptolemy has confused one section of them, called "Karâtai with a tribe of Saka race in east of Sogdiana".[331] It is perhaps, because of, all these historical developments that we do not find any perspicuity in ancient accounts, either Indian or foreign, about them.

However, the total picture about them is not gloomy. The statement of a French scholar that when the Aryans led by their warriors in course of their migration towards India via Balkh region and Hindukush, were passing through the mountain regions of Afghanistan, they felt scared of the attacks by the Kirâtas, who had occupied an extensive area in the territory of the Hazara and were well known for their predatory habits,[332] also indirectly proves their expansion at large scale in northern part of Afghanistan tentatively in the early Vedic age. It was this part of Afghanistan from where they, in course of time, had advanced towards Punjab and the Gangetic Valley. Their movements in the area occupied by the Arsanians (Urasa in Northern Afghanistan), to the West of Indus and in Punjab and Kashmir also get confirmation in the statement of a classical writer, Nonnus.[333]

It is believed that the Yaksas of Devaloka came to be known as Kirâtas.[334] The southern portion of Uttarakuru-Varsa (or Northern continent), north of mount Meru (plateau of Pamir), comprising all the lands from the Oxus and the Caspian Sea to the Arctic Ocean (Uttara-Samudra) i.e. Sogdiana, Bokhara and other adjoining areas, is identified with the *Purâṇic Devaloka.*[335] It is generally accepted view that the fertile valleys of Southern Uttarakuru or Devaloka were very favourable for the settlements of both Aryan and non-Arvan population in remote past because of water supply, irrigation, agriculture, animal transport facilities, etc. The Kirâtas may also be included among the races inhabiting this region. This also goes indirectly to support what Ptolemy and Wilson have stated in this regard. We may, therefore, have some ground to deduce that the expansion of races from this region further towards India definitely might have taken place even before the dawn of the Vedic age. It is not possible to subscribe to the view that "Austrics coming from the southeast spread over the whole country: they were known as Yaksas and Savaras".[336] Grierson and Hoernle have conclusively proved it that the Pisacas, Barbaras and mlecchas inhabiting the north-west of India and the neighbouring parts of the Himalayas, who were originally a rear people, were closely connected with the Yaksas, Nagas and Khasas.[337] The existence of the Paiúâcl Prakrt is so well attested to by literary references that there can be no reasonable doubt about its speakers being rear human beings.[338] The speakers of this language, known as the Yaksas including the Kiratas spread from Hindukush to Kashmir.

It has been surmised that the movements of the "Kirâtas in the later Vedic age" changed the course of the Âryan settlements in the north of the Himalayas and greatly affected the history of the Uttarakuru country.[339] The reference to their territory ("Kirâtakhanda") along with the Pahlavas, Kâmbojas, Sindhu-Saviras, Yavanas, Sûdras, Barbaras, etc.[340] can be taken as a distinct proof of their settlements in the north-west. It has also been suggested that the Kirâtas, Gândharas, Cinas, Úakas, Barbaras, Ramathas, Kâmbojas and others were living during the time of Mandhâtâ ("6101 B.C."), one of the powerful kings in the dynasty of Manu.[341] We have absolutely no evidence at our disposal to examine the historical relevance of this statement.

If the information supplied by Viúâkhadatta is taken trustworthy, it can be further added that the Kirâtas along with the Yavanas, Kâmbojas, Parasikas, Bahlikas and others came along with Candragupta Maurya (Sandrocottus of Megasthenes) and Cinakya before c. 322 B.C. from the north-west to Magadha just to help them to overthrow the Nandas.[342] There is every likelihood of their further expansion in the hilly regions of Magadha during the age of the Mauryas.

Their wide expansion along the Himalayan range in the north can be amply substantiated by the testimony of Kalidasa, as well as, by the data obtained from the researches carried out on his works by Indian scholars. Kâlidâsa, while showing Raghu's line of conquest along India's northern border[343] (from the east of Kashmir to the south-east of Tibet) refers to che Kirâtas,[344] who were positively the tribes of Ladakh (Sanskrit name Hasaka), north of 'Kashmere', Zanskar, Rupshu, Kailâúa-mountain in Tibet around the Manasarovara lake and the Brahmaputra Valley in the north-east.[345] Linguistically also their location in Ladakh and adjoining regions can be proved. In the frontier regions of India coterminous with Tibet different dialects of Kirâta group were spoken, which also included Baltic (of Baltistan) and Ladakhi (of Ladakh). It has been aptly remarked that "the Kiratas, whom Kâlidasa has referred to...were possibly the people, who stretched from the regions of Ladakh and Kâilâsa in the south-east of Kashmir to the extreme end of Kâmarûpa in the east. It is also a historical fact that these tribes from before the rise of Buddha ruled over the entire regions as organised groups constituting what may be called the present day republics..."[346] Mallinâtha (who belonged to the latter half of the 14th century) in his commentaries on the works of Kâlidâsa and Bhaṭṭoji Dîkṣita (a grammarian of the 17th century) have made it abundantly clear that the Parvatiya Ganas denote the seven tribes that inhabited the northern slopes of the Himalaya.[347] The Kiratas, Utsavasanketas and Kinnaras living within the range of the Himalayas, as mentioned by Kalidâsa, were perhaps included among the said seventh tribes. The Kirâtas whom Raghu met in the Himalayas can not be placed in Nepal as suggested by D.C. Sircar.[348]

Their settlements in the vast forest extending beyond the high mountain ranges on the northern frontier of India in trans-Himalayan region and leading to the mountain Kailâúa in Tibet is also corroborated by Bânabhaṭṭa.[349]

The Himalayan region on the southern side of the Kailasa was one of the main centres of their activities, where they became the followers of their lord, Siva, as evidenced by Bhâravi[350] and Mallinâth's commentary on him known as *Ghantâpatha.*[351] They have been described as low born mounlaineers and foresters. Their settlements in the upper range of the Himalaya in the north of Âryavarta has also been focussed.[352]

They had maintained their existence in the Punjab from ancient times to the late medieval period. The term Kirâta has been applied to the territory of Kiratapur in the Punjab.[353] The *Kulanta-PithaMahâtmya* provides some clues to their habitation along with their leader Úiva in the Kulu valley of the Kangra district of the Punjab.[354]

It is said that the Kirâta or Bhota (the people of ancient Tibet), as mentioned in Sanskrit literature came from the north-east and settled in the northern most fringe and after a lapse of centuries got mixed up with the locals.[355] On the basis of the data contained in the Sanskrit, Jaina and Buddhist texts, particularly *Mudrârâkṣasa* and *Pariúiṣṭa-paravan* it has been conjectured that the tropps collected by Chandragupta Maurya and Câṇakya from Punjab also included those Kirâtas who had settled in the Himachal hills[356] long before the foundation of the Mauryan dynasty. In the present state of knowledge this can neither be confirmed nor denied.

They like other non-Âryan races, were widely scattered over the hilly regions of Kashmir, as we know it from *Râjataraṅgini* of Kalhana. In the Central Himalayan region their expansion at large scale in the hilly tracts of Uttarâkhanda i.e. Garhwal and Kumaon below the Himalayas in the protohistoric period is a proven fact." It is not unlikely that the Râjis (Kirata) either came to Uttarakhanda as an advance party or belonged to the rear-guard of the migrant group who were driven into the jungles by the dominating force of the Âryans."[357] Further, the earliest immigrants into the northwestern parts of the countiv including Uttarakhanda, are believed to have been the Kirâtas and Nâgâs. The influx of the Âryans elbowed these tribes out to the eastern parts. In the process Kirâtas were pushed to the higher hills and Nagâs to the lower areas, where they still live as tribes in Arunachal Pradesh and Nagaland. Due to their intermixture with Kiratas and Nâgâs, the Âryans residing in Uttarâkhanda developed a religious outlook and came to be known as Khasa or Khasia.[358] They once lived to the west and east of the present settlements of Râjis in Askot. In ancient times they had extended from Jageswar to Tibet and from eastern Kumaon to western Nepal.[359]

The Pandukeswar (in Garhwal regions of the Himalaya mountain) inscription,[360] as well as, other epigraphic evidences of the ninth and tenth centuries A.D.[361] also confirm their settlements in Garhwal and Kumaon regions in ancient times. They were pushed to the eastern regions by the victorious Âryans. They occupied a much more extensive area in Nepal, which constituted an interal part of northern India in ancient times. The Nepalese tradition still gives the name Kirâta to the country between the Dudh-kosi and the Arun rivers. The whole, area occupied by them became popularly known as "Kirâta-deúa." They colonized the valley of eastern Nepal, north of Videha, in sub-Himalayan region after having conquered it and set up a dynastic rule, incontrovertibly, in pre-Christian era in succession to the Abhiras, and ruled for about twentynine generations, whose details are given in the forthcoming pages. It is not possible to accept the view of Raj Bali Pandey[362] that they come to Nepal after the ninth and tenth centuries A.D.

Their expansion in the Himalayan valley of Nepal and establishment of their political sway over them at a very early date can be supported by a number of reliable Indian and foreign sources.[363] They lived in the region from Nepal to the extreme east in the north,[364] which formed the nidus of their settlements. In fact, there were several branches of the Kirâta in north-eastern India. Lassen[365] has judiciously placed one branch of them on the South bank of the Kosi in Nepal and another in Tippera or Tripura. The descendants of the ancients of Morung to the west of Sikkim and situated between Nepal and Bhutan still preserve the memory of Belkakoth as having been the site of the capital of their ancient kingdom.[366] Among all the aboriginal hill-tribes of north-eastern India of former times, the Kiratas, who conquered and governed Nepal, are considered to be the most adventurous, brave race, independent and a powerful people.

Three main hordes of the Kirâtas are supposed to have invaded the valley of Nepal successively in course of three centuries preceding the beginning of its history, which has been tentatively fixed at c. 700 B.C.[367] They held sway over large part of the country between the Sapta-Gandaki and Sapta-Kosi. The ancient glorious kingdom, which was set up in the eastern Himalaya, is ascribed to them. It is believed that some of the adventurous groups among them penetrated into Nepal from north-east and west through different river routes. The geographical proximity of Nepal and Kâmarupa, on the one hand, and that of Nepal and Kumaon (called Kartrpura in Allahabad pillar inscription of Samudragupta, Fleet, CII; Vol. 3, 1 line-22), on the other, because of their contiguous boundaries cannot be overlooked. There were large stretches of territory in between these three frontier kingdoms, which were both forests and hills. Such a geographical position definitely might have facilitated their movements from one region to another in ancient times. Besides, the Kirâtadeúa—the land of Seven Kosi, was situated north of Varahaksetra region in north-east Bengal. The popular tradition still current among the modern Kirâtas, associates the history of their early rule over the valley of Nepal "with the population in the areas at middle reach of the Brahmaputra and its westerly tributaries in Assam which had another settlements of the Kirâtas in antiquity. The entire expanse of territory from the Bahmaputra to the Gandak was populated by the Kirâtas, who had ousted the aborigines."[368]

The possibility of a horde of Kirâta invaders making their way to Nepal valley through the course of the Bagmati, which was the most convenient route to penetration into this region from south in ancient past, cannot be precluded. They further expanded towards the east and west. There were successive waves of migration of Kirâta tribes in the valley of Nepal, one group of them entering the valley through the course of the Gandak might have possibly belonged to Kumaon region towards the west (Uttarâkhanda), where they had been living since the prehistoric period. It has been surmised that there were other groups, who penetrated into Nepal from Assam, as well as, from far off place like Kashmir.[369] On the basis of the study of ethnological data it has been suggested that "many of the tribes now inhabiting the hilly tracts of Assam, Nepal and Bengal belong to one race and some of them migrated to Nepal valley in the centuries before Christ... There was enough of intermingling of blood with the oriental settlers of the soil, where the Kirâtas had expanded into lower reaches of the Gandak, Kosi and the Arun rivers in the plains."[370]

Lassen, a German indologist, categorically and unequivocally states that the Kirâtas were a tribe of Sikkim. (*Ind. Alt.,* Vol. III, p. 38) He says that the Kirâtas belonged to the Bhota race whose name survives in the modern Bhutan. They are allied to the Tibetans. According to him, the Kirâtas were one of ten different tribes with several branches. The native capital of one branch of them was at Makwanpur in eastern Nepal. They were a warlike, uncultivated and polygamous race whose native animism yielded imperfectly to Brâhmaṇa or Buddhist teaching, and whose neglect of religious rites caused the Brâhmaṇa Hindus to reduce them to the rank of Sudras. (*Ind. Alt.,*Vol. I, pp. 441-50). He further adds that the Kirâtas belonged to the Bhota (Bhotadesa or Tibet) and are still found in Nepal and Sikkim. He places one branch of them on the south bank of the Koshi in Nepal. They according to him, were a widely diffused tribe. They had spread themselves in different directions in ancient times. They had wandered from their northern "Fatherland" to the eastern Himalayas and into the other regions long before the time (second century A.D.) in which the Greek geographer Ptolemy lived. (*Ind. Alt.,* Vol. III, pp. 235-37).

It appears that before the Kirâta invaders occupied the valley of Nepal, the people of Indo-Âryan origin had already settled there. The Austro-Asiatic tribe as well as, Indo-Âryans had been subdued by the Kiratas. About their expansion it has been correctly poisnd out that "Surely it must have been a tribal expansion that swamped our country at that time. Not only the ruling tribal heads but also their warriors, peasants and labourers might have constituted the hordes of emigrants. New emigrants mixed with Australoid and Dravidians, who had primitive culture. Kiratas emigrants certainly overwhelmed them, but the lower strata of them had also been in turn submerged with the toiling humanity of the land."[371] They "overwhelmed the local population because their number was larger than that of any other migrant section and there is no doubt that the latter absorbed them but in return accepted their language though everything worked under the dominant Sanskritic influence."[372] Their dominance over the Nepal valley is proved by the imposition of their language used in the inscription in the eleventh century and afterwards.[373] There are some gleanings from the chronicles or *Vaṁúâvalis* of the fourteenth century A.D. too about their occupation of the valley for several centuries.

Towards the sixth century B.C. the eastern Himalaya and the Tarais were brought under their control. In the mountainous tracts they were, however, supreme, but under the cultural influence of the Âryan victors. They were in the process of shifting from one place to another till the foundation of the Licchavi dynasty in Nepal. But, after being subjugated by the Licchavis sometime between the third and the fourth century A.D. they became confined to the valley, where some points are still maintained to remind us of the capitals of the invading-Kirata tribes of the early period, who are believed to be the ancestors of modern Limbu, Khambu, Yakthumba and Thadu. "The Kiratas of today occupy a region cut off by huge undemarcated forests and mountain range from the rest of the country and from the Newars of the valley of Kathmandu."

They were divided into a number of tribes. The east "Himalayish" had two main branches. Linguistically each branch had somewhat divergent languages or dialects, and the stock was somewhat scattered geographically. The Limbus, speaking a somewhat divergent dialect of the eastern branch, constituted one of the most important sections of the Himalayan Kirata.

According to one of their recorded traditions, there were ten brothers born in Vârinasi, who divided themselves into two groups, one going directly to Nepal and the other by way of Tibet.[374] Later they spread to the hill areas of present West Bengal and Sikkim. Quite distinguished from them there were some other branches of the Kirâta in Bhutan and its vicinity, where they were mostly known as the Bhotas because their earlier connection with Bhota country or Tibet beyond the Himalaya. Local tradition in Nepal not only ascribes to them an early rule over the valley of Nepal but also gives them an eastern extention to Bhutan. Perhaps the common boundaries of Nepal, and Uttarakhanda, and Videha and Nepal on the one side and that Assam, Bengal, Bhutan, Sikkim and Nepal, on the other, might have accelerated the pace of their movements from one region to another in ancient times. The frontiers of the Kirâtadeúa extended from Nepal to Prâgjyotiṣa at the eastern extremity of India.

A very important observation has been made about the movements of the early Kirâtas on the soil of India from the Vedic age down to the beginning of the Christian era. They are said to have entered India "through Assam, and their advent in the east might have been as old as that of the Âryans in the west at some period before 1000 B.C. By that time they might have pushed along the Himalayan slopes as far West as the eastern Punjab Hills. They came to be known to the Vedic Aryans as a cave dwelling people from whom the Aryans obtained mountain produce like drugs and herbs and the *soma plant* ... the passages in the *Yajurveda* and the *Atharvaveda* mentioning the Kirâtas are at least as old as that period. When the *Mahâbhârata* and the *Râmâyana* were taking shape, between 500 B.C. to 400 A.D., particularly 'in the pre-Christian centuries, they had occupied the southern tracts of the Himalayas, and the whole of north-eastern India, north Bihar contiguous to Nepal and to the north of the Ganges, the greater part of Bengal and Assam including the areas through which the Ganges passed into the Sea. Eastern Nepal and the Lauhitya or the Brahmaputra valley were the lands especially connected with them."[375] Further, their expansion in Northern India, in the valley of eastern Nepal and other eastern Himalayan tracts including Sikkim, Bhutan and other adjacent areas in the sub-Himalayan tracts as far west as Garhwal and Kumaon, and in the hill areas watered by the Satluj and the Beas, etc. earlier to c. 1000 B.C. has also been repeatedly mentioned.[376]

Prof. Chatterji's statement about the places of their dispersion and its approximate period is too clear to admit of any controversy. But a point of objection, which can be raised here, is to their identity. Actually, those who were moving from one place to another within the geographical limits of India during the Vedic and the epic ages were not the "Tibeto-Burmans" or "Mongoloids" as supposed by him without any valid ground, but the mountain dwelling tribes of Indian-origin. As a matter of fact, there was no such penetration of the Mongoloids within the frontiers of India either by way of Tibet or Burma or by Brahmaputra or along the southern slopes of the Himalayas through Assam before first millennium B.C. They (Tibeto-Burmans, later identified with the Kirâtas) might have possibly entered the northern and eastern Himalayas in the early centuries of the Christian era and not before that. This assumption may have some basis, because we do not have any authentic evidence to suggest their penetration into India from any corner prior to the dawn of the historical period. The whole root of confusion in this regard lies in his obsession with the "Indo-Mongoloid" theory like that of others.

One of the factors responsible for their expansion in the vicinity of the Eastern Himalaya was probably their defeats at the hands of the Âryans, who had victoriously marched on the territories in east and northeast directions. The Âryans were, from the remotest period surrounded on all sides by indigenous tribes from whom they differed both in mind and disposition. They were in touch with those, who had firmly established themselves in Assam and north and east Bengal, in north Bihar and in sub-Himalayan India, mostly in Nepal. They were known to the Âryans as Kiratas from Vedic times onwards. The Âryans had encountered them in course of their eastern expansion. They had to wrest from them, by force of their arms, the seats, which they had occupied. The Kiratas, of course, offered heroic resistance to their advancement, but were totally vanquished by them. Consequently, they had to take shelter in the hills, caves and forests in different directions. The Kirâta settlers, who had spread all over the Tarai region as far as the Ganges had to meet the same situation. It was, in fact, a contest between the Aryans and non-Âryans for further expansion in north-eastern India in which the former triumphed over the latter most of the times.

Coming to one of the most-important phases of their expansion in Madhya-deúa or Central region, mention may first be made of the Gaṅgâ-Yamunâ Doab of the later Vedic period, which is synchronous with expansion of the Âryans. During the period concerned, they settled along the banks of the Ganges, and occupied the mountain and forest tracts on the banks of the Yamunâ and Sarasvati. In post-Vedic times they spread to different other parts of this region, which can be proved without any doubt by the Purâṇic evidence.[377] It appears that they were living in the neighbourhood of the Kurus, probably in the north-eastern part of their territory, which extended from the Khandavavana on the bank of Yamunâ to the Kamyaka forest on the bank of the Sarasvati. We do not have any archaeological data to confirm their occupation of the forest tracts in the Upper Gangetic basin in the later Vedic period. But we do have literary evidence to show their settlements near Davitavana, which was the abode of the Pandavas in the epic age. They frequently visited the Kuru Desa as messengers of the Pâṇḍavas.[378] Between the Vedic and the Epic age they were moving from forest to forest and mountain to mountain.

Atkinson says: "There is every reason to suppose that the Nâgâs, Kirâtas and Khasas entered India by the same route as the Aryas, and that the Kiratas were the first to arrive then, the Nâgâs and then the Khasas. The earliest notices regarding the Kirâtas bring them westward as the Jumna in the first century."[379] He has further admitted that they occupied the vast tract of the Kuru-Jangala (waste land of the Kurus) and a place near the mount called Yamuna.[380] His statement except the date as suggested by him is near to the truth. They had moved towards the west and "occupied the Gangetic valley...of Madhyadesa before the time of the *Mahâbhârata*" as correctly pointed out by R. Shafer[381] and not in the first century A.D. The only mistake, which Mr. Shafer, has committed is that he has identified them with the "Sino-Tibetans".

The interpretation of the data as contained in the *Mahâbhârata*[382] shows that they had expanded upto Rampur-Busahar (close to the Valley of Spiti in present Himachal Pradesh) in the western side of the Kuninda-Pradeúa in the mountain tracts of Yamuna in Dehradun district. The total area occupied by them became popularly known as "Kirâta-deúa".[383]

In the trans-Yamunâ region (western), which was included in Madhyadesa of the Purâṇic period, they probably occupied "the southern part of the Aravalli hills" (the natural frontier region between the two valleys—the Indus and Ganges) in Rajasthan.[384] Their expansion in Rajasthan can also be corroborated by other sources. "That... Kirâtas once lived in Rajasthan and its neighbourhood, particularly its hilly tracts is shown by instances from later Rajput history, particularly by the name ... Kirâtakupa"[385] ('wells of the Kirâtas' or Kirâta Kuta=hillock). Their antiquity along with that of other non-Aryans has been pushed back to the "early Rgvedic times".[386] An inscription of 1235 Samvat era in one of the temples in the old city of 'Kirâdu' (now in ruins and connected with the ancient name Kirâta) in Jodhpur state in Western Rajasthan[387] is also a proof for our consideration about their existence in Rajasthan. From the Vedic age down to the early centuries A.D. it was occupied by non-Âryan tribal population. In the light of the above evidences, the statement of B.C. Law: "we have no information of the location of the Kirâtas in the Madhyadeúa"[388] stands disposed. The epic and Puranic traditions do not place them only in the eastern region, as mistakenly supposed by him, but in different other regions of India including Madhyadesa.

The *Sammoha Tantra* (List. 11, V. 5) also refers to the Kirâtas (Kilâtas) along with other countries of Madhyadeúa like Koúala, Kuntala and Sûrasena. They were also found in Matsyadesa (the extensive territory between the hills near the Chambal and the forests that skirted the Sarasvati of which the centre was Bairatin Jaipur). This lay to the south of the Kurus of Delhi region and to the west of the Úûrasenas of Mathura.

It is striking to note, that with the expansion of Âryans and the clearing of the forest in the Ganges valley in course of extensive urbanization in the first half of the first millennium B.C., the dispersion of the Kirâta population began in different directions including the Himalayan and Vindhyan region in search of new homes. Though we don't have either any literary or archaeological evidence to prove it, the trend, which was set in, provides some basis for us to warrant such conjecture.

They had their settlements in the eastern region as well. In the words of Romila Thapar: "The Kirâta are described as a non-Aryan tribe living in the hills and jungles of Magadh".[389] There seems to be some basis for upholding this view. In the early Vedic text[390] 'Kirata' appears to be non-Âryans. Yâska[391] also describes Kikâta as the name of a non-Âryan country (anarya-nivasa). Like Yaskâ the author of the *Brihaddharma Purâna*[392] also regarded Kikâta as an impure country, which, however, includes the name of Gaya as a holy region. It is quite apparent that the Kikata of the early Vedic period were the non-Âryans (the Kirâta) of southern part of Magadha. Kikata cannot be a synonym of Mâgadha as mistakenly supposed by many scholars because of their association with Gaya in later works. The name Magadha first appears in the *Atharvaveda* (v.v. 22.14.). Therefore, the observation of Prof. Thapar is absolutely correct.

Their existence in Magadha up to the times of the Palas can best be qualified in the words of M. Martin: "There can be little doubt that the Pâl-Râjâs,—powerful dynasty that appeared in Magadha, ... possessed the whole of Mithila and confined the Kiratas within the limits of their mountains".[393]

Mithila extending to the hill regions of Nepal on the north had become the strong base of the Kirâtas before the spread of the Âryan culture in the Brahmanic age (probably during the times of the *Úatapatha Brâhmana*). Both Mithila and its constituent parts of Nepal before being fully aryanised felt the deep impact of the Kirâta culture. Till the time of Lohangsena they were in the dominant position.

The evidence recorded in the *Mahâbhârata*[394] shows their gradual expansion in the vicinity of Mithila or Videha country in the epic age. While supporting this very evidence, H.C. Chakladar also observed that "the Kiratas were found also in other parts of India than the Himalayas".[395] But he has not provided any details about them. It seems that they had spread over a vast area extending from the boundary of Videha land to Indra Mountains, which were probably the mountain ranges of

Indrasthan to the east of so-called *Mahâbhârata Parvat* in the western side of the valley of Nepal in the Eastern Himalayan region. M. Martin on the basis of his study of both traditional and historical accounts of Eastern India has reasonably concluded that they were very powerful in Kamarupa, Mithila and Nepal.[396] Thus, in the middle Gangetic valley they spread over the whole of Videha region, north of the Ganga, extending to its east from the Gandak to the Kosi, and Magadha region, south of the Ganga, between the Son (on the west) and the spurs of the Rajmahal hills (on the east).

By the dawn of the first century A.D. they had not only extended to the west of the Ganges (West Bengal), in the regions to the north-east of Orissa, possibly in the Gangetic Delta, but also spread all over the plains of Vañia-deúa comprising mainly the southern and north eastern Bengal. They had settled in the extensive forest tracts of Orissa and another wild tract on the southern parts of Bengal signifying *Sunderbuns* bordering the sea. In the *Mahâbhârata*[397] and the *Purâna*[398] they have been connected not only with Videha but also with the Pundras, Vangas, Tamraliptakas, Bhargas, etc. They had occupied Sylhet, Mymensingh (to the east of Brahmaputra), Rangpur, Dinajpur (forming the part of ancient Pundra) and the neighbourhood in north-east Bengal in early period.[399] They had spread widely not only over 'Gangetic India but also over countries farther east. We find valuable references to their settlements in the valleys, hills and other parts of ancient Assam (the then Prâgjyotisa and Kâmarûpa) in the epic and Purânic periods. They were at the extreme east of the northern boundary of Bharata.

The earliest settlements of the Kirâtas as autochthones or aboriginals, not as immigrants, during the time of Bhagadat's father Naraka were in the Prâgjyotisapur near the Kâmâkhya hill (named Nalakûta = "Blue Moùntain") in the heart of Kâmarûpa proper or Gauhati, situated on the bank of Brahmaputra. But after being defeated by Naraka in a war they deserted the original place of their habitation and got dispersed in different groups and settled in different parts of ancient Assam including the frontier hill regions. They had spread over the area between the Karatoya in the west and the Dikkaravâsinî and Lalitakântâ in the east. Many of them had settled near the sea coast, which extended from the Lalitakanta in the east. Again many of them, particularly, those, who were opposed to the Vedas and Sastras, were driven out by him from the Lalitakanta.[400]

N N. Vasu has also mentioned that "the Kirâtas had one time occupied the whole of Assam, but subsequently losing hold over the country before the powerful Naraka they withdrew themselves to the coast of the eastern Sea".[401] Pargiter,[402] as well as, H.H. Wilson[403] referring to them as the dwellers of the eastern limits of India have also remarked that "in the centre of the country of Kâmarûpa, the sites of shrines of Devi, as Dikksavasint and Kâmakhyâ, were inhabited by the Kiratas. Thus, it is quite evident that during the time of Narâka they were forced to shift their place of residence from one place to another in both valleys and hills. It is remarkable that many of them went to hills from the valley of Brahmaputra.

During the time of Bhagadatta, the king of Prâgjyotisa—a country of eastern India, their number relatively increased, as we find from the *Mahâbhârata* that he was surrounded by a large number of the Kirâtas, Cinas and the dwellers of the marshy region near the eastern sea, known as Sâgaranupavasins.[404] The Kirâtas themselves were dwelling on the eastern coast.[405] Actually, they were living not only in the mountain regions of Assam, but also in the marshy lands on the shores of the ancient Lohitasâgara. This is an indication towards the small islands in the river Lauhitya. This can more or less be substantiated by other evidences.

It is suggested that "these marshy regions can only be the alluvial tracts and islands near the mouths of the Ganges and the Brahmaputra as they existed anciently" and "Prâgjyotisa comprised the whole of north Bengal proper."[406] The dwellers, of the sea coast were evidently the Kirata people living in the marshy regions of Sylhet, Mymensingh and Tippera. "The low lying parts of Sylhet and Mymensingh are still called haor (sagara). In the Bhatera copper plate inscription of Govinda Kesavadeva king of Srihatta (c. 1049 A.D.) the sea or sagara is mentioned as the boundary of certain lands granted"[407] The empire of Bhagadatta is believed to have extended upto the Himalaya on the north and the borders of China on the east.

On the basis of all the available evidences, which we have discussed we find that during the time of Bhagadatta the Kiratas had diffused in different parts of north and south east Bengal, which formed the integral part of Prâgjyotisa during the epic age. The Cinas were not the Chinese but the Tibetans, who were living on the border of Prâgjyotiṣa.

N.N. Vasu is also of the view that "there was a time when the Lohita-sagara of the *Râmâyana* and the Purvasagâra of the *Manu Saṁhitâ* and *Kâlikâpurâna* spread over a large part of eastern Bengal washing the feet of even the Garo, Khâsia, Jaintia and Kachar hills ... the Kirâtas inhabited the eastern shore of the eastern sea".[408] J.W. McCrindle's statement that "The country of the Kirâta, however, is placed in the great Indian epic, further, north in the neighbourhood of the Brahmaputra"[409] is absolutely correct.

The tribes living in Antargiri, Vahirgiri and Upagiri, conquered by Arjuna in course of his northern expedition[410] may possibly be the Kirâtas of the mountainous regions to the north of Prâgjyotisa (the hilly regions of present Arunachal Pradesh). The exact location of these areas are not yet well-ascertained. How ever, on the strength of *Mahâbhârata* it can be established that they must be lying within the boundary of Prâgjyotisa. This can be supported by the Purâṇic evidence too.[411] The location of the Kiratas there may not be surprising, because they were found in the inner, outer and upper mountain regions. Hence, they cannot be identified with the "lower slopes of the Himalayas and the Nepalese Tarai".[412] But V.S. Agrawala has suggested that the Vahirgiri Pradesh (called Cullahimvanta in Pali) inhabited by the Kirâtas was the outer range of the Himalaya, Mussoorie, Nainital, Shimla, etc. and Antargiri inhabited by the Bhotas included Kanchanjahgha, Nanda-devi and Dhaulagiri.[413]

They have been placed even in the most remote parts of the Himalays towards the mountain, where the sun rises in the mountain Karusa, which is at the extremity of the ocean or in the region of the Lauhitya or Brahmaputra.[414]

The Purânas place the Kirâtas at the eastern frontier of Bharatavarsa, the Yavanas at its western end and the Brahmanas, Ksatriyas, Vaiúyas and Úûdras in its centre.[415] In some of the Purânas it is clearly indicated that they were dwelling on the frontiers of Prâgjyotisa and Kâmarûpa, which have been called Purva-desa or Prâcẏa-desa.[416]

The Puranic division of Greater Bhâratavarṣa into nine Khandas or dvipas shows that India proper known by several names such as Bhârata dvipa or Bhârata-Khanda or Kumari-dvipa or Kumârikâkhanda (in *Skanda Purâna)* or Madhya-bheda (in *Agni Purâna),* was the ninth dvipa girted by sea (sâgarâsamvṛtah, Alberuni's Nagarasamvritta) extending over a thousand Yojanas (1 Yojana = 4 kosas) from north to south, to the east of which the 'Kirâtas have been placed.[417] Bhaskar-âcârya in his *Siddhânta Úromani* and Rajasekhara in his *Kâvyamimâmsâ* also divide the country in the same way as do the *Purânas.*

One of the Purânas, while giving the names of seventy-five countries of entire Bhârata-Khanda together with their gramas (villages), towns (pattanas) and harbours (velakulas), refers to the Kirâtadesa (Kirâta-vijayojaya) and the number of gramas (1/2 lakhs), contained in it.[418] We do not know how far the statement regarding the number of gramas is correct. This may, perhaps, be an interpolated version. On the authority of the Purânas it has been rightly suggested that the Kirâtas were inhabiting the mountain regions of eastern India and the hills to the north-east of Bengal.[419]

The directions, in which they had dispersed ever since the times of the *Mahâbhârata,* were mostly located in north-eastern India. They spread not only over the marshy lands on the eastern sea coast, the ancient Lohita sea, but also over the whole eastern frontier of India *i.e* Assam, Chittagong and the hill tracts of Tipperahs. One of the branches extended even to the south of Assam proper, i.e. Tripura (the Kirâta-deúa), who are also known as the southern branch. They also settled in the hill areas of Manipur and Nagaland.

By the time the two works—*Mârkandeya Purâna* and *Kâvyamimâmsâ*—were composed, the term Kirâta started losing its racial significance. The term merely signified uncivilized' mountaineers.

The earliest proof of their expansion in the south-western division of ancient India has been adduced in one of the Purâṇic texts. They have been associated with Ânarta,[420] which was the northern half of the Kathiawad peninsula, separated by the thickly forested mountain core of the peninsula. The wild tracts extending from Bânkut to Deogaḍh (now Deogaḍhbaria included in the tribal areas of Gujarat), as well as the western part of Gondwana (in Madhya Pradesh) are distinguished by the appellation, "Kirâta-Khaṇḍa", which denotes the territory of the Kirâta.[421] This was definitely their territorial expansion in the western and central regions of ancient times. The wild tracts of Gondwana is identical with ancient Mahâkântâra ("Greater Kântâra"),[422] If this identification is held correct, we can take liberty to suggest that the Kirâta tribes might have expanded over the greater part of the wild tracts of central India.

Their settlements along the mountain side in different parts of present Madhya Pradesh (possibly Mandla District of tribals) and in Gujarat in early medieval period can very well be ascertained from all the available indications.

Their penetration into Deccan sometime before the second century A.D. can only be attested to by Nâgârjunakonda inscription. One of the early Purânas refers to them in company with Dravidas, Pândyas, etc.[423] which can be taken as an indirect evidence of their early settlements in the south. From the manner in which the Kirâtas are described in the *Mârkandeya Purâna,* it appears that before this text was finally composed (5th century A.D.) they had already scattered themselves on the northern, eastern, western and even southern sides of the land in order to seek newer homes.

It is said that the Kirâtas were one of those Vana-vâsis or Âdivâsis who were driven away by the Dravidians.[424] But, unfortunately, details in this regard are totally lacking. And so we can only deduce that like the Âryans of the north the Dravidians of the south also might have vanquished them and pushed them away from the plains to the hills.

By the fifth century A.D. the concept of Kirâta-deúa (i.e. the country or a particular region where they had settled tensively) had distinctly emerged. Their expansion at a large scale in different parts of India by this time can best be illustrated by the statements of Varâhamihira.[425] While referring to them[426] frequently along with different other countries and peoples he has placed them specifically in south-west (Nairrita)[427] divisions of India which is strongly supported by Alberuni.[428] The author of the text (Br. Sam) has even referred to the Kirâta kings.[429] Their names are not distinct, but it is clear that the institution of kingship had also developed among themselves.

By the sixth century A.D. they had also colonized the Vindhyan forest region on the south of Âryavarta and made it their virtual home. Next to Nepal it was the Vindhyan region where they were well organised into one unit and remained in existence there for several centuries. It has been remarked that "Their migration may have been due to the expansion of the agrarian settlements in the Ganges valley... The Pulinda may have migrated from the Mathura region to the vindhyas for the same reason as did the Kirâtas.[430] They do not figure much in any literary text before the seventh century A.D. which is indicative of their fixed habitation in this region in the late period. For the first time Dandin[431] dealt with all the relevant aspects of their life and culture, which have been depicted in the present work in the places they deserve. But it does not mean that Vindhyan region was not the place of their settlement in the earlier period. They were previously more known as the Sabaras and the Pulindas than the Kirâtas. The name Kirata originally stood for a particular group of hill tribes, but later its meaning expanded so as to signify any hill tribe of Vindhya. That is why, all the three tribes of this region have been confounded in the early literary text with each other. The only noticeable change, which was witnessed, was that the Kiratas became the most dominant group amongst them by the late sixth century. The forest named Vindhyâtavi extending as far as the forests on the shores of both the eastern and western ocean and adorning the middle region was the seat of their activities. On the western bank of the sacred lake, called Pampâ (near Dandaka-vana) in the vicinity of great Vindhya forest their kindred tribe, Sabaras were also living. Bâñabhatta[432] in his works have described them under the name Sabara. In one of the famous medieval Tântric texts known as *Úaktisangama Tantra,* the "Kirâta-deúa" or Kirâta country, situated in the hill regions of the Vindhya range, is included in the list of fiftysix countries (Satpâncâsaddeúa-Vibhâga[433] of ancient India. R.P. Chanda also supports the settlements of the Kiratas, Pulindas and Úabaras, who have figured in the medieval Sanskrit literature, in the Vindhya hills.[434] They were found not only in the Himalayan region, but in the Vindhyan region as well.[435]

South Indian sources, both literary and epigraphical, also bear testimony to their survival in the Vindhyan region as late as the twelfth century A.D. Abhinava Pampa (12th century A.D.)[436] as well as, Nijagunayogi[437] have located them in this region. In the tenth century they received a serious setback at the hand of a Ganga king of Talkad on the Kaveri in the Mysore district, which is revealed by a grant of A.D. 973.[438] They were finally overthrown by the Hoysala king of Mysore in the first quarter of the twelfth century as indicated by an inscription dated A.D. 1117.[439]

Their penetration into southern India with special reference to Mysore apparently began in the first half of the twelfth century for exploring the new areas for their settlements. The habitation of the Kirâtas in some parts of Karnataka in the eighth century A.D. itself can very well be proved by a grant of a Ganga king Sivamara I dated A.D. 713.[440] But their number gradually increased after the process of migration of Vindhyan Kiratas towards Karnataka at a much larger scale began. They somehow maintained their existence further upto the sixteenth century as it is evident from the epigraphic records of Mysore.[441] Thus it appears that they were distributed in different regions of India.[442]

It was not only Tibet and China, but also a group of countries and islands known as indo-China, Malaya, Siam and Burma, constitutiug Greater India, which witnessed the expansion of Kiratas.[443] Now let us see who were they ?

From an astronomical work called *Jyotiṣtatvam* we know that the Kirâta country also constituted a part of Tibet which was known as Bhota in ancient times. Those who migrated towards Bhutan (Bhotanta i.e. the end of Bhota or Tibet= borderland of Tibet), Sikkim, Nepal and northern part of Uttarâkhaṇḍa after the spread of Buddhism in the seventh century became known as Bhotiyas. Those who settled in the hills and valleys of Assam were called Bodos (from Bod = Bhota), who are still included in the Kirâta group. During the eighth and ninth centuries which mark Tibet's expansion southwards and westwards several groups migrated towards the northern corner of the high Himalayan ranges i.e. the valleys of Lahoul and Spiti along the banks of rivers Chandra and Bhaga in present Himachal Pradesh. The contacts of Tibetans with the Chinese (not before the seventh century) led to the emergence of a new terminology—Sino-Tibetans, who are generally described as Mongoloids, about which we have already discussed enough. Later they were identified with the Kiratas of India without taking into consideration their identities, as well as, the periods.

"The lands to the east of India up to the China sea" were known to the Greeks and Romans as "India beyond the Ganges," which denotes "Farther India." Gerini thinks that the tribes who occupied at an early period the littoral as well as the adjoining islands of the Indo-Chinese coast...racially belonged to the same stock of the...Kirâtas, who are described in *Vâlmîki Râmâyaṇa* (*Kis. Kân*. 40, 27-28) as island dwellers in the region to the east of India.[444] If this statement is correct, the expansion of the Kirâtas in the *Râmâyaṇa* age can be proved or Vâlmiki's knowledge of their settlements in such a far-off place can be assumed. But we don't have any evidence to corroborate either of them.

In one of the oldest Cham (or Champa in Indo-China) inscriptions whose period is not known the people called "Vṛlah-Kirâta" have been identified with the Bhils of Central India. It is said that "from Central India to Cochin China they were called "Vṛlah Kirâta."[445] The mountaineers or hill tribes of the race "Vṛlah-Kirâta" of Champa became more or less blended with Negrito autochthones.

The "Austro-Asiatics" represented by the Mons in south Burma and south Siam, the Khmers in Cambodia ("who received Indian culture by both land and sea"), the Paloung and the Wa in Burma and several other small tribes in Indo-China and Sino-Tibetans or Tibeto-Burmans of Greater or Farther India became known as "Mongoloids" later identified with the Kiratas.[446]

They were also found in North Arakan (Burma), which was virtually the easternmost outpost of India. They widely diffused in the lower Gangetic regions and further split up into several group extending upto Arakan and Western Assam. The Kirâta peoples of north-Arakan like that of Chittagong were already Indianised or Brahmanised before the eighth century A.D., which is evident from some inscriptions of Arakan of the early period.[447]

Here it must be made clear that those who belong to Austro-Asiatic and Sino-Tibetan and Tibeto-Burman group (generally placed under the caption "Mongoloids") were completely separated from those who were in India proper at least up to the beginning of the Christian era. Because there is no evidence to record their contacts with the Indian Kirâtas during the centuries preceding the Christian era. They became a part of the Kirâta population of north-eastern India in the early centuries of Christian era and not before that. Before this period, the expansion up to Arakan was confined to those who were original inhabitants or non-immigrants of India. Hence, instead of mixing all the different branches of Kirâta together a line of demarcation should be drawn between the Kirâtas of India proper and Greater India. We do not know whether they set up any colony in Greater India as did the Hindu colonists, but those who were there came much under the influence of Indian culture.

The extension of Kitâtas' influence to Ceylon (now Úri Laṅkâ) can also be proved by some evidences.[448] It is impossible that a tribe so widely diffused in India and beyond could ever have become homogeneous.

Notes and References

1. Race and History (in the series, *The History of Civilization,* ed. by C.K. Ogden), p. 388, quoted in the Foreword by H. Berr to P. Masson-Oursel, AllC, xiii.
2. *Úukla*, YV, *Vâj. Saṁ.* XXX. 16; *Krṣṇa* YV; *Tai. Br;* 111. 4.12.1. AV; X, 2.4.14. See also Ralph, R.H. Griffith (tr.): TWYV; BK. XXX, V. 16 pp. 257-58; HAV; Vol. 1. BK V, XIII, No. 5, p. 208; Vol. II, BK. X. 4.14. p. 15; Devi Chand (tr.): YV; p. 369; W.D. Whitney (tr.); AV. Sam; p. 577; A.B. Keith (tr.); Tai, Sam. *(The Veda of the Black Yajus School* ed. by C.R. Lanman, Hos. 1914); Maurice Bloomfield (tr.) HAV; cf. SBE. (ed. by F. MaxMuller', Vol. XLII, p. 153; Macdonell and Keith, VI. Vol. 1. pp. 157-58; Dayananda Sarasvati (tr.): YV. p. 249; AV. p. 211 for different interpretations of the Hymns concerned with regard to the Kirâtas.
3. *Pañcaviṁúa Brâhmana,* XIII. 1.2.5. (the text reads Kirâta Kulyau. In connection with the story of Asamati it appears that two priests were opposed to the Gaupâyanas, Kirata, etc.); Sat.

Br. 1.1.4.14 (the text reads Kailatakuli); *Satyayanaka Brâhmana* cf Sâyana, RV. X 57. 1; 601; *Jaiminiya Brahmana,* III, 1.6.7. (In the Bohtlink's Dictionary based on the works of Sayana and in the Brhaddevata, VII. 86 Kilatakuli is an equivalent to the Kirâta Kula or Kiratakuli). See also JAOS, XVI, 1841, pp. 79-260; and E.W Hopkins, TCAAS; 15, 48, No. 1. cf. Macdonell and Keith, VI; Vol. 1. pp. 158.

4. VI; Vol, 1. pp, 157-58; Griffith, HAV; Vol. 1. p. 208; Vol. II. p. 16.
5. *Ait. Br.* VII. 18; *Rgveda Brâhmanas*: The *Aitareya* (tr. by A.B. Keith. HOS.), Vol. XXV XXXIII, 6. 45 & 307. See also *Sankhayana Srauta Sûtra,* XV. 26. 7: Zimmer, Alt, Leb. 101, 118 and Hillebrandt, *Vedische Mythologie,* 3, 276.
6. F. MaxMuller, HASL, P. 379; Louis Renou, *Vedic India* (tr. from the French by Philip Spratt) *Classical India,* Vol. 3. p. 126; R.G. Bhandarkar, EHD; p. 6; A.D. Pusaiker. *Aryan settlements in India;* HCIP. *The Vedic Age,* Ch. XI11, p. 264; R.C. Jain, EAB; pp, 100-102; Gustav Oppert, OIB; p. 86; R.S. Tripathi. HAl. P. 322, fn. 1. H.C. Raychaudhuri (PHAI; pp, 94 and 636) on the basis of Ait. Br. considers the Mutibas, Pulindas and Sabaras as Dasyu tribes.
7. Bau Dh. Su. 1.9; *Gau. Dh. Su.* IV.15; IV.17, 20-21; *Vaikhanasa Smarta Sûtra,* X. 12, 15.
8. *Val. Râm. Bâla Kânda,* 55.3. Also, Ram Kumar Rai VRK., p. 61. D.C. Sircar, SSAAM1., Vol. 1, p. 51, fn. 1.
9. *Vâl. Râm. Kiskindhâ Kânda,* 40, 27-28.
10. S.C. De, HRIAS., pp. 115 and 136. A. Weber's (IA- JOR.) Vol. IV, pp. 244f) explanations of the races enumerated in the *Valmiki-Râmâyaṇa* are not fully convincing.

    The Kol, Bhil, Kirâta and Khasa mentioned in the *Râmacarita Mânasa* (Ayodhyâ Kânda, Gorakhpur, Samv. 2043. 59.1; *Uttara Kânda*, Mathura, 1975, p. 8920) were the forest tribes of India.
11. Mbh. *Bhiṣma Parva,* 10, 12.
12. Mbh. *Adi Parva,* 165, 36.

    Also *Ibid.,* 165, V. 35; Ram Kumar Rai, Mbh. Ko. pp. 190-91.
13. Mbh. *Úânti Parva*, 65, 13-15, 17-23.
14. *Bhârata Savitri* (*Sânti Parva*), Vol. 3, pp. 60-63.
15. Muir, OST.. 11, pp. 365 and 491; A.C. Burnell, OM., (ed. E.W. Hopkins) p. 311, note 3; M.R. Singh GDEP., p. 182.
16. A.D. Pusaiker, *Aryan Settlements in India,* HCIP., *The Vedic Age,* ch. XIII, p. 253.

17. Griffith, HAV., Vol. 1, Bk. 1, VII, p. 95; E.B. Cowell, *The Brahmanical tribes and the Aborigines,* AL, p. 63; E. J. Rapson, AI. (from the earliest times to the first century A.D.), p. 21; Louis, Renou, *op. cit.* p. 76; M. Winternitz. H1L., Vol. 1, p. 63; Macdonell, HSL; p 153; Gustav Oppert, OIB., pp. 12-13; Muir, OST., Vol. 1,140; Vol. II (1871) p. 387; Gerini, RPGEA., pp. 185-186; Zimmer, Alt. Leb. pp. 117. 110; VI. pp. 347, 356-57; R.S. Sharma, *Conflict, Distribution and Differentiation in Rgvedic Society,* PIHC., (38th Session, Bhubaneswar, 1977), p. 178; IHR., July 1977, Vol. IV, No. 1, p. 2; R.C. Jain EAB., pp. 55f; V.N. Reu, *Rgveda Par Ek Aitihasik Drsti,* pp. 230-31, 233 fn. 1: A.C. Das, RI. Vol. 11, Preface, XI; R.P. Chanda, IAR., pp. 3, 245-46, notes-A: CHL, Vol. 1. *Ancient India,* p. 65; J.N. Talukdar, *The non-Âryans of the Rgveda',* JAS., Vol. XXI, Nos. 3-4, 1979, pp. 50f.
18. *Manu,* X. 45. Dayananda Sarasvati *(Satyârtha Prakâsa,* pp. 213-262) holds that Dasyudeúa and Mlecchadeúa were different from Aryavarta. The people of the eastern Himalayas, north-west and South were called Dasyus and mlecchas.
19. Mbh. *Úânti Parva,* 65, 13-14.
20. Mbh. *Anusâsana Parva*, 35, 17-18.
21. P.C. Roy (tr.): Mbh. Vol. II, pt, 1. Sec. IV p. 7; R.N. Saletore, EIC; Vol. II, pp. 750-51; B.A. Saletore, WTIH: pp. 14-15; Rangeya Raghava, *Prachin Bhâratiya Parampata aur Itihas,* pp. 224-25. Pargiter (AIHT; p. 132) has also admitted that "the Brahmana Kirâta was one of the rude Kirata folk".
22. *Manu*. X. 43-44.

    Also G. Buhler (tr,): *The Laws of Manu with Extracts from Seven Commentaries,* cf. F. MaxMuller (ed.): SBE; Vol. XXV, p. 412; A.C. Burnell, O.M.; pp. 310-11; N.V. Banerjee, SDSM; p. 67-V.S.A. Agrawala, IDM; p. 5.
23. IA. (JOR.) Vol. XLIII.
24. Mat. 114, 40-42 and VY; 45, 116-17.
25. Romila Thapar (AISH., pp. 164-65) placing her reliance on the texts-Mbh. and Manu. includes the Kiratas in the list of the tribes of indigenous origin, who were also known as Vratya or degenerate Ksatriya; see also her, *The Past and Prejudice,* p. 37; D.C. Sircar, SSAAMI; Vol. 1, pp. 48-49. 101-3 and 132 fn; SRAM1; p. 91; JARS., Sept. 1978, Vol. XIV, pp. 4-5; Research in Arunachal, (Proceedings of the Silver Jubilee Seminar organised by the Directorate of Research, Govt. of Arunachal Pradesh, at Shillong, 7-8 Sept. 1977), 1978, p. 33; P.V. Kane (Dh.

It., pp. 129-30) also supports both Mbh. 'Manu; M. Krishna Machariar, HCSL., Int. IX-IXi; R.P. Chanda (IAR., pp. 43-44) deriving authority from *Suddhitattva* of Raghunandana, a Bengali writer of the 16th century has upheld this view; Mangaldeva Sastri, DAG., pp. 308-9; S. Chat-topadhyaya, RENIT., pp. 32 & 73; G.S. Chaturvedi, *Purâr.a Parisilana,* pp. 44-45; Rângeya R.âghava, *op. cit,* p. 224; R.N. Rao, AAQ., pp. 95-96; V.N. Reu, *op. cit.* p-233, fn. 4-5; J. Vidyalankara, *Bhdratabhumi aur uske Nivasi*; B.A. Saletore, WT1H., pp. 14-15; M.R. Singh, GDEP., p. 199f Sylvain Levi, cf. PAPD., (tr. from French by P.C. Bagchi), pt. III. p. 89; Monier Williams (SED., pp. 283-84) thinks that the Kiratas were degraded mountain tribes who after having become Sudras were also known as mlecchas; Lassen, Ind. Alt. 1, pp. 441-250' M.A. Sherring, HTC. Vol. 1, Int. XVII; Muir, OST,, (1870), 1, p. 388; OST (1868), 1, p. 481; Zimmer, Alt. Leb., 32; VI., Vol. 1, pp. 157-58; B.C. Law, *Some Ksatriya Tribes of Ancient India,* pp. 26-29.

26. *A History of Assam* (1967), p. 12, fn. 2.
27. JASB., Vol. XVI, 1847; pt. 1, pp 27-28.
28. VSN.(SHMT), pp. Pref. IXIH, BK. 11, ch. Ill, pp. 161-62, BK. IV, ch. Ill, pp. 299-300.
29. Mârk (tr. BIS.) Vol. 11, p. 11, pt. 11, pp. 339 and 323; JASB.1897, Vol. LXVI, pt. 1, pp. 109-110.
30. *Kirâta-Jana-Kṛti* (AS., 1974). p. 28.
31. *The History of Civilisation of the People of Assam,* p. 97.
32. See the views of D.D. Kosambi, cf. JBBRAS,, 1952, Vol. 27, pt. 11, p. 183; K.C. Ojha, cf. JGRI., Vol. IX, 1951, pt. 1, p. 51; D.R. Regmi, AN. pp. 26, 27, & 29.
33. N.K. Dutt. OGCI., vol. 1, pp. 11-13.
34. HG., Vol. 11, pt. 1, pp. 279, 282-83, 363, 368-69.
35. *Vedavyâsa Smrti,* 1.11.
36. R.S. Sharma, SAI, pp. 44-45.
37. *Ibid,* pp. 33-41 and 280f.
38. Fick, *Diesociale Gliedtrung,* 202 et. seq. cf. VI; Vol. 11, p. 264,
39. *Amarakosa,* ii, X (Úûdravarga), 20.

    Also P.V. Kane, *Dh. It.* p. 129: Gustav Oppert, OIB., p. 17, fn. 19. Mallinatha (placed between 1325 and 1426 A.D.] in his commentary on the work of Kâlidâsa (The *Kumârasambhava* ed. M.R. Kale, p. 5, with reference to the above has given the characteristics of the mlecchas.

40. R.S. Sharma. SAI, p. 262.
41. *Gau. Dh. Sû.*, IV, 4; *Bau. Dh. Su.* 1.9.3; *Vas. Dh. Sû.* XVIII, 9.
42. —cf. Hazari Prasad Dvivedi, Kavira, pp. 17-18. But according to *Suta Samhitâ* (cf. P.V. Kane. Dh. It. p. 136) the mlecchas were produced through Brahmana mother and Vaisya father.
43. Romila Thapar, AISH., pp. 159-60, 165, 167, 172-73.
44. *Amarakoúa,* 11. 1 (Bhumivarga) 7.
45. S.C. Banerjee, Dh. Su. pp. 126-27, 234.
46. *Sabhâ Parva,* 47, 12.
47. *Ibid.* 20, 19.
48. *Mat.* 114. 11.
49. Wilson (tr.): Vsn., Bk. 1, ch. XIII, p. 84: Bk. 11, ch. Ill, p. 158.
50. *Bhag.* IX. 20.30. Also D.R. Patil, CHVP., pp. 307-8.
51. *Brah.* 110. 8.9,
52. Romila Thapar, *Op. Cit.* p. 220.
53. Pargiter, PTDKA., p. 65.
54. *Úat. Br.* 111. 2.1.24; SEE., Vol. XXVI, p. 32.
55. *Sumangala Vilasini,* 1, p. 176; *Sammoha-Vinodani* p. 388; G.P. Malalasekera, DPPN., 1, p. 607; *Prajnapana Upanga,* p. 397; *Jambudiva Paûnatti.* Also IA, Vol. XX, p. 374.
56. JRAS., 1900, p. 536.
57. A.K. Majumdar, EHID., Vol. 11, p. 411; Sudraka's *Mrcchakatikam* (tr. & annotated by M.R. Kale) Act VI, pp. 236-37, notes, p. 119.
58. *Arthaúâstra,* 11, 1; 111, 16; VII, 8; VIII. 4; IX, 1, 3.
59. Pad., 11, 27. 42-43. See also P.C. Roy (tr.): Mbh. XII, 59. 94-97, Romtila Thapar *op. cit.,* p. 307; H.D. Sankalia, *Prehistory of India,* p. 175 also refers to the Kiratas and Nisadas as they figure in the inscription of the 2nd century A.D.
60. IAR., pp. 5-6.
61. *Vsn.* 1.13; Wilson, *Vsn.* (revd. edn.) Vol. 1, p. 183.
62. *Bhâg.* IV. 14, 44. See also E.T. Dalton THEI., p. 128.
63. A.D. Pusalker, *Traditional History from the Earliest time .... The Vedic Age,* ch. XlV, p. 318.
64. *Mat.* 114, 34-36-,121, 49-54; Mat. cf. SBA.. 1. CXIV. pp. 307-8, CXXI, p. 327; VY., 45, 109-11; 47, 48-53.
65. *An Essay on the Sacred Isles in the West with other Essays connected with that work,* AS. Res. 1805, Vol. VIII, p. 331-32.

66. M. Krishna Machariar, HCSL., Int. IX, IXI; H.H. Wilson, Bentley, Wilford aid others, Mat, SBA., p. 307, note.
67. *Daíakumâracarita,* (text with tr. by M.R. Kale), Ucchavasa, 11, p. 24.

    Also *Ibid.,* Ucch. 1, text, pp. 13-16, tr. pp. 9-10, note, pp. 12-13; Ucch. 11. text. pp. 22-24. tr. pp. 15-17, note, p. 18; Varâhamihira (Br. Sam. IV. 23) also refers lo the Brahmanas of the mountainous, region.
68. JASB., Vol. XVI. 1847, pt. 1, p. 11.
69. R.C. Jain, EAB., p. 234.
70. M. Martin, HATSEI., Vol. IV, p. 39.
71. B.H. Hodgson, JASB., 1858, p. 448, E.T. Dalton, THEI., pp. 102-3.
72. Hodgson, 'On the Aborigines of the sub-Himalayas' JASB., Vol. XVI 1847, pt. 11, pp. 1235 ff; Atkinson, HG., Vol. 11, pt. 1, p. 365.
73. *The Periplus,* p. 253.
74. *Ind. Alt.* 1, 441-450.
75. For details see F. Haimendorf, *Inter-relations of Caste and ethnic groups in Nepal,* BSOAS., 1957, Vol. XX.
76. R.G. Latham, TR., Vol. 1, p. 84.
77. *Kirat Khambu Rais of Sikkim and Eastern Himalayas,* p. 12.
78. Shiva Kumar Rai, *op. cit.,* p. 5.
79. Charles McDougal *The Kulunge Rai* (1979), pp. 103ff, 124ff.
80. Martin Gaenszle, *Origins and Migrations of Mewahang* Rai (1991), p. 223.
81. Charles McDougal, *op. cit.*, pp. 2-3.
82. "On the Aborigines of the Sub-Himalayas", JASB, XVI, II (1874), p. 1235.
83. *Gurkhas,* p. 7.
84. Martin Gaenszle, *op cit.*, p. 4.
85. HATSEI, p. 39.
86. *Tribal History of Eastern India,* pp. 102-3.
87. *Ibid.*
88. H. Risley, *The Gazetteer of Sikkim,* p. 27.
89. *Op. cit.*, pp. 7, 8 and 12.
90. *Op. cit.*
91. E. Vansittart *op. cit.*, p. 137f.

92. Kumar Pradhan, *The Gorkha Conquest*, p. 161.
93. E. Vansittart, *op. cit.*, p. 137; also Iman Singh Chemjong, *History and Culture of the Kirat People* (1966), p. 86.
94. Cf. *Kiratavanshi Sunuwar (Mukhia) Koinch* (in Nepali), by Buddhiman Pradhan, Compiler Raghubur Mukhia (Gangtok, 1999), pp. 27-61, 94-97, 170-73; also Iman Singh Chemjong, *op. cit.*, p. 87; Vansittart, *op. cit.*, pp. 137-39.
95. Janak Lal Sharma, *Hamro Samaj: EK Adhyayan*, in Nepali, p. 298.
96. Namgyal Institute of Tibetology, Gangtok, text (P) 28.8.60, pp. 20 & 21 (g), Bombay, 1954.
97. *Ibid*; also Kumar Pradhan, *op cit*., p. 57.
98. *Sikkim: A Guide and Handbook p. 71.*
99. Suman Raj Timsina, "Nepali Community in India, The Sikkimese", *Gangtok Times,* Vol. I, No. XIV, Nov. 23-29, 1998, p. 22.
100. *History and Culture of the Kirat People,* pp. 70-71.
101. *Ibid*., 73.
102. *Ibid*., 74-75.
103. Cf. Santosh Allay, *Magar Juti Ko Itihasa Ani Samskriti*, Sikkim Ko Sandarbhama, in Nepali, pp. 2 and 13.
104. Tilak Pradhan, "Ancient Mangars of Indrakil", *Gangtok Times*, Vol. I, No. 11, Nov. 9-15, 1996, p. 4.
105. *Gorkha Magarharu*, in Nepali, p. 102, cf. Santosh Allay, *op. cit.*, p. 5.
106. *Op. cit.*, p. 7.
107. *Himalayan Journals*, Vol. I, p. 130.
108. *The Gazetteer of Sikkim*, pp. 10 and 38.
109. E. Vansittart, *op. cit*., pp. 84-86.
110. *Op. cit.,* p. 7.
111. *Darjeeling District Gazetteer* (1907), p. 43.
112. *Pahâd, The Study of Himalayan Society, Culture, Itihâsa and Ecology* pt. 11, pp. 145-46.
113. *Trails' Statistical Account of Kumann* (1823) pp. 19f. 57f. cf. As. Res. Vol. XVI, pp. 150f; Atkinson, HG., Vol. 11, pt. 1, pp. 365-67; M.M. Sharma, TCH., pp. 43-47.
114. Ch. 38 vv. 99ff; B.K. Kakati, *The Mother Goddess Kâmâkhyâ,* pp. 8f.

115. *Râjataraṅgini* (ed. M.A. Stein), pp. 60, 71 (No. 39) 358 and 417. Mr. Stein calls them aboriginal Indian tribes of Vindhya Hills and Rajaputana. Also the text (tr. by R.S. Pandit) p. 71.
116. E. Thurston and K. Rangachari, CTSI., Vol. 1, pp. 183, 185, 187ff; Vol. 11, p. 204; Vol. Ill, p. 294.
117. *Lassen's Review of the Reports of Ktesias concerning India's* tr. from his Ind. Alt. (2nd edn. 1874) Vol. 11, pp. 641ff. cf. J.W. McCrindle, AIK., pp. 65ff.
118. Frag. XLVI; Frag. 1 or an *Epitome of Megasthenes,* (Diod, 11. 35-42 cf J.W. McCrindle, A1MA., p. 35; *The Fragments of the Indika of Megasthenes,* collected by E.A, Schwanbeck, (Bonn 1846 tr. by J.W. McCrindle, cf. IA., 1877, Vol. VI, p. 121.
119. CR., October-December, 1844, Vol. 11, pp. 3-4.
120. *Op. cit.* pp. 228-29, 223f.
121. James Legge, RBK., pp. 14 and 34.
122. Thomas Watters, YTI., Vol. 11, p. 186; BRWW., 11, p. 196.
123. H.A.R. Gibb, *Ibn-Battuta's travel in Asia and Africa,* 1328-1354 (London 1929).
124. JASB., Vol. XVI, 1847, pt. 11, pp. 1235-44; JASB., Vol. XVIII,. 1849, pt. 1 pp. 451-60; JASB., Vol. XVIII, 1849, pt. 11, pp. 967-75.
125. IA., (JOR), p. 150; AIMA., pp, 74-75.
126. *Le Nepal,* Vol. 11, pp. 75ff.
127. *Pâli Sâhitya Kâ Itihâsa,* p. 295; *Purâtativa Nibandhavali,* p. 97.
128. (*a*) *Kirâta-Jana-Kṛti,* pp. 5, 15-16, 18-23, 26, 36-38, 41, 44, 58.
    (*b*) IAH., p. 49-50.
    (*c*) *Cul. Her. Ind.,* Vol. V, pp. Pref. XIX, XXIII, 659-61, 674.
    (*d*) IAC, Aril, 1954.
    (*e*) PAHCI., pp. 6, 9, 15-18, 31, 83.
    (*f*) IC. p. 9f. 17f.
    (*g*) *Non-Âryan Elements in Indo-Aryan,* JGIS., Vol. 11, 1936, No. 1, pp. 43-49.
    (*h*) *Race-Movements and Pre-historic culture, The Vedic age,* ch. VIII, pp. 143-45, 169-70.
    (*i*) ODBL., 1, pp. 77-79.
129. *Kirâta—A Study on Some Ancient Indian Tribe,* Le Monde Oriental, 1936, Vol XXX, pp. 97ff.
130. *Ibid*, pp. 100-23, 138-53.

131. EAI., pp. 124-25.
132. G. Bertrand, *Sacred Lands Where Women Reign,* p. 26.
133. B.S. Guha, *Racial Elements in the Population,* in *Oxford Pamphlets on Indian Affairs* No. 22 (1944), pp. 8, 16-17.
134. S. Chattopadhyaya, RENIT., pp. 2, 10, 72-73, See also S.K. Chatterji, *The Vedic Age,* pp. 143-45 and D.N. Majumdar, RCI., pp. 30-32.
135. S. Chattopadhyaya, *op. cit.* pp. 72-73, 104,; M. Govardhan Singh, *History of Himachal Pradesh,* p. 22.
136. IAR., pp. 68-69.
137. H.C. Chakladar, AOEI., p. 40.
138. Pargiter, AIHT., p. 292.
139. H.C. Chakladar, G.K., pp. 23-24; Pargiter, JASB., 1897, Vol. LXVI, pt. 1, pp. 85, 105,108-10; 1C., pp. 319f; Mark. (Eng. tr. BIS.), Vol. ll.pt. 11, Canto LVII, pp. 282-84, 319 322f; S.N. Majumdar Sastri, JBORS., 1922, Vol. VIII, pp. 41-42; P.C. Bhattacharya, *A Few Elements of the Indo-Mongoloid Boro Culture* JARS., Vol. XVI, 1962 (Pub. 1964) pp. 60-61; S.B. Choudhari, ESAI., p. 170; K.L. Barua, EHK., (2nd ed. 1966), pp. 2, 18-19; E. Gait, *op. cit.* (1967), pp. 3-6. See also G.T. Bettany, *The Tibeto-Burmese and Tibetans,* In. *As. Res.* VIII, pp. 110-112; W. Crooke, R.N. 1, pp. 31-32.
140. P.C. Sen, JARS., Apr. 1933, Vol. 1, No. 1, pp. 12-13.
141. EIC, Vol. 11, pp. 750-52.
142. Vsn. Bk. 1. ch. XIII, p. 84; Bk. 11, ch. 111. p. 42; Bk. V. ch. XXIX, p. 459.
143. V.A. Smith, EHI., (4th edn.), p. 38; OHI., pp. 15-16.
144. Paul Masson-oursel & c. AIIC., p. 13.
145. S.K. Chatterji, *Kirata-Jana-Krti,* pp. 7-8, 40-41, 45-47, 50-51, 121-24, 130-31, 140-41, 166-67.
146. Sylvain Levi, *Le Nepal.* Vol. 11, pp. 78-79.
147. NEB., (15th Edn., 1980), Vol. 8, pp. 885-86.
148. S.K. Chatterji, *op. cit.* 65; Campbell, JASB., 1840, p. 596: G.A. Grierson, LSI., Vol. 111, pt. 1, pp. 274f, 326f; D.R. Regmi, A.N. pp. 16-17, 24-27, 30-31; IAN: Vol. 3, pp. 191.
149. *Arthasastra,* ed. & tr. by V. Gairola, Prakarana 7, ch. 11. p. 33; Prakarana 16, ch. 20. p. 69.
150. A.N. p. 50.
151. EAI., pp. 124-25.

152. G.T. Bettany, In. As. pp, 111-12.
153. S.K. Chatterji, PAACI., pp. 9-10; Cul. Her. Ind, Vol. V, pp. 659-60; *Kriata-Jana-Krti,* pp. 5, 15, 26, Also Grierson, IG1, Vol. 1. pp. 384-85: E.J. Rabson (ed): CHI, Vol. I, *Ancient India,* pp. 35, 42; B.C. Allen, E.A. Gait & c. GBNEI., pp. 26 and 49; C. Chakraberti, CSARM., pp. 7 and 14.
154. W. Crooke. RNI., pp. 31-32.
155. EAI., pp. 14 and 124-25.
156. Cul. Her. Ind. Vol. V, pp. 659-60.
157. PAHCI., p. 9.
158. *Kirata-Jana-Krti,* pp. 26 and 36.
159. Ramdhari Singh Dinkar, *Samskrti Ke Car Adhyaya,* p. 4.
160. Owen and E. Lattimore, *The Making of Modern China* (The **Infantry** Journal), pp. 30-31, 35-39.
161. A. Nourse, *A Short History of the Chinese,* pp. 141f.
162. D.G.E. Hall, *Burma,* p. 28. Also, Hirth, *Ancient History of China,* pp. 6f; Richard, *A Comprehensive Geography of the Chinese Empire,* pp. 4ff. S. Sanang Setze in his chronicle *Mongol Kbadum Tog-Budji* has traced the Mongol's royal lineage to the Tibetans; I.J. Schmidt (tr. & ed. *Gesichte der Ostmongolen,* pp. 33f) has provided an elaborate account of the subject.
163. *Comparative Religion,* pp. 118, 175-76.
164. Robert Shafer. EAI., pp. 130-31.
165. In Sino-Tibetan family Chinese, Siamese, Burmese and Tibetan are included. This family is divided into six main divisions: Sinitic (Chinese), Daic (Thai), Bodic (Tibetan), Burmic (Burmese) Baric (Bodo, etc.) and Karenic (Karen)—Robert Shafer, *Introduction to Sino-Tibetan,* pp. 1-3.
166. *Tibet: A Political History* (1973), pp. 5-6.
167. Charles Bell, *Tîbet-Past and Present,* pp. 21f, 25.
168. (*a*) G.E. Harvey, *History of Burma from the Earliest times to 10th March,* 1824, pp. 6 and 338.

     British Rule in Burma, 1824-1942, pp. 9, 11, 70 and 85.

     (*b*) D.G.E. Hall, *op. cit.* po. 7, 10-11.

     (*c*) G. CCEDE's. *The Making of south-east Asia* (tr. from French by H.M. Wright), pp. 16f.

     (*d*) Ma-Myasein, *Burma,* pp. 6 and 9.

     (*e*) J.L. Christian, *Burma,* pp. 13 and 36.

     (*f*) P. Phayre *History of Burma,* pp. 1-5.

(g) Report on the Census of British Burma (Aug. 1872, Rangoon, 1875), ch. XI, pp. 26-27.

(h) G.P. Singh, *The north-east Indian Tribal races as described in Literary and Classical Sources,* PNEIHA (Shillong-1980), pp. 17-18

—*Traditional and Historical Accounts of early Tibeto-Burman Relations with Bihar and its cultural impact,* Journal of the Thinkers Forum, (Kohima, Nov. 1981), Vol. IX, No. 4, pp. 26-35.

169. D.G.E. Hall, *op. cit.* pp. 10-11.

170. Kal. 38, 98-147.

171. Mbh. Sabha Parva, 23, 19; Udyoga Parva, 19, 14-15.

172. S.K. Chatterji, *Kirata-Jana-Krti,* p. 28.

173. Macdonell and Keith, VI, Vol. 1, pp. 157-58.

174. B. Walker, *Hindu World,* 1 p. 555; H.H. Wilson, Vsn; Bk. 111, pp. 156-58, 162.

175. E. Gait, *A History of Assam,* p. 12.

176. D.C. Sircar (SGAMI., pp. 31, fn. -1, 46, fn. 2 and 200) has mistakenly identified the Kirâtas of the Purâṇas as well as of Kâlidâsa's Raghuvamsa only with the Kirâtas of Nepal.

177. (a) *Ratnâvali,* 2, 3.

(b) *Ibid.* (tr. & annot. by Ramchandra Mishra) p. 66. Also, *Raghuvaṁśa,* (tr. M R. Kale), p. 116;

(c) *Kumârasambhava,* Canto. l, v. 10; *Ibid.* 1, 6, 15; Wilson (tr.): Vsn. Bk. 1, ch. XIII, p. 84;

(d) Pãnâtantra quoted in *Raghuvaṁśa* (ed. N.R. Acharya, Bombay 1948), p. 104.

178. *Amarakośa,* 11, 4, 143.

179. S. Banerjee, JASB., 1873, p. 187; IA., 111, pp. 178-9.

180. EI., Vol. XX, pt. 1; B.C. Law, IETBJ., pp. 85-86; HGAI., pp. 73, 98-99.

181. El. XX, 22 fn, 11, p. 72; Vasudeva Upadhyaya, SAII 11, pp. 271-72.

182. R.D. Bannerji, *Lekhamalânukramani,* pt. 1, No. 210, p. 99.

183. Ed. Trenckner, IV, 8, 94, pp. 327 and 331; trans. from Pali by T.W. Rhys Davids, *The Questions of King Milinda*, in SBE, XXXVI, II (Oxford, 1894), pp. 203-04; R.D. Vadekar's edition: p. 321; M. Pelliot, JA., 1914, 11, pp. 379ff.

184. Sylvain Levi, IHQ., (ed. N.N. Law), Vol. XII. 1936. p. 126; D.C. Sircar, SGAMI., p. 232; S.K. Chatterji *op. cit.* p. 34; see GISO

Hemachandra's *Prakrit Grammar,* I, 183 cf O. Stein, *The Jinist Studies,* p. 100.

185. SBE., 1894, pp. 203-204 quoted in S.K. Chatterji, *op. cit.*

186. B.C Law, IETBJ., p. 86; HGAl., p. 73.

187. Motichandra, GESM., *Upayana Parva,* pp, 60-61; Alberuni, (E.C. Sachau, Alb. Ind. Vol. 1, pp. 201, 299-303.

Abul Fazl's *Ain-I-Akbari.* tr. Jarrett and Sarkar Vol. 11, pp. 118-19, 131-32; Pargiter, *Mark,* Vol. 11 pt. 11, pp. 284. 319 note and 322-23; B.C. Law, *Countries and peoples of India Epic & Pauranic sources,* ABORI., XVII, April, 1936, pt. 111, pp. 236-37; James Taylor JASB, VoL. XVI, 1847, pt. 1, pp. 29-30; K.L. Barua, EHK., 1966, p. 2; A.K. Majumdar EHID., Vol. 11, p. 423; urânas, VY. 1.45.118; 1.58.78-83; Bmd; 2.16.7; 18.46; 31-83; *Mark*. 57, 39: Vmn; 13.41; Mat. 114, 51-58; D.C. Sircar, SGAMI, p. 34; B.C. Law HGAI; p. 73 M.R. Singh (GDEP); p. 173. The Apadana ii, pp. 358-59; Robert Shafer, EAI., pp. 130-132; K.P. Jayaswal, *Hindu Polity,* pt. 1, p. 124 Note 33; S. Chattopadhyaya, RENIT., pp. 101-102; D.C. Sircar, SGAMI., pp. 80, 84, 103.

188. WTIH., p. 16.

189. J.W. McCrindle, AICI; P. Introd. XIV; C. Muller (ed): *Eragments of Hecataeus,* Geog. 1, 1-31.

190. McCrindle, AIM; pp. 3, 6fn; Bohn's, *Herodotus* tr. by Cary, Bk. III, 18.

191. Rennell, GSH; Vol. I, pp. 308f; E.H. Bunbury HAG; Vol. I., Ch. V, p. 142 and pp. 229-30; Wilcox- As. Res., Vol. XVII, p. 456; CHI; pp. 354-55. B.N. Puri, TLEGW; p. 5.

192. J. Taylor, JASB; Vol. XVI, 1847, Pt. 1, p. 13.

193. Lassen's Review of the Reports of Ktesias concerning India (tr. from his Ind. Alt; 2nd edn. 1874, Vol. II, pp. 641ff) cf. McCrindle.

AIK; pp. 87-90; Lassen, Ind. Alt; Vol. II, p. 657; *The Periplus;* (tr. by W.H. Schoff), pp. 253-54; C. Muller (ed): Ctesias (Frag; pp. 16-18; H.H. Wilson's, *Notes on the Indica of Ctesias,* Oxford, 1836).

194. McCrindle AICL; p. 61 fn. I; Fragm. XXIX, Strabo, XV. 1.57, p. 711 cf. McCrindle, AIMA; pp. 73-75. See also Wheeler, *History of India,* Vol. Ill, p. 179. *Arthasastra,* tr. C. Gairola, Pr, 16, ch. 20, p. 69.

195. AIK; p. 88.

196. IA; Vol. VI, p. 133, note and p. 135; Strabo's Geog. 57 cf. AICL; pp. 60-61.
197. AIK; p. 89-90.
198. IA; Vol. VII, p. 150.
199. Wilford (As. Res; Vol. VIII, pp. 331 f.) mentions the 'chipitanasika', snub-nosed, which is exactly the same as referred to by Varahmihira Br, Sam. XIV, 26.
200. V. Ball, PRIA; April 21, 1883, No. 572, p. 277.
201. FRAG. XXX—Plin. *Hist—Nat.* VII. 11.14-25, AIMA; p. 80.
202. R.C. Jain (ed); McCrindle's AIMA; p. 80.
203. *Ibid.,* p. 233.
204. FRAG. XV. B; FRAG. XXX 3, AIMA; pp. 73-74, 80,173-74, note and 177-78.
205. Schwanbeck. Ml; p. 66; Lassen, ZFKOM; 11.40,
206. R.C. Jain, *op. cit.,* Appx. 4, p. 230.
207. IA; 1876-77, Vol, VI, pp. 127f, 133f 349f.
208. St. Martin, *Etude;* pp. 195-97; Schwanbeck, MI., pp. 16f, 57f cf. McCrindle, AIMA; FRAG. LVI, Plim. Hist. Nat. VI. 21, 8-23. 11, p. 133.
209. AICL; p. 61fn.
210. Schoff, *The Periplus*; pp. 253, 266-67.
211. *The Periplus;* pp. 264-66.
212. R.M. Nath BAC; pp. 14-15.
213. JASB; Vol. XVI, Pt. I, pp. 46f.
214. F. Wilford, *An Essay on the Sacred Isles in the West;* As. Res. ; Vol. VIII, 1805 p. 338; As. Res; Vol. IX, p. 68; JAS 13; 'XVI; 1, p. 11.
215. Bostock-Riley *The Natural History of Pliny,* 11. pp. 59 Nos. 39 and 60.
216. V.A. Smith, EHI; p. 107.
217. Schoff, *The Periplus*; 62, p. 47; Vincent, *The Periplus;* Vol. II, pp. 523-28. He has also referred to this in his translation of Arrian's Journal. Also, McCrindle, CNES; p. 145; *Periplus Moris Erythraei* (tr. from the text as given in the Latin work *Geographi Groeci Minores* ed. by C. Muller) by McCrindle cf. IA. (JOR; ed. JAS, Burgess), 1879, Vol. VIII, p. 150; R.C. Majumdar, CAI; pp. 307, 312; JASB; XVI, 1, pp. 4, 10-11.
218. *Op. cit.,* p. 253.

219. Murray's *Ency, Geograh;* Pt. 1, Bk. 1, Ch. 11, Sec. VII.
220. F. Wilford, *An Essay on the Sacred Isles in the West;* As. Res; 1805, Vol. VIIl, pp. 337-38; *On the Ancient Geography of India;* As. Res; 1822, Vol. XIV, pp. 391 and 405.
221. IA; 1879, Vol. VIII, p. 150.
222. McCrindlc, AIP; pp. 70-71, 173 (sec. 80). J. Burgess *(Ibid,* pp. 353-54, notes) also locates Dasarnas in Orissa. Also AICL; p. 198 fn. 7 & 8.
223. Ind. Alt. Vol. Ill, pp. 135-37 cf. AIP; pp. 191f.
224. AICL; p. 199, fn. 8.
225. JASB; XVI, 1, pp. 8-11.
226. *Op. cil.,* p. 253.
227. Ind. Ait; 1 441-50.
228. *The Periplus.* (tr. by Schoff), pp. 253-54. Also JASB; XVI, I; As. Res; VIII and IX.
229. *Ibid.,* pp. 287-79. Motichandra, *(Sarathavaha,* p. 119).
230. Ind. Alt; III. 38.
231. *The Periplus*; pp. 48, 279.
232. *Ibid.* pp. 49, 256, 281 and 288.
233. Yule (tr.); TM; Vol. II, p, XIVI.
234. Schoff, *op. cit.,* p. 279.
235. McCrindle, AI; p. 180.
236. N.L. Dey, GDAMI; p. 26.
237. *The Invasion of India by Alexander the Great,* p. 156 note.
238. Drona Parva, 19, 11.
239. V.S. Agarwala, IKP; p. 455; Kielhorn, *Mahabhasya of Patanjali.* Vol. II, p. 282 cf. B.N. Puri, ITP; pp. 70-71.
240. Lasren, Ind. Alt; Vol. III, pp. 235-37, quoted in McCrindle, AIP; CAP. 2, pp. 191-194; AICL; fn. 1.
241. Lassen, *op. cit.*
242. AS. Res; Vol. XIV, pp. 444-45.
243. *Etude;* pp. 343-44, cf. AIP; pp. 191-94.
244. RPGEA; pp. 28, 256, note 1; Gerini *(Ibid.* Table-X).
    See also, R.C. Jain (ed): McCrindle'as AIP, APPx. 7, pp. 449 50.
245. RPGEA; p. 28.
246. *Ibid.* pp. 28-29. See also, Walter Elliot's NO; Southern India, pp. 9-15.

247. AIP; pp. 219-21 and J. Burgess' notes, p. 391.
248. *Ibid.* pp. 192-94, 219; Gerini, RPGEA; Table-X.
249. JASB; XVI, 1, pp. 11-12, 38-39.
250. AIP; pp. 192-94.
251. Ind. Alt; Vol. 1, pp. 279-85; Vol. II. pp. 555-61.
252. CPI; pp. 310-12.
253. RPGEA; pp. 51-52. (For further details about Tripura See PASB; Jan. 1874).
254. RPGEA; pp. 829-30 and Table-X. See also IGI; Vol. XIII. p. 175.
255. JASB; XVI, 1, p. 11.
256. AIP; CAP. 2, pp. 217-18.
257. RPGEA; pp. 53-54.
258. AIP; pp. 217-18.
259. Wilford, As. Res; Vol. XIV, p. 385.
260. AIP; pp. 217-18; JASB; XVI. 1, pp. 11f.
261. As. Res; Vol. XIV, pp. 390-91; R.C. Jain, *op. cit.,* Appx. 8, p. 452.
262. RPGEA; pp. 829-30 and Table-X.
263. AIP; CAP. 2, Sec. 17, pp. 219-21; CAP. 2, Sec. 24, p. 235; R.C. Jain, *op. cit.,* p. 255, and Appx. 8, p. 452.
264. McCrindle, CNES; pp. 23, 147-48.
265. JASB; XVI, 1, pp. 30, 32-33.
266. HGAI: pp. 98-99; TAI; Ch. LV, pp. 282-83; GAKW; p. 23.
267. GDAMI; p. 100.
268. HG; Vol. 11, Pt. I, pp. 357., 361f.
269. G.P. Singh, *The north-east Indian Tribal Races as described in Literary and Classical Sources,* PNEIHA; (Shillong, 1980) p. 16.
270. EHK p. 8.
271. BAC; pp. 20-21.
272. *A Few Elements of the Indo-Mongoloid Boro Culture,* JARS; Vol. XVI, 1962, (Pub. 1964). p. 61.
273. *Introduction to Manipur,* pp. 10 and 56.
274. *Rigveda,* Vol. 1, pp. 26-43.
275. *History of Manipur,* Foreword, V.
276. *Ptolemy's Geography,* BK. VI, CAP. 12, Sec. 4; McCrindle, AI; p. 277; H.H. Wilson, *Ancient Notices of Ariana,* Ar. Ant; Ch. iii, pp. 164-65 and also Index, p. 447.
277. AICL: p. 199.

278. *Bmd;* 2.16.60; *Mark;* (tr. Pargiter), Vol. II, pt. II, pp. 316, 335. 338.
279. D C. Sircar, SGAMI; p. 70, note 3.
280. Pargiter, *op. cit.*
281. Aranyaka Parva, 141, 25.
282. Pargiter, JASB; Vol. LXVI, 1897, p. 1, pp. 85, 105-9.
283. *Amarakosa,* II, X, 20-21; P.V. Kane, Dh. It., Vol. 1, pp. 129-30, 133.
284. *Arthasastra* (tr. by Shamasastry), pp. 46 and 49.
285. *Dasakumaracarita* (text), Purv. UCch. 1, pp. 13-16; Ucch. Ill, pp. 103-4; (tr. M.R. Kale), pp. 9-10 and note, pp. 12-13.
286. *Rājatarangini* (tr. R.S. Pandit), p. 71.
287. *Ibid.* Ill, 35, 39.
288. Vsn; (tr.), BK. 1, Ch. XIII, p. 84.
289. D.S. Sircar, *Text of the Puranic list of Peoples,* IHQ; (ed. N.N. Law), Vol. XXI, 1945, pp. 297-314; SGAMI; pp. 31, note, 1, 46, note, 2; K.P. Jayaswal, *op. cit.,* p. 124, note, 33; R. Shafer, EAI; pp. 124-25; Atkinson, HG; Vol. II. pt. 1, p. 365.
290. cf. Grierson, LSI; Vol. III. Pt. 1, p. 274.
291. *Ibid.*
292. *Ibid.*
293. Pargiter, JASB: Vol. LXVI, 1897, pt. 1, pp. 105, 108-10; 1C; p. 322 fr.; D.R. Regmi, AN; pp. 16-17, 24; R.N. Saletore, EIC, Vol. II, pp 750-52; Percy Brown, *Picturesque Nepal,* p. 30; Risley, TCB; Vol. 1, p. 490.
294. Sylvain Levi, *Le Nepal*; Vol. 11, pp. 72-78; Pt. Baldeva Pd. Mishra; *Nepal Kā Itihāsa,* pp. 7 and 20; Atkinson, NHH: p. 14; E. Gait, *A History of Assam,* p. 12.
295. D.R. Regmi, AN. pp. 55-56.
296. *An Account of the Kingdom of Nepal by Father GIUSEPEE Communicated by John Shore,* As. Res; (Delhi. 1979), Vol. 11, p. 253.
297. cf. Atkinson, HG; Vol. 11.pt. 1, p. 365.
298. *Ibid.,* pp. 364-65; JASB; 1854, pp. 595-96.
299. THEI; pp. 102-3 and 265.
300. S.C. Dutt, WTI; pp. 121-22.
301. B.H. Hodgson, *On the Aborigines of the Sub-Himalayas,* JASB; 1847, Vol. XVI, pt. 11, pp. 1235ff.

302. LSI; Vol. Ill, pt. 1, pp, 316-17.
303. *Ibid.*, p. 274.
304. E.T. Dalton, *op. cit.*, pp. 103, 105, 107-8.
305. D.R. Regmi, AN; pp. 55-56; N.B. Thapa, SHN; pp. 8-9.
306. *Ibid.*
307. IIH; pp. 89-90.
308. Risley, *op. cit.*
309. HG; Vol. II, pt, 1, p. 365, fn. 1.
310. HG; Vol. 11, pt. 1, pp. 365-68; Traills (first Commissioner of Kumaon) Report (1823), *Statistical Account of Kumaon* pp. 19f, 57f; Latham, *Ethnology of India*, pp. 11f, 16; Strachey's Journal at Garjjia (1846); M.M. Sharma, TCH; pp. 43-46.
311. Pritchard's Researches (3rd edn.). Vol. IV, pp. 206 and 231; *Ethnology of the British Colonies*, p. 132.
312. P. Carnegy, NRTCA; p. 1; D.R. Regmi, AN; p. 24; S.C. Dutt, WTI; p. 118.
313. HATSEI; Vol. IV, p. 39.
314. TR; Vol. 1, p. 84
315. HATSEI; Vol. IV, pp. 37, 39-40.
316. Charles Grant (ed); GCPI; p. 214.
317. S.K. Chatterji, *op cit.*, pp. 28-29.
318. AI. p. 515.
319. Vettam Mani, PE; p. 412.
320. E. Thurston and K. Rangachari, CTSI; Vol. 1, pp. 180-85; Vol. 11, pp. 203-4; Vol. Ill, p. 294 (Col. Wilks in his *Historical Sketches of the South India*, Mysore, 1810-17 also deals with them to some extent).
321. Narasimā Carya, *Kavicarite*, 11, p. 219, quoted by B.A. Saletore, WTIH; p. 25.
322. B.A. Saletore, *op. cit.*
323. Rice, *Mysore and Coorg from the Inscriptions*, pp. 5f; EC; VI, pp. 113-14; EC; VII, pp. 188.
324. *Sabha Parva*, 29, 15 or 32, 17: Śānti Parva, 65, 13-14; 207, 43; Anusasana Parva, 35, 17-18; R.K. Rai, Mbh. Ko; p. 241. Also H C. Chakladar GK; pp. 23-24.
325. *Vmm;* 13, 37-43; *Mark*; 54, 40; 55, 44-45 & 49-52; Pargiter (tr); *Mark.* Vol. 11, pt, 11, pp. 284, 369, 379 & 383; *Brah;* 27, 47-50; Vy; 1, 45, 119-20; 58, 81-83; *Mat;* 144, 44; *Bmd;* 49, 53-55; *Bhag;*

II, 4.18; IX, 20, 30; Pad. (Svargakhanda), 6.64, Also S.M. Ali, GP; p. 165; D.C. Sircar, SGAMI; pp. 32-35; M.R. Singh, GDEP; pp. 180-82; R.N. Saletore, EIC: Vol 11. pp. 750f. Chattopadhyaya's (RENIT; p. 104).

326. Geog. Bk. VI, Cap. 12, Sec. 4; McCrindle, AIP; pp. 35. 274. 77. 283-85 Gerini, RPGEA; p. 830, N.I, JRGS; Vol. XLlI, p. 327.

327. Ar. Ant; pp. 164-55; also Bunbury, HAG; Vol. 11, pp. 641-2.

328. TAI; Ch. LV, pp. 282-83; GAKW; p. 23. also his HGAI; pp. 98-99; IETBJ; pp. 71-72, 84, 86 and B.M. Barua's *Asoka and his Inscriptions* p. 100.

329. WTIH; p. 33.

330. Heeren, HRPNA; *Asiatic Nations,* Vol. I, pp. 277-79; H.H. Wilson, *op. cit.,* pp. 132-34.

331. McCrindle, *op. cit.,* p. 35.

332. Foucher, *Lancienne Route de L' Inde,* 11, pp. 184-85. "A mountainous country situated to the east of the Indus is called Halara—a name which retains some traces of old designation (McCrindle, AICL; p 34 fr. 2).

333. AICL; p. 199.

334. D.P. Mishra, SPHI; p. 23.

335. For details see *Ibid*; pp. 6, 18; M. Ali, GP; pp. 63-64; McCrindle, AIMA; pp. 78-79; P. Gupta, GNAIL; p. 126: N.L. Dey, GDAMI. p. 213; IHQ. Vol. 1, 1925, p. 457; IGJ; Vol. XX, No. 2; p. 55; Zimmer, Ait, Leb. pp. 101-2; Hopkins, JAOS. 1375, No. 7; Weber, Ind. Stu; 1, 165; Kern, *Manual of Indian Buddhism,* pp. 59-60: K.L. Daftari, ACAI; pp. 196-98.

336. C. Chakraberti, CSARM; p. 14.

337. cf. JRAS: 1950, pp. 285-88; ZDMG; 1912, pp. 72-77.

338. Pargiter, JRAS: 1908, p. 331 and 1912, p. 712; Oldfield's, *Nepal* Vol. 1, pp. 53 & 111.

339. H.C. Chakladar, AOEI: p. 40.

340. Br. Sam, XIV, 17-18.

341. D.S. Triveda, *Bharat Ka Naya Itihāsa,* p. 3.

342. *Mudrārāksasa* Act. II, p. 58. Also text with tr. by M.R. Kale, p. 26, note, pp. 24-25 and Satyavrata Singh, p. 89.

343. *Raghuvamsa,* Canto IV, 60-85.

344. *Ibid.,* canto IV, V, 76.

345. Bhagwat Saran Upadhyaya, IK; ch. Ill, pp. 61-63; M.R. Kale's Map appended at the end of his trans. & annot. work, *The*

Meghaduta of Kālidsa: B.C. Law, GAKW; p. 23; H.C. Chakladar, GK; p. 25; PTIOC (Sixth Session), p. 111. Also Pargiter (tr.): *Mark:* Vol. II, pt. 11., p. 322; JASB; 1897, Vol. LXVI, Pt. 1, pp. 108ff and B.C. Law, HGAI, pp. 28-99 for their location in Tibet.

346. KS: p. 153.
347. cr. M.R. Kale (tr.) ; *Raghuvamsa,* Notes, Canto IV, pp. 116-18.
348. SGAMI; p. 200.
349. *Kadambari:* Purv., pp. 144-45; text with trans. by M.R. Kale, ch. III pp. 7-8 and p. 123f; Kane, Purv. p. 270 & pp. 90-98, 331. Also Mahesh Chandra Bhartiya, *Banabhatta aur unki Kādambari* p. 76.
350. *Kirātārjuniyam,* Canto-XII, VV. 39, 82, 84-86; Canto-XIII. V. 36; Canto-XIV, W. 33-34, 45, 63-64.
351. pp. 2, 61, 104, 118-21 cf. *Ibid.*
352. Raj Bali Pandey, *Bhartiya Itihasa Ka Parichaya,* p. 5.
353. H.A. Rose, GTCP N.W.; 1, pp, 634-35; R.N, Saletore, EIC; Vol. II, pp. 750-52; B.A. Saletore, WTIH; p. 22.
354. K.K. Das Gupta, THAI, p. 77.
355. M G. Singh, *History of Himachal Pradesh,* p. 22.
356. *Ibid,* pp. 50-51.
357. M.M. Sharma, TCH; p. 45.
358. *Ibid.,* p. 29,
359. Atkinson, HG, Vol. II, p. 1, pp. 365-66.
360. *Ibid.*
361. EI; Vol. XXX, pp. 282-83; El; Vol. XXXI. p. 289 cf. D.C. Sircar, *Indian Epigraphy,* pp. 368-69.
362. *Op, cit.,* p. 113.
363. S. Levi, *Le Nepal,* II, pp. 72-78; Lassen, Ind, Ait. I, pp. 441-50; II, pp. 530-34; Schoff, *The Periplus,* p. 253; D. Wright, HN; pp. 89ff; Atkinson, HG; Vol. 11. pt. l, pp. 363-65; Pargiter, IC; p. 322 fn; M.M: Sharma, *op. cit.,* p. 45; B.P. Mishra, *Nepal Ka Itihasa,* pp. 2, 20 and 45; N.L. Dey, GDAMI, p. 100; R. Shafer, EAl; pp. 124-25; R.S. Tripathi, HAI; p. 332; R.C. Majumdar, AI; p. 351.
364. Pargiter, JRAS; 1908, p. 326.
365. cf. McCrindle, AIMA; pp. 177-78.
366. J. Taylore JASB; 1847, Vol. XVI, pt. 1, pp. 11-12: M. Martin, HATSEI, Vol. IV, pp. 38-39.
367. D.R. Regmi, AN, pp. 55-56; N.B. Thapa, SHN; pp. 8-9.

368. D.R. Regmi, *op. cit.,* pp. 57-58.
369. H.C. Ray, DHNI; Vol. I, pp. 272-80.
370. D.R. Regmi, *op. cit.,* pp. 15-17, 22. 57-58.
371. D.R. Regmi, *op. cit,,* pp. 57-58.
372. D.R. Regmi, IAN; Vol. 3, p. 192.
373. *Ibid.*
374. S. Levi, *op. cit.,* 1.p, 222.
375. S.K. Chatterji, *Kirata-Jana-Krti,* p. 36.
376. *Ibid.,* pp. 26, 28 and 58.
377. Mat; 114, 34-36; 121, 49-54; also Mat; cf. SBA; pt. 1, ch. CXIV, pp. 307-8; ch. CXXI, p. 327; Vy; 45, 109-11; 47, 48-53.
378. *Kiratarjuniyam* (with commentary of P. Pandey) Canto—1,VV. 1-26, pp. 1-17.
379. HG; Vol. 11, pt. 1, p. 363.
380. *Ibid.,* p. 364.
381. EAI; p. 14.
382. Āranyaka Parva, 141, 25.
383. V.S. Agrawala, *Bhārata Savitri,* Vol. 1-1, p. 268.
384. B.A. Saletore, WTIH; p. 19.
385. H.D. Sankalia, *Studies in Historical Geography and Cultural Ethnography of Gujarat,* cf. S.P. Gupta and K.S. Ramachandran (eds.): AIHA; p. 4.
386. *Ibid.*
387. S.K. Chatterji, *op. cit.,* p. 35.
388. ABORI, 1936, Vol. XVII, pt. Ill, p. 224.
389. AISH; p. 168.
390. RV; III, 4, 53, 14.
391. Nirukta, VI, 32.
392. Madhya—Khandam, XXVI, 20, 22, 47; Also VY; 78.22; Pad. (Patala—Khanda, XI, 45).
393. HATSEI; Vol. IV, p. 41.
394. Sabhā Parva, 27. 13.
395. GK; pp. 23-24.
396. *Op. cit.,* pp. 37-38.
397. Sabha Parva, 13, 19: R.K. Rai Mbh. Ko; p. 414; Bhisma Parva, 10, 49 & 55. Also R. Shafer, EAI; pp. 124-25.

398. Pad., 6. 64. See also B.C. Law. GEB; p. 33.
399. JASB; XVI, 1, pp. 8-12; M. Martin, *op. cit.*, pp. 38-40; Dalton, DEB; p. 103.
400. *Kā* I; ch. 38, VV. 99-133. Also B.K. Kakati, *The Mother Goddess Kāmākhya,* pp. 8ff.
401. SHK; Vol. I, 97.
402. *Mārk*; (tr.), Vol. II, pt. II. Canto—LVII, pp. 283-84, 322.
403. *Vsn.* (tr.), Bk. V. ch. XXIX, D. 459.
404. Sabhā Parva, 23, 19 See also Pargites, JASB. 1897, Vol. LXVI pt. IPP. 85 & 105-6; Pargiter, *The Nations of India at the Battle between the Pāndavas and Kauravas.* JRAS, 1908, p, 334; A. Barooah AGI: p. 68, P.N. Bhattacharya, KS; 1, pp. 23, 63, 120; IA; pp. 6.7; P.C. Sen, JARS; 1933, Vol. I, A.I, pp. 12-15: IGI, Vol. VI, p. 24.
405. Motichandra, *Sārthavaha*, p. 130.
406. D.C. Sircar, SGAMI; pp. 160-61, also 163-64.
407. EI: Vol. XIX, pp. 277-86. cf. K, L. Barua, EHK; pp. 1-2.
408. *Op. cit.,* pp. 42-44.
409. AICL; p. 61, fn. 1.
410. *Mbh, Sabhā Parva*, 24, 2-4, Also KS; pp. 23 & 31.
411. *Mat.* 114. 44-46; Vy; 45. 122-23.
412. B.C. Law, TAI: pp. 284-86.
413. *Op. cit.,* Vol. 2, p. 144.
414. *Mbh. Sabhā Parva*, 48, 8-11.
415. *Vmn;* 13. 11; *Kūr*; 1, 45, 25; *Mārk*; 54, 8; Pargiter (tr.) *Mark;* 54, 8; Pargiter (tr.) *Mārk*; Vol. 11, Pt. II, pp, 319, 322, 345-47, 369, 379 & 383 *Vsn*; 2, 3, 8; Wilson (tr.) *Vsn;* Bk. II, Ch. Ill, pp. 142-43; *Brah;* 19, 8; 27, 17; *Vy;* 45, 82; D.R. Patil, CHVP: p. 269; *Mat;* 114. 11; *Mat.* cf. SBA; Ch CXIV, pp. 307 & 311; *Agn;* pp. 155, 159, 162; *Grd;* 55.5; Pad; 6,46 & 52. *Bmd;* 2.16, 68; 3, 48-49; 4, 7,19. Also E.J. Rapson, *The Puranas* CHI: Vol. I, Ch. XIII, p. 271.
416. Vmn; 13, 44-46; Kūr; 45, 39: *Mark;* 54, 44: Vsn; 2, 3, 15; Brah; 19, 16; 27, 51-53; Vy; 45, 123; Mat 114, 46.
417. See, S.M. Ali, G.P; pp. 126-27; B.C. Law, HGAI; p. 10; *Geogrphical Essays,* p. 121; Raychaudhuri, SIA; pp. 82-83; S.N. Majumdar Sastri, JBORS; Vol. VIII, 1922 pt. 1, pp. 41-42; Pargiter, (tr.): *Mārk,;* Vol. II. Pt. II, Canto—LVII, pp. 283-4, 322.

418. *Skd:* (Mahesvara-Khanda, Kumarika-Khanda), ch. 39, VV. 127ff.
419. Wilford, *As. Res;* Vol. Ill, p. 38; Vol. IX, 68; R.P. Sharma, (PK; p. Ill) also adds that after being defeated by Raja Sagar they took shelter in the caves of the mountains.
420. *Pad.* 6. 64.
421. Bird, PSHG; pp. 10 & 104.
422. Motichandra, *Sārthavāha,* p. 172; R.S. Tripathi, HAI; pp. 242, fn. 2 & 392; V.S. Agrawala, *Harsacarila: EK Samskrtic Adhyayana,* p. 189; G. Ramdas (IHQ; 1,4. 684).
423. *Mark* ; 55, 31.
424. D.S. Triveda, *op. cit.,* p. 2.
425. *Br. Sam;* (text with tr. by B.P. Mishra), V, 35, 80; IX, 17, 35; XI, 54, 60; XVI, 2; XXXII, 19, 22. Also *Br. Sam.* (tr. Kern), pp. 90-92.
426. *Ibid,* XIV, 18.
427. *Ibid,* XIV, 30. Also S.B. Chaudhari; ESAI; p. 141.
428. Sachau, *Alb. Ind.,* Vol. I, pp. 301 & 303.
429. *Br. Sam,* IX. 17 (Kirāta bharttuh); XI. 54 (Kirata Parthivam) see also A.K. Sastri (IBV; pp. 82-83).
430. Romila Thapar, *op. cit.,* p. 168.
431. *Dasakumaracarita,* 1, 13-16; 11, 22-24, III, 103-4, VIII, 203.
432. *Kādambari,* pp. 37-38, 45ff; *Harsacarita,* Ucch, VII & VIII. Atkinson (HG; Vol. II, pt. I, p. 357).
433. Bk. Ill, patala (ch) VII, V. 29.
434. IAR; p. 6.
435. D.N.P. Kuttan Pillai, *Paurānic Sandarbha Kośa,* p. 181.
436. *Pampā Rāmāyana,* VII, VV. 109-15. pp. 193-95.
437. *Vivekacintamani,* pp. 423-24.
438. EC. II, p. 119.
439. EC. IV ch. 83, p. 10.
440. EC. Ill, md. 13, p. 51 cf. R.N. Saletore, EIC; Vol. II, pp. 750-51.
441. Rice, *Mysore and Coorg from the Inscriptions,* pp. 129ff.
442. See, B.C. Law, *Countries and Peoples of India* (Epic and Paurānic sources) ABORI; 1936, Vol. XVII, pt. IV, p. 332; also 1C; Vol. I. No. 3, pp. 381-82.
443. Vidyalankar, See also *Bhārativa Samskrti ka Vikasa,* p. 27.
444. RPGEA: p. 256. note-1.
445. Gerini, *op. cit.,* p. 257, No. I.

446. S.K. Chatterji, *op. cit.,* p. 178.

447. See E.H. Johnston, *Some Sanskrit Inscription of Arakan,* BSOAS; Vol. XI. 1943-46, pp. 357-85.

448. Malalasekera, DPPN; I, p. 607; IA; III, pp. 178-79.

BOOK THREE

LIFE AND CULTURE SINCE PREHISTORIC AGE

I

INTRODUCTORY REMARKS

The life and culture of the Kirâtas, both ethnographically and historically, constitute that complex whole, which incorporates their life-style, primitive habits, manners and customs, social system, economic condition, polity and administration, military activities, religion and philosophy, language and literature, knowledge, beliefs, arts, morals, laws, etc. The new empirical data obtained from researches into the early history and culture of mankind can be carefully examined and utilised for the purpose of historical reconstruction of the subject concerned. While investigating the successive stages of culture, which they passed through, the first step is to divide them into different parts and to classify them in porper groups. A detailed description of life and culture of a primitive community involves a study of all phases and facets of civilization, which they represent. The several faculties of civilization are knitted-together in such a manner that concentration on any one of them to the exclusion of all others is not only impracticable but also unfair. There are various factors, which determined the course of cultural evolution of primitive tribes. In this respect India has witnessed both independent and convergent evolution of culture.

The study of civilization or culture of hoary antiquity is, of course, a stupendous task, because, this culture finds little reflection in Indian and foreign accounts, contemporary sources, etc. Moreover, some of the events that took place in succession having some bearings on the life and culture of primitive communities have been recorded in a very ambiguous style. However, this task can be accomplished, to a certain extent by analysing the available data, by presenting the correct interpretation of the evidences, whatsoever they may be and by having a clear perception of sense underlying the varying statements.

The study of antiquity and growth of civilization is not only a branch of ethnological research but also of the historical research. The multi-dimensional approach to the problems concerned is *sine-qua-non.* While dealing with various levels of cultural advancements of the aborigines in ancient India, an equal emphasis is to be laid upon the ethnographic and historical data, which in some cases is indissolubly bound up. The partial application of historical method of inquiry into the subject and utter neglect of the ethnographical method will not give us any positive result.

Prof. Robert H. Lowie, a distinguished authority on primitive civilization has rightly observed that an "investigator of civilization must be a historian. Ethnologist must be a historian ..."[1]. There are some available data with regard to the Kirata culture, which need a fresh historical treatment.

It has often been found that higher civilizatian is investigated by a historian and primitive by an ethnologist. Here this fact should not be lost sight of that every higher civilization was at one stage simpler in its form and character. The higher culture has gradually been evolved out of the savage stage of mankind. Therefore, one cannot be properly understood in isolation from the other. The so-called simpler or lower culture of the primitive tribes in ancient India including the Kiratas served as a foundation for the growth of higher culture and civilization.

Whatever the historical traces have been found in the labyrinth of Indian antiquity are enough to indicate that it was tribe, who proved to be a milestone of Indian culture. The history of mankind really begins with primitive stage. We find that the arts and other appliances, which improve the human life were gradually invented by the primitive inhabitants of India. They represent very high culture with many new inventions and discoveries. In ancient times different Kirâta tribes developed different ways of life and different types of culture. According to the racial inheritance and capacity they built up their own society and civilization.

II

PRIMITIVE LIFE AND CULTURE

The differences exhibited by the various sections of the Kirâta tribe in their physical feature, socio-economic life, manners and customs, structure of language, religious doctrines, etc. may appear irreconcilable, but these can be attributed to the peculiarities of the localities they inhabited, the various occupations they followed and the socio-political status they enjoyed. Obviously various changes in their abode and position greatly affected their life-style, moulded their habits and regulated their actions. The lack of uniformity in the life-style and continuity in the cultural system of the races, who were widely different, was the general phenomena in ancient Indian history.

The scantiness of data, though, stands as barrier in the way of reconstructing the life-style and distinctive cultural patterns of the Kirâtas and establishing the antiquity of their civilization, yet, the literary and classical texts provide some valuable information regarding the primitive life-style, habits and manners, customs and usages and their beliefs both in general and particular, which can further be supplemented by some other reliable foreign accounts and amplified by going deep into them.

The earliest evidence of the primitive style of living of the Kiratas have been recorded in the *Vedic Saṁhitas* and *Brâhmaṇas*. In the *Vâjasaneyi Saṁhitâ* of the *Yajur Veda*[2] the name Kirâta has been applied in a generic sense to those 'people, who were the cave dwellers of the Himalayas. The dedication of the Kirâtas to the caves (guha) of the mountains, as described in this text, irrefutably proves this fact. From the *Atharva Veda*[3] and *Taittirîya Brâhmana*[4] it may be deduced that they were savage or wild tribes, barbarous and non-Âryans of degraded race inhabiting woods and mountains and supporting themselves by hunting.

Apart from the Vedic literature, there are some other reliable sources too, which depict a very simple picture of their life and culture, which can, undoubtedly, be connected with the prehistoric age. One of the rare French source of great historical value provides some indications about the predatory habits of the Kiratas of North-West India before the settlements of the

Vedic Âryans in the Gangetic plains. According to the evidence furnished by this non-Indian source we find that the Kirata people of Afghanistan frequently indulged themselves in the plundering activities, which were one of the means of livelihood for them particularly during the period of political upheavals and disturbances. They appeared to the Vedic Âryans as ferocious and aggressive. The Âryans, while crossing the Hindukush mountain and advancing towards Afghanistan in their attempts to enter Sindh and Punjab, were always sceptical of the invasions of the Kirâtas living in Hazara.[5]

The racial movement at a very large scale upset both the geographical and political balance in North Western India. As a sequel to this the Kirâtas never secured stability in their life. They remained nomadic for a considerable period of time. While leading their life in such a situation they had the propensity of attacking those, whose sudden appearance on the scene tended to pose some threat to their survival. Such practice was not very uncommon amongst the indigenous primitive tribes of India.

In the *Kiṣkindhâ Kaạḍa* of *Vâlmiki Râmâyaṇa,* an allusion is made to the Kirâtas as dwellers on the islands in the regions to the east of India and subsisting on raw fish. They have been described as cannibals and nomadic of fierce disposition.[6] This is the description of the primitive habits of the Kirâtas living near the sea-coast extending from the Lohit sea of North-East India to the regions of Sylhet, Mymensingh and Tippera. While giving a different interpretation of a passage quoted in the *Râmâyana* Prof. Lassen[7] points out that some of the Kirâtas were dwelling in Mount Mandara and others used this ears as a covering. Some of them looked like horrible blackfaced people with one foot, who could not be easily exterminated. They were chivalrous and cannibals. Mr. Schwanbeck[8] has also given his assent to this interpretation.

Some of the relevant passages occurring in the classical Indian literature as well as the Greek and Roman texts also give some idea about the place where the Kirâtas lived and their appearance, ways of living and simple life and culture during both the prehistoric and protohistoric periods. Here it must be made clear that much differences did not exist in their prehistoric and protohistoric life-style and culture in certain respects. Even during the historical period some of them retained those habits and manners that existed during the primitive age. We find only slight variations in the delineations of their life and culture in the literary and classical accounts. It will be appropriate to deal with them separately.

From the *Sabhâ Parva* of the *Mâhâbhârata* it is quite evident that the Kirâtas dwelling on the northern slopes of the *Himavat* (the Himalaya) and the mountains of the east, the mountains of the rising Sun in the region of Karusha on the sea-coast and on both sites of the Lauhitya mountain or on the banks of the Lauhitya river (Brahmaputra) having the golden complexion and pleasant looking wore their hair in a pointed topknot, dressed themselves in skins, lived mostly on wild fruits and roots, armed themselves with cruel weapons and kept themselves always engaged in cruel deeds.[9] The details provided here are concerning the Khâsi-Jaintias, the Garos, the Kacharis and the Tipperahs of North-East India, the Kiratas of Eastern Bengal, Tibet and Burma and other remnants of the Kirâta populatian of the Himalayan region, who might have passed into oblivion. V.A. Smith[10] also refers to them as wild race or savage, covering themselves with the kins of wild beasts, having claw like nails, strong enough to rip up raw fish and split the softer kinds of wood and ignorant of the use of iron.

The classical description of the primitive life and culture of the Kirâtas are also of great use for our purpose. Herodotus in his *Universal History* speaks of the Kallatai (Cirrhadai or Kirâta) as nomads inhabiting the marshes of the river and living on the raw fish, which they used to catch by going in the boats made of reeds and divided at the joint, making a canoe.[11] Since the knowledge of Herodouts about India was only confined to the remotest provinces of the Persian empire towards the east, we can take this as an account of the Kirâta tribes of North-Western region. But on the contrary, James Taylor[12] suggests that this is the account of an aboriginal tribe of low country beyond the Ganges or that of the ancient inhabitants of the marshes of Mymensingh and Sylhet. He further opines that the existence of cannibals in the hilly countries bordering on the eastern frontier of Bengal, generally admitted, was known to Herodotus. While connecting this account with the Kirrhadia or Kirâta he says that Herodotus also refers to their dress made of rushes which having mowed and cut they weave together like a mat and wear in the manner of a 'Cuirass'. He also mentions their age-old custom of killing the deceased man. The more aged among them were regularly killed and eaten. This practice was common among the cannibals and hill tribes of interior of Tipperah (appearing, to be anthropophagi of Ptolemy, and Chittagong as well as among the Tikleya Nâgâs of the northern part of Assam.

Ktçsias and Knidian in his *Indika* describes the Indians belonging to the race of the Kirâta as dwarfish, pygmies, diminutive and deformed, who inhabited woods and mountains in the interior of India and lived by hunting. They were degraded mountain tribes and barbarous. They had long hair and enormous beards. Somewhere they are described as the Bhuta people, who were beardless. They were excellent archers, brave hunters of wild animals like oxen and sheep. They used to eat the flesh of the animals. They learnt few technical arts. They dwelt in caves and kept goats and sheep in greatest number, that constituted their wealth. They hunted animals like hares and foxes not with dogs but with eagles, ravens, crows and vultures. They were accustomed to fight with vultures or eagits.[13] Some palpable exaggeration can be noticed in his account. Prof. Lassen in his review of the Reports of Ktesias concerning India has further elaborated this account of the Kirata in his monumental work in German. He says that they were protected by their inaccessible mountain in the event of a attack by their neighbours in war. They were just people.[14] J.W. McCrindle has also radiated some light on this aspect of Ktçsias' account in some other classical sources.[15] Dr. V. Ball in his paper read before the Royal Irish Academy in 1883 revealed that in the country occupied by the Kirâtas of Ktçsias there was a lake which produced oil and there were also many silver mines situated in the same region.[16] He has further pointed out that a hairy race of men of low stature are reported to be dwellers in the Upper Valley Irrawadi between Momein and Manipur.[17] He has seemingly not gone into details. Nor has he provided sufficient data in support of his contention. In absence of any confirmatory evidence it is not possible to give much credence to his findings.

Megasthenes[18] places the Scyritae or the Kiratas amongst the nomadic Indians of ancient times and compares them with Scythians, who did not till the soil but roamed about in their wagons as the season varied from one part of the Scythia to another. They were neither dwelling in towns nor having temples for worshipping gods and goddesses. They were so barbarous that they could wear skins of such wild animals which they killed and subsisted on the bark of trees. R.C. Jain[19] is of the view that Meghasthenes' Scyritae belonged to a race living on the confines of India on the east near the source of the Ganges.

Arrian in the first part of his *Indika* (chs 1-XVII),[20] chiefly based on the works of Megasthenes and Eratosthenes, asserts that no mutual intercourse was maintained between the tribes of ancient India and they lived in complete isolation from each other. Pliny (VIII.2)[21] has clearly stated that the Cirrhadae (Kirata) living on the eastern side of India near the source of the Ganges were having very rough and hairy bodies and covered themselves with the leaves of trees. "The Kirâtas of the Uttarapâtha are castigated as peoples who lived as criminal tribes with predatory habits like those of the hunters and vultures."[22]

The nomadic life, pastoralism, predatory habits, the customary practice of taking shelter in caves, the art of covering the body with skins and bark of trees, the method of subsisting on roots and fruits, the practice of hunting and food-gathering or the use of primitive from of agriculture, etc. as narrated in some of the Indian and foreign accounts discussed above point to the first stage of their civilization represented by the palaeolithic Age. During this age, which roughly falls between 8,000—5,000 B.C., they lived in a state of natural life without having any knowledge of developed art of life and metals like copper and iron. They used rude stone implements which consisted of axe-heads, digging tools, circular stones, scrapers, hammer stone, etc. They were devoid of any social custom. They had unsettled life. They were wandering from place to place. They remained at hunting and food-gathering stage till late period. They were moving from one place to another in search of new homes in both hills and plains. Their nomadic habit was not only confined to the pre-Vedic times. This practice continued even during the post-Vedic times. Some sections of them had of course settled during the Neolithic Age, but by and large, they remained in an unsettled position even during the *Epic age,* the *Paurânic age* and the Post-Christian era. From the Stone Age to the twelfth century A.D. they passed through various transitional phases in their life. One of the characteristic features of this age is that they preferred to live in caves for the sake of convenience and security.

The caves are the only surviving monuments of this age. They avoided their settlement in the forest because of the difficulty of clearing them with their primitive weapons. They moved from caves to hills and forest at later stage, which may be attributed to various factors. They changed their abode from plains to hills and forest or from one forest to another in ancient times according to the contemporary geo-political situation and other ecological factors. We have some glimpses of this truth in the Purânic accounts also. According to *Brahmâṇḍa Purâṇa* (3,48, 23-49)[23] the Kirâtas after having been subjugated by king Sagara fled away and took asylum in the caves of the mountains.

The discovery of some caves in the hill areas of North-East India prove the existence of some older branch of the Kirâta population in the prehistoric times. We have some recorded evidence of these caves existing in the Khâsi-Jaintia Hills, the Garo Hills, the North Cacbar Hills and the Nâgâ Hills of Manipur. In the Khâsi-Jaintia Hills the caves found near Cherrapunji, from the walls and roof of which quartzite chips, of which rough or unpolished stone implements were made, were available in ancient times, the limestone cave of Rupasor near the village Synden or the Syndai cave, the cave of Laitlyngkot with huge monolithic doors and dolmen containing the bones of dead as noticed by J.H. Hutton in 1926 and the cave at Lakadong with mural decoration and carvings as described by Ringwood in 1876 are worth mentioning.[24] In the Garo Hills a large cave near the Sizu or the Someswari known as 'Dobakkol' has been found. In the North Cachar Hills two caves representing the earlier patterns of tribal architecture was noticed by E.D.E. Frank in 1902. A cave near the Haflong is believed to have been the abode of the Kachari people.[25]

R. Brown refers to the caves of the Naga tribes living in the hilly areas of Manipur.[26] The archaeological exploration undertaken by the state Archaeology Department of Manipur in the recent past have brought to light five caves or rock-shelters of Tharon. The archaeological discoveries include edge-ground pebble tools and rock engravings. Besides, the four caves at Khangkhui with stone and bone tools and faunal remains and Handung caves in Ukhrul area have also been discovered.[27] These findings also go to prove the habitation of the Nâgâ tribes in the prehistoric times. The Greek source[28] also makes a mention of cave dwellings of the Nâgâs, the Garos and other Tibeto-Burman tribes like Kuki-Chin in ancient times.

The Raji Kirâta of Eastern Kumaon in Uttarâkhanda and Western Nepal were also basically the cave-dwellers in ancient times. It is believed that in absence of any natural caves they used to build one storey or double storeyed huts for their living, which is called as "makeshift" huts. They were naturally gifted with this skill. Hunting and fishing jhum cultivation, etc. were the principal means of the body with the leaves of the trees. They have age-old practice of moving down to the vallcysto engage themselves in the profession of making wooden jars. This has been the most popular profession of the Kirâtas all over the Uttarakhanda. The Limbu Kirâtas of Sikkim had more or less the same tradition. The various ingredients of the Himalayan rural culture are said to have been reflected in their life-style and primitive beliefs. Though, they were very much confined to the forest life in this part of the Himalayan territory, they never kept themselves isolated.[29] They cultivated the habit of maintaining cultural fellowship with their neighbours. Subsequently, they came within the pale of Âryandom, but they never lost the vitality of their primitive culture.

The scientific study of primitive people and the reconstruction of a culture that existed during the unrecorded parts calls for the study of prehistoric archaeology. With the help of this auxiliary science we can trace the antiquity of their civilization. The relics, discovered in caves, shell-mounds, burial mounds—serving as museum of early cultures, the Neolithic stone tools, the Megalithic structure including Menhirs, dolmens and cromlechs and some of other archaeological findings shed some light on the Neolithic culture of some sections of the Kiratas. Besides, some surviving antiquities also attest to the gradual progress which they made in their onward march towards civilization. The analysis of archaeological data available to us and other collateral evidences show that during the Neolithic Age, tentatively placed between 5000-2500 B.C., which was the second stage of civilization, some of the Kiratas achieved significant breakthrough in the series of experiments conducted in the prehistoric age.

The pre-Âryan settlements of the Kirâtas in North-Eastern India is attested to by advanced Neolithic cultures. The Neolithic Age really marked the beginning of civilization. The Kirata people of particularly North-East India made remarkable progress in different spheres during this age. A.H. Dani[30] has exhaustively dealt with the Neolithic cultures which flourished in the Khâsi-Jaintia Hills, the Garo Hills, the North Cachar Hills, the Nâgâ Hills of present Manipur and Nagaland and the Mishmi Hills of Sadiya Frontier Zone. He has classified the relics of Neolithic Age into different categories viz. stone celts, cists, chipped and grooved stones edges, shouldered axes, hoes, pecked and ground stone industry tools, faceted tools, stone implements of various types and the Megalithic monuments comprising dolmens, menhirs, cromlechs, upright stones, flat and horizontal stones, male stones, female-stones and other sepulchral and memorial stones. The neolithic remains have been studied by various other scholars also.[31]

The Nâgâs, the oldest branch of the Kirâta tribes and later designated as Negritos and Tibeto-Burman tribes, are believed to have been both in the Palaeolithic and in the Neolithic stage of culture. They were not equipped with the knowledge of agriculture and cattle breeding. They were food-gatherers rather than food-producers. They had nothing to contribute to the later civilization of India owing to their primitive stage, which was of longer duration. They were absorbed, to a large extent, by those people who followed them into India, particularly, the so-called Proto-Australoids. They had basically a rudimentary culture. They were dominated by those powerful peoples who were in a more advanced stage of culture. In the domain of culture they probably invented the bow, evolved a cult of the 'ficus' tree, which was adopted by the subsequent races of India and developed an eschatological belief (in the life after death). There age-old practice of head-hunting based on religious superstition and. other social and political considerations was a continuation of their primitive habits. In order to gain social superiority and high political status sometimes they resorted to this practice. Their intertribal feuds also resulted in the adoption of this primitive custom.

Another branch of the Kirâtas, the Khâsis, the so-called Nisâdas or Austric—speaking tribes of the Mon-Khmer group of the Austro-Asiatic section were also food gatherers in the Palaeolithic stage of culture like their compatriots, the Nâgâs. In the Neolithic stage of culture they made little progress worth the name. They had a distinct religious conceptions. The religious ideas giving rise to totemism and philosophical doctrine of transmigration and Karma even after the advent of the Aryans can be acknowledged as Kirâta's contribution to India. In a primitive society these people were leading very simple life based on primitive agriculture in their little settlements and had crude religious ideas. Their symbols of gods representing both benevolent and malevolent spirits in the shape of crude figures or blocks of stones formed very important part of their characteristic primitive culture. Their primitive practice also include sprinkling or smearing with the blood of the sacrificed animal or with vermillion and other red dye.

It is curious to note that the monuments of the Neolithic period are intimately connected with their socio-religious history. Their remains constitute the monumental evidence to their progress, which they made in the field of art and culture. The Megalithic monuments of the Kirâta tribes of the Neolithis Age also cast reflections, to a considerable degree, on their knowledge, beliefs, arts, technology and customs of the dim past. These relics also help us in determining the stages and extent of progress made by the Kiratas in the realm of civilization.

The Megalithic monuments have served as a Museum of early history and culture. The antiquities of the human race of by-gone age are considered as one of the fragments of a progressive series of civilization.[32] The surviving records and relics of the Stone Age can definitely be taken as highly impressive.[33] In this respect the Neolithic Age really marked a distinct phase in the progress towards civilization.

The structures of monuments of rudimentary character consist of huge rough undressed stones as well as elaborately dressed stones of sophisticated kind popularly known as menhirs, dolmens, cromlechs, stone circles, stonehenge, etc.[34] The statement made by B.C.. Alien, E. Gait. G.H. Alien and H.F. Howard that "Assam is somewhat destitute of archaeological remains"[35] is not tenable. The fact remains that both in the valleys and hills of North-East India large number of remains, of archaeological interest have been discovered. The Kiratas' wealth of Megaliths comprises several kinds of stones.[36]

The beliefs of the Kirâta people concerned in the doctrine of transmigration of soul or life after death and their social and religious practices, ceremonies and customs etc, constituted the base and further promoted the growth of Megalitithic cultures. The Megalithic monuments used to fulfil the threefold function i.e. funerary, commemorative and religious. Their utility for other utilitarian and ceremonial purposes was no less significant. One of the most prominent and striking aspects of the ancient history and culture of the Kirâtas of North-East (the Khasis, the Jaintias, the Nâgâs and the Cachari tribes) is the age-old practice of erecting various kinds of monumental stones, which are scattered generally on every way side. These are mysterious, solitary and clustered monuments of remote antiquity. These remarkable monuments of the Kiratas abounding in this region are similar to that of found in Europe and Western Asia. Some of them are puzzling and delightful for antiquarians The Megalithic stones were erected at different periods of history. But historically this practice can be traced back to Prehistoric age. They, no doubt, made a distinctive cultural contribution to the evolution of the Megalithic culture.[37]

The carvings, ornamentation and engravings of various rough designs and symbols on their monoliths are very impressive from both architectural and sculptural points of view. The Nâgâ monoliths are similar to that of Borneo, Philippines and Madagascar. One of the noteworthy features of the Megalithic culture of the North-East India is that it represents the living tradition of high antiquity, whereas the South Indian

Megaliths came to an end in the first Century A.D. These Neolithic stone monuments were associated with the cult of fertility, ancestor-worship, theory of sacrifice and worship of phallus (linga) and Yoni later associated with the Úaiva-Úakti cults of Hinduism.[38] One of the remarkable facts, which has not yet received recognition from the authorities is that the Kiratas' religious doctrines and artistic ideas associated with the Megalithic cultures greatly inspired the Hindu, Buddhist and Jaina religion, philosophy and art.

It remains to be examined whether the Megalithic culture of North-East India represents Northern Black Polished (NBP) were associated with Iron objects or Painted Grey Ware associated with Copper or Bronze implements. Since the black and red ware associated with iron objects or other metal like copper and bronze like that of Central and Southern India have not been discovered in the Megalithic burials of North-East India, it can be admitted that this region had not reached the level of distinctive ware cultures. This is a very puzzling question whether their Megalithic monuments of the Neolithic Age was associated with Iron objects or copper. The Khasis were the only tribes who acquired the knowledge of iron-ore, but it is very difficult to say as to whether it was connected with their Megalithic culture? The Khasis, presumably acquired the knowledge of iron in the post-Neolithic Age. History describes its antiquity to the first Century A.D.

To closer links and affinities of the tribal Megaliths of N.E. India with those of the Megalithic monuments of south—Western Coastal Strip of India, South-East Asia, Philippines, Farmosa. Madagascar, Africa, Mediterranean World and Pacific World, Asia Minor, Western Asia, France, Scandinavia and Denmark in respect of method and purpose, of course, stir our imagination. But they can never represent a single cultural phase as supposed by some scholars. Prof. Panchanan Mitra suggested that there arose Indo-Erythraean culture-complex and in the North-East strong culture stream came by seaboard which later passed over to another zone.[39] But this is merely a fanciful notion.

Its origin and antiquity are really debatable subjects. J H. Hutton, while delivering a lecture in the Indian Museum at

Calcutta in 1928 observed that its origin was from Indonesia and the Monkhmer speaking Khâsi tribe or Australoid or Austric Asiatic or Pre-Mediterranean Khâsis introduced this culture.[40] S C. Roy[41] and Haimendorf[42] seem to be inclined to endorse this view that Megalithic builders were Proto-Dravidians. Haimendorf as a Protagonist of the theory of its foreign origin has also observed that "they belong essentially to South-Eastern Asia—Indonesia, Oceania, the Philippines and Formosa."[43] Whatever be the truth underlying all these statements, it is almost certain that this culture was introduced in North-East India by the Khasis (so-called Austro-Asiatic immigrants) which is strongly supported by Sir Mortimer Wheeler,[44] an archaeologist of an international repute.

A.H. Dani[45] has suggested that this culture dates back to Prehistoric age. True, but we do not agree with him so far as this statement that, this can be associated with stone-tools of Neolithic Age, is concerned. The stone-tools and Megalithic monuments are archaeologically different from each other in respect of size, forms, structure, functions, utility, etc. This culture began much earlier but reached its high-watermark comparatively at later age.

As a matter of fact the Megalithic cultures of the Kiratas of North-East India constitute an essence of both indigenous and foreign elements. It would be unwise on our part to trace its origin and growth only under external influence. The identity of custom and striking similarities between the various practices do not always necessarily hint at their common origin. The contemporary geographical factors and natural environment in the different countries conditioned the evolution of the Megalithic culture in different ways. The antiquity of this culture may tentatively be ascribed to the Neolithic Age. Thus the Neolithic-phase of the Pre-historic Megalithic cultures of the Kiratas proved to be a cultural watershed in the early history of North-East India.

The settlement patterns of the Kirâtas during this age was quite different from that of the Palaeolithic Age. Some of them had a settled life but large sections of them remained pastoral. Some of them had their settlements in granite rocks which gave them natural protection from the rain and sun. Some of them were driven into the hills and forests by later invaders. This process continued even in the Protohistoric period. We have some evidence to show that in course of the extensive urbanization of the Gangetic Valley and the agrarian settlement of the Âryans during the second half of the first millennium B.C. large number of forests were cleared which affected the habitation patterns of the Kirâtas in more than one ways. But a considerable number of them continued to live in the large areas covering the forest especially nearer the hills which did not feel the impact of the Âryan agrarian economy. They had also the natural tendency to shift 'to the hills and forests.

The hunting and food gathering remained the chief occupation for them during this stage also. The hunting and food-fathering culture of the non-Âryans stand in sharp contrast to the extensive agricultural economy of the Âryans. They started domestication of animals towards the end of the Neolithic period. Ktesias the Knidian[46] opines that the sheep,. oxen and asses of the Kirâtas were very small. They also practised primitive system of agriculture. They began to produce crops, fruits and vegetables. Their food consisted of fruits, vegetables, roots, nuts, wild pulses, cereals, flesh of animals, raw fish, etc. The dress which they used were the barks of trees and skins of animals.

This age also saw the emergence of the religious conceptions among the Kirâta tribes in ancient India. The fundamental features of their religious system were the veneration of supernatural objects and the worshipping of the ancestral spirits. The animistic faith had also taken its root during this age. Their primitive fertility rites re-appeared in the form of the Tantric practice among the Hindus. They used to perform a large number of rites on the ceremonial occasions. The practice of stone-worshipping and human and animal sacrifice were also introduced by them. They provided the dead with all the amenities of life because of their unflinching faith in the soul. They also used urns for preserving the bones and ashes of the dead.

They also learnt the use of arrows and bows and the art of dance and music, graphic art, poerty, etc. One of the most striking features of their primitive life and culture was that each group of them had different dialects and languages, which were unintelligible to a greater extent.

On the whole we find that a variety of polished stone-tools of advanced workmanship, discovery of primitive form of agriculture, the settled life, domestication of animals, weaving, pottery, arts and crafts, Megalithic monuments, worship of phallic stones, the emergence of distinct religious conceptions and other technological advancement in the socio-economic field constitute the notable features of the Neolithic culture of the Kiratas of North-East India.

The transition from the Stone Age to Metal Age was a gradual process. Any attempt to establish the uniformity in the classification of the Metal Age will be futile. The Kirâtas of the North-East India had entered the threshold of the Chal-colithic civilization at belated stage. This age roughly placed between 2500 B.C.—1500 B.C. is marked by the development of metallurgical art, use of copper, smelting of iron ore, acculturation, development of the power of thinking, invention of alphabet and other technological developments. The Khasi tribes were in the Neolithic stage of culture and probably in India they learnt the use of copper and iron.[47] But it is very difficult to suggest the exact period during which they acquired the knowledge of these metals. But on the basis of the evidence furnished by Pliny[48] it can be affirmed that they learnt how to smelt the iron ore sometimes during the Pre-Christian era or before the dawn of the first century A.D. The Chutiya tribes living in the Sadiya region from time immemorial reached this stage not before the 11th or 12th century. They learnt the use of copper during this period which can be authenticated by some reliable evidence.[49] From the literary evidence it appears that the Kirâtas of the Himalayan region of the North-Eastern India had the knowledge of gold which they used to procure from the mountain.

The Prehistoric people have vanished from the face of the earth but some of their offspring still remain in the remote corners of India, who have made a marked progress in the field of civilization. They have developed some ideas, superstitions, rituals, customs, observances, attitudes towards life after death, etc., which have had great bearings on modern Indian society.

No materialist can afford to neglect the effect of their ideas and thoughts upon the course of the socio-cultural development of India.[50]

Here it is to be noted that except for North-Eastsrn and North-Western India, the Kiratas had settled in most of the parts of India during the Protohistoric period, which can be substantiated by the absence of details about them in the early classical Sanskrit literature and Greek and Roman texts. The literature belonging to these categories mainly deals with the Kiratas of North-Eastern and North-Western India. The Kiratas of Nepal, Videha, hilly country in Morung to the west of Sikkim (situated between Nepal and Bhutan), Uttarapatha or Udicya or North-West, Garhwal, Kumaon on Uttarakhanda Rajasthan, Gujarat, Kashmir, Vindhya region, Deccan Gangetic delta and other parts of Northern India figure comparatively in later Sanskrit texts and other historical records, which have been shown distinctly in earlier chapters. Somewhere it is very difficult to draw a sharp line of distinction between Prehistoric and Protohistoric cultures of the Kirâtas in general. However, some noticeable changes occurred in their life-style and cultural patterns, which varied from region to region. That is why, we don't find any uniformity in their life and culture. Further,' they had to struggle hard for maintaining their existence in the plains valleys, hills and forests because of the occasional inroads of the Aryans the Dravidians and other contemporary powerful and ambitious rulers into their countries and the consequent expulsions, subjugations, the occupation of their territories, or Janapadas, kingdoms and principalities, frequent migrations from one place to another etc.[51]

We have some more literary evidence to show their way of life and culture in Pre-and Post-Christian era. They were living in different natural surroundings carrying on some of their old primitive habits and simultaneously introducing some new innovations in order to improve their life condition. During the Buddhist period also their condition remained more or less the same. Because in the Pali Commentaries nothing such appears, as can be taken as an evidence of any change in their life. The Kiratas find mention in the Pali texts simply as 'a tribe of Jungle men.'

On the basis of a slender thread of evidence[52] it can be pointed out that the plundering activities of the Kiratas, which was one of the means of their subsistence continued down to the age of the Mauryas. Even during the Mauryan period the turbulent mleccha tribes called as Kiratas and wild forest-tribes known as Âtavikas were in the habits of preying upon trade for plunder. The trade was protected against them by state authorities.

Kâlidâsa has drawn a pen-picture of the primitive life-style of the Kirâtas in general. He has described their way of life, dress, manners and habits in an allegorical style. The description provided by him indicates that the Kiratas dwelling in the mountainous regions of the Himalayas were wild-tribes and great hunters. Their main profession was hunting, which was a kind of excursion for them. They had the practice of killing the wild animals. They used to wear girdles of peacock's feathers round their waists to accelerate their motion and the wind broke through them. It is very difficult to ascertain as to how far the feathers could have quickened their motion ? Perhaps they wore the feathers for the sake of ornamentation. The self-luminous roots and herbs served as light for the Kiratas at night living with their wives in the dark caves of the Himalayas.[53]

In the Post-Gupta period the Kirâtas living in the mountainous country of Northern India enjoyed the status of hunters. They were armed with arrows and bows. They were basically deer killers. They used to speak an incomprehensible language.[54]

By the dawn of the seventh century A.D. little changes were effected in their way of life. From the writings of Bânabhatta it is quite evident that the Kirâtas living in a vast range of forest adjacent to the Kailâsa mountain had settled life. Their dwellings in Suvarnapur town situated in the northern Himalayas testifies to their urban life[55] in a limited sense. This, of course, marks a departure from the earlier trend discernible in their life-style. Dandin affords an illuminating illustration of the forest life of the Kirâtas of Vindhya region. The Kiratas living in the heart of Vindhya forest were broadly divided into two classes, i.e. the civilized Brahmânâs and uncivilized barbarians. This is the forest which was earlier destitute of human habitation and fit for only wild beasts haunted by fierce animals. It was not out of danger to move about in the forest. Nevertheless, the Kirâtas dared settle in the woods and jungles of this area. The scars of wounds and weapons were found on their body. The civilized Kirâtas were ardent followers of Brahmanical culture. They always stood in defence of Brahmanas, who very often became the victims of the sinful acts of uncivilized Kirâtas in the forest. Once the Kirâtas saved Brahmanas from being killed by their associates, who were barbarous by nature. They rescued the Brâhmânas in vast wilderness.' In return the Brahmanas taught them the alphabet, explained *Sastras* and *Tantras* and gave instruction to regard the good conduct and observe truth and purity in life. This development of exceptional value had a soothing and a sober effects on the life and culture of the Kirâtas. As a result of the Brahmanic influence exerted on them, they started living in the group of families along with relatives, who were associated with them. Their descendants have been living in the Vindhya region since time immemorial. Their exact antiquity is unknown. The uncivilized class of Kirâtas residing in this region were also Brahmanas but only in name. They had not abandoned their primitive habits and cultures. They were in the habit of encroaching on the neighbouring countries, seizing the wealthy villages with their women and children and bringing them back to forest and putting them into custody taking all their wealth, etc. This practice indicates as to what extent some of them were leading the life of lawlessness and using all the cruelty that they possessed. This reality was exposed by the Kirâtas of the Vindhyas themselves while relating the story of their life to prince Râjavâhana, who was sent by: Magadha king Rajahamsa in the Vindhya region,[56] The other literary sources and epigraphic records also disclose the fact that the Kirâtas were living in the Vindhyas in a semi-barbarous condition till late medieval period.[57] *Sabhâsitâvali* by Vallabhadeva describes them simply as mountaineers living by hunting.[58]

On the whole, we find that that ways of their life were very simple. They were at the rudimentary stage of culture. In fact, their primitive ways of living continued to cast its shadow on the pages of ancient Indian history till late period. They were leading, by and large, wild, sequestered and unprogressive life.

They were not having all the paraphernalia of civilized life. They could not compete with the Âryans and the Dravidians in the race for making progress in the field of civilization, but did furnish, professedly, some of the elements, which became the base of the early Indian society and.culture.

III

SOCIETY AND ECONOMY

The Society and economy of the Kirâtas were inextricably interwoven constituting warp and woof of their life and culture. Both are treated here separately for the sake of analysis as well as convenience.

1. Social Life: The social life of the Kirâtas seems to have developed through a series of transitional phases. The process of chaage in the sphere of their social life was somewhat cumbersome. There is no objective criterion to be applied for drawing a clear picture of the subject. Nor is there any established principle by which a correct judgment may be formed about the progress in their social life. However, the clear understanding of the intricate dynamics of their social history may help us in dealing with the problems involved in the study of this aspect of their life.

After the appearance of the Âryans on the Indian scene the social history of the Kiratas took a very peculiar turn, and consequently dramatic changes occurred in their social position. It can be reiterated here that most of the Kirâtas originally belonging to warrior class or known as indigenous Ksatriya tribes were degraded to the rank of Úûdrâs and Dasyus before the time of Manu, because of the neglect of the *Vedas,* non-performance of sacred Brâhmanical rites or because of the wrath of the Brâhmanas. Thus they enjoyed the status of the Sudras and Dasyus in the early Indian society. The *Smrti* and the epic literature bear an eloquent testimony to the metamorphosis in their social status in ancient times. In the *Manu Smṛti*[59] we find a clear reflection of truth that the Kirâtas and other tribes, who were formerly Ksatriyas, became afterwards the Úûdras. Manu has also hinted at the idea that even the Brâhmanas, Ksatriyas, Vaisyas and the speakers of the mleccha and Âryan languages became the Úûdras because of the neglect of their duties.

V.S. Agrawala, while giving an authoritative interpretation of the statements made by Manu has pointed out that the country was divided into two great geographical units viz., Âryavarta and Mlecchadesa, which naturally pitched the Aryas versus the mlecchas or the Âryas versus the Anaryas or the Âryas versus the Dasyus. Some non-Âryan acted like Âryan and Âryan acted like non-Âryan. The fusion and admixture of non-Âryan elements with the body of Âryan population presented a formidable problem in Manu's time. Many tribes living on the borders of Âryavarta were known as Vrisala Ksatriyas. The distant population contained people some of whom spoke Âryan tongues and some mleecha tongues. They were all Dasyus, excluded from the community of the four castes. In the Âryavarta itself there were Dasyus and the Úûdras, who resemble very much that of the aboriginal tribes, who were living in sepulchral areas outside village, forests and mountains. Persons born of Dvijati (Brahmana, ksatriya and Vaisya) parents became apostates (vratyas) if they failed to perform their sacred duties and exercise their right of taking upavita up to the highest,limit fixed for it. The Vratyas had literally one birth and hence were equivalent to Sudras. They did forego their rights in caste and society. With the inrush of foreigners and the emergence of new social groups the Úûdra problem assumed a complicated character. It was because of the catholicity of the Hindu law—giver that he devised principles and methods by which the new comers were allotted place in the indigenous social structure without swamping the primitive culture ; they rather owed allegiance to the laws of their new home.[60] The *Vedavyâsa Smṛti*[61] also proves that the Kiâtas, the vaisyas (vanik) and the Kayasthas acquired the status of the Sudras because of their deviation from the original path and the neglect of duties prescribed and sanctioned by the society.

After delving deep into the *Úânti Parva*[62] of the *Mahâbhârata* we find that the Kirâtas were no other than the descendants of the ksatriyas, Brahmanas and the Dasyus. The Kirâta-Dasyu have been very often used in the text conjointly.

Romila Thapar[63] basing her conclusion on the *Mânavadharmasústra* and the *Mahâbhârata* has maintained that the indigenous mlecchas were originally of the ksatriya varna and their degeneration was due to the non-observances of the religious duties. She seems to be inclined to support the view that some of the tribes of indigenous origin like Kirâta, Dravida, Abhira, Úahara, Mâlava, Úibi, Trigarta and Yaudheya were the Vratya Ksatriyas or degenerate ksatriyas. The majority of such tribes were the inhabitants of the Himalayan and Vindhyan regions traditionally called the mleccha-desa.

On the testimony of the German account also the fact stated above can be authenticated. Prof. Lassen[64] has clearly stated that the Kirâtas—warlike and uncultivated were brought within the Brahmanical fold but their neglect of religious rites caused the Brahmana Hindus to reduce them to the rank of sudras. Such Kirâta tribes were also living in Nepal. Because of their lower position they were despised by the Âryan Hindus in the society.

They have been described in some of the classical Indian literature as tribes of low status. Actually, the determination of caste status in ancient India did not merely depend on the occupation of a group. "In some cases an entire tribe was ascribed a particular rank. Those speaking a non-Indo-Âryan language were frequently given a low rank and described as mleecha . . . Some of these tribes remained consistently of low status over many centuries such as the Kirâta and the Pulinda."[65]

The Kirâta, Úabara, Pulinda, Mutiba, the Matanga (of Vindhyan-region), Kinnara, Kikata, Nisada and many other technologically inferior tribes 'constituted another category which came to be included in the term mleecha'. The use of the world mleecha was extended to include speakers of an alien language, social groups ranked as mixed castes, technologically backward tribes and the people along the frontiers. The Âryans representing advanced urban civilization regarded the tribes living in the forests with hunting and food-gathering culture scornfully. The Himalayan region, the trans-Indus region, the Vindhyan region and the lands east of the Videhas were included in the mleccha-desa. The indigenous inhabitants of northern India at the time of arrival of the Aryan speaking peoples and the non-Aryan speaking peoples living close to the Tibeto-Burman area were all designated as mleecha.[66] In the light of the above facts it may be safely presumed that some of the indigenous Kirâta tribes living in these areas might have been granted the status of the mleecha by the Âryans.

The Kirâta tribes living in the Vindhyan region remained in comparative isolation up to the middle of the first millennium A.D. totally unconcerned with the mleecha status conferred upon their other counterparts by the Âryans. We have positive evidence[67] to show that the Kiratas of Vindhyan region were broadly divided into two classes viz., the Brahmanas and non-Brahmanas. The Brahmana Kiratas attained relatively higher degree of civilization and strictly followed the Brahmanical culture. They never neglected the duties of their caste. They believed in the sanctity of the Úâstras and Tântras. Actually, this change in the mode of their conduct and social behaviour was effected through the process of Brâhmanisation. But, on the contrary, there were some Kirâtas, who were uncivilized Brahmanas. They had not abandoned their primitive customs and led barbarous life. They were Brâhmanas only in theory not in practice. They were very much apposed to the study of the *Vedas* and other lore. They always ignored the observances of their tribe, who had accepted Brahmanhood. They set aside their religious and social duties.

Hiuen-Tsang's Ki-Li-to, which stands very much in approximation to the Kiratas of Kashmir had also experienced some changes in their social life. Hiuen-Tsang designates the people of Naga race of Kashmir as Ki-Li-to, which Prof. Lassen and Mr. Stanislas-Julien have identified with Krityas. They were also known as Kir-mlecchas or the 'Barbarian Kiras'. According to Wilson this appellation roughly corresponds to Kirah as the name of the people and Kira as a name of the valleys of Kashmir. The Kiratas of Kashmir, indeed, include the different races. They cared little for heretics and temples of the Brahmanical gods ; they were extremely hostile to the Buddhists. The neighbouring kings looked down upon the base Kashmiris and out of sheer contempt gave them the name of Ki-Li-to or Krityas or Krita.[68] The statement pertaining to changes in the social position of ancient Indian tribes can also be confirmed by the native chronicle of Kashmir,[69] which records the Kiratas as one of the low caste group along with the Kaivaratas and Candalas. Kalhana speaking of these Kiratas living in the forest mentions that there was no marked improvement in their primitive habits and customs. These are some of the notable examples of frequent changes in the social status of early Indian communities.

Taking over all view of the aforesaid description three possibilities may be suggested regarding the changes in the social position of the Kirâtas. Firstly, some of the Kiratas, who were the Pre-Âryan settlers of Prehistoric antiquity might have been later conquered by the Aryans and brought within the pale Aryandom, because the forces of the Aryanisation and Sanskritization were at work. But they might not have been in a position to reconcile to the altered situation and accept the norms of Sanskritic culture, because of their protest against imposition of new culture. That is why, they did not observe the Brahmanical rites and utterly disregarded the duties assigned to them. Some of the Kirâtas obviously fall within this category, about which enough evidence have already been cited in preceding pages. Secondly, some indigenous Ksatriya-Kirata tribes were excluded from the Âryan fold because of the neglect of their socio-religious duties and consequently degraded to the status of the Úûdras. The Âryans treated them contemptuously. Such Kirâta tribes were declared outcaste. As a result of their expulsion and degeneration their dispersion started towards the hills and forests in the Himalayan region. They adopted non-Âryan ways of living, customs etc. Their exclusion from tne Âryan fold and inclusion within the non-Âryan fold constitute one of the landmarks in the social transformation in the early Indian history. Thirdly, the possibility of the absorption of some of the Kirâtas in the Âryan community can't be precluded. They lost their tribal identity and became the part and parcel of the Âryan race. They adopted the language, culture and customs of the Aryans. They became indissolubly merged with the Indo-Aryan.

Mr. Johan Wilson[70] seems to be slighly disposed to admit the truth that the Âryans probably conquered the earlier inhabitants and it becomes manifest from the changed circumstances that it was from the conquest of the aborigines in the interior part of the country that afterwards name Úûdra was extended to the whole servile caste and enslaved classes of the country conquered by the Âryans in contradistinction to the more independent and more cordially hated tribes, such as the Cândalas. Some of the Úûdras and some of the more independent tribes in the interior land may have spoken a dialect not very dissimilar to that of the Âryas and may have been the descendants of prior Âryan immigrants.

The Kirâtas of North-Eastern and North-Western India were, by and large, Âryanised during both the Vedic and Post-Vedic periods following their contacts with the Âryans in their respective regions. By the dawn of the Puranic age large section of the Kirâtas were living outside the Âryan fold, which finds affirmation in the *Srimad-Bhâgavatam.*[71]

After having made a careful analysis of the data at our disposal the plausible explanation, which can be given here is that the Kirâtas on the whole belonged to the four categories', i.e. Brâhmana Ksatriya, Úûdra and non-Âryan Dasyus, so far as their social status is concerned. Therefore, any attempt to club them together blindly as non-Âryan or Mongoloid community of foreign origin will not only be unfair but also negation of a historical truth.

The social status of the Kiratas underwent frequent changes in ancient times with lot of regional variations. They also could not become an exception to the rules prescribed by Brâhmanical law givers regarding the social degradation of the members representing different strata of society. Their level of degradation largely depended on the nature and extent of the crime which they committed by violating the established social law and other norms. They were degraded from the original position of the Ksatriyas to the status of the Vrsala (i.e. Úûdra or outcastes). The changes in their status were very much in conformity with the well-established social tradition of degrading the tribes, not strictly following the purificatory rites to the rank of Úûdras. Those tribes, who paid scant regard to the contemporary Brâhmanical system were discarded and put into the lower orders of society. They were degraded from one position to another not only on the religious ground but also on the socio-economic and political grounds. In the Post-Vedic times some indigenous tribal groups were absorbed in the rank of Úûdras, but majority of them were accommodated in society as warriors of Ksatriyas, peasants or Úûdras. The tribes who were speakers of non-Indo Âryan languages were generally ascribed a low rank and described sometime as mleccha and sometimes as Úûdras Such tribes were adjusted into the caste hierarchy and assigned a caste status in olden days. This is what it exactly happened in case of the Kirâtas also. The Úûdras are said to have constituted a small servile class of defeated and dispossessed Âryans and non-Âryans in later Vedic times. The leaders of early Indian society as per established practice used to accommodate both the indigenous non-Âryans and foreigners representing the various grades of culture, suitably, in their conventional scheme of the fourfold classification or division of society. This was an open social system in ancient times. The incorporation of various tribal groups into the expanding Indo-Âryan-Varna system led to the formation of the mixed caste and emergence of various new groups including the Vratyas. Actually, the Varna system in ancient India was flexible enough to accommodate indigenous tribal segments at various levels. They were accommodated into Indo-Ârayan society not only as Úûdras but also as Vaisyas, Ksatriyas and Brâhmanas. Some of the aboriginal tribes after having become Hinduised claimed the status of ksatriya, though orthodox Brâhmanas were inclined to assign the position of degraded or degenerate Ksatriyas to them, but, on the other hand, the rank and file were classed as Úûdras in the newly emergent social system. After the assimilation of the aboriginal peoples in the Âryan society, the beliefs and practices of the former were adopted by the latter. This view has also been put forward that the settlements of the Brâhmanas in the aboriginal areas also led to the transformation of aboriginal tribes of peripheral regions into Úûdra castes, who later adopted agriculture as their avocation.

The expanding agrarian economy of the Âryans also quickened the pace of change in the status of the Kirâtas and other tribes. Those, who were accorded the status of a Úûdra, were assigned a new agricultural duty. It may appear as a hypothesis, but the general trend, which set in those days, indicates the every possibility of such social evolution. The Kirâtas by and large, remained at lower level in social hierarchy of ancient India.[72]

As a matter of fact, the concept of society of as such among the Kirâtas emerged comparatively at some later age. Their social structure was far different from that of the Âryans. The study of their social anthropology is of great help for shedding some light on the social structure of ancient Indian tribes. Among the Kirâtas both patrilineal and matrilineal forms of society existed. The thorough study of the subject reveals that in the beginning patriarchal form of society existed among the Kirâtas, governed by the rule of primogeniture. This might have been possible because of the impact of the social system of the Indo-Âryan on the earlier section of the Kirâtas. The growth of matriarchal organisation—the antithesis of the former system was the subsequent development which greatly affected the rules of inheritance. The primitive rules of inheritance had a lot of intricacies. The operation of the customary laws varied from tribe to tribe. The best known illustration of the matriarchal institution are furnished by the Khâsis amongst whom it still survives and the female-members enjoy all the prerogatives in the families. Different types of family existed among the different sections of the Kirâtas. Their family had a bilateral character. The bilateral family was absolutely a universal unit of human society in ancient times. The character of kinship usage is used to differentiate family among different Kirâtas tribes. They had no caste system as such. The rules of caste never prevailed upon them. But they were extensively divided and subdivided into exogamous and endogamous units, clans and tribes of heterogeneous character. The coalescence of several clan units led to the origin of tribes themselves.

Like other tribal societies their social organisation was also based on kinship relations determined by the rules of exogamy and endogamy. D.D. Kosambi, while discussing the tribal social structure in general has remarked that there was a classless society and pre-class social organisation among the tribes of India. "For the tribesman society as such began and ended with his tribe."[73]

The primitive form of marriage was determined by the rules of endogamy and exogamy. The marriage and lineage functioning through exogamous and endogamous kinship relations led to the growth of caste-oriented society, to some extent. The system of group marriage was in vogue. The theory of sexual communism as advocated by some appears to be purely hypothetical. Group-marriage practice did not pass through antecedent stage of sexual communism. The chastity of women was generally protected. The child marriage was not practiced. The system of paying the bride-price was nonexistent among them. Prof. Lassen[74] has rightly called all the Kirâtas as a polygamous race. On the basis of inferential evidence it can also be said that at one stage they were polyandrist.

Women's place in the society is a positive index of the cultural advancement of the communities concerned. In the case of the Kiratas women we find that they were never held in high esteem. They were treated like slaves. Yet there are some fragmentary evidence of the status enjoyed by the Kirâta women in the primitive society.

It is interesting to note that there was no segmentation of Kirâtas society in caste and gradation of ranks, nevertheless slavery existed among some sections of the Kirâtas. It is a fact to be reckoned with that slavery did not emerge as a social institution among the Kirâtas. It was an accidental phenomena in their society. We have some positive evidence of the slavery among the Kirâtas. The earlier evidence to this effect has been furnished by the *Mahâbhârata*. From the *Sabhâ Parava*[75] it is quite evident that the Kirâtas of North-Eastern Himalayan region presented ten thousand (myriad) serving Kirati-girls of their own race to Yudhiṣṭhira as slaves in the form of gifts at his capital Indraprastha after acknowledging his suzerainty. This particular literary evidence has been also corroborated by Vasudeva Sharana Agarwala.[76] Motichandra, while confirming the existence of slavery among the Kirâtas in ancient times on the basis of the evidence furnished in the said epic, has put forth that the Kirâtas used slaves as one of the articles of trade.[77] The kings of the Kirâtas (decked with ornaments) desirous of life had formely presented to Savyasacin together with many servants.[78]

The slavery was also in practice among the Kirâtas of the Vindhyan region as slightly reflected in the *Daśakumâracarita* of Dandin, already quoted. According to this text the Kirâtas of this region in course of their campaign against the neighbouring villages used to capture the women and children, brought them to the forest, put them into custody and probably behaved like slaves.

The epigraphy also confirms the existence of slavery among the Kiratas of the South. The Kiratas chiefs vanquished and ousted by the Hoysalas found themselves powerless and became, their servants as recorded in an inscription of A.D. 1117.[79] The slavery is believed to have existed also among the Nâgâ tribes of North-East region. It is believed that the war-captives were treated like slaves by the Nâgâs (the oldest section of the Kirâtas) in ancient times.

Thus on the basis of the literary and epigraphic evidences the slavery among the Kirâtas of the North and South may be conveniently proved. We have also an incontestable evidence of the Kirâta slavery in the German source. Prof. Lassen has emphatically asserted that the "Arian (Âryan) kings were accustomed to keep female Kirâta Slaves."[80]

The Kirâta women were also source of entertainment and pleasure for the kings in the South (Karnataka) as attested by one epigraphic record. In a grant or a record dated A.D. 713 of the Ganga king Sivamara-I, the praise of Nava Kama, the younger brother of Konguni Mahârajadhirâja, Bhûvikrama, has been bestowed on the Kirâta women. In the inner courts of the palaces of the kings the Kirâta women decorated their bodies with the "nectar from the temples of the elephants stain by the king and felt delighted after having a reflection of their joyous embraces in the jewelled courtyards."[81] The description provided by Kalidasa in one of his works[82] and further commentaries thereon also shows that the Kirâta women dwelling in the hill areas had to render their services to their respective kings in different forms. The Barbara-Kirâtas of North-Western or Uttarapatha region, are also said to have developed the practice of treating their women like slaves. Their serving girls were kept in a separate apartment (harem) maintained by the Indian rulets of that region.

From the foregoing description it is apparent that the women in the Kirâta society were, generally, accorded very low status. They never enjoyed significant position in the society. However, it may be unhesitatingly, admitted that slavery never assumed the character of a social institution. It was in operation in intermittent fashion.

II. ECONOMIC CONDITION

The economic life of the Kirâtas is based on the primitive system of agriculture, natural economy, food and crops, domestication of animals, land tenure system, production and distribution system, division of labour, arts and crafts, occupations and industries, trade and commerce and other archaic economic institutions. With the help of evidences, both recorded and unrecorded, some light can be thrown on this aspect of their life.

The Kirâtas have been depicted in classical Sanskrit literature as hunters *par-excellence* and not as agriculturists, but the fact remains that they had reached the rudimentary stage of agriculture. In course of time they had crossed the hunting and food-gathering stages which represent the earliest form of natural economy and gradually reached a new stage of primitive agriculture, popularly known as shifting or *Jhum* cultivation. Agriculture constituted the backbone of their economy. The availability of vast forest rendered it possible for them to resort to this system. The agricultural operation included clearing of jungle in a hill-slope, burning of the patch and planting of paddy and other vegetation. The jungles after having been cleared were used for a few seasons and then abandoned. They had a. well-established practice of selecting different sites for cultivation on a rotational basis, the duration of which varied from time to time and area to area. Generally they used to grow rice, millet and different kinds of vegetables under this system. Though being easier, the process did not yield sufficient production because of the poor fertility of the soil. However, being the primary source of livelhood, this primitive system of shifting cultivation became widely prevalert among the Kirâta tribes of North-Eastern India, Northern India and Uttarakhanda. The Raji-Kirâtas of Uttarakhanda named it *Katil* or *Khil*. Some of their socio-religious activities became intimately connected with the agricultural pursuits. This traditional system of agricultural operation was accompanied by religious ceremonies, festivals, songs and dances etc.

One of the characteristic features of the economic life of the so-called Austric group of the Kirâtas in the Neolithic period was the development of primitive system of agriculture in which digging stick (lag, lang, ling—various forms of an old work lak) and hoe were employed for tilling. Terrace cultivation of rice on hills and the cultivation of the same grain in the plains were introduced by them. They also introduced and developed the cultivation of coconut (narikela), plantain (kadala), betel vine (tambula), betel-nut (guvaka), turmeric (haridra), ginger (singavera), and some vegetables like brinjal (vatingana) and pumpkin (alabu) etc. Though not used to cattle-breeding they are considered to be the first people to tame the elephant and to domesticate the fowl.

In ancient times, for them, the land was the territory and not the property. The system of collective ownership of hunting grounds, forest land and agricultural lands was prevalent among them. They had no notion of private property or individual ownership. However, this assumption is demonstrably false. Full-fledged communism never occurred to the exclusion of personal right. The practice of communal ownership was not developed in the entire community. Among the pastoral people there was usually a highly developed sense of private ownership as regards their live-stock, but as far as the land is concerned, there was complete communism. This proposition is not seriously shaken but sometimes invalidated by testimony from number of distant regions. It is true that the production and distribution systems were fundamentally based on the principles of primitive communism. Food was shared by all in the community. There was division of labour among men and women. Women played a very important role in socio-economic field. In a society based on the principle of division of labour the importance of slaves increased. The goats and sheep, which they used to possess keep in large number, constituted the wealth for them.

The Vedic literature provides the earliest recorded evidence of the economic activities of the Kirâtas. The young maiden of Kirâta race (any hill-folk or aborigines) used to dig up the drug or remedy with golden spades or shovels (wrought of gold) on the high ridges of the mountains or hills[83] in the later Vedic age. The Kirâta women were also in the habit of exchanging Medicinal herbs for skin and mats with the Âryans.[84] The peculiar barter system, which formed an integral part of their internal trade and commerce, lasted for centuries.

On the basis of the description available in the *Aitareya Brâhmaṇa* the great Vedic scholar, Pandit Satyavrata Samasrami has concluded that, "It was from the Kirâta towns of Eastern India that the Âryans bought their Soma Plant".[85] In fact, the Kirâtas from Eastern Regions sold Soma in the markets of Âryan India. The cave dweller Kirâtas used to grow Soma Plant in the hilly tracts of their regions. It may reasonably be assumed that in the Vedic age this plant had many more customers among the Âryans. The sale of Soma was one of the forbidden things for the Âryans which can be attested to by the statements of Manu(iii, 180) and *Yâjñâvalkya* (1,223). As a matter of fact, the selling of this plant was considered as an offence for the Brâhmaṇas in the *Smṛti* literature. This vindicates the engagement of the non-Âryan Kirâtas in the selling of this plant.

The *Mahâbhârata* contains more picturesque description of the economic activities of the Kirâtas. Among the numerous tributary kings, who paid tributes to Yudhisthira after accepting his overlordship, were the numerous chiefs of the Kiratas dwelling on the northern slopes of the Himalayas and in the regions of the Karusa on the sea-coast or the marshy region on the sea shore on both side of the Lauhitya mountains of North-East India and the frontier regions. The tributes, which they once brought with them to Yudhisthira at his imperial place, Indraprastha included cargoes of sandalwood, agarwood or aloes wood, odoriferous black wood or black aloe, black pepper, agallochum, heaps upon heaps of skins of various animals, leather of good qualitiy, precious stones, heaps of gold of great splendour procured from mountains, silver and other gems of various sort like rubies, pearls, perfumes or incense, sweet smelling herbs, many beautiful animals and birds of remote countries and other charming presents of great attraction.[86] On the basis of the quality of gifts enlisted above Romila Thapar has formed the judgment that the Kirâtas were not as wild as sometimes they appear in the text (*Mbh.*—Sabhâ Parva). She has correctly observed that "If the gifts amounted to even a portion of what is described then the Kiratas cannot be said to have had a primitive economy."[87]

The Kirâtas dwelling in the hills and mountains of the east were, decidedly, rich in gold, silver and other gems, which they obtained from these mountains. The *Mahâbharata* shows, that the powerful epic hero received abundant wealth from them as well as the other mleccha kings dwelling by the shore of the sea. Till the age of the *Atharvu Veda* or even of the *Râmâyana* all the Kirâtas of the North-East except the Khasi tribe were ignorant of the use of iron and they used gold very largely. It goes without saying that during the age of the *Mahâbhârata* gold was available in abundance in their territories. Their natural wealth consisting of minerals and forest produce indicate their material prosperity.

Kâlidâsa also refers to their natural wealth. According to him the Kirâtas washed the gem with water, purified by fire and kept it in the box. They used to adorn their body with golden threads studded with gems hanging around the neck.[88] It is not very clear to which gem he is pin-pointing and to which section of the Kirâta it belonged.

Bânabhatta has given a vivid description of the economic life of the tribal people living in the Vindhyan region which was the famous place of the Kirâtas in the Seventh century. Actually, this is an eye-witness account of exceptional value. The people (Kirâta) had founded one village after clearing the forests in this region which was known as Vanagrâm (a village near the forest). The village was surrounded by the forest on all sides. Here the tribal people including the Kiratas had settled in large number. This was the place which was visited by Harsa in search of Râjyaúri. He spent many days in this region and saw with his own eyes the life-style of the people living along the forest area. Although the name Kirâta does not figure in the said account, which is of a general nature, yet we have every reason to believe that it deals with their life and culture, because they occupied very distinguished position among the foresters of this region. Moreover, the tribal people living in this region were collectively known as the Kirâta as evidenced from Dandin's *Daúakumâracarita.* Bâṇa has provided a pen-picture of both the primitive and progressive civilization of the Kirâta people of this region. They were in the intermediary stage of two civilizations, one represented by pastoralism and hunting and the other by agrarian economy. As described by Bâna, portion of the forest land was demarcated for *jhum* cultivation. They were basically agriculturists. Those, who were ignorant of plough cultivation, resorted to this *jhum* or shifting cultivation in which spades, which was their main agricultural implement, played very important part. Actually, there was no agricultural land for those farmers who practised this cultivation. They had to break a new ground with the help of their spades for sowing seeds therein which were scattered. They had to struggle very hard for making agricultural plots. They used to dig up the barren lands as well as forest lands with their spades and used them for cultivation. They had small plots of land which were lying scattered here and there. The hunting, forest produce, wild roots and fruits were the means of their livelihood. They had to lead a very hard life as they had nothing except forest in their neighbouring areas. Some of them were wood cutters. The rice was the staple food for them. The farmers belonging to this category were in the primitive stage of civilization. On the other hand there was another category of farmers, who had a system of the striking features of plough cultivation. One of the striking features of their economic life was that they had reached a stage of an agrarian village economy. One of the main concern of these farmers was to increase the productivity of the uncultivable and unproductive lands by using manures and pesticides which they used to carry by bullock-cart. This development marks the transition from tribal to peasant society. They had a big field of sugarcane. The houses in the villages lying along the forest areas were fenced with barbed wires inside which there was an excellent arrangement for dwelling, domestication of animals and storing forest produce, wild fruits, etc. for their subsistence. The forest produce included barks of trees, fruits and flowers, cotton, honey, wax, various kinds of woods, various types of plants whose roots were used for making perfumes and herbs, etc. The drinking water arrangement was really wonderful. They were using five different kinds of certain pots or wares for storing water. Their 'Gandkusul' is equivalent to ring-wells (baked) used for various purpose.[89] We find the striking similarities between their ring-wells and that of discovered in archaeological excavations carried out at Ahichatra, Hastinâpura, Kausâmbi, Râjghat and other places of hoary antiquity. They had considerable amount of knowledge of the use of coal and iron. They had blacksmiths among themselves. The natural surroundings, beautiful gardens, and the simple way of living of the Kirâta people of Vanagrâma in the Vindhyan region were so enchanting and captivating for Harsa that he decided to stay there for sometime.

The Kirâtas have a rich heritage of artistic craftsmanship; indigenous industrial art, metallurgical and technological art, etc. The Kirâta people of North-East had full knowledge of textile industry. The art of weaving was very popular among the Khasi-Jaintia tribes,[90] Dimaso Kacharis, Tipperahs and Mishmis[91] in ancient times. They were expert in the art of making coarse cotton cloths of various designs. Their cotton fabric were much in demand among the more civilized Hindus of the plains. Their descendants are still engaged in this occupation. Their age-old traditional art has not yet died out. R.M. Nath,[92] one of the popular authorities on the history of Assam has rightly observed that the Kirâtas of Assam first introduced the cultivation of silk of different varieties in ancient times. Almost all the hill-tribes were expert weavers of silk of different types.

The art of making rude or rough pottery and other earthenware were known to the Khâsi-Jaintias, Tipperahs and Mishmi-tribes of North-East. In absence of archaeological evidence it is not possible to throw any light on this point. However, their artistic skill employed in the art of making pottery constitutes one of the major elements of their archaic civilization. There are some available evidences[93] which prove that this art was very much popular in certain villages of both the Khâsi-Jaintia Hills and the Garo Hills. Their coarse rude pots had more durability than the fragile pottery vessels of the plains. Ishwari Prasad[94] has also observed that the ancestors of the Khâsis like that of the Santhals, Kols Mundas and the inhabitants of the Central Provinces and Nicobar Islands had attained perfection in the art of making pottery with the help of wheel and in the art of using the metals.

Some of their earthen pots were painted black with an infusion of bark called *sohlyia.* Their Iron-Age culture stands in marked contrast with N.B.P. ware culture which flourished in the Gangetic Valley in the first half of the millennium B.C. Some other minor industries associated with metal works in gold, silver, brass and iron were known to Tipperah tribes in ancient times.

The metallurgical art of the Khâsis of North-East associated with iron proves their technological advancement in ancient times. There is sufficient evidence of development of this art in the Kirata country. The Kirâtas' knowledge of iron-technology in ancient times is something very striking. In certain parts of the Khasi-Jaintia hills iron-smelting and forging formed the sole occupation of the people.[95] The iron smelters used to make various iron implements used for various purposes including agriculture. Lt. Yule[96] has surmised that the extraction of iron-ores in the Khâsi-Jaintia hills must have been the occupation of the people for last two thousand years. Perhaps this is not a plausible hypothesis but a correct discovery.

The most authentic evidence of their iron-work has been furnished by a classical writer, Pliny (73-77 A.D.). He has revealed the truth that their iron was of the best quality.[97] It is generally believed that the Khasis learnt the use of iron in the post-Neolithic age or before the advent of Aryans in India. But this may be merely a supposition. Deriving the authority from Pliny it can be conclusively established that this art must have been flourishing sometime before the first century A.D. The tradition also confirms the remote antiquity of iron industry in the Khasi-Jaintia hills. The Khâsis are also believed to have been acquainted with the art of manufacturing the swords, spears, bows, arrows, guns and other fire-arms. They used to work in other metals like gold and silver.

In North-East India, another Kirâta tribe known as the Chutiyas, was well-versed in the art of metal work in copper. Their Tamreswari temple (made of copper), tentatively ascribed to 11th—12th century A.D. whose ruins were found in the Sadiya region known as Sadayapur in ancient times constitutes the monumental evidence to their acquaintance with this art.[98] The cotton and iron-works were known to the Kirâtas of the Vindhyan region also. Of the essential features of their artistic creations was the well-established practice of making pottery and earthenware of various dotted designs and patterns. There is striking similarity between this form of art and that of one developed in the Gangetic basin. One of their specimens, called

Kantakit Karkari looks very much similar to those found in Ahichatra and Hastinapur in course of archaeological explorations.[99]

On the basis of some available evidence we find that the Raji-Kirâtas of Uttarâkhaṇḍa were not only engaged in the agricultural works, but also in some sort of arts and crafts, trade and commerce. They also knew the *jhum* cultivation and domestication of animals. They used to grow little rice, millet and vegetables in small jungle, which was cleared and used for few seasons. They believed in the system of communal ownership of production and distribution. They had the tradition of making the wooden bowls or jars, which were elegantly carved. The used to move from place to place in the forest areas of Chipula for selling the wooden jars. They hadalso the knowledge of barter system. They procured the grains of their requirements from the neighbouring people known as the Khasiyas by giving them in exchange wooden implements of husbandry and vessels, which they manufactured with some technical skill. This was an act of exchanging the commodities among themselves. The bartering, particularly of the wooden jars greatly helped them to meet their day to day requirements. Usually "they approached the villages at night and leaving jars in the vicinity disappeared in the woods. The villagers collected the jars as many as they required and kept as much grain in the same place as the jars could contain. The Rajis revisited the same place the next night and collected the items."[100] This kind of peculiar barter system lasted for several centuries. The Limbu-Kirâtas of Sikkim like that of the Raji-Kiratas also used to manufacture the wooden jars.

Broadly speaking, the most important aspect of the economic life of the Kirâtas was the internal and external trade system. There are few literary evidence, which show their internal trade and commerce. On the authority of the *Mahâbhârata,* Moti-chandra[101] has stated that the precious birds, animals and slave were the articles of trade for the Kirâtas of the frontier regions during the Epic age. An intelligent Kirâta or forest messenger from the Vindhyan region sold tiger skins and leather bags and gathered news as well in the city of Mahismati as described by Daṇḍin.[102]

From the *Harṣacarita* of Bâṇabhaṭṭa (already quoted) it appears that the Kirâtas living along the forest of the Vindhya Hills were also engaged in some sort of trading activities. Their men-folk carrying the load of forest produce on their head containing the barks of tree, flowers, various plants, whose roots were used for preparing perfumes and herbs, cottons, honey, wax, peacock feathers, etc. and women-folk carrying the wild-fruits used to sell them in the neighbouring villages. This kind of trade was one of the subsidiary means of their livelihood. From the non-Indian source (German)[103] also it appears that the Kirâtas exported to other Indians fruits of their trees. This probably must have been their wild fruits, which they used to sell frequently to their Âryan neighbours.

The classical writers have provided very valuable account of the external trade system of the Kirâtas of North-Eastern Himalayan region. Though their accounts are so confusing, conflicting and contradictory that they do not go well in accord with each other, yet, their value in any case cant't be dismissed. In order to remove the confusion and to present an account in perfect order the best and the safest course is to systematize them and to examine their credibility with the help of other supporting evidences comprising the travellers' accounts and other Indian and foreign accounts. The origin of their external trade system can be roughly traced back to the period preceding the Christian era. But the most authentic account of the subject is available from the records of the first century A.D. The important articles of their trade include cotton, silk, iron, *malbathrum* and other commodities.

The Kirâtas and their neighbours of the same stock in North-East India actively participated in the silk trade, which was carried on between China and India through Yunnan. North Burma and Assam in the early centuries of the Christian era. The Kirrhadai or Cirrhadae or Scyritae or Cirrahadoi or Cilata or Kallatai or Cirâta (as variously used by the classical writers with slight contraction) all standing for the Kirâtas were dealers in silk, called Seres. The Kiratas of Assam engaged in this trade have also been described in the classical records as Seres or Serica. It is they, who first introduced cultivation of silk of different varieties in Assam in ancient times. Most of the hill-tribes of Assam known as Kiratas were proficient in the art of silk weaving. After having firmly settled in Assam, they switched over to cultivation and due to their natural propensity carried on brisk trade with their original homeland and other parts of India on the one hand and Tibet, Burma and China on the other.

Pliny, the classical writer of the first century A.D. has clearly stated that the Cirrhatae or Scyritae had full knowledge of silk trade through Assam. He was equipped with detailed information about the Seres, who were no other than the people of the hill region of North-East India. They were well known for selling their products. The word Seres, applied to the people through whose hands the silk products both raw and manufactured were dealt in must not be understood always the Chinese proper themselves. At the same time the importation of silk from China by way of the Brahmaputra valley, Assam and Eastern Bengal in the early Christian era can't be denied.[104]

Changkien, the great Chinese general and explorer of Central Asia in 200 B.C. also testifies the commercial intercourse between North-Eastern India and South-Western China through Burma. It was through this route that the Kirata intermediaries carried on their trade with China in silk cloth down to the second-half of the first millennium A.D. The art of rearing, manufacturing and weaving silk first came to Assam and other parts of India through this route. The trade relations between Kirâtas of the Himalayan region and China, of course, existed anterior to first century A.D. E.G. Young[105] in course of his journey from Yunnan to Assam confirmed the commercial contact of Assam with China in ancient times.

In fact, the silk was originally produced in China and it was carried by merchants of Turkestan through Tibetan intermediaries to India and Assam in ancient times. The Chinese record of about 248 A.D. also speaks of the trade contacts of China and Assam and further mentions that there was trade route from Yunnan in South China through Shan states, Hukong Valley, the Brahmaputra or the Lauhitya river to Assam. The trade route through Lhasa generally took two months to reach Chounahat on the border of Assam. It does, not admit of any doubt that in ancient times traders from different parts of Tibet, Central Asia and China flocked to Assam through various routes and they mostly traded in silk. They have also been designated as Seres, Cirrahadoi or Kirata[106]. This fact can be further corroborated by other sources.

A meagre stream of trade from China is believed to have filtered through the Kirâta country into the ports of Gangetic India. A very important classical document on the trade and commerce of the Kirâtas with China in ancient times spells out that "the Chinese cotton was imported from the country of the Thinai Baktria to Barugaza (Bharoach) and by the Ganges to Bengal and thence to Dimurike (the country of the Tamils). In the North where the sea terminates outwards there lies somewhere in Thinai (Assam) a very great city not on the cast but in the interior of the country called Thinai from which silk whether in the raw state or span into the thread and woven into cloth is brought by land to Barugaza through Baktria or by the Ganges to Limurike. Few merchants rarely come from Thinai or Sinai having a large commerce in silk and woollen stuffs".[107] The ancient writers do not at all agree to its position. Colonel Yule[108] thinks that it was probably the city described by Marco-Polo under the name Kenjan-fu, which is an equivalent to Singan-fu, the most celebrated city in the Chinese history and the capital of the several of the most potent dynasties. It was the place which served as metropolis during the time of Shihwengti of the Tsin dynasty.

In order to make the picture clearer in this connection we can place our dependence on other reliable sources too. The silk produced by the people was generally known by the name of Seres in China and Japan. The general opinion places the region of Serica in Eastern Mongolia and the North-East of China, in Eastern Turkistan, in the Himalayas towards the sources of the Ganges and also in Assam and Pegu or Burma. This name was first used by Ktçsias the Knidian in the 4th century B.C. Actually, the name Seres seems to have been vaguely used to designate the inhabitants of the different regions producing silk or Seres.[109] The merchandise brought from Thinai or Assam was brought to Balkh or Bactria and ' purchased there by merchants, who were proceeding or who were there on way to India and who afterwards sailed down the Indus to Barugaza or Guzarat where they took shipping for Red-Sea. The another route mentioned by Arrian down the Ganges and thence by sea to

Limurike, as referred to also by Dr. Vincent is Brahmaputra. The merchandise from Thina or Serica brought by the channel to the Gangetic mart in the vicinity of Dacca was thenceforth shipped to the Limurike. It consisted of silk-raw and manufactured, skins, iron, etc. All these were exported from Assam or countries bordering on it to distant lands including principally Berhampore and Dacca.[110] The import of silk from China has also been supported by J. Ware Edgar,[111] who extensively travelled in the frontier areas of Tibet and Sikkim. S.K. Chatterji[112] is also of the opinion that the Kiratas of Assam imported raw silk, silk yarn and silk cloth from Thinai or China. The Kiratas' trade with China in silk is also be confirmed by an observation of Romila Thapar. To quote her, "...contact with the Chinese goes back to the third century B.C. through trade in silk...they are, often associated with the...Kirâta and eastern India—the two regions from which trade with China was conducted in the early period".[113]

The antiquity of the silk industry in India is uncertain. The trade in silk yarn and silk cloth started in Northern India soon after the Âryan settlement. Silk is mentioned several times as gifts from foreign countries in the *Mahâbhârata*, the *Râmâyaṇa* and the Institute of Manu. However, it may be inferred that the Kirâtas might have come into contact with China through trade in silk sometime between the third millennium B.C. and the first century A.D. Both the Greek and Roman writers appear to have fallen into the grip of confusion about the actual place which was the emporium of silk trade. Some of them hold that the Kirâtas of Assam were exporting silk to the Chinese, whereas on the contrary, some of them believe that the silk was imported by the Kirâtas from China. Moreover, the names Thinai, Seres and Serica have been used in the context of both Assam and China. But in most of the cases Seres and Serica distinctly appear to be Assam. This really appears to be paradoxical. However, we can strike a reasonable balance between the conflicting views. Though the weight of evidence seems to be in favour of import of silk from China by way of the Brahmaputra river and its tributaries, the Ganges and also through the upper courses of the Irrawady, Mekong, Chindwin and other rivers of Burma, as well as, though Assam, Eastern Bengal, Bhutan, Tibet and other parts of Burma. We can not ignore the fact that the

Chinese also imported silk from the Kiratas of North-Eastern Hill region to a certain extent. The exchange of the silk cloth between the two seems to be true. That is why, both China and Assam, which were equally famous for silk industry in ancient times, have figured under the same denomination, though confusedly, in the classical records. Furthermore, their accounts suffer from ambiguity regarding the mode of operation of the silk trade between the Kirâtas of North-East and China. Most probably this trade might have been carried on through Tibet, and Burma because of the geographical proximity of the places for both Assam and China. Many of Tibeto-Burmans, who belonged to the Kirata section might have been playing the role of intermediaries in this trade. Because in ancient times it was a well-established practice that the goods received from Assam by them were passed on further to the Chinese. Secondly, the Kiratas' silk brought down by the Ganges might have been shipped to China from the part of Bharoach in Gujarat which seems to be less probable. Anyway the journey of the Caravan definitely might have been undertaken in ancient times through both land and sea routes.

Pliny[114] has categorically mentioned that the articles of Chinese commerce were silK, iron, skin and other clothes, which were exported from Serica or Assam. He has also stated that the iron of Serica is considered to be the best in India. Actually, this refers to the iron-ores of the Khasis which they exported to other countries. In ancient times their hills abounded in iron. The other commodities were also exported by the Kirâtas of Assam to China and other countries. He has indicated that the Romans imported these goods for the, manufacturers of their sherds. While emphasising the importance of Indian iron Herodotus (VII-65) refers to the similarly of Iron-arrow heads of India and Rome which implies that the Iron constituted an important commodity of India and it was exported to Rome during his time that is the fifth century B.C.

Ktēsias, the classical writer of the fourth century B.C., has revealed that the Kirâtas (the hill people of the North-Eastern Himalayan region or *black aborigines*) used *Siptakhora* fruit as their food and an export commoditiy as well. They carried on trade with the civilized Indians in their neighbourhood and maintained a free relationship with the Indian king. They brought him annually two hundred and sixty talents of dried fruits of the *Siptakhora* tree on rafts, as many talents of a red dye-stuff and one thousand of *elektron* or the gum exuding from the *Siptakhora* tree. In exchange they received bread, oatmeal, cotton-clothes, bows and lances, required for hunting of wild animals. Every fifth year the king presented them hundred bows, three thousand lances, one hundred and twenty thousand small shields and fifty thousand swords.[115]

The above description throws some light on the relations these *Indian aborigines* had with the Âryans. It also brings to light the intercourse of the civilized Indians with thier barbarous countrymen and the civilizing influence which the former exercised upon the latter. Secured from subjugation in their inaccessible mountains, they must have felt satisfied to live in peace with the neighbouring kings and to propitiate them by offering presents. Notwithstanding, the Aryans made them feel the superiority of their power. Moreover, because of the means of subsistence and occupation, which they procured from their civilized neighbours, the *aborigines* were obliged to accustom themselves to have intercourse with them and to afford them an opportunity for opening a new door for the administration of their doctrines and laws among them.

On the authority of Ktçsias and Aelian, Taylor[116] mentions that the *Siptachora* includes not only the silk lac and other dyes but also the musk, ivory, gold, silver and iron, which were exported by the hill-people of Assam to India via the Brahmaputra in exchange for bread, coarse cloth, etc. The Khasis used to bring to the mart on the borders of their country cotton, iron ore, honey, wax, orange, ivory and cassia for selling as well as exchanging them for rice, tobacco, spirits, fish etc. They as well as, other hill tribes on the eastern frontier of Bengal carried down their goods in large conical shaped baskets or hampers called *tapas* by the Khasis. The Sasatae (Kirâtas) coming to the established mart on the borders of Thina were accompanied by their wives and children carrying heavy burdens wrapped in mats. The mode of conducting traffic leaves no doubt that the Sasatae are one of the hill-tribes of Assam. The Garos also brought down to the plains large baskets of load containing cotton and exchanged them for rice, dry fish, betel nut, salt and gold ornaments.[117]

The gold was another prized article of trade, which was exported by the Kirâtas of both Assam and Tripura to other parts in India as well as abroad in ancient times. The gold was brought to India through the rivers of Assam and Burma. It was obtained chiefly from the river washings of Assam and Northen Burma in ancient times. The proof in support of the Kirâta trade in gold has also been adduced in one of the classical texts.[118] The gold was brought to India through the Tipperah country about 60 miles east of the Ganges delta. The coarse gold was obtained from the gold mines in the hilly country of Tripura in former times and exported to China in exchange for silver.[119] This can further be confirmed by the native tradition as well as the travellers' account. Tavernier observes "that both silk and gold were sent overland to China and the merchants of Tripura trading in the Deccan, took back valuable commodities."[120] He has also referred to coarse silk, iron, gold, silver, steel and leads which were produced in the hill-areas of Assam and exported to neighbouring countries.[121] It is to be specifically noted here that the Kirâtas of North-East Hill region were exporting both iron and gold to foreisn countries.

The classical scholars unanimously speak of *tezpat* or *malabathrum* as the principal article of the Kirata's trade but regarding the identification of the tribes engaged in this trade and the exact location and position of the trade emporium the difference of opinion exists among them. The tribes allied to the Kirrhadai or Cirrhadae or Kirâtas of the Eastern Himalayas and the Gangetic delta (the people of the Khâsi Jaintia Hills, the Garo Hills, Sikkim and Eastern Bengal) exporting *malabathrum (Cinnamomum albiflorum)* to China have been designated both as Basatae (Besadai) and Sesatai (Sasatae) in the classical literature. Ptolemy with greater accuracy has assigned to them an island position eastward of the river Ganges which was the greatest source of supply. He describes their country as one of *India extra Gangen,* situated higher up than a range of mountains called Maiandros, which is the Garo range of the hills to ths east of Sylhet and Mymensingh.[122] The same position has been assigned to it by D' Anville.[123] Ptolemy further places Besadai above the Maiandros and from this as well as other indications we must take them to be the hill-people in the vicinity of Sylhet, who are in all possibility the Khâsi-Jamtias and Garos. The country of the Kirrhadae or the Kirâta living on the Eastern frontier of Bengal was celebrated for its *Malabathrum*—species of *Cinnamomum albiflorum,* which abounds in the valleys along the base of the mountain range of Sylhet. According to him the best *Malabathrum* was produced in the country of the Kirrhadia.[124] It was grown on the Southern slopes of the Khasi Hills and a considerable trade was carried on by the people of the district of Sylhet. The country of the Kirrhadia as mentioned by him can, undoubtedly, be identified with the country inhabited by the Kiratas from the foot of the Garo and Khasi Hills to the hilly areas of Tipperah along the eastern coast of the Brahmaputra estuary. G.E. Gerini, who has carried out an extensive researches on Ptolemy's Geography, has conclusively proved that the best *malabathrum* was produced by the Kirrhadia people of Sylhet, Cachar, Eastern Assam, Sheila, Shillong, Sadiya and Bisa.[125] We do not see any reason to doubt the correctness of this statement.

In confirmation of the views expressed in the preceding pages the discussion can be lengthened little more. It is true that the trees from which different kinds of oil and spice and other laurel were prepared are not to be found in about at the present day in this country, however, it can never be denied that in Sylhet and its neighbouring areas which is not very remote from Chaturgrama, *Malabathrum* was produced in large quantities.[126] We can take it as a definite indication towards the borders of the Khasi and Garo Hills, which were very famous for export of *tezpat* even in ancient times.

According to the testimony of those writers, who have dealt with the subject, to a considerable extent, we can affirm that *malabathrum* is not betel but consists of the leaves of one or more kinds of the *Cinnamon* or *Cassia* tree. We may profitably, quote the following passage: "Cinnamomum albiflorum is designated taj.—*tajpat* in Hindustan; the former name being generally applied to the leaf and the latter to the bark of the tree; taj, *tejpate* or *tejapatra,* by all which names this leaf is known, is used as a condiment in all parts of India. It is indigenous in Sylhet, Assam, Rangpur (associated with the Kirrhadia of Ptolemy) and in the valleys of the mountain range as far as Mussoorie. The dry branches and leaves are brought annually in large quantities from the former place and sold at a fair which is held at Vikramapura. Tej however is a name that is also given in the eastern part of Bengal to the bark of a variety of *Cinnamomem Zeylanicum* or *Cassia lignea,* which abounds in the valleys of Kachar, Jyantia and Assam."[127]

The following interesting passage describes the mode in which the Kirâtas of North-East India traded in this article with the Chinese in ancient times. Every year on the confines or borders of Thinai an annual fair was held on the established mart, which was the emporium of trade. The fair was attended by the merchants from China, who used to come very rarely and the tribal people known as Besatae and Sesatai who were of diminutive size with their broad face and in appearance they looked like "wild beasts". Some of them were almost entirely uncivilized, but most of them were quite mild and gentle in disposition. Their place of assembly was between their own borders and those of Thinai, which was in all probability situated along the foot of the hills on the eastrn frontier of Bengal. The Kirâta tribes used to visit this fair along with their wives and children carrying heavy loads of goods or produce wrapped up in mats and plaited baskets resembling in outward appearance the green grape leaves or the young leaves of vine. Here spreading out the mats they squatted on them and exhibited their goods for sale and then resorted to fest which was held for several (seven) days after the conclusion of which they returned to their own places in the interior and the Thinai. And then the natives watching them came into that place after their departure and gathered up their mats, which had been purposely left behind and extracted from the braids of the fibres, called *petri* or *petroi*, which was used for weacing, and then took the leaves, folded them double and rolled them up into balls through whcih they passed the fibres of the calami or which they pierced with the fibres from the mats. Three kinds of *malabathrum* were made and designed according to the size of the leaf from which they were made. Those made of the largest leaves were called the large-ball *malabathrum*; those of the smaller, the medium-ball and those of the smallest, the small balls, which were also known as hadro, Meso and *Mikros-phalron*. Hence there existed three kinds of *Malabathrum* which were brought there by the manufacturers.[128] The Kirâtas are also recorded to have exchanged their merchandise the *malabathrum,* at the marts or hauts (established on the eastern frontier of Bengal or on the borders of their forest) for the produce of plain. The barter was effected either by signs or through persons understanding their language and acting as brokers on behalf of the Thinae or people of plain.[129]

The Kiratas of Sikkim are said to have maintained trade relations with China. The *malabathrum* was also sold near Gangtok. Lassen has identified the Besatae of "Periplus and Besadae of Ptolemy with the Cirrhadae or tribes of Sikkim.[130] We are informed by the author of the *Periplus* that "the Cirrhadae (Kirâta), a tribe of squat figure with their broad face and flat nose but mild in disposition, used to come to the border of Thinai (China) for their trade in *malabathrum* (*Cinnamomum albiflorum*) with the Chinese. On the basis of the information supplied by some noted authorities[131] on trade and commerce Mr. Schoff has suggested that "the location of their annual fair must have been near the modern Gangtok (27°20′ N. 18°38′ E.) above which the Cho-La or the Jelap-La pass leads to Chumbi on the Tibetan side of the frontier from which the overland route led across the table-land to Koko-Nor. Siningfu and Singanfu. Other passes through Nepal are possible, particularly that by the Aruna River, but the route through Sikkim involves the least deviation from the direct line from Koko-Nor to the Ganges ; while from Gyangste to the source of the Arun a pass must be scaled higher by 3000 feet than Jelapa-La."[132] Pseudo-Callisthener (III, 8) refers to the Bisadae "who gather a leaf. They are a feeble folk of very diminutive stature and live in caves among the rocks. The understand how to climb precipices through their intimate knowledge of the country and are thus able to gather the leaf. They are small men of stunted growth, with big heads of hair which is straight and not cut."[133]

On the basis of relative position assigned to the country of Kirrhadia, Taylor[134] has rightly included the Kirâtas of Morung lying the west of Sikkim and situated between Nepal and Bhutan among the traders in the Himalayas. Motichandra (an acknowledged authority on ancient Indian trade and Commerce), while corroborating the account recorded in the *Periplus* (63-65) has included Tâmra-lipti—the modern Tamluk and the Hughli estuary and other district of Bengal in the rivers districts and towns of the Ganges, shown in the said text. He further asserts that the *tejpat* or *Malabathrum* of the Himalayas and China, the silk cloths of China etc. were articles of trade in this region. In the northerly direction of the Ganges, China and its capital 'Thinai' (perhaps 'Naking') was the centre of the trade from where, silk, cloths, tezpat, etc. were exported through both land and sea routes, but the Chinese traders seldom visited India. The Besatae, identified with the Kirâtas, used to bring *tejpat* once in a year from China and they sold it near Gangtak surreptitiously.[135]

Some discrepancies appear to have occurred in the above statement, because the Kiratas were not the importers but the exporters of *malabathrum.* The Indian and Chinese articles of trade enumerated in a list prepared on the basis of eye-witness account of an Egyptian Greek merchant of Berenice (the first man to make the vovage to India in the middle of the first century A.D.) and appended at the end of the *Periplus*[136] clearly shows that the *malabathrum* was the merchandise of export in both the Himalayan mountains and the Ganges delta, and the Chinese were the exporters of only raw silk, silk yarn and cloth. *The Periplus* further records that the *"malabathrum (Cinnamomum tamala)* is native in this part of the Himalayas, being one of the principal trees".[137] It was extensively cultivated in the Himalayan region of India and therefore, it was an article of export to China but not import therefrom. On the basis of this discovery the view of Suniti Kumar Chatterji[138], that the tribes allied to the Kirthadai or Kirâta known to the Greeks as Besatai or Sesatai used to import *malabathrum* from China in baskets carrying them on their backs, can be disposed off.

Marco Polo in his account of "Tebet" has stated that *Cinnamom* also grows there in great plenty."[139] The author of the *Periplus* locates the Besatai Kiratas also "on the borders of the land This" (Thinae—probably as the genitive of 'this'—the western state of China) and indicates that "Tibet was then subject to China."[140] The *malabathrum* of the Himalayan mountains exported to China also includes those of Tibet. The Tibetans are the fragments of a great primitive population that occupied both the northern and southern slopes of the Himalayas at some very remote prehistoric times. The descendants of the Kirâtas of Tibet are found in Burma, Siam and China. Depending on the version of Ptolemy (VII.II. 16), that the best *malabathrum* was produced in the country of the Kirrhadia, J.W. McCrindle[141] has conjectured that this commodity was exported from Nepal (where it was called *tezpat)* as well as Rangpur. More or less on the same supposition, Vincent[142] holds that the malabathrum as referred to by Ptolemy was cultivated by the Kirrhadae of Arracane and the country about the mouth of Megna, but he takes it for betel leaf, which James Taylor has contradicted and pointed out that *malabathrum* is not betel but it speaks of *Cinnamomum albiflorum* which abounds in the valleys along the base of the mountain range extending from Sylhet to Mussoori.[143] But the contradiction is not a valid one for which justification will be given little later. Here it will suffice to mention that Taylor's own statement is not absolutely correct.

The *malabathrum* and *Spikenard* have been used together by Taylor as articles of Chinese commerce. According to him the former was exported or procured from Sylhet and Assam and the latter from Rangpur.[144] The statement is true, but the explanation is not satisfactory. Because, he has not given identification of *Spikenard.* Nor has he provided the details about the nature and course of trade in the commodity. Moreover, the place, from where the said article is claimed to have been procured, is not confirmed.

The *Periplus* helps us in this regard. According to the information supplied in the text *Spikenard* was a kind of leaf, which was obtained from the mountains. It was perennial herb of the Alpine Himalaya, which extends eastward from Garhwal and assends to 17000 feet in Sikkim. In India it was largely used as an aromatic adjunct in the preparation of medicinal oils.[145] According to Pliny (XII, 26) it was a leaf whose price varied according to its size. It was also of three kinds. The *hadrosphaerum* consisting of the larger leaves was sold at 40 denarii per pound. The smaller leaves were called *mesophaerum* and sold at 60 denarii. But which is considered the most valuable of all was known as *microsphaerum* and consisted of the very smallest of the leaves sold at 75 denarii per pound.[146] This goes very well in accord with the explanation given about the size and kinds of *malabathrum* by different scholars including Taylor himself. Thus it confirms our beliefs that there were different species of leaf—from the Himalayan mountain which were exported outside. This further shows that this leaf was exported by the tribal people of Garhwal and Sikkim, but not Rangpur as erroneously supposed by Taylor.

Pliny further observes that this "leaf or *Spikenard* held the first place in Rome among the ointments of his day".[147] Taylor believes that the *malabathrum* of Assam was imported into Rome but leaf is not identical particularly with betel-leaf.[148] This can be further confirmed by the statements of other scholars. Pliny says that "the *malabathrum* which entered so prominently into Roman perfumes should have a smell like *Nard (Spikenard)*.[149] But, other Roman writers seem to have confused it with the Ganges *Nard* mentioned in the *Periplus*. Watt also opines that it was not the betel-leaf but some other leaf which might have entered into international commerce in the Roman period.[150] Schoff has given the most convincing explanation of the subject discussed here at length. He has clearly stated that the Romans knew the...... *Cinnamon leaf,* a later article of commerce, under the name of *Malabathrum* as a product of India and Tibet... *malabathrum* and *Spikenard* were the two most treasured ingredients of the ointments and perfumes of the Roman empire."[151]

The fact which is worthy of our notice is that the Romans knew the commercial value of the *malabathrum* (the product of the Kirâtas of India), which was exported from various parts of the Himalayan mountains and other parts of India. At least in one case the *malabathrum* was the leaf from the same tree that produced variety of *Cinnamon*. The *Periplus* (56 & 63) confirms the export of *malabathrum*. This seems to be an indication of a trade monopoly of very ancient date and it was through enforcement that the bark only went for trade purposes to the other country while the leaf was an open article of trade to India.[152] Lind give remarks that this is the striking instance of the secrecy with which the ancients conducted the more valuable portions of their trade.[153]

Several derivations from the word *malabathrum* have been suggested by scholars which have made the confusion worse confounded. Heeren, Vincent and McCrindle translate it as a 'betel' and thereby accuse the *Periplus* of a blunder committed in sections 63 and 65 where the substance is described as coming from the Himalaya mountains. The translation rests on an assumption that the petros of the text (65) is the same as the betel. The author of the *Periplus* is misled by a fancied resemblance to the Greek petros, fibre, whereas the word is the Sanskrit patra, leaf. Otherwise, the description of the preparation of the *tamala* leaves is correct, being corroborated throughout by Pliny. And so is the case with McCrindle, a renowned authority on the classical texts, who sometimes speaks in affirmative and sometime in negative tone about the identification of the *malabathrum* with the betel-leaf. Taylor[154] also seems to be bit hesitant to subscribe to the views expressed by Salmasius[155] and Vincent.[156] We have also taken *malabathrum* as betel-leaf. Taylor has always acclaimed that it was purely a species or leaf of *Cinnamomum albiflorum,* which is not necessarily true. This fact should not be lost sight of that betel-leaf as distinguished from *malabathrum* was also produced in both the plains and hills of Assam. Till today this practice is still being continued. Schoff has rightly pointed out that "the leaf coming from the Himalaya mountains was principally from the *Cinnamomum tomala,* which was native there.[157] McCrindle himself admits that the word *malabathrum* is a compound of *tamala* (the Sanskrit name of *Cinnamum albiflorum}* and *patra-a.* leaf."[158] Here we intend to prove that not only *tezpat* but also the betel-leaf was an article of commerce for the Kirâtas. Betal-leaf was, of course, an article of internal trade and commerce for them. In support of our contention we can record one valuable evidence from the document on ancient commerce and navigation based on information supplied by the author of the *Periplus* and Arrian, whose account is primarily based on the *Journal of the Voyage of Nearchos.* "The *Malabathrum (Tamalapatra*—the leaf of the *Laurns Cassia* or betel-leaf) obtained from Thinai (Assam) from the Kirâtas or Sesatai tribe was exported from the interior of India to Mouziris and Nelkunda.[159] The *malabathrum* was not only a masticatory but also an unguent or perfume."[160]

The Latin text of the *Periplus* also confirms that near the source of the Ganges on the eastern side as located by Ptolemy and in the northerly direction beyond Dasarene (whose location has already been discussed in the previous chapter) there were variety of 'barbarous tribes' including the Kirrhadai. On the mouth of the river there was a great trade emporium from where *malabathrum,* cotton and other commodities were exported by the Sesatai tribe to different parts of India and Thinai (China).[161]

While extracting the truth veiled in different accounts and statements discussed above, we can affirm that the Kiratas of Northern and Eastern Himalayan region and the Ganges delta including the tribes of Khâsi-Jaintia Hills, the Garo Hills, Sikkim, Tibet, Nepal and the Marshy regions near the sea cost extending up to Sylhet and Mymensing were taking part in the trade in *malabathrum (tejpat)* which was the chief article of export to China. Their external trade was well organised as evidenced from their commercial activities carried on regularly at their metropolis. The Kirâtas of Tibet and Burma must be acting as intermediaries between the Chinese and the other Kiratas of India. In all probability they might be exporting the different varieties of the leaf procured from their respective mountains and jungles and other forest" produce to the market towns of the Gangetic India and the Deccan. Their export of betel-leafs to the port towns of Southern India can very well be confirmed by the testimony cited above. Their all merchandise except *tezpat* were the items of internal trade. They were the importers of only silk from China by both land and sea routes.

The general trading activities of the Sesatae (Kirâtas) of Assam as referred to in the *Periplus* have been spoken of very highly in different classical texts. Pliny and Pomponiues Mela (III, Viii, 60) for instance, describing the country of the Seres (Assam) and the silent trade of the Himalayas have bestowed a great amount of praise on them for their qualities, which they used to exhibit in course of their trade and commerce. They used to carry their merchandise for exchange with different merchants and procured everything of their necessity and requirements. This occupation proved to be very much lucrative for them from social, economic and cultural standpoints.[162]

Nonnos, a classical writer of fifth century A.D. in his Greek epic poem in hexameter verse called the *Dionysiaka* or

Bassarika has stated that 'Cirradioi' (Kirâta) of the North-West living by the side of the other tribes of the maritime region immediately west of the Indus (or between the Indus and Hydaspes of Jhelum) were great navigators and warlike race. He has also mentioned the names of the Kirâta chiefs.[163] From this little hint we can infer that in the North-Western region also they must be having some commercial dealings. with the people of neighbouring countries. The reference to their boars and naval warfare is indicative of their active engagements in the maritime trade extending from the Indus up to shores of Bengal, eastward of the mouth of the Ganges. The details are wanting in this regard.

The Barbara-Kirâtas of North-West were also having some trade activities. The *Periplus* clearly indicates that on the mouth of the Indus the tribes living on the lower having ferocious character. The *Barbaricum* was their metropolis. This port was known as Bahardipur in ancient times which still survives in the modem Indus delta. The name is evidently Hellenized from some Hindu ward—Shah-bandar (Royal Ports) formerly accessible to men of war and now lies far inland to the east of the present main channel of the Indus. The inland behind the small island later became the metropolis of Scythia, known as Minnagara. But in ancient times the river had seven mouths, very shallow and marshy and not navigable except the one in the middle, at which stood the market town, Barbaricum by the said of its shore.[164] This was the colony of the Barbara Kirâta where they had commercial contacts with both the Indian and Chinese traders. Some of them possibly carried on their trade up to ancient Sindhu or Taxila.[165] The Seric skins, which appear as one of the articles of export in the list given in the *Periplus* probably came from the Barbara-Kiratas at this metropolis. Because their territory abounded in skins and there was a geographical proximity of their territory and the said market town. However, this may be taken as suggestive but not conclusive. In absence of any positive evidence it is neither possible nor fair to elaborate it.

During the period of the Kirata rule in Nepal the trade also flourished to some extent. The Kiratas of Nepal who were very simple in manners and customs carried on both internal and external trade. During those days Nepal had become a trade centre for the Kirâtas traders. They came into commercial contact with the traders of other parts of India as well as that of distant countries like Tibet and China. This contact led to their material progress.[166]

IV

POLITICAL ORGANISATION, ADMINISTRATIVE SYSTEM AND MILITARY ACTIVITIES

The existence of political institution or organisation among the Kirâta tribe during the ancient period can't be denied. There has been a persistent attempt on the part of Morgan to establish that the primitive people lacked political organisation because they had no territorial extension. But such view can be falsified on the basis of the functioning of their age-old political institutions, time— honoured practices, popular traditions and beliefs and some realiable sources, help us to a reasonable extent in having a clear understanding of the system which was prevalent among them during the early period. His basic contention is that the political organisation in the narrower sense is a relatively recent development at a very high cultural level. The primitive people, according to him, deal with an individual as a member of kinship group through personal relation, whereas the civilised state deals with him through the territorial relations. This contention does not always hold good. The harmonious development of both tribal (kinship) and political (territorial) elements in ancient times can be taken some cognizance of. The judicious combination of both in their political system is a factor which is worthy of our attention. The present author pays respect to widely acknowledged view that the primitive political institutions were invariably bonded with the kinship factor. It is, indeed, a fact that the history of political ideas and institutions begins with the assumption that kinship constituted the sole possible ground of community in political functions. The kinship was always a pivotal point in all governmental relations of ancient times. A rudimentary form of administrative system introduced by the Kiratas was by and large, based on democratic principles. After making an intensive inquiry into the subject concerned we find the note of diversity in their political system. The polity and administration or the pattern of political organisation differed fundamentally from tribe to tribe. But the basic democratic spirit was always maintained. Their military activities also deserve our notice.

The political evolution of the Kirâtas was preceded by social evolution as the law of nature. Their kingdom or rashtra. contained tribes (Jana), tribal units or clan, (Vish), family (Griha or Kula), and village (grama). History records that the first stage of political evolution of the tribal people was their clan organisation which was subsequently followed by creation of families bound together by ties of kinship and formation of a village, which constituted as a nucleus of the whole system. This proved to be a stepping-stone of their organised civil administration. Each of the village belonging to a group of families or household was governed by a chief or headman. Several clans constituted a larger group, subsequently known as the tribe, the head of which was popularly known as chieftain. The phratry was the cementing force between the family, the clan and the state. Their political evolution resembles to some extent, to that of the Aryans of the early Vedic Age and of the Greek before the advent of the city states in Hellenic Age. The trend of their political evolution more or less forms the "Social Contract Theory" postulated by Rousseau. The magnificent superstructure of their indigenous democratic system of government has been built up on a foundation which was laid in the primitive age. They had independent or semi-independent tribal forms of government.

It is worthy of note that before the formation of tribal states in early Medieval period and the germination of sophisticated political ideas and institutions, the villages were the pivot around which their whole administration revolved. In the primitive days the open assembly was held in which everything was decided on the basis of collective wisdom. The villagers used to assemble in groups; they used to sit on different stones placed in different rows in an open ground and both male and female members used to take part in the deliberations. In the beginning they had no conception of Chieftaincy or Kingship. The evolution of their political institutions on well organised basis and the growth of various political ideas can very well be traced back to a protohistoric period saw many new changes in their political system. But during the prehistoric period their collective will and wisdom constituted the bedrock of their administrative organisation.

The emergence of the institution of Chieftainship, which constituted the most important element in the political system of the Kirâtas-was an event of great importance in the political history of ancient India. The prevalence of the Chieftainship system among them goes, as far back as the age of the *Mahâbhârata.* From this literary text it appears that the Kirata tribes of the North and East had their own Chiefs or Kings. From the Sabha Parva[167] it is quite evident that Pulinda and Sumana, the two illustrious and virtuous Kshatriya chiefs of the Kiratas and their numerous other chiefs attended the imperial assemblage of Yudhisthira along with other kings.

The classical account of India bears witness to the fact that the Chieftainship had existed among the Cirradiois (Kiratas) of North-western region much before the 5th Century A.D. The Kirâtas living in the areas adjacent to Ariana and Caspeiri or Kashmir, west of the Indus territory lying between the Indus and *Hydespes* (Jhelum) were headed by their two Chiefs named Thyamis and Olkaros, who happened to be sons of Tharseros the rower, which can be confirmed by the statement of Nonnos as recorded in his *Dionysiaka* or *Bassarika* (A Greek Epic Poem).[168]

The epigraphic evidence also helps us to prove the existence of this popular political institution among the Kirâtas in ancient times. The Kirâtas dwelling on the outskirts of the Vindhyas, which divide north and south, were living with their chiefs from 10th to 12th century A.D. as gleaned from the inscriptional records of Karnataka.[169] The Kirâtas of North-East, i.e. the Khasi-Jaintias, the Garos the Kacharis, the Nâgâ tribes and the tribal people of Tripura had also well established Chieftainship system. The Kirâta Chiefs were nominal heads. They were not acknowledged as the chiefs in the real sense of the term rather they were appointed as spokesmen of the villages known as Elders without enjoying much power. They were assisted by advisers, Councillors and other local officials in running day to day administration. Any decision pronounced in the Village Council was considered to be the mandate of the whole population. They used to manage their affairs in accordance with the republican principles of the government. On the whole they had democratic and oligarchic or republican system of government.

The Village Panchayat System constitutes the most significant aspect of their local Self-Government. The head of this institution played an important part in managing the affairs of the community with the help of Council consisting of elders. Their chiefs were elected by all the villagers even in the olden days. Their village organisation was fundamentally based on the democratic principle of the government. The self-governing villages were the corner-stones of political system of both the Aryans and non-Aryans.

The role played by the entire population in the conduct of administrative business in the Village Council—an open Assembly and a supreme Parliament of the people, remarkably testifies to the existence of their long standing democratic tradition. A.S. Altekar has rightly stated that "in historic times republics were flourishing in ancient India in north-western and in a north-eastern Zone."[170] K.P. Jayaswal also affirms that the Parvatiya Ganas were republican communities.[171] The paurânic and the Epic accounts of the Parvatiya Janapadas of the Kirâtas, as already referred to in earlier chapter confirm this statement. The Kirâtas of the Himalayan region from Ladakh and Kailasa in the South-east of Kashmir to the extreme end of Kamarupu in the east ruled over the entire regions even before the rise of Buddha as organised groups constituting what may be called the present republics. V.A. Smith[172] is of the opinion that the customs of hill-men give the best clue to working of all Ganas. His appreciation of the tribal republics of so-called Mongolian origin is very striking. The essence of republican forms of government of the Kirâta people was that the decision was taken on the basis of free and frank discussion in public meetings or in open councils and assemblies.

The administration of justice furnishes an illuminating example of their developed sense of democratic system of government. There was a complete absence of Central authority. Kinship groups became the judicial body. They had a rude but mature jurisprudence. They had disproportionately small body of Civil law in ancient times under archaic conditions. The civil jurisprudence, penal law, the unwritten customary law etc. were generally obeyed far more willingly than written code obeyed spontaneously. Henry Maine's observation that "the penal law of ancient communities is not the law of crimes; it is the law of wrongs or to use the English technical word of Torts"[173] is absolutely correct.

Their customs, conventions, usages, ancient practices ethical codes, precepts, fables, antecedents, etc. formed the part of their customary laws which can be fairly compared to *Dharma-Sûtras* (600—300 B.C.)—a record of social customs and usage on which civil and criminal laws were based. The tribal justice was guided by the customary laws exactly in the same way as in ancient India in Pre-Kautilyan age. Hindu system of justice was guided by *Dharma-Sûtras.* Their village councils used to function as an open court where disputes were heard and decided according to established customs and practices. The village councils constituted as a supreme court of justice. The chiefs, their advisers, councillors and other local ofticials in collaboration with each other used to administer the justice. They used co decide the civil and criminal cases according to ancient practices. In ancient times they used to hold open courts for dispensing the justice through arbitration, mutual reconciliation persuasion and other means. Their judicial procedure, crimes and punishment, oaths and ordeals were based on traditional beliefs.

It is worthwhile to note that the political institutions of the Kirâta people stand in marked contrast to the *Vedic bicameral* bodies Sabhâ and Samiti, the Parisad of the Brâhmanic or Upanisadic period, the Samgha and Gana of the age of Panini and Patanjali, the Gaṇa-Râjya of Buddhist India, the Hellenic Institutions known as *Yepovia* or *Senatus,* the folk-assembly *Ayopa* of Homeric age, democratic and oligarchical institutions of Pericles age, Public Councils of Burma known as *Hiuttaw* and *Byedaik,* the minor republics of Chumbi valley in Tibet and other folk assemblies, Senates and Tribunals of western countries.[174]

The espionage and diplomatic activities of the Kirâtas may also be mentioned here. The Kirâtas were employed by Yudhisthira as messangers or duta (Kiratas Dutam) during the Epic age, whose primary duty was to equip him with information about the moment, strategy and planning of Duryodhana as stated by Abhinava Pampâ in his Kannada work called *Vikramârjunavijaya* or *Pampâ Bhârata*[175] composed in the Saka year 863 (A.D. 941). They were actually appointed to supply the detailed information to Yudhisthira in Dvaitabana about the dealings of the ruler of Kurudesha with the subjects or common people. The Kirâtas described as foresters, *Vanaichara,* used to narrate the whole details to Yudhisthira. They used to perform their duty very sincerely. They were the most trusted followers and messengers of Yudhisthira. They were guided by the philosophy that an appointed messenger should not deceive his master.[176] They expressed their gratefulness to Yudhisthira for receiving the training in the field of learning the secrets of politics through observing the war strategy of Duryodhana for usurping kingdom by deceitful means. During the Maurya age also the Kirâtas rendered their services to the kings both as a guard and as a spy.[177]

Their military organisation was of a simple nature, but there was some sort of uniformity in this system. Their interest in war and politics and qualities as valiant soldiers and expert warriors are also worth mentioning. They had natural tendency to help their masters as well as neighbouring kings as warriors. Right from the epic age they were recruited as soldiers in the army of their contemporary kings. Bhagadatta, the king of Pragjyotisha was surrounded by large army consisting of the Kirata and Cina soldiers and many others dwelling on the Sea-coast of the marshy regions. In course of the northern expedition launched for subjugating various kings and their countries for the purpose of establishing the empire of Yudhisthira, when Arjuna attacked Bhagadatta, the Kirata soldiers along with others fought on his behalf and resisted the attempt of the Pandava hero to conquer them. The battle of resistance lasted eight days but eventually Bhagadatta recognised the supremacy of Yudhisthira and agreed to pay taxes. Later Bhagadatta joined the Kaurava side in the war of the *Mahâbhârdta* and ceded one Aksauhini of soldiers, mostly Kiratas and Cinas endowed with a golden complexion.[178] After having subjugated the king of Pragjyotisa, Arjuna marched towards North and conquered mountainous tracts and their outskirts and hilly regions. Having conquered all the mountain kings reigning there brought them under his political sway and exacted tributes from them. The Kirâtas of Vindhya have been referred to by Abhinava Pampâ (12th century A.D.)[179] as countless army in the retinue of the Mleccha king named Raudrabhuti.

The Greek and German accounts also confirm the military activities of the Kirâtas in general. Three thousand of them were in the retinue of the king during the classical period and" later they adopted the laws of the Indo-Aryans [180] These accounts are not in any great detail so nothing definite can be made out of the meagre evidence supplied by them. However, it can be positively stated that their valour and powers prompted the Indian rulers to utilize their services as soldiers.

The bravery and heroism displayed by the Kirâta men and women in the war fought between Úiva, their lord and Arjuna their opponent on the Himavat also prove the fact that they were excellent warriors. Siva, assuming the form of the Kirâtas or attired in the dress of the Kirâta accompanied by large number of the Kirâtas fought with Arjuna. The quarrel flared up between Arjuna and the Kirâtas over the issue of taking the credit of killing a demon named Muka, son of Ditj. When this demon was pierced by the arrows of both the Kirâtas and Arjuna simultaneously, the latter was taken to task by a Kirâta who was a messenger of one of their chiefs. Arjuna was advised to meet their chief. The Kirâtas fought with their primitive weapons, arrows and the bows, shafts, etc. There was a continuous fight between the Kirâtas under the leadership of Siva and Arjuna. The bodies of the former had been afflicted by the multitude of arrows showered on them by the latter. They are stated to have swallowed many arrows struck by Arjuna. The army of the Kirâtas gathered from the forests on all sides swooped over Arjuna with their arrows in order to help Úiva and defeat him, their powerful adversary. Lord Úiva has been called charming Commander of Kirâta legion or as a leader of Ganas having body of Kirâtas constituting huge army -of foresters. This battle ended in the victory of the Kirâtas over Arjuna. This incident is believed to have occurred somewhere in the northern Himalayas, probably on the summit of the mountain in the Kâilaúa region.[181] The importance of this episode should not be dismissed purely as a mythological account. At least their soldier like quality finds some reflection in such story as narrated in ancient Indian literature.

The description provided by Kâlidâsa,[182] of Raghu's conquest of the mountain tribes inhabiting the northern slopes of the Himalayas, also helps us to ascertain that several Kirâtas chiefs living in the Himalayan mountains of the Kâilâúa (Tibet) region took part in the fierce battles with the army of the former. Raghu had to face the array of attacks from the Gana army of the hills and mountains. Hc had to quell the resistance of the Kirata tribes. In the battles which took place between him and the mountain tribes fire flashed forth as the iron darts and the stones flung by means of slings clashed together. They had steel arrows. It also shows the great skill of the mountaineers in throwing stones with slings. The Kirâtas had to face their discomfiture in the Himalayan war waged during the time of Kâlidâúa.

V

RELIGION, PHILOSOPHY AND ART

Religion, philosophy and art as a whole constitute very important section of life and culture of the Kirâtas. Geographical barriers kept the Kirâta tribes apart in ancient times, nevertheless, they evolved religious and philosophical ideas and artistic traditions of their own in isolation which as an impregnable force could not be destroyed by science. It is very striking to note that in spite of the absence of temples, idols or shrines and religious scriptures or written Sastras in the primitive age they evolved a very developed religio-philosophical system. They have had a definite notion of religion and philosophy conforming to the canons laid down in Spengler's theory of "Magian Culture". Each section of them has had religious faiths, mythological beliefs, philosophical conceptions and idealistic imaginations regarding their gods and goddesses, life and soul and other material and immaterial aspects as accepted by all celebrated anthropologists, ethnologists and classical historians.

Animism, Hinduism and Buddhism are the three cornerstones of the religio-cultural and philosophical system of the Kirâta people. The original religion of the Kirata tribes is popularly known as animism. It includes the faith in the classic doctrines of souls, spirits, transmigration, future life, etc. Such faith is generally based on rudimentary mythic conception. This also signifies the attribution of spirit or soul to inanimate objects. This is the crude form of religion in which magic is the predominant element. The polytheistical beliefs, which constitute the essential component of the cult of animism, comprise the propitiation of both benevolent and malevolent spirits, natural and supernatural objects and other innumberable gods and goddesses having an anthropomorphic attributes. This seems to be based on magico-religious system. The classic art of the worship of rude objects is a characteristic feature of the animistic system of mankind. The veneration of such objects is of remote barbaric antiquity. Primitive magic and fetishism, animal worship and belief in demons are often combined with the worship of more or less personal gods, as we find in mysticism, asceticism and abstract and profound theological system or esoteric doctrines. Natural evolution of religious ideas broadly based an primitive animistic doctrine cannot be invalidated. This doctrine embodies, the very essence of spiritualistic and metaphysical philosophy. It can be positively asserted that in ancient times there was some sort of unbroken continuity in the growth of the philosophy of natural religion. However, it can't be denied that the commingling of various races led to the fusion of Âryan and non-Âryan elements, which greatly shaped the foundation of the religio-cultural traditions of India. The distinction between the various levels of popular belief and that of elaborate ritual technique, and philosophical speculation of both the Âryans and non-Âryans can very well be marked by many stages of transition, modification and variation in the patterns of co-existence.

In the lower level of civilization the objects worshipped by the Kirâta tribes may be arranged in the following five categories: (*i*) Parts of nature, great or small ; (*ii*) Spirits of ancestors and other bodies; (*iii*) Objects supposed to be haunted by spirit, i.e. Fetish worship; (*iv*) Supreme Being and (*v*) a Principal deity to whom the minor deities were subordinated (the system based more or less on monotheistic belief). It appears that the idea of oneness of god existed among all the ancient nations. Yâska's remarks as recorded in his *Nirvkta* (7-4) that "all Gods are but the limbs of one Supreme Soul" finds the clear reflection in the traditional reigio-cultural system of the aboriginals of India.

While dealing with aspect of the subject, it necessarily needs to discuss the general character of Kirâta pantheism based on traditional and popular religious faiths. With reference to the religious beliefs of the Kirâta tribes of northeast India it can be categorically stated that the Khasis and Syntengs (Jaintias) believed in the existence of the Supreme Being (the creator of the world) and in the propitiation of good spirits of ancestors (resembling to Shamanism), the God of the state, the God of water, the God of wealth (snake worship), inferior spirits residing on hills or in rocky dales or in groves, tutelary deities of the village and other minor deities or evil spirits. The general practice, which they followed relating to another worship, was the erection of memorial stones. They were the followers of purely animistic religion in the beginning.[183] The Garos also believed in the Supreme God known as Saljung, who has been compared by Mr. Elliot with Mahadeva, but we do not find any affinity between Saljung and Úiva, usually called by the Brâhmans as Mahâdeva. The heavenly bodies, sun, moon and stars and spirits, who presided over hills, woods and rivers were considered to be agents employed by Saljung (residing in the heaven) to manage the affairs of the world. They also believed in the spirits of the hills, rivers and forests, and other evil spirits.[184] This statement has been further corroborated both by L.A. Waddell[185] and Montgovcry Martin.[186] Like the Khâsis and Syntengs they also believed in ancestor worship. The Dimasa Kacharis were also animists. Their beliefs regarding the earth, heaven, creation and hell are more or less identical with those of Gâros. Every village and every clan had its own deity. They believed in the existence of both Supreme God and minor or subordinate gods. It is said that *Sibrai* was worshipped as the common god by all of them.[187] It can be further added that the malignant demons of the hills, streams and lakes, as well as, malicious spirits, which used to infest the houses were worshipped by them much more frequently than the great good spirit, but without any palatable offerings and rejoicing.

The Kirâta tribes of present Tripura, popularly known as the Tipras, also believed in both beneficent and malignant spirits. They had firm faith in the existence of Supreme Being and in the worship of various elements and objects of nature e.g. trees, stones, animals, etc. They used to worship various gods and goddesses including "the God of water, the God of' fire, the God of forests, the Earth Goddess", etc.[188] The royal chronicle[189] of Tripura furnishes the detailed list of the original Tipra names of the various gods and goddesses worshipped by them. They are as follows :

(*i*) "Matai—Katar-Tipra Matai—'God' Katar-'Great, Supreme.' The Deity of the Tipras who has been identified with Úiva Mahâdeva".

(*ii*) and (*iii*) "Lam-Pra-twin deities, Sky and Sea (Khabdhi-Khab and Abdhi in Sanskrit-or, rather Earth and Sea Ksma and Abdhi: Pra means the Sea)".

(*iv*) "San-grama or the Himalaya Mountains. Lam-Pra and San-grama are looked upon as most potent or living deities".

(*v*) "Tui-ma or Ganga (the Ganges) especially worshipped in the month of Agrahayana and generally at all other times. The priest of Tui-ma declare the cause of illness after consulting the deity while performing worship in her honour. (Tui-ma='Water Mother')."

(*vi*) "Mailu-ma—The Goddess of Rice, identified with Sri or Laksmi".

(*vii*) "Khulu-ma—The Goddess of the Cotton plant".

(*viii*) "Burha-cha—The God who is worshipped especially to cure illness. Bengali='Old Child'(?)."

(*ix*) and (*x*) "Bani-rao and Thani-rao: Two brothers, sons of Burha-cha. (Bengali rao=Skt. rava, rava,'shout, roar"?

(*xi*) to (*xvii*) "The Seven Budiraka sisters. Six of them are married and the 7th is a Goddess who like the Goddess of Love in many mythologies, attracts men and grants them her favours. They are called Dakinis of Yoginis by the Hindus (or the Seven Pari or Fairy Sisters,, among Muslims of Tripura)."

(*xviii*) and (*xix*) "The two brothers Goraiya and Kalaiya (Bengali names—"the Fair one" and "the Dark one") who are worshipped on the last day of the Hindu year (Caitra Sankranti), when the Tipras drink much rice-beer in their honour for two or three days."

The pre-Hindu or pre-Âryan tribal religion of the Kirâtas (or so-called Indo-Mongoloid of Bodo group) of Hill-Tipperah was greatly modified by Hinduism after they come under the pervasive Hindu influence and inspiration. This modification led to the final transformation of the Kirâta pantheon (which mainly consists of a group of 14 gods and goddesses, chiefly based on superstition and mythological tradition) into the orthodox Hindu pantheon of the Puranic antiquity, probably as early as the thirteenth century A.D. Their fourteen gods[190] and goddesses identified with the major deities of the Brâhmnical pantheon are the following: (1) Hara or siva—the destroyer in Hindu trinity. (2) Umâ or Durgâ—the consort of Úiva, (3) Hari or Vishnu—the presérver in the Hindu trinity, (4) Ma or Lakshmi. the consort of Vishnu and the Goddess of prosperity, (5) Bâni or Sarasvati—the Goddess of learning, (6) Kumara or Kartikeya — the God of war and the commander-in-chief of the Gods, (7) Ganapa or Ganeúa—the God of wisdom, (8) Biddhu or Chandra—the moon, (9) Ka or Brahma—the creator in Hindu trinity, (10) Abdhi—the God of Ocean or water, (11) the River Ganges (Ganga)—the most sacred river of the Hindus, (12) Sekhi or Agni—the God of fire, (13) Kama—the God of love and (14) Himadri—the Himalaya mountain (sometimes the Earth Goddess is also included in the above list).

The following Sanskrit verses quoted by Kâli Pra-Sanna Sen[191] from the *Râjâ-Mâlikâ* and the Sanskrit *Râjâ-mâlâ* are of considerable value, so far as the identification of deities of Kirâta pantheon is concerned :

Haroma (=Haratuma), Hari-ma, Vani, Kumaro, Gana-pa, Vidhih:

Ksmabdhir, Ganga, Sikhi, 'Kamo, Himadrisca Caturdasa

(Râjâ-mâlikâ)

Úankaranic Úivaninca Murârim Kamalan tatha |

Bharatinca Kumâranca Ganesam Vedhasam tatha ||

Dharanim Jahnavim Devim Payodhim Madanam tatha |

Hutasan Ca Nagesan Ca Devatas tah Subhâvahah ||

(Sanskrit *Râjâ-mâtâ).*

The fourteen vertical lines on the reverse side of Ratna-Manikya's coin, dated Saka 1386 (which is a piece of numisatic and epigraphic evidence) stand as a glaring example of stylistic representation of the fourteen deities (the Caturdasa-devatas) of the Kirata people of Tripura.

It is believed that Lord Úiva, while promising Tripur's (one of the ancient kings) widowed Rani a son, stipulated that Úurya and Chandra or the Sun and the Moon, as well as, the Chaudevatas should be duly and regularly worshipped. According to royal chronicle, *Râja-Mâtâ* "these deities were installed by a legendary ruler of Tripura,—Râja Trilocana, who was supposed to be a contemporary of Yudhisthira of the *Mahabharata.*"

According to S.K. Chatterji, "this form of worship of the fourteen gods and goddesses is the outcome of the transformation of the religion of the Indo-Mongoloid people under Hindu inspiration, where the non-Brahman high priests, the Contais, ministered to the old pre-Hindu gods and retained the old rites and rituals, they gradually absorbed the important Brahmanical deities and their national pantheon was transformed into the Caturdaúa-devatas. Subsequently these fourteen deities have been identified with the Brâhmanical names, and thus the absorption of the tribal religion by Hinduism was complete. The use of the heads alone in lieu of full images is only something very unusual in the Hindu iconographic system . . . and this may have some connexion with a primitive cult of the Head which appears to have prevailed among Indo-Mongoloids and Austrics."[192] From the Assamese Tripura-Buranji it appears that before the installation of fourteen gods and goddesses, various birds and animals, e.g. buffaloes, methans or wild bisons, pigs, dogs, ducks, pigeons, goats, deers, etc. were sacrificed in non-Brahmanical way, but after coming into close contact with Brahman priests, their rites and rituals were also modified.

The Kirâtas' gods and goddesses identified with the Brahmanical deities have been compared with the 14 deities of Greek pantheon "as given on the pantheon frieze-Zeus, Hero, Iris, Ares, Demeter, Dionusos, Hermes, Athene, Hephaistos, Poseidon, Apollon, Artemis, Aphrodite, and Eros and the 12 chief deities of the Romans given in the Old Latin Saturnine verse-Juno Vesta Minerva Ceres Diana Venus Mars Mercu-rius Jovi Neptunus Volcanus Apollo."[193]

In common with other Kirâta tribes of North-east India the Nâgâs had also faith in natural objects, supernatural forces, ancestor worship, stone worship, etc. Their religion, which was basically animistic, seems to be a manifestation of worship of nature and propitiation of minor deities, benevolent and malevolent spirits, etc. They also believed in the existence of Supreme Being. They worshipped the stones by chanting the mantras or incantations. Some of them used to worship both the Sun and the Moon as good and evil spirits. Their religion was based on philosophy of worship of devils and, therefore, every spirit was propitiated by offerings of different objects.[194] They usually believed in more powerful and less malicious spirits in comparison to other. J.H. Hutton[195] refers to the fundamental unity in the diverse religious beliefs and practices of the Naga tribes.

The religious system followed by the two most ancient frontier Kirâta tribes (also known as North Assam tribes living in present Arunachal Pradesh), known as the Mishmis and the Akas, was chiefly based on animistic beliefs. The religion of the Mishmis was confined to the propitiation of demons for the sake of warding off illness and misfortune. They had no notion of Supreme Being and benevolent deity. They used to worship Mujeedagrah—a god of destruction (which resembles the Hindu God, Úiva or Mahadeva), Damipaoni—the god of knowledge and Tabla—the god of wealth.[196] The Akas also believed in the existence of various gods and evil spirits. Their three gods, Fuxu—the god of jungle, Firan— the god of war and Situ—the household god were propitiated by resorting to sacrifice.[197] Their religion consists of invocations to the malignant spirits for protection of human lives, cattle and crops. The religion of these Kirata tribes appears to be polydemonism. The different people propitiated the malevolent spirits, that caused sickness or death, in different ways. They called it the spirits of the earth, water and trees. But the underlying fear was the same, which bears a striking resemblance to the old belief that still exists under the veneer of Buddhism in Tibet. The propitiation to avert the anger of some demon was the keynote of their religion and these propitiatory rites played a prominent role in their lives. The influence of Tibet on them was naturally more apparent. They worshipped numerous malicious spirits residing in trees, forests, waters, mountains, etc.[198]

A careful investigation of the subject indicates that their religious mechanism predominantly resembles Rig-vedic religious system in respect of propitiation of various gods and evil spirits. The most important feature of their religious system is that the Mishmis like other frontier tribes believed in the Cult of *Donyi-Polo* (the Sun and the Moon respectively). This traditional faith goes back to remote antiquity. According to V. Elwin[199] *Doini-Pollo* (Sun-Moon God) was the supreme God and upholder of truth. This system shows the comparison with sophisticated religious practice of the civilized group.

The Kirâta religion in the initial stage was primarily based on superstitious beliefs and was connected with the practice of sorcery, exorcism and magic. It represents a synthesis of theism, animism, supernaturalism and polytheism. Most of the North-Eastern Kirâta tribes, unlike the aboriginals of Peninsular India evolved a religio-philosophical system, which bears a close resemblance to the Vedic religious system, the Mayan civilization of Mexico and polytheistic beliefs of the Chinese, Egyptians, Greeks and Romans.

The tree-worship, the worship of Earth-Goddess, the cult of Mother-Goddess and Candika Devi, snake worship, stone worship in the form of linga or the worship of the cult of phallus, the worship of memorial stones and magic witchcraft, etc. held very important place in the Kirata families in ancient India.[200] The aborigines or the mountain tribes of the country, who have not yet come into contact with Brahmans or other civilized Hindus do still rever an invisible supreme spirit, various other evil spirits, minor deities, etc.

The village gods and goddesses as of the Kirata tribes were held in high esteem and venerated at large scale even by the Brâhmanas in ancient times. The Brâhmanas openly participated in the ceremonies and festivals held in connection with the reverence of village goddesses including the Kirâtadevi. The *Grâmadevatâpratistha* mentions Kirâtadevi, Úabari, Yaksas Bhutas, Pretas, Piúacas, Rudra, the harassing followers of Úiva, demons, yoginis, various kinds of Úaktis made of wood, stone and clay and various other gods and goddesses as Gramadevatas, which signify the deities of the village. Bopadeva (a grammarian of 13th century and author of two books—*Mugdhabodha* and *Kavikalpadrumd)* also includes Kirâtas, Bhillas and others in the list of Grammadevatas.[201] The

Grâmadevata represents the principal national deity of the non-Âryan population (including the Kirâtas) of India. The *Âgamasmrtisâra* contains a sloka, which clearly assigns the Gramadevatas to thc Sudras.[202]

The Kirâta concept of Gramadevata, particularly the female deity was intimately connected with the veneration of evil spirits. Every village contained a shrine dedicated to Kirâtadevi (the female village deity of the Kirâta). She by her power used to protect her devotees from diseases, plagues and other calamities. As a result of mutual contacts of the Âryans and non-Âryans in the Vedic age both the pure Vedic doctrine and non-Âryans tenets underwent a significant change and the form, method and practice of worshipping the Grâmadevatâs (both village gods and goddesses) were greatly modified. The Gramadevatas were revered throughout the length and breadth of India not only by the non-Âryans but also by the Âryans.

The religions of the Kirâta tribes represent some surplus material not yet built into the temple of Hinduism. Mr. Lassen has stated that the native animism of the Kirâtas yielded imperfectly to Brâhmanism or Buddhist teaching and their neglect of religious rites caused the Brâhman Hindus to reduce them to the rank of Úûdras.[203] The credibility of this statement can't be put to doubt.

The religious history of the Kirâtas took a different turn in the proto-historic period, when they came under the influence of Âryans. It is very difficult to say as to when the process of Âryanisation of the Kirâta tribes started. However, we have some indications to show that this process started in the epic age and continued roughly upto the Gupta age. This ddes not necessarily mean that this age marked the termination of this process. This was a long continued process, so far, as transition from animism to Hinduism and the co-existence of both for the aboriginals of India are concerned. However, this fact cannot be set aside that between the epic age, and the Gupta age the religious beliefs of the Kirâta tribes were greatly modified because of the impact of Âryan culture on them. S.K. Chatterji is of the opinion that the Kirâtas started coming within the pale of Hinduism from the late Vedic period.[204] We don't have any concrete evidence to support this view. It is true that they were known to Vedic Âryans as it appears from the Vedic texts, about which we have already discussed. However, this does not mean that the process of their Âryanization had begun in the later Vedic age. Moreover, the Hinduism, worth the name had not taken its root in the soil of India during this age in the real sense of the term. The Vedic religion itself contained the elements of tribal culture.

Further, the worship of gods and goddesses by the Kirâta which subsequently occupied prominent place in the Brâhmanical pantheon is not a testimony of an impact of Brahmanical religion on their religious system, which they evolved in the begininng, but an instance of the originality and purity of their religious ideas, which they maintained as well as, of their contribution, which they made to evolution of Hindu religion and culture in ancient India. Hence, it will not be perfectly justified to say that right from the Vedic age they were being brought within the fold of Hinduism. What we propose to establish here is this that the process of their Hinduisation went on in an intermittent fashion. The Kirâtas of Assam, Bengal, Bihar, Orissa, Nepal, Vindhyas and Uttarakhanda were brought within the fold of Hindu religion and culture by the end of the 7th century A.D., whereas the Kirâtas of the Deccan accepted Hinduism later. On the whole, bulk of the Kirata population were absorbed within the fold of Hinduism by the first millennium A.D. It is because of the expanding and absorbing power of the Brahmanical Hinduism that the original elements of the Kirata religion and culture haye been pushed into the background. But the fact remains that many of the Hindu gods and goddesses were originally worshipped by them. Their religious systems were, of course, moulded to a greater extent after coming within the fold of Hinduism. And so is the case with the religious system of the Hindus. That is why, we find a synthesis of both Âryan and non-Âryan elements in the religious system of India. Both the Âryans and non-Âryans influenced each other in the spheres of religion and philosophy. There are manifold stages in the evolution of the religious system of both. What it concerns us most is that both their indigenous system as well as what they accepted after coming under the influence of Âryans, and that of the followers of Brâhmanical Hinduism, flourished side by side. We notice striking similarities in the mode and method of worship and the nature of deities of the Kirâta tribes and those of Âryans, who came in touch with them.

Indian tradition ascribes the origin of an institution of Brahmanism to non-Âryans. This finds confirmation in the statement of Mr. Pargiter: "Brâhmanism then originally was not an Aila or Âryan institution. The earliest Brâhmanas were connected with non-Aryan peoples, and were established among them when the Ailas entered,"[205] He was unequivocally referred to "the brahman Kirata...of the rude Kirâta folk."[206] The Kirâtas along with Yavanas, Cinas, Gândhâras, Barbaras, Sakas. Tusâras, Sabaras, Pahlavas, Pulindas and others (altogether eighteen designated as Dasyus, were Âryanised during the epic age. This Âryanisation led to their conversion to Hinduism, Mandhâtâ asked Indra as to how shall these Dasyus (as noted above) follow their religion ? and how shall they be initiated to a new religion?[207] While responding to these two questions as put by Mahdhâtâ, Indra provided, detailed information about their religious duties. The statement furnished by him shows that they were indoctrinated regarding their duties and obligations. All Dasyus were asked to pay regards to their elders, preceptors, sages and saints, and to follow the Vedic religion. They were also instructed to follow a new code of conduct. They were taught to speak the truth, to follow the principle of Ahimsa or non-violence and to adopt the religious doctrines postulated by the Brâhmans in the past. As a result of this development the Kirâtas and so-called other Dasyus became the followers of Brâhmanical religion explained to them, as it appears from the epic literature.[208] This literary evidence can be further corroborated by the statement of Vasudeva Sharana Agrawala. He also holds that many indigenous and foreign races, who had settled in India before the dawn of Gupta age had neither accepted the Indian social system nor the prevailing religion and culture. Hence they were persuaded to follow the trend, which was slowly emerging in the arena of Brahmanical culture. The eighteen different Dasyus including the Kirâtas were not fully assimilated into the Âryan fold. Therefore, it was a question before the contemporary Indian rulers as to how to bring them within the fold of Âryandom. However, they gradually came under the influence of Âryan civilization and became the followers of Brahmanical religion and culture to a considerable extent.[209] .

The Kirantis, in spite of being subjected to the Brâhmanical priesthood, on the one side, and the more indulgent exhortations of Buddhist monks, on the other, strictly adhered to their primitive paganism. They had no name for God and no recognised order of priests. The priesthood system gradually developed among them. The office of the priest became hereditary. The Kiranti priest was called *Nakchong*. The Limbus believed in the existence of Supreme God. who was called *Sham-Mungh,* the God of the Universe, and worshipped other deities named *Mhang Mao, Takpaka, Hem-Sung-Mung,* etc. They did not build temples or make images of their gods but propitiate them by sacrifice of animals. The Kirantis believed in all kinds of sorcery, witchcraft, exorcism, etc.

Úaivism, Úaktism, Tantricism and Visnavism—the four important sects or forms of Hinduism also became popular amongst the Kiratas. It is very difficult to ascertain the exact period, which marked the emergence of Úaiva, Sakti and Tantric cults as popular religious cults in the Kirâta society. The origin, antiquity and evolution of Úiva and Sakti worship is, of course, a very controversial subject. However, on the basis of information contained in the literary texts and other collateral evidence it can be easily affirmed that a large section of the Kirâta population in ancient times had abiding faith in the worship of Úiva, Mother-goddess or Úakti and Devi, par-excellence and in the Tântric practices. Some of them came under the impact of Bhagavata cult too.

While making an attempt at systematic presentation of evolution of the above mentioned cults among the Kirâtas we beam with Úaiva cult. Úiva, generally conceived as a non-Arvan deity, secured a prominent place in the Kirâta pantheon. It is very difficult to determine the relevancy of the supposition that the history of Úaivism as the most ancient living faith in the world dates back to the Chalcolithic Age. However, it can be roughly asserted that Siva worship must have begun among the Kirâtas in the mountainous regions of the Himalayas in pre-Vedic times before the advent of the Âryans. That is why, Úiva (Kirâteúvara = the God of the Kirâtas) has been considered as ore-Âryan God. It is true that Úiva worship was the most popular form of religion in early times both amongst the aboriginal and the Âryanised people. But stating the fact more precisely and specifically it can be pointed out that in the pre-historic legendary period Úiva appears to have been the more popular God amongst the aboriginal people. Úaivism in some 'gross form was the prevailing religion of the aboriginal Kiratas. It is quite probable that they were under the protection of Úiva.

On the basis of an episode as described in the *Mahâbhârata,*[210] as well as, the *Kirâtârjunîyam*[211] of Bharavi the Kirata can be identified with Siva, and further it can be suggested that Siva was their popular deity. From the details as furnished in both the literary texts it transpires that the god Úiva in the disguise of the Kirâta followed by several others Kiratas and the mlecchas entered into a protracted battle with Arjuna in the northern Himalayas, which resulted in the victory of the former. This event is indicative of the dwelling of Úiva in the mountainous region and his worship by the Kirâtas. Romila Thapar,[212],while supporting this literary evidence, has also admitted that, in all likelihood, the Kirâtas were worshippers of Úiva.

The worship of Úiva-God of the Himalaya mountain by the non-Vedic Kirâtas can be proved in more than one ways. Some of the competent foreign scholars have also acknowledged the truth that Úiva was a patron god of aboriginals,[213] Megasthenes has also referred to two Indian deities under the names of Dionysus (identified with Úiva) and Herakles (identified with Krishna).[214] Different authorities, while trying to prove the validity of the identification of these two deities as mentioned by a classical scholar, have clearly stated that the former was worshipped as the highest god on the mountains and the latter was adored in the plains.[215] It thus seems probable that these two cults took shape about the 4th century B.C. At that time the worship of Úiva was also prevalent in northern India. Prof. Lassen, on the basis of observations made by Megasthenes, has inferred that Úiva worship was prevalent in the hill regions of India antecedent to the reign of Chandragupta. For sometime the Brâhmanas resisted this innovation and refused to extend their patronage both to Úiva and his worshippers, but it proved to be ineffective, because the popular current of non-Úryan worship of Úiva was very strong.[216] Here, as so often, exact chronology fails us in the early history of these sects, but it is clear that the practice of worshipping Siva might have begun considerably anterior to the Christian era, even though the Kirâta people did not call themselves Saivas.

Mrs. Speir, while dealing with Úiva's character and history on the authority of Kâlidâsa's work *Kumârasambhava,* Cantos I-IV, translated by Griffith under the title *The Birth of the war-God* has also confirmed the worship of lord Úiva on the hills.[217]

The most valuable confirmatory evidence, which can be adduced here is that Chandrapida, the sovereign prince of Ujjain, in course of his expedition against the Kirâtas and the kindred tribes inhabiting the vast tract of forest extending beyond Suvarnapura (their headquarter in the Himalayas lying at the northern extremity of Bhâratavarsa), as far as, the mountain Kâilasa (the abode of Úiva) in Tibet, saw both Úiva temple and a cave in its southern direction, as recorded by Banabhatta in his famous work, *Kâdambari.*[218] This is a definite indication of Úiva worship in the Kirâta region of the northern Himalayas. In all probability, it were they who first introduced the practice of worshipping Úiva, dwelling on the summit of the Kaliasa mountain. The concept of Siva worship undeniably, first flourished among the primitive tribes living in the hills and forests, the Vrâtyas, Nisâdas and other non-Âryans.[219]

All the available evidences indicate that in the centuries preceding the Christian era the Vedic or Brâhmanic religion was not the only form of worship and philosophy in India. There were some other popular deities and rites of the aboriginals, which the Brâhmanas were not originally associated with. Nor were they opposed to them, rather they countenanced them when it suited their interest. When some aboriginal divinities became important because of their popular character, which was reflected, and the prosperity of the tribe or locality with which they were connected, they were recognised by the Brâhmanas and admitted to their pantheon, perhaps as an incarnation of some personage more generally accepted as divine. The greater this trend grew up, the more brighter was the prospect for fusion and borrowing. What takes place in India today took place then. The name Úiva is euphemistic and it means propitious and, like Eumenides, is used as a deprecating and complimentary title for the god of terrors. It is not his earliest designation and does not occur as a proper name in the Rgveda, where he is known as Rudra, a word of disputed derivation, but probably meaning the roarer. The Rudra of the Vedic pantheon (as depicted in the *Yajur Veda* and *Atharva Veda)* is not Brahmanic he is not the god of priests and orderly ritual, but of wild people and places. But the main conceptions of which the character of the later Úiva is built existed in Vedic times. The Âryanised conquerors held this religion (Úaivism) in disdain and placed it under a ban. At the same time to secure easy recognition by aboriginal people they brought to prominence another cult—the cult of Mother-goddess worshipped in various manifestations as opposed to the cult of Siva worshipped more in the symbolic form (the phallic symbol) than in any other form. The phallic worship among the aboriginal tribesmen including the Kirâtas is really very striking. They used to worship Úiva in the form of phallus symbol or Linga, which found an indirect expression in the symbol of stone pillar erected in large numbers in the pre-Vedic period. In fact, the origin of concept of phallicism in the pre-historic period is greatly attributed to the Kirâta tribes. The instances cited of phallic worship among aboriginal Kirâta tribes are not particularly numerous or remarkable. Nevertheless, it can't be denied that such worship as prevalent in ancient India was not only confined to any particular place, rather it flourished in all parts of India even in Assam and Nepal. It was definitely a non-Âryan practice. The old theory, that it was borrowed from aboriginal, as well as Dravidian tribes, can't be totally discredited.

The outline of Úiva is found in Vedic writings and the later centuries posterior to Vedic age added new features to his cult, chief among which is the worship of a column known as the Linga, the emblem under which he is now most commonly adored. But it does not mean that the conception relating to Úiva and his worship in a phallic symbol was conspicuous by its absence among the Kirâta tribes in the pre-Vedic times. The only noticeable change, which took place is that it later distinctly emerged as a popular religious cult. The Vedas do not countenance this worship and it is not clear that it was even known to the Vedic Âryans. It is not certain whether the Úisnadeva, whom Indra is asked to destory in *Ṛgved*[220] were worshippers of the phallus. But it is generally admitted that the worshippers of Úisana or Linga as described in the said text were hostile to Vedic Âryans and a orthodox section of them disapproved of the phallic cult. This shows that it was originally an aboriginal cult and the Linga was worshipped as a deity by those pre-Âryan people. It is my firm belief that the worship of Âiva Linga (in the form of large size of stone considered to be the natural lingas of divine origin) was prevalent among the primitive tribes before the commencement of the Vedic period. It is first enjoined in the *Mahabharata* (Anusasana Parva) in which there are some passages, which show that Úiva was venerated under the emblem of the phallus. The tentative inference, which can be drawn here is this that it was accepted as part of Hinduism just about the time, when the present edition of the *Mahâbhârata* was compiled. The possibility of the adoption of the cult of phallus by the Âryans from their counterparts—non-Âryans can't be dismissed. The evidence suggests that this cult grew up among Brahmanical Hindus in the early centuries of our era. Actually, Linga worship found its strong exponents in the post-epic age. In spite of the fact, that the royal patronage was extended to the propagation of Mother-goddess cult, Úaivism continued to be the popular religion among the Kirâta people.

Some Kiratas living in the heart of Vindhya forest were also the devotees of Siva—the moon crested god. Actually they learnt the art of worshipping this god from Brahmans with whom they were closely associated. The religious transformation made them followers of Brahmanical Hinduism.[221] They started meditating upon one God, which suggests their faith in monotheism.

The worship of Úiva also became popular among the Kiratas of the eastern Himalayas, it is true that they received Brâhmanical culture quite belatedly, but those in the Nepal valley were under Brâhmanical influence from the very ancient times. The old text of the chronicle refer to Brâhmanas and their gods, rituals, etc. The Kirâtas worshipped Úaivite phallus, as well as, Vaisnavite deities. It is said that *Gopâla Vamúavali* with a

Saivite bias refers to the Kirâtas as votaries of lord Úiva who protected them by taking the shape of Kirata himself (Kirâteúvara).[222] Practically nothing is known about the religious beliefs of the Kirâtas of Nepal up to the second century A.D. But about the third century A.D. they are believed to have reached to a stage of highly developed culture. It is very difficult to say, as to what kind of culture flourished there at the time of advent of the Licchavis. But some indications are available about the co-existence of both Hinduism and Buddhism, whose stamp on the religious outlook of the Kirâtas of Nepal is found. The epigraphic evidence also testifies to the prevalence of Úaiva form of Hinduism among the Kirâtas of western Rajasthan. An inscription of Samvat 123: found in a Siva temple in an old city of Kirâdu (Kirâta) provides some clues to this effect.

The Raji Kirâtas of Ultarâkhanda were not only the worshippers of their local deities residing in a cave, but also of god Úiva. The trident or *trisul* of Úiva kept in front of their huts for warding off evil spirits shows their devotedness toward this god. Striking similarities have been noticed between their religious practices and that of the Hindus.[223] The popular tradition also confirms their beliefs in Úiva worship. Several legendary stories relating to Úiva-Parvati are still current among them, particularly, in the Kumaon region.

It is worthy of note that the concept of Úaivism and Úaktism flourished concurrently. The Sakti cult was intimately associated with the cult of Úiva. It will not be correct to regard Úaktism as a 'mere offshoot of Saivism,[224] though both are identified with each other. Úiva was usually worshipped as father god along with the mother-goddesses by the Kirâtas like all other pre-Úryan people of India. The cult of the mother goddess occupied an important place in the religious life of the Kirâtas people. The mother-goddess or Úakti was worshipped by them under various names—Devi, Pârvati, Umâ, Durgâ, Kâli, Cândika, Ambika, etc., represented in Indian mythology as consort of great god Úiva. Though the Úakti of Úiva is theoretically one yet she assumes many forms; sometimes many deities are combined into one and sometimes a sovereign is attended by a retinue of similar female spirits. The Durgâ and Pârvati have been rightly consisidered tribal deities originally worshipped by the mountaineers in the

Himalayan region. The name 'Kirâti' as mentioned in the *Harivaṁúa* (10, 248) has been taken as an epithet of Durgâ or Uma worshipped by host of Kiratas and others.[225] Many female deities were worshipped but the worship of a Mahadevi was widespread amongst the Saiva Kiratas.

The Úaktism identified with the active female principle (Prâkrti) of Sâmkhya philosophy or with the Mâyâ of Advaita philosophy, defined as energy and co-existent with Brâhmanas was manifested in one or other form of worship of Úakti or Úiva's spouse under various names in accordance with the rites prescribed in the Tantras. The *Tântrasaútra* accords the highest place to the adoration of the female divinities. The mother-goddess cult was not only popular but dominant cult in the Kirata society. The male god was given a subsidiary position in the Kirata pantheon. The pre-dominance of the female principles in all the primitive societies of the Neolithic Age proved to be a responsible factor for the popularity of worship of mother-goddess. In almost all Indian religious sects, particularly the Tantric sects of tribals, Hindus and Buddhists the Úakti concept was all-pervasive. The prevalence of Úakti worship was connected with the principles of creation, preservation and destruction.

Saktism is reckoned as the most remarkable religion among the principal sub-divisions of Hinduism. It is believed to be a revelation from Úiva himself, but considered historically, it appears to be compound of Hinduism with non-Úryan beliefs. It acquired great influence among the Kirâta people of North-Eastern India but without producing personalities of much eminence as teachers or writers.

An aboriginal goddess identified with a 'black' or fierce aspect of Siva's spouse, popularly known as Candi was worshipped by the Kirâtas. Sometimes this goddess is considered as identical with the wood goddess Basuli, worshipped in the jungles of Bengal and Orissa.[226] It is generally held that goddesses like Candike Devi, Kali, Bhairavi and Durgâ are not products of purely Hindu imagination, but represent earlier stages of amalgamation in which both Hindu and aboriginal ideas are compounded. The derivation of Úaktism from lower cults can't be doubted. Actually, the cult of Úakti personified as a female is far more primitive than other cults. The history of Indian religious thought supports the view that Hinduism incorporated certain ancient ideas originally conceived of by the aboriginals, but without purging them sufficiently to make them acceptable to the majority of Hindu scholars.

The earliest forms of the mother seem to be connected with mountains. The goddess *Umâ-Haimavati,* daughter of the Himavat or Himalayas and Parvati of the mountains were the objects of worship for the Kirâta tribes in ancient time. From an interesting passage of the Kena Upanisada (iii, 12.25 & iv. 1), it distinctly appears that *Uma-Haimavati* did not have any acquaintance with Brâhman and she was originally worshipped by the dwellers of the Himalayan region. Jacobi writes that she was apparently an independent female goddess of the mountain in the Himalayas, and was later identified Rudra's wife.[227]

Úiva's consort has many forms classified as white or beniguant and black or terrible. Uma belonged to the former class and Kâli, Durgâ, and Cândika to the latter. The Kirâtas used to worship Úiva's spouse mostly in the latter's form. Among many forms of the Úakti of Úiva we find the ten *Mahâvidyâs* or personifications of her supernatural knowledge; the Mâhâmatrs, Matrikas or the Great Mothers, allied to the aboriginal goddesses, the Nâyikâs or mistresses, and the Yoginis or sorceresses. But the most popular of her manifestations are Durgâ and Kâli who found adherents among the Kirata tribes in early times. The forces of nature are identified under separate personalities known as Divine Mother and old ideas are revived with fresh and more impure association. The ritual of the sect prescribing blood offerings and other abominable libidinous rites found in the Tântric treatises embodying cruder form of belief are old as *Atharva Veda.* Later it left its indelible mark on Buddhism.

The ancient Indian traditions testify to the evolution of the cult of mother-goddess on the principle of mother right in the matrilineal sciety of the Kirâta tribes. In the primitive Kirâta society the concept of paternity was indistinct, but in case of mother the ideas was clear. The women and her organs and attributes became the obejcts of propitiation since the beginning of Upper-Palaeolithic Age. Ever since then the followers of Sakti school started looking upon women as the symbol of goddess.

It is quite true that like the mother-goddesses of Sumerians Babylonians, Egyptians, Semites and that of Syria, Asia Minor, Greece and Italy (particularly, of Western Asia), the pre-Âryan cult of the Indian mother-goddess originated in the matriarchal form of society.[228]

The worship of the mother-goddess as the goddess of fertility, which symbolize the Earth-Goddess of Prithvi was widely prevalent among the Kirâta tribes in hoary past. The fertility cult or the cult of Earth or Bhumi occupied an important place in their village cults. The importance of sanctity and propitiation of Earth-Mother was realised after their settlements as agricultural communities in primitive age. The Earth was propitiated by them with sacrifices and magical rites.

The three forms of Sakti worship—ordinary form, fierce form associated with animal and human sacrifice and the sensual form—were widely prevalent among the Kirata tribe in ancient times. With the publication of Tantra literature about the 9th or 10th century A.D. the worship of female energy took a grosser form. The Sâktas became the adherents of Tantric rituals and the female organ became the direct object of worship.

Úiva and Úakti were worshipped not only in the human form but also in the symbolic form of the Linga and Yoni, the former representing procreation and virility (based on the conception of the god Siva as the father or procreator) and the latter (Pudendum Muliebre or the female organ of jreproduction or generation symbolizing motherhood) and fecundity or fertility. The Kirâtas were devoted to the worship of both the mother goddess and the phallus (Lingam). The seat of Úakti worship also became famous as a centre of Úiva worship. The place where the Devi or the Úakti was worshipped became known as the Sakta Pîthas or Pithasthânas and the Tantric Tirthas. According to a mythological story the association of the female organs with certain localities gave rise to beliefs regarding the mother-goddess.[229]

The Kirâtas of the Himalayan and Vindhyan regions used to worship their popular deity, the mother goddess or Devi in various manifestations. The worship of a goddess, identified with the mountain deity (conceived as a female), presiding ever the Vindhya hills, by the Kirâtas and other kindred tribes is well attested to, especially, in the Purânic and Tântric texts. In the *Vârâha Purâṇa* this female deity is addressed as Kirâtini, which implies Kirâta women[230] and the *Abhidhanacintamaniparisista* of Hemacandra Kirati is given as one of her names. In the Prakrta poem *Gaudavaho*[231] of Vakpati, a contemporary of Bhavabhuti, the goddess is addressed as Savari, meaning a Sabara women. The Tantra text also alludes to the worship of the goddess, called Úavara.[232] Actually, both the Savaras and Kiratas, living together in the Vindhya hills, were the devout worshippers of the mother-goddess. From the Harivamúa (a work of the 4th century A.D.) it appears that the mountain goddess, Vindhyavasini (the deity of the Vindhyan forest), also identified with Narayanî and Durga (all manifestations of Siva's consort) was commonly worshipped by the Savaras, Barbaras (savage Kirâtas) and Pulindas according to Tantric rites associated with sacrifice of animals, eating of meat and drinking of wine.[233] This can further be corroborated by the statements of Dandin and Bana made in their respective works.

Dandin has described the goddess Vindhyavâsini as the principal deity worshipped by the Kiratas and their associates and identified her with Durga as well as saviouress.[234] Bana, (the writer of the 7th century A.D.) has also adduced proof of the worship of Durgâ (Cândi or Câmundâ Devi) by the Kirâtas, Úabaras and other mleccha tribes of the Vindhyas. He has provided detailed description of temple of the goddess Durgâ and her propitiation associated with offering and sacrifice. The pedestal of the image of Durgâ found in the vicinity of the great Vindhya forest was of black stone with an iron buffalo in front of it bearing marks of red sandal paste made on it. While speaking of an architectural style of this temple he says that its door was made of tusks of wild elephants and was endowed with an iron-arch.[235] The worship of this goddess connected with the Kiratas-Sabara-Nisadâ culture became widely prevalent in the whole northern India, probably in post-Harsa period. It was not only the deity of the Kirâtas, that was an object of adoration, but even the Kirâtas themselves have been deified in Hindu literature.

The celebrated Úakta work entitled *Candi* incorporated in the *Mârkaṇḍeya Purâna* also bears evidence to the cult of the goddess Vindhyavâsini.[236] The *Kubjika Tantra* refers to the Vindhyan region (Vindhyagiri) as one of 42 Úakta Pithas—the resort of the celebrated non-Aryan mother goddess, Vindhyavasini,[237] whose temple new stands near Mirzapur (U.P.). Another Tantra text, *Prânatosani Tantra* includes Vindhyan cave with symbol of *Nitamba* or back in the list of 108 Pithas or holy places associated with the worship of mother-goddesses.[238] The *Tântrasara* identifies the goddess Vindhyavasini possibly, with 'Sulini' and associates it with the Pitha-centre of Úakti worship in the form of a limb, prista or back.[239] In the list of 51 Maha-Pithas (of greater importance) and 26 Upapithas (of lesser importance) enumerated in *Sivacarita* and analysed by N.N. Vasu in *Visvakoúa Vindhyaúekhara* has been associated with the limb Vamapadariguli and Devi Vindhyâvâsini. A sacred place known as Kiritakena has been connected with an organ Kirita and Devi Bhuvane's.[240] Vindhya region also figures in the list of 51 Sakta Pithas given in *Jñânarnava Tantra,* in the manuscript of *Tântracudamani*[241] and in Brahmananda's *Sâktânanda-tarangini*[242] The Gaudavaho[243] identifies Vindhyavasinî with Kâli and Parvatî worshipped by the Vindhya tribes, Úabanis, Barbaras (Kirâtas) and Pulindas and associates her with human sacrifice, wine, flesh, etc. Jacobi has also observed that "A similar mountain-goddess had her home in the Vindhyas ; she was of cruel character, as might be expected from a goddess of the savage tribes living in those hills. Her name is Vindhyavasinî and she too is identified with Siva's wife."[244] This refers to the propitiation of the goddess Durgâ (Vindhyeúvarl), residing on the Vindhya mountains by the Kirâtas and other hill tribes. The above statement can also be supported by other evidence.[245]

The primitive form of Durgâ is the result of syncretism of a mountain-goddess worshipped by the dwellers of the Himalayas and the Vindhyas. This goddess was worshipped by the Kirâta as a war-goddess. "As her votaries advanced in civilisation the primitive war-goddess was transformed into the personification of the all destroying time (Kâli), the vegetation spirit into the primordial energy (Âdya Úakti) and the saviouress from Samsara (cycle of rebirths) and gradually brought into line with the Brâhmanic mythology and philosophy."[246]

The antiquity of the worship of the goddess Vindhyavâsini can be traced back tentatively to pre-Harsa period and not to c. 730-53 A.D. as suggested by D.C. Sircar.[247] Because Harsa (A.D. 606-647) during his sojourn in the forest region of the Vindhyas witnessed with his own eyes the temples of Durga (variously known as Câmunda Devi, Cândi, Vindhyâvâsini) and transmitted everything to his court poet Banabhatta, who described them in his two noted works. *Kâdambari* and *Harṣacarita.* On the basis of the details furnished in the contemporary literature it can be suggested that the worship of this goddess among the Vindhya Kirâtas must have been in vogue from very ancient times which was brought to focus in the 7th century A.D. during the time of Harsa. It does not mean that the practice of worshipping the mountain-goddess was never before there. Moreover, the pre-Vedic antiquity of the mother-goddess cult, which first flourished among the t mountain tribes is now a proven fact.

The Devi, having the largest number of votaries among the Kirâtas and the kindred tribes in ancient times, was popularly known as Cândika, another manifestation of Úiva's consort Durga in the fierce form. This can be confirmed both by literary evidence and epigraphical records. The description provided in detail in the *Devi Mâhatmya* (an important work on the mothor-goddess cult, assigned to the seventh century A.D.) proves an independent origin of the goddess Cândika or Durgâ in an eastern region.[248] She is an embodiment of the energy of the gods and represents the female principle of universe.

The origin of Cândika or Durgâ, worshipped by the Kirâtas, is said to be similar to that of Târâ Bhâgawati (or Târini-saviouress or deliveress, recognised by the Buddhists as the mother of all Buddhas and Bodhiúattvas and the consort of Avalokitesvara), the celebrated Buddhist goddess of Mahayana School, born in the Tibetan regions.[249]

The place of the origin of the goddess Caṇḍikâ being located more or less in the Kirânta-deúa gives definite indication of the truth that she was primarily a Kirâta deity. From the activities of a celebrated Buddhist theologian and a great propounder of Tantricism in Tibet and India known as Nagarjuna or Nagasena (contemporary of Indo-Greek ruler. Menander and Kusana ruler

Qaniska and hence placed sometimes between 2nd century B.C. and 2nd century A.D.), it has been suggested that he was chiefly instrumental in popularizing the worship of essentially the Kirâta deity Candika and the Buddhist goddess Târâ in India. The tradition also affirms the propitiation of the Câandika Devi by himself.[250] It is generally accepted that the Tântric mode of worship introduced from Tibet either in the Second century A.D. or a little later reached its zenith of progress in the 6th and 7th centuries, when the cult of Târâ spread far, beyond the shores of India to the distant islands in the Southern Seas. We don't have any positive evidence to prove that prior to the age when Buddhist cult of Târâ was introduced from Tibet, there existed here Brâhman, cal counterpart Câandika or Durgâ among the deities of the Hiudus We have already seen that it was somewhere in the 6th century or so that the Kirâtas moved gradually from their eastern and northern homes towards the Aravali Hills and especially in the direction of the Vindhyan forests. We can only assume that consequent on their dispersion over the western and southern parts of Aryavarta, their deity too must have been popularized till she was admitted into the fold of the Hindu divinities and elevated to the status of a premier goddess. The Buddhist Târâ was only the precursor of the Brâhmanical Câandika or Durgâ both in respect of time an a homage. However, it is unworthy of any serious consideration.

Some of our suppositions may be questioned but it can be denied that the Câandika or Durgâ was intrinsically a Kirâta deity. The narratives of, particularly, Dandm clearly show that the Kirâtas used to worship Câandika, enshrined in a beautiful temple located in the Vindhyan region resorting to human sacrifice to ensure success of their wild deeds. The name given by him to the goddess Câandika or Durgâ (dweller in wilderness) in later passage is also Vindhyavâsini,[251] whose perpetual abode is in the Vindhya hills and who is fond of spirituous liquor, flesh and sacrificial victims. Etymologically Durgâ means one, who is approached with difficulty. Bânabhatta has described in detail the temple of goddess Candika, widely scattered over the Vindhyan regions.[252] We have every reason to believe that this Vindhyan deity had travelled as far as the Sahyas or the northern part of the western Ghats.

The epigraphical record dated A.D. 943 of the Pallava king Diliparasa testifies to the fact that the Kirâta kings of the Vindhyas were worshippers of Cândika Devi.[253] In addition to this there are some other inscriptional records[254] of the south, which help us to prove this fact to a substantial degree.

All the available evidence confirm our surmise that Cândida was the most favourite deity of the Kirâtas, who had permanently settled in the Vindhyan forests before the dawn of the 7th century A.D. The goddess Durga or Candi secured the place in the Hindu pantheon not before the dawn of early medieval period.

The worship of Úiva and Úakti in various forms by the Kirâta tribes of N.E. India in both pre-and post Naraka period can also be testified to by some of the trustworthy accounts as recorded in the Upa-Purâna, Tântras and other related sources. Úaivism and Úaktism were undoubtedly the most popular forms of religion among the Kirâtas tribes of this region in ancient times. The Úaiva-Úakti cult was originally practised by them quite independently and later under Brahmanic auspices. Again the three most esteemed scriptures the *Kâlikâ Purâna*, the *Yogini Tantra* and the *Mahânirvana Tantra* set the guidelines for the further practice of this cult.

Before the advent of Naraka the aboriginal Kirâtas of Pragjyotisa were basically the followers of Saiva cult. But at the same time the Úakti worship was prevalent among a considerable section of them. The mother-goddess or Devi Kâmâkhyâ manifested in the form of Yoni symbol and representing Úakti or procreative force of the female was an object of veneration for those Kiratas, who were the devotees of the creed. It is traditionally believed that the genital organ of *Sati* fell on Kamagiri, i.e. the Nilachal hill near Gauhati, and ever since then this place has been held sacred to Kamakhya, the goddess of sexual desire. It seems quite probable that at initial stage the Kirâtas might be worshipping her organ of generation in a small shrine (situated on the top of this mountain), which was the genesis of the temple constructed later during the time of Naraka and dedicated to the goddess Kâmakhyâ. This holy shrine containing the said organ became the sacred spot for the Kirâta tribes. In course of time it became famous as one of 51 Úakta Pithas. It can scarcely be denied that it were they, who initiated the worship of Úakti in this form. That was the stage when there was no temple, no Brahman priest and Tantra text. It was Naraka, who after having conquered Prâgjyotiúa and its original inhabitants, the Kirâtas brought to prominence the aboriginal cult— the cult of mother-goddess worshipped in the Yoni symbol as opposed to the cult of Úiva worshipped in the phallic symbol. No wonder, the Kâmâkhya was an embodiment of the fusion of both Âryan and non-Âryan beliefs and practices. The Kirâtas continued to worship the mother-goddess Kâmâkhyâ till they were driven away by Naraka from the plains to hills. However the remaining section of the Kirâta population who had settled in the Pragjyotisa after enjoying his grace continued to adhere themselves to this sect. That is why, the origin of the mother-goddess cult is generally ascribed to the Kirâtas. In the post-Naraka period the goddess was worshipped both according to old Kirâta custom and Purânic rites.

It is accepted that, Úaivism in some gross form mixed with varied forms of Tantric rituals was the prevailing religion of the Kirâtas of ancient Assam. The mother cult of Kâmâkhyâ originally belonged to certain matriarchal tribes like the Khâsis and the Gâros. Besides, many other rough tribesmen also followed this cult. Later, in order to win over them for getting their support and allegiance as well as to propagate the Âryan ideas and customs royal patronage was extended to the local cult of Kâmâkhyâ.[255]

The evolution of the conception of the pre-Âryan cult of the Indian mother goddess, like that of the mother goddess of Western Asia in a female dominated society has been widely acknowledged. The worship of the mother-goddess by the two matriarchal tribes of N.E. namely, the Khâsis and the Gâros has been specifically emphasised by others. The interesting parallelism between the ancient socio-religious system of the Khâsis and that of Western Asia and Egypt has also been pointed out.[256]

The association of Kâmâkhyâ with the Kirâta tribe, the Khâsis (the so-called Austric), can be further confirmed by the linguistic data. The name of the goddess Kâmâkhyâ is traced to

Austric word *Kamei-Kha* (Kamoi=demon, Kamoit=Devi, etc. in Khâsi). After the process of Sanskritisation began, it was called Kâmâkhyâ by the Hindus.[257] Further, the Bodos (the Gâros, the Kacharis, the Hill-Tipperahas and the Chutiyas) are said to have installed the phallic emblem of their worship near the Austric *Kâmeikhâ*. This emblem was given the name of *Umei-Ludai-Fia* (Mei-Mother, Ludia=Male genital organ and Fia=pha=God) by the Austrics. The name *Umâluda* underwent transformation and consequently became *Umânuda* which is now known as *Umânanda* (representing Úiva-Lingam and traditionally believed to be the consort of Kâmâkhyâ), situated on the Bhasmachal hill—a small island in the bed of the river Bhrahmaputra north of Gauhati. The Úiva-Lingam on this hill is still an object of worship). The Bodos called the Austric *Kâmeikhâ* (representing the genital organ of mother Earth) *Kâmei-Fria* (Fiar=female God).[258] This evidence suggests the amalgam of Úaiva Úakti principles in the religious beliefs of the ancient Kirâtas. The holy shrine of *"Kâmâikhâ"* was particularly associated with two "Austric" tribes, the Khâsis and Syntengs (Jaintias).

The evidence as recorded in the *Yogini Tântra* irrefutably proves that the religion of the Yogini Pitha (i.e. Kâmâkhyâ) was purely of Kirâta origin (Siddhesi Yogini Pithe dharmah Kairâtajahmataḥ").[259] This finds support in other source also.[260]

The *Kubjikâ Tantra,*[261] the *Kularnavâ Tantra,*[262] the *Brhan-Nilatantra* (Patala-VI), the (*Rudrayâmala Tantra*, the *Jñânanaua Tântra* the *Tantracúdamani* (pp. 515-16), the Brahmananda's *Úaktânandatarangini* (ch. 15), *Hevajra Tantra* and the *Úadhanamâlâ* of the Buddhist, and *Mahapîthanirupana* the *Sivacarita,*[263] the *Kâlikâ Purâna,*[264] the *Matsyapurana,*[265] *Devi Bhagavata,*[266] and the *Mahâbhârata*[267] attest to the importance of Kamarûpa and Kâmâkhyâ as one of the premier Úakta Pithas (whose number varies from 7 to 108) and to the worship of Devi Kâmâkhyâ in the Yoni symbol. The celebrated Kâmâkhyâ temple hallowed by its association with Yoni symbol attained popularity as a centre of Tântric culture. The prevalence of Úakti worship in ancient times in accordance with Tântric practices has been copiously dealt with in different Tântric texts.

In one of the faithful records it is clearly mentioned that the Kâmâkhyâ temple of Úakti (Úiva's consort) situated in the heart of Pragjyotisa was very famous in ancient times and it was a great centre of bloody or sensual form of worship as inculcated in the Tantras.[268]

Since time immemorial the Kâmâkhyâ or Kâmâksa on a hill standing on the banks of the Brahmaputra has been considered as a chief sanctuary of Úaktism. Several shrines on the hill dedicated to various forms of the Úakti have been found. In the depths of the shrine a cleft in the rock representing an image of the goddess is still adored as the Yoni of Úakti. The Kirâta's method of performing the worship of Úakti formed no part of the Âryan religion in the contemporary situation It is remarkable that this barbarous and immoral worship though looked at askance was by no means confined to them. The Kirâta's Úaktism of the earliest stage should not be looked upon as a mere survival of barbaric practices. After all, their union with the female spirit for liberation of Mukti can't be denied.

As a proto-type of *Kâmeikhâ,* which was the holiest shrine of the Khâsis and the Jaintias, a shrine was established in the southern slope of the Jaintia Hills, which was named Griva-Kâmâkhyâ, representing the shoulder of the Supreme Mother. A massive Úiva-lingam was also installed near the rock, which was named Hatakeúwarat. Jayanta (ascribed to the 7th century A.D.), one oi the Jaintia kings established another Kâmâkhyâ on the South-eastern part of the kingdom and named it Bama-Jangha Pitha, which represented a shrine containing the stone emblem of the left thigh of the Supreme Mother.[269] This evidence supports the prevalence of both Saivism and Saktism among the Jaintias. Úiva was worshipped in the phallic symbol and Devi (a manifestation of Durga) in the left thigh symbol. The lower part of the left thigh is said to have fallen at Faljur in the Jaintia Pargana in Jaintiapur, the erstwhile capital of the Jaintia Kings. Here it is significant to note that the Jaintias were one of those Kirâta tribes, who at the time of dispersing in different groups from Prâgjyotisa (Gauhati) into hills after facing the defeat at the hand of Naraka carried away with them the cult of mother-goddess as a replica of their past life.

The Jayanti Devi also finds mention in th e Puranic, Tantric and other sectarian literature. The *Yogini Tantrâ* (1.11.67), the

Jñânarnavo Tântra, the *Tantrasara,* the *Mahâptthanirupan* and *Siva-carita* clearly associate this Devi (Jaintesvan) with the left thigh *('Vâmâjangha')* symbol. The native chronicle[270] also refers to the worship of Mahamaya Bhagavati Goddess Durga amongt the Jaintias. H. Yule[271] has clearly stated that side by side with gloomy Mahadeva (Siva) the worship of Kâli to a certain degree also spread into Khâsi-Hills and a spurious Hinduism was grafted on their original demon worship. It has also been observed that the so-called Austric tribes adopted to a large extent, the religious practices, customs and manners and language and scripts of the Âryans.[272]

Some of the Garos were devoted to the worship of Visnu.[273] According to the *Rgveda* Brahma, Visnu and Rudra or Siva are the different attributes of the same. Actually Sakti worship was common to both Saivas and Vaisnavas. Saktism was also associated with the principles of toleration and liberalism. The archaeological evidence (the terracotta fragments belonging to the 5th—12th century)[274] also bears evidence to the Garos' worship of Úivalingam in early times.

Úaiva, Úakta and Vaisnava forms of Hinduism also flourished among the Kirata tribes of North-Cachar Hills. On the basis of some reliable evidence it can be affirmed that the worship of Phallic symbol of Úiva was widely prevalent among them in ancient times. The rock-cave temple of Hara-Parvati on the Bhubaneswar Hill originally constructed by the Tipperah kings and the Visnu temple at Chao-Bung (Subang) near Vikrampur originally constructed about the 7th century A.D. were sacred places for them. The worship of Úakti in various forms—Kâli, (identified with Ramcandi) and Durgâ and that of the image of Visnu were also very popular among them.[275]

Úaivism was the most prominent religion of the Kiratas of Tipperah hill (the hill region of the present Tripura). The worship of Úiva in the Tipperah hill was greatly associated with human sacrifice.[276] The association of Úiva with human sacrifice in the general way has been traced back to the days of the *Mahâbhârata.*[277] The worship of Úakti in the form of Umâ or Durgâ (consort ot Siva) Visnu and various other Hindu gods and goddesses by the Kirâta tribes of Tripura along with their tribal deities mark the notable features of their religious system. The list of Sakta Pithas enumerated in the *Mahapîthanirupana* and in *Úvacarita* also includes Tripura associated with the limb, Daksinapada of Tripuri Devi.

J.H. Hutton has clearly stated that both the Linga as a simple cone the Yoni as a triangular prism are somewhat though not realistically presented by the Angami Nâgâs of Kohima and the pre-historic monoliths of Dimapur. But his view, that the Phallic worship is connected with that of Khmer of Java and of Japan,[278] is not based on any valid logic.

The archaeological discoveries also prove the existence of crude form of Úaivism among the Kirâta tribes of North-East frontier region (present Arunachal Pradesh) before the emergence of the Mother-cult. The Âkas (tribal group) were ardent devotees of Lord Úiva. The discovery of various Sivi-lingam (Phallic stone) and sculptured images of Hindu Pantheon like Daúabhuja Durgâ, bull—nandi (the vehicle of Siva), etc. in the archaeological explorations carried out in the late sixties and the early seventies of the present century conclusively proves the prevalence of both Úaivism and the cult of Mother-goddess, in this region. By the middle of the 7th century A.D. The Kiratas of this region were completely brought within the orbit of Hinduism. The Úkas, the Mishmis and the Chutiyas came under the influence of Brahmanical philosophy of Hinduism.

The worship of mother-goddess become widely prevalent among some of the primitive tribes of ancient Assam in the early medieval period. The Kirâta tribe who brought the goddess to awful prominence was known as the Chutiyas, who were reigning at Sadhayapuri (the old name of Sadiya region) at the beginning of the 13th century. Their most favourite deity *Kesai-Khati* (the eater of raw flesh), popularly known as Tâmresvari Devi (the goddess of copper temple), was identified with Kali who was worshipped in its most dreadful form in accordance with the Tantric rites. It is said that in this copper temple (which contained the goddess, known as Tâmreúvari Devi) human sacrifices were annually offered by the Chutiya priest, which continued for several centuries.[279] The rites of these deities were originally performed by tribal priests, but as Hindu influence spread the Brahmans gradually took charge of them without modifying their essential character.

The Tâmreúvari temple as well as the Phallic symbol of Siva installed near by the Paraúuramakunda were in centres of worship for not only the Idu Mishmi Kirâta tribes, but all the hill-tribes of that region in early medieval times. The epigraphic evidence also proves the existence of this temple. The Tâmreúvari temple or Dikkaravasim temple inscription of prince Muktadharmanaray an a dated Saka (1364=A.D. 1442)[280] constitutes the monumental evidence to the fusion of Sakti-cult of non-Âryan origin and mother-goddess concept of the Hindus.

After Saivism and Úaktism mixed with varied forms of Tantric rituals attained great popularity, Tantricism developed in full form among some Kirâta tribes of North-Eastern India. It represents a system of magical or sacramental ritual, which professes to attain the highest aims of religion by such methods as spells, magic, sorcery, witchcraft, exorcism etc. It also signifies a happy blending of monism, unitarianism, syntheticism and universalism. It emphasises absolute self-surrender to the will of Úakti or Mâhâmayâ for the liberation and enjoyment of the divine bliss. Theoretically it appears to be the development of the Vedic Karmakânda, but practically it differs from the Vedic sacrifices in method rather than principles. It is very difficult to accept the view that Úaktism is the Vedic Hinduism as modified by the Shamanistic tendencies of the non-Âryan converts. After c. 630 A.D. it was infected with Buddhism. Many Tantras present it in a refined form of Saktism and modified form of Âaivism in conformity with ordinary Hindu usage. But other features indubitably connect it with aboriginal cults. It has been suggested by some scholars that both Tantricism and the ghastly rites of the Kâpâlikas originated from Saivism and the Vedic Âryans in India found a crude form of Saivism associated perhaps with human sacrifice. Subsequently the Tantric form of Hindu religion got intermixed with the Vajrayana cult of Buddhism. The adherents of this sect base their observance on the Tântra ceremonies, incantations, etc. Various goddesses like Durgâ, Kâli, Cândika, etc. were worshipped by the Kirâtas in their shrines according to Tantric practices. This cult remained dominant till it received a check from the followers of Vaisnava cult.

The growth of both Úâkta and Tântric forms of Hinduism extensively associated with magic, witchcraft, sorcery, animal and human sacrifices, occult practices, esoteric beliefs and practices, etc. the ancient times in the North-Eastern part of India has been recorded in a very valuable source.[281] In the Tamreúvari temple human sacrifices were performed at the altar of the goddess by the Chutiya priest in accordance with Tantric rituals. The temple priests were the Idu Mishmis. In the words of L.W. Shakespear "Tamasari Mai was dedicated to KamakhyS and the Yoni but Úiva and Linga were also worshipped with barbarous rites and human sacrifice."[282] The worship of various form of Kâli by the tribal priests of the Chutiyas and that of the Jayanti Devi with ghastly system of human sacrifice as laid down in the *Kâlikâ Parâna* have been frequently mentioned in some reliable sources.[283] The Tântric cult spread among the Synteng or Jaintia tribes at a much wider scale. Jayantia has been mentioned in the *Yogini Tantra* as one of the sacred places to the Devi. In Hill-Tipperah also the Tautric rites of sacrifice were performed by the Kirâtas. Besides, the temples dedicated to Úakti some other temple of Úiva were also in existence in the N.E. region where animal sacrifices were performed according to the tribal customs. The worship of Tâmreúvari of the Chutiyas, Jaintessvarî of the Jaintias, the Ranacandi and Mahamaya of the Kacharis and that of the fourteen Devatas of the Tipperahs was associated with human sacrifice in early medieval times.[284] It is also believed that the Kirâtas used to offer sacrifices to their Grâma-Devatâs or village deity enshrined in the sacred grove particularly on an occasion when any exceptional calamity befell them. The purpose behind such practices was to propitiate the deity for the protection and welfare. These pre-Âryan beliefs have not yet completely died out. These are still practised by them on such occasions with exorcism and divination. However, the system of sacrifice as followed by them in remote past was undoubtedly a barbaric practice and voluptuous aspect of Hinduism. This barbarous and immoral worship may be glorious in their holy places from their points of view, but so far as the theology and metaphysics are concerned, any defensible argument will not be plausible. Stein's view, that the practice of human sacrifice was imported into India from Asia Minor by the Mediterraneans or their predecessors—the proto-Austroloids can very well be disputed.[285]

Since the Kirâtas as they figure in the Vedic texts *(Yajur-Veda* and *Atharva-Veda)* were known to the Vedic Âryans, it would not be unreasonable to suppose further that there was every likelihood of the Âryans speaking followers of the Vedie religion and the Kirâtas with their primitive religion influencing each other in certain aspects of their socio-religious life. The elaborate nature- of animal sacrifice of the later Vedic age and that of the Kirâtas of northern and eastern India including Nâgâs are somewhat similar. The Nâgâs' *Feasts of Merit* involving animal sacrifices bear some resemblance to that of the Aryans of later Vedic age.

Thus on the basis of all recorded evidences and popular traditions this can be proved beyond doubt that both Úaiva and Úakti cults were prevalent among the Kirâta tribes of N.E. India. The great controversy centres round the place where the cult of Úakti and Tântric form of Hinduism originated. However, this can be settled with the help of some authentic evidence adduced in this connection.

The birth place of Úaktism and Tantricism—the predominant forms of Hinduism—was North-Eastern India or Assam,, when there was no ancient Brahmanic settlements, and no ancient centres of Vedic learning and Puranic traditions. It is generally recognised that Assam has been the land of magic and incantation since time immemorial and particularly Kamakhya was the original centre of Tantric culture.[286] On the weight of evidence the views of N.L. Day, that Tantricism as an offshoot of Buddhism of Mâhâyana School developed about the ninth century under the Pala rulers of Magadha and it was the Buddhist University of Vikramasila (the centre of Tantric doctrines) from where Tantricism probably spread in Kâmarûpa[287] and that of Spooner, who has traced the origin of the conception of Sakti to a Persian (Magian),[288] can be disposed off. Further it is not reasonable to suggest that the mother cult arose in eastern Bengal and Assam about the 5th century A.D.,[289] because it has already been proved that this cult had become popular much before this date.

The strange inconsistencies of Saktism are of the kind which are characteristic of Hinduism as a whole, but the contrasts are more violent and the monstrosities more conspicuous than elsewhere; wild legends and metaphysics are inextricably mixed together, and the peace that passes all understanding is to be obtained by orgies and offerings of blood. In some aspects Úaktism is similar to the erotic Vaisnav sects but there is little real analogy in their ways of thinking. The essence of vaisnavism is passionate devotion and self-surrender to a deity and this idea is not prominent in the Tantras.

The Bhâgavata tradition in Vaisnavism, chiefly based on personal devotion or the cult of bhakti, which emerged in the early centuries A.D. also attracted the Kirâtas. Their acceptance of the Bhâgavata sect of Hinduism can be proved by the Puranic evidence. The chronology fails in tracing the early history of this sect. However, it was not before the 5th or 6th century A.D. that they came within the pale of Bhagavatism.

The description provided in *Úrimad Bhâgavata Mâhâpurânam* is a clear indication of the truth that the Kiratas along with other degraded Indian and foreign race, notably the Abhira, the Pulinda, the Khasa, the Hunas, the Yavanas, etc. became devotees of Visnu (an incarnation of Krisna) for their purification.[290] This shows the impact of the Bhagavata cult on them. Actually both Visnu and Siva are believed to have been the offspring of philosophic and poetic minds playing with a luxuriant popular mythology but the sectarian tendency is stronger in Vaisnaism than Úaivism. The doctrine of Bhakti common to both, is very much similar to that of Sânkhya and Vedânta.

Some Sanskrit inscriptions of Arakan supply valuable evidences as to Hinduisation of the Kirâta people of north Arakan (the eastern-most outpost of India) and Chittagong before the dawn of the 8th-century A.D.[291] As a result of influx of Brâhmanas and Ksatriyas from different prats of Bihar and Bengal into Arakan the earlier settlers—so-called Indo-Mongoloid population came under the impact of Brâhmânical and Buddhist culture during the early years of Christian era. The establishment of several Brâhmanical dynasties there, between the second and the tenth century A.D., facilitated the onward transmission of the Brâhmanical and Buddhist culture of India to the Kirâtas ot Brâhmadesa (Burma) and the adjacent areas.

Although the Kirâtas' faith in Jainism and Buddhism is very obscure aspect of ancient Indian History yet some available epigraphic, as well as, other reliable evidences, go to prove that some sections of the Kirâtas either embraced Jainism and Buddhism or came under their influence. To start with the subject chronologically Ashoka's inscriptions, probably issued between 257 and 256 B.C. can be mentioned. The 13th Major Rock Edict found simultaneously at Girnar in Kathiawar in the west, Kalsi near Dehradun, Yerragudi in the Kûrnool district and Mansehra near Abbotabad and Shahbazgarhi near Peshawar in the North-west clearly shows that Aúoka'in pursuance of his paternalistic policy instructed his officials to persuade all the Vanavasis (forest tribes) and other tribal peoples to accept the principles of Dhamma and to join the fold of Buddhism.[292] But it is not very clear as to what was the process of their conversion to this religion how far did they respond to such appeal and to what extent Aúoka got accomplished his mission. However, we have every reason to believe that there was some impact of the gospels of Buddhism as propagated by him on his tribal subjects. It is true that the name Kirâta nowhere distinctly figures in his inscriptions, but the names of some as the Pulinda (the cognate of the Kirâta) of the Vindhya hills (also the abode of the Kirâtas and Sabaras) is very much there. From this indication we can infer thac the Kirâtas who formed very important section of his Vanavasi subjects definitely might have come under the influence of Buddhist culture.

During the time of Aúoka, the Kirâtas of Nepal directly came under the influence of Buddhist culture. It is very interesting to note that they were brought within the fold of Sanskrit culture by both Brahman priests and Buddhist monks, whereas in Assam only by the Brâhman priests. That is why they «mbraced both Brâhmanism and Buddhism. According to the most reliable version of the Nepal *Vamsâvalî* they participated in the development of Brâhmanical and Buddhist culture. The Kirati period proved to be the first of the milestone in the long march towards the cultural progress in Nepal.

Both the *Vamúâvali* (composed in the 14th century) and *Svayambhu Purâna* (a Buddhist text composed in the 15th century) tradition confirm the visit of Maurya emperor Aúoka and his daughter Carumati to the valley of Nepal during the time of the contemporary fourteenth Kirâta king, Sthunka and the establishment of four Buddhist shrines in Lalitapuri (Patanyangala), the then capital of the Kirâta rulers. In the early medieval period this capital became the centre of Buddhist learning.[293] The Buddhist Chaityas existed side by side with the shrines dedicated to deities to Hindu pantheon. We find that the Kirâtas inhabiting the vast tracts, extending from Sikkim to Nepal represented by the Limbus, the Lepchas and the Bhotiyas by and large became Buddhist and the Parbatiyas remains followers of Brâhmanical culture. The acceptance of Buddhist religion brought about a new intellectual awakening among them in both social and religious fields. But it can't be denied that Hindu elements remained predominant in their religion. Actually their religion became singularly mixed with Hinduism with several castes and divisions.[294] In their worship they made frequent use of flowers and fruits as offerings and usually resorted to sacrifice of goats, buffaloes, cocks, etc. at their shrines. The blood was sprinkled on the shrines and the flesh was consumed by the worshippers. Formerly much barbarity was practised in the performance of these sacrifices.[295]

The traditional religious beliefs and practices and rites, rituals and ceremonies of the Kirâtas of Nepal and Sikkim bear the stamp of tribalism. The animism, shamanism, ancestor-worship, polytheistical and eschatological beliefs, the practice of warding off the malevolent spirits etc. which are purely tribal in origin, still co-exist with their new faiths whether Hinduism or Buddhism.

The Úunga-Úâtavâhana phase (second century B.C. to third century A.D.) is very important, so far as the history of Brahmanism, Jainism and Buddhism is concerned. It was a phase of cultural revival and synthesis. This period not only witnessed the revival of old Brâhmanical culture, but also the survivals of Jainism and Buddhism. The Úunga and Satavahana rulers were ardent followers of Brahmanical culture but on the other hand they were also tolerant towards the followers of Jaina and Buddhist culture. They extended their liberal patronge to Buddhist Bhiksus or Monks and provided adequate facilities for their maintenance. It was because of the catholicity of their outlook and benevolent attitude that some of the converts among the Kirâta tribes professed and practised their religions quite freely.

One of the stone railings of the Great Stupa of Sanchi of Úunga Period (185-73 B.C.) containing the expression="Chiratiya bhicchunodanam."[296] constitutes monumental evidence to the fact that some of the Kirâtas became Buddhist monks or Bhiksus during this period, received grants and cash endowments and enjoyed the patronage of the rulers. The Buddhist faith of the people of this age has been reflected through the stone sculpture. Actually the various scenes connected with the life and teachings of Buddha have been graphically depicted in the reliefs on the pillars, gateways and on the railings through panels of sculpture. The Sanchi Stupa was looked upon as a symbol of Buddha and his devotees were in the habit of paying visits to this place in order to pay their fervent devotion to it. The snub-nosed relief images of both Sanchi and Bharhut have been correctly identified with the "Kirâtas".[297] With the available evidence it can be deduced that a considerable section of the Kirâta population of Madhya Bharat came under the influence of Buddhist culture sometimes between second and first century B.C. and were patronised by their contemporary rulers.

The most important inscription from the point of view of chronology and history of Jainism is the Hâthiguphâ Cave Inscription of King Kharvela of Kalinga (contemporary of the Sungas) dated first century B.C. which was obtained from Udayagiri on the Kumari Hill located in Bhuvaneswar (Orissa)*. The word Kirâtas distinctly figures in the inscription which begins with an invocation of the Arhatas and the Riddhas in the Jaina style. It also proves that Jainism had spread in Orissa and probably became the state religion within hundered years of death of Mahâvira. Since the inscription is damiged, it is not possible to make full use of it. However, it is obvious that a large number of people including the Kirâtas came under the influence of the Jaina culture, during the time of this King who was a lover of peace, follower of law of piety and tolerant towards

* The present author had an opportunity to visit this cave on 29th December, 1977.

Jainas.[298] But we are not sure whether they were converted to Jainism or not.

The first two centuries of the Christian era appear to be glorious epoch in the history of Buddhism in Deccan. The Nagarjunakonda inscription of the Iksvaku king Virapurusadatta, (the successor of the Satavahana) dated 3rd century A.D. proves beyond doubt that the Kiratas, Cinas, Yavanas and other tribes were taken into the fold of Buddhism. From the inscription it is quite evident that the dedicated Buddhist teachers of the Theraveda Sect were gladdeners or converters of the Cina-Cilâta (—Kirâta), Yavana, Vanavasi (dwellers of forests), Tosali, and other tribes of different regions extending as far as Kashmir and Gândhâra. This is further strengthened by the fact that the Kirâtas alongwith other visitors used to attend regularly the religious discourses of the Arhats at Nagarjunakonda, which was the most important seat of Buddhist culture during the times of the Iksvakus.[299] There is also an evidence to show that during their times both Brahmanical, as well as, Buddhist religions were popular. But during the time of Iksvaku king, Virapurusadatta, Buddhism became more popular than Hinduism. The Mahayana form of Buddhism was largely followed by the people. The worship of the image of Buddha became popular among the followers of this sect. Among all the sects prevalent at Nâgârjunakonda Aparamaha-vanaseliya sect was the dominant. They promoted Buddhism by granting land and making donations to the monks and other adherents of this religion.[300] It is not at all clear that which sect of Buddhism the Kirâtas of Deccan belonged to, but there is no denying the fact that some of them embraced Buddhism during this period. The scene depicting Buddha's sermon at Nâgârjunakonda also shows the importance of the place in context of Buddhism.

The philosophical ideas of the Kirâtas were fundamentally based on the doctrines of Atmân or soul, law of Karma and of metempsychosis. One of the noteworthy features of their religious philosophy is their firm belief in the existence of other world wherein the spirits of the dead live. They believed in the existence of a spirit which after death spends sometime in another sphere before getting reincarnated. They believed in the transmigration of soul as a state of reward or punishment. Their eschatological beliefs were connected with the idea that the attainment of heaven or hell after death depends on the acts of piety or sin (law of to Karma) performed during the life on this earth. Their eschatological concepts exactly coincided with the Upanisadic doctrines, Buddhist philosophy, Koranic princal pies, Biblical precepts, Zoroastrianism and the ideas propounded by Dante in his *Divine Comedy.* These concepts of the Kirâtas of North-East differ fundamentally from that of prevailing in Middle India. But the characteristic features regarding the belief in a soul of the psyche—type appear to be the same. The moral basis of such philosophical conception was not fully developed among the primitive Indo-Âryans. In fact, the commingling of the Âryans, Dravidians, Austrics and the Kirâtas gave birth to a new conception, which was later incorporated in the religio-philosophical system of the Hindus.

The age-old practice of erecting the memorial or monumental stones by the Kirâta tribes of North-East India, which became popularly known as Megalithic monuments, constitutes the earliest example of their knowledge of art, inspired by the philosophical conception. These monuments, which were dedicated to the spirits of dead include the large upright stones or menhirs or vertical stones table stones or dolmens and stone cromlechs or cairns serving the purpose of ossuaries. After death bones were collected in earthen pot and eventually placed in common sepulchre of clan. The idea associated with the spirit of the dead was gratified by these stone memorial. This practice also denotes their belief in ancestor worsh'p. The upright menhirs and sitting stones have been interpreted in different ways. They also represent phallic memorials through which the soul-matter of the living or of the dead assists the fertilization of nature ; the upright stones also represent the male and the flat ones the female principles. The hallowed monoliths represent a specialised form of phallic ancestor—cult which was widely prevalent among the earlier Mongolians of south-east Asia.[301] All the remarkable, mysterious, solitary and clustered monuments and oblong; pillars of unknown origin not only excite the admiration of the antiquarians but also throw some light on the socio-religious history of the Kirâta tribes. Sir Mortimer Wheeler a celebrated archaeologist has rightly observed that...the Buddhists, Jains and Hindus imitated free-standing structures in cutting their cave temples and monasteries..."[302]

Their artistic talents also find expression in the sculpture, iconography, decorative arts and paintings. The Kirâtas' sculptural style and features in the hill-regions of North-East India are akin to the East India tradition. The primitive style of utilitarian-cum-religio-magical value in the form of wood works and stone works, the early medieval sculptural style in the form of human figures and other non-iconic figures and the Eastern School of art of Bihar, Bengal and Orissa in the form of wood carving, image work of varying degree, etc. can be noticed in their art. The pivot of their sculptural art is the traditional beliefs and religious practices. Sculpture of human forms including gods and goddesses, sculpture of animal forms, sculpture of geometric floral and symbolic designs and other sculptures found chiselled on stone slabs, rocks and terracotta plaques are worth-mentioning.

The carving on the monoliths of simple circle with petaliform pattern, the statue of an elephant carved out of solid rock and the rock carvings representing the sun and the moon and other emblems like images of warriors, animals and other animate and inanimate objects in the Khâsi-Jaintia Hills bear testimony to their artistic perfection in this branch of art.[303] The fantastically carved grotesque figures, ornamentations representing wooden images, animals, various kinds of fruits and vegetables on the post and beams of the houses in the Garo Hills constitute the most conspicuous example of the art, which flourished among the Gâro-tribe.[304] The stone and wood carvings of an exquisite beauty, found in Nâga Hills prove the acquaintance of the Nâga tribes with this art. In some parts of the Nâga Hills the front view of the houses were carved in slight relief representing various conventional designs, execution of life-size human figures, etc. The pillars of their Morungs were elaborately carved with human heads, horn-bills, tigers, elephants, some other natural objects, etc. They were no doubt skilful wood carvers.[305] The paramount glory of the sculptural art of the Naga tribes lies in the techniques, symbolism and variation based upon the adopted themes. The wood carvings of the Mishmis are one of the finest specimens of the sculptural art which flourished among the Kirâtas of the frontier region.

The art of making images was not very popular among them in ancient times. However, the images of three major cults—Saiva, Sakta and Vaisnava were mostly chiselled on rocks and stones. The Hindu shrines in the Jaintia Hills were adorned with images of Mahadeva, Durgâ, Kâli and Krsna. The archaeological record[306] also confirms the traditional evidence. Some terracotta pieces containing the figures of Úiva seated on bull, Ganeúa, Kârtikeya and other human figures belonging to the 11th—12th centuries A.D. have been found near Bhaitbari, which confirm the familiarity of the Garos with the art of iconography, which flourished in ancient times. The terracotta fragmentation bear close affinity with the late Pala and Sena arts.[307] In the Hill-Tipperah the life-size figure of some of the tutelary gods and goddesses like Úiva, Durga, Visnu, Lakshmi, Sarasvati, Ganesa and Brahma ascribed to the early centuries of the Christian era, were very much worshipped by the Kirata tribes.[308]

The worship of Candikâ Devi in an anthropomorphic form in the Vindhya Hills, the temples of Durgâ found in the vicinity of its forest and its door made of the tusks of wild elephants and the pedestal of the image of Durgâ, which was of black stones as described by Bânabhatta (already referred to) bear witness to the high degree of excellence, which the Kiratas of this region achieved in the realm of sculpture and iconography. The wood carvings of the Râji Kirâtas of Uttarakhanda also deserve mention here.

The intense passion for beauty and artistic work inspired the Kirata tribes of N.E. Uttarâkhanda and the Vindhyas to decorate and paint almost everything used in daily life. The houses and shrines were decorated with carvings and paintings of rough geometrical patterns as circles, squares and oblong lozenges. Their colourful designs and beautiful patterns are really of artistic value. The representation of different animals and designs on the Naga clothes indicates their emotional attachment to this art. They really excelled others in this branch of art. This art shows a tendency towards abstraction or geometrical forms. It is more or less an applied art in its origin and form. The art is akin to the art of primitive and unsophisticated peoples of the world. The basic beliefs behind this art is magical because of being connected with cults. This art was practised to redeem the primitive emotion of fear. There has been an unconscious tendency in this art to be utilitarian.

VI

LANGUAGE AND LITERATURE

1. The Historical Background of Evolution of Language and the Method of Learning

While carrying out a historical enquiry into the genesis and growth of Kirâta culture it has been felt necessary to make a thorough examination of structure and patterns of various languages or dialects, which they used in ancient times. In fact, the question relating to the origin of human speech still stands unsolved. Yaska in his *Nirukta* has described the language as a gift of the God. The language also affords a glimpse into the various grades of culture of the primitive tribes. An objective and dispassionate study of the various elements of which their spoken language is made up, is very essential. This we can do with the help of linguistic palaeontology, a science which not only unravels the origin of man but also traces the original character of its culture by making a comparative study of the meaning, force and application of words in its language. There are different stages in the evolution of the Kirati language. The original formation of language took place among the mankind in a primitive stage of culture that has survived to our day to some extent. Thus it constitutes one of the elements in the development of civilization of any human race. The civilization of the Kirâta people also finds some reflection in the mirror of changes that occurred in the field of the language at different periods of history.

The origin, antiquity, form and use of all archaic scripts Or alphabet in ancient India, is a very controversial subject. While dealing with the subject the oriental scholars as well as, script-historians have generated a lot of controversies. From the very beginning an attempt is being made to create an impression that before the 6th century B.C. or even in pre-Asokan period the Indians were ignorant of the art of writing so they borrowed it from different other foreign countries. Some of the noted scholars, who followed this line of enquiry during the 18th and 19th centuries were Sir William Jones, Wilford, Cope, Lapsius, Sterling, Burnouf, James Prinsep, Senart, Weber, Benfey, Sayee, Lessen, Burnell, Issac Taylor, Whitney and others. Most of them tried to prove that the Indian alphabet are more or less an imitation or adaptation of Cuneiform Assyrian inscriptions and alphabet of Greek, Phoenician, Aramaeon or Aramaic, Egyptian, Babylonion and Semitic origins. They have ignored the originality of Indian scripts.

But, on the other hand, Prof. J. Dowson, Cunningham, Prof. Wilson and Max Muller found that the system of writing prevalent in ancient times was an invention of India. This view got wide currency that there was hieroglyphic writing in India and Asoka's letters were fashioned in imitation of them. We also find concrete evidence of archaic script in our Sanskrit, Jaina and Buddhist texts. The *Nirukta* (philology) of Yaska, *Chondogya Upanisad, Taittimya Samhitâ,* the Brâhmanas—*Úatapatha* and *Gopatha,* Santi Parva of the *Mahâbhârata,* the Dharmaúâstras like the Smrtis of Manu, Yâjnavalkya, Narada and Brhaspati, the *Dharma* Sutras of Baudhâyana and Gautama, the Purânas—*Padma* and *Garuda,* Vararuci's *Kâvya Prakasa* and the works of two noted Grammarians like Pânini and Kâtyâyana—all irrefutably prove that from time immemorial India had its own system of writing. The Brâhmi was the earliest lipi or alphabet of the Deva Âryans and mother of all other scripts in Asia. George Buhler, the most outstanding among the scholars, already noted above, in his two famous works *Indian Brahma Alphabet* and *Indian Palaeography* has also dealt with this aspect of the subject. Different forms of speech were current among the Âryans and non-Âryans. Indra, Chandra and Mahesha were the three inventors of ancient Indian scripti. Out of all these three the Maheshwari script was very important. This can also be noticed in some of the historical writings of the early twenties of the last century. The researches of Shree L.S. Wakankar, a great lipikâr, carried out in the past have now conclusively proved the existence of pre-Aúokan Maheshwari inscribed writing of the Ganapati tradition or pre-Asokan Maheshwari Brâhmi writing in ancient India (vide *Some Doubtful Areas in the Chronology and Factual History of India,* Pub. by GARSI., Bombay, 1983, pp. 48-49). The decipherment of a pre-Asokan writing found engraved on a Babylonian Brahmi Tablet *(JBBRAS.,* N.S. Vol. 29, pt. I, pp. 62-65 cf.-*ibid)* also leaves no doubt about the existence of writing system in pre-Asokan period.

The Jaina Sûtra known as *Sama- Vâya Sûtra* and *Nandi-Sutra* deal with eighteen and thirty-six kinds of writings respectively. The Sixty-four kinds of writings enumerated in the Buddhist text *Lalitavistara* include the scripts of both the Âryans and non-Âryan Kirâtas, particularly the Nâgas and the Khâsyas. A fresh historical survey of the evolution of writing system of both the Âryans and non-Âryans in ancient India is very essential. The alphabet provides key to the history of mankind. There were 1,800 roots of Sanskrit in ancient times.

There is a general impression that the tribal people in ancient India had neither any dialect nor any system of writing of their own. But in the light of a few evidences, which have come to fore, this impression can be dispelled. No doubt, they had their own scripts and writing system, which in course of time passed into oblivion due to reasons unknown to us. This is supported by their folktales and traditions. The Kiratas extending from the Himalayas to the Vindhyas have age-long traditions of their ancient system of writing. Actually, they lost it exactly like that of the "ancient tribes of America, who were mercilessly wiped out and their scripts were deliberately destroyed by the ruthless invaders". Who knows the Indian tribes also might have met the same fate. However, this is a well-known fact that the British, in order to, introduce the Roman scripts among certain sections of the Kirata tribes (particularly of N.E. India) and to bring them within the pale of Christianity tried to belittle the importance of their historical traditions by creating an impression that they never had any script or system of writing in the remote past.

According to Wakankar the primitive tribes used Phemonics in the beginning but later their ideas were associated with simplified pictures as in Chinese system of writing. In the ideographic writing thousands of signs were used. *A Handbook of Asian Scripts* published by the British Museum in 1966 shows that the South East Asian scripts of Tibet and Burma, the script of Limbus of Sikkim, etc. are all derived from *Hiregana,* which symbolises the use of signs as in Sanskrit

The intermixture of different dialects and languages spoken by the Kirata people of the Himalayan and sub-Himalayan regions and the blending of one into the other renders it difficult to make an attempt at their classification. The absence of any specimen of their dialects and alphabet of unknown antiquity afforded an opportunity for scholars concerned to explain the things in a fantastic manner. Several theories have been propounded so far by the Indian and foreign linguists in this regard. It is necessary here to examine their credibility without any prejudice or pre-conceived notion. The lack of unity in their approaches to the problems and a general consensus among themselves create several problems in our way of dealing with the subject concerned in a historical outline. The linguistic analysis provided by them are not very satisfactory, nor does it reflect any historical basis. The philological records available at our disposal are so scanty and defective that it becomes difficult to present our view-points in a very convincing manner. However, we find wide scope for treating the subject following a different line of enquiry and making a fresh interpretation of the data, which have come to light. We can't remain contented by simply having a cursory glance at the subject-matter currently discussed. The historical analysis of the data obtained from the linguistic researches so far is very necessary. It helps us to lift the veil of mystery befalling the origin of the ancient system of writing.

The linguists or philologists have committed one common error that is to connect the language of a particular group of people with race and that is why their findings do not appear to be very much convincing. We have already proved that racially the Kirata people as a whole do not belong to only Mongoloid group likewise, linguistically, they do not fall within only one category of language i.e. Sino-Tibetan or Tibeto-Burman as supposed by many. Each section of the Ganas (mountaineers) including the Kirâtas were speaking some language or the other in ancient times before the evolution of Tibeto-Burman group of language. For the primitive people there was not only one but various sources of language. Their linguistic formations influenced by various factors and all of them cannot be blindly connected with the one group of language. The structure and forms of their languages further bear testimony to this truth. The traditional classification of their language like that of the race is not perfectly justified. The use of the terminologies i.e. Sino-Tibetan, Tibeto-Chinese, Tibeto-Burman, Austro-Asiatic etc.

like that of Indo-European are very confusing. The basis of such classification is not very rational. The evaluation of the linguistic data in this connection is also very necessary in order to judge the relevance of the use of all these terms. Actually, the Tibetan language is more akin to the Burmese than the Chinese. Thus, the combination Tibeto-Chinese is not correct. Moreover, the Himalayan tribes in India never spoke Chinese group of language. Only some section of the Kirâtas, particulary, those who migrated from Tibet and Burma adopted Tibeto-Burman group of language at later stage. We, therefore, don't find any justification to connect them with the Sino-Tibetan group of language. Moreover, all the Kirâtas have not come either from Tibet or from Burma. Many of them had independent group of language. Further, the Tibeto-Burman language comprises several dialects in an old form, which goes back to at least 7th century. It is absolutely unwarranted and unreasonable to suggest that the Tibeto-Burman language has got the common script or common origin. The scripts of their languages are greatly based on the scripts of the Âryan language because of the colonization of their lands by the Buddhists and expansion of their culture. The Tibetan script was itself derived from the Brâhmi and Gupta scripts of India, which is as early as A.D. 350. Similarly, Burmese language contain many words of Sanskrit and Pâli. Their languages still bear the stamp of Indian influences on their scripts, culture and religion. Wherever the Buddhist missionaries went to propagate their religion, they left their mark on the script of that country. The Kirâta tribes even placed under Tibeto-Burman groups assimilated variout Âryanised and semi-Aryanised words into their linguistic system as a result of their contacts with the Âryan population. This opens up a new vista of knowledge about their cultural and linguistic history. The progress made in the arena of linguistic researches, so far as this aspect is concerned, is not very satisfactory. This sub-group of so-called Tibeto-Chinese family in respect of assimilation exactly looks like Indo-European group of language, which includes Greek, Sanskrit, Avestan, Go thic and other ancient Germanic, Old Irish, etc. The similarity between Sanskrit and European languages was first emphasised by Philippo Sassetti, an Italian trader of the 16th century who had lived in Goa for five years (1583 to 1588). He discovered this similarity 200 years before Sir William Jones (1784). The next scholar was Benjamin Schults, a German, who harped on the same tune in 1725. Since then this similarity is being frequently quoted by every scholar. But the truth runs far from it. Recent anthropological discoveries have proved that the Âryan races in Europe and in Asia viz., the Teutons, the Celts, the Slavs, the Hellenes, the Persians and the Hindus are not all actually descended from the same stock although they speak languages derived from the same ancient tongue of which the Sanskrit language is the oldest. So race and language are not the same. No strenuous endeavour has ever been made to trace out the impact of Âryan form of speech or Sanskritized dialects on the non-Âryan forms of speech and *vice-versa.* The Austro-Asiatic group of languages does not embody all the scripts of Europe and Asia. Like the supporters of Indo-European group of language the protagonists of this group of language thought that like Âryans the Austric spread from Pacific Islands to India and spread Austric language. These are only the assumptions and nothing else. The Mon-Khmer group of language, which flourished in South-East Asia also contains lot of Sanskrit and Pâli words because of their contacts with the Âryans who disseminated their culture in this Zone. It is ridiculous that the speakers of the Non-Khmer group of language, notably the Khâsis (very important section of the Kirâtas in N.E.) have been connected with the Austric sometimes racially and sometimes linguistically. This does not appear to be a consistent approach from the point of view of looking at the problem from only one angle. In any case, the racial theory should not be made the sole basis of the linguistic analysis.

Our historical enquiry gives us the result, which is quite different from that of the accepted one. They represent the different groups of language. We have examined the issues involved in the present study in the light of the data obtained from the linguistic researches carried out very diligently in the recent past. Their language never remained static rather it had to undergo transformation from time to time. Various geographical and historical factors influenced the course of the evolution of their language. From all the available historical and other interspersed evidence we find that the natural barriers disintegrating the tribal society into innumerable groups and keeping them isolated from each other for centuries gave rise to countless dialects, whose quantification is an impossible task. The currents of acculturation and various assimilative forces, modified their scripts. For obtaining more accurate knowledge of their scripts we shall have to see as to what language did they speak before the formation of well-known Tibeto-Burman .group of language generally ascribed to all Himalayan tribes. It is for the experts of linguistics to make more detailed and useful inquiry into the subject concerned. It is neither desirable nor necessary to introduce the subject at any more length here. In the subsequent part of the discussion the controversial and unwanted elements have been deliberately discarded so that, history should not be guilty of either encroaching upon the privileges of the philologists and linguists or making forcible intrusion in their jurisdiction.

The Kirâtas (Pre-Aryan) had some form of speech or the other even during the pre-historic period for the purpose of communicating with each other among themselves as well as with their neighbours. They must be having some commonlink language as a medium of expression, otherwise, it would have been impossible for them to survive. That's why Mr. Buhler[309] and other German scholars[310] have referred to an archaic language of India, which was probably also spoken by some section of the Kirâtas in ancient times. Professor Gordon Childe has correctly remarked that "The primitive culture must be the stage of development reached by several peoples while living sufficiently close together to communicate".[311] Daniel Wright,[312] while speaking of the Kirata group of Nepal also observed that all races had different language or a dialect of their own.

It is very striking to note that the Kirâtas of Kurâ-Jângal area and the Gangetic Doab, as well as, of the North-Eastern region used to converse with the Pândava heroes and other civilized neighbours during the epic age. As already discussed, the Kirâtas of Dvaitbana, described as vanaichar in the Kirâtarjunîyam had to pass on the information to Yudhisthira, which they used to collect as an appointed messenger. Now the question follows, as to what was the medium of communication between the two? It is not possible to answer the question satisfactorily, unless and until it is presumed that they had acquired the technique of expression and their language was quite intelligible.

It is very difficult to assume as to what might have been the earliest form of their speech in ancient times. But as recorded in the Buddhist and Jaina literature it can be said with great amount of confidence that they used to speak mleccha languge, which can be amply substantiatede by other evidence too. From the Pâli, Sanskrit and Jaina sources it is quite evident that the Kirâtas of the Northern and North-Western frontier region (Uttarapatha) and some other parts of India were the speakers of the mlecha language.

Buddhaghosa (5th century A.D.) in his two famous Pali commentaries—one on *Digha Nikaya*[313] and the other on *Abhidhamma Pitaka*—[314] has recordd that the language of the Kirata fall in the category of *Milakkhânambhâsa*, the language spoken by all the mlecch as (Milakkhas). In the latter work he speaks of the eighteen *Milakkhabhasas* and includes in it the Kirata, Oddaka, Andhaka, Damila, Yavana, Okkala, and the like. He has classed the dialect of the Kirâtas with those of the Ottas (oddas), the Andhakas (the Andhras), the Damilas (Tamils)—the non- Âryan people of the Peninsula and the Yonakas (Greeks). The Jaina Canonical text, known as *Jambudvipa Prajnapatih* also—spilled as *Jambudiva Pannâtti*—a Upanga commentary by Âcârya Amitgati (first half of the 11th century) also refers to the mleccha language of the Kirâtas and others, which were thirteen in number.[315] Other Jaina texts[316] also mention the mlecchas (Milikkas) and Ariya (Ârya) as the two earliest people and refer to the mleccha language of the former. The said texts place the Varvaras (Barbaras), the Sarvaras {the Úabaras) and the Pulinda tribes under the denomination of Milakkhu and enjoin that the Buddhist monks and nuns should dissociate themselves with them.

B.C. Law[317] has not given by satisfactory explanation of this language as recorded in the Buddhist and Jaina texts. R.N. Saletore, has explained it in different way. He finds that this language of the Kirâtas must have been a peculiar one. It was characterised as the language of the 'Milakkhas' i.e. non-Âryans. While supporting the details as provided in the Pâli literature, he has also classed their language with the Ottas (Oddas),

Andhakas (Andajas?), Yonakas (the Greeks) and the Damilas (Tamilians).[318]

The *milikkha-bhasa* was not only spoken by the less civilized tribes like the Kiratas and the Pulindas, whose language was sometimes incomprehensible, but also by those Aryans who had lost their status, as for example, the Kâmbojas of the North-West and those foreigners such as the Yavanas or Yonas, who had of course the high status but spoke an alien language.[319] From the Buddhist sources it appears that the language was the most important criterion of differentiation. The Buddhists were very conscious of the mleccha-bhasa because of their close association with the mleccha regions. Even Aúoka (3rd century B.C.) could not disregard the tribal people in his empire. The list of these people as recorded in one of his inscriptions[320] tally with the lists of the mleccha Peoples mentioned in other sources, although he does not call them mleccha. The language, spoken by the Kirâtas of the Uttarapatha, the people of Orissa and Andhra, the Tamilians, in the South, as well as the Yavanas or Yonas (Yavana-bhâsa with Yavana lipi) has been actually, described as the Milakkhas.

The evolution of the mleccha language of the Kiratas goes back to the later Vedic or the Brâhmanic age. An example of barbarian speech quoted in the *Úatapatha Brâhmaṇa* (3.2.1. 23-24) "tesura attavacaso helave iti vedantah, parabaphubuh..." stands for the speech of Asuras (asuryah or demoniac or hostile in nature), the anti-Vedic people of the Prâcya or eastern region (XIII.8.1.5.). Helava,—Helava words are of Asura Origin. Brâhmanas could not speak like mlecchas. In the *Úatapatha of* Kanva recension it is "Helo-Helah". This is further discussed by Patanjali in his Vyâkarana *Mahâbhâsya,* 1.1.1. "tesura helayo helaya iti Kurvantah Parbabhubuh......" The Helayo-Helaya is the mleccha word. The said, Brahmana used the term in the sense of a barbarous form of language spoken by the people of the mleccha or Asura race.[321] Actually, the barbarous tribes of the mleccha-deúa surrounding, the Âryavarta were the speakers of the barbarian language. The above example is also an index of the truth that the barbarian speech was also a Prâkrit dialect of eastern India. It should be noted here that the hill tribes have been designated as both mlecchas and Asuras in our classical Indian literature.

This can further be substantiated by the facts recorded in the literary and other sources. Prof. Vasudeva Sharana Agrawala also admits that the Indians were .familiar with themleccha language right from the time of *Úatapatha Brâhmaṇa*. In support of his contention he quotes the *Mbh.* (*Âdi Parva*, 2/103), which refers to the talk between Vidur and Yudhisthira in mleccha language. The latter explained the mleccha. language to Kunti in Sanskrit, because it was indistinct for her. During the epic age some people having acquaintance with the Asuras used to speak their mleccha language.[322]

The *Jaimini Dharmaúâstra* (1.3.10) mentions certain mleccha words i.e. pika, nema, sata, and tamaras meaning respectively a bird, a half, a vessel, a red lotus, which are sanskritized versions of words used in the Dravidian languages.[323] It means that the mleccha words were in use among the non-Aryans. As a matter of fact, all the barbarian tribes of India including the Kiratas described in the Sanskrit, Buddhist and Jaina sources as the mlecchas used to represent the barbarian stage of speech, which was not very distinct. The word mleccha most frequently used in Sanskrit stands for all the barbarian tribes. The etymology of the word has been derived from the root 'vac' (speech), which was for those, who were not familiar with the known speech or it was of alien speech.

Different categories of speech have been demarcated in the Vedic Samhitâs and Brâhmanical literature.[324] The speech was also one of the means for making distinction between the civilized race and uncivilized or barbarous people, which mostly includes the tribal people like the Kiratas. That is why, Manu (X.43) distinguishes between mleccha vac and Arya-vâc. The territorial demarcation was also made on the basis of the differentiation in language. The areas represented by the speakers of the mleccha—bhâsa (language) was regarded as the mleccha-desa or country of the mleccha tribes or the barbarians and the areas dominated by the civilized Aryas representing noble speech and speaking more intelligible language was known as the Âryavarta, which roughly corresponds to the Ganges-Yamuna Doab and the plain of Kurukshetra or probably the entire Indo-Gangetic plain.[325] The Purânic evidence[326] also reveals the truth that the mlecchas, who had no regard for ethical code and whose origin is unknown, used to speak an unintelligible language—the Paiúâcika-bhâsa. The Kirâta, Pulinda and Sabara of the mountainous country of the Vindhyan region described as mleccha[327] were speaking an unintelligible language.

The antiquity and origin of this language have generated great controversies among Indian and foreign scholars. It has been pointed out that the word mleccha has been derived from 'Me-lub-ha' which stands for the Sumerian name for an eastern land. The Pali word milakkha is phonetically related to the Sumerian version. The etymology of the word also points to the indigenous inhabitants of northern India, who were the contemporary of the Âryan speaking people.[328] The derivation of this word from the proto-Tibetan word 'mltse' meaning 'tongue' and the Kukish 'mlei' has also been attempted. This shows the association of the word with the non-Âryan speaking peoples living close to Tibeto-Burman area.[329]

The literal meaning of the word Mlecch is to speak indistinctly. It was an 'onomatopoeic' sound imitating the harshness of an alien tongue. Retroflex consonants are believed to have been assimilated into Indo-Âryan from Dravidian.[330] The possibility of the assimilation of some Kirâti words also in the Âryan from of speech can't be precluded. The noted grammarian Panini[331] uses this word in the form of mlista, which was spoken indistinctly or barbarously. He has shown it in the noun form as indirect speech or a foreign language.

Romila Thapar in her scholarly article[332] has exhaustively dealt with the subject-matter in a very logical and convincing manner. But, so far as, this statement, that "......mleccha represents a cultural event rather than a linguistic fact"[333] is concerned, we find it little self-contradictory. The barbarian form of speech of the Kirâta and other less civilized tribes as recorded in our literature as mleccha—bhâsa is a proven fact. The word mleccha not only indicates the grade of their culture but also the quality of speech.

K.P. Jayaswal has expressed the view that the mleccha is not a Sanskrit, but a Semetic word. The Pâli form of the same word is Milakkha (Childers) and the Jaina Prakrt, malikkhu (also milukkha, milekkha milikkba milakkha and Hindi malichchka). 'Helva' is a Semetic Vocative—he-ellu=holy (Assyrian), 'elo wah', God.[334] While supporting the analyses of Mr. Jayaswal Vasudeva Sharana Agrawala has said that the word mleccha is of Assyrian origin. He has identified the Helava of *Útapatha Brâhmana* with 'ellu' of Assyrian language. In support of the identification he has argued that ancient Asuras were Assyrians and a comparative study of their words and phoenecian and Hebrew words indicates the possibility of assimilation of their words in the Sanskrit. The Pali word milekkha and the Prakrt malikkhu have been also assimilated in our Buddhist and Jaina literature from the Assyrian source,[335] which is nothing but mere-supposition.

With quite a disagreement to the views of both Shree Jayaswal and Shree V.S. Agrawala, it is noticed that the word mleccha as described in the Sanskrit, Pali and Prâkrt sources as well as the barbarian form of speech are purely of Indian origin, because all the uncivilized mountainous tribes speaking indistinct language have been distinguished from the more civilized Âryan and placed under the category of the 'mlecchas'. And so were the Kiratas. Their derivation from Assyrian or Sumerian stock is not acceptable.

In the famous list of sixty-four kinds of writings (lipi or alphabet) as enumerated in one of the later Buddhist text in Sanskrit known as *Lalitavistara*[336] (a magnified life or Buddha), a special kind of writing has been attributed to the Kirâtas, which proves beyond doubt their knowledge of script and palaeography. The alphabet described in the Buddhist text are named, Khasya, China, Nâga-Asura, Sankhya, Kinari, Uttarakuru, Lekh-Pratilekha, Daksina, Anga, Benga, Magha, Darada, Nâga-Yaksa, Kinnara, etc. One of the Kirâta kings of Mithila region, named, Lohangasena introduced Kirâta script among the Kirâtas of Mithila and Nepal, which also confirms their knowledge of the art of writing.[337] This also indicates that they had reached to a stage of learning the scripts or alphabet.

The most significant stage in the evolution of their language in general was the stage of Prâkṛt. The evidence recorded by Vararuchi (375-413 A.D., contemporary of Chandragupta Vikramaditya) in his monumental work, *Prâkṛt Prakâúa*[338] (based on the extract of chapter seven of Bharata Muni's *Nâtyaúâstra)* in this connection is very concrete and of inestimable value. From this text it is evident that the Kiratas had adopted the Prâkrt form of language before the time of Bharata Muni (who may be ascribed to either the second or the third century A.D.). Further, the Bahlikas Udicyas, Khasas, Sabaras, Abhiras, Barbara-Kiratas and other foresters (vanacharen') were the speakers of one of the forms of the Prâkrt. But their language was not used in the Sanskrit drama or play because of its unintelligibility, as stated by Bharata Muni. In his *Nâtyasastra* (XVII. 37, 54-56), he has assigned the local dialects (Vibhâsas) to various tribes, who were representing lower grade of culture and not speaking Sanskrit. The Prâkrt tongue (vulgar form of speech) has been described by him in contrast to refined tongue (Sanskrit spoken by members of higher class).

Whatever be the truth, it can't be denied that the Prakrt was their lingua-franca at one particular stage. But the question follows what was the nature of this language ? In answer to this question it can be plainly stated that this was original, natural, uncultivated, unmodified and unrefined language spoken by the common people in ancient times. It was derived from the Prâkrti (nature). It was a vernacular provincial dialect derived from Sanskrit. Thus it is akin to Sanskrit.[339]

The old form of Prâkrt reappeared in the form of Pali during the time of Buddha and Asoka. Subsequently its several modified forms were evolved region-wise. This form of speech gained popularity in the regions extending from Hindukush to Bengal for nearly four centuries preceding the Gupta age. Even in the wooden plate inscriptions in Scrindia or modern Chinese Turkestana the North-Western form of Prâkrt has been used.

The "oldest contemporary notice of a prâkrtic habit of speech in India" is found in the *Tândya* or *Pañcaviṁúa Brâhamâna,* (XVII, 4) which runs as follows: aduruktavâkyâm duruktamâhuh... a diksita, diksita-vacam vadanti'. While speaking of the Vrâtyas this *Brahmana* proves that "they call an expression which is not uttered with difficulty as being uttered with difficulty, and also they speak the language of the initiated (i.e. into Brâhmanism) although they are not initiated."

The Vrâtyas, according to this Brahmanical text "call a sentence difficult to utter, when it is not difficult to utter" and "although they are not initiated into the Vedic religion, they speak the speech of the initiated". This is interpreted to mean that they unlike the Âryan speakers of the Midland and the North-West, who were building up the Vedic religion and culture found difficult to utter the compound consonants and other phonetic traits which characterised the Âryan speech or in other words they had presumably developed Prakrt habits of speech in which conjunct consonants were assimilated. This Brahmana story repeated by the sages and grammarian Patñjali in his *Mahâbhâsya* (2nd—century B.C..) of the Asuras of the East, that they mispronounced the Sanskrit word arayah (=the enemies) as alayo or alavo, is an evidence of the notice which the Western (Udicya) people took of the eastern (Prâcya) habit:of pronouncing 'r' as 'i'.[340] The Prâcya or eastern region, which was inhabited by the Kirâtas Vratya Âryans, Kol Dravidas and others, was the main centre of the Prakrtic form of speech. It was the East from where this form of speech gradually spread to the North-West and West.[341]

Phonetically, the Âryan language of the eastern region was profoundly influenced by the Kirâta form of speech. In the Videha region the vocabulary and the articulate speech of the Âryans were slightly modified because of their contacts with the Kiratas. The phonetical changes, which had occurred in the language of the Âryans of the Videha because of their contacts with the Nisâdas, Kirâtas and others, can be very well traced back to the time of Yâjñavalkya much before Panini. The Kirâta group of people of Assam and Manipur used to pronounce was 'eha' as for example, sat (seven) as 'chat' and 'ansu' (tears) as 'anchu'.[342] The Paisacika form of Prâkrt, which was one of the most antique languages of India was spoken by the Barbara-Kirâtas and Piúacas of the areas stretching from Kashmir to North-West frontier region. The evolution of this form of language goes back to early medieval period, but from sixth century onward, this language started gaining popularity among the Kirata people of Northern and North-Western region.

Dr. Hoernle proposes to identify phonetically sound equation with Piúâcas. They were according to him, original people, probably, of non-Âryan origin in North-West India and neighbouring parts of the Himalayas closely connected with the Khasas, Nâgas and Yaksas (the three-Kirâta tribes).[343] The existence of the Paiúâcic-Prâkrt is sp well attested by literary references that there can be no reasonable doubts about the speakers as being the real human beings in North-West.

The Piúâca characteristics are not only confined to dialects of Kashmir and Hindukush, but also found in most of the outer Indo-Âryan language. Much wider area than the North Western India comprising Punjab, Vindhya hills and the country of the Bhils was represented by this form of speech. The Piúâca peculiarities are probably derived not only from the speakers of the Piúâca language, but also from the stock of languages spoken by the invaders akin to Homo-Alpines of Eastern Turkestan. The dialects of the Hindukush and Kashmir retain a greater number of these peculiarities, because they have been more or less influenced by the midlandic Indo-Âryan language than the other outer-Indo-Aryan language. The whole of Punjab is the meeting ground of two entirely distinct languages. The Piúâca form of speech is also believed to have extended from the Indus Valley towards the East—the place of so-called Piúâca language in the Âryan family. This language also includes the Shina-Khowar group, who occupy a position intermediate between the Sanskritic languages of India proper and the Eranian languages further to their west. They, thus, possess many features that are common to them and to Sanskritic languages. But they also possess some features which are peculiar to themselves and others in which they agree rather with the languages of the Eranian family.[344]

On the basis of literary evidence it can be proved that the Kirâtas living in the heart of the Vindhya forest learnt the alphabet from the Brahmans with whom they were living in close association during the 6th and 7th century A.D. The Brahmanas used to teach them Úâstras, Tantras, etc. This truth is based on the statement made by the Kirâtas themselves, which can be easily confirmed by the text dealing with it in detail.[345]

The Rajis or Râjya Kirâtas living in northern, eastern and central Himalyan regions extending from the forest area of

Askot in Kumaon (Uttarâkhanda) to the foot-hills below the province of Doti—the westerly district of Nepal and the area lying between Jageswar in Chaugarkha, the ancient Amaravana and Tibet, commonly known as the Rajis of Hindu origin, still have a dialect of their own, which is known from very ancient times as Kirânti dialect like that of Nepal. Some of them communicate with their civilized neighbours in a language which is known as *Pâhâdi Hindi.* The Copper Plates of Katyur Pawar and the princes of Lunar race, discovered in this region, also throw some light on the indigenous Pahadi language spoken by them. The scanty vocabulary of the language of the Rajis of Kumaon collected in the 19th century supports their connection with the Kirâta tribes of Nepal speaking Kiranti dialect. Linguistically they are placed between the Kirantis of Nepal and Khasas or Khasiyas of Kumaon, who equally pronounce somewhat Âryan form of speech.[346] According to other accounts the Râjis have fairly developed language, which is known as *Râwt.* Its sound is believed to be something like twittering of birds and is entirely different from the local Kumaoni or Hindi. This indicates a different origin of the Khâsias of Kumaon. Some words of their language have been found similar to the local dialect of Nepal, which also suggest their common origin. Some influence of Hindi is also noticeable in their language. A few specimens of their Rwati language are given below.[347]

English	*Rwati*
What is your name ?	Ni nami huen ?
Where are you going ?	Goha gasyan ?
Where do you live ?	Nang gabju cher ?

One of the peculiarity of the linguistic structure of the Râji Kirâtas is that it constitutes the synthesis of the Indo-Âryan group of language, the language of Mon-Khmer and Munda group of Austric family, Tibeto-Burman group of language, Kirâta-Skandhîya form of speech and Dravida language. They are surrounded on all sides by the speakers of Bhotiya language of north, the Khâsa-Úaka-Gurjara and the speakers of the Âryan language. Notwithstanding, they have preserved their indigenous archaic language till to-day, which is a glaring example of their linguistic consciousness. Linguistically, the Âryan influence has been predominant in their areas. The Jyoha or Johari of Bhotiya group of the north are also the speakers of Âryan (Kumaoni) group of language. But the Râjis speak both Kumaoni and western branch of the Kirânti language of Nepal as their link language. But in their forest-belt they still speak fundamentally their own archaic language. As the number of speakers of this language is numerically less and as there is complete absence of literature among them, it will be more proper to call it as dialect. They don't have any script, but it is a means for them to communicate with each other. Their pronunciation of words of Âryan and Kirâta-Skandhîya groups are unintelligible to their own neighbours to some extent. Some of their words are not all analogous to the Âryan and northern Bhota speech of the adjacent area. Sometimes it does not tally either with Kirâta-Skandhiya form of speech or with Kumaoni of central Himalayas. The languages spoken in central and eastern Himalayan regions do not necessarily belong to Sino-Tibetan family of language.[348]

B.H. Hodgson after having collected complex pronominalized language of Nepal under the head of Kirânti comprising Yakhas, Khambus, Limbus, Thulung, Kulung and other Kirata people of Eastern Nepal and its neighbourhood (Sikkim) so-called Kirânt country of the Central region of the Eastern Himalaya concluded that they had their own dialects called 'Kirânt dialects'.[349] The analysis of the data reveals that in ancient times the people of Kirâta country stretching from Nepal to Sikkim had in their own archaic dialect, which might have been subsequently modified after coming in touch with new comers —the speakers of Tibeto-Burman group of language. That is why Mr G.A. Grierson[350] placed them under Tibeto-Burman family. Edward Gait's statement that 'the dialects of so-called Kirânt group are closely related to dialects spoken by tribes, who have never claimed to be Kirântis',[351] can outrightly be rejected. The Limbus of both Nepal and Sikkim and likewise Lepchas and Bhotiyas inhabiting the hill-regions of modern Sikkim and Darjeeling are also generally classed with Tibeto-Burman family. Actually, they picked up Tibeto-Bunnan group of language at later stage. They also had their own dialect. But, the people of Bhot race is an exception to this. Because they originally belong to the Bhot, the most ancient name of Tibet (Trivistap) and hence from the very beginning they used to speak

Tibetan language. While speaking of the north-eastern aborigines and Mongoloids of Tibeto Chinese family, Hodgson has observed that the sub Himalayan dialects differ from the trans-Himalayan standard, but both can be identified with it.[332] His arguments are not very clear.

The languages spoken by the Khambu-Rais, Gurungs, Sunuwars, Magars, Yakhas (Dewans) and Bhujels belong to the eastern Himalayan branch of Tibeto-Burmese family. Each ethnic community has its own script and language. The Khambu-Rais are the speakers of the language of both Tibeto-Burman sub-family and Tibeto-Chinese family. The indigenous script of the Gurung is called "*Khema*" and their language *Tamu* is of Tibeto-Burman group. Sunuwars' Kirat script is based on Cuneiform letter and their language called "*Koinchlo*" is of Tibeto-Burman origin. The archaic script of Magars is called *Akkharika*, and their language belongs to Tibeto-Burmese family. *Bhujikura,* the language of the Bhujels, is also placed under the branch of Tibeto-Burmese family. The yakhas like the Rais have also own dialect (Kirant) and language. They, of course, speak Nepali language but just to communicate with the members of Nepali community.

D.R. Regmi candidly admits that the "Kiratas had dominated even culturally by way of introducing their linguistic hegemony." They greatly affected the texture of social life in the valley of Nepal. Their life and society are not much known but "the Newari language and culture shows certain features that are distinctly pre-Mongoloid".[353] He further states that the native chronicles and the Puranas clearly reflect the truth that the Kirâtadeúa was in touch with the Madhya-deúa from time immemorial. The influence of Sanskrit on the Kirâti language of Nepal was, of course, very rare. This also betrays the profound influence of Sanskrit on their vocabulary. In all probability, the Kirata had succeeded, to a considerable extent, in imposing their language on the people of the valley. They speak the Newari of Tibeto-Burman family of language.' The Kirâta victors were absorbed by the conquered in their society. But, except the similarity of language the two societies of the Kiratas and Newaris differ from each other. "The Kirâtas had yielded to the indigenous settlers of the valley in cultural sphere". They represent the lower order of civilization. They were subjected to powerful cultural force after coming to Nepal. It was so because they came into contact with the people of valley, who were culturally advanced and superior to them. However, their language could hold ground, but they were exposed to the factors tending to modify their language both morphologically and semantically.[354] Consequently, they lost much of their originality in the linguistic and cultural spheres.

Sylvain Levi is of the view that they are the speakers of the Tibeto-Burman group of language as proved by the names of their kings, such as, Ya-Lamb=a, Ba-Lamba. Thunka and Khim-bu.[355] But, the careful study of the dynastic chart provided the present work also shows some Âryanised names of their kings. One of the common features of the dynastic list of the Kirâtas, wherever they had established their fule is that the same king had both Âryan and non-Âryan names, which give more clues about their mutual contacts with the Aryans as well as, about the impact of the Âryan form of speech on their language.

Tne Geographical, historical and social factors have profoundly influenced the evolution of the so-called 'Kirânti or Kitantish' language generally placed under Sino-Tibetan and Tibeto-Burman groups of languages. The Tibeto-Burman languages have evolved from the ancestral language-proto-Tibeto-Burman at their own pace in consonance with the geographical and social factors, that have determined the fate of Central and South-Asian peoples. Some tribes have' been stationary and others have swept over huge areas. As a result, the archaic or conservative features do not occur in only one contiguous part of the language area. The nearest genetic relations are often not identical with the closest typological one. Old Tibetan pronunciation can be very well reconstructed by making a comparison of modern dialects and through the very archaic alphabetic script of Indian origin that dates back to the 7th century A.D. and found its present form in the 9th century. Old Tibetan is one of the most archaic of Tibeto-Burman language. Himalayish languages are in certain respects as archaic as Tibetan. An influence from contiguous region seems possible but not certain. The Burmese language of the Myazedi Inscription of 1113 A.D. shows that the writing system was taken over from the Mon people, who had developed their writing from 'Pyu' (—a Sino-Tibetan language known in Burma from c. A.D. 500). It is alphabetic of an Indian type, but represents a separate southern line of development. Old Burmese is phonetically further from proto-Tibeto-Burman than is Tibetan.[356]

The people living within the Indian territory in close proximity to the Tibetan frontiers are mainly the speakers of the language of the Kirâta family. The Baltistan and Laddakh areas, notably, represent the Kirâta group of language. In the northern frontiers of Assam several tribes (Akas, Defla, Miris, Mishmis and others and the tribes by ordering the eastern frontier of Bhutan) speak the Kirâta language. In the Brahmaputra or Lauhitya valley also there are some tribes, who can be classed with the language of the Kirâti group."[357] The number of the speakers of the Munda and Kirâta-group of languages are, of course, very few. This language has neither any script nor alphabet. Actually, the Kirata language has neither any script nor any alphabet. Actually, the Kirata language spoken in ancient times was a kind of Pahadi-bhasa, which developed under archaic condition.

The dialects of the diverse Kirâta communities of North-East can be classified broadly under the following heads, viz., Austric family, which includes the Khasi-Jaintia people, Tibeto-Burman sub-family (division of so-called Tibeto-Chinese family), which is further divided and sub-divided into different branches, i.e., Tibeto Himalayan including the Limbs of Sikkim and Nepal, North Assam Branch including two important frontier Kirâta tribes, the Akas and the Mishmis, Bodo or Boro group including the Garos, the Kacharis and the Tipperahs, the Naga group including the Western, Central and Eastern Naga tribes, etc.

Different philologists have classified the languages of the Kirata tribes of North-Eastern Himalayan region in different ways. Generally, the speeches of the Sino-Tibetan or Tibeto-Chinese family have been placed under different branches of which Tibeto-Burman group forms the most important section. The speeches of Tibetan (Old Tibetan or Bod, c. 650 A.D.) group, Himalayan groups (non-pronominalised or pure Tibeto-Burman group and pronominalised group with Austric influence with some modifications), north-Assam group, Assam-Burma group and Bodo—(Boro) Naga group constitute the most important branches of Tibeto-Burman group of languages. The Bodic (Tibetan) including Himalayan dialects, Baric (Bodo and Naga) and Burmic or Burmese are considered to be important branches of Sino-Tibetan family too. In the extreme North-East the hill-tribes speak the languages having an affinity with the great Tibeto-Burman sub-family, which have been divided by philologists into two main branches, i.e. the Tibeto-Himalayan and the Assam-Burmese and North-Assam branch. The speeches of the Akas and Mishmi Kirâtas have been placed under north-Assam branch.[338] Linguistically, sometimes all the Himalayan tribes are put under Tibeto-Burman group, which can't be accepted in toto from the standpoint of general classification. The traditional classification of the speeches and dialects of the Himalayan tribes as generally given by the Indian and foreign linguists are neither scientific nor historical, and, hence, it need not necessarily be accepted.

S.K. Chatterji, while placing the Kirâtas, so-called Mongoloid tribes, under the Sino-Tibetan family has suggested that they were the speakers of the Sino-Tibetan forms of speech. t He has based his arguments on the theory of their Mongoloid origin. He has put forth the views that they started speaking Sino-Tibetan forms of speech in their original homeland—Western China from where their migration towards South and West started in pre-historic times and continued upto the early part of the first—millennium B.C. We have conclusively proved that all the Kiratas were neither Mongoloids nor of Chinese origin. Hence any attempt to connect them linguistically or racially with Sino-Tibetans will be futile. He has further classified the Sino-Tibetan languages into two groups or branches—Tibeto Burman and Siamese-Chinese. Tibetan and its various dialects spoken in a wide area extending from Baltistan in the West to Khams in the east covering Ladakhi, Chang, Central Tibetan speech, Kham or Eastern Tibetan and Den-Jong-Ke or Sikkimese Tibetan, as well as Lho-Ke or Bhutanese; the Himalayan group of dialects spoken in the Himalayan regions of Nepal and Sikkim. e.g. Kiranti, Lepcha or Rong, Newari, Magar, Gurung, Murmi, Surwari, etc. of Pure Tibeio-Burman origin; the pro-nominalised Himalayan dialects of Tibeto-Burman—slightly modified through influence of the Austric speeches falling into two groups, a western (Kanawari spoken near Simla, Lahuli and nine other dielects current in the Eastern Punjab Himalayas) and an Eastern (current in Nepal like Limbu, Yakha, Khambu, Rai, Vayu, etc.; the North-Assam group of Tibeto-Burman speeches comprising Akas, Mishmi, Miri, Abor and Dafla; the Assam-Burmese groups—Tibeto-Burman speeches of North and East Bengal, Assam and Burma including the Bodo speeches: the Naga dialects of Ao, Angami, Sema, Tangkhul, Songtem, Konyak, Lotha, Mao and Kabui Nagas; the Kuki-Chin speeches of Manipur, Tripura and the Lushai Hills, as well as Burma, the Meithei or Manipuri; the Kachin-Lolo group of Northern Burma and finally the Myamma or Burmese dialects have been included in the former.[359] We find that Newari, Magar, Gurung, Murmi, Sunwari of Nepal, Miri, Abor and Dafla of North-Assam group and speakers of Kuki-Chin group of language of Manipur, Tripura and Lushai Hills, the Meithei or Manipuris, etc. do not fall within the category of the Kiratas and hence they are beyond the purview of our treatment. The Siamese-Chinese branch of Sino-Tibetan includes on the one hand the Chinese in its various dialect, derived from a single un-divided Chinese speech, which was current till about 6500 A.D. and on the other hand Siamese and the various forms of speeches and dialects connected with it like Thai, i.e. Siamese proper, and Lao, Shan, Khamti and Ahom—the language of the Shan conquerors of Assam who entered the country in the second quarter of the 13th century. We have already pointed out that the Thai or Siamese, the Khamtis and Ahoms have unnecessarily been included the Kirata tribes.

The Bodic (Bod—or Tibetan) branch and Bodish—the Tibetan speech and Burmic representing the entire Burman group and Burmish standing for the Burmese speech constituting the important branches of the Sino-Tibetan family as suggested by Robert Shafer roughly correspond to the practice followed in the classification of the Indo-European languages in English, e.g. Celtic, Italic, Germanic, Hellenic, Slavic, Baltic, Indic, branches and Irish, Spanish, Polish, languages.

With the single exception of the Khâsis and Jaintia or Syntengs of North-East all other Kirâtas or 'Mongoloid' peoples are erroneously believed to be the speakers of the Sino-Tibetan or Tibeto-Chinese form of language. This is the branch of the most widely diffused linguistic family in the world.

The Khasi-Jaintias linguistically belong to the Mon-Khmer family of Austro-Asiatic group of language. The linguistic researches of Peter Schmidt and Sten Konow enable us to trace the affinities of the Austric or so-called Nisadas with other speakers of this group of the language. Mr. Schmidt in his *Die Mon-Khmer Volker* has established an intimate relationship between the Mon-Khmer group of language and various other speeches of Indo-China, South-east Asia, Pacific Ocean as far as Easter Island off the coast of South America and other places. This group of language according to him embrace Mon, Khmer, Palaung and Wa of Burma, Riang of Salween, basin, cham of Cochin-China, Munda and Khasi languages, of India and various other minor forms of speech and aboriginal dialects of Cambodia, Annam, Malay-Peninsula, Assam Upper Burma, Nicobar Islands, Salween and Mekong, etc. This, important group of language was neither Tibeto-Burman nor Sinitic, but was independent of both while on the other hand it was closely connected with the Khasi in Central Assam. The Mon-Khmer-Malacca-Munda-Nicobar-Khasi tongues have been grouped by Schmidt as Austro-Asiatic language, which is neither Aryan nor Tibeto-Sinitic but form an independent group. He has included the languages of Indonesia, Melanesia, and Polynesia under Austro-Asiatie language.[360] We have thus got a clear evidence that the Khasis are linguistically identical with Mundas, Mon-Khmers of Cambodia, Nicobarese, Wa, Palaung, Reang, Cham, etc. Mr. Schmidt regards the "Austro-Asiatic" as a section of the family of "Austrie" languages and finds connecting link between the people or Central Asia and those of Austronesia. A connecting link is certainly there : but have they any connection with a wider family? J. Przyluski an excellent Judge in the field of linguistic is of opinion that "the theory is still only conjectural, for it is rash to place agglutinative Munda and Monosyllabic Annamite in the same group. This linguistic stratum must lie on the top of other still older languages, of which vestiges survive in Malaysia."[361]

S.K. Chatterji in some of his important writings has mentioned that the Khâsis-Jaintias are by race Indo-Mongoloid or Mongoloid people but their language is different. They have adopted the language of the earlier race, the Austrics (or Proto-Australoids known to the Âryans as Nisâdas) after their dispersion from the Tibeto-Burman area. The Austric language represents the oldest family speech in India. This language constitutes one of the valuable relics of the past link of India with Burma, Indo-China, Malaya, Indonesia, Melanesia and Polynesia. The Khâsis might have changed their speech to Austric or Mon-Khmer while they were in Burma and further after their settlements in the Khasi-Jaintia Hills, successfully resisting all possible attempts of the Bodos who attempted at dislodging or absorbing them. They are said to have been congeries of diverse Tibeto-Burman speaking tribes in the Kthâsi-Jaintia Hills and in the plains of Sylhet who settled among original Austric speakers whose language they adopted for the sake of convenience, as their own tribal dialects were too numerous and diverse. This linguistic change over possibly occurred before the expansion of the Bodos. They have preserved this linguistic uniqueness among the surrounding so-called Tibeto-Burmans (Bodos) and speakers of the Aryan language. The Austric tribes preserving their language had mixed with other races, Mongoloid, Dravidian and probably also Negritos, the Kol or the Mundas. The Austric speech-family originally belongs to the Proto-Australoid group of language. The Proto-Australoids were probably modified in India and labelled as 'Austrics'. The Austric speech, religion and culture are believed to have been characterised within India. The Austric branches of the original Kirâta people of India carried their language to the South and East to Malaya and Indonesia (Sumatra, Jâvâ, Bali, Borneo, the Philippines etc.) and from Indonessia to Micronesia and Melanesia (Caroline Islands, Marshall Islands etc.) and to Polynesia (Samoa, Tonga, Cook Islands, Society Islands, Tahiti, Tuamotu Archipelago, New Zealand, Easter Island, etc.). All these languages were spoken in the Islands of Indonesia, Micronesia and Melanesia and Polynesia from the Austronesian branch of the Austric family. The original Austric stock was considerably modified in the Islands through intermixture with other races, notably the Mongoloid race in Indonesia and the Negrito race in Micronesia, and with a 'Caucasian' race in Polynesia. Some sections of the Austric tribes in Indo-China became the Mons, the Khmers or Cambodians, the Chams, and the lesser known tribes like the Paloungs, the Was and others. One group of them sailed into the Nicobarî Islands and became the Nicobarese. Other groups, i.e. the ancestors of the Khasis and others penetrated into erstwhile Assam. The Continental Austrics in contradistinction to the Island Austrics or Austranesians were known as Austro-Asiatics. "This Austro-Asiatic branch of the Austric includes the Mon-Khmer languages (Mon Khmer and a few other speeches of Indo-China Khasi of Khasi-Jaintia Hills, the Indian Kol or Munda languages and dialects, Cham of Cochin China, and Paloung of Burma, Nicobarese, and the Semang and Senoi (Saki) dialects spoken by aboriginal Negritos of Malaya.[362]

We are not certain about the kind of language, which was spoken bv Proto-Australoids. Some observations are nothing but highly speculative thoughts. It is very likely that the Austric speech family was greatly associated with the Proto-Australoids and their descendants.

The Austric dialects spoken by the Kirâtas of North-Eastern India (the Khasi-Jaintias) mainly fall into two groups (1) "Austro-Asiatic", which covers the speeches current in India, Burma and Indo-China i.e. the mainland of Southern: and South-eastern Asia (the Munda speeches of India, Nico-barese of the Nicobar Islands, Khasi of Assam, Paloung and Wa of Burma, Mon or Talaing of South Burma and South Siam, Khmer of Cambodia ; Cham of Cochin-China, Stieng Bahnar and other speeches of Indo-China and Sakai and Semang of Malaya) ; and (2) Austronesian, which includes (*a*) Indonesian—Malay, Javanese, Sudanese, Madurese, Balinese, Sassak the Celebes, speeches, Tagalog, Ilocano Visayan and other Philippine Islands speeches and Malagasy of Madagascar, (*b*) Melanesian in the Islands of Melanesia like the Solomon Islands, New Caledonia, New Hebrides, Viti or Fiji, etc. and Polynesia-Samoan Togan Tahitian, Tuamotuan, Marquesan, (*c*) Maori of New Zealand, Hawaiian, etc.[363]

L. Rabel Berkley[364] on the basis of his findings has discovered that imitatives, which play an important role in the Khasi language are very much parallel to German or English usages.

But all the authorities concerned have failed to trace the impact of Âryan language on the Austric speech family. Nor are all the explanations absolutely correct, so far as the connection of Mon-Khmeer group of language with other forms of speech is concerned. In support of their connection with the Âryan form of speech some positive evidence can be furnished. According to one reliable source[365] it can be pointed out that Khasi combnes to a certain extent with a 'Indo-Aryan Vocalism' and has many points of interest with their diffusion phenomena.

Reginald Le May unravels a truth of great historical value that "according to Sten Konow, Blagden and Schmidt we get specimens of old Khmer from inscription going back to 629 A.D. Sanskrit has introduced into Khmer language a large number of words into science, religion, administration... Thc Khmcr alphabet is derived from the Pallava or the East Chalukya alphabet of South India."[366] The Khasis, being an isolated group speaking a monosyllabic tongue cannot be identified with any particular group of family. In order to prove that the Mon-Khmer is Monosyllabic a few specimens of this tongue can be given here, e.g. Linga=Lin, Visa (poison) = Pis, Vela (Time) = Pel, hasta, etc. (this is derivation in North India too).

Actually the Khasis linguistically belong to Mon-Khmer race, who were subsequently absorbed in Tibeto-Burman family. In ancient times the speakers of Mon-Khmer language spread over a vast region extending from Madhy-desa or Midland, Pracya or eastern region and Gangetic belt to Cambodia. Before the great Bharata war the hill-areas around the Kamakhya temple in modern Gauhati witnessed the synthesis of the Âryan, Munda, Tibeto-Burman and Mon-Khmer forms of speech.

The main centre of Mon-Khmer language was Cambodia or Kampuchea. As a matter of fact, the Mon-Khmer belongs to the Kamboja group of language, which started taking its formation in the North western region or Udicya right from the epic age on a different footing. It was later on included in the Austric group of language. The-Khasis racially and linguistically are associated with the Kambojas. After the Turko Afghan invasions of Kamboja region some sections of them migrated towards Assam and some of them towards South East Asia. The linguistic and cultural identity between the speakers of the Austric and

Mon-Khmer speeches may be primarily attributed to their mutual contacts in course of their migrations, movements and expansion, which continued for centuries. But initially the evolution of the Mon-Khmer and Austric languages took place in isolation from each other. At subsequent period of history both were connected with each other. The sources of the origin or formation of both the groups of language were originally different. In the Austro Asiatic group of languages many speeches of Australia and Asia are not incorporated. The Aryans, Dravidians and Mundas have played equally an important role in the formation of Austro-Asiatic group of language. That is why many linguists do not accept the independent existence of Austro-Asiatic group of language. The Khasi language should not be blindly linked with Austro Asiatic language. Mon Khmer language was originally Sanskrit and Pali oriented.

The word 'Gula' used in the archaic Mon language signifying the people of India became 'Gala' in modern Mon language and 'Kula' in ancient Burmese language, which is derivation from Pali 'Kulaputta' and Sanskrit 'Kulaputra'. The synonyms of Kula standing for Kulaputta can be found in the speeches current in the area stretching from Burma to Kampuchea. The 'Par' (fly) use in the archatic Mon language is based on Sanskrit 'Parana' or Para; the Pava used in modern Mon language is derived from 'Pava' or 'Pavana' of Sanskrit; the Khmer=Tula (cotton) is identified with Tola of archaic Mon language and 'Tova' of modern Mon speech. The Sanskrit-Tana' (weave) corresponds to Taana' of archaic Mon speech and 'Tanga' of Khiner and 'Tenon' of Malaya, etc.[367] The further researches in the various forms of speech current in South-East Asia will, expectedly, reveal their connections with the Indo-Aryan group of language.

The impact of Austric form of speech on the Indo-Arayan group of language can also be noticed. Sylvain Levi, Jean Przyluski and Jules Bloch have candidly admitted the influence of Austric on Sanskrit.[368]

The Austric or Austro-Asiatic section of Kirâta tribes, while spreading over the whole of northern India right up to the Punjab and penetrating into the central and south India greatly affected the Indian forms of speech. Their settlements especially in the valleys of the great rivers in northern India provided an avenue for them to come in close contact with the indigenous Aryans. The name of the river Ganges, Ganga is believed to be an example of Sanskritisation from some Ancient Austric word found in Indo-China as Khong (Me-Khong, i.e. Ma Ganga-=Mother River) in Siamese as Me-nam (== Mother Water) in old Chinese as Kiang and in northern Chinese dialect as Chiang (Gang) meaning just a river. The traces of the Austric form of speech in the great plain lands of northern India now survive in the original notions in the folk or village ults of the Hindus, who appear to be Âryanised in speech and transformed outwardly. They had mixed with the Dravidians who come after them, as well as with the Âryans. The Austric elements representing various stages of culture are also represented by the lower strata of Indian society and those who fled towards central Indian highlands as a result of Âryan pressure.[369]

"While adopting the Âryan speech *en masse* it would be natural to expect that certain changes would come inco the language of their adoption and these changes would naturally reflect their original language—in sounds, wherever possible in forms, in syntax, in idioms and turns of expression and in words. The Austric dialects in this way supplied one of the backgrounds for the transformation of the Âryan speech in India. In all the points of material culture—there is evidence of Aryan borrowing from Austric—apart from subtler and deeper influence of Austric on Aryan phonetics, syntax and idiom."[370].

The importance of Austric and Bodo forms of speech in the formation of the Assamese language has also been accepted. The Kâmeikhâ is believed to be the Austric word, which was later transformed as the Kâmakhyâ. The Umei-Ludai-Fia (Mei = Mother; Ludai = Male gential organ, Fia=pha=God) was later known as Umaluda or Umanuda, which is equivalent to Umananda.[371] Several Austric and Bodo words found their places in the Assamese vocabulary.

The linguistic influences of the Austric Khâsis, the Bodos and the Nagas on the development of the Âryan Assamese language have been recognised by a number of scholars. The Austric Khasi speech of the 'Indo-Mongoloid' Khâsis and Syntengs or Jaintias (one of the important sections of the ancient Kirâtas of N.E.) has similarly influenced the Âryan language of the contiguous region. Prof. Banikanta Kakati in his valuable work,[372] while discussing the matter in detail has given the lists of words and toponyms of Khâsi or Austric and Bodo origin, which helped the formation of the Assamese language. He has proved that the name of the shrine of the Great Mother Goddess at Kamakhya and the place names such as Kâma-rûpa, Kamata and Kamilla (Comillal) are all of pre-Âryan Austric origin.

A good number of Assamese words of Indo-mongaliod provenance are also to be found in Bengali language because of the Bodo-influence as suggested by the late J.D. Anderson. A case study of the evolution of Bengali and Assames syntax in comparison with the Bodo and Khâsi speeches will further reveal some points of contact between Indo-Âryan and Indo-Mongoloid. The Bodo element Kam or Kam occurred in the name of the most western tribe of the Bodo. The Kawomca or Kamoea was sanskritized as Kamboja in the 10 century in a north-Bengal inscription. Evidently by 1000 A.D. Aryan were spoken side by side in the Assam and north-Bengal plains.[373]

We can also have some glimpses of the relationship between the Kiratas ("Indo-Mongoloid") and the earlier Austrics and Dravidians and the Âryan speaker in North-eastern and eastern India with reference to Assam and Nepal in the Âryanised form of Sino-Tibetan dialects and speeches. In some cases so-called Austric speech of the Khasi has triumphed over Sino-Tibetan. In the Nepal valley the so-called Mongoloid dialects have apparently ousted the Austric speeches; but the latter somehow managed to influence the former only to some extent. In eastern Nepal, Kumaon and Garhwal and further to the west as far as Chamba the two groups of Tibeto-Burman dialects represent the so-called "Pro-nominalised Dialects" (the incorporation of the pronoun with the verb) e.g. Limbu Peg—ang=went—I (I went); hip-tu-ng=strike-him-I (I strike him); hip-ne-ni-ng=strike-you-two-I (I strike you two); hip-a=he strikesme (I am struck); me-hip-a=they strike me, etc. This is the common characteristic of Kol or Munda languages of the Austric family, which got mixed with two New Indo-Aryan speeches i.e. the Maithili and Magahi of Bihar. Austric dialects spread along the Himalayan regions, and like two Aryan speeches, i.e. Magahi and Maithili of the plains a number of Tibeto-Burman Himalayan dialects (approximately twenty-one) like Limbu, Lahuli, Kanauri or

Kanawari, Kirânti (Dhimal), etc. adopted some of their characteristics as a sub-stratum or acquired new feature after coming into contact with Austric speeches. The Kirânti or Kirât group of people in eastern Nepal as they were called in all likelihood by the Âryan speakers as Kiratas used to speak pro-nominalised dialects, which also proves their early contact with Austric speakers in the Himalayan tracts probably during the pre-Christian era. The Austric characteristics of the Kirânti dialects also testifies to the remote antiquity of the Kirâtas. The number of speakers of the "Pro-nominalised Himalayan languages" amongst the eastern Kirântis rose up to more than thousand in ancient times. All the Kirâtas ("Indo-Mongoloid") have been shown as speakers of the various dialects and languages of both the Tibeto-Burman and Siamese-Chinese branches of the Sino-Tibetan speech-family. Some of the earlier tribes who formed the nucleus or basis of the 'Himalayan Mongoloids' of Nepal were speaking languages like Newari, Lepcha. Magar and Gurung and the Pro-nominalised languages like Dhimal or Kiranti Khambu, Kanawari and others. The speakers of the 'Pro-nominalised' dialects are believed to be the earliest group of people and the Newars, Lepchas, Magars and Gurungs, etc. represent later arrivals. "In addition to the 114,000 Himalayan Tibeto-Burmans speaking Pro-nominalised dialects there are some 102,000 people who employ the non-pronominalised dialects" including 25,000 Rong or Lepchas.[374]

One form of Austric speech is believed to have penetrated into the north beyond Kashmir, which roughly corresponds to the tract forming the present day state of Hunza-Nagyr, represented by Burushaski speech, which followed its own line of development in isolation, but possibility of it being an offshoot of Austric or its agreement with Austric speech can't be precluded or ruled out. The Austric speech is also understood to have gone further to the west beyond the northwestern frontier of India. The present-day Austric languages deviated to some extent considerably from the original Austric speech, which has not yet been reconstructed. "There are Austric speeches like the Indonesian languages, which show a polysyllabic inflexionless structure, although using some prefixes, suffixes and infixes; there are other ones like Mon, Khmer and Khasi which show a tendency to Monosyllabism (as if the proximity of the Monosyllabic Tibeto-Chinese speeches has helped to bring this about)...[375] "The date when the Austric peoples began to filter into India is not known, but it must have taken place several thousand years B.C. and certainly long anterior to the advent of the Aryans from the west and probably also to that of the Dravidian speakers from the same direction."[376] Linguistically the Lepchas living in the hill-areas of Sikkim and Nepal from time immemorial have been connected with the Nagas inhabiting the present Nagaland State by Robert Shafer.[377] In the present state of knowledge we can't say anything about the correctness of his findings. However, the tradition does not support it.

The Himalayan Kirâtas or "Indo-Mongoloids" are believed to have mixed with Âryan speakers in the East Punjab Hills too. The Khasas representing an Âryan speaking tribe later on absorbed some of the "Indo-Mongoloid" features both racially and linguistically. The Kunindas living in the Hill-areas of Eastern Punjab in ancient times, probably in the early centuries of Christian era were the Âryan-speaking tribes, who are described as Hill people of mixed Indo-Âryan and Indo-Mongoloid origin. The Kunet community of the Simla Hills and the Trans-Satluj areas lying between the Beas and the Satluj and in the states of Kahlur, Mandi and Suket are considered to be the descendants of the ancient Kunindas. These areas inhabited by the Kuninda-Kunet people also adopted the Tibeto-Burman and Austric forms of speech. The Tibeto-Burman-ti-di (=water or river) came in use in the Kunet area ; e.g. 'Rawa-ti=Ravi River', 'Nyung-ti=-Beas', 'Zang-ti=Satluj' Para-ti=Para river', etc. The Sânskritised names of rivers like Irava-ti, Goma-ti, Parva-ti, etc. contain the Tibeto-Burman elements.[378]

The languages of the Akas and the Mishmis — the two important Kirâta tribes living in the present Arunachal Pradesh from very ancient times have been put by Grierson and other linguists under North-Assam Branch of Tibeto-Burman Family. The Akas speak a language, which is nearly allied to that of the Abors ; half of the words can be found alike in both the languages: one fifth of the words agree with the Mishmis and considerable number of the words with the Burmese, Singphos and Manipur.[379] C.H. Hesselmeyer has put forth his views that "the language of the Aka however tells a tale and so does their national character. The language contains mere words, which can be traced to the valleys south of the Patkoi ranges joining the Shan and Manipuri countries than words in dictating a closer affinity with the Dafla and Abor tribes. He is ignorant of the art of reading and writing and though he covets the production of art, which Assam and Bhutan supply including Tibetan oil-paintings of Buddhist deities yet does he look down upon books."[380] Grierson[381] supporting both the statements calls it Tibeto-Burman language and further mentions that its vocabulary shows points of contact with Dafla, which do not seem to be due to borrowing. The language of the Muslims bears some affinity with that of Abors and Miris. Robinson has written the grammar and vocabulary of both the Miju Mishmis and Digaru Mishmis.[382] The Taera Mishmi language belong to Tibeto-Burman family shows some dichotomy in grammer.[383]

Here it must be confessed that the North-Assam Branch of the Tibeto-Burman sub-family is a haphazard collection of languages grouped on geographical rather than on philological principles. The speakers of this group of languages can be classed neither as Tibeto-Himalayan nor as Assam-Burmese, though they are slightly connected with them. There should be a separate classification of languages falling under this group. We can best qualify our statement in the words of Professor Konow "these languages are called Tibeto-Burman forms of speech, although in many of them we can observe several features, which are not in accordance with Tibeto-Burman principles."[384] Due to the existence of an old heterogeneous substratum of the population they have spoken dialects belonging to a different linguistic family. The impact of Âryan language on the Himalayan philology can never be due to their cultural intercourse since second millennium B.C. The classification of the Himalayan languages is still gaining ground because the new discovery in the field of linguistic researches still await recognition. The Tibeto-Himalayan languages are sometimes connected with the Assam-Burmese and sometimes with Bodo-Naga-Kuki-Chin and Kachin and other several groups.

The Assam-Burmese Branch is further sub-divided into the groups i.e. the Bodo, Kuki-Chin, Naga, etc. Here we are mainly concerned with the Bodo and Naga groups. The four Kirata tribes of the N.E. India, namely, the Dimasa Charis of North-Cachar Hills, the Gâros of the Gâro Hills of present Meghalaya, the Chutiya tribes of erstwhile Sadiya region and the tribes of Hill Tipperah (present Tripura): considered to be the speakers of so-called Bodo group of language. Grierson opines that "the Dimasa of North-Cachar and the Bodo of Kamrup formed one tonality till about 1540 A.D.[385] Though the" differentiation he ween Dimasa and standard Bodo has probably taken-place but form the point of view of history, tradition, legend and cu1ture common characteristics in their languages can be noticed. These two are really not so nearly connected as French and Spanish. Grierson has categorically stated that the "language in its original form is strictly an agglutinative one, but a gradual process of deglutinisation has for some time been going on."[386] The Aryan forms of speech are also known to them. The Garo language, so far its construction is concerned is allied with the buts as stated by Robinson. But this is contradicted by Hodgson, because he does not find any analogy between the two. The linguistic affinities are decidedly with the Bodo' the Mech and the Chutiya. They have no written language. The altered form according to circumstances gives but little clue to their early history.[387] While the Kacharis have yielded to the influence of foreigners, the Garos have remained to a greater degree unaffected by them and have retained their tongue and manners. The Garo language unlike the Kachari represents the primitive form of the Bodo tongue. Atkinson[388] refutes this view and suggest that the Garo ('pagan') language has affinities with Aryan dialect spokeu in the north, south and west, though the language has Tibetan basis. The dialect spoken by the Chutiya race proves the linguistic affinity wrth that of the Garo and Bodo. As a matter of fact, their language Iike that of religion and custom dates back to one hundred years antecedent to the Ahom invasion of Assam, which took place in the second quarter of the thirteenth century. Their constant contact with the Âryans for several centuries greatly modified their linguistic structures.

The remaining important language of the Bodo group is found among the Kirâta tribes of Hill-Tipperah. It shows point of connexion and agreement with both Dimasa and Gâro. The admixture of Âryan and non-Âryan dialects forms the basis of their language. The Tripuri dialects are generally placed under the Bodo group of Assamese-Burmese branch of Tibeto-Burman family. The Maghs have got their own language with a separate script, which according to Grierson's classification belongs to Assam. Burmese Branch, the Riangs' dialect also belongs to Tibeto-Burman sub-family of so-called, Tibeto-Chinese group of language. Some of the dialects were originally written in Burmese characters in ancient times. W.W. Hunter has fairly stated that the Tipperahs have a distinct language of their own but they have no written characters. The language of the Hallams is mere dialect of Kuki.[389]

We are in perfect agreement with Grierson[390] so far his view that "the most important invasion on the Bodo country was that of the Âryan culture from the west and with its language it has occupied the parts of Cachar, Garo Hills and Hill-Tipperah forming the Âryanised population" is concerned. Thus we find the semi-Âryan form of speech in different Bodo areas, which is resultant of inter-cultural attacks of more than two centuries before the Ahom invasion of Assam in the 13th century.

Among the ancient Kirâta tribes of present Manipur and Nagaland represented by only the Nâga tribes the numerous dialects have been recorded. The dialects of the hill-people of Manipur have been broadly classified into following two groups on the basis of their affinity: i.e.=(*a*) the Naga group consisting of Thangal, Maram, Kabui, Kacha and Thankhur and (*b*) the Kuki-Chin family represented by the Kuki-Chin tribes. This classification can't be accepted as absolutely correct for, great similarities among the Kabui, Thadou, Mizos, Methei or Mithei (Manipuri) and others can be noticed. None of these tribal dialects has any script. However, we are here concerned with the linguistic history of only the hill people of Naga-groups. From the materials made available by the pioneers of linguistic and ethnological investigation it is evident that the languages of sub-Himalayan tribes bear some affinities with other dialects of their areas, so far as their vocabulary and linguistic structure is concerned.

Deriving the authority from T.C. Hodson (one of the noted authorities on the Naga tribes of Manipur) Grierson[391] refers to a group called Nâga-Bodo group, which lies between Angami

Naga and the Bodo form of language bridging over the differences between the characteristic features of the two forms of speech. This is very much similar to another group called Nâga-Kuki, which falls between Angami Naga and the Kuki languages. The Nâga-Bodo group also consists of two main languages viz. Mikir and Kacha Nâga.

As already stated, the classification of Kabui group of languages is arbitrary, for, they have connection with the Bodo form of speech and show many points of contact with the Kuki. According to Grierson, the Naga-Kuki sub-group includes Sopvema or Mao, Naga, Maram, Miyangkhang, Knoirong or Liyang, Lukupa or Luppa languages, viz. Thangkul and Maring.[392] Their languages are partly related to the Bodo dialects and partly Naga language containing Kuki elements. The fact, that the old Kukis used Thadou as a lingua-franca, is possibly an indication of the manner in which the earlier Kuki immigrants were overrun by the later one. It is not written language, which accounts for variations of pronunciation and phraseology, that differ, although very slightly in some cases from village. How far this traditional belief is reliable that very long ago the Thadou Kukis, the Nagas and the Manipuri had a separate language, written on skin, we do not know. In this particular zone there are, apparently rich variety of dialects, which can be attributed to the effects of the confluence of various streams of language. The more detailed philological examination of the said dialects will display more variety and show the remarkable gradation and prove the series of development.

Among the different Naga tribes there is current tradition that in the beginning the deity gave the knowledge of reading and writing both to the Naga in the Hill and the plainsmen of Assam; the former were given a book of skin and the latter the stone or paper to record their writings. It is believed that they had in their possession the written language and they were well acquainted with the art of writing in remote past, which may not be a mere supposition. Sir G. Duff Dunbar and others have also casually mentioned about this secret of writing but there is no authentic historical evidence to confirm this tradition. It is very difficult to say whether such belief is based on myth or reality. However, it can scarcely be denied that even without knowing the art of writing they somehow managed to retain the purity of their dialects, which have, presently, reached a high state of development.

Grierson has classified the Naga language proper into three sub-groups a western, a central and an eastern. The western Naga sub-group includes Angami, Sema, Rengma and Kozham. The most important is Angami with its two dialects, i.e. Tonglma and Chakroma. There are other numerous sub-dialects among which the principal ones are dzuma. Khhona and Nali.[393] Captain Butler holds the view that the Angamis have a singularly expressive manner of emphasizing the messages. A similar use of symbolism to convey or to emphasize a message is common among Sema Naga too. The commonest symbols used by them are Punji, a burnt stick and a chilli.[394] The symbolic message reminds us of a passage in the story of Herodotus, which relates as to how the Scythians sent a message to Darius. The Nâga dialects vary both in vocabulary and in pronunciatin from village to village. The Rengmas are divided into two linguistic groups distinguished from each other. The southern villages use the languages, known as *Tseminyu* and the northern as *Inseni-kotsenu*. It is worthy of noticc that other Nâgas readily borrowed new words in the past from the Assamese or so-called Hindustani and assimilated them into their own tongue. Apart from it the Angamis also invented a few words of purely Angami character or form.

The central Naga sub-group includes Ao, Lontha or Lhota, Tengsa Nâga, Thukumi an Yachumi but the principal members of this group are Ao and Lhota. The two well-marked dialects known as Chungli and Mongsen are spoken in the north-east of the Nâga Hills-District. Both dissyllabic and Monosyllabic features are present. They use the poetical language and traditional and archaic words, which reflect their deep attachment to the primeval cultural elements. There is a marked similarity between Sema and Lhota vocabularies. Tengsa, Thukumi and Yachumi are spoken by tribes beyond the Dikhu about which no clear data is available.

In the eastern Nâga sub-groups are included the dialects of all other Naga tribes known as Angwanku, Chingmegnu, Banpara, Mutonia, Mohengia, Namsangia, Chang, Assi-ringya, Moshang and Shamgge found in the tract east of the Ao country extending to the Kachin country on the east and bounded on the south by the Patkoi range. This group of language as spoken by them is unintelligible to others. Within twenty miles of the country five or six dialects are often to be found. The information available is scanty but it proves the strong affinity, which existed among all of them. The Chang language is grouped with Konyak tribes.

The discussion would hardly be complete without a remark that the Assamese language, which served as an excellent - vehicle for reproduction of Nâga idioms and expression and interpretation of speeches and thoughts, proved to be a far better lingua-franca, for some of them than any other Hindustani language.

Here it is to be noted that the linguistic distinction between sub-groups hardly corresponds to any sort of racial distinction, as far as the as Nâga tribes are concerned. Further, the Monosyllabic language like those of the Naga groups grew apart from one another very rapidly, particularly under the condition of isolation. The two different Naga villages are no more connected with one another than two different nations. J.H. Hutton's observation is worth placing here. According to him "there is no part of the world with so much linguistic variations in so small a population or in so small an area." He further adds that the development of about thirty languages as different as those of different nations in Europe in an area of the size of the Wales is strange feature of their linguistic history. "The Naga languages are all agglutinative and have been described as monosyllabic at all early stage in the process of becoming dissyllabic."[395]

The Naga group of dialects, on the whole, are more closely related to Tibetan than to Burmese. In the south and west the Naga dialects are connected with the Bodo and Kuki-Chin languages by means of several intermediate dialects. We find the dialects of the North-Assam group merging into the Naga and further into the Bodo and Kuki-Chin forms of speech and further we can also trace a line from Tibetan through the Himalayan language culture across the Bodo and Kuki-Chin groups of language. Max Muller in his letter to Chevalier Bunsen attempted at classification of the Tibeto-Burman group of language by sub-dividing them into two groups, which he called "Sub-Himalayan or Gangetic and Lohitic" respectively. The latter sub-division broadly comprises the Burmese and the dialects of the north Assam, Nâga, Bodo, Kachin and Kuki-Chin groups.[396] The further investigation shows the connection of the Naga-Bodo sub-group with other forms of speech indicates the independent position of some other groups.[397]

T.C. Hodson, while referring to the Tibeto-Burman dialects tried to eastablish the links among different tribes, such as Dimasa, Garo, Tippera, Chutiya, Mikir, Mishmi, Ao and other frontier tribes as well as among the Naga groups,[398] whose detailed explanation does not fall within our purview. But we can embrace the opportunity to point out that all these details are fundamentally based on philological and ethnographical principles devoid of genuine historical altruism.

The Nâga tribes are linguistically connected with the Bodo speakers. The Bodo form of speech spoken by the Kirata Bodos popularly amongst both the Âryans and non-Âryans of north eastern and eastern India, particularly Assam and Bengal. The movement of the Bodos over the wide areas covering the whole of Brahmaputra valley, north-Bengal, east-Bengal and the hill-areas of north-east rendered it possible for the extension of their language, which further became very rich after the collection of the folk-poetry and tales. But the Nâgas remained isolated and primitive in their culture and ways of life for a long time as a result of which they could not absorb the Âryan speech of their Âryan speaking neighbours much in their linguistic system. They are split-up into a number of mutually exclusive tribes in such a manner that they do not always understand each other's dialects or speeches. This constitutes one of the unique feature of the linguistic and cultural milieu of the Nâga tribes of the Hill areas in the present Nâgâland. The Âryan form of Assamese speech in a broken form known as Nâgamese t subsequently became the lingua-franca for various Nâga, tribes. In Manipur the Nagas were absorbed linguistically and culturally among the Meithei or Manipuri people to certain extent in ancient times. The archaic language of the Nâgas, on the whole, has unfortunately, not survived on the soil of North-East India. Because of their geographical situation, they were not in a position to influence the languages which came into prominence in India subsequently. The Negrito speech was covered up by two other linguistic strata, the Austric and the Dravidian before the evolution of the Âryan speech. That is why the original form of Negrito speech did not survive. Some of the words like pet, wet, met, wed, wat, etc. forming elements of the aboriginal languages of Malaya and Indo-China of the Austic stock were spoken by the Negrito tribese—e.g. tra-pet, sa-pet, ham-pet, sa-met, ha-met, ka-wet, ka-wed, etc. The original Negrito speech of India, whatever it was seemingly survives among the Andamanese in the form of an isolated language of dialect-group.

The Tibeto-Burman group of language spoken in the eastern part and the Himalayan regions of India has been grouped together by Ram Vilas Sharma"[399] under the Nâga language. His linguistic explanation, to a considerable extent, is based on the researches of P.K. Benedict, who has added a new dimension to the Sino-Tibetan form of speech. He has visualised an archaic language as a source of the speeches falling under the Sino-Tibetan family. Mr. Sharma on the basis of his findings claims, that the Naga language spoken in the areas extending from eastern Himalayan region to the Northern part of Kashmir also appear to be a combination of Âryan, Dravidian and Kol elements. In support of his view he quotes Grierson and Konow who on the basis of striking similarity between the Nâga and Kol languages had inferred that Himalayan region, where the Naga dialects are spoken, there, the speakers of the Kol language were living in former times.

We find quite a different picture in the case of North-Eastern Hill region. The Nâga Bodo group of language is related to Tibeto-Burman family but not the Chinese family. In those parts of northern or Udicya region, where Kharosthi script was in use upto 5th-6th century, the Naga community were also living and the ruling class of people used the Âryan form of speech which was very much akin to lower grade of Prâkrt speech. Nothing definite can be said about the actual process followed in the formation of the various forms of Naga-Bodo speech spoken by the Kirata people.

The manuscript's photocopies of Bhuvan Pahâd Stone Inscriptions recently discovered from the caves near Haflong

(North-Cachar Hills, Assam) and partly deciphered and transcribed by Shri V.S. Wakanker, a renowned archaeologist, gave me the impression that the indigenous system of writing existed among the Kacharis of North Cachar Hills, the Nâgas and other Kirâta tribes of the adjacent areas in ancient times. The close resemblance between these inscriptional writings of early times and the Gupta Brahmi and Sankha script of Central West Bharat has been also established.* This discovery invalidates the theories propounded by linguists, anthropologists and historians concerned that these Indo-Mongoloids were only the speakers of Tibeto-Burman group of languages.

Just for the sake of an instance it can be added that the archaic script used in Manipur is still claimed to be of Kuki-Chin group of Tibeto Burman branch of Sino-Tibetan family of languages. But it distinctly appears as a mixed form of Devanagari and Brahmi scripts of Indian origin. This is one of Indian origin. This is one of the specimens of old script, which they have preserved till today. Their alphabet like that of Tibetan and Burman scripts are believed to be modification of Indian (Sanskrt) system of writing, which was adopted in early times. But its exact antiquity and provenance are not known to us. Some Manipuri chronicles have been written in the archaic script, which undoubtedly proves its use before the 1st century A.D. This gradually fell into disuse among the Manipuris after they adopted the Bengali script in the 18th century. The specimen of this alphabet is given in *LSI.*, Vol. Ill, pt. Ill, p. 12. The Manipuri alphabet appears to be different from the Chinese and the Burmese. It is very much akin to Devnagari.

With the exception of Khâsi all other non-Âryan dialects of North Eastern region are placed under the Tibeto-Chinese family and the Tibeto-Burman sub-family. Among the various groups of language spoken by the Kirâtas in the North-East, the Bodo-group represented by all the surviving non-Aryan

---

* I am extremely grateful to Prof. K.N.P. Magadha for making the said Manuscript copy available to me. I am also thankful to L.S. Wakankar, great Lipikar, for his valuable suggestion (vide his letter dated 27th Jan., 1987 written to me). I was also in close touch with Shri V.S. Wakankar in 1987 through correspondence. I got the facsimile of the said inscription deciphered by some epigraphists of Dharwad University (Karnataka) in 1988. Some similarities between the scripts of the said tribes and the Brahmi was confirmed. I hope that the future researches on this point will unfold some more hidden truth.

languages of the Brahmaputra valley, the Garo, the Kacharis, the Chutiyas and the Trippera section of the Kirâtas occupied the prominent position. All the explanations given in connection with the Sino-Tibetan or Tibeto-Chinese family are not acceptable because of the reasons which will find little reflection in the discussion to follow.

The language of the Kirâtas of Sikkim has been greatly influenced by the Tibetan dialects, which fall under the Himalayan languages of the Tibeto-Burman family. The Sikkim dialect is popularly known as "Den-Jong-Ke", which is akin to 'Lho-Ke' of Bhutan. They are considered to be the modifications of the U (Dbus) or Lhasa-speech of Central Tibet. No literature is available in these Tibetan forms of dialects. The Lepcha dialect current in Sikkim and Darjeeling has been connected by Robert Shafer with the distant Nâga-group of the Tibeto-Burman speech family in the east of Assam. We don't have any positive historical evidences to trace the development of this branch of Tibeto-Burman speech family. But it is believed that the people of Kirâta-group in Sikkim including Limbus and Lepchas had an archaic script of their own in ancient times, which was subsequently modified by the Tibetan script. Till recently its immediate affinities were not known. We do not know on what basis Mr. Shafer identified it with the Nâga group of Tibeto-Burman speech family. However, it is a proven fact that, the dialects of Kirâtas of Nepal and Sikkim in ancient times were evolved out of their indigenous traditions but because of their disuse in subsequent period and the pre-dominance of various other group of languages on them. Because of intermingling or commingling of various races the line of enquiry followed by philologists went in different directions and consequently the results obtained from it became very confusing.

The language of the Kiratas have been placed under different linguistic families because of their wide expansion in the different parts of Himalayan and sub-Himalayan regions. There has been a general tendency on the part of linguists to connect their languages mainly with Tibeto-Burman sub-family of Sino-Tibetan group and to call them Indo-Mongoloids merely on the assumption they emigrated from China, Tibet and Burma and settled in different parts of India. Historically, we find picture which is little different from them. The bulk of Kirâta population living in the mountainous regions, different hill areas and along the forests in India right from the pre-historic days have had distinctively their own traditions, religion, culture and languages. They had their own archaic dialects as attested to by their traditions, but unfortunately some of them have been lost because of the reasons unknown to us. Some of them were further modified by the Tibeto-Burman dialects of those sections of the Kiratas who originally belonged to Tibet and Burma and later shifted to the Himalayan regions of India. As a result of this historical development and synthesis of various elements in their linguistic structure they lost their originality. This provided a host of avenues to the linguists and other scholars to examine the formations and structures of their languages and to propound different theories. This led to the creation of different linguistic families and their different classifications and consequently the language spoken by the Kirâtas mainly fall under different sub-groups i.e. the Austric or Mon-Khmer, Boro, Nâga-Bodo, Kachin, Meithei, Kuki-Chin, North-Assam group, Lepchas, Newari, etc. Quite contrary to it, their languages or speeches fall under different groups, as we have discussed in this section. However this can't be denied that the Kirâtas linguistically and culturally affected the formation of the Âryan and Dravidian forms of speech. The Âryans are believed to have learnt the art of writing from their non-Âryan compatriots. Later, the people of mixed Âryan and non-Âryan origin too adopted the non-Âryan systems of writing, which was obtained in India in the initial stage of the development of Âryan language! Anderson has also accepted that in Assam and Bengal the Âryan forms of speech was profoundly affected by Bodo language. It was the Bodo medium through which the Kirata influence percolated up to lower level. The Kirâtas' influence on the Himalayan vocabularies and speeches is perceptible. In Nepal, Sikkim, Uttarakhanda, Himachal Pradesh, Kashmir, etc. the Kirâta languages were in a flourishing stage. Some Tibeto-Burman and Chinese words, e.g. Tuni, Tokma, etc. are believed to have found their place in Nepalese vocabulary through the Kirâtas. The over-all impact of the Kirâtas on the linguistic structure of India can, of course be professed.

Though the vocabulary is the most trustworthy guide for establishing the exact relationship between Aryan and non-

Âryan languages like that of the relationship of Latinized, English, Urdu, Semitic or Eranian and Sanskrit languages with other linguistic groups yet it will not be unwise to follow a historical line of enquiry for illustrating the close resemblance that exists among various linguistic groups because of their commingling during both prehistoric and historical periods. In our attempts to do so we are sure to fall in confusion and to face some insurmountable problems. However, our continuous efforts will definitely lead us to success.

The observation made by Dhrubanand Mishra (a Brahmin scholar of Bengal) in the early forties of the 19th century is of great historical value. To quote him :

> "there is a commixture of the original wild dialects with the polished vocabulary of *Vedas* and *Puranas.* They have also undergone similar mutations in men and language with its insular mistress of the west where the Saxons and Normans amalgamated with the aboriginal savages, though they were driven into inaccessible mountains and forest".[400]

In the present context, it will be quite befitting to remark that while dealing with the linguistic history of the Himalayan Kirâtas, the factors influencing the formation of Tibeto-Burman group of languages should not be lost sight of. This will reveal the mystery which shrouds the origin and development of Tibeto-Burman speech family. The languages spoken by the Kiratas in most cases are placed under Tibeto-Burman group of Sino-Tibetan family merely on the assumption that they belong to "Indo-Mongoloid" stock and came from China, mixed with Tibeto-Burman population and assimilated in their original Chinese language many Tibeto-Burman elements. This is the conventional explanation, which is often repeated by many. At best, we can partially accept it, but not in toto. Because these are highly speculative thoughts or fanciful notions of the scholars concerned. We have proved that a larger section of them developed their language, religion and culture along their own genius and traditions. Only some sections of them later migrated from Tibet and Burma and left behind their impression on their indigenous linguistic systems. The gravity centre located in the sphere of Tibeto-Burman language conforms to the Âryan and Dravidian languages but not the Chinese. In any case their languages can't be linked with the Chinese. The Sino-Tibetan combination is misnomer. The impact of Âryan forms of speech and Sanskritised dialects on the non-Âryan forms of speech has been pushed into background. The Kirâta tribes placed under Tibeto-Burman groups including the Bodo and Nâga groups as a result of their contacts with the Aryan population right from the epic age absorbed various Âryanised and semi-Aryanised words into their own dialects.

There is an amazing similarity between Tibeto-Burman scripts on the one side and the Brahmi and Gupta scripts on the other. The extension of particularly the Brahmi script, which was similar to the pictorial script of the Indus valley, in the greater part of India can be ascribed to the 3rd century B.C. This was widely used between post Asokan period and the 4th century A.D. Thus scripts of not only India but Tibet and Burma and whole south east Asia evolved out of the Brahmi script. The script of Tibetan language is fundameatally based on the scripts of Indo Aryan group of languages. The Tibetan language contains not less than ten per cent of the Sanskrit words. The composition of *Sambhota Vyâkarana*—the oldest grammer of Tibet—is itself based on Pâṇini's *Aúṭâdhyâyi.* From Aúokan inscriptions of circa 250 B.C. and from the writings of a well known grammarian, Pâtañjali (circa 150 B.C.) also it is evident that the Âryan speech mixed ' with several dialects was employed in north India too. While speaking of the Sabara Pulinda speech family of Vindhya region, which is connected today with Austric family including the Mon Khmer language, Raj Bali Pandey[401] has clearly stated that there are some influences of Sino Tibetan languages on the Kirâta speech family of upper regions of the Himalayas as well as the extreme eastern region of India but the vocabulary of this family is replete with or full of words of Âryan speech family. All the languages of India derived from the archaic Brahmi script are written in Devanagari and other local scripts. This statement can be further supported by other sources also. It is stated that the two great languages spoken by the tribes (Kirâta) of the Himalayan tracts are Tibetan and Burmese—each of which has an alphabet of its, own akin to Devanagari, as well as an extensive literature. Tibetan is one of the several dialect-groups under the general name, 'Bhotia', which is a derivation from the word 'Bhot', the ancient Indian name of Tibet.[402] The alphabet of Indian origin have left their stamp on both these languages widely spread among the Himalayan tribes. The influences of Sanskrt, Brahmi and Gupta scripts on the Tibetan script, which began in the second century, 4th century and 7th century A.D. have not been given due importance by the linguists, as a result of which, their analysis in most of the cases are not found absolutely correct.[403]

Similar is the case with the Burmese language. The Burmese got their alphabet from Hindu colonists of India. Their script is also based on Sanskrit and Pali. The Indian influences on their script can be traced back to first century A.D. The earliest recorded inscription of the third century discovered at Annam Coast was in Sanskrit language, used both by the Burmese and the Siamese. This can be confirmed by the Burmese chronicles of early Medieval period. Even the Burmese chronicle of 850 B.C. bears witness to the introduction of Sanskrit language in Burma. The Burman traditions also attest the high antiquity of the colonisation of Bruma both north and south by Ksatriya princes from India. Despite the fact that the Burmese is a monosyllabic tonal language closely akin to Tibetan in general and blend of four main types—Mon (Tai alphabet tinged with Indian speech-Sanskrit spoken in the country of lower Burma under the Hinduised name, Ramannades'a influenced by Indian culture), the language akin to that of Khmer (Cambodian), Shan language and the Arakanese of the coastal strip with an admixture of Indian blood, almost all classical, technical and other terms have been derived from Pâli language, which was the most popular language in the Magadha region.[404] This can be amply testified to by the statements of two renowned authorities on the history of, Burma, G.E. Harvey[405] and G.E. Hall.[406] They have alsa professed that the Burmese language, akin to Tibetan was an unwritten language in the beginning. The Burmese got their scripts from the Indian Brahmanical colonists. Their language and literature were profoundly influenced by the Pali language. Before the Burmese became a written language during the Pagan period (1044-1287) the Mon Alphabet, which they learnt about 832 A.D. was adopted by them for use. Their Medieval chronicles even go to the extent of proving that the Burmese themselves came from India.

S.K. Chatterji, while advocating the Indian origin of Burmese language has also pointed out that the oldest Pali and other inscription in Burma date back to 5th-6th centuries, on the basis of literary evidence it can be well assumed that the Raman (Mon or-Talaing) inhabitants of south and central Burma, who are racially and linguistically kinsmen of the Austrics of India, received by land, sea routes Indian culture and Indian speech even before the Christian era. The first thousand years after Christ was a period of intense Âryanisation of the Mon or Raman people. "This Âryanisation was carried on through the introduction of the Indian script and the Sanskrit and later on the Pali languages apart from the Prakrit vernaculars".[407]

It is because of the progressive Indianisation of several Tibeto-Burman (generally called Indo-Mongoloids) and Austric tribes were later absorbed in the indigenous Kirâta population of India, that they carried along with them their alphabet bearing the Indian influences.

The language also bears an ample evidence of the imporance of the synthesis that took place in India of two prominent cultures—Âryan and non-Âryan including the Kirâta, the Nisada and the Dravida. This synthesis led to the evolution of different Âryan and non-Âryan languages. The Aryan language within a few centuries after its evolution and gradual adoption by masses of non-Âryans began to take a new shape. Likewise the synthesis of the best elements in the Âryans and pre-Âryans ("Mongoloid, Dravidian and Austric") led to the development of Sanskritic Indo-Âryan speech. The importance of non-Âryan elements in the Vedic and Sanskrit languages can't be dismissed. The possibility of borrowing vocables from the languages of the Kirâtas the Sabaras, the Nisâdas, the Pulindas, the Kollas, the Bhillas and other aboriginal tribes by the Âryans can't be ruled out.[408] This is the most fertile field for carrying out a historical investigation.

It will not be a digression to add that like race, religion and culture, the language or the Kirâta too was not pure in ancient times. After having a deeper insight into the various trends, which followed one after another in the historical evolution of the Âryan and non-Âryan languages, we find that India has always been a repository of composite culture with vehicle of expression, which is combination of the Austric, the Kirata, the so-called Tibeto Burman Mongoloid, the Bodo, the Dravidian and Aryan elements. All the archaic scripts in ancient India developed in concert or league with each other. The influence of one language on the other can be attributed to racial fusion, cultural interactions between diverse racial groups, expansion of Aryan and non-Âryan religion and culture in and outside India, their mutual contacts through trade and other historical factors. This is true in case of both the pictographic Harappan script, which is sometimes connected with Dravidian or the Proto-Dravidian or eastern Mediterranean language and sometimes with the Sumerian language and ancient Indo-European languages like, Sanskrit, Greek, Avesta, Gothic, ancient Germanic, Italian, Spanish, French, Teutonic, Scandinavian, etc. Most of the Asiatic scripts like the Sharada script of Kashmir, the Siddham of Tibet, Nagari of Central Indian regions, the ancient Brahmi, and many other Cambodian, Vietnamese. Thai, Tibetan, Mongolian, Burmese and other scripts follow a Sanskrit based phonological order in their alphabetical letters and orthography. Here we find tht common source for diffusion of ideas about the script.

Taking an over-all view of the preceding discussion it can be postulated that the ancient dialects spoken by the Kiratas in India extending from the northern and eastern Himalayas to the plains in the south constitute a synthesis of an archaic dialect of unknown identity, mleccha-bhâsa, Prâkrt form of speech, piúâca prâkrt, Aryo-Dravidian forms of speech and Tibeto Burman group of language with Indian (Sanskrit, Pâll, and Brâhmi) influences. Hence the theory connecting the Kirâtas only with the Tibeto Burman family of Sino Tibetan group of languages can no longer he held as tenable.

In the light of linguistic data also we do not find any justification to call them "Indo Mongoloids" as it has become a general fashion to call them. The historical researches into the primeval civilization of the primitive people of by gone age is still in its infancy. The linguistic researches conducted by Grierson, Sten-Konnow, Schmidt, Hodgson, Przyluski,. Burrow, Benedict and others in this connection should be further pursued. The researches in the field of historical linguistics have also not made much progress since the time of W.P. Lehmann, a pioneer in this field. There is a need of making a comparative study of philology and scriptology of ancient India. The historical and linguistic researches into the original linguistic structure of the Himalayan primitive population, as well as, the inter-disciplinary approaches to the problems involved will open up a new vista for the cultural and linguistic history of India.

II. Literature

The literary efflorescence of the Kirâta people greatly merits our attention. Their genius in literature found an expression in folktales—oral and traditional literature, folk-lore legendary episodes and lyrics. This kind of literature, which they possessed in ancient times, may appropriately be called a narrative literature. The history of the primitive literature bears witness to the fact that oral literature has always preceded the written one because of the absence of a particular script. The oral tradition continued for a pretty long time because it took many years to invent scripts. This is a treasure-house of valuable information about their past history, tradition and culture. This is also a kind of historical science which deals with several experiments conducted from the primitive stage to the higher stage of culture. These have not been generally preserved because many of them were unacquainted with the art of writing.

The folk-lore of the Kirâtas, indisputably forms an invaluable part of the literary, cultural and historical traditions of our country. The historical value of both recorded and unrecorded folk-lore of the Kirâta tribes of India can neither be belittled-nor wholly dismissed. The subject is, of course, as vast in its entirety as extensive in its scope. However, we can begin with this fundamental assumption that myths and legends, tales and stories, facts and fictions, tradition and mythology, manners and customs, beliefs and practices, folk music and dance, fairs and festivals, fables, lyrics and ballads, folk art and architecture and several other related matters, which have bearings on the lives of the people, from an inseparable part of their folk-lore or oral literature. Besides, it is also a repository of simple truth, high ideals, grand imagery, naive and unsophisticated expression, delicate ideas, ethnological conceptions and so on. The Kirata folk-tales as a whole, appear to be a strange mixture of cosmological principles, ethnographical and sociological theories, geographical and historical themes, religio-cultural and philosophical ideas, theological doctrines, artistic traditions, aesthetic beliefs and other episodes connected with natural and astronomical sciences, etc. These folk-tales are marked by their simplicity, originality, nobility of thoughts, elegance and charm, realism and emotionalism and poetic expression devoid of any ornmentation and embellished thoughts. The correct understanding of the history and culture complex of the primitive races of any country pre-supposes an intensive study or their folk-lore. Their folk-tales, myths and legends of the pre-scientific age constituted the bedrock «f the history of the later age ; their folk-literature provided the basis on which higher literature was developed by the later writers and poets ; their fine or applied arts and folk-arts became an inexhaustible source of inspiration for the subsequent artists and architects for developing the national form of art and the first secrets of nature discovered by their creative genius proved to be a beacon of light for the later scientists to invent some astonishing and miraculous laws of nature.[409]

The earliest evidence alluding to the subject under discussion has been adduced by the *Atharva Veda Samhitâ.* One of the hymns of this Vedic text expressly states that the narratives and stories were held in high esteem exactly like that of the Purânas and Itihâsa (history).[410] But this evidence, because of being wrapped into haziness, undeniably, appears to be of dubious character. Kâutilya (4th century B.C.) was probably the first Indian classical scholar to distinctly recognise the historic value of folk literature in broader context by affirming that "Purânamitivrtta-mâkhyayika Dharmasastra Arthasastra Ceitihasa" (the Purana record of the past, tale, illustrative story, the secular literature and *Arthasúâtra* all are Itihasa (History).[411]

In all the ancient countries of the world the narrative literature has been reckoned as one of the dependable sources for depicting the vivid picture of the different aspects of the history and culture of the people. India, Greece, Persia, Arabia,

Egypt, Babylon and Germany are believed to have maintained a glorious tradition of preserving folk-lore, rich in both forms and substance. The folklore finds expression not only in the Vedic literature, the Epic and the Pauranic traditions, the Buddhist-Jatakas and Jaina Dhamma-katha, the classical literature of the Homeric Age and Hellenic Age, but also in the writings of Herodotus (5th century B.C.)—the so-called "father of history", in the 'SAGA' literature of Germanic races of the early centuries of the Christan era, the Sagas of Teutons, etc.

The narrative literature of some of the non-Âryan races of India also deserves mention. The folklore of the Kirâta people of North East India also contains substratum of historical truth with regard to certain aspects of their past lives. It provides some clues which can be safely relied upon to a reasonable extent for tracing their lineage and ascertaining the exactitude of their racial affiliations, extractions etc. It can be reasonably suggested that while dealing with the origin, ethnology and antiquity of various Kirâta tribes of ancient India, anthropologists, historians and other social scientists should give weightage to a considerable degree, to those folk-tales and time honoured traditional beliefs which are in full accord with other trustworthy recorded evidence. Absolute reliance can of course, not be placed upon those tales which are purely of hypothetical nature. The manners and customs, various socio-economic practices, the material culture, political set-up with reference to the customary laws and judicial practices, traditional religious faths, pantheistic beliefs, doctrine of Âtman (soul) and Karma (action), eschatological beliefs, the priesthood, sacrifices, divinations, religious incantations or Mantras, folk songs and dances, fairs and festivals, folk art including carving, paintings and decorative arts, etc. of the Kirâta tribes have been shaped, moulded and regulated by their folklore since time immemorial. The regional cultural patterns may be diverse, but the basic laws framed by the authors of various folklore, which govern the Kirâta society, religion and culture are manifestly identical in nature. It will not be an exaggeration to say that the greater part of the history and culture of particularly the Kirâta people are primarily based on their folklore.

The oral or the traditional literature, transmitted to us from generation to generation right from the time, when writing was not invented, represents the most valid and appropriate expression of religious, mythological, historical and cultural milieu of the tribal folk. It was the only form of literature that existed among them in ancient times. The source of the folk literature cannot be traced to any single author. The folk-literature has been enriched by the anonymous folk songs which appear to be rich miniatures representing the lives, the joys and sorrows of the village folk within a wide canvas. Steeped in antiquity the folk customs and beliefs revealed in the vital form of folklore afford us an opportunity to conjure up a vision of the development of human mind. The songs and dances, which belong to the community, convey to us an aesthetic sense of the people. The authorship of the songs is not known to us; they are preserved by oral tradition.[412]

The Kirâta tribes of north-east India are credited with having a wealth of both recorded and unrecorded folk-literature which contain various enchanting stories and thrilling legends about the mytho-historical origin of tribes, their primitive existence, attachment to natural objects, early economic life, and early socio-cultural contacts with the people of the plains, origin of the world, sky and planets and other interesting episodes concerned with natural phenomenon. Some of their folk-tales bear resemblance to the stories recorded in Indian classical literature including the *Vedas,* the *Râmâyana* the *Mahâbhârata,* the *Purâṇas* the Buddhist *Jatakas* and the secular literature.

The folk-tales of the Khâsi-Jaintias elaborately deal with the historical aspects with regard to the various trends of racial movement and migration, war and peace, victories and defeats and evolution of culture; political aspect regarding the formation of society, growth of state and other institutions, religious and philosophical aspects concerning the traditional beliefs, practices and usages and pantheism and geographical aspect relating to metamorphic changes and effects of geography on history. The Gâros have also large number of verses, stories and tales and songs handed down from generation to generation by word of mouth, which come under the categories of oral literature. The Gâro story of *Gunal and his wife—the bird-maiden Singwil* as recorded by Playfair in his book on the Gâros is very famous. The stories narrated in prose style are usually in spoken dialects but the verses are in an archaic diction which is very difficult to comprehend.

In North-Cachar hills, the Dimasa Cacharis have a long, tradition of recording some interesting stories from the classical literature, particularly the *Râmâyana*. Their folklore contains some other religious stories too. But, unfortunately, we do not have any authentic evidence at our disposal to confirm this tradition. Mr. S. Endle has referred to the Cachari story of the Merchant lad.[413] The few specimens are the favourite Indian form of a sequence, well known in Sanskrit literature and in general folklores in Europe. Some of their folk-tales like the Mikir folk-tale of *Harata-kinwar* are in some respect comparable to that of Pururavas and Urvasi story which forms a part of Indo-Âryan myth.

In the hill-areas of Manipur none of the tribal dialects has any script, but from time immemorial the Naga tribes have maintained the tradition of preserving their rich folktales consisting of anecdotes, legends and myths, which constitute the branch of primitive history. Some of their folk-tales have recorded in the report of the Linguistic Survey of India[414] reveal their old religious views and beliefs and their mythological conceptions about the creation of man, heavenly bodies, etc.

The folk-tales of Nâga tribes of present Nagaland handed down from father to son for untold ages refer to large number of versions mixed with myths and legends, which throw a little light on the origin and migration of the clan, vis-a-vis tribes, origin of the universe, heroic deeds of their ancestors, their customs and beliefs, etc. Many tales are common to the tribes. These tales are little scraps of unreliable history of purely local interest. However, some of the historic tales, such as, Ao's story of *Magician,* Sema's story of *The battle of Birds and Creeping things,* Angami's folk-lore about *The Male and Female Islands* described by Marco Polo and other stories resembling to the Biblical story of the Tower of Babel and Lhota's story of a *Cace in Wokhahills* painted with picture of every sort of men and animals with mysterious inscriptions are worthy of our attention. J.H. Hutton[415] has recorded that Angami folk-lore is parallel to perhaps Moi version of the Tower of Babel. The Moi like all Nagas have universal story of the Amazons, who used to slay their male children. The folk-tales common to all the Kirata tribes of N.E. India exhibit their natural talents and literary splendour.

Sir Richard Temple made a pioneering endeavour to publish the famous folk-tales of the aboriginals of India in 1866. The folk-tales collected by G.H. Damant from some parts of N.E. India also appeared in the *Indian Antiquary* (Vols. I—IX) published between 1872 and 1879. The myths and legends and folk-lores and folk-tales of the Kirâtas have been profusely narrated in some of these works. In the closing decades of the last century Willam Crooke, Rev. A Campbell, Rev. J.H. Knowles and other spared no pain to study and collect the various folk-tales of the Kirâta people of N.E. India. The works done by late Verrier Elwin in this field in the present century are worth appreciating. India can boast of a royal folklorist named Hala of the Satavahana dynasty of Andhra (ascribed by the tradition to the early decades of the first century of the Christian era) who by compiling an anthology of 700 verses known as *Gâthâsaptaиatî* set a noble example for future folklorists of India and western countries.

The Kirântis, the Limbus and other Kirâta tribes of Eastern Nepal and Sikkim have also got oral or folk literature. The religious and mythological traditions of the Kirântis have been collected and published under the title of *Kirât Mundhum* or *Kirât Koved* (the Religious, Social and Historical traditions and Usages of the Kirânti people). The work originally collected in Kirânti language was later published in the Nagari character with a Nepali translation from Patna in 1971 by Iman Singh Chemjong.[416]

One of the striking features of the folklore traditions of the pre-Aryan and pre-Dravidian Kirâta people of N.E. India is an indelible stamp which they have left behind on the pages of the classical literature of the Âryans. Some of the oldest folktales, stories, myths and legends, which were woven into the very web of Paurânic literature may be traced back to the great non-Aryan ideas and beliefs. It is believed that not only the Paurânic story but even the Râmakatha is based on the folk-tales of the so-called Austric people. The Âryans or the Hindus are believed to have borrowed some of the folktales of proto Australoids and the

Kirâtas of North East India, which find clear reflection in the Vedic, the Paurânic and the Epic traditions.[417] The Kirâtas also contributed their share to the evolution of Hindu myths, legend and cults. S.K. Chatterji has aptly remarked that "there is no doubt that Dravida and Nisada and Kirâta stories have lived on even after the Âryanisation in language and Hinduisation in religion of these peoples. A great many of the Pre-Aryan myths and cults have found a place within the fold of Hinduism. The Cosmogonic conceptions of Hinduism are largely of pre-Âryan ("Nisâda and Kirâta") origin".[418] It is because of the cultural intercourse among the Âryans, Dravidians, Austrics-, and other non-Aryans that we find the general characteristics of their folk literature almost the same.

There are some motifs which we find in common with the Kirâta folk-lore, Aryan folk-lore and Austric folk-lore. For instance the oldest versions of the motif of a goddess reciprocating the love of a human lover may be found among the Indian Aryans, the Greeks and others. The story of Pururavas and Urvasî in the *Rig Veda,* in the *Ùatapatha Brâhmaṇa*, in Kâlidâsa's works and in the *Purânas*, that of Santanu and Ganga and of Samvorana and Tapti as in the *Mahâbhârata* and of Aphrodite and Ankhises and Eros and Tithonos in the Greek legend may be quoted. In Roman mythology also we have the story of King Numa and the Nymph Egeria like that of Germanic legend about Welant (Volundr) and his brothers and the Valkyries, and Sigurd and Brynhild. This motif captured the imagination of many folklorists of the greater part of the world. The Japanese *No play of Hagoramo* and the *Arabian Nights* story of Hosan and Basra about divine or fairy women, heavenly nymph or angel etc. are some other instances. The so-called great *Epic cycle of legendary stories* of the Tibetans (so-called Indo Mongoloids) relating to the hero king Gesar or Kesar or Gling is comparable to the Sanskrit *Mahâbhârata* epic, the old Greek Homeric epics, the Rustam cycle in the Iranian *Shahnama,* the Gilgamesh epic of ancient Babylonia, the Sigurd Brynhild epic of the ancient Germanic peoples and the Concobar Cycle of the ancient Irish.[419]

The general trend, which followed all over the world in connection with borrowing of some folk-tales from each other really appear to be something fantastic. Both Max Muller[420] and Max Donell[421] are of the view that the folktales of the East found their way to the west and *vice versa*. We find that the *Iliad* and *Odyssey* of Homer are replete with those romantic stories which figure in our Epic tradition. Only the *Pañcatantra of* Visnu Sharma caught the imaginations of the folklorists of Persia, Arabia, Syria, Spain, Germany, Italy and England. The *Arabian Nights* according to Arabian historian Masudi (10th century A.D.) is a collection of Persian, Greek and Hindu tales. *Sindabad—the* best known stories of Arabia is purely of Hindu origin containing many Indian references. Many ideas originally borrowed by the Indians from the west found their way back to Europe in an Arabic guise.

The myth is nothing but a primitive history. Actually, the eternal quest of man to know the truth in the natural surroundings led him to invent the myths in which the rudiments of history can be seen. Aristotle also was of the opinion that the "myths were the inventions of law". "The purpose of the myth is to explain matter in the science of pre scientific age".[422]

It may be deplorably observed that some of us today are not inclined to attach an importance even to a slightest degree to the quasi-historical and historical truth underlying the folklore. The truth of yesterday is very often misquoted, misconceived and misrepresented as fables of today. This practice will inevitably lead to the projection of distorted image of races and cultures of the primitive age.

Notes and References

1. *Primitive Society,* pp. 4-5.
2. XXX, 16. See also Ralph T.H. Griffith (tr.); TWYV., Bk. XXX. 16, pp. 257-58.
3. X. 4.14. See also Griffith, (tr.); HAV., Vol. I, p. 208. Vol. II. p. 16; A.A. Macdonell and A.B. Keith, Vol. I, pp, 157-58.
4. iii. 4.12.1.
5. *Hancienne Route de l' Inde,* Vol. II, pp. 184-85 ref. to Motichandra. *Sârthavaha,* p. 38.
6. 40, 27-28.
7. ZFKDM., 11.40.
8. ML, p. 66.

9. *DyutaParva,* Ch. 48, Vs, 8-11. See also Pratap Chandra Roy (tr.): Mbh. Vol. II, pt. I, Sec. Li, pp. 103-4; G. Bertrand, *Secret Lands Where Women Reign*, pt. I, pp. 26-27.
10. EHL, pp. 93, 107.
11. Ref. to J.W. McCrindle, AICL., pp. 1-5. See also Bunbury, HAG., Vol. I. pp. 226-30.
12. JASB., 1874, Vol. XVI, pt. T. pp. 13-14. See also Rennell, GSH., p. 308; Wilcox. As, Res., Vol. XVII, p. 456.
13. J.W. McCrindle, AlK., pp. 88-90. See also C. Muller (ed.), The *Fragm. of Ctesias,* pp. 16-18; Wilford, As. Res., Vol. VIII, pp. 331f; IA., Vol. VI. pp. 133-35, Vol. VIII, pp. 15Of.
14. Ind. Alt. Vol. II. pp. 641ff. cf. AIK., pp. 90f.
15. AICL., p. 61, fn. I; AIMA. (Fragm. XXIX, Strabo XV. i. 57, p. 711) pp. 73-75, fn. I.
16. PRIA., April 21, 1883, No. 572 p. 277.
17. *Ibid.*
18. J.W. McCrindle, AIMA. (Fragm. XXX, Pliny Hist. Not. VH. 11-14-22), p. 80.
19. (ed): AIMA., p. 80.
20. AIMA., p. 119.
21. Cf. Schoff, *Periplus,* pp. 266-67.
22. B.C. Law, GAKW., p. 23; HGAL, pp. 98-99; TAI., pp. 282-83 ; B.M. Barua, *Asoka and his Inscriptions,* p. 100.
23. Cf. PK, p. 111.
24. J.H. Hutton, JPASB 1926 (Calcutta 1928). New Series, Vol. XXII. pp. 333-346; JASB., 1844, Vol. XIII, pt. 4, p. 616; ADG., Vol. X. pp. 6, 9; JARS., Apr. 1939, Vol. VII. No. I. pp. loff .
25. JASB., 1902, Vol. LXXI. Pt. III. p. 37; JARS., Apr, 1933, Vol. i. No. pp. 4-5.
26. SANSM., p. 37.
27. A Report of the State Archaeology Department, 1983.
28. *Periplus,* pp. 272-79; McCrindle, *Ancient India,* p. 180, see also Jacques De Morgan, *Pre-historic Man,* pp. 154; Handerson, *Prehistoric Man,* 133 ff; Dawson, *The Age of the Gods,* p. 45.
29. See M.M. Shartna, TCH., pp. 43 44; Capt. H. Strachey's Journal at Garjjiaghat (1846) cf. E.T. Atkinson, HG., Vol. II, Pt. I, pp. 366-68; *'Pahad': A Hindi Journal on Himalayan Society, Culture, History and Ecology,* Pt. II, pp. 145-46

30. PPHEI., pp. 41-72. See also F.R. Allchin, *Review of Pre-history and Proto-history of Eastern India* by A.H. Dani, BSOAS., 1961, Vol. XXIV, pp. 696-98.
31. C. Brown, CPAIM., pp. 130-33; J.H. Hutton, *JPASB.,* Vol. XXIL p. 133; JP. Mills and Hutton, *JPASB.,* Vol. XXV. pp. 295-97; Hutton, Man. (JRAD, 1924, pp. 20-22; Peal. *JPASB,* Vol. LXV, III, p. 20; J. Cockburn, JASB., 1879. II, pp. 133ff; PASB.. 1871, pp. 83f; H.C. Dasgupta, JASB., Vol. IX (New Series), pp. 291-93 ; G. Hesseldin, JASB, (New Series), Vol. XXII, p. 133; Hutton, JRAI., Vol. LVI, p. 71; Hutton, MI (QAJ.), 1928-29; J.P. Mills, JARS., 1833, Vol. I, No. I, pp. 4-5; H.D. Sankalia, PPIP., pp. 283-98; P. Mitra, *Pre-historic India,* pp. 327ff.
32. Taylor, *Primitive Culture,* pp. 38-62.
33. Will Durant, *The Story of Civilization, Pt.* I, *Our Oriental-Heritage,* pp. 97f.
34. See *Ancient India* (BASI.), 1947-48, No. IV, pp. 5, 147f.
35. GBNEI., P. 43.
36. *JARS.,* April 1933, Vol. I, pp. 4-5; *JARS.,* April 1939, Vol. VII, pp. 10-18.
37. G.P. Singh *Researches into the Origins. Antiquity, Nature and Functions of the Pre-historic Megalithic cultures of the Hill-people of North-East India,* PNEIHA. Sixth Session, Agartala, 1985, pp. 24-25.
38. For details see B.C. Alien, ADG., "1905-8, Vol. X pp. 53-54,124 Gurdon JASB, 1904-5, Vol. LXXiii Pt. Ill, pp. 64-65; JASB., 1879, Vol. XLVIII, pp. 133-37; Yule, CR., 1868, Vol. XXXViii, pp. 274f; JARS., 1939, pp. 4-12, 33-40; Gait, *Census of India* ACR., 1891, Vol. I, p. 261; Gurdon, *The Khasis,* pp. 145f; Haimendorf, MI (QAJ.), 1945, Vol. XXV, pp. 73-86; Yule, JASB., 1844, Vol. Xiii; Pt. 2, pp. 617-18; Hutton, JPASB., 1926, Vol. XXII, pp. 333-46; JRAI., 1926, Vol. LVI, pp. 71f; MI (QAJ.), 1926; pp 74f; JRAI., 1922, Vol. LII; JRAI., 1965, Vol. 95, pp. 28f; J.P. Mills, MI (QAJ.), 1930, pp. 34-35; Hodson, *The Naga-Tribes of Manipur,* pp. 86ff; *Geographical Society,* 1904, 31-32; JSA., Vol. LXXX, 550; Hooker, HG., 1854, Vol. II, pp. 66ff; Austen, JASB.. 1874, Vol. XLiii, Pt. I, pp 1-6; Sankalia, *Indian Archaeology Today,* pp. 100-2; JASB., 1931, Vol. XXVII, pp. 1-96; L.W. Shakespear, *History of the Assam Rifles,* pp. 260-62.
39. JARS., April 1939, Vol. VII, No. I, pp. 1-18; JARS. July 1939, Vol. VII, No. 2, pp. 35-40.
40. Cf. Bagachi, PAPDI., Introd. XVII-XVIII.
41. Cf. JARS., July 1939, p. 35.

42. *New Aspects of the Dravidian Problem, cf. Tamil Culture,* 1953-11.
43. *The Problem of Megalithic Cultures in the Middle India, cf. MI* (QAJ.), 1945, Vol. XXV, pp. 73-86.
44. EIP., p. 150.
45. PPHEI., p. 41.
46. AIK., pp. 88-90.
47. IAH., pp. 37-38.
48. Lib. XXXIII, C. XIV, cf. JASB., 1847, Vol. XVI, pt. I, p. 73.
49. JASB., 1845, Vol. XIV, Pt. 2, pp. 477-78; JASB, 1848, Vol. XVII, pt. 1, pp. 462-68.
50. D.D. Kosambi, CCAL, p. 28.
51. L.J. Trotter, *History of India From the Earlier Times to the Present day* pp. 2-3, 23-24.
52. B.N. Luniya, *Life and Culture in Ancient India,* p. 265. Kautilya, *Arthaúâstra* (trans. by Gairola), Prakarana, 7, Ch. II, p. 33; Also II.I; III. 16; VII. 8; VIII. 4; IY. I; IK. 3; X. 2. (quoted in Romila Thapar, AIH., pp. 163, 185 & ref. n. 57).
53. Kalidasa, *Kumârasambhaua* (ed. by M.R. Kale, with commentary of Mallinathta) Canto-I, Vs. 6,10,15, pp. 4-6,8-6, See also B.C. Law, HGAI., pp. 83-84.
54. *Amarakosa,* VII. 21.
55. *Kâdambari* (original text), Purvabhaga, pp. 144-45, trans. by M.R. Kale, pp. 123ff, Ch. Ill, pp. 7-8.
56. *Dasakumaracârita,* Ucchavâsa, 11, pp. 22-24, trans. by M.R. Kale, pp. 15-17.
57. *Pampâ Râmâyânâ,* Nijagunayogi's *Vivekcintâmani,* pp. 423-4; *Chikka Deva Inscription of the seventeenth century of Rice, Mysore and Coorg from its Inscriptions,* p. 129.
58. Cf. V.S. Apte, SED., pp. 149-50.
59. X. 43-45, 51-73.
60. IDM., Ch. Ill, *Social Life,* pp. 16, 17 and 19.
61. 1. 10-11.
62. 65, 13-15, 17-22. See also Mbh. Anusâna Parva, XXXV; Sabha XIV, LII Âúvamedha Pasva, XXIV.
63. AISH., pp. 164-65.
64. Ind. Alt. Vol. I. pp. 441-450 ref. to *Periplus,* p, 253.
65. Vâj. Sam, XXX. 16; Tai. Br. 111. 4.12.1; AV., X. 4. 14; Manu. X. 44; *Raghuvamsa,* XVI. 57. The Pulindas are referred to in the Ait. Br,, *Srauta Sutra* XV.20. *Asoka's Thirteenth Major Rock*

Edict; Manu X. 44; *Kathâsarâasâgara* quoted in Romila Thapar *The Study of Society in Ancient India,* Presidential Address, Ancient Indian History Section, PIHC. XXXI Session, Varanasi, 1966, AISH. pp. 220, 236 & ref. no. 37.

66. Romila Thapar, AISH., pp. 153-162.
67. Dandin's *Daúakumarâcarita* (original Sanskrit text), Ucchavâsa, 11. pp. 22-24, tr. pp. 15-17.
68. A. Cunningham, AGI., pp. 78-79; Thomas Walters, YCTI., Vol. I. p. 265.
69. *Râjatarangini,* viii, 358.
70. *India Three Thousand Years Ago,* p. 56. Jayachandra Yiyalankar's *Bhâratabhûmi our Uske Nivâsi* 'pp. 5ff.
71. 11.4.18.
72. Romila Thapar, *Ethics, Religion and Social Protest in the first Millennium B.C. in Northern India,* Daedalus. JAAAS., Spring 1975. Vol. 104, No. 2, pp. 119-33 cf AISH., pp. 47f.
73. ISIH., pp. 21-22, 27.
74. Ind. Alt. Vol. I. pp. 441-450.
75. Dyuta Parva, Ch. 49, Sl. 10.
76. Bharata Savitri, Vol. I, p. 171.
77. GESM., Upayana Parva, pp. 123-13 quoted in his Sarthavaha, p. 69.
78. Mbh. Drona Parva, CXII. pp. T321-2cf. Saletore, WTIH., pp. 23-24.
79. EC., IV. Ch. 83, p. 10.
80. *Ind. Alt.* Vol. II, pp. 641ff, cf. AIK., p, 90.
81. EC. Ill, Md. 13, 113, p. 51, vide R.N. Saletore, EIC., Vol. II, pp. 750-52; B.A. Saletore, WTIH., p. 35.
82. Raghuvamsa (ed. by N.R. Acharyya with introduction by Prof. H.D. Velankar, llth Edn. Bombay. Saka, 1870) Canto-16, V. 57, p. 415–416.
83. AV., X. 4.14; Rlaph T.H. Griffith (tr.): HAV., Vol. II, p. 16; A.A. Macdonell and A.B. Keith, VI., Vol. I, pp. 157-58; Bloomfield, SBE., Vol. XLII, p. 153.
84. Vide, R.N. Saletore, EIC., Vol. II. pp. 750-52.
85. Vide *Ait. Br.* (Asiatic Society edition), Vol. IV. Introd.; Haug (tr.): Ait. Br. 1.3.7.
86. *Sabhâ Parva.* Dyûta Parva, Ch. 08, SL. 8-11.

    See also *Ibid.,* Chs. 30, 26-28 & 47,19; Pratap Chandra Roy (tr.): Sabhâ Parva, Vol. II, Pt. I, Sec,—Li, pp. 103-4; Vasudeva

Sharana Agrawala, *Bharata Sâvitrî,* Vol. I, Upayana Parva, Chs. 43-51, p. 171; Motichandra, GESM., Upayana Parva, pp. 84-85 ref. to *Sarthavaha,* p. 69.

87. AISH. p. 168.
88. The *Vikramoravasiyam* (original Sanskrit text with trans. by B.R. Arte), 3rd edn., Act-V. vs. 5, 20-21 pp. 131, 140, 144.
89. *Harsacarita,* Ucchavasa-VII, 227-230 cf. V.S. Agrawala, *Harsacarita. Ek Samskrtika Adhyayana,* pp. 182-88 & illustration 90.
90. B.C. Alien, ADG, 1906, Vol. X. p. 86.
91. Dalton, DEB., pp. 11, 15-16, 24-34.
92. BAC, pp. 14-15.
93. IGI.Vol. VI, p. 73, Vol. XV, pp. 262-63; GBNEI., pp. 83. 491, 509; SAA., Vol. II, pp. 167-68, 235; ADG., Vol. X, p. 39.
94. *A New History of India,?.* 15.
95. CR., 1863 & 1861, Vol. XXXVIII, p. 278; IGL, Vol. VI, p. 73, Vol. XV. pp. 262-63; GBNEI., pp. 81-84, 491, 495-97; Hooker. HJ., (London, 1854), Vol. II, pp. 66ff; JARS., 1939, Vol. VII, No. 2, p. 40; S.K. Chatterji, I AH., pp. 37f; SAA., Vol. U, pp. 235f; Gurdon, *The Khâsis,* pp. 57f; JASB., 1832, Vol. I, pp. 150-51.
96. JASB,, 1842, Vol. XI, Pt. II, pp. 853f.
97. Quoted in James Taylor, JASB., 1847, Vol, I, pp. 68-69, 73.
98. Vide. JASB., Vol. XVII, p. 476. PI. XXX.
99. V.S. Agrawala, *Harsacharita: Ek Smskrtic Adhyayana,* pp, 183, fn. I, 185-87 & illustration 87.
100. Atkinson, HG., Vol. II, Pt. I, pp. 367-68; M.M. Sharma, TCH. pp. 43-44.
101. GESM., *Upâyana Parva,* pp. 112-13cf. *Sarthavaha,* p. 69.
102. *Daúakumâracarita,* Ucch. VIII, p. 203.
103. Lassen, Ind. Alt, Vol. II, pp, 641f cf. AIK., p. 90.
104. Pliny, *Nat. Hist.* VII. 2; Schoff, *Periplus,* pp, 164-67; Watt, CPI., pp, 992-1026; CNH., VI, 375; *Ammsanus Marcellinui,* XXii, VI. XXIII, VI; Bunbury, HAG., Vol. I, p. 565, Vol. II, pp. 166, 658; Vincent, *Periplus,* II, pp. 523f; J.L. Whiteley *The Periplus.* pp. 134f; Taylor, JASB., 1847, Vol. XVI Pt. I, pp. 29f. For further studies see D'Anvilie, RGHSA.. (1768) in MARIBI., XXXii, 573-603; Tozer, HAG., pp. 281f.
105. GJ. (JRGS.), 1907, Vol. XXX, pp. 152f.
106. R.M. Nath, BAC., pp. 14-15; P.C. Bagchi, *India and China,* pp. I8f.

107. J.W. McCrindle, CNES., pp. 12, 23, 146-148.
108. TM, Vol. II. p. 21.
109. J.W. McCrindle, AIMA., Bk. II. Fragm. XXV, Strabo XVI, 35-36 . (p. 702.), p. 66.
110. James Taylor, JASB., 1847, Vol. XVI, Pt. I, pp. 32,35.
11. RSTF., 1873 (BHS. I), Vol. 2, p. 46.
112. PAHCI., pp, 32-33.
113. AISH., p. 174.
114. Lib. XXXiii, C. XIV ref. to Taylor, JASB., 1847, XVI, I, pp. 21-22, 68, 73. See also JIH., 1981, Pts. 1-3, Vol. LIX, p. 54.
115. J.W. McCrindle, AIK.., pp. 85-87. See also Lassen, Ind. Alt. Vol. II, pp. 641ff; Wilford, As. Res. Vol. IX. pp. 65f.
116. JASB., 1847, Vol. XVI, Pt. I pp. 47f. See also Heeren, HRPNA. Vol. II, Asiatic Nations, IV, App. p. 380.
117. Taylor, JASB, 1847, Vol. XVI, p. 35.
118. Schoff, *Periplus,* pp. 47-48, 258-59.
119. Taylor, *op. cit.* p. 25; *Periplus,* p. 259.
120. V. Ball, *Travels in India* (tr. from original French edn. of 1670 ed. by William Crooke), Vol. II, pp. 220, 275, 281; *Tavgenier,* III, XV-XVII; Ball, EGI., pp. 231ff. See also Pliny, Xii-18; B. Srivastava, TCAI., pp. 297.
121. V. Ball, *op. cit.* pp. 220, 27f, See also CR., 1853, Vol. XXI, p 411;: Mommesn, *(Provinces of the Roman Empire,* Vol. II, pp. 299-300 cf. JIH. 1981, Pts. 1-3, Vol. LIX. p. 56.
122. J.W. McCrindle, AIP., pp. 217-19; James Taylor, JAS8., 1847, Vol. XVI, Pt. I, pp. 11-12.
123. RGHSA., *Vide,* MARIBL., XXXII, pp. 573ff.
124. J.W. McCrindle, AIP., pp. 193-94; 217-18; JASB., 1847, Vol. XVI pp. 11-12; Ptolemy, VII.J1.16 ref. to J.W. McCrindle, CNES. p. 23. W.H. Schoff, *Periplus,* 63-65, pp. 256, 278-79.
125. RPGEA., p. 53 & Table-X.
126. J.W. McCrindle, AIP., (CAP. 2), pp. 192-94.
127. J.W. McCrindle, AIP., pp. 219-21; JASB., Vol. XVI, pp. 38-39.
128. Schoff, *Periplus* (Cap. 65), pp. 41-49, 288; J.W. McCrindle, AIP., pp. 219-21; J.W. McCrindle, CNES. (Being a translation of the *Periplus Marts Erythraei, Arrian's account of the voyage of Nearkhos etc.).* pp. 148-49; James Taylor, *Remarks on the sequel to the Periplus of the Erythraean Sea and on the country of the Seres as described by Ammianus Marcellinus"* cf. JASB. 1847,

Vol. XVI, Pt. I, pp. 4-6, 32-35; Vincent, *Periplus,* Vol. II. pp. 523-28; J.L. Whiterley, *Periplus,* pp. 134-38; R.C. Majumdar, CAI., pp. 308-9.

129. JASB., 1847, Vol. XVI, Pt. I. pp. 36f.
130. Ind. Alt., Vol. III, p. 38.
131. Freshfield, *The Road to Tibet, GJ.* (JRGS.), Jan. and March, 1904, Vol. XXiii; *The Highest Mountain, in the World GJ.,* March J903,. Vol. XXi; O'Connor, *Routes in Sikkim;* Louis, *Gates of Tibet*— all quoted in *Periplus,* p. 279.

    Periplus, pp. 47-48, p. 278-79, note; CNES, pp. 145, 148; AICL, p. 199 notes 8; CAI, p. 307.
132. *Periplus,* pp. 47-48, 278-79, note; CNES, pp. 145, 148; AICL, p. 199, note 8; CAI p. 307; See also Hue (RJTTC, 1844-46).
133. Vide McCrindle, *Ancient India,* p. 180.
134. JASB, 1847, Vol. XVI, pp. 11 12.
135. *Sarthavaha,* p. 119.
136. Cf. Scoff, p. 288.
137. *Ibid.,* p. 281.
138. *Kirtâ-Jana Krti,* p. 37.
139. Yule (tr.): TM., II, XLvi, vide H. Cordier (ed. : *Cathay and* the *way Thither,* Vol. IV.
140. Vide. Schoff, *Periplus,* pp. 261, 279. 281.
141. CNES., p. 23.
142. *Periplus.* Vol. II, pp. 523-28.
143. JASB., 1847, Vol. XVI. pp. 11-12.
144. *Ibid.,* pp. 21-22.
145. Vide. Schoff, *op. cit.* pp. 42, 45, 112,170, 188-89, 217, 251 & 273.
146. Cf. Schoff, *op. cit.* pp. 18-889. For further reference see Lassen, Ind. Alt., Vol. I, pp. 288-89.
147. Ref. to Schoff. *op. cit.* p. 189.
148. JASB., 1847, XVI, pp.
149. Ref. to Schoff. *op. cit.* pp. 216-17. See also Lassen Ind, Alt. Vol. I, pp. 279-85. Vol. II, pp. 555-61; Horace, II, Vii, 89.
150. CPI., pp. 891f.
151. *Op. cit.* pp. 89, 217.
152. Schoff, *op. cit.,* p. 217.
153. HMSAC. Vol. I, pp. 156-7.
154. JASB., 1847, XV), pp. 22-23.

155. *Exercitations Plinlanae,* pp. 853ff.
156. *Periplus,* Vol. II, pp. 523-28.
157. *Op. cit.,* pp. 216, 281. See also *Tavernier Travels,* II, Xii.
158. AIP., pp. 219-21.
159. *The Periplus* (tr. by Schoff), pp. 44,128, 203-5, 208, 212, 233.
160. J.W. McCrindle, CNES., p. 23. Schoff, *op. cit.* p. 256.
161. Anonymi (Arriani ut Fertur) *Periplus Marts Erythraei,* trans. from the text (as given in the GGM. ed. by C. Muller, Paris 1855) by J.W. McCrindle *vide.* JAS Burgess (ed.): IA., (JOR), 1879, Vol. VIII, pp. 150.
162. See Taylor, JASB., 1847, pp. 43ff.
163. Cf. J.W, McCrindle, AICL. p. 199.
164. Cf. Schoff, *op. cit.* p. 270, See also pp. 37, 39, 128 and 165 for different explanations regarding the geographical position of Barbaricum town in ancient times.
165. See V.S. Agrawala, *Ithihasa-Darsana,* p. 67.
166. See N.B. Thapa, *A Short History of Nepal,* p. 14. J. Ware Edgar, RSTP., 1823, BHS. 1, Vol. 2. pp. 45f.
167. Trans. by P.C. Roy. Vol. II, *Sabhâkriya Parva,* Section W, p. 7; *Dputa Parva,* Sec. Li, pp. 103-4; See also Mbh. Ko., pp. 109-91; R.N. Saletore, EIC., Vol. II, pp. 750-52.
168. Ref. to J.W. MeCrindle, AICL., p. 199.
169. EC. Vol. II, p. 119; EC. Vol. IV, Ch. 83, p. 18, Cf. R.N. Saletore EIC., Vol. II, Pp. 750-52.
170. *State and Government in Ancient India,* p. 118.
171. JBORS., Vol. L. pt. II, pp. 1,73-78.
172. IA. 1905, pp. 233-35; See also K.P. Jayaswtl, *Hindu Polity,* pp. 170f.
173. Lowie, *Primitive Society,* p. 385.
174. See G.P. Singh 'A Study of the Tribal Republic of North-East India' *North-Eastern Affairs,* QSTE, Annual 1976, pp. 79-103; *The Tribal Administration of Justice Tribal Institutions of Maghalaya.* pp. 345, 357-58.
175. VII. p. 152, Rice, Bangalore, 1898.
176. Bharavi's *Kirâtârjuniyam* (with Parameshvardin Pandey's *Commentary)* Canto-I, VS-1-4, pp. 1-3; See also VS-5-7, pp. 4-5.
177. Vachaspati Gairola (ed: & trans.): *Arthaúâstra of Kautilya,* Park. 16, Ch. 20, p. 69.

178. Mbh. *Sabha Parva, Digvinaya Parva,* Ch. 23, Sl. 17-18, 20; V.S. Agrawala, *Bharata Savitri,* Vol. I, p. 151, Vol. 2. p. 40; IAA., Pt. II, pp. 6-7; K.S. pp. 23-24.

179. *Pampâ Râmayâna,* VII, Vs. 109-115, 193-95 (Rice, Bangalorfe 1892).

180. J.W. McCrindle, AIK., pp. 88-90; AICL.. p. 61, FN. I; Lassen Ind. Alt. Vol. II, pp. 641f.

181. Mbh., *Âdi Parva,* 1, 109, ii, 107; *Âranygka Parva,* 40, 25, 11, 13, 17-18, 20-21, 25-26, 30-47; V.S. Agrawala. *Bharata Savitri,* Vol. I, P- 223; P.C. Roy, *Vana Parva,* Vol. II, Pt. I, *Kairata Parva,* Sec. *XXXIX,* pp. 186-89, *Indralokagamana* Parva, Sec. XLIX, p. 107. *Âúvamedha Parva,* 72, 24.

    See also, *Kirâtâ-juniyam* of Bhâravi (based on *Vana Parva,* Chs. 27 to 41 of the Mbh. and *Mahâ Úva Purâna)* with Mallinotha's commentry ed. by S.N. Sen Canto-XIV; V. 33, pp. 60-61; V. 64, pp. 118-19; Canto XII, V. 39, p. 61, V. 82, 84, 85, 86 pp. 86-72; Canto XII, V. 36, pp. 75-76 and N.L. Day Civ. An. Ind. pp. 90-91.

182. *Raghuvama* (Trans. and annotated by 'M.R. Kale), Canto-IV, vs. 76-77, pp. 95-96, See also pp. 27-33, Notes, pp. 116-17.

183. JASB., 1904-5, Vol. LXX111, "pt. Ill & IV, pp. 57-74; JASB., 1844, Vol. XIII, pt. 2, pp. 627f; CR., 1863, Vol. XXXV111, p. 280; ADG., 1906, Vol. X, pp. 64-65; Dalton, DEB., p. 64; Robinson,. DAA, d. 412; Gurdon, *The Khasis,* pp. 65-96.

184. Hamilton, *A Descriptive Account of Assam,* pp. 95-96.

185. JASB., 1900, Vol. LXIX, pt. Ill, p. 57.

186. HATSEI., Vol. V. p. 694.

187. B.N. Boddoloi, *District Handbook, United Mikir and North Cachar Hills,* Tribal Research Institute, Gauhati, 1972, p. 17.

188. W.W. Hunter, SAB., Vol. VI, p. 482; Daltin, DEB., p. 110.

189. *Râja-Mâla* (tr. by Kailas Chandra Sinha), pp. 24-28 cf. S.K. Chatterji, *Kirâta-Jana-Krti,* pp. 137-38.

190. Somerset *Playne's* Report, BABO., pp. 463: S.K. Chatterji, *op. cit.* pp. XXII, 136 .

191. *Râjâ-mâlâ* (Agartala, Tripura Era 1336 = A.D. 1926), pt. 1, 131-132 cf. S.K. Chatterji, *op. cit.,* p. 138.

192. *Op. cit.,* p. xxii.

193. S.K. Chatterji, *op. cit.,* p. 138.

194. S.E. Peal, JASB., 1872, vol. XLI, p. 28; T.C. Hodson, *The Naga Tribes of Manipur,* pp. 125f; Robinson, DAA., d. 396.

195. JRAI., 1965, Vol. 95, pts. I & II, p. 29.
196. Dalton, DEB., p. 20; E.A. Rowlatt, JASB., 185, Vol. XIV, p. 487.
197. C.R. MacGregor, PASB., 1884, No. XI, pp. 198ff.
198. MASB. 1913-17, Vol. V, pt. I, p. 67; JASB., 1900, Vol. LXIX, pt. 16; JASB., 1913, Vol. IX, pp. 108ff.
199. *A Philosophy for NEFA.,* pp. 79f.
200. Rangeya Raghava, *Prachin Bharatiya Parampara aur Ithihasa,* pp. 103, 115.
201. Cf. Gustav Oppert, OIB., pp. 455:56, fn.
202. *Ibid.,* p. 450, fn.
203. Ind. Alt. vol. I, pp. 441-50.
204. PAHCI., p. 16.
205. AIHT., p. 306.
206. *Ibid.,* p. 132.
207. Mbh. *Sinti Parva,* Ch. 65, 51, 1 3-15.
208. *Ibid., 51,* 17-23.
209. For details see *Bharata Savitri,* Vol. 3, Santi Parrea pp. 60–63.
210. *Aranyaka Parva,* 40, 2-47; (See also *Vana Parya*, chs. 38-40); *Âú*vamedha Parva, 72, 24. In *Drona Parva* (chs. 80-91) and *Anusaana* Parva (ch. 14) also Siva has been depicted as dweller of Himalaya mountain.
211. Canto XIV, Vs. 33-34, 45, 63-64; Canto XII, Vs. 39, 82, 84-86.
212. AISH, pp. 168, 187, ref. n. 83.
213. Weber, Ind. Stu., 2, 22 Indian *Literature,* 110, 111 ef. MacdonellandKeith, VINS,, Vol. II, pp. 149-50.
214. J.V. McCrindle,AIMA., pp. 97f.
215. Macdonell, HSL., pp. 115, 154; E.J. Rapson (ed.); CHL., Vol. I, *Ancient India*, p. 437.
216. Cf. C. Speir, *Phases of Indian Civilization,* p. 374.
217. *Ibid.*
218. *Purvabhaga,* pp. 144-145. .
219. R.G. Bhandarkar, *Vaisnavism, Úavism and Minor Religious Systems,* pp. 131-32.
220. Vii. 21.5 and X. 99.3. Sec also J. Muir. OST., Vol. IV. pp. 345-46.
221. Dandin *Daiakumârcarita,* (Sanskrit text) Ucchavasa-II, pp. 22-24, (trans. text, pp. 15-17).
222. D.R. Regmi, AN., pp. 25-26 & 81.

223. E.T. Atkinson, H.G., Vol. 11, pt. 1, pp. 363-67; M.M. Shanna, TCH., p. 47.
224. Monier Williams, *Religious Thought and Life in India,* p. 184.
225. M. Bloomfield, AJPH., Vol. XLVII, 3, No. 187, p. 220, fn.
226. See, JA., 1873, p. 187.
227. ERE., Vol. 11, p. 813 a. E. Gait, *A History of Assam,* p. 12, fn. 2.
228. S. Piggott, *Prehistoric India,* pp. 217f; J. Marshall, *Mohenjodaro-and the Indus Civilization,* vol.1, p. 51; E.O. James, *Pre-historic Religion,* pp. 153; O.R. Ehrenfels, *Mother Right in India,* pp. 18-35; J.G. Frazer, *The Golden Bough,* pp. 135-36; R. Briffault. *The Mother,* Vol. Ill, pp. 196-209; V.G. Childe, *New Light on the Most Ancient East* pp. 48ff; E.B. Tylor, *Religion in the Primitive Culture,* pp. 5ff. R. G. Bhandarkar, *Collected Works,* Vol. IV. p. 208; N.N. Bhattacharya, *Indian Mother-Goddess,* pp. 6-8 and 25; ERE, vol. 1, pp. 227-28; vol. 11, pp. 115f and R.P. Chanda IAR., pp. 149-50.

229. Rv. X. 61.5.7; Ait. Dr., 111.33-34; Sat. Br., Mâdhyaudina Version 1. VII, 4, 1-8; Kanva Version 11 VII. 2. 1-8; 1.2.5.5-6; Tand. Br., VIII. 11, 10-18; Gop. Br., 11.1; Mbh. XII. 282-85; Brah. p. ch. 39; Mat. p., ch. 12; Pad p. S$_i$stikhada, ch. 5; Kur. p. 1, ch. 15; Brahd. P., ch. 31. Bhag. p. IV. 20-21; *Devi Bhâgavata,* VII. 30; Kâlidâsa's *Kamara-sanbha»a* 1.21; Kal. p. XVlI, 42-49; 18, 42-51 ' *Yogini Tantrâ,* Patala-IX; *Brhan Nilatantra-Patala- VI; Rudrayamala Tantra; Kubjika Tantra,* PâtalaVIl; *Jñânarnava Tantra; The Tmtrasari; Prdnatosani Fantra, p.* 236; Gop. Br. (pub. in Nos. 215-252, BIS.), pp. 30-35.

230. 28, 34.
231. V. 305.
232. *Merutantra* (Pvrascâryarnanva, Benares, 1901, p. 22)
233. 11, iii, 7-8, 12; 11, 22, 53-54, 58-59; 6-1; 59, 32:34-Savarai barbarrai Scaiva Pulindaiúca Supûjitâ.).
234. *Daúakumâracarita,* Purv. Ucch. 1, 14-15; (Ucch; VI,. 149; Ucch, VIII, 204, 206.
235. *Kâdambari(ir.* by M.R. Kale), pp. 331; (tr. by Kane) PP- 94-98; (tr. by Mahesh Bhartiya!, pp. 169-70; *Harsacarita* (tr. by V.S Agrawala, *Harsacarita; EK Sâmskrtik Adhyayan),* p. 183. An eleventh century literary text. *Kathâsaritasâgara* (IV. 22) also speaks of an adoration of a Devi in its terrible form by the Pulindas (kindred tribe of the Kiratas) of the Vindhyan region.
236. Ch. 21, Vs. 37, fn. 1.
237. MS. (No. 3175), RASB., Patala-VII, also in JRASB., Letters, 1948, Vol. XIV, No. I.

238. *Vasumati* (ed.), pp. 234-36.
239. p. 193.
240. Cf. D.C. Sircar, *The Sâkta Pithas,* pp. 19-23, 25-26, 39-41. (The above three are also quoted in the same work).
241. Pp. 515-16.
242. Ch. 15.
243. Verses-285-347, ref. to D.C. Sircar, *op. cit.,* pp. 20-21.
244. ERE., Vol. 11, 815a.
245. Romila Thapar, AISH. p. 178; C. Eliot, *Hinduism and Buddhism* Vol. 11, 277; Crooke, *Popular Religion of Northern India,* 1.63 and Monier-Williams, *Brahmanism and Hinduism,* p. 57.
246. R.P. Chanda, *op. cit.,* p. 148.
247. *Op. cit.* p. 20.
248. Mark. p. ch. Lxxzsii, Vs. 10-18; Ch. 11, V. 107. Pargiter (Mark, p. Intr., pp. xiii-xiv) See also El. Vol. xi, p. 302; Romila Thapar,. *op. cit.,* p. 178; Rangeya Raghava, *op. cit.,* pp. 103f, 115.
249. B.A. Saletore, WTIH., p. 26.
250. B.A. Saletore, *op. cit.* pp. 27-28. See also Hirananda Sastri, MASI. No. 20, pp. 12 and 16; Foucher, *Iconagraphic Bouddhique* p. 78; JASB., 1873.. 11, p. 116 cf. Saletore, *op. cit.*
251. *Daâakumaracarita,* 1, 14-15; VI, 149; VIII, 206.
252. *Kadambari,* p. 331.
253. EC., XII. 28. p. 92; Rice, *Mysore; A Gazetteer* (revised edn.), p. 307.
254. EC., VII. 137, p. 104; Rice, *Mysore and Coorg from the Inscriptions,* pp. 72-73; EC., XII, 61, p. 55; *Madras Epigraphical Report for the year 1901; South Indian Inscriptions,* VII, No. 328, p. 168; EC., VIII, 13, p. 165.
255. B.K. Kakati, *The Mother Goddess Kâmâkhyâ,* pp. 10-16. See also GBNEL, p. 53.
256. Rangeya Raghava, *op. cit., pp.* 103 and 115; C.J. Lyall's Introd. to Gurdon's, *The Khasis,* pp. xxiiif. 82f; Playfair, *The Garos* pp. 80f; *Giros,* pp. 80f; ERE., Vol. 11. p. 115; Bhattacharya, *Saktism and Mother-Right,* cf. D.C. Sircar (ed.): *The Sakti cult and Târâ,* pp. 65-67; J. Marshall, *op. cit.* p. 51.
257. B. Kakati, *Assamese -.Its formation and development,* p. 53; D.C. Sircar, *The Sakta Pithas,* p. 15.
258. R.M. Nath, BAC., pp. 4, 17 & 95.
259. 2.9.13.

260. B.K. Kakati, *The Mother Goddess Kâmakhya,* pp. 9 and 47; JARS., 1962, (Pub. 1964), Vol. XVI, p. 61.
261. MS. (No. 3174) RASB., Patala VII, also in JRASB., Letters. 1948 Vol. XIV, no. 1.
262. DCSM., RASB., VII, pp. 110-11.
263. The above texts quoted in D.C. Sircar, *op. cit.,* pp. 12-26, 35-41.
264. 18 42-51.
265. Ch. 13.
266. Vii. 39. 5-30,
267. VI. 23.
268. IGI., Vol.VI, p. 23.
269. R.M. Nath, *op. cit.,* pp. 97, 99 & 105.
270. *Deodhai Assam Buranji,* pp. XXIK, 169-175.
271. CR., 1863, Vol. XXXVIII, p. 283.
272. Jayachandra Vidyalankar, *Bhâratabhumi aur Uske Nivasi,* Pariccheda, 41.
273. M. Martin, HATSEL, Vol. V. pp, 665 and 690.
274. JARS., Vol. XX, 1972, (Pub. 1972-73), pp. 8-13.
275. R. M. Nath, *op. cit.* pp. 71 & 75; JASB., 1900, Vol. LX1X. p. 45; JARS., July 1936, Vol. IV, N. 2. p. 38; JASB., 1902, ol. VLXXI, pt. III, pp. 36-37. L.W. Shakespear, *History of Assam Rifles,* pp. 256f.
276. James Long, JASB., 1850, Vol. XIX. Nos. 1 to VII, pp. 533ff; S. Playne's Report cf. BABO., p. 463; B.K. Kakati, *op. cit.* p. 64; Dalton. DEB., p. 110.
277. J. Muir, OST., Vol. IV, 1863, pp. 245f.
278. MI (QAJ) 1922, Vol. 11, No. 3. p. 150.
279. B,K. Kakati, *op. cit.* p. 62; E. Gail, *op. cit,* p. 268; K.L. Barum, EHK., p. 180f; D.C. Sircar, *op. cit,* pp. 15-16 1 IGI., Vol. VI, p. 36; C. Eliot, *op. cit,* p. 279; JASB., 1845, Vol. XIV, pt. 2, pp. 477-78; JASB 1843, Vol. XVII. pt. I, pp. 462-68.
280. D.C. Sircar, JARS., Sept. 1978, Vol. XVI, p. I.
281. BPP., (JCHS.) July-Dec. 1934, Vol. VXL11I, Nos. 95-96, p. 38.
282. *Op. cit,* pp. 264-65.
283. E. Gait, *op. cit.,* p. 268; IGI, Vol. VI, p. 36.
284. JARS., April, 1938, Vol. VI, No. 1, pp. 7-8; JARS., July 1938, Vol. VI, No. 2, pp. 55f.
285. 1C., Vol. VI, p. 288.

286. C. Eliot, *op. cit.,* pp. 278-79, see also p. 137 of the same for antiquity of Saiva and Vaisnava cults, which have also been connected with N.E.; see also his article "Hinduism in Assam", JRAS., 1910, Pt. 11, pp. 1155-1186; E. Gait, *op. cit.,* pp. VII-VIII, 15 and 58; see also his report, *vide.* Census of India, 1891, Assam, Vol. I, pt. II, Ch. I, p. 51, Ch. Ill, pp. 80-81; R.P. Chanda, *op. cit.,* p. 157 (he supports the views or Mr. Wilson); K.L. Barua, *op. cit.,* pp. 9-10.
287. JPASB., (new series) 1914, Vol. X. p. 346.
288. JRAS., 1915, p. 81.
289. IGI., Vol. l,p. 427.
290. Bhag., 11-4-18.
291. E.H. Johnston, BSOAS., 1943-46, Vol. XI, pp. 357-84.
292. Janardan Bhatt, (ed.): *Inscriptions of Asoka,* pp. 35, 45, 55, 64 and 74: B.M. Barua, *Asoka and His Inscriptions,* pp. 100f.
293. A.K. Warder, IIH., pp. 89-90.
294. Daniel Wright, HN., pp. 30-32; Baldeva Pd. Mishra, *Nepal Ka Itilwsa,* p. 37; D.R. Regmi, AN., pp. 25-26; N.B. .Thapa, SHN., p. 14; E. Atkinson, H.G., Vol. II, pt. 1, pp. 364-65.
295. Daniel Wright, *op. cit.* p. 33.
296. R.D. Banerji, Lekhamalânukramani, pt. 1, 210, p. 99.
297. K.P. Jayaswal, CHN., cf, JBORS., Sept. 1936, Vol. XXII, pt. III, pp. 157-264.
298. For details see EL, Vol. XX, pp. 72f; IHO., 1938, pp. 461-82.
299. EL, Vol. XX, pt. 1, pp. 22ff; D.C. Sircar, Sll HC: Vol. 1, p. 235.
300. K. Raghunath, *Religion of the Ikshvâku Times,* JIH., Dec., 1978, vol. LVI, pt. Ill pp. 429-435.
301. JASB., 1844, vol. XIII, pt. 5, pp. 617-18; JASB., 1904, vol. LXXIII, pt. Ill, pp. 57-74; E.A. Gait. *Census of India,* 1891, Assam, Vol. I, Report, c. 261.
302. *Early India and Pakistan,* pp. 158-59.
303. JASB., 1974, Vol. XLVIII, p. 5; Archi Br. 'B' Progs. June, 1910, Nos. 7-9.
304. Dalton, DEB., pp. 61ff.
305. L.W. Shakespear, *op. cit.,* p. 262; Report on Archaeological Tour in Assam, 1905; DEB., pp. 11-16, 24, 31, 39 & 42; Hodson, *The Naga Tribes of Manipur,* pp. 42f.
306. Arch. Dr. 'B' Prog, June 1910, Nos. 7-9, File No. 24, AG-10, E-13.

307. JARS., 1972, XX, pp. 8-13.
308. Somerset Playne's Report, vide BABO., p. 463.
309. Vide, *Grundriss,* Ind. Pal. plate-IV. Co.-VIl.
310. Vide ZDMG., pp. 77, 651.
311. *The European Inheritance* (1954), Vol. I, p. 84.
312. HN., p. 28.
313. *Sumañgalavilasini,* 1, pp. 176f cf. B.C. Law, IFTBJ., p. 86. See also G.P. Malalasekera, DPPN., 1, p. 607.
314. *Sammohavinodani (Vibhânga Commentary),* p. 388 cf. B.C. Law, IETBJ., pp. 86 & 271. See also Manoratha—*Purâni, Anguttara Commentary,* 1, 409; *Apadâna,* 11, 359; *Sutta Nipâta,* 977.
315. B.C. Law, IETBJ., p. 86.
316. *Prajnapana Upanga,* p. 374; *Acârnâña Sutra,* 11, 3.1; 11.11.1.7. See also I.A. XX, p. 374; SBE., XXVI, p. 32.
317. IETBJ, pp. 86, 271.
318. EIC., Vol. II, pp. 750-52.
319. See Jataka, VI, 208, 210; Manu, X. 44; *Sumangalavilasini,* 1,276; *Sammohavinodini,* 388 cf. Romila Thapar, AISH., pp. 162-63.
320. Major Rock Edict-XII, J. Bloch, *Les Inscriptions d' Asoka* pp. 130 *ff. cf Ibid.* p. 163. His list includes the Kâmbojas, Nabhaka, Andhra, Yona, Pulinda, etc.
321. SBE., Vol. XXVI. pp. 31-32, n. 3; V.S. Agarwala. *Itihâsa Darúana,* p. 68; Romila Thapar, AISH., pp. 155, 182 & n. 18.
322. *Itihâsa Darúana,* p. 69.
323. Romila Thapar, AISH., pp. 153, 181-82 and ref. no. 8.
324. Sat. Br. IV, 1.3.16; *Kathaka Samhitâ,* 1, 1.5.; Tai. Sam. Vi. 4.7.3; *Maitrâyâni Samhit,* 111.61. ref. to Romila Thapar, *op. cit.* pp. 153, 181 and ref. no. 4.
325. Manu. 11.23; X. 45; 11. 17-74. Also cf. V.S. Apte, SED; p. 450.
326. *Padma Purâna, Srsti Skandha,* ch. 57.
327. The *Amarakosa,* ii. 10.20 The Mleccha-desa in this lexicon has been located not in Central India but in Northern India.
328. Romila Thapar, AISH., pp. 158, 181 and ref. nos. 6 & 7.
329. R. Shafer, EAL, p. 23; Romila Thapar, *op. cit.,* pp. 153, 182 and ref. no. 9.
330. Romila Thapar, AISA., p. 154.
331. *Astâdhyâyi,* VII. 2.18.
332. *"The Image of the Barbarian in Early India",* AISH., pp. 152-181.

333. *Ibid.,* p. 153.
334. JBORS., 1920, p. 197.
335. *Itihâsa-Darsana,* pp. 68-69.
336. p, 125. See also A.K. Majumdar, EHIDS., Vol. II, p. 549.
337. The present author deeply laments his failure to recollect and trace the source from which this valuable information was collected over a decade ago. This explains as to why its details have not been provided here.
338. p. 1, facing p. 6, vs., 57. See also vs. 49-56.
339. Hemachandra has stated that many of these dialects are spoken by the female characters and inferior personages of Sanskrit plays. Dandin in his *Kâvyadarśa,* 1.33-35, has also referred to this aspect of the subject, cf. V.S. Apte SED., p. 374.
340. Weber, *Indian Literature,* pp. 67-68; S.K. Chatterji, ODBL., p. 47; IAH., p. 61.
341. ODBL., p. 48.
342. L. Jha, *Pashchim Bengal Men Maithili Ki Vibhasa Khutta Ka Bhasasastirya Adhyayana* (unpub. Ph.D. thesis) 1985, pp. 6, 10, 38.
343. JRAS., 1959 pp. 285-88.
344. For details see G. Grierson, *The North-Western group of the lndo-Aryan Vernaculars,* vide, IA., XLIV, pp. 226f, 257; ZDMG., (1912), pp. 77 f; R.P. Chanda, IAR., pp. 77-78, 246-47 (Note-B).
345. Dandin's *Daśakumaracarita,* ucchavasa II, pp. 22-24 (trans. pp. 15-17).
346. For details see Latham, EL, pp. 11-16; *Traill's Report on Kumaon* (1823), *vide.* SAK., pp. 19, 57; As. Vol. XVI, pp. 150 f; Capt. H. Strachey, *Journal at Garjjiaghat* (1846), cf. E.T. Atkinson, HG. Vol. II; pt. I, pp. 365-68.
347. M.M. Sharma, TCH., pp. 47-49.
348. For details See Shovaram Sharma's research article, *Râji Boli: Ek Bhâsa Vaijnânik Adhyayana'* cf. Pahad based on the study of Himalayan Society, Culture, History, Ecology, etc. 2, pp. 145-56.
349. ELLRNT., Pt. II, pp.29ff; *Comparative vocabulary of the languages of the broken Tribes of Nepal,* JASB., 1857-8, Vol. XXVI, pp. 333ff; Vol. XX VII, pp. 393ff (for Kiranti language of Nepal); MEIS., 1880, Vol. I, pp. 176f, 320 f; LLRBNB.; LSI., Vol. III. pt. I, pp. 274; LSI. Vol. I, pt. I, p. 58. See also As. Res., 1828, Vol. XVI, pp. 410-11.
350. LSI., Vol. Ill, pt. I, pp. 274, 326.
351. Vide, LSI., Vol. Ill, pt. I, p. 274.

352. JASB., 1849, Vol. XVIII, pt. I, pp. 451-60; JASB., 1849, Vol. XVIII, pt. II, 967-75.
353. AN., pp. 57-58.
354. *Ibid.* pp. 25-32,
355. *Le Nepal,* Vol. 11, pp. 78-79, See also Robert Shafer, EAL, pp. 124-55.
356. Grierson, LSI., Vol. 3 (1909); Frank M. Lebar, G. Hickey and J.K. Musarave, *Ethnic groups of Mainland South-East Asia* (1964): Voegelin, *Language of the World: Sino-Tibetan; Anthropological Lingusotics,* Vols. 6 & 7 (1965-65); R. Shafer, *Introduction to Sino-Tibetan,* 3 Vols. (1966) and *Bibliography of Sino-Tibetan Languages (*2 Vols. 1957-63), cf. EB. (New Series V 16 (1980), pp. 803-6.
357. Satyaketu Vidyalankar, *Bhâratiya Sanskrti Kâ Vikâs,* p. 27.
358. Grierson, LSI., Vol. 1, pt. 1, pp. 60ff; Edwin T. Atkinson, HG., Vol. 1, pt. 1, pp. 17-20; Robert Shafer, JAOS., Sept. 1940; P.K. Benedict, *Sino-Tibetan: A Conspectus,* pp. 4-6; S.K. Chatterji *Kirata-Jana-Krti,* 'pp. 22-23; Cul. Her. Ind. Vol. V, pp. XVIII, 659-61.
359. *Op. cit..* pp. 22-23.
360. JRAS., 1907, pp. 187-91; Grierson, LSI., Vol. 1, pt. 1, pp. 15, 53; B.C. A ADG., Vol. X, pp. 59f; Gurdon, *The Khasis,* pp. 200-1; See also Edward Gait, *A History of Assam,* pp. 5-6.
361. Quoted in Paul Masson—Oursel, AIIC, p. 11, fn. 2.
362. (*a*) *Kirâta-Jana-Krti,* pp. 8, 50.
    (*b*) IAH,, pp. 36-41.
    (*c*) Cul. Her. Ind. Vol. V. pp. 669-70, 674-75.
363. *Kirâta Jana Krti,* p. 8.
364. *Khasi a language of Assam,* pp. VIII, 116, 179.
365. MRAS., London, Octob., 1962, Vol. LXII, Nos. 253-55, 294-99, p. 188.
366. *The Culture of South East Asia,* pp. 25-44, 279-287.
367. For details see. G.H. Luis, *Lingua,* (IRGL.), 14; Ram Vilas Sharma, *Bhârata Ke Prâchin Bhâsa-Parivâr aur Hindi,* Vol. 3, pp. 86-87, 98-100 & 111.
368. Vide PAPDI. (trans. from French by P.C. Bagchi), pp. 4, 25, 99 & 122f.
369. S.K. Chatterji, IAH., pp. 38-39.
370. *Ibid.,* p. 40.
371. R.M. Nath, BAG., pp. 4, 17 & 95.
372. *Assamese, Its Formation and Development,* pp. 25-27, 32-33, 42-56; See also Nagendra Nath Vasu, SHK. pp. 176 f for non-Aryan or Tibeto-Burman names from Assam and north Bengal Inscriptions.

373. S.K. Chatterji, ODBL., Vol. 1, p. 69, Appendix—E pp. 179-181, Vol. III, pp. 35-40.
374. S.K. Chatterji, *Kirata-Jana-Krti,* pp. 39-41; IAH., pp. 40-41.
375. IAH., pp. 40-41.
376. IAH., p. 42.
377. *Classification of Some Languages of the Himalayas vide* JBRS., 1950, Vol. 36, pp. 192ff; *The Classification of the Northernmost Naga Languages, vide* JBRS., 1953, Vol. 39, pp. 225-264.
378. A. Cunningham, AS1AR., 1878-1879, Vol. XIV, pp. 125-33.
379. Robinson, DAA., p. 352.
380. *The Hill Tribes of the Northern Frontier of Assam,* JASB., 1838, Vol. XXXVII, pp. 192ff.
381. LSI., Vol. I, pt. 1, p. 60.
382. V. Robinson, *Notes on the languages spoken by the Mi-Shmis,* JASP., 1885, Vol. XXVI, pp. 307-24; *Notes on the Languages Spoken by the various tribes inhabiting the valley of Assam and its Mountain Confines,* JASB., 1849, Vol. XVIII. pp. 183 ff. See also Grierson, LSI., Vol. 4, pt. l, pp. 60f.
383. S.K. Ghosh, MI. (QAJ.), Octob. 1968, Vol. 48, No. 4, p. 331,
384. Cf. Grierson LSI., Vol.1, pp. 55-56. See also S. Konow, *Note on the Languages spoken between the Assam Valley and Tibet,* JRAS., 1902, pp. 128ff;B.H. Hodgson, *On the Aborigines of the sub. Himalayas,* JASB., 1847, Vol. XVI, pp. 1235ff; *On the Aborigines of North-Eastern India,* JASB., 1849, Vol. XVIII, pp. 421ff; *Aborigines of the North-East Frontier,* JASB., 1850, Vol. XIX, pp, 310-16.
385. LSI., Vol. 1, pt. I, pp. 63-64.
386. LSI., Vol. iii, pt. ii, pp. 1-117.
387. Vide Dalton, DEB., p. 96. .
388. HG., Vol. 1, pt. I, p. 22,
389. SAB., Vol. VI, pp. 488-89. See also the views of Grierson and Sten-Konow, vide, IA. (JOR. ed by Richard Carnac Temple Bart) Bombay, 1902, Vol. XXXI, pp. 3-5.
390. LSI., Vol. I, pt. I, p. 92.
391. LSI., Vol. iii, pt. ii. pp. 379f.
392. LSI., Vol. iii, pt. ii, p. 451.
393. LSI., Vol. 1, pt. I. pp. 66-68. See also N. Brown, *Specimens of the Naga language of Assam,* JAOS., 1851, Vol. 2, pp. 157-65.
394. JASB., 1875, Vol. V, p. 317.
395. *The Mixed Culture of the Naga Tribes,* vide. JRAI, 1965, Vol. 95. pts. I & II,p. 19.

396. Grierson, LSI., Vol., III, pt. I, pp. 11-12.
397. ——LSI., Vol. iii, pt. ii, pp. 380ff.
398. JRAS., April 1913, Vol. XIII, pp. 315-23.
399. *Op. cit.* pp. 17-19, 27, 34-38.
400. CR, 1844, Vol. ii, pp. 4-5.
401. *Bhartiya Itihasa Ka Parichaya,* p. 7.
402. IGL, Vol. 1, pp. 387-87; Buhler, Ind., Pal., Plate-IV, Vols-I-VIi.
403. G.P. Singh, "Traditional and Historical Accounts of Early Tibeto-Burman Relations with Bihar and its cultural Impact" *vide, The Thinker, Journal of the Thinkers Forums,* Kohima, Nov., 1981, Vol. IX, No. 4, pp. 30-31.
404. *Ibid.,* pp. 33-34.
405. *British Rule in Burma* (1824-1942), pp. 16, 70.
406. *Burma,* pp. 16, 32 34.
407. IAH., pp. 71-72.
408. *Ibid.,* pp. 82, 97-98.
409. G.P. Singh, "Flok Lore of North-East India: Some Historical Observations." In S. Sen (ed.): *Folklore in North East India,* Delhi, 1983, pp. 224f.
410. 15.1.6, 11-12.
411. *Arthasastra,* BK. I, ch. 5.
412. See MI. (QAJ.), 1943, Vol. XXIII. pp. 405-6.
413. *The Kacharis,* pp. 115-21.
414. Vol. ii, pt. ii, pp. 423f, 479f.
415. MI. (QAJ.), Sept. 1928, Vol. II, No. 3, pp. 146-7. See also LSI., Vol. III, pt. II, 218-20.
416. S.K. Chatterji, *Kirata-Jana-Krti,* p. 79.
417. R.S. Dankar, *Sanskriti Ke Char Adhyay* (Four Chapters of Culture), pp. 75-78.
418. *Op. cit.* p. 182.
419. S.K. Chatterji, *op. cit.* pp. 179-81; A.H. Franck's, *A Lower Ladakhi Version of the Kesar Saga,* RASB. Calcutta 1905-1941 (with introd. by S.K. Chatterji) contains many interesting folk-tales.
420. *On the Migration of Fables,* Vide Chip from German Workshop, IV, 412; *Selected Essays.* 1, 500.
421. *India's Past,* pp. 129-29, 175-93.
422. Maria Leach (ed.): *Standard Dictionary of Folklore, Mythology and Legend,* (New York 1950), Vol. II, p. 778.

BOOK FOUR

THE EMERGENCE AND FALL OF JANAPADAS, KINGDOMS, PRINCIPALITIES AND TOWNS (FROM THE SPIC AGE DOWN TO THE TIMES OF THE HOYSALAS)

I

PREFATORY REMARKS

The transition from the prehistoric nomadic life to the protohistoric settled life had some impact on the social structure and political set-up of the Kirâtas. Their settlement patterns, obviously, started changing from the later Vedic period onwards. They developed a tendency towards the permanent settlement in a particular area. The territories, on which they had settled, gradually evolved into compact units leading to the emergence of the Janapadas and kingdoms. The formation of territorial units or Janapadas constituted a significant landmark in their pplitical life. Their strength, powers and influence increased after they had settled in their respective Janapadas. With the ecological changes, the socio-political changes and the other geo-political factors the Janapadas gained their identity.

Their claims to larger territories led to the transformation of the Janapadas into kingdoms which had well defined political boundaries. The Kiratas, like the other tribes, not organised as a nation, formed several kingdoms. Their kingdoms and principalites in northern, eastern, and central regions and in Uttarâkhanda deserve our notice. Apart from the Janapadas, kingdoms and principalities the Kirâtas had one urban site on the northern frontiers of Bharatavarsa. But, it is strongly noticed that they could not achieve territorial stability. The obvious reason being their frequent sub-jugation by the contemporary rulers. This process of frequent subjugation started right from the epic age and continued till the times of the Hoysalas .in the 12th century. In the following pages an attempt has been made to thoroughly investigate their Janapadas, kingdoms, principalities and town as mentioned in literary texts, epigraphic records and other sources.

II

THE JANAPADAS IN THE EPIC AND PURÂṆIC TRADITIONS

The data contained in the *Mahâbhârata* and the *Purânas* about the Kirâta- Janapadas are supplementary to each other. However, the Purâṇic classification of the Janapadas is comparatively wider than that of the epic, so far as, the coverage, meanings or sense and the clarity are concerned. Moreover, it also conveys an idea that the Purânakâras had better conception of the subject than that of the author of the said epic. A comprehensive list of Indian Janapadas (both Âryan and non- Âryan) containing about 175 names is preserved in the Bhuvanakoúa chapters of the *Purâṇas.* The best possible way of obtaining the satisfactory result is to interpret the data as a whole by placing our reliance on the combined testimony of both.

The Janapadas of the Gangetic Doâb in Madhya-Deúa or the Middle Country

One of the oldest Janapada of the Kirâta tribes was situated in the Gangetic Doab (Gaṅgâ- Yamunâ Doâb) of Madhya-deúa.[1] This can be testified to by the evidences recorded in the *Mâhâbharata,* the *Purâṇas* and such other reliable sources. Actually, they had occupied the Gangetic valley, the richest part of Madhyadeúa or Central region before the time of the *Mâhâbharata.* This region comprised the upper and middle Gangetic basin and the Yamuna. There were, of course, forest tracts in the whole upper Gangetic basin, but the settlement of the Kirata was not only confined to it. They alike the Âryans settled on the banks of the rivers (Gaṅgâ, Yamunâ and Sarasvati) that is why, their Janapadas have been included in the Âryan Janapadas of the Purâṇiclist.

The Purâṇic description of various Janapadas situated on the river banks of India is very reliable. The Kirâta Janapada of Madhyade–a has been mentioned along with the Janapadas of Kuru (with capitals at Hastinâpur in the present Meerut Dist. and Indraprastha in the Delhi region), Pâñcâlas (with their capital at Ahicchatra and Kâmpilya), Sâlva (in Punjab and the adjoining regions), Jâñgala (Kuru Jângla near the Sarasvati) Bhadrakaras (Madrakâras-a branch of Úaiva tribe inhabiting the north eastern part of the Punjab). Úûrasenas (a branch of the

Yadavas living near Mathura), Pataccaras (who occupied parts of Allahabad), Matsy (Jaipur-Alwar region or Vatsa in Allahabad region), Kulyas (the people of the present Kulait region on the upper Ravi), Avantas (Avantis in West Malwa with their chief city at Ujjayini), Kuntis (a branch of the Yadava tribe living not far from the Mathura region), Kâúis (people of Varanasi), Kosala (Uttara Kosala with its capital at Ayodhyâ) and the like.[2]

The Âryan Janapadas of the Kirâtas, Pulindas, Kuru, Pâñcâla, Matsya (Virâta), Magadha, Añga, Vanga, Kimpurusas, Suhma, Kauúika, Tamralipti, etc. were sanctified by the sacred water of the Ganges. In the same context it has been further mentioned that the Hlâdini, one of the seven streams of the holy Ganges originating from the Himalaya and striking against the Vindhyan hills runs eastward and after passing through the territories of the Kirâtas, Nisâdas, Dhlvara, Nilamukha, Kekaras, Kalanjara, Vikarna, etc. falls into the southern sea.[3] This shows that their territories situated on the banks of the Ganges were watered by its eastern stream represented by the river Hlâdini.

The settlements of the Kirâtas in the Ganga-Yamunâ Doâb can be confirmed by other evidence too. It is said that Iúvara, the king of the Kirâtas ruled between the Ganges and the Yamunâ and that the territory of the Kurus lay to the south of this kingdom.[4]

The Purânic texts refer to the Kirâtas as northern neighbours of the Kurus. The *Puranas* describe the river Ganges as watering the Kirâta territory before reaching the land of the Kurus. Thus, they appear to be the immediate neighbours of the Kurus.[5] In all probability they might have settled in the forest belts in the north of Kuru Janapada or in the adjoining areas of Kurujâñgala.[6] The, testimony of the *Mahâbhârata* also states that they were the dwellers of the Kuru-Jâñgala or 'thicket-Kuruvarnakas'. The 'Kirâtas, Tamasas and Sudeshitas' have been placed near the mount called Yamunâ.[7] This goes well in accord with the statement of Atkinson: "the earliest notices regarding the Kirâtas bring them westward as the Jumna in the first century."[8] But this is partly true because they had settled here long before the century. During the period of the *Mahâbhârata,* the territories of the Kirâtas and the Tanganas were in the Visaya of Subâhu (the king of the Kunindas) on the south of which the mount Yamuna was situated. The Kunindas or Kulindas were the inhabitants of the Himalayan region.[9] They have also been placed somewhere to the east of the river Sutlej.[10] The territory of the Kunindas has also been located in the mountain tracts of Yamunâ in Dehradun District whereform their coins have been discovered. In the northeast of the Kunindas the Janapada of the Tangans and in the west the Janapada of the Kirâtas were situated.[11] The extensive domains of Subâhu situated on the Himalnyas abounding in horses and elephants were densely inhabited by the Kirâtas, Tanganas and the Pulindas or Kulindas. King Subahu was the lord of all these tribes, whom he received at the frontiers of his dominion paying them respect on honour. His influence extended upto the mountain Himalayas and the mountain of Gandhamâdan in Kailâúa side in Tibet.[12] The *Mahâbhâraia* mentions also the Kirâta Janapada along with the Janapadas of the Kâúi, Kosala Anga and Tanganas.[13]

We are better informed by the classical writers about the exact location of the Janapadas of the Kirâtas and other tribes with whom, they are associated as represented in the *Mahâbhârata* and the *Purânas.* Ptolemy, while proceeding to describe the interior of trans-Gangetic India begins with the tribes or nations that were located along the banks of the Ganges on its eastern side. The Ganganoi or Tanganoi (Tanganas) occupied the regions along the eastern banks of the upper Ganges. Their territory probably stretched from the Ramganga river to the upper Saraju (Sarabos). They have been placed between the Kirâta and the Kulinda in the highlands, which protected the plains of Koúala on the north. They were all barbarous tribes, whom the Brâhmanic Âryans in course of their conquest of the region to the east of the Ganges and Yamuna drove back into the Himalayas or towards the Vindhyas, where their descendants of the classic times Were noticed later.[14] Their position can't be more precisely explained with certainty.

The Janapadas of Udicya (Uttarâpatha) or the North-Western India

The Udicya or Uttarâpatha in a narrower sense denotes north-western position of India, but its customary designation is north as a whole. The *Mahâbhârata* as well as the Purâṇas furnish evidence of the Kirâtas' settlements in North-Western India. In the *Mahâbhârata* they have been placed with the Yavanas, Pahlavas, Sakas, Barbaras, Gandharas, Cinas, Daradas, mlecchas arid others.[15] Further from description it is quite evident that their Janapadas were situatedin the countries of Tomaras, Haṁsamârgas and the Karamañjakas.[16] They had their settlements in North-Western Kashmir.

The Uttarâpatha Janapadas of the Kirâtas have been described with some variations in the different *Purânas* along with the territories of the tribes inhabiting the north western region of India viz. Lampakas (modern Laghman in Afghanistan), Culikas (Sogdians living to the north of the Oxus or Vamksu river). Jâguda (southern Afghanistan with its capital at Ghazni), Aurasa (people of Urasa, modern Hazara Dist.), Puskala (people of Puskalavati), Taksasilas (people of Taksasila), Pahlavas, (the Pahlavis Sassanians of Persia), Gândharas (the Rawalpindi and Peshwar Dists. with ancient capitals at Takfe&la in the Rawalpindi Dist and at Puskalavati, Char-sadda near Peshawar), Yavana, (Indo-Greek settlements in west Pakistan and adjoining lands including Kandhhara region), Sindhu Sauvira (Sindh to the west and Sauvira to the north and east of the lower Indus), Madras (the people of ancient. Sakala or Sialkot), Kambojas (having settlements in the land extending from Kashmir to Kandhar and near the Badakhshan beyond Hindukush). Daradas (living round Daratpuri in the upper valley of the Kisheng Ganga in Northern Kashmir), Tusaras (people living in Bactria and in the mountainous country on both sides of the middle Oxus as far as Badakhshan), Hamsamargas (Hunza in North western Kashmir,) Kâshmira (people of the upper Vitasta valley), Kulûtas (of Kulu in the Kangra Dist.), Vahikas of the Punjab, Bahlikas (living in Balkh area in the northern part of Afghanistan), Hfinas (somewhere about the Western Punjab), Darvas (people of Darvâhisârar which roughly comprised the Punch and Naushera regions between the Jhelum and the Chenab), the Khasas (identified with modern Khakhas, living in Punjab and Kashmir), Cînas, Barbaras, Ambasthas, Malavas, etc.[17]

On the basis of the data presented above, we can tentatively decide that the Kirâtas occupied the territories for their settlements in different parts of North-Western India which include, Punjab, Kashmir, with adjoining region, Afghanistan, Taksasila, Hazara Dist., Gandhara, West of Indus and the mountainous country on both sides of the Oxus or Vamksu river as far as Badakhshan beyond Hindukush.

The Janapadas of Prâcya—Deśa or the Eastern Country

One of the principal Janapadas of the Kirâtas in the eastern region of Bhâratavarṣa was in the hilly region of Prâgjyotiṣa as it appears from the *Mahâbhârata* and the *Purâṇas.* Actually, they had occupied the territories in different parts of the Prâgjyotiṣa before the Great Bhârata War. At the initial stage their territory was only confined to the hilly region adjacent to present Kâmâkhyâ temple in Gauhati. But after the defeat at the hand of Naraka, they dispersed in different directions and settled in the region lying further east. Their settlement in Prâgjyotisa first find mention in the *Mahâbhârata.*[18]

Their settlements in the eastern country with special reference to Prâgjyotisa or Kâmarûpa situated on the bank of river (Lauhitya or Brahmaputra) have been referred to in the number of *Purâṇas.*[19] Prâgjyotiṣa, Videha,' Magadha, Anga, Vaṅga Pundra, Tâmralipti, etc. have been clubbed together as Janapadas of Pracye-desa. They are classed together with the Pundras, the Bhargas and the Sudesnas in the *Mahâbhârata*[20] as well as in the *Purâna*[21] more or less in the similar fashion. They are described in different sources as the eastern neighbours of the Kirâtas.

The *Mahâbhârata* in particular supplies very valuable information about their position in Eastern India. One of the very popular kings named Paundraka Vasudeva has been depicted as the ruler of Vaṅga, Pundra and the Kirâta kingdoms.[22] This implies that the Kirâtas had their territorial settlements in north and east Bengal. The Kirâtas' settlement in the north of Videha (the sub-Himalayan tract of Nepal) also figures of course indirectly in the epics[23]. All these evidences go to prove that in Eastern India the Kirâtas had settled in different parts of Assam, north and east Bengal and in the north of Videha in the epic and Purâṇic period.

The Janapadas of Dakṣiṇâpatha and Aparânta or the Southern and Western Regions

The Kirâta Janapada along with that of Niṣâda, Niṣadha and Ânarta has been placed in Nairrita,[24] which is almost equivalent to South West from the geographical point of view. This can better be confirmed by Varâhamihira's[25] and Alberuni's[26] references to the territory of Kirâta (Kirâta-khanda) of south west. Further their southern Janapada appears together with Paradâs, Pandayâs, Dravidas and Úûdras,[27] Colas, Madras, etc.[28] The indication to their settlement in the south has also been provided in the *Mahâbhârata.*[29]

The exact location of their Janapada in the south can be determined by other Purânic evidence. As a matter of fact, in the Puranic period their settlement in the Daksinâpatha was only confined to the Vindhyan region, and at that time they were more popularly known as the Pulindas and Úabaras living in the Vindhyan region than the Kirâtas. In the epic and Puranic literature, the Pulindas, have often been associated with the Kirâtas. In the *Mahâbhârata*$_t$ particularly, the Pulinda has been shown as one of the kings of the Kirâtas.[30] The Pulinda, as described in the Purâṇas[31] has been clearly identified with the "Kirâtas living near the Vindhyas of Aparanta region."[32] The Pulindas and the Úabaras have been mentioned *(Mârk. Vy. Bmd Mat.* and *Vmn.*) as dwellers of the forests (âtavya) of the Vindhyan region in the Dakṣinâpatha. In some of the *Purâṇas (Vy. Bmd. & Mat.*) the Kirâtas and the Pulindas have been mentioned together. There is every possibility that they all might be kindred tribes in the hills and forests of the Vindhyan region.

The Janapadas of Parvatiya Deúa or (the Mountain Regions

The Parvatiya Janapadas of the Kirâtas were located in the northern, eastern and central or middle Himalayan regions of India. In the *Mahâbhârata*, one of their such Janapadas has been placed with that of Videhas, Tâmraliñga (Tamraliptakas), etc.[33] They have also been described as the dwellers of the Himalayan fort.[34]

In the *Mahâbhârata (Udyoga Parva,* 64, 21; *Bhiṣma Parva,* 10, 49-55; *Karṇa Parva,* 73, 19-20; *Droṇa Parva,* 4, 7), the Kirâtas have been described as dwellers of the Himalayan regions, particularly the eastern Himalayas.

In the *Purâṇas*, they have been depicted as Parvatâúrayins or the mountaineers living on the mountain slopes along with Haṁsamârgas (of the Himalayan region having settlement in

North west Kashmir), Khasas (of Kashmir), Kupatha (Himalayan locality), Kuthapravaranas (situated in the Himalayan region probably in the eastern Himalayas, Urna or Hunas in Uttarapatha somewhere about the western Punjab), Darvas (people of Darvabhisara roughly comprising the Punch and Naushera region between the Jhelum and the Chenab). Tanganar (at Tangana-Pura near Joshimath in the Garhwal Dist. U.P. *(EI,* Vol. XXXI, p. 286), Kasmiras, Suhukas, or Huhukas or Suhudaka (of the Himalayn region), Trigarta (modern Jalandhar region), Malavas (cis-Satluj Dist. of the Punjab together with some Himalayan country, Tamra, or Tomara, etc.[35] The Puranic texts relates that the Kirâta kingdom was also situated on the mountains. The Parvatâúrayin Janapadas of the *Purâṇas* find pointed mention in Pânini's *Asṭâdhyâyi* (IV. 91 Parvatâyana) as the mountainous tracts of north west.[36]

In fact, they inhabited the high mountain ranges of the Himalaya in North India including that of the Kailâúa in Tibet. Apart from it they had their settlements in the mountain regions of Prâgjyotisa, Nepal (north of Videha) Uttarâkhaṇḍa (Garhwal Kumaon region), Central region with reference to Vindhyan hills, Punjab, Kashmir and the hilly region of north-west and south-west. Their Himalayan territories with reference to that of the mountain Kailâúa and of the region around the Manasarovara have been given due prominence."[37]

III

THE PRINCIPALITIES AND KINGDOMS OF NORTHERN AND EASTERN INDIA

The Kirâtas' principalities and kingdoms of both pre-and post-Christian era in the valleys and hills of Northern and Eastern India can broadly be divided into the following four sections :

The Seven Principalities : North of Videha

The Seven principalities of the Kirâtas situated in the Eastern Himalayan region on the north of Videha rose to prominence during the epic age. It is stated that Bhima marched towards the eastern direction with the assent of Yudhiṣṭhira for the conquest of kingdoms and principalities. After having subjugated many other Âryan and non-Âryan rulers he conquered Videha country which was under the sovereignty of Râjâ Janaka. During his sojourn in Videha ne launched an expedition against the Kirâtas and finally defeated their seven kings (chiefs) living close to Indra mountain (Sikkim) and ruling over a vast dominion.[38] It is worthy of note that they were of indigenous origin. Thereafter he conquerred Vaṅga and Tâmralipti and exacting tributes from all he advanced towards Lauhitya region in Assam and subdued all mleccha kings dwelling in the marshy region on the sea coast and received many valuable things from them in the form of tribute. After having successfully completed his task he returned to Indraprastha where he handed over to Yudhisthira all valuable wealth which he had collected from different rulers.

The seven principalities of the Kiratas along with other eastern kingdoms conquered by Bhima went to form the part of Yudhiṣṭhira's empire. The epic account of Kirâtas' principalities conquered by Bhima has also been supported by others.[39] It has been rightly observed that "The Great epic-*Mahâbhârata* mentions several principalities all along the border land of the Himalayas ruled by the Kirâta kings with whom the rulers of Delhi and come into conflict".[40] Varahmihira has also placed Kirâta along with the dwellers of Videha region (Kirâtavaidehakâna)[41], which shows their juxtaposition.

The exact location of the said principalities has not yet been determined with any degree of accuracy for want of details in the original source. The subject needs some more verification. While making effort in this direction we can be helped, to a certain extent by the indications, which have incidentally appeared in some stray accounts. The territories of seven Kirâta kings are said to have been located between the Seven Gandakis and Seven Kouśis which roughly corresponds with the ancient Kirâta country in the eastern Himalayas comprising the greater part of the mountain regions of present Nepal.[42]

We find that along the northern fringe of Videha the mountainous country extending to the borders of Nepal formed one geographical unit. It was not well demarcated because of being coterminous. To put it in another way, on the north Mithila extending to the hills and there bound by Nepal constituted an old division of India subject to Raja Janaka. The ancient Videha kingdom is also believed to have comprised a part of Eastern Nepal.[43] It cannot be denied that in the mountain regions of Eastern Nepal there were Kirâta principalities in the epic age.

The exact location of all the seven needs some more investigation at the hands of the scholars to get a clearer picture of the subject.

In all probability, the Kirâta kingdom in the east might have split into several petty principalities out of which these seven might have been noted as one. There is every possibility that the so-called seven principalities might have been in the mountainous country between Nepal proper and Bhutan. There is also an evidence to support it. As reported by the Kirâtas themselves Belkakoth in the hilly country of Morung to the west of Sikkim and situated between Nepal and Bhutan was the site of the capital of their 'kingdom' in ancient times.[44]

This also corresponds with the tradition whicn was current all over the mountainous principalities of Nepal and Morung throughout Mithila till the first half of the last century. According to this recorded tradition. "Bhimsen, the son of Pandu and one of the brothers of Yudhisthira" was sent to the snowy mountains. He had his dominion in that part of the country. He was the king of 1,10,000 hills that extended from the sources of Ganges to the boundary of the people of Bhutan. Further Bhimsen is described as a prince, who lived at one particular point of time at Belkakoth (near the Kosi), which was in a centrical situation, convenient both for his dominions in the hills and for those in the lower country. He .governed both Nepal and Mithila. In the Kirâta country of Morung several old princes and chiefs are recorded to have maintained their principalities.[45]

In any case the reliability of this tradition can't be doubted. Bhimsen, who has been mentioned here as a prince, is different from that of son of Pandu. It is exceedingly doubtful that both are the same. Actually, he was a Kirâta chief governing the mountainous country concerned. This name might have been given to him probably because of their cherished desire to retain the memory of the visit of Pandava here to their land in the past. .Moreover, we have come across another Kirâta chief, named Lohangasen, who was well known in Mithila and Nepal. Thus, the possibility of a Kirata dynasty of such kings can't be precluded.

However, it is not possible to form any rational conjecture about the time, when they might have ruled in this region.

Further the Kirata chiefs represented by Rai are still found in association with Limbus in the hilly areas of present Nepal, West Bengal and Sikkim. They still have an age-old seven clans among themselves. Some of them represent the posterity of the seven Kirâta chiefs of the epic age. After analysing the data contained in the *Mahâbhârata* itself we find that as Bhima proceeded from Videha towards Nepal, Bengal and Assam in course of his eastern wanderings, these seven Kirata kings, whom he met might have been in different directions of the Eastern Himalayas. The historical relevance of the data can well be judged in the context of ancient India. Thus combining both tradition and history into one the existence of seven Kirâta principalities in Eastern India in ancient times can't be denied.

The Purâṇic Account of the Kingdom of Prâgjyotiṣa

The ancient kingdom of Prâgjyotisa (corresponding to an extensive high hill adjacent to Kâmâkhŷâ, situated in the heart of Gauhati town) situated on the extreme eastern fringe of Bharatavarsa was under the suzerainty of Ghataka, the king of the Kirâtas during the epic age. The subject under discussion still stands as one of the most obscure aspects of the political history of ancient India in general and ancient Assam in particular. The numismatics and the epigraphy help us very little in recasting the ancient political history of the tribal people of this region. However, the epic and Puranic traditions are of immense help for confirming the truth that the Kirâtas were the earliest inhabitants of this land and a very powerful race.

The puranic account, no doubt, testifies to the existence of the Kirâta kingdom in Prâgjyotisa during the time of Naraka who was the ancestor of king Bhagadatta. In the common parlance he is known as mytho-historical figure, but actually he was the foster child of Raja Janaka (of Kshatriya origin) of Videha. He came from Videha to Prâgjyotisa as a political adventurer at the age of sixteen in pre-Bharata war period (roughly ascribed to 3102 B.C.) or before the commencement of Kali Yuga or Iron Age and after having inflicted a crushing defeat on the Kirâtas in a fierce battle conquered the land, installed himself on the throne of Prâgjyotisa (later known at Kamarupa), proclaimed his political supremacy, laid the foundation of first Âryan kingdom and paved the way for the infiltration of Âryan ideas and culture, which gradually led to the evolution of synthesis of the Aryan and non-Âryan culture in North East India.[46]

Before the advent of Naraka the whole Praâgjyotisa was brought under the political sway of the famous Kirata chief named Ghataka. Lord Visnu found him a very majestic ruler. He was famous for his glory and splendour. After having got firmly convinced that Naraka's purpose is to usurp his throne, king Ghataka marched with his army and started showering arrows after arrows on his political adversary. The war started between the Kirata king and Naraka. Naraka being a redoubtable warrior fought gallantly with arrows, bows and other weapons. In this war all the chiefs of the Kirâtas, their commander-in-chief and other prominent soldiers were killed. Their most beloved king Ghataka was beheaded. Naraka captured twenty five thousand elephants of the Kirata king, his cavalry, army, jewels, ornaments of women, their colourful costumes, state's banner, etc. After overthrowing the mleccha king Ghataka, Naraka unfurled the banner of victory over newly besieged kingdom of Prâgjyotisa. After the death of Ghataka, many of his Kirata subjects deserted the country and fled away eastwards to the sea-shore. Those who survived the massacre submittd to invader or surrendered at the feet of triumphant Naraka. After this historic event, which cnstituted a land mark in ancient history of north east, the Kirâtas were pushed back to the hills from the plains. Naraka provided shelter to those, who voluntarily submitted to him. Actually, it was Lord Visnu who asked Naraka to exterminate the Kirâtas running away towards Dikkaravasini and to protect those who have taken shelter. Naraka is stated to have pushed the Kirâtas to the other side of the river (modern Dikrang) which later became associated with Devi Dikkaravâsini of Saumara Pitha. Many other Kiratas were driven away towards the eastern side lying at the end of the sea or marshy region. The Kirâtas unable to withstand the oppression of Naraka settled on the eastern side of the Dikkaravasini. Subsequently through the intervention of Visnu it was settled that their possession should extend from the eastern sea to Lalitakânta, while the country from the west of Lalitakanta to the east of Karatoya river was to be the jurisdiction of the Goddess Kâmakhya or Naraka. Actually this was the divsion of territory between Naraka and the Kirâtas. Between rivers Karatoya and Lalitakanta large number of Brahmanas well versed in the *Vedas* were made to settle. The Puranic text[47] bears an eloquent testimony to the aforesaid facts.

Similar information is supplied by a Tantric text[48] of late medieval period which helps us, to some extent, to corroborate the Puranic account. It is said that Lord Visnu conferred on Narakâsur the title of Raja, allowed him to settle at Kâmâkhy then known as Prâgjyotiṣa and granted the kingdom of Kamarupa as a reward for his victory over the Kirâtas.

The evidence furnished in the *Kâlikâ Purâna* and the *Yogini Tantra* can be partly supported by the statements recorded in some other sources.[49] This particular context has been expressed by D.C. Sircar as ".....Naraka, son of the god Visnu and the goddess Earth, was taken to Prâgjyotisâpur near the temple Kâmâkhyâ in the heart of Kâmârûpta. He drove out the Kiratas, inhabitants of the country from the area between the karatoya in the west and the Dikkaravasini (located at the Dikrang near modern Sadiya or ancient Sadhyapuri) and Lalitakanta (associated with the hill streams of Sandhya, Lalita and Kanta not far from Gauhati) in the east for settling the twice born, while the Kirâtas were rehabilitated in the sea coast extending from Lalitakanta in the east...."[50] The settlements of the Kiratas near the sites of shrines of Devi and Dikkaravasini and Kmkhyâ during the time of Naraka can also be confirmed by other source.[51]

Here it must be made clear that Dikkaravasini as mentioned in the Purânic and Tântric texts was the eastern most boundary of ancient Kamarupa. This region has been mentioned in the *Yogini Tântra* as Saumara Pitha (one of the four Pithas). B.K. Kakati seems to be perfectly justified in suggesting that Naraka drove away the aboriginal Kirâtas from his kingdom upto the point in north-east frontier tract which is at present inhabited by various tribal groups—the Abors, the Miris, the Mishmis, the Khamptis and the Mataks.[52] In ancient times certain Âryan colonies were established there, as it appears from the literary evidence and archaeological remains. The Kirâtas taking shelter there possibly might have been Aryanised and absorbed by the other tribal groups. There is a reason to believe that the Kiratas after having lost their ancestral kingdom might have dispersed in different groups, settled in the neighbouring hill regions and mixed with other tribal people. There is every likelihood that they might have consisted of some sizable section of the Khasis, the Gâros the Jaintias, the Mishmis, the Kacharis and the Chutiyas.

The historicity of Ghataka, the ruler of the Kirâtas, can be proved both by local tradition and archaeology. He is said to belong to the same dynasty of Asuras or Danvas to which his predecessors, Hatak (asur), Sambar (asur) and Ratna (asur) belonged. That is why, he was also known as Ghatakâsur. Because of being non-Âryan he is also known as mleccha king. After he was overthrown by Naraka a new dynasty was founded. Some historical records of this dynasty, which were, the first in order, are claimed to have been found. It appears, that the kings of the dynasty ruled over Pragjyotisa for a considerable length of time. According to the popular tradition Ghatakasur's capital was situated on or near the Sarania hill close to Gauhati town. "When the top of this hill was cleared in 1917-18 two big stones—slabs with lotuses, cut in each were found besides scattered broken bricks and a figure of Ganeúa on all sides of which are mystic diagrams cut into the rock. To the north-east of the hill is the site of an ancient ruined city, about a square mile in area which seems to have been inlaid throughout with bricks about 3 ft deep."[53] Unfortunately, no verticle or horizontal archaeological exploration of the site has been undertaken. This will certainly arouse some curiosity among the archeologists and other interested scholars to conduct further inquiry and investigation.

After the annihilation of the Kirâtas, who did not recognise the authority of the *Vedas* and *Úâstras,* the Dvija or twice born people—followers of the Sanatana Dharma were allowed to settle. The Vedic rites and rituals were revived. Naraka adopted Maya, daughter of the Raja of Vidarbha as his queen and thereafter his coronation ceremony took place. This ceremony was attended by his God father Janaka, who came from Mithila to Prâgjyotisa along with his queen and retinue to establish his son as a feudatory chief of the newly conquered kingdom. He stayed for some time in Pragjyotisa, blessed his enterprising foster child, enjoyed his hospitality and left for Videha after some time.[54] Janaka had certainly some affection for him otherwise he would not have visited the new kingdom. Actually, the visit of king Janaka to Prâgjyotisa constituted the milestone towards the real beginning of politico-cultural contacts between these two eastern kingdoms. The early historical tradition can fairly be attested to by the following observation that "in imitation of the custom of the family of the God father new king assumed the title Nara-Ka (protector of men) as Jana-Ka (protector of men) was the title of the royal family of Mithila. The capital was established near the present Gauhati town and its old name Prâg-Zuh-this was rejoined as Prâgjyotispur."[55] Prâgjyotisapur looking like Indrapuri was regarded by Naraka as Amrävati.

Naraka became the reputed founder of the ancient and famous city (pur) of Prâgjyotiṣa (Prâgjyotiṣapur=modern Gauhati). According to popular tradition he ruled from Kara-toya river to the extreme east of Brahmaputra valley.

After Naraka came to power and rose to prominence the name of the kingdom was changed from Prâgjyotisa to Kâmarûpa, which became the part of Âryavarta and came within the pale of Âryandom. "Pragjyotisa and Kamarupa, though very closely associated at one time, formed two distinct Janapadas. Kamarupa in later time came to be regarded as the name of the kingdom or Janapada of which the pura or head quarter had the name of Prâgjyotisa." It marked the beginning of the process of Âryanisation. The Brâhmans coming from Mithila and other parts of the Âryavarta to Prâgjyotisa were granted the royal patronage, which marked the beginning of the process of Âryanisation in North-East India. It has been correctly stated that the "New kingdom was gradually extended and the people from Mithila were brought to man and administer the country."[56] This paved the way for the spread of Maithili language and culture in ancient Assam. Naraka is also believed to have introduced and popularised the cult of Úakti which was very much associated with Austric elements.

The association of Kâmarûpa known in ancient times is Prâgjyotisa with Naraka and the Kiratas goes back to the epoch of Mahâbhârata war. The Âryan name was extended to this region directly from Videha and Magadha long before central or lower Bengal became either habitated or Âryanised.[57] It has also been mentioned that after having killed the Kirâta king Ghataka and conquered Prâgjyotisa Naraka allowed the Âryans to settle in his new kingdom before the Bhârata war.[58] This has also been substantiated by E. Gait.[59] Naraka period is marked by the genesis of synthetic culture—Âryan and non-Âryan-represented by the Kirâtas.

The earliest tradition connects the history of Kâmarûpa with Naraka and Lord Krsna. It is said that Krsna appointed him guardian of thee temple of Kâmâkhyâ. But because of being a great oppressor and worshipper of river God Úiva he was put to death by Krisna. About the death of Naraka the Purânic tradition relates that Lord Krsna in one fierce battle fought in Prâgjyotisa cut Naraka to pieces with his discus, a celestial missile.[60]

It is of course, very difficult to determine the exact antiquity of the Kirâta kingdom in Prâgjyotiṣa. The interesting episode as depicted in the literary text provides some clues to this effect. However, the suggestion put forth that the forward limit of Naraka's time could not be later than the end of the fourth century and backward limit cannot be earlier than the third century cannot be accepted. The further suggestion that Naraka of Mithila established himself sometime between 200-500 A.D.[61] can also be dismissed. The anoth er statement that Assam ruled by Ghataka, the Kirâta chief, was invaded by Narakasura about 2200 B.C.[62] is also not a reasonable postulation. We cannot find ourselves in agreement with such chronology. Naraka's acquisition of the Kirâta kingdom of Prâgjyotisa in the east can be tentatively placed before the battle of Kuruksetra in which his son Bhagadatta took part. Thus he must have flourished in the period preceding to it.

The Hill-Principality in Tripura

The ancient name of Tripura was 'Kirât'. But it was more popularly known as Kirâtadesa. This can be amply substantiated by the available evidences.[63] On the testimony of classical sources too the 'Kirrhadia' or Kirâta has been precisely equated with the ancient Tripura.[64] There is still a surviving tradition to support this ancient name.

The statement that 'Kirât' was a person of that name meaning "the hunter of the Lunar or Indo-Scythian race, the brother of Puru,.."[65] seems to be absurd and paradoxical. Neither the ancient Indian literary texts nor the classical sources refer to the Kirâta as a name of a particular individual. All the sources concerned distinctly refer them as a tribe or race living mainly in the northern and eastern Himalayas. The Kirâtas, because of being inhabitants of the hill ranges of Tripura, became also known as Tipperahs. The tradition tells Asahgo as their first king.[66] They are probably allied to some of the hill tribes of present Tripura. In the genealogical list furnished in the royal chronicle[67] of Tripura also, 'Kirât' has nowhere been shown as a person. The Kirâtas have rather figured in the text as one of the early rulers of Tripura.

The views held by some scholars that, the Tipperahs came originally from the Bodo home in Central Asia and they, like the Cacharis and other tribes of Eastern India, were of Tibeto-Burman [or Mongoloid origin[68] seem to be untenable in view of the fact that they are of mixed origin and none of them came from outside. Racially, they have been placed under the "Indo-Mongoloids" and linguistically identified with the Tipra section of the Bodos[69] which is not perfectly justified. Further, the Kiratas have been indiscriminately amalgamated with the rulers of the royal family.[70] It has been rightly suggested that"... the early members of the family were leaders of some aboriginal tribes of neighbouring hilly region... it is not however, possible to think that they were outsiders like the Mongoloid".[71] The name Tripura is undoubtedly the sanskritized form of a tribal name Tipura born by the aboriginal people inhabiting the eastern fringe of south east Bengal to which the royal family of Tripura belonged.[72] It is also believed that the name Tripura was given by the Aryan speaking immigrants from upper India.[73]

The transformation of name from Kirâtadeúa to Tripura not only shows the domination of the Kirâtas in the early phase of history and their subordination to the later Âryan immigrants, but also the emergence of two different dynasties on the early political stage of Tripura.

This is further confirmed by the truth that king Druhyu as recorded in ancient Indian historical tradition and in the native chronicle after being sent into exile by his father Yapati of Lunar race came to north-eastern part of India, then known as Kiratadesa and after defeating the king of the Kirâtas set-up a new dynasty in Tripura. The local tradition also confirms it. The royal family of Tripura claims their descent from him. It appears from the sequence of events that the Kirâta rulers of the hill region survived side by side with the rulers of Indo-Aryan stock of another dynasty.

It is said that it was Pratardhan, twenty sixth in descent from Druhyu, who conquered the Kiratas and established a new kingdom with the capital known as Trivega on the bank Kapili river.[74] His descendent known as Daitya, who was an efficient and powerful ruler further defeated the Kirâtas and enlarged the frontiers of his kingdom which included the hilly country to the east as far as the border of Burma. Tripur, his successor and fortieth in descent from Druhyu, who is believed to have given the name Tripura, was a follower of the Kirâta culture.

From the genealogy of Tripura rulers provided in the said' chronicle it is quite evident that the two different dynasties, one having the Sanskrit names and another with Bodos (the modern term used linguistically for the tribal people) names ending with 'Pha' or 'fa', flourished in ancient times. Most of the rulers appear to have assumed both the names Sanskrit as well as Bodo, e.g., Harihar alias Chuchung-pha, Chandrasekbar alias Machi-Chang-pha, Dungar-pha alias Hari Roy (640-670 A.D.), Kritidhar alias Cheng-Thun-pha 1240 A.D.) and likewise. This is a pointer to the Hinduisation and Sanskritization of the Kirâta tribes (so-called the Bodos) because of their mutual contacts with the Âryan rulers. A major section of them might have been possibly absorbed by their superior neighbours. The chiefs bearing the title 'pha' were definitely no other than the non-Âryan tribes living in the hills.

One of the notable events in their early history was the grant of the whole of Pañcakhnda to certain Brahmanas from Mithila sometime between 640 and 641 A.D. by Dungarpha, a contemporary of Bhaskarvarman of Kamarupa. It is also pointed out that after the downfall of the Varman dynasty due to uprising of the mlecchas or Bodos, a batch of Brâhmanas migrated from Kâmarûpa to the kingdom of the Tipperahs during his reign and settled at Pancakhanda. This is further evidenced by the fact that Copper Plate grants of Bhaskarvarman to Nagar Brahmanas have been found at Nidhanpur near Pancakhanda. The Copper Plate inscription is lost but an extract therefrom can be seen in *Vaidika Sangvadini*'.[75] The Brahmanas of Mithila, no doubt, were made to settle in Kamarupa, Tripura and Sylhet in ancient times.[76] It is a fact to be reckoned with that from the time of Druhyu of Lunar dynasty to the 12th century A.D. the Kirâtas somehow maintained their petty hill principality co-existing with the rulers of different dynasties that sprang up during the period concerned, and acknowledging the supremacy of the rulers of royal family.

The Kingdom in the Valley of Nepal

The foundation of the Kirâtas' rule in the Himalayan Valley of Nepal, which was one of the outlying kingdoms of ancient India, was laid in the pre-Christian era. Traditionally it is believed that Nepal was at first under the rule of eight kings of Gopâla dynasty. They were overthrown by the rulers of Ahira or Abhira dynasty, which was also powerful in Westtern India. They were succeeded by the Kirâtas. Thus the Kirâta dynasty was third in succession. Nepal was finally conquered by them during the reign of the third king of the Abhira dynasty. The number of the Kirâta kings, who ruled over the valley of Nepal, varies from twentytwo to twentynine. But, the thorough examination of all the available records shows that they were twentynine in number. They consisted of both Aryans and non-Aryans. On the whole, their rule in Nepal continued up to the first quarter of the 8th century A.D. During the period of their rule they shifted their capital from one place to another according to the changing situation. One of their famous capitals was at Gokarna in the north of Nepal valley. In the third century B.C. during the reign of Sthunko, the fourteenth ruler of this dynasty Nepal was visited by Aúoka.

The early centuries of the Christian era are marked by several events, which adversely affected the prospects of their dynastic rule in Nepal. During their rule the country was conquered by a Katriya prince from India named Nimisa. With the advent of the Licchavis in Nepal from Videha sometime between the first and second century A.D., the contest for political supremacy between the two powers ensued. Thfr Kirâtas were ultimately conquered by them between the 3rd and 2th century A.D. Consequently, their power gradually began to decline. However, this was not the end of their rule, but the beginning of real struggle for existence.

With the dawn of the 6th century A.D. the Kirâtas' attempt at revival of their power and restoration of their fallen virtues began. The wheel of the fortune took turn in their favour. The beginning of the 7th century A.D. marked the internal dissensions power of the resuscitation of the power of the Abhiras or later Guptas, who were the feudal chiefs during the times of the Licchavi ruler. The period falling in between the 6th and the 7th century A.D. saw the eruption of hostility between the Licchavis and the Abhiras. Taking advantage of the situation the Kirâtas decided to test their fortune once more. They entered into conflict with the Abhira Guptas during the period concerned. Actually this was the period of tripartite struggle for sovereignty over Nepal.

The Kirâtas were finally dethroned by the Âbhîra Guptas by the end of the 7th century A.D. or the beginning of the 8th century A.D. With this their power and prestige completely eclipsed. The apparatus of their kingdom started falling apart. But they themselves did not become extinct. They only lost their status as rulers. Their successors continued to survive there for ages. They were brave, warlike race, independent and powerful people in former times.

IV

THE JANAPADAS AND KINGDOMS OF DAKṢIṆÂPATHA (VINDHYAN & TRANS-VINDHYAN REGION)

The Vindhyan and trans-Vindhyan region, known as Daksinapâtha in ancient times saw the emergence and decline of several tribal kingdoms and Janapadas. One of the most popular Janapadas of this region is the Kirata Janapadas as it appears from the literary, epigraphic and other dependable records.

The geographical application of the Sanskrit name Daksinâpatha or Daksina, which roughly corresponds with the

Deccan, varied from time to time. It was often loosely used in ancient times for whole of the Indian peninsula lying to the south of the Narmada just as Uttarapatha vaguely designated the country to its north between the Vindhyas and the Himalayas. It was one of the cradles of early tribal culture in India. Right from the epic age this region has been the source of attraction for both Âryan and non-Âryans. The territorial units of the Kirâtas, and that of their kindred tribes popularly known as the Pulindas, the Úabaras and the Mutibas were located within the geographical limits of this region. In the *Mahâbhârata*[77] and the *Purâṇas*[78] they have been referred to as Daksinapathavasinah. From the definition of Madhya-deúa as given in the Dharmasûtras[79] it seems that Daksinâpatha lay to the south of Paripatra or Pariyatra, which covered the considerable portion of the Vindhyan range. The Pali texts, the *Mahâvagga* (V. 13) and *Cullavagga* (XII. L) of the *Vinaya Pitaka* and another Buddhist text, *Divyavâdâna* place Daksina Janapadas to the south of the town of Úatakarnika. In the *Sumaṅgalavilâsinî* (1.265) the whole tract of land lying to the south of the Ganges and to the north of Godavari has been designated as Daksinapatha. In the Allahabad pillar Inscription[80] Samundragupta Daksinâpâtha râjya is used as a name of South India as opposed to north called—Âryavarta. The Brahmanical tradition as contained in the Kâvya-mimmhsa of Rajaúekhar indicates Daksinâpatha region to the south of Mahismati, which has been identified with Mañdhâta on the Narmada.

The Kirâtas were living in the vicinity of the Vindhya mountains which were entirely covered with forests. The Vindhyas constituted the southern limit of Aryavarta. In fact, it was the natural frontier between the Aryanised nations of the north and the Dravidians of the South. That is why, it is sometimes placed in Mid-India too. The people inhabiting the neighbourhood of the Vindhya has been called as Vindhyântavâsinah and placed in the south-eastern (Âgneya) division.[81]

The forest was called in Sanskrit Araṇya or Atavî, which implies an impervious wood. And in the fitness of things the extensive forest tract of the Vindhyas has been used in a much wider sense in ancient Indian literature as Vindhyâtavis, which extended as far as the forests on the shores of both the eastern and western Oceans. The forest kingdoms situated in the Vindhya region was known as 'âtavikarajyas' in ancient times. The forest tract or Atavi has also been described as Âtavyas, which represent both as a people and territory of Janapada of Dakṣinâpatha.

The existence of Janapada, as well as forest kingdom of the Kiratas in the Vindhyas at different periods of history can be confirmed by several sources. It should be made clear that all the tribes, notably, the Kirâtas, the Pulindas, the Úabaras and the Mutibas inhabiting the forest region (Atavi) of the Vindhyas have generally figured in the literary texts and inscriptions as Âtavyas with little variations. The geographical boundary of their kingdoms never remained the same because of political upheavals. The earliest reference to Atavi as a city in the Deccan occurs in the *Mahâbhârata.*[82] Some of the *Purâṇas*[83] also refer to Âtavyas, as the foresters represented by the Sabaras, dwelling in the forest region. The Puranic references to Âtavyas signifying the aboriginal tribes of Central India, as well as, the Vindhyan Janapadas of Southern region or Daksinapatha have also been supported by others.[84]

In the Buddhist texts it has been described as "Vinjhâtavi", which represents the forests surrounding the Vindhya range.[85] The Jaina text, *Jambûdiva (Jambûdvipa) Pannâtti"* unequivocally speaks of the eighteen settlements of the aboriginal tribes along the 'Vaitadhya' of Vindhyas.[86]

During the times of the Mauryas and the imperial Guptas their status was reduced to vassal tribes. The tribes of Âtavi (mentioned along with others in Aúoka's Rock Edict XIII)[87] have been correctly identified with the peoples of the Vindhya forest living in his dominion. In all likelihood the Kiratas along with the Pulindas and others were under his rule. The forest kingdoms of the Himalayan region were undoubtedly, included within his empire.

The early texts speak of the Kirâta Janapadas and kingdoms in the north and east, but the later texts refer to the same in the Vindhyan region. The reasons are not far to discover. In the early phase their settlements were mainly confirmed to the north and east and no such forest kingdom bad come into existence in the Central India and the South. But by the middle of the 4th century A.D. or the early part of the 5th century A.D. they had established powerful kingdoms in the northern, north-eastern, central and southern parts of India, which can be indirectly proved by the statements recorded in the literary texts composed between the fifth and middle of the 7th century A.D. and in the epigraphic records.

The atâvikarâjyas (collectively used as forest states as mentioned in the Allahabad pillar Inscription[88] possibly included the forest kingdoms of the Kirâtas and other tribes of the Vindhyas. From the said inscription it appears that atavirâjya and Mahâkântâra had appeared on the Indian map as two distinct separate geographical regions. The tribal states, which were just like the small city-states of Greece, emerged as very powerful states during the Gupta period. The kings of the forest states of Central India like that of the monarchs of Daksinâpatha and other tribes could not escape the attention of Samudragupta. They were compelled to acknowledge their allegiance to him, which has been discussed in detail in the subsequent section of this work. Here it will suffice to state that the Kirâta state too like other forest rajyas had risen to prominence during his time.

History is, unfortunately, silent as far as the exact location and identification of these forest states and other details are concerned. However, there is an inscription, dated A.D. 528-9 of the times of the Mahârâjâ Sanksabha, which clearly proves the existence of eighteen forest kingdoms ("aṣṭadaúa-âtavi-râjya")[89] in Central India. With the help of this epigraphic evidence it can be postulated with considerable amount of confidence that the Kirâta kingdom situated in the Vindhyas formed the part of these eighteen Atavi states or forest kingdoms during the period extending from the middle of the 4th century A.D. to the 6th century A.D.

It is perhaps some of these which Varâhamihira speaks and further includes among the 'Vana-rastra' (forest countries) and 'Vanarâjya' (forest kingdoms) of northern and eastern parts of India.[90] Further he places Vindhyâtavi along with the Kirâta, the Pulinda and the Úahara in the list of the countries lying towards Narmada.[91] He has depicted in his work both the Janapadas and kingdoms of the Kiratas in different parts of India.

The earlier position could not contine for a long time. It was sometimes between the 6th and 7th century A.D. that the Vindhyan kingdom of the Kirâtas attained indepdendent status. From this period onwards till their subjugation by the contemporary rulers they maintained their kingdom along the tribal customs and traditions.

The first authentic historical account of the well-organised Vindhyan kingdom of the Kirâtas has been provided by Dandin. The Vindhyan region during the period concerned was the stronghold of the territories of the Kirâtas, the Pulindas and the Úabaras. Their kingdoms were located in the heart of Vindhya forest. The Kirâta group consisted of both Brahmanas and non-Brâhmanas. But basically there was domination of the former group because of the prevalence of Brâhmanical religion and culture. The majority of them had been Brâhmanised by that time. But many of them were leading the savage life of the foresters. The son of one of these became famous by the name of Matanga. The Kirâtas. were in a very commanding position. They used to harass the neighbouring villages, and often forced them to acknowledge their authority and supremacy. Some of them became undisputed leaders. One of the leaders of the mountaineers has been described as "Kirâta-bhartri". They had their own system of trade and commerce. It seems that they had some positive sense of diplomacy. Trade was also the means for the intelligent Kirata forest messengers to gather news. This is what they used to do in the neighbouring city of Mahismati.[92]

The name and fame of this region as a reputed home of the Kirata spread for and wide by the middle of the 7th century A.D. Even Bânabhaṭṭa and Harṣa became attracted towards this region. The description provided by them supplement Daṇḍin's account.

While giving an exhaustive account of Vindhyâtavi (the forest region of Vindhya) Bâna mentions that the king of this region was called Âtavika Samanta. One of the kings of this region along with the Sabaras had met Harsa while he was moving in this region in search of Rajyasri. The explanation of the prevailing political system in this region as given by him shows that the position of Âtavika kings was equivalent to that of the feudatories. The geographical frontiers of the *Atabika* states in the north of Vindhyacal comprised the areas extending from Chambal and the middle regions of 'Sindhvetavakena' in the west to Sona in the east. He has vividly portrayed that this whole forest region at one point of time was under the control of the Úabaras who had their own chiefs and Senapati (commander). Some of their names have also been mentioned. They had extended their political sway up to Mahakosala or Greater Kosala and Kalinga.[93]

The Kirâtas and Úabaras had no separate identity during the time of Dandin because he has equated one with the other. But during the time of Bana as it appears, the Úabaras were more well-known than the Kirâtas. However both were kindred forest tribes of the Vindhyas. His description of the forest kingdom of the Vindhyas does not only apply to the Úabaras, but to the Kirâta as well living in this region.

The *Úakti Sangama Tantra* also refers to the small country of the Kiratas in the Vindhya range. But the details are wanting.

The large extent of the Kirâta's territorities in the Vindhyas and beyond also figure in the historical traditions of South India. The *Pampâ Râmâyanâ*[94] of Abhinava Pampâ (12th century A.D.) states that the Kirâta warriors were living in the Vindhya forest together with other mleccha kings. They were maintaining countless army to help the neighbouring kings of this region.

The annals of the ancient Karnataka kingdoms of the south and the west also refer to them. Nijagunayogi, a Kannada writer in his work[95] mentions the Kirata kingdom of Dakṣinâpatha. Another Kannada poet, Virabhadra Râja (circa A.D. 1530), only refers to the activities of the Kirata women of this region,[96] which indirectly goes to prove their settlements on a large scale.

The post-Harsa inscriptions of both Northern and Southern India also testify to the existence of the Kirata Janapadas in the Vindhyan and trans-Vindhyan India.

The stone inscriptions of Yaúovarman, ascribed to the 8th century A.D. reads as follows: "whose pleasure mound was that

Vindhya, the peaks of which are charming with the sweet notes of his excellencies sung by Kirâta women seated on spotless lotuses".[97] This indirectly points to the inter-relations of the Vindhyan Kiratas and the Varman rulers of Kanauj during the period concerned.

The Janapadas of the Daksinâpatha have prominently figured in the South Indian epigraphic records of both early and late periods. The records of the kings of Ganga dynasty, which was founded by Kongani-Varman sometimes in the 4th century A.D. transmit very valuable information in this regard. The kingdom of the Gangas comprised the greater part of Mysore and was called after them Gangavadi.

A Grant of Ganga king Sivamara-I, dated A.D. 713 shows the presence of the Kirata women in the inner courts of the palace of Navakama the younger brother of Kongani Mahar-ajadhirja Bhuvikram.[98] An inscription dated, A.D. 973 ascribed to the king Konguni Varman Dharmamaharaja of the Ganga dynasty records the settlements of the Kiratas on the outskirts of the Vindhya forest.[99]

There are some indications to their survival till the 12th century A.D. on the outskirts of the Vindhyas. Their dispersion from the Vindhyan region and settlements in the far south, by and large, might have possibly started after the 12th century A.D. as it appears from the available records.

The Pallava records of the 10th century, the record dated A.D. 1007 ascribed to Chola king Rajaraja Deva (c. 985-1014 A.D.) and the 12th century records of the Hoysala kings of Southern India prove that they had an extensive territories in the Daksinapatha during the periods concerned. But their relations never remained cordial. Because the Pallavas, the Cholas and the Hoysalas were very much hostile to the Kirata chiefs.[100]

Even the Grant of A.D. 1641 also shows that they were living in the south. Later they penetrated into the kingdom of Keladi rulers of Mysore.[101]

South Indian sources as late as the 17th century continue to refer to them as living in the Vindhyan and trans-Vindhyan region in a "Semibarbarous condition". It is worthwhile to note that they could not achieve territorial stability in the Southern

Peninsula because of their ouster by the contemporary rulers from one region to another and consequent obstructions in their permanent settlements.

V

THE MINOR PRINCIPALITIES OF UTTARÂKHAṆḌA

The existence of numerous petty tribal principalities in the hilly tracts, forest region and mountain fastness in ancient times, cut-off from the main currents of political life, to a greater degree, because of geographical barrier, constitutes an important feature of Indian history. Here it is neither desirable nor possible to enumerate all such tiny states that flourished and decayed in the early period. But quite a few deserve our notice as the relics of the past which were fast disappearing.

One of these worth-mentioning is the territorial units of princely Kirâtas (popularly known as Râji-Kirâtas), situated in the Uttarakhanda. The literary and epigraphic evidence, popular tradition and other reliable records based on historical researches help us in this regard.

To proceed first with the epigraphic evidence, one of the Pandakeúvara inscriptions of Kumaon provides a glimpse of the Kirâta Rajya, which, decidedly, stands for Kumaon and Kârttikeyapur. Because of having in their possession large territory in this region, they also became popularly known as "Rajya Kirâta", which literally means the kingdom of the Kirâtas.[102]

The Charters and Grants of Lalitasura (middle of the 9th century) and Padmata (middle of the 10th century) also testify to the settlements of the Kirâtas in Garhwal— Kumaon region. In the said epigraphic records the Kirâtas of this region have been repeatedly addressed to.[103]

They have been described in different records under different names. One of these is said to be the "Kirâtas of Rajya". But, collectively they became most popular by the name of the 'Rajis' because of their claim of royal descent.

The Kirâtas once lived in the forest region to the west and east of the present settlements of the Râjis of Askot in Kumaon. That is why, it is connected with the whole Askot Pargana of Pithauragadh, the eastern Janapada of Uttarâkhanda, situated on the confluence of Gori and Kali (Sarda) rivers. The whole area inhabited by the Raji Kirata is also designated as "Râjya-Kali-Kumaon".

It is said that Rajis represent descendants of one aboriginal prince of Kumaon, who with his family fled to jungles to escape the destruction. The Râji Kirâta to whom the various petty dynasties of eastern Kumaon are attributed, preceded the 'Chand' (Candravamsi, the descendants of Manu) dynasty as mentioned in inscription and supported by tradition.[104]

There are some contradictory accounts as regards the antiquity of princely kingdom of the Kirâtas. However, they are worthy of consideration. The legends and traditions handed down from generation to generation ascribe the origin of Raji Kiratas to a prehistorical king of Asoket, who had two sons. The elder one, being an ardent lover of nature and fond of hunting spent most of his time in jungle. And, therefore, after the death of king, the throne was usurped by the younger brother who ordered the elder one to stay out in the forest. The fear of the treacherous brother kept the prince on the move. The Rajis are believed to be his descendants. According to mythological belief they are the descendants of a Candravamsi king named Wahin.[105]

Grierson has identified Garhwal-Kumaon region with the district mentioned in the *Mahâbhârata* as containing settlements of the Kirâtas.[106] But, the details are wanting. However, the settlement of the tribal population can definitely be pushed back to the epic age on the basis of this evidence, though insufficient it may be. In the Ramayanic age the Kirata Rajya of Uttarâkhaṇḍa was lying within the territorial limits of Uttarakoúala.

The Uttarâkhaṇḍa does not have ancient historical records, the reasons for which are not far to seek. But it does have its own age-old tradition which bespeaks the antiquity of the Kirâta kingdom. The tradition connects the princely Kirâtas with the ancient Rajya Kirâtas of the Puranas, one branch of which is represented by the Rajis of today and others had almost merged in the Âryan population of Uttarâkhanda, which later came to be called as the Khasa or Khâsia.

The names of fourteen rulers of the Khasa race in Kali-Kumaon are very much similar to that of princely Kirâtas in character because of the blending of one with the other. Thus there can be little doubt of close connection between them. Possibly there is a living link between the Kirâtas and the Khasas of equally pronounced Âryan form.[107]

The *Vârâha Sahṁitâ* also refers to the 'Vana-Râjya-Kirâta',[108] which is placed between Amaravana and China or between Jagesvara and Tibet and connected with princely Kirâtas.[109] This shows either the extension of their sway over the large territory bordering Tibet or the rule of another powerful branch of the Râji Kiratas over the areas lying beyond Uttarâkhanda.

The available evidences as cited above give us an impression that the settlements of the Kirâta in the hilly region of Uttarâkhanda had already begun in the prehistoric age itself, but their kingdoms and principalities did not come into existence at that time. It was in the epic and Puranic periods that the concept of a territory to be ruled by a particular tribal prince or chieftain had emerged among the Kirâtas. Further, they consolidated their position sometimes between the 5th and the 10th century A.D. It is worth-noting that the princely Kiratas maintained their existence throughout the history, which is supported by the surviving tradition of today.

VI

TOWNS OR NAGARAS OF THE HIMALAYAN REGIONS

Different sections of the Kirâtas after being driven away from the plains to the hills took shelter in the most inaccessible forest regions of the Northern and Central Himalayas for their self-protection and defence. They occupied the remote areas for their permanent settlements and peaceful living. Subsequently, they carved out their own separate territory, which emerged in the form of a Janapada in the epic and Purânic periods. They also erected some impregnable *durgs* or forts for the purpose of war and defence and founded towns or *nagaras* or cities, as evidenced by the details provided in the *Mahâbhârata,* the *Purânas* and other literary texts. The Himalayas have also preserved the remnants of the most primitive form of urban culture and civilization of the Kirâta and other tribes.

In order to check the advancement of the hostile forces and to prevent their entry into their own territory the Kirâta tribes, who happened to be expert warriors, constructed forts in the

Himalayan regions. The *Mahâbhârata* records one such, fort in the middle Himalayan range, which was captured by Karṇa.[110]

One of the cities or nagaras of the Kirâtas as situated near the slopes of the Himalayas has also been referred to in the text: 'Himâcalopatyakâyanstu Kirâtanagare Úubhe."[111] The Kirâtas, the Khasas, the Nagas, the Cînas and others of the Northern Himalaya has maintained a high degree of civiilization in the pre and post Vedic periods. They lived in forts and walled towns.[112]

However, it was not before the 7th century A.D. that the Northern Himalayan region saw the emergence of the urban centre of the Kirâtas. The vast territory extending from Suvarnapura (a magnificent town situated on the northern frontiers of Bharatavarsa) to the forest region near the mountain Kailâúa was inhabited by the Kirâtas, who were called 'Hemajakûtas'. Suvarnapura, the noted urban centre in the Northern Himalaya, was the stronghold of the Kirâtas and the Kinnaras. It was the last boundary of India at that time.[113] The fact can indirectly be supported by other statements like that of Pragiter who goes to state: "The chief territory of the Kiratas was among the mountains Kailâúa, Mandara and Haima i.e. the region around the Mânasa sarovara (Mânasarovara)."[114]

VII

SUBJUGATION AND ANNIHILATION

The period extending from the time of the *Mahâbhârata* to the times of the Hoysalas of the south saw not only the subjugation but also the destruction of the Kirâtas living in the vast areas stretching from the Himalayas on the north to the trans-Vindhyan region on the South. It became almost a convention in ancient India, particularly, for the minor kings to subjugate the tribal chiefs, who happened to be their weaker neighbours, and to extend their sway and influence over them. The said kings were guided by the ambition and actuated by their desires to claim suzerainty over vast areas of the Indian sub-continent, which are reflected in both literatures, and inscriptions. The frequent subjugation and defeats of the Kiratas in various battles with their contemporary rulers could not provide stability to their Janapadas, kingdoms and principalities, whose rise and fall became a recurrent feature. The following pages present an account of the subject in a chronological order.

The Epic and Purâṇic Periods

During the epic period the Kiratas of north-eastern and western regions were in a very strong position. But they were conquered both by the Pandavas and Karvas. The Pândava heroes wanted to bring them along with others under their sway just to compel them to acknowledge the sovereign rule of Yudhisthira. That is why, Arjuna in the north, Bhima in the east, Nakula in the west, and Sahdeva in the south marched for *digvijaya* or conquest of both Âryan and non-Ârayan Janapadas, kingdoms and principalities. Whereas, on the other hand, the Kaurvas wanted to keep them as their subject to utilize their services in the war against their opponents. But their participation in the Great Bhârata war proved to be suicidal for them. Because they invited the wrath and cupidity of the Pâṇḍavas. Consequently they received blow after blow at their hands and ultimately met the tragic end. Thus, because of their divided loyalty, they could not consolidate their position. And ultimately, most of them rallied round the imperial banner of Yudhiṣṭhira.

Among the Pâṇḍavas Arjuna was greatest subjugator of the Kirâtas. In pursuit of his attempt in the northern direction he attacked the kingdom of Prâgjyotiṣa, which was surrounded on all sides by the Kirâtas. After having suffered a humiliating defeat at the hands of Naraka, they had accepted the supremacy of his son, Bhagadatta, which is confirmed by the fact that they along with others joined his army. The Kirâtas along with the Cînas and other soldiers who were dwellers of the marshy regions on the sea-coast, fought on behalf of Bhagadatta, (the king of Prâgjyotiṣa) with Arjuna for eight days. But they were defeated and finally Bhagadatta agreed to recognise the supremacy of Yudhisthira and pay tribute to him.[115] The defeat of the Kirâtas in the war led to their sequestration. It is believed that the Kirâta who fought for Bhagadatta were living on the banks of the Brahmaputra or on the both sides of the Lauhitya.[116] Bhagadatta has been repeatedly described as the master of the Kirâtas and the dwellers of the sea-shore.[117] He accompanied by the Kirâtas, the so-called mlecchas and other mountain chiefs came to Yudhiṣṭhira with some presents.[118]

After having subjugated the king of Prâgjyotisa, Bhagadatta, and his follower Kirâtas, Arjuna conquered all the chiefs of the mountainous tracts and their outskirts. The regions conquered by him included Antargiri, Vahirgiri and Upagiri[119] comprising the hill territories of Prâgjyotisa and beyond probably up to the hilly areas of present Arunachal Pradesh. He brought all the mountain chiefs reigning there under his sway, exacted tributes from all and established suzerainty of Yudhisthira over the hilly areas of north.[120] He is said to have defeated king of Lauhitya along with ten minor chiefs of eastern frontier.[121] It is obvious that the Kirâta of both the plains and hill sin the north were subjugated by Arjuna.

Large number of the Kirâtas including the followers of Bhagadatta who came from Prâgjyotisa and northern hills or from the fastnesses of Himavat to take part in the battle of Kuruksetra on behalf of Duryodhana[122] were vanquished by Sâtyaki and Arjuna. About one thousand of them were annihilated by Sâtyaki alone and the rest by Savyasâcin. They were well accomplished in the art of fighting. The Kirâta kings, riding on elephants well protected with armour, fought very effectively in the battle, but finally they were crushed by the Pândavas. Bhagadatta himself was killed by Arjuna.[123]

In spite of their discomfiture in this battle they remained undaunted in their courage and indomitable in their spirit. They, like other Yavana, the mleccha and Âryan rulers, fought with Arjuna even in the post war period,[124] but were defeated once again. While going for Digvijaya with Sacrificial horse Arjuna first conquered Mâgadhas and the Cedis and thereafter proceeded, from the southern direction, towards the Janapadas of the Kirâtas, the Khâsis, the Angas, the Koúalas and the Tanganas and finally brought them under his sway.[125]

Bhîma in course of his expedition to Eastern India also subjugated the Kirâtas. After having defeated their seven kings on the confines of Videha, he defeated the kings of Pundra, Suhma, Vañga, and Tamralipti. In his expidition he reached Lauhitya region and subdued the mleccha kings and dwellers of the sea-shore (sâgaranûpavasins) and forced them to pay taxes.[126] There is every reason to believe that the people defated by him were no other than the Kirâta tribes of Prâgjyotisâ.

In pursuance of the imperial policy of conquering the

Eastern Himalayan kingdoms he might have conquered regions inhabited by the Kirâtas. It has been rightly observed that "Bhima conquered the whole Eastern India including Bengal, Tripura, Bihar, Kamarûpa, IIimalaya countries and the hill people living on the sea-coast in the marshy region and subjected them to pay tribute."[127]

Nakula going for conquest in the western direction, also subjugated the fierce mlecchas residing on the sea-coast and the wild tribes—the Kirâtas, the Pahlavas, the Barbaras, the Yavanas and the Úakas.[128] This is, the substantial evidence of the Pandava's conquest of Kiratas in the west.

Sahdeva in course of his southern expedition is stated to have conquered the Nisâdas, who were evidently the kindred tribe of the Kirâtas.[129] In the present state of our knowledge it is very difficult to confirm the resemblance between the two kinds of wild tribes in the present context.

The Kiratas, after having been fully subjugated by the Pandavas acknowledged the sovereignty of Yudhisthira by paying tributes, giving presents, offering services and extending their allegiance to him. All the valuable gifts, presents and tributes collected by the Pândavas from the Kiratas added to the wealth of Yudhisthira at Indraprastha.

It is stated that quite a good number of chiefs of the Kirâtas (armed with cruel weapons and attired in skin) living on both sides of the Lauhity mountains (the mountainous regions on both sides of the Lauhitya river, on the northern slopes of the Himavat and on the mountains from behind and in the Karusa on the sea-coast) brought with them tributes for Yudhisthira at Indraprastha as a token of submission.[130]

The Rajasûya of imperial sacrifice performed at Indraprastha, was attended by various tribes of the Kiratas, the Yavanas, barbarous mleccha of the sea-coast, the chiefs of the frontier or outlying states, kings of Pahlavas, the Dardas, the kings of Anga, Vañga, Pundra and many other kings from different parts of the country. They performed various duties on this memorable occasion.[131] Pulinda, or Kunindra, Sumana and Subahu (who commanded both the Kirâtas and Tanganas)—the three noted kings of the Kirâtas along with other kings and illustrious rulers were always present there to offer their services to Yudhisthira.[132]

The Seven states of the Kirâtas, Pragjyotisa, the whole Lauhitya region, Kimpurusa (Nepal), Hataka (near Manasarovara), Uttara Harivarisa (Tibet), the five ganârajya of the north, Pulinda nagar (Bundelkhanda), Pancala Videha, Daúarna, Magadha, Pundra, Tâmralipti, the regions inhabited by Nisada, the Barbaras, Bahlikas, etc. formed the parts of Yudhisthira's empire.[133]

The Kiratas living within the precincts of the Himalayan fort and well known for their qualities as expert warrior and vigorous fighters were conquered by Karna (king of Añga) for Duryodhana.[134] Those, who tendered their submission before the Kaurvas, must have belonged to the Eastern Himalayan region.

The *Purâṇas* supply interesting information about their subjugation by the Brâhmanas. It is said that Pramiti and Kalki of Paraúara gotra, known as Visnuyasa raised an army consisting of armed Vipras or Brâhmanas to annihilate the Kirâtas, Cinas, Daradas, Dravidas, Gândharas, Pahlavas, Khasas, Pulindas, Ândhrakas, Paradas, Yavanas, Sakas, Tusaras, Barbaras, Pârthivas. mlecchs, irreligious Vrsalas, Udîcyas, Madhyadesas, Vindhyas, Dakúinâtyas, etc.[135] They have been described as the people as well as the Janapadas. The Kiratas and other mlecchas out of fear fled to forests. We find some interpolation and discrepancy in the Purânic data. Because the reference as have been made to their annihilation by both at the end of the Kali Age. Again it is mentioned that Kalki will be led by Yâjñavalkya to annihilate them with his discus. Whatever, may be the truth, we find some positive indication to their subjugation by the Brahmana at different times.

There is an evidence of a very reliable nature to show their destruction by Bharatâ, son of Dusyanta. It is categorically stated that Bharat in course of his digvijaya or conquest killed the Kirâtas, Hunas, Yavanas, Ândhras, Kankas, Khâsas, Úakas, mlecchas and also others, who were anti-Brâhmaṇas.[136] He was undisputed ruler of India at that time.

It is obvious that the Kirâtas were well known for their anti-Brâhmanic and anti-Vedic attitude since the time of Manu. This was the main reason of their conquest by the Brâmanical rulers. Because of this phenomena they lost their territories or the Janapadas.

Raghu's Conquest of the Kirâtas as described by Kâlidasa

The Epics and the Purânas mention the name of Raghu, as one of the kings of Ayodhya. He has been described as the son of king Dilipa-II of Iksvaku line or Solar race, but nothing is mentioned about his activities. It is Kâlidâsa, who has provided the details of his conquest of the Kirâtas and other mountain tribes. He has given description of his conquest or expedition from the Northern Himalayan region down to the kingdom of Kâmarûpa.

After subjugating the Pârasîkas or Sassanians and the Yavanas in the western region Raghu proceeded towards the northern areas of Bharatavarsa. He first conquered the Hunas on the banks of the Sindhu (Vamksu or Oxus) in the Bahlika country or Bactria (Modern Balkh). Next he subdued the Kâmbojas in the north-west[137] and then escorted by his formidable cavalry he ascended the Himalaya mountains where the soldiers rested for a while. At these halting places the *devadaru* trees with barks rubbed off by the neck-ropes (with which the elephants were tied to them) indicated to the Kirâtas the height of his elephants. Thereafter a fierce battle ensued between the mountain tribes including the Kirâtas and his forces. He had to face the array of attacks from the Gana army of the hills or Parvatya Ganas. But finally the mountain chiefs were vanquished and brought under control.[138]

The ferocious Kirâta tribes had fled away out of fear when Raghu approached them in the Himalayas. They ventured fourth from their lurking places only when they found that Raghu had left. In this connection Kâlidâsa mentions the names of two classes of wild tribes Utsavasanketar and the Kinnaras, who were conquered by him. After defeating the mountaineers or Pârvatyas, the Kirâtas, Utsavasanketas, Kinnaras and other hill tribes and accepting the services and the presents of the Himalayan people he descended from the Himalayas and finally reached the kingdom of Prâgjyotisa or Kamarûpa by crossing the Lauhitya or Brahmaputra river.[139]

Unfortunately, the evidence is too vague to project a clear picture of the subject. After all, it is a poetic description. However, the modern researches on the works of Kâlidâsa, as well as, the interpretations of the data contained in the original text by different annotators lend support to the theory of subjugation of the Kirâtas living on the Himalaya mountains by Raghu.

Bhagavat Saran Upadhyaya[140] strongly supports this view. The Pârvatya Ganas or mountain tribes as referred to by Kalidasa have been classified into seven groups that inhabited the northern slopes of the Himalayas.[141] It has been further mentioned that these seven mleccha tribes, dwellers of the mountain regions of the Himalayas were defeated by him.[142] The Kirâtas, who were also known as the mlecchas inhabiting the Northern Himalayan region, must have been one of these seven tribes, who were defeated by him. Furthermore, the style of presentation of the facts by the poet shows that Raghu conquered these tribes in course of his ascent on the mountain which evidently refers to the Kâilâúa mountain in Tibet.[143]

We have already explained that this was one of the main centres of Kirâtas habitation. Thus there is every reason to believe that he must have subjugated the Kirâta chiefs too along with others. The tribes living in the north of Kashmir or in the north-east of Ladakh and in the south east of Tibet were the main victims of his attack.

Did Alexander (c. 327—325 B.C.) Conquer the Kirâtas ?

It is true that Alexander the Great, in course of his Indian expedition in the 4th century B.C., had conquered many wild tribes living in the mountainous region of North-Western India, but it will not be reasonable to suppose that all the mountaineers vanquished by him belonged to the Kirâta groups.

The statement made by B.A. Saletore[144] based on the vague evidence furnished by V.A. Smith,[145] that the Kiratas were also conquered by him, is not based on the facts. The validity of the statement is questionable. Because there is no such evidence in the original Greek source related to Alexander's invasion of India[146] which leads us to warrant such belief. The word Kirrhedia or Scyritae or Ciratae, invariably mentioned in other Greek works, does not find even a single mention throughout the whole text. Obviously, they were not present there to offer any resistance to Alexander. Hence, there is hardly any reason to believe that the Kiratas were ever conquered by Alexander.

The theory of Alexander's conquering the Kiratas seems to be a far fetched imagination of the said authors.

Subjugation by a Sâtavâhana king of the Deccan ?

The epigraphic records of the Sâtavâhana kings of the Deccan establish their claims as the lords of Daksinâpatha or south India lying beyond the Vindhyas. Gautamiputra Úatakarṇi (c. 106—30 A.D.), the great king of this dynasty claims to have been the lord of Vindhya Pariyatra, which covered the greater portion of the Vindhyan range.[147]

If this information is correct we may have ground to presume that the Kirâtas, who were living within the Vindhyan range, also might have come under his sway. But, nothing definite can be said in favour of or against this presumption.

Samudragupta's (c. 335—380 A.D.) Conquest of Forest Kingdom

All the Standard historical texts on ancient India records that the Mahâkântâra the wild tracts or extensive forest region) of Vyâghraraja, one of the monarchs of Daksinâpatha, was conquered by Samudragupta but it is not yet fully known has to how many other forest kingdoms or principalities of tribal chiefs were subjugated by him. The matter concerned is yet to be examined thoroughly and critically.

The people and the countries conquered by him have been divided into five groups. Group three (3) includes the forest kingdoms. We find that all the kings of the "forest countries" were subjugated by him. Line—21 of the Allahabad pillar Inscription:—"Paricarakikrta-Sarvatavika-rajasya" (râjyas)[148] bears testimony to the fact that he made the rulers of the *atavika râjyas* or the forest states, his servants. This is also supported by some noted authorities.[149] Here we are confronted with the problems of location and identification of these forest states. In this connection it can be reasonably suggested that the wild tracts situated in the Vindhyan region, popularly known as the Vindhyâtavi in Central India, where powerful Kirata chiefs have established their kingdoms by the middle of the 4th century A.D., might have been brought under his control. There is every possibility of tendering of submission of the Kirâta chiefs ruling over their forest kingdoms to him after being made servants.

Ancient Indian history is completely silent about the policy of Gupta emperor towards the forest chiefs. However, it can be surmised that they might have simply acknowledged his supremacy and complied with his imperious commands i.e. giving all kinds of taxes and obeying his orders, etc. It does not seem probable that they might have been deprived of their possessions in the forest region by the emperor. In the post-Gupta period they might have re-asserted their independence.

Prof. B.A. Saletore strongly supports the subjugation of the Kiratas and other forest tribes of Central India by the Gupta emperor.[150] This can be further substantiated by other views. V.A. Smith has categorically stated that Samudragupta "controlled the wild tribes of the Himalayas and the Vindhyas...."[151] H.G. Rawlinson has also clearly stated that "he did not attempt to extend his empire south of the Vindhya mountains, but he carried out wonderful military raid into southern India which occupied two years... Marching through the thick jungles of the Vindhya mountains he went beyond and "on his return journey he received the submission of the rajas through whose territory he passed together with huge sums in the way of tribute, but made no effort to annex them permanently...."[152]

The above two statements do not leave any doubt about the submission of the Kirâta tribes living in the forest regions of the Vindhyas. It is well known that one of the principal forest kingdoms or principalities of this group of tribe was located in this region which constituted the dividing line between the north and south.

The location of the forest states, whose kings submitted to him in Central India has also been supported by some.[153] The identification of the *âtavika râjyas only* with Dabhala or the Jabalpur region[154] on the basis of his Eran inscription is not absolutely justified. In the earlier chapter it has already been proved on the basis of an inscription of the sixth century A.D. that there were altogether eighteen forest kingdoms in the Central India. Thus its identification with only one is not advisable. The mighty Gupta emperor is said to have brought under the imperial sway all the forest regions which in all probability also included that of the Vindhyas.

Actually, the aim of the Gupta emperor concerned was to bring about the political unification of India and to make Himself an Ekarat (single sovereign) over this united empire. The epigraphy confirms it. He has been mentioned as 'Sarva Prthvi-Vijayajanita',[155] which implies that he conquered and ruled over the whole earth. He extended his political sway from the foot of the Himalayas on the north to the Narmada on the south. However, there is no denying that he did not annex the tribal territories of Central India to his dominion like that of parts of Aryavarta lying within the Gangetic basin. Nor did he extend the same treatment to the forest chiefs, which he did in case of the rulers of Northern, Southern and Eastern India and that of the tribal states of North-Western India and frontier kingdoms of Assam and the Gangetic delta.

Subjugation by a Ruler of the Vâkâṭaka Dynasty of the Deccan

Prithvisena II. (c. 470-490 A.D.), son of Narendrasena, was one of the prominent rulers of the Vakataka dynasty. He was ruling over the Deccan contemporaneously with the Guptas, who were the masters of Central India. From the epigraphic evidence it appears that he established suzerainty over the mleccha (mleccha-desa), 'Kirâta-Cîna' and others. As the Cîna-Kirâta[156] figure together in most of the inscriptions and literary sources, we can safely assume that here also both are the same. But it is very difficult to say as to how and when they were subjugated by him and which area they belonged to.

The inscription and the Purânas testify to the truth that the rulers of this dynasty in the hey day of their glory exercise suzerainty over their weaker neighbours and dominated over Bundelkhand, Central provinces, Northern and Western Deccan. This meagre evidence leaves this clue only that most probably the forest tribes of the Vindhya Hills and south of it might have also been brought under their control sometimes between the last quarter of the fifth and the second quarter of the 6th century A.D.

Subjugation by a Prince of Avantideúa

Bâṇabhaṭṭa has adduced a concreate evidence of subjugation of the Kirâtas of Northern Himalayan region by a prince of Avantideúa.

When the Prince Chandrapida, son of sovereign ruler named Tarapida of the celebrated city of Ujjain (the capital of Avanti) set out with a vast army on an expedition for the conquest of the world, he also moved towards the north. He subdued the Kirâtas inhabiting the northern frontiers of the Himalayas and occupied their famous city Suvarnapura. All the Kiratas dwelling in the vast forest region extending up to the mountain Kailasa and called Hemajâkûtas (Hemâkutas) were subjugated by him.[157] In course of his three years' expedition, he conquered many kings and their countries. He resisted all those who were hostile to him, but he re-established those, who yielded or succumbed afterwards.

Submission in Post-Harṣa Period (c. A.D. 647-1200)

The post Harṣa period of the subjugation of the Kirâtas includes two-fold submission by them. First mentionable is their submission to Yaúovarman and the imperial Pratiharas of Northern India and second to the rulers of south India.

It is well known that political unity of Northern India achieved under Harṣa was broken. The details of the exploits of Yaúovarman (c. 725-752 A.D.) are given in the *Gaudavaho,* a Prakrt work of Vâkpatirâjâ, his court poet. This text credits Yaúovarman with extensive conquests as far as the south. It is also mentioned that he reached the Vindhya mountains. It is not possible to say as to how far the poet is right. But, we get confirmation and certain information from the epigraphic record about the extension of his sway up to the forest region of the Kiratas in the Vindhyas.

The stone inscription of Yaúovarman[158] in an eulogical style indicates that the Kirâtas living in the vicinity of the mountain Vindhyas had come under his sway. Because this inscription distinctly refers to the praise bestowed by the Kirata women on him.

Nâgabhatta II (c. 805-33 A.D.), the famous Pratihara monarch, made every possible attempt to retrieve the fallen fortunes of his family in the beginning. The Gwalior inscription proves beyond doubt that he won victories over the "Kirâtas" (of the Himalayan regions'), Turuskas (Arab settlers of Western India), Ânartta (Northern Kathiawad), Malavaor Central India, the Matsyas (of eastern Rajputana), etc. and occupied their hill-forts.[159] His suzerainty was certainly acknowledged up the foot of the Himalayas.

When Râjyapala (c. 991-1018 A.D.) succeeded to the throne about the decade of the 10th century A.D. the power and prestige of the Pratihara family were on the wane. But he re-established the supremacy of his family by conquering different countries in different directions. It is said the Krita Cîna (Kirâta-Clna), Anga, Vañga, Kalinga, Odra, Suhma, etc. had accepted his suzerainty.[160] These conquests did not lead to any permanent results.

Next, the Kirâtas of the Vindhyan and trans-Vindhyan India frequently came into conflict with their contemporary rulers and were defeated by them, which called a great setback to their Janapadas and kingdoms. Satyavâkya Kongani Varman, the king of the Ganga dynasty is said to have subjugated and destroyed the groups of Kirâtas dwelling on the outskirts of the Vindhya forest in the 10th century. This is testified by an inscription dated A.D. 973 ascribed to the said Ganga king.[161] Actually the aggressive activities and the turbulent nature of the Kirâtas necessitated the extension of Ganga arms in the forest of the Vindhyas. The Ganga king exercised control over a small area of the Kirâtas. In spite of being subjugated they continued to cause havoc to the rulers of this dynasty.

A Record dated A.D. 943[162] of the Pallava king Diliparasa of Kanchi also shows that Nolambavadi rulers of Mysore (Chitaldrug & Bellary Dists), who were the minor princes also conquered some of the Kirâta kings who were worshippers of the goddess Chandika, which means that they were also the dweller of the Vindhya forest.

The great Chola king Rajarâja Deva also destroyed the nill-chiefs as evidenced by the record dated A.D. 1007[163] but the picture is very faint. Thus nothing definite can be said about this.

Punisa, the most famous general of the greatest of the Hoysala kings, Visnuvardhana Bittideva (c. 1110-40 A.D.) ousted the Kirâta chiefs of the Vindhyas in course of establishing his authority over an extensive territory in the far south. The conquered Kirâta chiefs were reduced to the status of the Vassals, and consequently they owed allegiance to him. But, on the other hand, he gave protection to those who were left with no power. This is proved by an inscription dated A.D. 1117.[164]

As a result of the frequent defeats at the hands of South Indian rulers, the power and strength of the Kirâta chiefs of the Vindhyas were shattered, which they were endowed with. For sometime their glory was eclipsed but their history did not pass into oblivion. One of the direct results of the frequent attacks of the rulers concerned on the Kirâta territory was their dispersion from the Vindhyas to the trans-Vindhyan region or the far south approximately in the twelfth century A.D.

In the Southern Peninsula also they continued to occupy an influential position in the post-twelfth century which is evident from the epigraphic records of the sixteenth and the seventeenth centuries. The Keladi rulers of Mysore like Venkatapa a (A.D. 1582-1629) and his grandson Vîrabhadra Nayaka and tne celebrated monarch of Mysore named Cikka Deva inflicted crushing defeats on the various groups of the Kirâtas in several battles because of their penetration into their kingdom. The details are provided in the epigraphic records dated 1641 and 1680 A.D., etc.[165]

Notes and References

1. For details see *Manu*, 11.21; *Bau. Dh. Su.* 1.1.2.9; *Vas. Dh. Su.* 1.8; *Mahavagga,* F. 12-13; *Divyâvadâna,* 21-22; Asvaghosa, *Saondarananda Kâvya,* 11. v. 62; *Kâvyamimâṁsâ,* p. 93; B.C. Law, IEIBJ., pp. 20-21; AGAI, pp. 12-13; PK., 396.
2. *Mat.*, 114. 34-36; *Vy.*, 45, 109-11 (Kirâta+Kisasna). See also *Mat.*, cf. SBA., pt. 1, ch. CXIV, pp. 307-8; S.M. Ali (GP., p. 163) and D.C. Sircar, (SGAMI, pp. 30-31).
3. *Mat.*, 121, 49-54; Ey. 47, 48-53. See also SBA., CXXI, p. 327 and D.C. Sircar, *op. cit.,* pp. 70-71.
4. *Vis. Dh. Mah.*, I, ch. 207, vv. 1-4 cf. M.R. Singh, GDEP., p. 199.
5. M.R. Sihgh, *op. cit.* pp. 29 and 199.
6. For details see B.C. Law, IETBJ., pp. 31 and 24; GEB., p. 18; GAK W., p. 3; F.E. Pargiter, AIHI., p. 76; H.C. Raychaudhuri, PAAI., pp. 21 ff; Panini (iv. 1. 172j cf. F.S. Agrawala, IKP., pp. 55-56.
7. Muir, OST., 11, pp. 365 & 491.
8. HG., Vol. 11, pt. 1, pp. 363-64.
9. Mbh. Âraṇyaka Parva, 141, 25. See also *Ibid.,* 141, 26 & 29; *Mbh. Ko.* pp. 190-91; M.R. Singh, *op. cit.* p. 199. In the *Sabhâ Parva* (4.21-22).

10. Allan, CO.A.I, p. cii. Also Cunningham, CO.A.I, p. 71.
11. V.S. Agrawala, *Bhârata Sâvitri,* vol. 1, p. 268.
12. P.C. Roy (tr.): *Mbh.* vol. 111, *Vana Parva*, pt. 11, *Tirtha-Yatra Parva*, see. cxl, p. 288. Varâhamihira, *Br. Sam.* 14, 29-30.
13. *Asvamedha, Parva*, 84.4; *Mbh. Ko.*, pp. 194-91.
14. McCrindle, AIP., pp. 210-11. See also Saint Martin, *Etude;* pp. 327-28.
15. *Âdi Parva*, 165, 35-36; *Sabhâ Parva*, 29-15 (in some versions 32. 17); P.C. Roy (tr.): *Sabhâ Parva* XXXII, p. 94; *Úânti Parva*, 65, 13-14; 207.43; *Mbh. Ko.*, p. 241; *Anusâsana Parva*, 35, 17-18.
16. *Bhiṣma Parva* 10.67 (Jambukhaṇḍa Nirmana Parva contains the list of janapadas).
17. *Vmn.,*13,41 & 42; ch. 13, vv. 37-43.
18. *Sabhâ Parva.* 23, 17-19; *Udyoga Parva,* 19,14-15.
19. *Vmn.*, 1311, 44-46; *Kur.*, 1.45. 25 & 39; *Mark.* 54.8 & 44;- *Vsn.* 2.3.8 & 15; *Brah.*, 19.8 & 16; 27. 17, 51-53; *Vy.*, 45.82 & 123, *Mat.*, 114.11 & 46.

    Ibid., cf. SBA., 1.CXIV, pp. 307-8; *Agn.*, 1.118.6; *Kal.*, 38. 100-47; *Pad.* (Svargakhanda) 6.46 & 52; Grd., 55.5. See also Pargiter (tr.): *Mark.* Vol. 11, pt. 11, pp. 284, 319 & 322; H.H. Wilson, *Vsn.* Bk. 1, ch. XIII, p. 84; Bk. Ill p. 142; Bk. V, ch. XXIX, p. 459; D.R. Patil, CHVP., p. 269; Dutt. *Agn.* 1, CXVIII; Sachau, *Alb. Ind.* vol. 1, ch. XXIX, p. 303.
20. *Bhiṣmâ Parva*, 10, 49; See also ch. 10, V. 55 P.C. Roy (tr.): *Bhîṣmâ Parva*, vol. V. Sec. IX, pp. 22. 32-33.
21. *Pad.*, 6.64.
22. *Sabhâ Parva* (Mantra Parva), 13.19. See also Mbh. Ko. p. 414.
23. *Sabhâ Parva*, 27.13.
24. *Pad.* 6. 64.
25. *Br. Sam.*, IV, 17-18. See also D.R. Patil, CHVP., p. 250.
26. Sachau, Alb., vol. 1, ch. XXIX, pp. 301-2.
27. *Mârk.* 55.31.
28. cf. Pt. Giridhar Sharma Chaturvedi, *Purâṇa Pariúìlana,* p. 348.
29. P.C. Roy, *Âúvamedha Parva*, LXXXIII, p. 203.
30. P.C. Roy (tr.): *Sabhâ Parva*, Sec. IV. p. 9.
31. *Bmd.*, 1.16. 60.
32. M.R. Singh, GDEP., p. 315.

33. *Bhîṣma Parva*, 10. 55.
34. *Droṇa Parva*, 4.6.
35. *Vmn.*, 13.57; *Mark.*, 54-57; Brah., 27. 63-64; *Vy.*, 45. 135-36; cf. Pt. Giridhara Sharma Chaturvedi, *Purâna Parisilana,* p. 348; *Mat.*, 114, 56. 57. Also *Mat.*, cf. SBA., 1. CXIV, p. 310; Pargiter, (*Mark.*, pp. 345 & 347; *BMd.* (1.16.68; 3.48-49; 4.7.19 cf. PK., p. 111. Pad., Patâlakhanda, ch. 19 cf. M.R. Singh, GDEP., p. 199. See also M.R. Singh, *op. cit.* pp. 180-82; S.M. Ali, GP., p. 169; D.C. Sircar, SGAMI., pp. 45-46; Sachau, *Alb. Ind.*, p. 300; 1C., 1. p. 299.
36. Von Otto Bohtlingk, PG., p. 161; V.S. Agrawala, IKP., p. 42.
37. B.C. Law, HGAI., pp. 14f; Pargiter, *op. cit.,* p. 322 fn.
38. *Mbh. Sabhâ Parva* (Digvijaya Parva), 27.13. See also *Ibid,* 27, 12, 14; V.S. Agrawala, *Bhârata Sâvitri,* Vol. 1, p. 156; *Mbh.* (Eng. tr. by P.C. Roy); *Sabhâ Parva*, vol. 11, pt. 1, Sec. xxviii-xxix, pp. 56-61 and R.K. Rai, *Mbh. Ko.* pp. 190-91.
39. M. R. Kale (tr.): The *Raghuvaṁśa* or Kâlidâsa, p. 116, note; Rangeya Raghava, *Prâcin Bhâratiya Paramparâ aur Itihâsa,* pp. 225-26; J. Taylor, JASB., 1847, vol. xvi, pt. 1, p. 12; A.K. Majumdar; EHID., vol. 11, p. 397.
40. R.M. Nath, BAC., pp. 13-15.
41. *Br. Sam.*, xx xii. 22..
42. V.S. Agrawala, *op. cit.* p. 156; D.R. Regmi, AN., p. 22; Hodgson, JASB., 1847, vol. xvi, pt. 11, pp. 1235ff.
43. For details see Pargiter, JASB., 1897, pp. 89f & *Suruci and Gandhara Jâtakas,* 489 and 406 respectively.
44. JASB., 1847. vol. xvi, pt. 1, p. 12.
45. *Ibid.,* M. Martin, HATSEI., Vol. iv, pp. 38-40.
46. G.P. Singh, *"The Puranic Account of Naraka's conquest of Ancient kingdom of Prâgjyotisa and the Kirâtas in North-East India,"* PNEIHA. (1983), pp. 16-23 and also *"Some Aspects of Politico-Cultural Contacts between Assam and Bihar and its Impact from the Early Vedic Age..."* PNEIHA., (1981), pp. 63-64.
47. *Kal.*, ch. 38, vv. 100-118. 125-128, 134-36.
48. *Yogini Tantra,* 1. xii. 6.

    See also Jivananda Vidyasagara (ed.): *Yogini Tantra,* Purvakhanda, Patala-12, p. 65.
49. M.R. Singh, GDEP., p. 229; R.P. Chanda, IAR., p. 68; N.N. Vasu, *op. cit.* pp. 38-43; E. Gait, *A History of Assam,* pp. 12-13; K.L.

Barua, *op. cit.,* pp. 14, 18-19; B.K. Kakati, *op. cit.,* pp. 37 & 56; R.M. Nath, *op. cit.,* pp. 13-15; KS., pp. 11-12. 83.

50. SGAMI., pp. 162-63.

1. Pargiter (Eng. tr.): Mark. vol. 11, Canto LVII, pp. 282-84 & 322.

52. *Op.cit.* p. 56 See also G.P. Singh, *The Genesis and Growth of Tribal Culture and Civilization in North-East India* (from prehistoric times to the 12th century A.D.), JISR., vol. 1, 1981, No. 1 p. 30.

53. K.L. Barua, EHK., pp. 18 and 231.

54. *Kal.*, 38, 128-147.

55. R.M. Nath, *op. cit.,* p. 26.

56. *Ibid,* p. 27.

57. JIH., vol. XII, 1933, pts. I-II, p. 303.

58. K.L. Barua, *op. cit,* pp. 20-21, 27, 29-30.

59. *Op. cit.,* p. 13.

60. Robinson. DAA., 146-48.

61. B.K. Kakati, *op.* cit., p. 29; Farquhar, ORLI., pp. 122f.

62. R.M. Nath,,op. cit., pp. 13-15.

63. James Long, JASB., vol. XIX, 1850, Nos. I to VII, pp. 533-37; JASB., 1873, 187; IA., Ill, pp. 178-9; B.C. Law, TAI, pp. 282-83; E. Gait, *A History of Assam,* p. 12.

64. J.W. McCrindle, AIP., pp. 191-94; R.C.'Jain (ed.): McCrindle's AIP., p. 194; G.E. Gerini, RPGEA., pp. 51-52.

65. James Long, *op. cit.* E.T. Dalton (DEB., p. 106) supported this view without examining the validity of the statement.

66. G.P. Sigh, "*The History and Culture of Ancient Tripura: A Re-Appraisement,*" PNEIHA., Shillong, 1980, pp. 27-39;" *Tipperah—The Ancient Hill Kingdom,*" *North-Eastern Spectrum*, Gauhati, 1977, Vol. 1. Nos. 11-12, pp. 24-33.

67. Rajmala (ed. by K.P. Sen) Vol. pp. 38f, vol. 11, pp. 9-12.

68. W.W. Hunter, SAB., Vol. VI, p. 483; R.M. Nath, BAC, p. 77; S.P. Gupta, JRAI., Vol. XXXVIII, 1958, pt. 1, p. 109; Ghulam Hussain Salim, *Riyazu-s-Salatin,* p. 12; B.K. Barua, *A Cultural History of Assam,* Vol. 1, pp. 67.

69. S.K. Chatterji, *Kirâta-Jana-krti,* pp. 130-31.

70. *Ibid.,* pp 131f.

71. DC. Sircar. JASL., vol. xvii, 1951, Nos. 1-3, p. 80.

72. D.C, Sircar, *op. cit.,* S.K. Chatterji, *op. cit;* K.C. Sinha, *Râjmâlâ,* (1896), pt. 11, ch. 1, pp. 2f; R.C. Majumdar, *Banga Desher Itihasa,* Vol. 11, (1973) p. 480.
73. W.W. Hunter, *op. cit.* pp. 357-51.
74. JARS., Vol. Ill, 1935, No. 3, pp. 93-95; R.M. Nath, *op. cit.,* p. 77.
75. JARS., Vol. III, 1935, pp. 96-97; R.M. Nath, *op. cit.,* p. 79.
76. For details see Bhandarkar, *The Cagar Brâhmanas and the Bengal Kayasthas,* IA., Vol. LXI, 1932, pp. 41-55 & 67-71.
77. Xll 207. 42.
78. *Mat.*, 114. 46-48; *Vy.*, 45, 126; *HV.*, LVIII, vv. 6-8; *Brahd.* 1.2.16.60.
79. *Vas. Dh. Bau. Dh. Su.* 1.1.2 9. etc.
80. CII., Vol. III. p. 7, Line 20, & p. 13, fn. 5; Vasudeva Upadhyaya, SAII, p. 312.
81. *Br. Sam.*, XIV. 9.
82. 11.31, 13-15, 71-72; 11, 28, 48. (The *Mbh.* like the Allahabad Prasasti distinguishes the Âtavika from the Kântârakas).
83. *Vy.*, 1.45. 126; *Mat.* 114.48; *Brahd;* 11.16. 57; *Mark;* 57, 47; Vmn. (13.47-49) reads *Ârayanyas.* See also D.C. Sircar, SGAMI., p. 37, fn. 2. and B.C. Law, IETBJ. p. 173.
84. S.M. Ali, GP., pp. 167-68; ABORI., vol. 17, p. 322; *As. Res.* vol. 14, p. 391.
85. *Mahâvaṁsa* (Geiger's edn. and tr.), xix, 6; *Dipavamsa* (tr. by Oldenberg), xvi. 2; The *Úarabhanga Jataka.* V. pp. 134, 267ff. *Majjhima Nikâya,* 1, p. 378 *Mahâvastu.* 111. p. 353f: *Sâmantapâsadika* 111. p. 655 ref. to B.C. Law IETBJ., pp. 33 and 106. See also DPPN, 1, p. 295.
86. B.C. Law, *op. cit.,* p. 107.
87. CIL, Vol. 1, p. 22.
88. CIL, Vol. III, No. 1, pp. 7-13, line 21; Vasudeva Upadhyaya, SAIL, p. 312, line-21; D.C. Sircar, SIIHC, pp. 254ff See also EL, vii, p. 126 and H. Luders, List, No. 1195, Vide EI, Vol. X. App. (for Atavi's identification).
89. CII, Vol. Ill, pp. 113-16; EI, viii, pp. 284-87. From this inscription it appears that Mahârâjâ Sanksabha born in the line of Hastin (of epic fame as the founder of Hastinapur) had inherited the kingdom of Dabhala (or Dhabala=modern Bundelkhand) together with all the countries included in the eighteen forest kingdoms and properly governed them.

90. *Br. Sam.* XIV. 29-30.
91. *Ibid.*, XVI. 2-3: See also IX. 13, 17.
92. *Daíakumâracarita* (text with tr.) ucch. 11, pp. 22-24; See also pp. 15-17; ucch. 1, pp. 14-15; ucch. III, p. 104; ucch. VI. p. 149 ucch. VIII, pp. 203-6.
93. *Harṣacarita.* VII, VIII pp. 227-233. See also V.S. Agrawala, *Harṣacarita Ek Sâmskrtike Adhyayana,* pp. 182-90; *Kadambari* (text with tr.). Purvabhaga, pp. 37-38, 45-57 & 61 also pp. 2cff, ch. 1, pp. 3-4; Harsadeva, *Ratnâvali,* 12. 29, p. 21.
94. VII. vs. 109-15, pp. 193f.
95. *Vivekacintâmani,* pp. 423-4.
96. Vide Narasimhacarya's *Kavicarita,* 11, p. 219.
97. EI, I, p. 131.
98. B.C., 111. p. 51.
99. EC, p. 119; R.N. Saletore, EIC. Vol. 11, pp. 750-52.
100. EC., Xll. 28, p. 92; EC., Ill, 44, p. 76; EC, IV, 83, p. 10 R.N. Saletore, *op. cit.*
101. EC, VII. 2, p. 3; R.N. Saletore, *op. cit. Mysore Inscriptions,* p. 310 Rice, *Mysore and Coorg from the Inscriptions,* pp. 129-30; Robert Sewell & C, HISL, No. V, 1932; R.S. Panchamukhi, *Karnataka Inscriptions* (KRS.), 1941.
102. Atkinson, HG., Vol. 11, pt. 1 pp. 365-67. Some of his findings are also based on the study of four copper-plate grants preserved in the temple of Pândukesvara near Badrinath.
103. EI, Vol. xxx, pp. 282-83, Vol xxxi, p. 239 cf. D.C. Sircar. *Indian Epigraphy,* pp. 368-69.
104. George William Traill's Report, on Kumaon, vide *Statistical Account of Kumaon,* pp. 19f, 57 cff. Atkinson, *op. cit.,* AS. Res. Vol. xvi, p. 152.
105. M.M. Sharma, TCH., pp. 44-45.
106. JRAS., 1925 No. CI, pp. 234-36.
107. Atkinson, *op. cit.* pp. 364-65.
108. xiv, 30.
109. Atkinson, *op. cit.*
110. Mbh., *Drona Parva*, 4.6.
111. *Pad* (Uttarâkhanda), 213. 8.
112. Atkinson, H.G. Vol. 11 pt. 1, p. 363.

113. Bana's *Kâdambari* (the text with tr. by M.R. Kale), Purvabheâga, pp. 7-8, 123f, 144-45; Kane (Bombay edn. 1914) p. 90; Maheshchandra, Bhâratiya, *Bânabhatta aur unki Kadambari,* pp. 74-76.

114. Pargiter (tr.) *Mark.*, p. 322 fn.

115. *Mbh. Sabhâ Parva* (Digvijaya Parva), 23, 17-26; *Mbh. Ko.* pp. 190-91, 460.

116. V.S. Agrawala, *Bhârata Sâvitri,* Vol. 1, p. 151.

117. *Mbh. Karna Parva,* 5, 15-16, 29.

118. *Mbh. Sabhâ Parva*, 47-12; P.C. Roy, (Eng. tr.), *Mbh. Sabhâ Parva*, Vol. 11, pt. 1, Sec. xxxiii, p. 71.

119. *Mbh. Sabhâ Parva*, 24, 1—4; P.C. Roy (tr.) *Sabhâ Parva*, Vol. 11, pt. 1, sec. xxvi, p. 57.

120. KS., pp. 23, 31.

121. P.C. Roy, *op. cit., 'see* also Hayunthal Copper plates of Harjara Varman of middle of the 9th century A.D.Y. JARS., vol. 1, pp. 109ff; IAA., p. 91 and KS., p. 63.

122. *Mbh. Bhiṣma Parva*, 20, 13; *Udyogâ Parva*, 19. 14-15.

123. *Drona Parva*, cxii, pp. 321-2; cxix, p. 349; Karna Parva, Ixxiii p. 271; Mbh. Ko. pp. 190-91: B.A. Saletore WTIH., pp. 23-24 and 32. See also *Droṇa Parva*, 19, 17, 20; 25, 31, 35; 26, 2, 4; 27. 14, 26; 28. 1,6,9-11.

—*Mbh. Âúvamedha Parva*, 72. 24.

124. See also *Mbh. Ko.*, pp. 28-29, 109-91.

125. Âúvamedha Parva, 84. 4; P.C. Roy (tr.) Asvarnedha Parva, Lxxxiii, p. 209; Mbh. Ko. pp. 29.

126. *Mbh. Sabhâ Parva*, 27.13-28. See also HATSEI., Vol. iv. p. 40.

127. Pargiter, JASB., Vol. Lxvi; 1897, pt. 1, pp. 108ff.

—*Sabhâ Parva*, 29. 15 or 32.17.

128. See also *Mbh. Ko.*, pp. 190-91; P.C. Roy (tr.): *Sabhâ Parva*, Secs, xxxi, pp. 67-67; xxxii, p. 94; A.K. Majumdar, EHID., Vol. 11, pp. 400, 402-3.

129. P.C. Roy (tr.): *Sabhâ Parva*, Sec. xxxi, p. 87.

130. *Sabhâ Parva*, 48, 8-11; V.S. Agrawala, *Bhârata Sâvitri,* Vol. 1, p. 171; P.C. Roy (tr.): *Sabhâ Parva*, Vol. 11, pt. 1, Sec. Li, pp. 102-4.

131. *Sabhâ Parva* (Râjasûyârambha Parva), 31, 6-13, 14-25; 47, 10-16; P.C. Roy (tr.): *Mbh.* Vol. 11, pt. 1, Sec. IV. pp. 7-9; XIV, p. 33; Li, pp. 110 and 155; *Mbh. Ko.,* pp. 190-91.

132. *Sabhâ Parva*, 4, 21-22; *Mbh. Ko*. pp. 190-91.
133. Rangeya Raghava, *Prâcin Bhâratiya Paramparâ aur Itihâsa,* pp. 224-26.
134. *Drona, Parva*, 4. 4.6.
135. *VY.*, 58, 78-83; 98, 106 9 cf. D.R. Patil, CHVP., pp. 73-77, 292-93, 307-8.
136. —*Bhâg* IX.20.30. See also PK., p. 370.
137. The *Raghuvaṁúa* canto-IV, vv. 60-73.
138. The *Raghuvaṁúa*, canto-IV, vv. 76-77
139. *Ibid,* vv. 78-81.
140. IK,, ch. Ill, pp. 62-63. See also KS., pp. 136-38 & 153.
141. Cf. M.R. Kale (tr. & ed.): *The Raghuvamsa,* canto-IV, p. 116.
142. Brahma Shankar Mishra (tr. & ed.): *The Raghuvamsa,* canto-IV p. 115.
143. S. Hedin, THDAT., p. 198 cf. KS., pp. 137-38.
144. WTIH., p. 33.
145. EHI., pp. 93f.
146. McCrindle, *The Invasion of India by Alexander the Great.*
147. D.C. Sircar, SIIHC., (1942) vol. I, pp. 196ff, and also VIII, pp. 59-62, 73-74.
148. Fleet, CII., Ill, pp. 13f; Vasudeva Upadhyaya, SAII, p. 312.
149. H C. Raychaudhuri, PHAL, p. 357; B.C. Law, MAI, p. 19; R.S. Tripathi, HAL, p. 242; RG. Basak HNEI, pp. 23 and 26; B.A. Saletore WTIH, pp. 34-35; Buhler, JRAS, 1899, pp. 315f;V.A. Smith EHI, pp. 283-4.
150. *Op. cit.*
151. OHI, (revised by H.G. Rawlinson), p. 66.
152. CHIP., p. 61.
153. R.S. Tripathi *op. cit.* p. 242; HC. Raychaudhuri, *op. cit.* p. 543; VA. Smith, *op, cit.,* R.G. Basak, *op. cit,* p. 26.
154. CII, iii, p. 114; El, viii, pp. 284-87.
155. D.C. Sircar, SIIHC., Vol. 1, (1942), p. 259.
156. Balaghata plate of Prithvisena 11, FL, ix, p. 273 cf. Romila-Thapar, AISH., pp. 175 and 190, ref. no. 120. See also V.V. Mirashi (ed.): CII., Vol. V (1963) for inscriptions of the Vakatakas.
157. M.R. Kale (tr.): The *Kâdambari, Purvabhâga,* pp. 144-45; See also pp. 123f and ch. Ill, pp. 7-8; Kane (tr.) *Kadambari,* Bombay 1914,

Purv. p. 270 and p. 90; Maheshachandra, *Bhâratiya Bânâbhaṭṭa aur Unki Kâdambari,* Purv., p. 76.

158. EI, 1, p. 131.
159. EL, XVIII, pp. 107fT; D.C. Sircar, SIICC Delhi 1983, Vol. 11, Line-8, p. 245: see also R.S. Tripathi, HAI, p. 321 and Romila Thapar, *op. cit.,* pp. 174, 190, ref. no. 121.
160. Bhaturya Inscription of Râjyapala, EL, XXX, III, p. 150cf. Romila Thapar, *op. cit*; pp. 175, 190 ref. no. 120.
161. EC, 11, p. 119.
162. FC, xii, 28, p. 92; Rice, *Mysore: A Gazetteer* (revised); 1, p. 307.
163. EC., 111, 44, p. 76.
164. EC., iv, 83, p. 10. See R.N. Saletore, EIC., Vol. 11. pp. 750-52 and BA., Saletore, WTIH., pp. 35-37 (for ref. Nos. 5 to 8).
165. EC., vii, 2, p. 3.; KHR., Vol. iv, January-July, 1937, Nos. 1 & 2, pp. 98f; *Mysore Inscriptions,* p. 310; Rice, *Mysore and Coorg from the Inscriptions,* pp. 129-30. See also *Mysore Epigraphical Report for the year 1901; South Indian Inscriptions,* vii, No. 328, pp. 168ff. cf. B.A. Saletore *op. cit.* and Robert Sewell & C, HISI, No. V. 1932.

BOOK FIVE

RISE AND FALL OF THE DYNASTIC RULE IN NORTHERN INDIA (NEPAL) (FROM THE APIC AGE C. 3102 B.C. DOWN TO THE SEVENTH CENTURY A.D.)

I

INTRODUCTORY REMARKS

The epic age constituted a significant landmark in the early annals of India. This age witnessed the occurrences of many significant events in political and cultural history of ancient India. It was, no doubt, an eventful era in ancient history of Northern India too. The period under review saw the dawn of dynastic rule, worth the name, of the Kirâtas in the valley of Nepal, the most ancient glorious Himalayan kingdom of Bhâratavarṣa. The Kirâtas laid the foundation of the dynastic rule at a very crucial stage of their history which remained consolidated for a considerable period of time.

The ancient Indian historical tradition or the local chronicles (or the *Vaṁúâvalîs*) and some other trustworthy sources fairly substantiated by available epigraphic records help us to a considerable extent in providing the details relating to the dynastic history of the Kirâtas in Nepal. Some scholars without going for an exhaustive investigation of all such sources have assumed that there was no dynastic rule of the Kirâtas as such in Nepal and hence they found themselves contented with a very meagre and sketchy details of the subject under notice. While others when providing only an outline or a sketch of the Kirâtas in general, have passed over this aspect in silence. However, a fresh attempt has been made to recast the subject by placing reliance on authorities, who have highlighted the subject to a considerable degree the early dynastic rule of Kiratas over the valley of Nepal, which formed the part of Northern India, stands supported by both the tradition and the history.

The dynastic rule of the Kirâtas in Eastern Nepal with their capital at Mokwanpur (or Makwanpur) from the age of the *Mahâbhârata* down to the seventh century A.D. can conclusively be proved by the evidence recorded in local chronicles or *Vamúávalis* (originally composed in the fourteenth century), works on the history of Nepal, and some other historical works.

II

THE RULERS AND THE EVENTS

The Chronicles of Nepal and other authoritative works on the subject under discussion have furnished a list of names of Kirâta rulers that vary from 26 to 32 in number. But after thorough examination of all the relevant sources we find that there is general agreement among the authorities about the existence of 29 rulers who ruled over the valley of Nepal from the beginning of *Kaliyuga* to the 7th century A.D. Admittedly, it is not possible to suggest an acceptable date for the beginning of their dynasty. Because in the treatment of a subject in ancient Indian context anachronism has been noticed as a general phenomenon. However, on the basis of some political and cultural events associated with the Kirâta rulers anterior to the outbreak of the Bharata war in general participation of one of their kings in this war testify to the foundation of their dynasty roughly in the epic age. Unfortunately, we do not have any chronological chart of the rulers as we find about the Licchavi rulers of Nepal, which has also been confirmed by their inscriptions and coins. However, on the basis of all the available sources[1] we can deal with the subject to a reasonable extent.

James Taylor has correctly observed that "one of the ancient dynasties of Rajas that governed Nepal, belonged to the Kirata tribes of Eastern mountaineers."[2] But his conclusion (based on Prinsep's Genealogical Tables, *Essays on Indian Antiquities,* London, 1858) that it comprised twenty seven princes, the first of whom reigned about B.C. 640[3], is not confirmed by other sources.

Lassen, while referring to their dynasty in the Himalayan valley, points out that their native Capital was at Mokwanpur in Eastern Nepal.[4]

The *Vamúávalis* or the local chronicles testify to the rule of the Abhiras, Kirâtas, Somavamúis and the Úuryavamúis, but their chronology is not very much reliable.[5] It is believed that twenty-nine Kirâta kings ruled in Nepal when the country was conquered by a Kúatriya prince from India named Nimisha.[6]

To start with presenting the systematic account of Kirâta rulers in Nepal, Yalambara (Yellung or Yellamba or Yalamba or Yalambhang) was the first king who laid the foundation of the Kirâta dynasty in Nepal which formed an integral part of India in ancient times. He reigned for about thirteen years. During this period he extended the frontiers of his kingdom from Tista of Bhutan to Trisuli in the west. No other details of his achievement are available.

Pabi (Paivi or Pambi or Yanchihang) was the second ruler during whose reign the astrologers had announced that the *Kaliyuga* had entirely overspread the earth, and the mankind were bent upon committing sin. His period is believed to have marked the end of the *Dwâparayuga* associated with the period of Gods and the beginning of the first quarter of *Kaliyuga*.

He was succeeded by his son Skandhara, (Dushkhan or Yalan or Dhaskan or Skandhahang) who happened to be the third ruler. He was further succeeded by his son Balamba (Yalamba or Ballancha or Malam or Balambhang). The fifth and sixth rulers are recorded as Hriti (Hritti or Hritihang or Chamin) and Hunati (Humati or Hanantat or Dhaskam or Humatihang) respectively. During the reign of 6th ruler popularly known as Humati, the Pândavas were destined to reside in forests and Arjuna fought with Mahadeva, who was found in the form of Kirâta, and pleased him by his skill in archery. This is the only event which has been recorded in the *Parbatiya Vaṁúâvali.*

With the accession of Jitedasti, (Jitadesi or Jitadastihang), the son of Humati, to the throne of Nepal, the history took a new turn. He was the 7th ruler of this dynasty. He was the most prominent among the early rulers of this dynasty. The king after being persuaded by Arjuna went to Kuruksetra, took part in the war of Mahâbhârata on behalf of the Pândava against the Kauravas and lost his life. According to Pt. Bhagwan Lall Indraji[7], he had ascended the throne five hundred thirty six years later than the Gopala dynasty who had ruled over Nepal for five hundred twenty one years.

He was followed by Gali (Galimja or Galinjhang), Pushka (Tuska or Hurma), Suyarma (or Syaswahang), Parba (Pava or Parbahang), Bunk a (Pancha or Panchahang) and Swananda

(Thomoo or Dasti Chamba or Thouka Kemka). All these rulers probably ruled sometimes between 3102 B.C. and 6th Century B.C.

The Buddhist tradition records that during the reign of 7th king Jitadasti Gautama Buddha visited Nepal. This tradition is not supported by history, moreover his visit during the reign of this Kirâta king seems to be unbelievable. However, the Parbatiya *Vaṁúâvalî*[8] has recorded that Buddha came into Nepal from Kapilvastu city situated in Terai and having visited Swayambhu Chaitya and Manjuúri Chaitya fixed his abode at Puchkagra Chaitya, which was lying to the west of Swayambhu hill. He accepted the worship and offering of a female Bhiksu named Chuda and thereafter started proselytissing activities. He is said to have converted 1350 persons including Sariputra, Maudgallyayana, Ananda and others belonging to the Brahmana and Ksatriya castes. He then visited Guhjesivar and after that the Namobuddha mountain situated at the distance of about twelve miles east of Bhatgaon. Here he discovered and showed to his disciples certain ornaments belonging to himself buried under the Chaitya. He preached his doctrines to the people for quite sometime. When he found the time of his death approaching he went to the city of Kasi or Benares. Some of his followers remained in Nepal and professed his religion.

About 250 B.C. during the reign of Sthunko, the fourteenth ruler of this dynasty, Asoka, the Mauryan king of Pâṭaliputra having heard of the fame of Nepal as a sacred place and having obtained the permission of his spiritual guide named Upagupta Bhiksu came on a pilgrimage to Nepal accompanied by his family and large number of his subjects. Here he built several monasteries and Chaityas. In order to commemorate his visit to Lumbini the birthplace of Buddha. He also got his edicts engraved on rocks and pillars and installed them at Kumindehi, which is the ancient Lumbini of Nepal. At present this place is in Taulihawa district of Nepal. Later he also came to the valley of Kathmandu and gave his daughter named Chârumati in marriage to Devapâla. She settled near Pasupati and founded the town called Devapatan in memory of her husband Devâpala. She also erected Charumati Vihâra after her name which is known as Chabahil. The erection of four stupas at the four cardinal points of Patan constitute monumental evidence of Aúoka's visit to Nepal during the reign of the fourteenth king of the Kirâta dynasty. It is believed that these Stupas were erected by the missionaries of Aúoka in the 2nd century B.C. The Nepalese Mahâyâna Buddhistic tradition about the visit of Mauryan Emperor, Asoka of Magadha to Nepal and founding of the city of Patan or Lalitapatana or Lalitapuri with the four Buddhist Shrines during the time of the said Kirâta king can be corroborated by a number of reliable evidence.[9]

The historic visit of Aúoka to the Kirâtadeúa in the 3rd century B.C. will go down in the latter's history as the most memorable and significant event. During this period some section of them might have embraced the Buddhism which flourished in Nepal. The *Aúoka Avâdna* in Buddhist Sanskrit preserved in Nepal as referred to by Rhya Davids[10] may possibly throw some light on this aspect.

The first and second parts (VI & VII) of *Gopalaraja Vamúâvali* discovered by Bendall only refer to the names of the rulers of the Kirâta dynasty. The chronicles composed comparatively at later age deal with the participation of the Kirâta king in the Mahâbhârata war, visits of Buddha and Aúoka to Nepal during the rule of the Kirâtas.[11] "The Vamúâvalis have sought to synchronise some of these Kirâta kings of Nepal with Indian Âryan kings, legendary and historical e.g. with the Pândavas with Buddha and with Aúoka" as stated by S.K. Chatterji.[12] But none of them was legendary figure as erroneously supposed by him. The historicity of all the three can be proved without any difficulty. The Kirâta rulers had their capital at Gokarna in the North of the Nepal valley. This place was famous as a seat of government of the Kirâta rulers in the contemporary Age.

The reign of Sthunko contemporary of Aúoka of Magadha, is associated with some other interesting events of considerable historical importance. He is believed to have successfully resisted the Indian encroachment on the Nepalese territory by breaking the horse statue in the column capital over the Aúokan pillar cut Lumbini to pieces. This episode appears to be an expression of reaction of this Kirâta king against the tenets of Buddhism. This is further evidenced by the fact that an another horse image was carved and placed in the panel of the sculpture of Trivikrama Visnu. Trivikrama's association with his horse symbolizes the activities of the Kirâta king Manadeva, a Licchavi ruler ascribed to 5th century A.D., being inspired by the patriotic fervour and glorious past of the Kirâta age in the ancient history of Nepal set up a base relief of Trivikrama Visnu or Vikranta image of Visnu with a clear conception of Vâmana in it. It is contended that the conception of Vamana in the base relief metaphorically represented the short stature of the Kiratas. This also supported the Kirâta affinity with the principal image in the relief.[13]

The conception of Vâmana does not convey any idea about its racial affinity with the so-called "Indo-Mongoloid" Kirâtas. The logical arguments put forward by Mr. Regmi for rejecting this hypothesis merit our attention. He has argued that there is no historical data to prove the existence of Sthunk and other rulers of this dynasty as well as to show that the former was the contemporary of Aúoka. He has raised some questions which we must ponder over. Why did Sthunko an alleged Buddhist Kirâta king break the Asokan pillar erected at Lumbini to honour the memory of the lord? Was it not a sacreligious act? Why did he deem it fit to strike only at Lumibini pillar and not the Rampurwa and Lauria Nandangarh pillars of Aúoka that lie much closer to his seat of power in the Nepal valley? What was the necessity for Mânadeva to take upon himself the task of glorifying the Kirâta people? Has Sthunko left behind any trace of his exploit as it was open to the Kirâta king to inscribe in the said pillar whatever he did? Further Manadeva has not said anything about the Kirâtas in his inscription. There was no need for Mânadeva to invoke the so-called glory of the Kirata to prove his own greatness.

Some questions are of course very pertinent which still await proper solution. But some explanations sought for are not very reasonable. We can't deny the existence of Sthunko and other Kirâta rulers of this dynasty, because the local chronicles or *Vamúâvalis* bear an eloquent and glowing testimony to their rule in the valley of ancient Nepal. Moreover, after examining the historical validity of the statements contained in the said chronicles the existence of this dynasty has been confirmed by other noted authorities also as already quoted. Regmi has unnecessarily lamented the absence of historical data in this connection. Here it is to be noted that the data furnished by the chronicles are no less than the said historical data. For reconstructing the history of any ancient kingdom or dynasty of a particular region we shall have to place our reliance on the historical data, whatsoever they may be, as supplied by the native chronicles. The culture and civilization of a contemporary age also find some reflection in the chronicles. However, it is true that we can't accept everything blindly. There are some data which must be critically examined for extracting the truth. But this task should be undertaken not for the sake of convenience but for discovering the truth without any bias and prejudice. It is also undeniable that any attempt either to magnify the deeds of rulers or to glorify the achievements will not be appreciated. It is always better to strike a balance between the two extreme views. The contemporaneity of Sthunko and Aúoka should also not be made a subject of doubt on the basis of the conspicuous absence of the details concerned in the historical records other than the chronicles. It must always be kept in mind that various threads of our missing knowledge are lying scattered hither and thither which can be collected and 'restored with the help of all the available documents not only one or two. The absence of any inscribed pillar as a proof of the exploits of Sthunko does not strike any wonder, because he was neither equipped with that skill nor keen to leave behind any such record. The attempt on his part to break the Aúokan pillar at Lumbini was nothing but his inability to reconcile to the new state of affairs. He is also believed to have pillaged the Aúokan relics at the Lumbini with an avowed intention to avenge the conquest of the same place by Aúoka. a king of hallowed memory. At that stage he might have been the follower of Hinduism and hence the possibility of a fair contest between the Hinduism and the Buddhism may not be precluded. We do not have any positive evidence about the impact of Buddhism on the Kirâta dynasty at any given time. But in broader perspective the impact of this new doctrine on the Kirâta rulers for sometime can't be denied.

Sthunko, the fourteenth king of this dynasty was succeeded by his son Gighri (Gidhrinhang). He was further followed by Nane (Nanyahang), Luk (Shimkhu or Lukchang), Thor (Thora or Thamo or Thorhang), Thoko (Thokohang), Barma (Varma-or Brahmahang) Guja (Gmja or Gunjahang), Pushka (Puskara), Kesu (Keshuhang), Suja (Joosha or Sunsasunga or Sungahang), Sansa (Samsu or Sansahang), Gunan (Gunam or Magamam) and Khimbu (Khemboo).

The above mentioned Kirâta kings used to live in an inaccessible "Durbar" or palace built in the Jungles of Gokarna, which was their noted Capital. The *Parbatiya Chronicle*[14] records that these Kirâta used to kill the jackals which infested the place. These animals took refuge at Gupteswara on the banks of the Bagmati. They raised a small mound which was called Jambuka Dobhani or Hillock of Jackals which was lying near Gokarna between it and Pashupati.

The twenty eighth king named Patuka; son of Khimbu, was repeatedly attacked by Somabamsi Rajputs from the west. As a result of this attack he left his capital at Gokarna and moved towards Sahankhamula Tirtha at a distance of four *Kos* to the south, where he built a new capital. The ruins of his new palace in the form of mound are still seen. This is supposed to have been the remains of the palace, of the Kirântis. The last king named Gasti of this dynasty being hard pressed by the invasions of the Somabamsis fled from new capital. There the Somabamsis, after having subdued the Kiratas, built a new palace near Godavari at the foot of the Phulocheha mountain. Nimikha or Nimicha was the first Somabhamsi Raja who after having conquered the Kiratas founded the Somavamsi dynasty a round 205 A.D. 15 K.P. Jayaswal[16] takes Nimisha as the dynastic name and suggests that Manaksha or Mataksha was the first ruler of the Somavamsi dynasty. But we have no evidence to corroborate this supposition.

We find that the closing years of the last Kirâta ruler proved to be fatal for the Kirâta dynasty because of the repeated invasions of the rulers of the new dynasty known as Somavamsi. This conquering dynasty belonged to the Solar family of the Licchavis. The Licchavi's conquest of the Kirâtas roughly during the early centuries of the Christian era heralded the dawn of a new Age in the ancient history of India, but it must be noted that this was not the ultimate collapse of ths Kirâtas' rule. They had not disappeared completely from the scene. This was just the beginning of the end of the Kirâtas' rule. This aspect will be dealt with separately in the following pages.

The existence of the Kirâta dynasty can further be attested to by the available epigraphic evidence, whatever its nature may be. A long Stone Slab, forming a part of the platform of the Degutale temple in the Hanumandhaka palace complex bears an inscription[17] in five lines which appears to be mutilated to certain extent and runs as follows:

"Kirâta Varṣadhara Chirantanam Lichchhaviraja Kâritam Purâtana brittibhuja rupeksam."[18]

The above inscription has been interpreted by different scholars of Nepal in different ways. However, the word 'Kiratavarsadhara' constitutes the cornerstone of the said inscription. On the basis of this the existence of the Kirata dynasty, which ruled over the valley of Nepal, can be irrefutably proved. The statement recorded in the chronicles, that the Kirata dynasty was very much in power before the ascendancy of the Licchavis, can be confirmed by this inscription without any hitch and hesitation. This dynasty might have come into power after the Mahispalas. Surprisingly enough, D.R. Regmi[19], a popular authority on the history of Nepal, does not appear to be very much confident in his approach with regard to the existence of the Kirâta dynasty. He has made again and again contradictory statements. On the one hand, he professes that the people of the Kirâta origin were living in the valley and they ruled over the country in the hoary past for quite some time before the foundation of the Licchavi dynasty. On the other, he has denied their domination in the valley. It does not find any reliable evidence to support their dynastic rule. He further observes that as they have left an indelible impression on the history and culture of ancient Nepal, it is difficult to assign them any proper place in the political and cultural history of the country.

The historical importance of all available details can't be set aside merely on the basis of the assumption that they are fictitious and hypothetical. On the combined testimony of the Chronicles and epigraphy the Kirâtas' rule over the valley of Nepal can be, undoubtedly established.

The script of the inscription represent late Brahmi of Northern variety belonging to the 7th century A.D. This inscrition probably belonged to the Age of Amúluvanna, the most prominent ruler of the Licchavi dynasty, who, according to all available epigrapbic and other records, ruled sometimes between 640 and 652 A.D.[20]

The local annals of Nepal ascribe to the Kirâtas a dynasty that ruled the valley for twenty nine generations. Man Mohan Sharma's statement[21] that twenty two Kirâta rulers ruled over the valley of Nepal for ten thousand years, is not absolutely correct. It is very difficult to calculate the total period of reigns of the rulers of this dynasty. Because nothing positive in this regard is available. The availability of the chronological chart would have simplified our task in making a scientific study of the genealogical chart. But, unfortunately, we are not in possession of any such helpful aid. Another difficulty which we are confronted with is the absence of an authentic record about the continuty or discontinuity in the dynastic rule, which was in existence both in proto-historic and historic periods. However, it is roughtly estimated that they ruled for "ten thousand years in the *Dwâparayuga.*"[22] Such kind of statement appears to be purely imaginary, hence it is not possible to accept it. There are other varying statements in this regard which are not less fenciful than this. But we will refrain ourselves from dealing with all these data, because no purpose will be served by undertaking a fruitless exercise.

According to *Vaṁúâvalîs,* one thousand one hundred eighteen (1118) years, Sylvain Levi, one thousand one hundred seventy eight (1178) years and Kirkpatrick one thousand five hundred eighty one (1581) years have been assigned to twenty nine rulers of this dynasty as a total period of their reign. We do not know the basis for making such calculations. At the same time it is also very difficult to ascertain as to which data is the most correct and acceptable. Thus we find ourselves in a very embarrassing position, so far as the fixation of the total period of their reigns is concerned. Further, the computation of time that intervened between the rulers of this dynasty is another difficult task. However, the reconcilement of several contradictions in varying statements may be of some use for our purpose. D.R. Regmi[23] after having found gross exaggeration in the above suggested dates applied his own method to overcome the problem concerned. Here he accepts that this dynasty had unbroken period of reign. In order to ascertain the total period of reign he has assigned an average twenty five years to each twenty nine rulers. And hence 25 multiplied by 29 (25x29) becomes equal to 725 years. Such kind of guess-work is unavoidable in our ancient history. However, they ruled over the valley of Nepal tentatively for more than one thousand years in both pre and post Aúokan period.

From their dynastic genealogy it appears that 28 or 29 rulers belonged to the Kirâta dynasty. The regnal year (length of reign) of each ruler and total duration of their rule find mention in the *Vaṁshâvali* of Kirâtavaṁshi Sunuwar (by Ram Bahadur Sunuwar, Samvat 2013 = AD 1956). According to this genealogical record, 28 Kirata chiefs ruled in the valley of Nepal altogether for 1655 years.

On the basis of Aúoka's visit to Nepal in 3rd century B.C. (roughly 240 B.C.) during the time of Sthunko or Thumko the fourteenth Kirâta ruler as recorded by the chronicles, Mr. Regmi[24] has fixed early 6th century B.C. as the initial period of the Kirâta rule. The basis for such speculation may be the visit of Gautama Buddha to Nepal in the 6th century B.C. during the time of one of the Kirâta rulers not exactly known. Contradicting his own statement, he suggests that 7th century B.C. probably marked the beginning of the Kirâta's rule and not 3102 B.C., the initial year of the *Kaliyuga.*

Actually various dates i.e. 1739 B.C., 900 B.C., 7th century B.C. and 6th century B.C. have been suggested by different authors as the beginning of the Kirâtas' rule. None of these dates is correct. Because it has alteady been proved that much before all these dates the Kirâta rulers were in -occupation of the valley of Nepal as evidenced by the participation of one of their kings in the Mahâbhârata war. Hence in the ultimate analysis 3102 B.C. which marked the beginning of *Kaliyuga* is hereby accepted as the initial year of their reign. As a matter of fact, many scholars hesitate to suggest such dates as it is the general practice only because of their lack of confidence in the data available about our own chronology based on astronomical calculations, according to which the four *yugas* have been divided and assigned the period concerned.

The dynastic rule of the Kirâtas had some impact on the social, political, religious and cultural history of ancient Nepal. After their appearance on the stage of Nepal many significant changes took place. Politically they dominated the scene by overwhelming the indigenous population of the pre-Kirâta Age who are generally described as Australoid, Dravidian, Indo-Mongoloid, etc. The Kirâta rulers in course of their expansion were accompanied by their warriors peasants,and labourers. The commingling of the pre-Kirâta people and the old and the new hordes of the immigrant Kirâta population paved the way for evolution of a synthetic culture in ancient India. Their cultural domination is proved by the linguistic hegemony which they established there. Their socio-cultural life underwent metamorphosis. The primitive culture entered upon a new phase of orientation. S.K. Chatterji has correctly stated that "These Kirâtas kings were undoubtedly preparing the way for Newar and other Ind-Mongoloid domination in the affairs of Nepal and for their fullest participation in the development of its Hindu (Buddhist or Brahmanical) culture in centuries to come".[25] At later stage large section of them were absorbed in the indigenous population of the land.

III

STRUGGLE WITH THE LICCHAVIS FOR POWER AND POLITICAL SUPREMACY FIRST TO THIRD CENTURIES

(The period of subjugation and decline of the rule)

The appearance of the Licchavi dynasty of the Solar race of the Ksatriyas, popularly known as the Somavaṁsî in the local annals of Nepal, on the political stage of ancient Nepal in the early centuries of the Christian era turned the very face of the Kirata history. A new age of the struggle or contest between the members of these two dynasties—the Kirâta and the Licchavi for power and political supremacy begaa in who the former was vanquished and subjugated by the latter. After having crowned themselves with victory, the Licchavis conquered Nepal and established their dynasty with capital in the extreme south of the valley at Godawari. The foundation of this new dynasty of the Licchavîs struck a challenge to the Kirâtas.

Here it must be made clear that the Kirâta dynasty did not disappear completely from the scence after their defeat at the hands of the Licchavîs. But their popularity, of course, was on the wane. It was the period of the decline of their rule. In spite of being conquered by the Licchavis in the early centuries A.D., they continued their struggle till the 3rd century A.D.

The most reliable version of the *Gopâla Râja Vamúâvali* of the 14th century A.D. confirms the Licchavi conquest of the Kirâtas and the role of the former from first century A.D. down to the end of the 8th century A.D.[26]

Here it must also be made clear that the Licchavis, who conquered the Kirâtas were no other than one of the eight clans of Vajjian or Vrijjian confederacy of Vaiúâli which was the seat of their government right from the latter half of the sixth century B.C. to the first century or 3rd century A.D. The Licchavi territory lying north of the Ganges may have extended as far as the Nepal Hills. They belonged to Ksatriya clan not the Mongolian extraction as already proved. Their power began to decline after their conquest by Ajâtúatru (492-460 B.C.) the king of Magadha, who extended his political sway over the regions lying between the Ganges and the Himalayas. Later in the first century A.D. during the time of Kushana rule they* out of fear of fresh wave of attack, began to migrate. Thus one branch of the Licchavi of Vaisali started their immigration to Nepal from 1st century A.D. which continued probably up to the beginning of the 3rd century A.D.[27]

A great controversy has been sparked off about the founder of the Licchavî dynasty in Nepal. The primary reason for this is the different interpretations of different inscriptions discovered by different scholars. Of all the available inscriptions,. No. 15 collected by Pandit Bhagwan Lall Indraji,[28] a popular authority on the history of Nepal, has been acknowledged the most reliable, because it gives the systematic, complete and anthentic picture of the dynastic history of ancient Nepal. According to the said inscription Jayadeva—I, ascribed to the 1st century A.D., was the founder of this dynasty. This discovery has been further corroborated by other scholars.[29]

Suniti Kumar Chatterji has rightly observed that the Kirâtas were suppressed by a new dynasty known as Surya-Vams or Solar Licchavîs who came from Bihar and conquered Nepal. The historical period of Nepal begins with them. But his statement, that they ruled from c. 350 A.D. to the end of the 9th century

A.D. as evidenced from their inscriptions and coins,[30] does not appear to be very much convincing. Because they started their rule much earlier than the date highlighted by him. Their own inscriptions speak this truth.

In the twilight of this finding it can be stated with confidence and accuracy than the first chapter of Kirâta-Licchavi struggle was opened in the first century A.D. during the reign of Jayadeva—I. The first Licchavî ruler made a serious attempt to conquer the Kirâtas to establish his own dynasty on the ruins of the former dynasty.

Mr. Regmi's work[31] transmits the information that Mataksa and Kakavarma (2nd to 3rd century A.D.), followers of Kirata had launched a struggle or pursued their resistance against the Liechavis for regaining the power and establishing supremacy. Puspadeva or Pusparekha; probably the 4th king according to him inflicted a crushing defeat on the Kirâtas and consolidated the position of his dynasty. During the period extending from 2nd to 3rd century A.D. the Kiratas were repeatedly attempting to regain power, but ai they received blow after blow from the Licchavis, their position became gradually weak.

According to the evidence furnished by Bhaskardeva, the 5th king also conquered the Kirâtas before setting out on his victorious march to the south. He struck a severe blow to the imperial power, prestige and authority of the Kirâtas. He successfully put down the resistance of the Kirâtas to the Licchavi power.[32]

Strikingly enough, the names of the Licchavî rulers as shown above do not figure either in the list of Pandit Bhagwan Lall Indraji or in the list of Dr. Fleet. The existing discrepancy in the epigraphic records as well as the chronicles may create some doubts in our mind about the historical authenticity of the facts as stated above. Hence, in order to set this doubt at rest it must be made clear that the names of many rulers are missing in almost all the available inscriptions on the Licchavi dynasty.

This has been confessed by the discoverers of the said inscriptions themselves. Thus if the epigraphic records and the chronicles are treated as supplementary to each other, we can arrive at any definite conclusion, thest with-standing, their discernible deficiencies. In the light of above facts the genuineness of the above details should not be viewed with a sceptical eye.

In this connection K.P. Jayaswal's findings can't be passed over in silence. According to him about 200 A.D. Nepal was annexed to the dominion of the Licchavis who had their capital at Vaisali and they ruled over the territory of Nepal in that fashion for seven generations. It was Jayadeva—1 (c. 340-350 A.D.) who shifted himself to the valley of Nepal and started his rule confining himself within the newly conquered area. Since the Vaiúâli and Nepal broke away from each other and the latter was absorbed in the Gupta Empire at the subsequent stage.[33]

The above theory propounded by K.P. Jayaswal contain some substratum truth as well as error. The presentation is not in order. The said annexation is followed by the accession of Jayadeva—I and his transfer of seat of power. It should have been in reverse order. There is no justification to ascribe the date—c. 340-350 A.D. to Jayadeva—I, because this date does not figure in any other relevant source. Moreover, in the list of rulers shown by Pt. Bhagwan Lall Indraji on the basis of epigraphic evidence Râja Mânadeva (Samvat 386-413 or A.D. 329-356[34] or Saka 386-413=A.D.. 464-491) was the ruler somctimes between the fourth and 5th century A.D. Hence the date suggested by him seems to be a hypothetical one. It has already been proved that Jayadeva—I conquered the Kirâtas in the first century A.D. and founded a branch of the Licchavî dynasty in Nepal. So far the annexation of Nepal to the Licchavî domination of Vaisali in 200 A.D. is concerned, it can't be denied that Nepal remained under the paramount control of the Licchavis for quite some time. We also find that by 3rd century A.D. the power of the Kirâtas and completely declined which might have facilitated the extension of political hegemony of the Licchavis to the Kirâtas' territory.

From the foregoing discussion the conclusion is that with the dawn of the 3rd century A.D. the power of the Kirâtas had completely declined. In fact there were various phases of the decline of their rule. The process of the decline might have possibly begun in the 1st century A.D. when one branch of the Licchavîs of Vaiúâlî had entered the Kirâtas' territory and it was completed when their another branch might have tightened their grip over them. However, it must be remembered that the

3rd century A.D. marked the decline and not the downfall of their rule.

IV

REVIVAL OF THE GLORY AND EXTINCTION OF THE DYNASTY

(From the fifth Century to the reign of the Âbhira Guptas in the Seventh Century)

The 5th century A.D. was a period of upheaval in the history of the Licchavîs and a period of revival in the history of the Kiratas. In order to refurbish the tarnished image of the earlier 3rd century A.D. the Kirâta rulers, actually, left no stone unturned. The local annals of *Vaṁúâvalis* and epigraphic records are silent over this point. As a matter of fact several vacuum are found in them. The Kirâtas were on the look out for a suitable opportunity to restore the fallen virtues of their dynastic rule. The conflict between the Licchavis and the Guptas provided the long awaited opportunity to them to do so. The emergence of the rulers of the Gupta dynasty caused great setback to the authority of the Licchavîs. During the rule of the Guptas (500-625 A.D. in Terai area up to Janakpur, the earlier capital of Mithila) which virtually began with Jayagupta some interesting events of considerable importance took place. Both the Licchavi and Gupta dynasties ruled over Nepal simultaneously, but most of the times the relationship between the two remained hostile or strained. Taking advantage of the hostility between the two, the Kirâtas made a fresh attempt to revive their glory and fame.

K.P. Jayaswal on the authority of a very important Tibetan Text[35] ascribed to the 9th century A.D. has highlighted hitherto, an unrecorded—fact relating to the history of the Kiratas. The translated passages of the Tibetan text, *Mañjusri Mûlakalpa* will help us to fill in the vacuum in our existing knowledge about the Kirâtas. According to the text after Mânadeva—I the Licchavî ruler of Nepal the Kirâta dynasty of the Abhira branch contemporaneously flourished.

Various missing names of the Kirâta rulers along with the names of some Licchavî and Gupta rulers of Nepal occur in this text. The post-Mânadeva period has been described as the period of Mleccha kings named Vabisa, Subrsa, Bhavasu, Subhasu, Bhakrama, Rudakrama, Kamala followed by Ghagupta, Vatsaka,

Bhasvam in the west and Udaya, Jisnugupta etc. K.P. Jayaswal is of the opinion that the names up to Kamala belonged to the Kirâta dynasty. They have been described as Mlecchas only because of the fact that they had been declared degraded for not observing their customary rites and rituals. After Jisnugupta Nepal passed under suzerainty of Tibet as recorded elsewhere also. K.P. Jayaswal's identification of the Mleccha kings with the Kirâtas appears to be objectionable to D.R. Regmi.[36] He finds that this identity does not rest on any firm ground and the word Mleccha may imply anything. But we find that the basis for his objection to this identity is not justified, because the text concerned gives the names of these rulers along with other rulers of the Licchavi and Gupta dynasty of Nepal, who may be no other than the Kirâtas. George N. Roerich,[37] who seems to be familiar with the said text, has mistakably associated all the names from the Licchavî Mânadeva to Jisnugupta with the Tibetan kings. We do not find any justification for this, because epigraphy is ready to prove the association of all the names with the history of Nepal.

After Manadeva—I the Nepal valley was invaded by the Kiratas under the inspiring leadership of Vabisa. The example set by him was followed by his successors. But the Licchavis were not ousted. They remained in power. The last ruler named Kamala tried to revive the rule of the past by opposing the Guptas. The Kirâtas were defeated by the Gupta rulers which weakened their strength. K.P. Jayaswal is the great protagonist of the theory of the Kirata revival in the last quarter of the 6th century A.D. There may be some contradictions and weak points in his theory as referred to by Mr. Regmi, but we think that it is a great discovery which will constitute a valuable addition to our existing knowledge.

Piercing through all the haziness enveloping the subject under discussion it can be affirmed that like the Âbhîras, the Kiratas also invaded Nepal towards the closing decades of the 6th century A.D. and entered into struggle with some Gupta rulers. The Âbhîras after their victory in the struggle with the Licchaîs ruled for sometimes by ousting the latter. But they were ultimately defeated by Amúuvarma of the Thakuri dynasty. Thereafter, struggle ensued between the Kirâtas and the Âbhîras. The Abhîras (5th to 8th century A.D.) were the feudal Chiefs during the time of the Licchavî rulers.

The Kirâtas were finally dethroned by the Âbhîra Gupta rulers in the 7th century A.D. The 7th century witnessed only the fall of the dynastic rule of the Kirâtas and not their extinction.

Regmi observed that "...although there was a Kirata revival during the last reign of the first Licchavi Dynasty, it is not at all certain that the revival was effected by the Yellung Kirâtas. It is possible that a revival in question signified a series of raids carried out by a ferocious tribe rather than any event of historical importance."[38] This is not a correct judgment. Because their struggle for power and attempt for revival can't be equated with raids only. The value of events should be assessed in the context of contemporary situation.

Notes and References

1. (*a*) *Parbatiya Vaṁúâvali* (originally composed in the 14th century in parbatiya with an admixture of Sanskrit and Newari, trans. by Munshi Shiva Shankar Singh and Pandit Shree Gunanand, both native scholars of Nepal, some time before 1877); *Gopâlarâja Vaṁúâvali* (a composite work in three parts, VI, VII and VIII, originally written in the 14th century partly in Sanskrit and partly in old Newari, discovered by C. Bendall during 1884-85, and preserved in the Darbar Library Kathmandu).
   (*b*) Daniel Wright, HṆ (primarily based on the Eng. trans. of the *Parbatiya Vamúâvali*), pp. 109-12.
   (*c*) D.R. Regmi, AN, pp. 56-59.
   (*d*) Kirkpatrick, AKN, pp. 259ff.
   (*e*) Sylvain Levi, *Le Nepal,* Vol. II, pp. 78-79.
   (*f*) Bhagwan Lall Indraji, "Some Considerations on the History of Nepal", *Ind. Ant.,* Vol. XIII, 1884, pp. 411-12.
   (*g*) K.P. Jayaswal, "Chronology and History of Nepal 600 B.C. to 800 A.D.", JBORS, Vol. XXII, Pt. III, 1936, pp. 260-64.
   (*h*) H.C. Ray, DHNI, Vol. I, Ch. IV, pp. 183-234 and also 272f.
   (*i*) IP (1955-56), Vol. I, pp. 133ff.
   (*j*) Robert Shafer, EAI, pp. 124-25.
   (*k*) N.B. Thapa, SHN, pp. 8-9.
2. JASB., Vol. XVI, Pt. I, 1847, p. 11.
3. *Ibid.*
4. Ind. Alt. 1, pp. 441-50 cf; *Periplus,* p. 253.
5. R.S. Tripathi, HAL, p. 332.

6. R.C. Majumdar, AI., p. 351.
7. *Some considerations on the History of Nepal,* Quoted by Pt. Baldeva Prasad Mishra, *op. cit.,* p. 45.
8. Quoted in Daniel Wright, HN, p. 110.
9. (*a*) A.K. Warder, IIH, pp. 89-93.
   (*b*) Suniti Kumar Chatterji, *op. cit.* pp. 63-64.
   (*c*) Edwin Atkinson, HG. Vol. II. pt. I. p. 364.
   (*d*) Man Mohan Sharma, *Through the Valley of Gods,* TCH., p. 45.
   (*e*) Pt. Baldeva Prasad Mishra, *op. cit.,* pp. 45-46.
   (*f*) V.A. Smith, (CAL, CC1M., Section, XIX, pp. 280-81) and Raj Bali Pandey, BIP, p. 113.
   (*g*) Sir John Houlton, BHL, p. 100.
   (*h*) N.B. Thapa., SHN, pp. 8-9.
   (*i*) Percy Brown, *Picturesque Nepal,* pp. 6-13. R.S. Tripathi, HAI; p. 331.
10. BIP. 276; R.L. Mitra's SBLN, ASB, 1982.
11. D.R. Regmi, AN, pp. 58-59.
12. *op. cit.,* p. 66.
13. Vide Kaisar Bahadur, *Nepal Guardian: A Miscellany,* pp. 11-21 quoted in D.R. Regmi, AN, pp. 136-37.
14. Danicl Wright, HN, p. 112.
15. (*a*) *Ibid.*
    (*b*) N.B. Thapa, SHN, pp. 9, 15.
16. JBORS. 1936, Vol. XXII, Pt. III, pp. 261-64.
17. Dhanavajra Vajrâchârya, LKA., N. 91 quoted in D.R. Regmi, IAN., Vol. I, IXXXV, p. 85.
18. D.R. Regmi. IAN. Vol. 3, p. 155.
19. *Ibid.,* pp. 155-56.
20. For a detailed study about the period of reign-of Amsuvarma and the different characters of the Licchavi inscriptions the following monographs, records and documents will be very much helpful:— Bhagwan Lall Indraji, *Twentythree Inscriptions from Nepal;* Bhagwan Lall Indraji and Dr. Buhler, IN., Ind. Art (JOR.), 1880, Vol : IX, pp. 163ff; R. Gnoli, NIGC. (S.O. Roma, X. 2); Bendall, JLAR. pp. 71-79; Ind. Art. 1884, Vol. XIII, pp. 411-427; Dr. Fleet, CII. Vol. Ill, p. 177ff, plates XII and XXXII. B, JASB. 1889, Pt. I, Synchranistic table; Dr. Buhler's *Gundriss* (Ind. Pal.) IV tafel; Prof. Max Muller's letter, cf. TICD., (Leiden, 6th session) pp. 124-128; AO., Vol. I Pt. III, p. 64; Dr. Buhler's *Remarks on the Hariuzi Palmleaf,* MSS. (Anecoxon's Vol. I, Pt. III, p. 65; Ind. Art., 1881, p. 424; Seals, BRWW. Vol. II, p. 81: El. Vol. I. pp. 68-73; Ind.

Art.; V.A. Smith, CAI (CCIM.), pp. 280-83; A Cunningham, AGI., p. 380 and Thomas Walters, YCTI. Vol. II, p. 84.

21. TCH., p. 45.
22. E. Atkinson, HG., Vol. II. Pt. I, p. 364.
23. AN, p. 56.
24. *Ibid.,* pp. 55-56.
25. *Op. cit.,* pp. 65-66.
26. (*a*) D.R. Regmi, AN. pp. 61, 63, 74.
    (*b*) A.K. Warder, IIH. pp. 89-90.
27. For a detailed study Licchavi's origin, location, position, migration, conquest of Nepal, Inscriptions etc. please see the following :— A. Cunningham, AGI., pp. 380-81; D.R. Regmi, AN. pp. 25-31; R.G. Basak, HNEI. pp. 359-63, 376; Thomas Walters, YCTI. Vol. II, pp. 83-84; A.C. Raychoudhuri, PHAL, pp. i 18-26; B.C. Law. IETBJ., pp. 124-25, KTAI. Ch. II, Sec. V, pp. 26-27; Vinaya Texts, SBE., II, 171; SBE., XIV, 339; *Majjhima Nikâpa* II. 101 : DPPN. (Malalasekara), II, 781-82, 814, Lefmann, *Lalitavistara* (BIS.); Ch. Ill, p. 21; 1C., Vol. II, pp. 808-10; Mr. 1918, pp. Soff; V.A Smith, EHT., pp. 155ff; K.P. Jayaswal, JBORS., 1936, P. 14 pp. 258ff; *Hindu Polity,* pp. 172-82; IHQ., 1933, Vol. IX, pp. 429-40. R. Gnoli, NIGC., S.O. Roma, X. 2.7. Nos-1-VIII; Sylvain Levi, *Le Nepal, Vol. I,* pp. 14f; H.C. Roy, DHNI, pp. 188ff; H.N. Jha, *The Lichchhavis of Mithila and Nepal* and Upendra Thakur. *Mithilâkâ Itihasa,* pp. 94-95.
28. Ind. Ant. (JOR.), 1884, Vol. XIII, p. 427; See also Bhagwan Lall Indraji and G. Buhler, IM., Ind. Ant. 1880, Vol. IX., pp. 165ff; Bendall, JLAR., pp. 71-79; Dr. Hoernie, JASB., 1899, Pt. I, Synchronistic table and R. Gnoli, NIGC., No. I-V.
29. Fleet, CII. Vol. III. Introd. p. 136 : A. Cunningham, AGI. pp. 380-81; HNEI, pp. 359-63.
30. *Op. cit.,* p. 66.
31. AN. p. 74.
32. *Ibid.,* p. 78.
33. CHN., JBORS. Sept. 1936, Vol. XXI, Pt. III, pp. 258-59.
34. *Ind. Ant.* 1884, p. 427, Nos. 1, 3 and 15.
35. AMM (ed. by Ganapati Sastri, Trivandrum Sanskrit Series), vv. 554-559; trans. by K.P. Jayaswal, JBORS., Sept., 1936, Vol. XXII, ap. 211ff.
36. An, p. 144.
37. (Trams): *Blue Annals or Deb-ther, Snun-Po by* Gos—10—*Stsa—ba—gzon-nn-dpa* (1392-1481 A.D.) Pt. I, pp. 44ff quoted in Regmi, AN, p. 145.
38. AN, pp. 56 See also pp. 144-147.

BOOK SIX

THE ROLE AND CONTRIBUTION OF THE KIRÂTAS

I

GENERAL REMARKS

The study of the exact nature of genesis and growth of Indian Civilization can't be conducted in isolation from what the non-Âryans have contributed to it. D.D. Kosambi, a great champion of the study of tribal elements in India history, has correctly observed that "the entire course of Indian History shows tribal elements being fused into a general society."[1]

It is worth-while to mention that the Austric and Dravidian elements in Brahmanical Hindu civilization, which started taking its shape from the Vedic period onwards and further flourished after coming into contact with other non-Ârayan cultures, have been, undeniably, discussed by a number of competent scholars. But the Kirâta (so-called Sino-Tibetan or Mongoloid) elements in Indian culture and civilization have not received the attention of oriental scholars and indologists, which it deserves. The Kirâtas, by far, made their presence felt in Indian history. The contributions which they started making right from the dawn of history to the various aspects of Indian life, thoughts, beliefs and practices, have very often been underestimated. A general appraisement of the roles of the Kirâta peoples in the development of composite Indian culture can be regarded as one of the important aspects of indology. The following treatment of the subject will confirm that the Kirâtas, one of the very important sections of pre-Âryans population made significant contribution to Indian culture and civilization and played notable role, to some extent in the political history of ancient times.

II

ROLE OF THE KIRÂTAS IN THE EARLY ANNALS OF INDIA

We have got both mythological and historical accounts of the role played by the Kirâtas as warriors on different occasions in the early annals of India. They played their role both conscientiously and unconscientiously. *Vâlmikis Râmâyana*[2] furnishes the earliest evidence of their role during the protohistoric period. The long standing hostility between great sage Vasistha and Viúvâmitra, well known for his ostentation, vanity, and chivalry furnished the occasion for various races to display their war-like qualities and bravery. Actually, after having received the persuasion and guidance from Vasistha, various mlecchas got ready to fight against Viúvâmitra. The Kiratas along with the Paundra, the Barbasa, the Dardas, the Pahlavas, the Úabaras, the Yavanas, the Sakas the Kambojas and other miecchas joined the army of Vasistha and played very vital role on his behalf in the destruction of the Visvamitra, which consisted of infantry, cavalry, elephants and chariots. This can also be confirmed by the details provided in the *Mahâbhârata.*[3] In fact, Vasistha wanted to shatter the pride, glory and military powers of his opponent, Visvâmitra with the help of the Kiratas and other contemporary Indian races.

But after having critically examined the credibility of the foregoing account as recorded in the epics we find that it does not bear the historical character and further suffers from lack of coherence, continuity and clarity. Nor does it present an impressive record of the performances of the Kirâtas in Indian history during the early period. However, their participation in various episodes and their gallantry, which they occasionally exhibited, gave new turn to the early history of India.

The Kirâtas have been, admittedly, a history factor in the early annals of our country. They had very much appeared on the scene, particularly, in the age of the *Mahâbhârata.* We have very clear and ample evidence of the role, which they played during the epic age. Their participation in the Bhârata war or the battle of Kurukṣetra as an ally of the Kâuravas can very well be confirmed by the details narrated in the *Mahâbhârata.*[4] According to all available evidences, it can be proved that Bhagadatta, the mleccha king of Prâgjyotiṣa (later Kâmarupa) accompanied by the unassailable troops consisting mostly of the Kirâtas and Cinas soldiers endowed with golden complexion and many others drawn from the sea shore took part in this war joining the side of the Kaurvas. One *akúauhini* of soldiers led by Bhagadatta mostly included the Kirâtas of North-East India. The Kirâtas and Cînas were all looking like figures of gold and assuming a beauty like that of a forest of Karnikara trees. They fought on behalf of Duryodhana against the Pandavas. After having been defeated by Pandava heroes, they fought along with other non-Âryan and Âryan races against Arjuna. It appears from the details of events that they played very effective role in this war. Here it can be reasserted that when Arjuna launched his expedition against the rulers of north-eastern region in connection with the establishment of an empire of Yudhisthira, the Kirâtas along with others fought against him under the inspiring leadership of their ruler, Bhagadatta continuously for eight days, but ultimately accepted the defeat and acknowledged the supremacy of Yudhisthira. The Kirâtas along with others were defeated by Arjuna. It is also recorded that Bhagadatta was killed by Arjuna.[5] Some more valuable and interesting details as regards the Kiratas' participation in the said war have been provided in other Parvas of the *Mahâbhârata*. We find that the Kiratas associated with the Sakas, the Yavanas and the Pahlavas also joined the army of the Kauravas and fought in this war.[6]

Several Kirâta kings and other mlecchas of Northern Himalayas riding the elephants—all cased in armour and decked with ornaments, achieved marvellous feats of actions, while fighting against Satyaki in the battle. They were well accomplished in the art of fighting from above elephants. They were well-equipped with arms and weapons. They fought very effectively in the battle. Satyaki urged his charioteer to take him to the place of war where these Kirâtas and Daradas, the Barbaras the Úakas, Tamraliptas and other countless mlecchas armed with bows and arrows were stationed.[7]

On the seventeenth day of the memorable battle Krsna told Arjuna that a great number of soldiers comprising the Kirâtas, the Yavanas, the Khasas, the Tusâras, the Darvabhisâras,' the Daradas, the Úakas, the Kâmathas, the Ramathtas, the Tanganas. the Andhrakas, the Pulindas. the mlecchas and the mountaineers hailing from the seaside—all of terrible deeds and exceedingly fierce nature, well armed and endowed with great "wrath and prowess gotunited with the Qurus and fought wrathfully for Duryodhana's sake. They were incapable of being defeated by anybody except Savyasacin (Arjuna).[8] They were ultimately defeated by him.

The rulers of the Kiratas, the Daúârnas, the Daserakas, Anupakas, etc. were placed in the neck of *Krauncaruna array* formed by Yudhisthira.[9]

Here it is to be noted that the primary reasons for the participation of the Kiratas and other races in the Bharata war on behalf of the Kauravas may precisely be attributed to various attempts of the Pandava heroes to usurp their ancient Janapadas and kingdoms in the epic age.

They played very notable role in the Indian history during the time of Chandragupta Maurya (c. 322-298 B.C.). The role which they played in overthrowing the Nanda dynasty (c. 413-322 B.C.) and in the ascendancy of Chandragupta as a ruler of Magadha still stands unrecorded in ancient Indian History. The combined forces of Chandragupta, including the Kiratas, the Sakas, the Yavanas, the Kambojas, the Pârsikas, the Bahliks and other soldiers collected from North-Western India through the diplomacy of Cânakya and that of the kings of the mountain regions (Parvateúvara), blocked the city of Kusumapura or Pataliputra on all sides the then Magadh Capital under the direction and guidance of Cânakya, resembling the oceans with their water in wild commotion, besieged the city on all sides defeated the forces of the Nandas assisted by the Raksasas and other mlecchas, ruined the kingdom and paved the way for the establishment of the Mauryan empire. Chandragupta, undeniably, inflicted crushing defeat on the Nandas with the help of the Kirâtas and other soldiers, who formed the part of his retinue, captured Pataliputra and proclaimed the establishment of the Mauryan empire.

Thus the Kirâtas helped Chandragupta, to a considerable extent, in making him crowned with victory and in his elevation to the throne of Magadha after the fall of the Nanda dynasty. On the basis of the positive evidence as reflected in Viúâkh-adatta's historical play[10] it becomes quite apparent that they played very important part along with other kindred tribes in the foundation of the Maurya dynasty in the 3rd century B.C. Actually, they contributed their share to the fall of the Nanda dynasty and the rise of the Mauryan empire.

The above literary account has also been supported by other scholars.[11] B.C. Saletore[12] has mistakenly linked this episode with the interference of the Kiratas and the kindred tribes in the Mauryan politics. As a matter of fact, it was not an act of intervention but a glaring example of positive response of one of the popular races of ancient India—the Kiratas to the call given by Canakya for dethroning the rulers of Nanda dynasty.

McCrindle[13] a popular authority on the classical treatises and Mr. Schwanbeck in his authoritative work[14] have cast doubt on the historicity of the literary account as recorded in the Indian comedy *Mudrârakúasa* on the ground that this drama was written in the tenth century after Christ or tenth centuries after Seleucus. Both the authorities have expressed their doubts about the historical authenticity of the account only because of being influenced by the fanciful notion about the later date of composition of the text. Further, Schwanbeck has derived his authority from Wilson. The view held by McCrindle, that "when even the Indian historians have no authority in history, what proof can Drama give written after many centuries", can outrightly be rejected. He seems to have pronounced his judgment without taking care to understand the historical importance of this play in context of the Mauryas. Furthermore, this drama was not written in the 10th century A.D. It was composed sometime between the sixth and the seventh century A.D., as amply substantiated by the authorities on the work concerned. The validity of the statements is, not judged by the period during which they were recorded but by the impartial examination of the truth contained in the statements. It appears to be paradoxical that McCrindle on the one hand, admits this drama favours the Indian expedition undertaken by Chandragupta Maurya assisted by the Kiratas and other soldiers for capturing the city of Kusumpura, but, on the other hand, attempts to belittle the importance of the proof adduced by this drama about the role of the Kirâtas played during the Mauryan age.

The role of the Kirâtas as a class of warrior is indirectly proved by the German source. Lassen[15] has opined that the Kirata people even in later times appear to have joined the royal retinue or Army of the Indian emperors as confirmed by the

Greek report on this point. He has further stated that they had adopted the laws of the Arian or the Âryans of India.

The role of the Kirâtas as warriors during the time of Raudrabhuti, a mleccha king of the Vindhya forest is also worth-mentioning. On the basis of an evidence provided by Abhinava Pampa (12th century A.D.) in his famous work, called *Pampâ Râmâyana.*[16] We can state that they always helped Raudrabhûti, in winning over the rulers of the neighbouring areas. There is a solitary instance of the help extended by the Kiratas to the king of the Vindhayan forest. They said mleccha king was helped by the countless army of the Kirtas in defeating Valakhilya, the ruler of the town of Kuravakas and taking him as prisoner.

Thus we find that the Kiratas concerned played little role in ancient Indian history. From the above discussion it is evident that they were chivalrous and courageous. They used to respond to an appeal made by the rulers for taking part in the war. The saga of their gallantry displayed on few occasions constitutes an addition to the examples set by other tribal warriors in ancient India.

III

CONTRIBUTION OF THE KIRÂTAS TO THE EVOLUTION OF INDIAN CULTURE AND CIVILIZATION

The Kirâtas of Northern and Eastern India made substantial contribution to the evolution of Indian culture and civilization. Their contributions in socio-economic, political, religious, cultural, literary, artistic and various ocher fields appear to be very much impressive. They have left distinct and indelible imprints on the manners, customs, thoughts, beliefs, practices, religious system, language, art and culture of the Âryans. All aspects of Indian culture—material, moral and spiritual have been enriched by them, which can be perceived even today. Among the various races the Kiratas also profoundly influenced the evolution and transformation of the culture-complex of India. The pre-historic archaeology philology, anthropology, sociology, epigraphy and the prevailing religious and cultural systems in contemporary India of proto-historic periods bear a glowing testimony to the share contributed by different sections of the Kirâtas to the common store-house of Indian life and civilization.

The prehistoric period is marked by many significant contributions of far-reaching importance made by the non-Âryan groups of the Kirâtas of North-East India, which in subsequent periods formed the basis of Indian culture. These non-Âryans, like that of the Âryans, by building up a distinctive advanced culture of their own came within the orbit of Indian fusion of various races, viz., the Austrics or so-called Nisadas, the Negritos, the Bodos, the Dravidians, the Mongoloids, the Âryans and the Alpine Âryans in both pre-and post-Vedic periods and their cultural contacts with the Mediterranean Pundras of Northern and Central Bengal, who had the Chalcolithic civilization like the dwellers of Indus valley led to the evolution of the synthesis of cultures, which greatly influenced the various levels of Indian social structure. The importance of the Kiratas' contribution to the evolution of synthetic culture in prehistoric Assam can't be denied. According to S.K. Chatterji[17] this may be looked upon as the great contribution of Assam in prehistoric period. The first remarkable and impressive record of their contribution begins with the Neolithic period.

One of the very important sections of the Kiratas of North-East India, popularly known as the Khasi-Syntengs (the Jaintias) made several distinctive cultural contributions, such as Megalithic burials, Neolithic shouldered hoe, terraced ricecultivation, iron smelting and matriarchy, all indicative of advanced culture and civilization.[18] The stone celts and Megaliths associated with burial urns erected in the memory of their deceased representing the phallic worship, the use of iron implements, the developed animal husbandry, the formation of groups under the leadership of headman, the art of cultivation, the primitive system of Jhum cultivation, the introduction of matriarchal principles in the matter of administration and inheritance, the belief in the immortality of the soul or the spirit, the worshipping of the mother cult, etc. were some of the practices of the Khâsis and the Jaintias in the Neolithic period, which constituted the fundamental base of the socio-economic and cultural life of India.[19]

One of the curious features of this aspect of the subject is that the Neolithic stone monuments are associated with the cult of fertility, ancestral worship, theory of sacrifice, the worship of

Phallus—Linga and Yoni, later personifield as the mother-goddess and Úiva principles of Úaktism. G. Bertrand has also pointed out that "the Khasi monoliths comprising memorial stones, menhirs and dolmens like those of Western Europe, Northern Africa and Western Asia are doubtless the emblems of that Phallic cult of standing stones, which were so widespread in ancient times. These monoliths in the shape of Linga found in India are associated with the worship of Úiva."[20]

It is significant to note that "The stone worship among the Hindus seems a survival of rite belonging originally to a low civilization, probably a rite of the land, whose religion largely incorporated into the religion of the Aryan invaders, has contributed so much to form the Hinduism of today."[21] Later, there developed the classic doctrine and classic art of the worship of the same rude objects, whose veneration, no doubt, dates from remote barbaric antiquity.

About the importance of the stone memorials Sir Mortimer Wheeler a distinguished archaeologist has correctly stated that "the Buddhists, Jains and Hindus imitated free-standing structures, in cutting their cave temples and monasteries.[22]

The contribution of the tribal people to the evolution of the philosophical thoughts of the Hindus, Buddhists and Jains has not yet received the serious attention of scholars.

Their notion of life after death and idea of the plurality of the souls are believed to have given a new line of speculation to the Brahmanical thinkers and the Âryans, who had no acquaintance with the doctrine before.

The Neoliths and Phallic Megaliths of various sections of the Kirâtas of North-East India, known as the Khasis, the Jaintias, the Garos, the Kacharis and the Nâgas, generally associated with tbe worship of Phallus linga and Yoni, later personified as Siva and the mother-goddess, soul-matter magic, fetishism and animism led to the evolution of various minor and major religious cults and laid the foundation of socio-religious fabric of India. The ideas connected with the worship of memorial stones throughout the length and breadth of our country was brought to prominence first by the non-Âryans including the Kirâtas. J.H. Hutton[23] informs us that the Phallic worship is connected with the Linga—a simple cone and 'yoni' —a triangular prism. Both are somewhat realistically presented by the Nagas in their prehistoric monoliths. The Megalithic monuments of the Kirâtas representing Úiva-Úakti. principles and other stone memorials are believed by some savants to be evidence of ancient Phallic worship.

We find an unmistakable evidence of transition from primitive paganism of the Kirâta people to an elaborate Hinduism, the former symbolise:! the great monoliths of unhewn stones and latter symbolised the Hindu temples with the images and carvings.

Generally speaking, the discovery of agriculture, the advanced workmanship, weaving, pottery, farming, technological art, introduction of art of culturation, megalithic monuments, art. paintings, worship of phallic stones, totemic religion and other revolutionary innovations in socio-economic and cultural fields constitute the distinguishing features of their contributions made in the prehistoric times. Some of the primitive practices were absorbed by the Âryans at comparatively later age.

The *ophiolatry* or serpent worship widely prevalent in most parts of India, particularly Southern India and Eastern India including Bihar, Bengal and Assam may be originally connected with the Austric group of the Kiratas known as the Khasis tribes. Dr. Hutton remarks that.

> "the Austro-Asiatic *Finnougrians* clearly prceded the Mediterraneans in India and therefore *ophiolatry* is to be put down as the distinctive cultural contributian of the former."[24]

Their contribution to the evolution of the religious and philosophical system of India is of paramount historical importance. On the basis of all trustworthy historical evidences we can establish the truth that the contribution of the non-Âryans including the Kirâtas to the growth of Saivism, Úâktism and Tântricism in gross forms are important from both religious and cultural points of view. The popularity of three important religious cults, i.e. Úaiva, Úakta and Tântric among the Hindus may be fairly ascribed to the Kirâtas of North East India. Úaivism and Úâktism were the prevailing religions among the Kirâta people, especially the Khâsis, the Jaintias, the Garos, the

Cacharis, the Tipperahs, the Chutiyas, the Âkâs and the Idu-Mishmis in pre and post Naraka period. Actually, all these tribes known as the Kirâtas in the epic age were worshippers of mother-goddess, Kâmâkhya, the chief sanctuary of Úâktism. No wonder the Kâmâkhya was an embodiment of the fusion of the Âryan and non-Âryan beliefs and practices in the early times. These tribes lived in ancient Prâgjyotisapur, where the holy shrine of Kâmâkhya is located. Undeniably these cults were, first of all, popularised by the pre-Âryans including the Kirâtas. The Âryans later on imbibed the important attributes of these popular cults from the non-Âryans, who were the precursors in this field. The Kirâtas left some unmistakable imprints of their religious practices on the Brahmaputra valley. After being subjugated by Naraka in the war in Prâgjyotisa in pre-Bhârata war period, the Kirâta people dispersed in different groups carrying with them the cults of mother-goddess as replica of early life and settled in hills, mountains and jungles. Some sections of them popularised this cult as far as the Dikkarav-asini (the present Sadiya region). The Âryanised colony of the ancient times in the north-east frontier has been referred to in the Purânic literature as Dikkaravâsini and in the Tantric literature as Saumera Pîtha. Here also, there was synthesis of cultures embodying the elements of the Kirâta or so-called Indo-mongoloid culture and Âryan culture which was completed by the end of the 11th century A.D.[25]

The basic elements of Úaivism, Úaktism and mother-goddess cults identified wilh the active female principle (Prakrti) of Sankhya philosophy or with the Mâyâ of Advaita philosophy co-existent with Brahman as manifested in one or other form of worship of Úakti or Úiva's spouse under various names, Devi or Parvati, Durgâ and Kâli in accordance with the rites prescribed in the Tantras were deeply rooted in the religious system of the Kirâtas in the pre-Vedic and pre-Bharata war periods. On the basis of literary and other sources[26] we can state with certain amount of confidence that the Kirâtas installed the Phallic emblem of their worship near the Austric Ka-Mei-Khâ (Kâmâkhya), which, later on, became very popular centre of Saktism. They used to worship the mother-goddess in the Yoni symbol as opposed to the cult of Úiva worshipped in the Phallic symbol in pre-Naraka period. The Kirâtas lived in Prâgjyotisa containing the holy shrine of Kâmaikhâ or Kâmâkhyâ.

The absorption of non-Âryan beliefs and practices connected with these two cults in the religious system of the Hindus at the subsequent periods of history, posterior to the Âryan occupation of Prâgjyotisa, later known as Kâmârûpâ, was an epoch-making event in the religious and cultural history of ancient Assam.

Sir Charles Eliot, a popular authority on Hinduism and Buddhism, has observed that from historical standpoint Kamakhya appears to be compound of Hinduism with un-Âryan beliefs. It acquired great influence both in the courts and among the people of North-Eastern India but without producing personalities of much eminence as teachers or writers.[27]

These non-Âryan cults embodying cruder form of belief are as old as *Atharva Veda,* which subsequently developed and later left its indelible mark on Buddhism. Dr. Bhandarkar is also of the view that all the thoughts and beliefs associated with the cult of Saivism may be taken as the contributions of the non-Âryans including the Austrics. Their clear conceptions of Úaivism may be confirmed by other evidences too. The combat between lord Siva in the disguise of the Kirata Arjuna as referred to earlier is an interesting example of association of Úiva with primitive non-Âryan tribe. The Archaeological Report of Dr. T. Bloch[28] and the discovery of numerous objects in recent archaeological explorations clearly testify to the prevalence of Úaivism and the cult of mother-goddess in north-eastern frontier region in ancient times.

Dr. D. Sharma[29] and K.L. Barua[30], placing their reliance on the views of John Marshall, have tried to establish that the cult mother-goddess or the cult of Linga and Yoni are certainly of pre-Âryan Dravidian origin. The Austrics and the Bodos came under the cultural influence of the Mediterraneans—the authors of the pre Aryan Indus Valley culture and perhaps borrowed this custom from them. There are apparent contradictions in such statements, which are not purely based on facts. How far it is true that the Austrics or Nisâdas and other Kirâta tribes of north-eastern region imbibed this tradition from Dravidians of Mohenjodaro and Harappa or *vice-versa,* it is very difficult to ascertain. Because, we do not have any positive proof of cultural links or contacts between the two civilizations. At the same time it is also not possible to affirm that some section of the Austric group of the Kirâtas of North-East India were dwelling in the Indus Valley and later on accepted the Aryânised faith. The problems involved in such kind of investigation can't be finally solved. Rather, it will be futile to establish any link between the Kirata culture of north-east and the Harappan culture of north-west. The fact remains that both the cultures emerged and developed independently. However, it can definitely be asserted that as a result of mutual contacts and cultural fellowship between the various groups of the Âryans and non-Âryans in India the cults of Úaivism and Úaktism further flourished. The contribution of the Kirâta people like that of the Dravidians to the evolution of the said cults can, of course, be acknowledged. Actually different races played their roles in different ways in the history of the cultural growth of India.

Their contribution to the popularity of worship of Úiva both in the human form and in the symbolic form of the Liñga or Phallus needs our special attention. The concept of Saivism was, no doubt originally envisaged by them. Úiva, originally a Kirata deity worshipped by the dwellers of the Himalaya mountains later secured a prominent position in the Brâhmanical pantheon. They were the people, who first of all realised the dreadful and destructive aspects of this god. This idea was later imbibed by the Vedic Aryans from them. The pre-Âryan Kirâtas' Father, God-Úiva was in the process of amalgamation with Âryan Rudra even in the early Vedic period.

The Rgvedic Rudra, is believed to have absorbed aboriginal elements from the very beginning. As the later Úiva with his Phallic symbol became more like a Dravidian demon than an Aryan god, likewise, the Rgvedic Rudra became the most demoniac of all the early gods.[31] The concept of Rudra-Úiva in a combined form based on both the Kirâta and Âryan elements gradually evolved as one of the popular religious cults of the Hindus in ancient India.[32] The borrowing of the cerebral consonantal sounds from the non Âryan speech resulted in the modification of the Rgvedic god Rudrâ and in the germination of the concept of theism. Thus a non-Âryan institution (in the mixed Aryo-aboriginal form) was later completely absorbed in Indian religious life.[33]

An allusion to Sisnadevah (the worshipper of the god Sisna or Phallus) in the Vedic text[34] has been interpreted by different scholars in different ways. It is very difficult to determine as to whether the worshippers of this god were Âryan under the influence of pre-Âryan cults or non-Âryans in origin or Barbarians. However, this has been suggested that the worshippers of this god were considered hostile to Aryans. Because the warrior Indra was slaying all those hostile forces whose god was the Sisna.[35] If this interpretation of the Rgvedic evidence is correct, we have every reason to believe that Liñga as a deity was worshipped by the pre-Âryan people, who were at war with the Brâhmanas. Anyway, the disapproval of the Phallic cult by the orthodox section of the Rgvedic Âryan vindicates the worship of the Phallus by the Pre-Âryan aborigines. The conception of Siva as the Supreme Being, and of Phallus worship arose outside the pale of Vedism. Macdonell, while supporting this view observed "The Âryans in course of time adopted the cult of Phallus from the non-Âryans and started worshipping them".[36] The worship of Siva in the form of Phallus represents a remnant of the ante-Brâhmanical religion of India. Linga worship became quite popular before the commencement of the Christian era. However, the Phallic worship among the pre-Âryan Kirâta tribes in the form of stone is in approximation to the truth, if it is not conclusive.

The history of the origin of the Phaliic emblems is a veiled in mystery. It renders it extremely difficult to present a clear account of its origin. Its origin was more philosophical than mysterious.[37] The Phallic symbol of Úiva is intimately associated with the mysterious upright conical stones (set up on the ground like the Menhirs), the Cylindrical stone pieces, the Phallus stone fixed in a Yoni, burial stones, dolmens and other megalithic stone memorials of the Kirâta tribes of prehistoric Age. This practice represents the pre-Vedic and pre-Brahmanic tradition of India. The Phallic cult is also believed to be of Austric or proto-Austroloid origin. The remains of various stone objects in North-East India belonging to Austric Khasi and other Kirâta tribes constitute an evidence of the existence of cult of linga and yoni in the Neolithic Age. Jean Przyluski has suggested that the word Liñga is equivalent to 'Lakuta' and 'Langula' of Austric origin. The *Zoomorphic divinities* or the lower animals typifying the forces of nature and supplying symbols or figures for the supernatural or the god-head seems to have been known to the Aryans to a limited extent. The *Zoomorphic deities* came into prominence in the days of Purânic Hinduism. As a matter of fact, there was a gradual shift from abstract symbolism to anthropomorhic iconography. The aboriginal practice was symbolized in a modified form and incorporated into Hinduism.

The non-Aryan tribal practices of worshipping the Phallic emblem was very much similar to the worship of the Phallus of Orisis in ancient Egypt, Priapus in ancient Greece Mylitta (the goddess of fertility), in ancient Babylon and of the phallic emblem Mutinus in ancient Rome.[38]

The clear conception of Úiva arose in the Upanisadic age. Siva has been, for the first time, explicitly mentioned as an Âryan god in the *Úvetâsvatara Upaniṣad* in the background of Yoni-Linga relationship.[39] Herein Rudra is equated with Siva and Mahesvara. There are some vague references to this god in the *Maitryânîya Upaniúad* too. He is abundantly extolled in many parts of the *Mahâbhârata*. We don't find any positive evidence of the worship of Phallus symbol or Úva in ancient Indian literature anterior to the *Mahâbhârata*. The assimilation of the Kirâta god-Úiva was not even complete in the age of Patañjali. Because in his commentary on Pânini's *Aúṭâdhyâyi*[40] he, instead of including Úiva in the list of main gods mentions him as a folk god or *laukika-devatah*. He has not referred to the Phallic cult, which indicate that linga-worship was not widely prevalent during his time. It can be deduced that by the first century B.C. the worship of Úivaliñga became acceptable, to a large section of the Indian people.

If the literary evidence furnished above is properly analysed one can get the result that before the Vedic, Upânisadic, epic and later concepts of Úiva in both human and phallic forms emerged amongst the Âryans and the Hindus, the non-Aryan Kirata tribes had adopted the Úaiva and phallic cults.

The growth of Úiva-Liñga concept was in the ascending order from the lower level to the higher level. Úva was gradully exalted to higher position in the Hindu pantheon.

The views held by Sir John Marshall[41] and others[42] that the ancient Úaiva, Phallus and mother goddess cults are of pre-

Aryan Dravidian origin of Chalcolithic Age and the Aryans borrowed these cults from Dravidians, are not absolutely correct. This can't be accepted in toto, because the Indo-Aryan, not only came into contact with the Dravidians but also with other non-Aryan Kirâta group of people.

Thus it will not be very logical to suggest that only the Dravidians were the founders of these cults. We have already seen that the pre-Dravidian Kirata tribes had popularised these cults much earlier.[43]

It is true that one of the seals discovered in an excavation at Mohenjodaro showing the figure of one male god looking like Úiva seated in Yogic posture surrounded by animals with three visible faces and two horns adorning the head having the marking of ithyphallic (urdhva lingâ) as well as the archaeological discovery of other objects at Mohenjodaro and Harappa to attest to the prevalence of proto-Saiva cults, phallic cult and mother-goddess cult, but they apparently explain the later conception of Úiva (based on Pâúupata cult) representing the earliest school of Saivism and that of other cults. We find that there were different phases and schools of the growth of Úaiva cult. Historically speaking, the worship of Úiva became popular in different forms at different times. K.A. Nilakantha Sastri has rightly stated that "Úaivism is not a 'single cult, but a federation of allied cults."[44] And one of these cults also flourished among the mountainous Kirâta tribes at a stage when the idea of any particular school of religion was conspicuous by its absence.

N.N. Law has also maintained that the "Mother-Goddess Cult is pre-Aryan elements in the Indian culture. The cult of Liñga and Yoni (Úaiva-Úâkta principle) worshipped is an anthropomorphic, form is older than the Chalcolithic age of Mohenjodaro. Phallus worship played an important role in the religious and magical ideology of the pre-Aryan and non-Aryan peoples of India. The cult of Liñga became embedded in Brahmanism in the Epic period."[45]

It is now an accepted fact that the non-Aryan or non-Vedic and aboriginal elements largely contributed to the worship of Úiva and Úakti or mother-goddess by the followers of the Brahmanical religion and culture. The Úakti and mother-goddess cults of the Hindus are largely based on the traditions followed by non-Aryan Kirâta tribes. The history of evolution of the Úakti cult, goes back to pre-Vedic times. The concept of Úakti identified with the cult of mother-goddess flourished in all ancient societies, particularly in the Neolithic society. The pre-dominance of the female principles in the tribal societies of the Neolithic Age became very helpful factor in the popularity of worship of the mother-goddess among the Hindus. The cult of the mother-goddess as such was originally known to the matrilineal aboriginal Kirâtas, but not to the Aryans, who were basically a patrilincal people. The origin of the idea of the female principle can be traced back to the pre-Vedic tribal tradition. That is why, it is generally admitted that the cult of mother-goddess is a legacy of the pre-Vedic culture. The historical development of the Úakti cult clearly shows, that the Phallic emblem and its feminine counterparts sublimated into symbols of energy helped in the growth of the higher forms of Hindu religion.

It has been rightly observed that in the later Vedic and historical periods there were definite attempts at assimilating the mother-goddess cult based on primitive conception and giving it a definite shape. Significantly enough, the mother-goddess initially worshipped in symbolic forms in the caves and forests by the non-Vedic and non-Brahmanic peoples living in the forests and hilly regions of India found expression in various iconographic forms worshipped in the Puranic and Brahmanic traditions. That is why, it is said that the Hindus are indebted to them for the popularity of the cult of Úakti.[46]

The Úakti was particularly worshipped by the chief aboriginal races like the Kirâtas, Úabaras, Pulindas, and Barbaras (Barbara-Kirâtas) of Northern, Eastern, Central and Southern India. Thus they supplied a strong foundation for the supposition that the cult of Devi or of the Female Energy arose among the non-Âryan aboriginal tribes and was not imported into this country by the victorious Âryans. The Úakti cult became known to the Âryans later and made an entry into their philosophical theories naturally in a considerably modified form.

The 'Mongoloid' Kirâtas of North East India are credited with having started several Tantric practices in the early period. The

Tântric religion based on aboriginal ideas and forms of worship further flourished among the Hindus and Buddhists in ancient India. The antiquity and original provenance of Tântri-cism and Úaktism arc of course, debatable questions. However, it will be a mistake to suppose that the 'Sakta system began to appear from a time not very much earlier than the 6th century A.D.[47] In this connection the observation made by R.C. Hazra that the Úakta philosophy and Tântric system which often went against the Brâhmanical ideas and practices attained recognition not earlier than the 9th century A.D.[48] seems to be more convincing. Because the tribal system prevailing earlier to these centuries were further systematized, developed and perfected by the time of composition of Tântra literature.

Úaivism and Úaktism, mixed with varied forms of Tântric rituals attained great popularity among the Kirâta tribes and further paved the way for an emergence of Tântric cult. The non-Âryan Tântric cult—a system of magical or sacramental ritual associated with magic, sorcery, witchcraft, exorcism, etc. conditioned the development of the doctrine of Vedic, kârmâkanda, which after being accepted by the Aryanised race further got manifested in the Vajrayana cult of Buddhism. Tantricism got intermixed with Vajrayana cult of Buddhism probably during the 8th to 12th century A.D. P. Bhattacharyya[49] observes that it was during the Pala rule that Kâmâkhyâ became the centre of Tântric Buddhism.

The theory propounded by Nandlal Dey,[50] that the Tantricism as an offshoot of Buddhism of Mahayana School developed about the ninth century under the Pala rulers of Magadha and from the ancient Buddhist university of Vikram-úilâ (near Modern Bhagalpur in Bihar) the Tantric doctrines spread into Kâmârupa and Tibet, can fairly be disputed on the basis of the statements made by E. Gait[51] and Charles Eliot,[52] who held that this doctrine originated in North-East India. Both the scholars have contradicted the former's view and stated that the birth place of Úaktism and Tântricism as definite sects seems to have been North East India, which was inhabited by tribes belonging to Monkhmer (the Austric khasi) and Tibeto-Burman families. This region was neither a land of ancient Brâhmanic settlement nor a centre of Vedic and Purânic learning. This is indeed, a fact that the Kirâta people of North-East India played a positive role in shaping the structure of the Brâhmanical, Vedic and Purânic doctrines in the realm of religion and philosophy.

The Tântric cult, of course, received great impetus from the Kirâta people of North-East India in the beginning. The Aryans became familiar with this cult afterwards. Many Tântras present it in a refined form of Úaktism and modified form of Úaivism in conformity with ordinary Hindu usuage. Some of its features are indubitably connected with aboriginal cults. Both Tantricism and the ghastly rites of the Kapalikas originated from Úaivism and it is now accepted by most of the scholars that the Vedic Aryans coming into India found a crude form of Úaivism associated perhaps with human sacrifices.

E. Gait[53] confidently remarks that the Úâktism was the predominant form of Hinduism in Assam. Its adherents base their observances on the Tântras—a series of religious works in which the various ceremonies, prayers and incantations are prescribed in a dialogue between Úiva and his wife Parvati. The fundamental idea behind it is the worship of the female principle, the procreative power of nature as menifested by personified desire. It is a religion of bloody sacrifices from which even human beings were not exempted. He further observes that "the old tribal beliefs are gradually being abandoned and the way in which Hindu priests established their influence over non-Âryan chiefs and gradually drew within their fold is repeatedly exemplified in the pages of Assam history."[34]

S.K. Chatterji has also expressed the view that "these Kirâtas or "Indo-Mongoloids", i.e. Mongoloids of India might very well have come to India before the Âryans and they contributed a great deal in the evolution of Hindu history and culture in North-East and Eastern India."[55]

The statement made by N.N. Vasu is. befitting to the context in which the subject matter has been explained. To quote him :

"Assam may be looked upon as a federation hall, where the most ancient and the most modern, the most antiquated and the most up-to-date are found to meet together upon terms of perfect cordiality. The followers of all the schools of philosophy —the Vedic, the Purânic and the Tântric have thrived here equally well and people of all races, Âryans and Non-Âryans, Hindus and

Non-Hindus have equally contributed to the building up of the social fabric of Kamarupa. In a word, with the ancient history of this glorious land is indissolubly bound up the social, religious and the rational history of the whole of India."[56]

It is worthwhile to note that the religio-cultural and philosophical patterns of India distinctly appear to be a curious blend or queer mixture of both the Âryan and non-Âryan elements. The assimilation of non-Âryans' (including the Kirâtas) religious conceptions embodying polytheistical beliefs, animistic beliefs, superstitious beliefs, propitiation of both benevolent and malevolent spirits, supernatual objects, heavenly bodies, natural phenomena and other innumerable gods and goddesses having the anthropomorphic attributes based on magico-religious system, eschatological belief, the crude forms of worship, esoteric beliefs, totemism, the ideas connected with transmigration, monotheism or in the words of Max Muller, henotheism, the doctrine of Âtman, the law of Karma and metempsychosis, ritualism, priesthood, sacrifices, fetishism, omens and divination and other indigenous faiths into the Aryan religious system seems to be a cardinal feature of Indian civilization.

Úaivism, Úaktism and Tantricism, which emerged as popular religious cults in ancient India co-existed with the aboriginal forms of worship and further flourished after coming within the pale of Âryanisation. The Âryans further systematized, perfected and popularised the system. A large number of scholars is of the opinion that all the ideas connected with Hindu religion and culture are conspicuous by their absence in the Vedas can be attributed to the non-Âryans. Most of the non-Âryan faiths and ideas were absorbed by the Aryans. As a result of this cultural interaction a new concept emerged in the domain of religion, populalry known as *proto-Hinduism* which combined in itself the intermittent character of Hinduism. We have every reason to believe that the concepts stemming from pre-Âryan civilization have found their way into Hindu doctrines, thoughts and scriptures exactly like that of assimilation of the concepts of orthodox Hinduism into the religious system of the primitive tribes of our country. Several Upanisadic, Vedic and Puranic doctrines and even the Vedantic philosophy have got pre-Aryan features.[57]

The literary, religious and cultural traditions of India have many masters. The Vedic system of religion represents the growth of many centuries and the deities of Vedic pantheon are the deities of many tribes. Some of them are simply personifications of the phenomena of nature clothed with a thin veil of anthropomorphic form. For an instance, the Mother-Earth or Earth Goddess worshipped by the Kiratas was very much worshipped in the Vedic system. The combined primitive religious and social ideas of the Kirâtas and Vedic Âryans found expression in the classic form of Brâhmanic culture.

The moulding of early Vedic society, religion and culture by different races has already been accepted.[58] The classical scholars have also recognised the fact that religion and philosophy with all its blessed advantage to man, flourished long ago among the barbarians diffusing the light among many.[59] "The Indian philosophical ideas and Upanisadic doctrines, which are the results of long period of elaboration, represent the highest phase of interpreted by Âryan and the lowest phase of essentially non-Âryan pre-dominated."[60] The Vedic religion absorbed, embodied and preserved the types and rituals of other cults. Instead of destroying them it adapted them to its own requirements. It took so much from Dravidian and other inhabitants of India that it is very difficult to disentangle the original Âryan element from the other."[61]

The positive contribution of the Kirâtas in the long historic process of building up the socio-cultural fabric of India and giving the concrete shape to Indian civilization appears to be the distinguishing hall-mark of their history and culture. The truth contained in the statement finds reflection in the remarks of S.K. Chatterji. He observes: "When the Âryans came into India, the country was not a no-man's land—it was already populated by some races or peoples which had risen to a high level of civilization...the new materials and the new orientation show that the credit for building up Indian civilization is not the Âryans' alone, but that the non-Âryans in India had a share, and that too, the larger share, in supplying the bases, the latter in some parts of the country having been in possession of material civilization far in advance of what the Âryan, who was but a nomadic barbarian in front of the town-dwelling, non-Âryan, could show. It is now becoming more and more clear that the non-Âryan contributed by far the greater portion in the fabric of Indian civilization, and a great deal of Indian religious and cultural traditions, of ancient legend and history, is just non-Âryan translated in terms of the Âryan speech—as it was the Âryan's speech that became the dominant factor, although non-Âryan elements made very large inroads into as 'purity...the ideas of *Karma* and transmigration, the practice of Yoga, the religious and philosophical ideas centering round the conception of the Divinity as Úiva and Devi and as Viṣṇu, the Hindu ritual of Puja as opposed to the Vedic ritual of homa—all 'these and much more in Hindu religion and thought would appear to be non-Âryan in origin. A great deal of Puranic and epic myth, legend and semi-history is pre-Âryan; much of our material culture and social and other usages—e.g. the cultivation of some of our most important plants like rice and some vegetables and fruits like the tamarind and the coconut etc. the use of the betel-leaf in Hindu life and Hindu ritual, most of our popular religion, most of our folk crafts, other nautical crafts, our distinctive Hindu dress (the *dhoti* and the *sari),* our marriage ritual in some parts of India with the use of the vermillion and turmeric—and many other things would appear to be a legacy from our pre-Âryan ancestors."[62] He has expressed more or less similar views in his other works.[63]

The truth relating to the contribution of the non-Âryans in general to the evolution of Indian religion and culture has also been confirmed by other competent scholars like S. Radhakrishnan,[64] Tylor[65], Atkinson[66], Romila Thapar[67], P. Mitra,[68] S.K. De,[69] Ramdhari Singh Dinkar[70] and others.

The non-Âryan forms of belief having origin in or beyond the Himalaya have influenced the religious system of India from the earliest ages to the present day. The structure of non-Indian Hindudom is largely based on the primitive beliefs. The Âryan religion has been modified not only by Dravidian elements but also by Austric, Mongoloids and the Kirâta elements, to a considerable extent. There are sufficient indications of the non-Âryan influences exerted on the growth of Hindu civilization. The Austric section of the Kirâtas also described as the proto-Australoid contributed a major share to the introduction of many new religious practices and the evolution of new concepts, which were later adopted by the Âryans. The origin of many Brahmanical Hindu gods and goddesses as well as the emergence of the cult of mother goddess may be traced back to the primitive age, which in characterised by many new religious experiments conducted by the non-Ârayan people described in classical and Indian literature as the Kirâtas. Many gods and goddesses of the non-Âryan Kirâtas later on got recognition in the Hindu pantheon of the Âryavarta. The beliefs, practices and religious thoughts as recorded in the Vedic literature contain both the Aryan and non-Aryan elements. The synthesis of Âryan and and non-Âryan faiths constituted the backbone of the Hindu philosophy.

The manners and customs unrecorded in the Hindu scripture but practiced by the Hindus, are mainly the non-Aryan. The heterogeneous elements are not only discernible in the population structure of India, but also in its religious and cultural system. The assimilation of different races in the Hindu religion and culture led to the evolution of polytheism. The practice of worshipping the female energy and Úakti, Candika "Devi, trees, spirits of hills, forests, rivers, streams, the custom of disposing of the dead body by exposing it to the wind, the system of sacrifice and offerings etc. are all the remnants of the Kirâta civilization, which spread from Bengal to Arakan. The Âryans subsequently accepted these faiths in a considerably modified form. J. Talboys-Wheeler[71] has strongly supported this view. He has remarked that the origin of the religion of the Âryans is quite different from that of the Dravidian people. The Âryan religion may possibly have been a development of the ancient worship of the *genii-Loci*—the spirits of hills, forests, glens, etc. The religious practices of the primitive hill tribes find the highest expression in the doctrines of the Âryans.

One of the noteworthy features of their contribution to the development of Hindu religion and culture is the adoption by the Brâhmanas of the system of worshipping the Kirâta devî and Gramadevata or village gods and goddesses propitiated by the Kirâtas in ancient times. The Grâmadevatapratistha[72] mentions as Grâmadevatas the Kirâtadevi, Bhûtas, Pretas, Piúacas, Yaksas, Rudra, and other village gods and goddesses. A closer inquiry into this subject discloses the fact that the Gramadevta, the principal tutelary deity of the village adored by the Kiratas, is the personation of the Female Energy as represented by Mother Earth, the power, i.e., Úakti and other superior forces venerated in different localities retaining their local supremacy. The concept of the worship of the Grâmadevatas first became popular among the Kirâtas. This exercised a considerable influence on the Brâhmanic element. It has forced its way gradually into the very heart of the Âryan worship which eventually underwent a thorough change through amalgamation of various other popular.doctrines. The Âryan and non-Âryan practices got blended in such a manner that the purity of its system disappeared and it became difficult to keep the two currents asunder and to discover the original source. A new belief in the Brahmanic religion of our day which partly rests on non-Aryan ideas was substituted in its stead. The Brahmanas were found openly participating in the unhallowed proceedings at the festivals of the village-goddesses and defending their action. As a result of influx of non-Âryan tenets in the pure Vedic doctrine and contact of the Kirâtas with the Âryan ideas not only have males intruded into the once exclusively female circles of Grâmadevatas, but also a motley of queer figures have crept in forming, indeed, a very very strange gathering. The existence of the Grâmadevatas (originally conceived by the Kiratas) among the poorest class of the Hindu population, where the most faithful devotees, can be proved by the popularity, which it acquired in great number of their shrines, their temples, sacred grove and hamlet located both within and outside the village. Every villager, man or woman started taking personal interest in the worship of Grâmadevatâs. Visnavas, Sâktas, Kapalikas and Ganapatas became the devotees of the Grâmadevâta. Actually, such kind of practice percolated to the lower levels in the society.

E.A. Gait,[73] while supporting this idea, has observed that pre-Âryan beliefs have not yet completely died out which is shown by the fact that even now many villages have their sacred grove and their Gramadevatâs to whom they venerate with sacrifice.

It is also worth-mentioning that the contact of the non-Âryan population with the Âryans since the dawn of the Vedic age provided an opportunity for both to be influenced, by each other in the domain of religion and culture. Since the Kirâtas, later described as "Indo-Mongoloids," have been mentioned in both thi *Yajurveda* and *Atharvaveda,* it would not be unreasonable to assume that the Âryans—the follower of the Vedic religion, and the Kirâtas might have borrowed the essence of the religious and cultural ideas from each other. It can also reasonably be pointed out that as a result of this mutual contact and cultural intercourse not only the beliefs and ideas of the Âryans were affected, but the chief features of their deities were also modified to a considerable degree by the pre-Âryan population of the primitive age Thus, the Âryan faiths further underwent transformation. Some of them are not easily perceptible.

Atkinson observes that the hill tribes of Northern Himalaya the Kiratas, the Khasa, the Nâgâs, Cinas and others had attained to certain degree of civilization in some respect superior to that reached by the Âryans of the Vedic age.[74] But this statement smacks of some exaggeration. Because, the question of superiority of one culture over the other cannot be raised in context of ancient Indian History. Each race contributed its might to the evolution of composite culture of India. Moreover, that was not the age of competition but rather of co-ordination and cultural interaction between the people of various races representing different grades of culture.

The process of Âryanization which set in the greater parts of Northern and Eastern India tentatively in the first millennium B.C. facilitated the commingling of both the Âryans and the non-Âryans. Many non-Aryan elements in the field of religion and philosophy were Aryanised and later incorporated in the body of composite Indian culture. The early contacts of the Kirâtas with the Vedic Âryans contributed several factors to the synthesis of culture. This synthesis went on at a faster speed throughout the pre-Christian centuries and it was well-nigh complete before the dawn of the historical period In order to avoid confusion, and mis-understanding it must be made clear that the composite culture in India had not taken the shape unifonnally. It had taken its earliest shape in North-Eastern India, but in other parts of India this culture flourished at comparatively later age, so far as the impact of the Kirâtas' contribution on the Âryans and Hindus are concerned.

The Kiratas' influence on Hindu religion and culture can be discussed from different angles. Not only North-Eastern region, but also some parts of Northern and Southern India were affected by the Kirâta culture. The Hindu pantheon entered upon a new phase of orientation after being modified by the non-Âryan neighbours. The most abiding gift of intrinsic value, which the Kirâta gave to this country, was in the shape of a new deity to the Hindu pantheon. The epigraphic records as well as literary evidences confirm this truth. It is quite obvious that the goddess, with the Kirâtas and the Kindred tribes worshipped was Candika, which finds expression in the fierce forms of Durgâ and Kâli. The Candikâ and Vindhyavasin were the favourite deities of those Kirâtas, who had settlement in the Vindhyan forest. The epigraphic record[75] dated A.D. 943 of Pallava-king Diliparasa supplies indirect evidence of worship of Candika among the Kirâtas of South.

The Kirâtas of Videha, Nepal, Uttarakhanda and Rajasthan also played conspicuous role in the growth of the cult of Úaivism, which can be fairly attested to by their religious rites and rituals performed in primitive style to propitiate Lord Úiva. The method and style of their worshipping the gods and goddesses, their custom of sacrifice and offerings, etc., were handed down to the Aryan Hindus in a much more refined form. This development, was effected by a two-fold reason. Firstly, the Âryans in the wake of their frequent contacts with the non-Âryans borrowed from them such religious beliefs as were very much popular and such customs as were very much in vogue among them. Secondly, after the Âryan occupation of the areas, which were the seats of the Kirâta culture, the religious practices of the non-Âryan population found some place in the newly modified form of Hindu religion.

The Indian society and economy are also based to some extent, on non-Âryan elements. The food habits, dress pattern, social customs, manners and practices, etc. of the Âryan were greatly modified as a result of widespread racial mixture. The head turban and loin-cloth which later came in popular use are believed to have been bequeathed to the Hindus by the non-Âryan population. However, we don't have any positive proof of their contribution to socio-economic development of India.

In the political field the early Kiratas' conceptions of exogamous units, clans, families and villages laid the firm foundation of organized civil administration and it influenced the political evolution of the Vedic ¿ryans regarding their formation of groups, the family (grha or Kula), the village (grama), the canton or clan (vis), the people (Jana) and the country. This became possible only due to their early mutual cultural contacts. It may be quite heartening to note that the age old and time-honoured self-governing republican institutions of the Kirâta tribes, unaffected by manifold social changes and political turmoils in course of long passage of time covering many centuries or millenniums and practically escaping the fall into general complex dynamic process of transition from monarchy to aristocracy and on to democracy—a thesis, antithesis and synthesis, greatly influenced the Hindu and Buddhist polity and administration from the Vedic Age down to 600 B.C. in particular and the political system of ancient India in general.

We have some recorded evidence to show the contribution of the Kirata people to the artistic growth of India. It is worthy of note that the Indian art and architecture in ancient times was fundamentally based on traditional system. The Kirâta tribes laid the foundation of an artistic culture, non-Âryan in form with little touch of Hindu art, on which edifices of other schools of art and architecture have been erected. They carried most of the arts of common life to high perfection. The relics, monoliths and monuments of the Kirâta tribes of ancient Assam, (particularly that of the Khasis and the Jaintias)—consisting of sepulchral monuments like cairns, dolmens, menhirs, cromlechs, upright stones and other huge blocks of stone or memorial stones popularly known as Megaliths bearing carving of figures, geometrical patterns, animals, birds, etc. and depiction of interesting drawings and designs of antiquarian interest constituted the earliest specimens of art of Neolithic Age. This became the source of inspiration for the Âryan population, who followed them and came into their contact. The architecture and sculpture also received the impetus from the Kiratas of Nepal to a considerable degree.

Generally speaking, the early artistic experiments conducted by the non-Âryan population further led to the evolution of various architectural and sculptural designs. It will not be an exaggeration to state that the attainment of their high degree of perfection in the field of architecture, graphic sculpture, drawings, art, iconography, decorative arts, pottery or ceramic arts, etc. contributed a lot to the enrichment of Indian art and architecture. Striking similarity between the non-Âryan art of ancient Assam and the contemporary Eastern school of Bihar, Orissa and Pala-Sena art of Bengal can be noticed. They carried most of the arts of common life to high perfection.

While highlighting the participation of contribution of the 'Indo-Mongoloid' Kirâtas in the evolution of Indian history and culture, S.K. Chatterji has opined that one can find certain types of artistic expression in the fine arts and the crafts, architecture, sculpture and painting, decoration, textile arts (in both cotton and silk), etc. of the advanced section of the Indo-Mongoloids like the Newars, the Tipras, the Kacharis and others.[76] The mentality, attitudes towards life and emotional quality of the Indo-Mongoloid peoples are reflected in the changes that occurred in the history of Hindu art and culture.

The Indian art is apparently, a synthesis of both Âryan and non-Âryan elements. S. Kramrisch,[77] has correctly pointed out that the various racial factors have determined the art history of India as a whole.

Their contribution to the growth of language and literature in ancient India are also of considerable importance. Quite a good number of words from the Austric or Mon-Khmer language basically spoken by the Khasis (one of the important sections of the Kirâtas of North-East India) got absorbed in the Indo-Âryan language and literature primarily because of the synthesis, that took place in India, of different cultures represented by both Âryans including the Kirâtas. Before the advent of the Âryans in India, the Austric language was in use. Thus, in all probability, the Âryans might have adopted the language of their predecessors, which can be seen in their vocabulary concerning flora and fauna. It began to take a new shape few centuries before Christ. We don't have clear cut proof of the influence of the Kirâta language on the Vedic Sanskrit. However, this development opened up a new vista in the linguistic and cultural history of India. The contribution of the

Kirâtas to the development of Prâkrt speeches in ancient India has not yet received its due recognition. The development of the Prakrt dialect is ascribed entirely to the inability of the conquered population to reproduce precisely the speech of the invaders.[78]

The different forms of speech used by pre-Dravidian Kirâta tribes were borrowed by their successors. Several Austro-Asiatic words were borrowed by the Aryans from the so-called Austric tribes.[79] The growth of Austric language (e.g. spoken by the Khâsis of north-east) is described as one of the specific contributions of primitive races of India to linguistic and cultural elements.[80]

The languages belonging to four different families—the Âryan, the Dravidian, "the Sino-Tibetan or Mongoloid Kirâta" and Austric developed side by side by the dawn of third millennium B.C. and profoundly influenced each other, as a result of which the basic character of various forms of speech were subsequently modified.[81]

The absorption of Tibeto-Burman speaking Kirata tribes into an Aryan speaking Indian body-politic inevitably resulted in the evolution of Âryan language in Assam, Bengal and Nepal.

B.K. Kakati in his thesis has clearly stated that both Austrics and Bodos have contributed words to Assamese vocabulary. Kâmâkhya and Kâmarûpa may be sanskritization of non-Âryan words "Khamoch" and "Kâmarût" respectively.[82] Thus we find that the words used by the non-Âryan people went a long way in the formation of the Aryan language. The French indologists, named Przyluski, Block, S. Levi and others, notably, Prof. T. Burrow, have also dealt with the Austro-Asiatic influences on Sanskrit.

Equally great is the influence which they exerted on the Indian Historical tradition and secular literature. The Vedic and Puranic myths and legends are not only the inventions of the Aryâns' mind, but the joint creation of the Kirâtas and the Aryans. The stories as narrated in the Puranic literature, the Upanisads, the Smrtis and the Buddhist Jâtakas are principally based on the folk-tales and legendary episodes of different Kirata tribes, particularly the Austric group. The historical traditions, ballads and songs current among the non-Âryans were recorded in the vernacular forms of the Âryans and then altered to Sanskrit, which formed the nucleus of the *Puranas* and the *Mahâbhârata*.

It does not strike any wonder as to why the Kirata stories have survived, notwithstanding, their Âryanisation in the linguistic field and the Hinduisation in the realm of religion. A great many of the pre-Âryan myths and cults found a secured place within the fold of Hinduism in an accidental manner. The cosmogenic conceptions of Hinduism are largely of pre-Âryan or Kirata origin. The beliefs connected with the aboriginal forms of worship, rites and rituals, sacrifices and offerings, etc. were incorporated in the body of the Purânic tales.[83]

The myths and legends, folklores and folk-tales, the poetry and songs of the Kirâtas paved the way for the evolution of Hindu myths, legends and cults as found in the legendary history of India. The Kirâta genius in literature found expression in folk-literature and lyrics, which are primitive and unsophisticated. The folk-tales of Mikir tribe relating to Harata Kunwar comparable to that of Pururavas and Urvaúî found in Indo-Âryan myth, Kachari story of the Merchant lad, Garo story of Gunal and his wife the bird maiden singwil, the folk-tales of the Nâgâs, etc. are some of the interesting examples of the Kirata folk-tales of North-East India, which found their place in Hindu mythology. Some scholars have gone to the extent of presuming that even the story of Rama is also based on the popular folk-tales of the Austrics.

However, it is undeniable that as a result of commingling of the Âryans, the Austrics, so-called Nisâdas the Kirâtas, so-called Indo-Mongoloids and the Dravidians, their folk-tales were given recognition by each other which no doubt, influenced the *Itihasa-Purâna Smrtis, Daúanas* (philosophical thoughts) and the Sanskrit literature, to a limited extent.

"Sino-Tibetan mongoloid" Kirâtas living in India from time immemorial like other primitive races furnished in India a slight "Modicum" of folk literature, songs, tales legends, etc. The tradition developed in these languages but these were never written down as the practice of systematic writing had not evolved.[84]

One of the notable contributions of the Kirâtas to Indian History and culture was the introduction of the system of writing. The Buddhist text, *Lalitauistara,* in its famous list of 64 writings, attributes special writings to the Kiratas. The literary evidence can be further confirmed by the statement of Sylvain Levi, which runs as follows : "In fact, the Kirâta attributes to their hero Srijanga-the invention of special writing.[85]

Lohangsena, a Kirâta chief of Mithila region, is believed to have introduced the Kirâta script in Mithila and Nepal the two another premier centres of Kirâta culture in early India. But it is not yet known as to what extent this change affected the course of the growth of Âryan language in these belts and how long this script was in use? Because no positive evidence is available to this effect.

Though the evidence adduced here in support of the contribution of the Kiratas to Indian Palaeography does not seem to be satisfactory yet the importance of their early system of writing will secure a place in the history of evolution of writings in ancient India.

From the foregoing account of the subject it is quite evident that the Kiratas, by and large, contributed in the different fields of Indian History and culture. The views put forth by S.K. De in this regard deserve our attention. According to him "not only in the socio-economic sphere but also in the more important branch of the religious beliefs, nay in the whole field of Indian culture, the non-Âryans have really contributed to and laid the foundation of Modern Hinduism whether in India or Assam and many-survivals of non-Aryan cults may still be traced".[86]

Notes and References

1. ISIH., p. 27, see also his CCAI., p. 28.
2. (*a*) *Bâla Kâṇḍa*, 55, 3-4.
   (*b*) VRK.; p. 61. See also M. Krishnamachariar, HCSL., pp. Intr. IX-ixi.
3. *Âdi Parvâ,* 165, 36-38.
4. (*a*) *Sabhâ Parvâ* (Digvijaya Parva), 23, 17-20.
   (*b*) *Udyoga Parva*, 19, 14-15.
   See also V.S. Agrawala, *Bhârata Sâvitri,* Vol. 2. p. 40.
   (*c*) *Aśvamedha Parva*, 72, 24.
   (*d*) *Mbh. Ko.,* pp. 28, 190-91, 460.
5. *Drona Parva;* 19, 17-20; 25, 31, & 35; 26, 2 & 4; 27, 14 & 26; 28, 1,6,9, 10-11, 44.

6. *Bhisma Parva* (Bhagavad Gita Parva), 20.13. See also P.C. Roy (Eng. tr.): *Mbh. Bhisma Parva,* Vol. V, See XX. p. 45.
7. PC Roy (Eng. tr.): *Drona Parva,* CXII, pp. 349f.
8. *Karnâ Parva,* (XXII, p. 271).
9. *Bhisma Parva,* L.P. 186.
10. *Mudrârâksasa* (Trans. by Satyavrata Singh with Sanskrit and Hindi commentaries), Act. ii, p. 89; See also the text trans. and annotated by M.R. Kale, f.n. pp. 24-26.
11. (*a*) IA. JOR., (edtd. by JAS. Burgess), 1877, Vol. VI, pp. 113ff.
    (*b*) B.A. Saletore, WTIH, p. 34.
    (*c*) A.K. Majumdar, EHID., Vol. II, p. 512.
12. WTIH., p. 34.
13. AIMA., Introd., f.n. pp. 11-12.
14. MI., p. 18.
15. Ind. Alt. Vol. II, pp. 641ff. cf. AIK., p. 90.
16. VII, VS. 109-115, pp. 193-95, ref. to B.A. Saletore, WTIH., p. 22.
17. PAHCI., pp. 6, 11.
18. JARS, July 1939, Vol. VII, No. 2, p. 35.
19. G.P. Singh, *"The Genesis and Growth of Tribal Civilization in North India"* (From Pre-Historic times to the 12th century A.D.), cf. QRHS., 1980-81, Vol. XX, No. 4, pp. 13-14.
20. *Secret Lands Where Women Reign,* pp. 13-14.
21. E.B. Tylor, *Primitive Culture,* Vol. II, p. 164.
22. EIP., pp. 158-59.
23. MI., (QAJ)., 1922, Vol. II, No. 3, p. 150; T.C. Hodson (*The Naga tribes of Manipur,* pp. 70f).
24. Quoted in JARS, July 1939, Vol. VII, No. 2, p. 37.
25. (*a*) G.P. Singh, *The Genesis and Growth of Tribal Culture and Civilization in North-East India* (From pre-historic times to the 12th century A.D.), JISR., Jan., 1981, Vol. I, pp. 29-30.
    (*b*) B.K. Kakati, *The Mother Goddess Kamakhya,* pp. 5-6, 10-16, 37.
    (*c*) R.M. Nath, BAC., pp. 4, 17, 95, 97, 99, 105.
    (*d*) G. Bertrand, *op. cit.,* pp. 171-73.
26. (*a*) KAL., (Original Sanskrit text with Parallel Hindi trans. edtd. by Chamanlal Gautam), Vol. I, vs. 100-118, 125-26, pp. 497-501.
    (*b*) JARS., 1962 (pub. 1964), Vol. XIV, p. 61.

(*c*) B.K. Kakati, *op. cit.,* pp. 100-18.

(*d*) R.M. Nath, BAC., pp. 4, 17, 95.

27. *Hinduism and Buddhism,* Vol. II, p. 274.
28. RATA., 1905 cf. Home 'B' Progs nos. 702-708. File No. V.A.8.
29. JARS., 1962, Vol. XVI, (pud. 1964), pp. 22-23.
30. JARS., July 1938, Vol. VI, no. I, pp. 8-9.
31. H.D. Griswold, RRV., p. 293.
32. R.G. Bhandarkar, VSMRS., pp. 102f; De La Saussaye, MSR., pp. 639f.
33. D.C. Sircar, *The Sâkta-Pithas,* pp. 100-101.
34. RV., VII. 3. 21. 5 ; X. 8.99.3.
35. J. Muir, OST., Vol. IV, pp. 345-46.
36. H.S.L., p. 154. Mr. Stevenson, JRAS., Vol. VIII, pp. 330-339. See also Prof. Lassen-Ind. Ait., Vol. 1, pp. 924-925, old edition p. 783.
37. Edward Moor, *The Hindu Pantheon,* p. 301.
38. D.R. Thapar, *Icons in Bronze,* pp. 77f.
39. 111,14; IV, 10; IV, 11 and V. 11.
40. IV. 1.49: IV. 1. 112 ; V. III. 99.
41. MIC., Vol 1, ch. V, pp. 48-60.
42. M. Wheeler, *The Indus Civilization,* pp. 108-9; EIP., pp. 93f E. Mackay, *Further Excavations at Mohenjodaro,* Vol. 1, pp. 335-37; V.G. Childe, NLAE., pp. 222f ; H. Heras, SPIMC., Vol. 1; K.N. Dikshit, *Prehistoric Civilization of the Indus Valley*; D.C. Sircar, SRAML. pp. 94f: Charles Eliot, *op. cit.,* Vol. 1, pp. 211-15; A.K. Coomaraswamy, H IIA., pp. 5-7; J.H. Hudson, *Caste in India,* pp. 152-54, 224-30.
43. E. Mackay, *Early Indus Civilization,* pp. 54-75.
44. Cul. Her. Indus., p. 63.
45. IHQ., 1934, Vol. X. No. 1, pp. 14-20.
46. B.P. Sinha, *Evolution of Úakti worship.in India,* cf. D.C. Sircar (ed.): *The Úakti Cult and Tara.* pp. 51-55.
47. J.N. Farquhar, ORLI., pp. 167f, 256-57.
48. SPRHRC, p. 91.
49. JARS., 1962, Vol. XVI, p. 56.
50. JARSB., (New Series), 1914, Vol. X, p. 346.
51. *History of Assam,* pp. VII-VIII, 15, 58.
52. *Op. cit.,* pp. 278-79. Also, Wilson (quoted by Dr. Spooner), JRAS., 1915, p. 81.

53. *Op. cit.,* p. 58.
54. *Op. ett.,* pp. VII-VIII.
55. IAH., p, 50
56. SHK, Vol. I, pp. 1-2.
57. G.P. Singh, *The Contribution of the Non-Aryans of North-Eastern Region to the making of History and Culture of India, through the Ages,* cf. JNEICSSR., April 1981, Vol. V, No. 1, pp. 19-20. Also, JISR., Jan 1981, Vol. 1, No. 1, p. 31.
58. L.D. Barnett, AI (AHCAH), pp. 3ff.
59. AIMA., p. 104.
60. G.W. Brown, SIPI, pp. 82-83, SHB., pp. 75ff.
61. Radhakrishnan, ERWT, p. 308.
62. IAH, pp. 32-34.
63. (*a*) *Kirāta-Jana-Kṛti,* pp. 53-54, 62-63.
    (*b*) *Race-Movements and Prehistoric Culture* cf. HCIP., (The Vedic Age), Vol. 1, ch. VIII ; pp. 148, 167-171.
    (*c*) *Non-Âryan Elements in Indo-Âryan* cf. JGIS. 1936, Vol. II, No. 1, pp. 43-49. See also P.T. Srinivasa Aiyangar, LAIM., pp. 125-26.
64. See his *Hindu View of Life.*
65. *Primitive Culture,* Vol. II, p. 164.
66. HG., Vol. I, pt. 1, Preface.
67. *A History of India,* Vol. 1, pp. 43-44, 48-49.
68. *Pre-Historic India,* Preface IX.
69. *The Beginning of Indian Civilization* cf. Monthly Bulletin, Ramakrishna Mission Institute of Culture, Octob. 1951,11, (No. 10), p. 152.
70. *Smastkrti Ke Câr Adhyaya* (four chapters of culture), pp. 49-52, 76-78.
71. *India from the Earliest Ages,* Vol. Ill, p. 15.
72. Ref. to Gustav Oppert., OIB., pp. 455-56.
73. Census of India 1891, Assam, Vol. 1, Report. Ch. HI, p. 82.
74. HG., Vol. II, pt. 363.
75. EC., XII, SI. 28, p. 92 ; Rice, Mysore, the Gazetteer (revised), I, p. 307.
76. *Kirâta-Jana-Krti,* p. 54.
77. *Ancient Indian Sculpture,* pp. 127-28. See also P. Mitra, *op. cit.,* pp. 327, 330-36, 340-43 and F.B. Jevans, *Pre-Historic Antiquities of the Aryan people.*

78. Petersen, JAOS., Vol. XXXII; pp. 414ff.
79. J. Bloch, BSL., Vol. XXV, pp. Iff ; J. Przyluski, *Ibid,* pp. 66f, vol. xxiv, pp. 118f, 255f; W. Schmidt, *Die Mon-Khmer Volker* (1906).
80. Radha Kumud Mookerji, AI., pp. 28-29.
81. S.K. Chatterji, Cul. Her. Ind. Vol. v, pp. xix-xx, xxiv 670.
82. *Assamese, Its Formation and Development,* pp. 25-33.
83. Ojha, JBORS., Vol. xxviii, p. 59.
84. S.K. Chatterji, *Cul. Her. Ind.,* Vol. v. pp. 659f.
85. Quoted in D.R. Regmi, AN., pp. 23-24.
86. *Op. cit.*

CONCLUSIONS AND OBSERVATIONS

CONCLUSIONS AND OBSERVATIONS

The Kirâtas, one of the most popular races in ancient India, constituted the largest tribal group in ancient times extending from the pre-Vedic age down to the 12th century A.D. Those who had been living in caves, mountain and forest regions of particularly Northern and Eastern Himalayan regions ever since the Prehistoric Age and known as the *Âdivâsis* (aborigines) were called for the first time as 'Kirât' by the later Vedic Âryans. The tribes of other parts of India including the trans-Himalayan region in the north having more or less the same pattern of settlements appeared in ancient Indian, Greek and Latin texts under the same denomination. Even the tribes of the Gangetic India whose settlement pattrns were completely different from that of others received the same name.

The over-all analysis of the data contained in ancient historical and semi-historical records as well as some of the very important modern works leads us to plausibly draw the conclusion that they belonged not only to the non-Âryan social group as hitherto believed by many but to the Âryan as well. They were by and large of indigenous origin. Their racial ethnology differed from region to region. The non-uniform racial characteristics point to the fact that they belonged to different stocks. A considerable section of them were the descendants of the Brâhmaṇas and Kṣatriyas, but owing to non-observance of their own caste rules and neglect of study of the *Vedas, Brâhmanas* and *Sâstras* and other social and religious duties they were expelled from their own communities and consequently took shelter in different caves, hills and forests, and eventually turned to be a non-Âryan tribal community. Many of them became tribes from the castes between the age of the *Vedas* and *Manu Saṁhitâ,* because of their socio-cultural transformation. There is an abundant evidence in the *Yajurveda* to show that the Âryans, while assigning the duties of and the place for residence to their own respective social group deputed the Kiratas for caves.

Those, who were enslaved or conquered by the Âryans, and of low mentality, were called Dasyus or Dâsas. Those, who were reduced to lower status or placed at a lower social order, were designated as Úûdras. Those, who were barbarians and speakers of unintelligible language, were placed in the category of the mlecchas.

From the point of view of origin they can broadly be divided into two categories. The inhabitants of north-west, Madhya-deúa, Vindhyan region, western and southern region were purely of indigenous origin. Moreover, the dwellers of "Madhya-deúa and Vindhyas were not only non-Âryan tribes, bu also those, who were of Âryan extraction. Those, who we are living in northern and north-eastern region, can further be sub-divided into two sections. One section of them, who did not mix-up with any foreign immigrants, can be called the early Kirâtas and those, who lost their indigenous tribal identity after being absorbed by the later immigrants from Tibet Burma, China and other parts of Greater India, can be called the latter Kirâtas.

The geographical distribution of the Kirâtas, as a whole, does not warrant the assumption that all of them came from east of China, Tibet and Burma and were Mongoloids. Actually, they were of mixed origin. Thus, to put them under one particular category is neither fair nor accurate in ancient Indian historical context. After getting all the available evidences thoroughly examined, we can easily conclude that there was no migration of the Kirâta population from outside India before the beginning of the Christian era.

Historically, linguistically and culturally the word 'Kirâ' underwent several transformations in ancient times. Different appellations have been used for them in Sanskrit. Pali and Prâkrt languages in inscriptions of different times and in Greek and Roman texts, which are interchangeable. They were known by different names in different regions. They had racial affinities with other tribes in most of the parts of the country. However, they formed a series of allied, yet distinct tribes or clans.

The Himalaya has been their homeland since time immemorial. That is why, they have been generally described in early texts as the people of the Himalayan borderland. But, the fact remains that they spread not only along the whole range of the Himalayas, northern, eastern and central, but also over other parts of India, including the Gangetic provinces. In the Western and Central India their expansion was as much wide as that of the Bhils. But, the latter remained throughout dominant and maintained longer existence than the former, who have become almost extinct now. This may be because of the absorption of the former by the latter, and it is perhaps because of this reason that sometimes both are identified with each other.

The life-styles and cultural-patterns of the Kirâtas in ancient times varied from region to region and time to time. Like all other primitive non-Âryan tribes they had to pass through several stages from prehistoric Age to the early medieval period. Different settlement patterns, different manners, customs and habits, nomadism, pastoralism, hunting and food-gathering, etc. constitute the essential features of the prehistoric culture, which flourished in the Himalayan and sub-Himalayan regions. The urban culture, which flourished particularly, in the northern Himalayan Kirâta region by the 7th century A.D. was, of course, a striking historical development of that period. It is significant to note that even at the prehistoric stage of their life, they conducted several such experiments, both out of necessity and compulsion, that furinshed the base of early Indian society and culture.

After the appearance of the Vedic Âryans on the Indian scenes dramatic changes took place in their social position. They, being the speakers of non-Âryan language were assigned low rank in the society by the Âryans. Their social status was comparatively lower than that of the Âryans. This position remained unchanged for many centuries. Different designations, such as mleccha, Dasyus, Úûdras, etc. were applied to them by their Âryan counterparts. The Âryans representing, so-called higher phase of civilization looked down upon all the forest tribes, who were at the hunting and food gathering stage and represented the lower level of culture.

But the case of the Vindhya Kirâtas is completely different from those of other parts of India. They remained greatly unaffected by the mleccha status, which was usually being conferred upon others. Some of them belonged to the category of civilized Brâhmanas and some of them to uncivilized non-Brahmanas. The pre-Âryan settlers were, by and large, conquered and brought within the pale of Âryandom. But many of them were in a position to reconcile themselves to a new emerging situation. They were not prepared to accept the new Sanskritic culture, which was emerging out of the Âryanisation and Sanskritization process which was started little later. They vehemently opposed the imposition of Aryan culture on them. Consequently, some of the original Ksatriya Kirâta tribes were degraded to the rank of the Sudras because of neglect of the Vedas and Brahmanical rites. Some of them, were declared outcastes. On the other hand, some of them were excluded from the non-Âryan fold and absorbed within the Aryan fold. As a result they got inextricably mixed up with the Âryans and adopted their ways of life and culture. It became increasingly difficult to distinguish one from the other. On the whole the Kiratas of both indigenous and foreign origins represented different sections of society, *viz.*, non-Âryan primitive tribes, Brahman, Ksatriya, Sudra, and Dasyus". Their social status frequently underwent changes.

The urbanization process, which had begun with the expansion of the Aryans in the upper Gangetic basin in the later Vedic period greatly affected the settlement-patterns of the Kirâtas. The clearings of the jungles compelled many of them to move here and there in search of new homes. This indirectly resulted in their expansion. The bulk of Kirâtas of North-East, North-West, Vindhyas, Nepal and Uttarâkhanda were Aryanised in the post-Vedic times. They had both patriarchal and matriarchal forms of society. The rigidity of caste system never existed in their society. But they were extensively divided and sub-divided into exogamous and endogamous units, clans and tribes. The position of women in their society was very low. The slavery was very much in existence, but it never took the form of a social institution.

With the passage of time they shifted from their natural economy represented by hunting and food-gathering to a primitive system of agriculture commonly known as shifting (Jhum) cultivation, which marks a tradition in their socio-economic life. The land was the common property for them. The collective ownership system prevailed for a considerable period of time. The production and distribution system was fundamentally based on the principles of primitive communism. The division of labour was a common feature of their economic life. The Vindhya Kirâtas, particularly, had reached to a stage of agrarian economy. Generally speaking, the mountains and forests supplied all the essential items of their daily requirements for their subsistence. Keeping in view the abundance of their natural wealth, the forest produce and various precious gems including gold and silver, which were presented a tributes by the Kiratas especially of northern and eastern Himalayan region to Yudhisthira in the epic age we can affirm that they had crossed the stage of primitive economy at a particular point of time and reached to a stage of developed economy. The forest produce and various medicinal herbs and perfumes which were prepared from the roots of hill-plants were supplied by them to their Âryan neighbours in exchange for the products of plains. They had different arts and crafts. Their artistic craftsmanship, indigenous, metallurgical and technological art, the art of weaving and that of making the rude pottery fairly attest to their technological advancement. They had a well-organised internal and external trade system. The hill and the forest products were the main articles of their internal trade in general. The cotton, silk, gold, iron and *malbathrum* were the articles of external trade for the Kiratas of north-eastern Himalayan region in particular. The *Malbathrum* was the principal article of trade. They had external trade relations particularly with China and Rome which had practically begun in the centuries preceding the Christian era. Between the 1st century A.D. and the 5th century A.D. this trade was in a very flourishing stage.

The trend of the political evolution was quite similar to that of the Âryans On the whole, different forms of Govt. i.e. monarchical, democratic, oligarchical and republican existed among them. The village Panchayats in their case were the most popular self-governing political institution. Their interest in the war and diplomacy was immense. They presented a good account of themselves both as diplomat, security guard and spy during the Mauryan period. They were recruited as soldiers in the army by their contemporary Âryan kings. They set up several Examples as an excellent warriors between the epic age and the early part of the 13th century.

Religion was not only the chief bond of their society but also one of the powerful factors in the regulation of their affairs. Religion also indicates their position in the scale of civilization. The nature of their religion should be judged by the standard prevailing in their contemporary society. The animism, monotheism, polytheism, propitiation of both benevolent and malevolent spirits and various other gods and goddesses including the Gramadevatas having the anthropomorphic attributes, superstitious beliefs, eschatological doctrines connected with the transmigration of soul, magic, witchcraft, divination, sacrifices, ritualism, priesthood, etc. constitute the cardinal features of their religio-philosophical system.

Out of the four religious cults—Úaiva, Úakti, Tantric and Vaisnava—which emerged in early times, the former two became relatively more popular among all sections of the Kirâtas. The cult of Siva was particularly the most prominent one. Úiva worship in the Phallic symbol was widely prevalent among them. The mother-goddess or Sakti was worshipped in different manifestations, i.e. Uma, Parvati, Durgâ, Kâli, Candi or Candika Devi, Kirâta Devi, Kirâtin and Kirâti, represented in Indian mythology as consort of Úiva. The worship of Úakti in various symbols representing her organs or limbs in respective regions, where they fell was also in vogue. The publication of Tantra texts, which began from the 9th century onwards, greatly modified the character of Úakti worship. It was more associated with Tântric rites including animal and human sacrifices, particularly in north eastern Bengal and Assam as it appears from Tântras, both Buddhist and Brâhmanical. A close study of these texts is still a desideratum from the point of view of their participation in the religious and cultural evolution of India. The religious milieu that developed on their background is apparent, to some extent in the life of their descendants. Some sections of them (unidentified) by the 5th or 6th century A.D. also came under the influence of Bhagavata cult. They, like that of other degraded Indian and foreign race become devotees of Krisna for the purification of their soul. A considerable section of them were Âryanised sometimes between the epic age and the Gupta age, which eventually resulted in their conversion to Hinduism. They gradually became the followers of Brâhmanical religion and culture. Their religious beliefs were modified by later Hinduism, which led to the transformation of their pantheon. Their gods and goddesses were identified with the deities of Brahmanical pantheon.

In the centuries preceding the Christian era the Kirata of Orissa region came under the impact of Jaina culture, whereas, on the other hand the Kirâtas of Nepal, Central India and Deccan embraced Buddhism sometimes between the 3rd century B.C. and the 2nd century A.D.

In the field of Megalithic monuments of Neolithic Age, sculpture marked by both wood and stone carvings, iconography, decorative arts and paintings of north-eastern Kirâta tribes excelled those of Vindhya region. Uttarâkhanda and peninsular India.

They also played conspicuous role in the evolution of different groups of language spoken in ancient time. They don't represent only Sino-Tibetan or Tibeto-Burman family as mistakenly supposed by many philologists. At the initial stage their system of expression was symbolical, which was sometimes of course, unintelligible to others. Every civilized or uncivilized community in ancient times had some or the other means of communication to survive in the society and to transact the affairs of their daily life. The Kirâtas of northern and north-eastern parts (Uttarâpatha) of India were basically the speakers of mleccha-bhasa, which came into use for the first time in the age of Úatapatha Brâhmana. They had their own script and dialects. They were probably acquainted with the art of writing. In course of time many of them lost their original scripts for the reasons, which are not known to us, but they somehow could be able to retain their different dialects. By the 3rd or 4th century A.D. they had adopted the Prakrit form of speech, which later got mixed with several other dialects. The Piúâca-Prakrt was spoken only in the north-western frontier region. The Vindhyan Kirâtas had learnt the alphabet and the Úâstras from the civilized group of Brâhmanas amongst themselves. The Kirâtas of Nepal and Mithila regions had their own scripts and system of writing. In the whole Uttârakhanda (Garhwal and Kumaon regions) and Kirântadesâ or Kirâta-desa stretching from Sikkim to Eastern Nepal Kirânti dialect was usually spoken. In the northeastern regions there have been the diverse linguistic groups among the Kirâtas. Linguistically they belong to Tibeto-Burman sub-family to Tibeto-Chinese group and Mon-khmer language of Austro-Asiatic group, Bodo language, etc. In northern and central India the mixed Indo-Âryan and Âryo-Dravidian forms of speech were prevalent among them.

The adoption of Brâhmi and Gupta scripts in Tibet and Burma between the 3rd century B.C. and the 4th century A.D. profoundly affected the Tibeto-Burman linguistic structure. And so was the impact of Pali and Sanskrit on this group of language. That is why the Kirâtas falling under this group adopted many words of Indian origin. The Tibetan grammar was broadly based on Pânini's Sutras enunciated in his Astâdhyayi and not on the Chinese words. Thus, in the fomation of different language groups in Indian sub-continent they also contributed their share.

Their narrative literature serves as a repository of several ethnographical, historical, sociological, religious and cultural data.

In ancient times the Kirâtas had their Janapadas or territorial units in the Gangetic Doab (situated in Madhyadeúa), northern, eastern, central and southern parts of India and in the mountain regions of northern and eastern Himalayas. Their social formation, political organisation and chieftainship system working in unison facilitated the emergence of principalities and kingdoms in North-Eastern India, Uttrâkhanda and the Vindhyan region in Mid-India. But, they could not achieve political stability between the epic age and the 4th century A.D. It was the middle of the 4th century A.D. that they had established powerful kingdoms in northern, north-eastern and central parts of India. Their frequent migrations from the plains into the Hills caused by the attacks of strong Âryan neighbours and other rulers created a feeling of insecurity among them. Thus, for the flake of their protection and defence they resorted to the practice of erecting forts particularly, in the mountain regions of nothern-eastern Himalayas. One of their noted urban centres called Suvarnapur in the northern Himalayas was situated on the northern frontiers of Bharatavarsa. The vast forest region just opposite of this town extending up to the mountain Kailâúa was the principal habitat of the Kirâta tribes. This is the typical example of their territorial settlement in the northern mountain regions.

The transformation in their life-style at different stages of history provides a glimpse of their gradual progress achieved by them in social and political fields. The interplay of the compulsion of situation and their natural instincts brought about tremendous changes in their socio-political life. But these changes were not ever lasting. They had to experience several ups and downs in their life because of changing situation. Like other tribal groups they had also strong internal tendency to split up into numerous communities. A number of such small independent communities, under its own chief or king in a limited sense came into existence. There was neither strong national spirit nor other cohesive elements amongst them like that of others. They became victim of their own situation. Taking advantage of the prevailing, disintegrating tendency among them some of the powerful and ambitious rulers of India, in order to establish their sovereignty and to make themselves master of the whole country by usurping their territories or petty kingdoms and principalities either conquered them or reduced them to subjection. Some sections, of them lost their territories, kingdoms and principalities because of the lack of stability and some of them were absorbed into adjoining communities.

The process of their subjugation and destruction had virtually started in the epic age and it continued up to the times of the Hoysalas in the 12th century A.D. And even beyond it. The Pandava heroes of Tndraprastha, in order to bring them under the overlordship of Yudhiúthira subjugated them in the northern, eastern and western regions. The participation of north-eastern

Kirâtas in the Great Bharata war on behalf of the Kurus resulted in their destruction, which is mainly attributed to Ârjuna. In the Purânic age they weremainly subdued by the Brâhmans and the Ksâtriyas. Even the prince of Avanti could not lag behind; he went up to the Himalayas in the north to subjugate them. Between the 3rd and the 8th century A.D. the Kirâtas of Nepal were conquered by the Licchavis and the later Guptas. The Pratihara rulers had vanquished them in different regions in the Post-Harsha period.

The Vindhyan Kirâtas were the worst sufferers. They sustained greater loss than those who belonged to northern and eastern India. Because right from the time of Samudragupta in the 4th century A.D. to the time of the Hoysala king Bittideva in the first half of the 12th century A.D. they were defeated several times by several rulers. Besides the Gupta, Vâkâtaka and Varman rulers, the Ganga king, the Nolambavadi rulers (during the times of the Pallavas) the Hoysala king and other rulers of southern Peninsula defeated them one after another which caused an irreparable loss to them. They were dislodged by south Indian rulers from their Vindhyan territory by the end of the 12th century. Thereafter, they started their penetration in the far south, where also they could not escape the attention of the hostile rulers. By the 17th century they were either crushed by them or absorbed in the local tribal communities.

The establishment of dynastic rule of Kirâtas in the Sub-Himalayan tract of North-Eastern India roughly from the fourth millennium B.C. down to the 7th Century A.D. forms an important Chapter of our ancient history. Twenty-nine rulers of this dynasty ruled over the valley of Nepal uninterruptedly for about one thousand years. From the preceding discussion it is evident that they appeared on the political stage of ancient Nepal at two different periods of history, one prior to the commencement of the Kaliyuga (3102 B.C.) and other during post Kaliyuga period. The exactitude of the total duration of their reigns can't be ascertained from some considerable reasons already dwelt upon. However, this can be stated with great certainty that they held undisputed sway over the Eastern and Central Himalayan regions of ancient India for a considerable period of time. The participation of one Kirâta king in the *Mahâbhârata* war and their contacts with Gautama Buddha, and emperor Aúoka during the course of their visits to this land, appear to be of pan-Indian importance. Hence they can be assigned a proper place in ancient Indian history.

The appearance of the Licchavis of the solar race of the Ksatriyas on the political stage of ancient Nepal in the 1st century A.D. from Vaiúâli region proved to be detrimental to the existence of the Kirâtas. The period extending from the 1st Century A.D. to the 3rd century A.D. was the period of their struggle for power and supremacy. They received blows after blows from the Licchavis, which led to the gradua decline of their rule. In this contest for power, the Kirâtas lost the ground and were ultimately conquered by the Licchavî in the 3rd century A.D. However, they always remained undaunted in their courage, undeterred in their spirits and unflinching in their convinction. They continued the struggle against the Licchavis again and again for regaining lost power and prestige. But they could not subdue the Licchavis, rather they themselves were subjugated by them. The internal dissensions, among the Licchavis and the hostility between the Abhira Guptas and themselves turned to be a blessing in disguise for the Kirâtas. Taking advantage of this situation, which was very favourable to them, they spared no pain to revive their power and glory between 4th and 7th century A.D. But this time also fortune did not favour them. Their all attempts ended in fiasco.

The rulers of the new dynasty, known as the Gupta dynasty, which appeared on the scene in the intermediary stage in a very dramatic manner, missed no opportunity to resist the attempts of the Kirâtas to seize the throne. Ultimately they were badly defeated by the Abhira Guptas sometimes between the 6th and 7th century A.D. which saw the extinction of the Kirâtas' dynastic rule in ancient Nepal. We will close the present discussion with this remark that it was only the end of the dynasty not the total annihilation of the Kirâta population. The present day Kirâtas popularly known as Kulung, Thulung and Yellung are supposed to be the descendants of those important twenty nine rulers of the ruined dynasty, who ruled over Nepal in ancient times.

The Kirâtas' role in Indian history and contribution to Indian culture have not been properly estimated. The thorough "examination of all the fragmentary (both recorded and unrecorded) evidence, which we have at our disposal, reveals the truth that they also like other pre-Åryan races played positive role in building up the early socio-religious political and cultural fabric of India. They also added some threads to the texture of Indian civilization characterised by its unity in diversities. They were the great transmitters of the culture which they received from the Hindus of the plains. Their contributions to the history of India right from the Neolithic Age down to the early medieval period were in several fields, *viz*; socio-economic, political, religious, cultural, artistic, linguistic, literary, etc.

The part which the played in the political and cultural evolution of ancient India was not doubt very conspicuous. For quite some time they became successful in moulding the course of ancient Indian History. The role, which the Kirâta population of North-Western India played during the Mauryan Age by extending their unstinted support to Chandragupta Maurya for overthrowing the Nanda dynasty and occupying the throne of Magadha, was, of course, very important. This, is the only concrete instance of their participation in the political history of ancient India.

They always played their role, whatsoever it may be, the political field as a class of warriors, which may definitely be considered as one of their notable qualities. Whenever, they were approached by their Âryan and non-Âryan rulers of the neighbouring areas for fighting on their behalf in war against their foes, they did so. They rendered their services to their contemporary rulers, whenever necessary by joining their army. The role played by them particularly in the Vindhyan region bears witness to this fact. Thus, some place can be assigned to them in the political and administrative history of ancient India.

Far greater was the contribution, which they made to the religious and cultural history of India, during the period concerned. It is very difficult to determine with any degree of accuracy as to what extent the Kirâta elements influenced the growth of Hindu religion and culture. However, it can be taken for granted that the Hindu religion and philosophy were greatly modified by aboriginal elements as a sequel to their mutual contacts and cultural fellowship. That is why the present day Hinduism contains both Âryan and non-Âryan elements. The Kirâtas' contribution is not so extensive and deep, but nevertheless it is very much there in the history and culture of ancient Assam, North and East Bengal and Nepal.

The earliest religious ideas of the Âryans were broadly based on the concept of primitive animism. Most of the basic things in Hindu religion including myths, legends, superstitions, ritual of sacrifices, priesthood, theological doctrines, philosophical system, etc. are derived from the pre-Âryan Kirâtas to a certain extent. The Kirâta cults and customs, speeches and ideologies, etc. were engrafted on the Indo-Âryan stock of culture. However, the pre-Âryan culture never triumphed over the Âryan culture. At best, we can acknowledge that it did modify the pattern of Âryan religion and culture. The assimilation of non-Âryan religious beliefs and practices within the folds of Âryan as well as the Hindu culture and vice-versa later became the twin pillars of composite Indian culture and civilization. As a result of cultural intercourse amongst the various racial groups a common pattern in respect of society, economy, polity, art, religion and culture was evolved.

In order to present a clear picture of the subject it is necessary to mention that some pf the Kirâta people of North Eastern India made greater contribution to Indian history and culture. They played very important part in the evolution of the common culture of north-eastern and sub-Himalayan India. The contribution, which they made, particularly in the field of religion by giving fillip to the cults of Úaivism, Úaktism and Tantricism, is really of great historical value. Their contribution to the growth and development of Indian art and architecture is also very noteworthy. The, aboriginal art, inspired the growth of Hindu art to a greater extent. Their monolithic marvels dating back to later Neolithic Age, pre-historic finds, ancient monuments and relics of pre and post Christian era, sculptural and iconographic art, decorative art, paintings, etc. later on became an object of attraction and specimen for emulation for their Âryan successors. Their artistic perfection still finds expression in many pieces of the Hindu art of today. In the light of the evidence already adduced and the treatment of the subject made, it warrants us to dispose of the theory propounded by E.J. Rapson that "Assam is country which at most periods of history has remained outside the Indian civilization."[1] The truth runs contrary to this remark.

The Kirâtas of distant northern frontiers of. India, Central and Eastern Nepal (the Khambu, the Yakha, the Limbu and other Kirânti peoples), Central India, and North-Bihar made proportionately less contribution to our history and culture as evidenced by the traces which they have left behind and the vestiges, which are visible.

Animism prevailing in the crudest form among the compact well-organised forest tribes in early times formed the basis of the developed religions, largely represented in modern Hinduism. Different tribal faiths, creeds and deities were merged and identified with those of the Hindus. At a later stage all religious duties were monopolised by the Brahmanas under whole influence, the cults developed with all that luxuriance, which becames manifest in Oriental faiths.

Generally speaking, the Kirâtas were one of the builders of cultural tradition and founders of schools of religion, particularly, Úaiva, Úakti and Tântric, which formed the part of principal sub-divisions of Hinduism. A consideiable section of them were the progenitors or harbingers of many of the essentials of Hindus culture. Many of the Kirâtas'cults, i.e. the cults of Úaiva, Phallus (Liñgam), Yoni, Úakti or mother-goddess (represeming Durgâ, Umâ, Kâli, Candikâ, Kirâtini or Kirâta Devi), fertility, earth-goddess, village goddess, priest, etc. were slowly absorbed into the main currents of Hindu religion. These cults are not merely a survival of barbaric practices but originally the products of aboriginal conception. The most abiding gift which the Kirâta gave to the country was in the shape of new deity — Candika (fierce form of Durgâ), who later secured an important place in the Brâhmanical pantheon. These cults in the modified and refined forms found a place in the classical Hinduism. These cults began to play a more positive role in the evolution of Hinduism in the period following the 5th century A.D. Along with the cults, many of their religious beliefs, rites and rituals were incorporated into the Brâhmanical religion.

Hinduism in the initial stage, remained vague and amorphous for quite sometime, and it had not emerged as a distinct faith. In the past it embraced many beliefs and practices from the highest to the lowest level. In its broadest connotation, "starting from the Vedas, Hinduism has ended in embracing from all religions... It is all tolerant, all comprehensive and all absorbing."[2]

It has been rightly pointed out that "Hinduism has not been made, but has grown. It is a jungle, not a building..."[3] Further "Hinduism is an unusual combination of animism and pantheism, which are commonly regarded as the extremes of savage and of philosophic belief. In India both may be found separately but frequently they are combined in startling juxtaposition... The bottles of Hinduism have always proved capable of holding all the wine poured into them..."[4]

It is difficult to draw a sharp line of distinction between popular Hinduism and tribal religion. The age-long processes, facilitated by a tendency towards fusion have led to an assimilation of many local beliefs, popular tribal cults and regional traditions into pan-Indian Hinduism,[5] often described as proto-Hinduism.

We can't deny that the contacts between the tribal communities and Hindu population have extended over countless centuries. And thus we have every reason to believe that the concepts stemming from pre-Âryan aboriginal civilization have found their way into Hindu doctrines, thoughts and scriptures just as the concepts of orthodox Hinduism have been assimilated by many of the primitive hill-tribes of our country. Several Vedic, Upanisadic, Brâhmanic and Purânic doctrines and even the Vedântic philosophy have get un-Âryan features. The influence of tribal religion on Hindu religion and philosophy is similar to the impact of Hinduism on Buddhism, and that of Buddhism on Christianity and influenced of Sufism and Greek philosophy on Islamic theology. This represents a kind of tradition of religious cofraternity, which had evolved in course of several millennia and centuries.

In the long historic process of making the classical Indian tradition and giving the concrete shape to ancient Indian culture and civilization the contribution of the primitive or aboriginal Kirâtas tribes falling under Tibeto-Burman "Indo-Mongoloid", Austric, Bodo and semi-Âryanised groups cannot be underestimated.

After having made a general assessment of their contribution to Indian history and culture we can plausibly draw the conclusion that Indian religion, and philosophy, art and culture, etc. still bear the stamp of Kirâta influences. Ancient India moved from one epoch to another carrying the veneer of non-Âryan Kirâta culture. The Hindu World of today still acknowledge the indebtedness, which they owe to the Kirâtas, who supplied the foundamental base or pedestal of their religious beliefs and ideology. The assimilation of Kirâta agreements in Hindu religion and culture of North and East Bengal, Assam, Mithila, Nepal and Vindhyan region is of primary importance. On the whole, their positive contributions towardt the making of the composite culture and civilization of India is of pan-Indian significance.

Here it is indispensable to put the views of S.K. Chatterji, who is one of the recognised judges of the non-Âryan contribution to Indian history and civilization. After having made a short survey of the nature of Kirâta or "Indo-Mongoloid" participation in Indian history and their contribution in the evolution of Hindu or Indian culture for the last 3,000 years, in his own style, he observes that "the Kiratas or Indo-Mongoloids from the Vedic times onwards have been the fourth basic element in the formation of the Indian people and we find them taking their share in Hindu history, beginning with the battle of Kurukshetra, from the 10th century before Christ, Kirâta or Indo-Mongoloid influences may have affected the life and religion of the Vedic Âryans as well... we can see that at least in the areas where they established themselves, they furnished a new and a fourth element, and quite a powerful one, in the formation of medieval Hindu religion and culture. Closely interlinked as the various groups of the Indo-Mongoloids were with the affairs of India for over 2500 years,, and considering also the brilliant part they played in becoming the champion of

Hindu culture and fighters in the protracted war for Hindu political freedom in North and East Bengal and Assam, they have become an integral part of the body-politic in India, from the deathless story of which land it will never be possible to minimise or relegate to oblivion their services and their contribution. Can we think of Indian History and civilization, particularly in Eastern India, without the contributions of the... Kachari, Tipra and other peoples,... the Jaintias and the Manipuris ?"[6]

The present line of inquiry, we are sure, will open fresh avenue for conducting further historical investigation into the subject under our notice.

Notes and References

1. CHI, Vol. I, pp. 11-12.
2. Monier Williams, *Hinduism,* p. 12.
3. Charles Eliot, *Hinduism and Buddhism,* vol. I, p. 41.
4. *Ibid.,* pp. 167-68.
5. EB, vol. 8, p. 898.
6. *Kirâta-Jana-Krti,* pp. 183-84.

GENERAL BIBLIOGRAPHY

GENERAL BIBLIOGRAPHY

1. Original Sources: Texts, Translations and Commentaries

The Vedic Saṁhitâs

Atharvaveda Saṁhitâ; Ed. by R. Roth and W.D. Whitney, Berlin, 1856.

——: Ed. with Sâyaṇa's commentary by S.P. Pandit, Bombay, 1895-8.

——: Eng. trans. with a popular commentary by R.T.H. Griffith under the title *The Hymns of the Atharvaveaa*, 1st Nov. 1894, Banaras, 1897, reptd., The Chowkhamba Sanskrit Studies-Vol. LXVI, 2 Vols., Varanasi, 1968.

——: Eng. trans. by W.D. Whitney, *HOS*. (ed. by C.R. Lanman), Cambridge, 1905, 2nd Indian rept., Delhi, 1971.

——: Eng. trans. by M. Bloomfield, *Hymns of the Atharvaveda SBE;* (ed. F. Max Muller), Vol. XLII, OUP; 1897, Delhi, 1973.

——: Hindi trans with a commentary by Dayananda Sarasvati, Dayananda Saṁsthân, Delhi, VS. 2032.

——: Ed. and trans with Sâyana's comm. by Ram Sharma Âchârya (in Hindi), 2 Vols. Bareilly, 1973. 1975.

Ṛgveda Saṁhita: Ed. with Sâyaṇa's commentary by F. Max Muller, 2nd edn. 1890-92; Saṁhitâ texted by Th. Aufrecht, 2nd edn. Bonn, 1877.

——: Trans. by R.T.H. Griffith, Banaras, 1896-97.

——: H.H. Wilson. Vols. I-VI, London, 1866-1888.

——: Ed. and trans. with Sâyaṇas' commentary by Ram Sharma Âchârya (in Hindi), 4 Vols. Bareilly, 1974-75.

Yajurveda: Taittiriya Saṁhita, ed. by A. Weber, Ind. Stu. XI and XII, Berlin, 1871-72; with the comm. of Madhava, Calcutta, 1854-99; Trans. by A.B. Keith under the title *The Veda of the Black Yajus School, HOS*. (ed C.R. Lanman), XVIII and XIX, 1914, Delhi, 1967.

——: *Vâjasaneyi Saṁhitâ* (of the *Úukla Yajurveda*), ed. with Mahidhara's comm. by A. Weber, London, 1852; Trans. by A.B. Keith, Cambridge, Mass. 1914.

——: Trans, with a popular comm. by. Griffith under the title, *The Texts of the white Yajuryeda*, Banaras, 1899, The Chowkhamba Sanskrit Studies, Vol. XCV, Varanasi, 1976.

——: Eng. trans. with a comm. by Devi Chand, Delhi, 1980.

——: Hindi trans. with a comm. by Dayananda Sarasvati, Delhi VS. 2032.

——: Ed. and Trans. by Ram Sharma Âchârya (in Hindi). Bareilly, 1974.

The Brâhmaṇas

Aitareya Brâhmaṇa: Ed. by Th. Aufrecht, Bonn, 1879.

——: Trans. by A.B. Keith, *HOS.* (ed. C.R. Lanman), Vol. XXV, Cambridge, Mass. 1920, first Indian Rept., Delhi, 1971.

——: Ed. with a trans. by M. Haug, 2 Vols. Bombay, 1863.

——: Ed. with Sayana's comm. and tr. in part by U.S. Sharma, Varanasi.

Jaiminiya Brâhmaṇa: Ed. by H. Oertel with Irani, and notes, *JAOS;* XVI, 79-260.

——: Ed. by W. Caland, Amsterdam, 1919.

Pañcaviṁúa Brâhmaṇa: Ed. by A. Vedanta-Vagisa, Calcutta, 1869-74.

Satapatha Brâhmaṇa of the Sukla or White Yajurveda in the Madhyandina recension (complete Vol.): Ed. by pt. A Chinnaswami Sastri, pt. p. Sastri and pt. R.N. Dsksita, 2nd, edn, Varanasi, 1984.

——: Ed. by A. Weber, London, 1855, 1885.

——: Trans. by J. Eggeling, SBE; Vols. XII, XXVI, XLI, XLII, XLIV, Oxford, 1882-1900.

Taittiriya Brâhmaṇa of the Black Yajurveda.: Ed. with Sayanas Comm. by R. Mitra, 3 Vols. *BIS;* Calcutta, 1855-70.

——; Ed. by N. Godabole, Poona, 1898.

Dharmasûtras

Baudhdyâna Dharmasûtra (also called Dharma-úâstra): Ed. by E. Hultzsch, Leipzig, 1884; A.C. Sastri, Banaras, 1934. *Gautama Dharmasutra:* Ed. by A.F. Stenzler, London, 1876.

Vasiṣṭha Dharmasûtra: Ed. by A. A. Fuhrer, Bombay, 1883, 1916.

——: Trans. SBE, (Oxford), Vol. XIV.

Trans. of the *Dharmasûtras* of Apastamba, Gautama, Vasiṣṭha and Baudhâyana by G. Buhler, SBE; Vols. II and XIV, Oxford, 1879-82.

The Dharmaúâstras (Smṛtis)

The Manu Smṛti or Mânava Dharma-Úâstra: Ed. by J. Jolly, London, 1887; N.N. Mandlika with commentaries, Bombay, 1886.

——: Ed. by Pt. Gopala Úástri Nene and Trans. with the commentary of Kulluka Bhatta and Hindi commentary by Pt. H.G. Sastri (The Chowkhamba Sanskrit Series, Dhanna Sastra section No. 3), Varanasi, 1970.

The Manu Smṛti or Mânava Dharma-Úástrâ): Trans. by A.C. Burnell under-the title *The Ordinances of Manu*, completed and ed. by E. W. Hopkin's, London, 1884, 2nd edn. Delhi, 1971.

——: Trans. by G. Buhler under the title, *The Laws of Manu with Extracts from Seven commentaries, SBE;* (ed. F. Max Muller), Vol. XXV, OUP, 1886, Delhi, 1964.

——: Trans. by William Jones, Calcutta 1794, Revd. Calcutta and London, 1796; G. Jha, 5 Vols. 1922-29.

Vedavyâsa Smṛti: Trans. by Ram Sharma Âchârya in his *Twenty Smṛtis*", (texts with Hindi tr.), 2 Vols; Bareilly. 1979-80.

Yâjñavalkya Dharma Úástra: Ed. by A.F. Stenzler, Berlin, 1849.

——: *Smṛti*—ed. by H. Apte, Ânandâ-srama Skt. Series, Poona, 1903.

The Dharma Úástra Samgraha ed, by Jivananda Vidyasagara (Calcutta, 1876) contains the texts attributed to Viṣṇu, Yâjñavalkya, Âpastamba Bṛhaspati, Vasiṣṭha, Gautama and others.

The Epics

The Mahâbhârata of Krishna Dwaipâyana Vyâsa: Ed. with trans. by Pt. Shree Pada Damodar Satavalekar & Shrutishil Sharma fin Hindi), Paradi (Gujarat):

——: (1) *Âdi Parva*, 1968.

(2) *Sabhâ Parva*, Úaka, 1903 = a.d. 1981 (pub. 1982).

(3) *Âraṇyaka Parva*, 2 Vols. 1969.

(4) *Udyoga Parva*, 1969.

(5) *Bhiṣma Parva*, 1972.

(6) *Droṇa Parva*, 1975.

(7) *Karṇa Parva*, 1973.

(8) *Úánti Parva*, 2 Vols., 1979-80.

(9) *Anùsâsana Parva*, 1978.

(10) *Âúvamedha Parva*, 1977.

——: Ed. by V.S. Sukthankar and S-K.

Belvalkar, BORI, Poona: —

The Sabhâ Parvan, Vol. 2, 1944;

The Âraṇyaka Parvan, Vol. 3, 1942;

The Udyoga Parvan, Vol. 5, 1940;

The Bhisma Parvan, Vol. 6, 1947;

The Drona Parvan, Vol. 7, 1958;

The Sânti Parvan, Vol. 12, 1961.

The Mahâbhârata: Trans. by P.C. Roy, Calcutta, 1884-96; also P.C. Roy, *Sabhâ Parva* and *Vana Parva*, Vol. 2, Pt. 1, 3rd edn., Delhi, 1973; *Vana Parya*, Vol. 3, Pt. 2, Delhi, 1974; *Bhiṣma Parva*,, Vol. 5, Delhi. 1,9,73.

Vâlmiki—Râmâyaṇa: Ed. by D.R. Mankad, Oriental Institute, Baroda, 1965.

——: Eng. trans by R.T. Griffith, London, 1870.

——: Bala Kanda trans. by Pt. Yudhisthira Mimâṁak, Amritsar, VS. 2025.

——: Kiskindhâ Kaṇḍâ trans. by Pt. Akhilânanada, Amritsar, VS. 2021.

(Also the *Râmacaritamânasa* of Tulsidas, *Uttarakâṇḍa*, ed. with trans. by Pt. Jwala Prasad, Ist edn. 1953, Mathurạ, 1975; also Gorakhpur edn.,VS. 2043).

The Purâṇas

Agni Purâṇa: Ed. by R.L. Mitra, Calcutta, 1373-79.

——: Trans by Tarinisa Jha, Allahabad, Saka, 1907; S.D.

——: Gyani *Agni Purana: A Study*, The Chowkhamba Sanskrit Series, Vol. XLII, Varanasi, 1964.

——: Ram Sharma Acbarya, Vol. I, Bareilly, 1973; M.N. Dutt, 2 Vols. Calcutta, 1903-4.

Bhâgavata Purâṇa: Bombay, 1889, 1905; Eng. trans. by M.N. Dutt, Calcutta, 1895.

——: Hindi trans. 2 Vols. Gita Press Gorakhpur, Sarhvat, 2040.

Bhaviṣya Purâṇa: Bombay, 1910.

Hindi trans. by Ram Sharma Acharya, 2 Vols. Bareilly, 1978, English trans. by R.K. Arora, "*Historical and Cultural Data from the Bhavisya Purâṇa*" Delhi, 1972.

Brahma Purâṇa: Ed. by H.N. Apte, Anandasrama Press, Poona, 1895, Hindi trans. by Taranisa Jha, Prayag, 1976.

Brahmânda Purâṇa: Venkatesvara Press, Bombay, 1906. 1913.

Garuda Purâṇa: Bombay, 1906. Eng. trans. by M.N. Dutt, Calcutta, 1908.

Harivaṁśa: Ed. by N. Mukbopadhyaya, ASB, Calcutta, 1858; R. Kinjawadekar, Poona, 1936.

Kâlikâ Purâṇa: Venkatesvara Press, Bombay, Saka, 1829.

——: Ed. by Visvanarayan Sastri, Varanasi, 1972.

: Hindi trans. by Chamanlal Gautama, 2 Vots. Bareilly, 1973.

Kurma Purâṇa: Ed. by Anandaswarupa Gupta and trans. by Shree ghaudhari Shree Narayana Singh (in Hindi), Varanasi, 1972.

Mârkaṇḍeya Purâṇa: Ed. by K.M. Banerjee, BIS, ASB, Calcutta, 1862.

——: Eng. trans. by F.E. Pargiter (Vol. II, Pt. II), *BIS:* ASB, Calcutta, 1904.

——: Ed. and trans. by Dharmendranath Sastri (in (Hindi), Meerut, 1983.

Matsya Purâṇa: Anandasrama Skt. Series, Poona, 1907.

——: Ed. by Jivananda Vidyasagara, Calcutta, 1876.

——: Ed. by Jamna Das Akhtar and trans. (in English) with notes by B.C. Majumdar, S.C. Vasu, H.H. Wilson, Bently, Wilford and others, *SB A;* Delhi, 1972.

——: Hindi trans. Vol. I, Gorakhpur, Jan, 1985.

Padma Purâṇa: Venkatesvara Press, Bombay, 1895.

——: Ed. by V.N. Mandalika, Anandasrama Skt. Series, Poona, 1894.

Úva Purâṇa: Hindi tr. Gorakhpur, Jan., 1962.

Skanda Purâṇa: Hindi tr. Gorakhpur, Jan., 1951.

Vâmana Purâṇa: Ed. by Anandaswarupa Gupta and trans. by G.C. Vedanta Sastri, Shree Chaudhan Shree Narayana Singh and Gangasagar Rai, Varanasi, 1968.

Vâyu Purâṇa: Anandasrama Skt. Series, Poona, 1905; Ed. by R.L. Mitra, 2 Vols. *BIS;* ASB; Calcutta, 1880-88.

——: Eng. trans. by D.R.Patil, *Cultural History from the Vâyu Purâṇa*, 1st edn. Poona, 1946, rept. Delhi, 1973.

Viṣṇu Purâṇa: Ed. by J. Vidyasagar, Calcutta, 1882.

—: Eng. trans. by M.N. Dutt, Calcutta, 1894.

——: Trans. by H.H. Wilson (Vols. I—V, ed. Fitzedward Hall, Vols. VI—X), London. 1864-70; also H.H. Wilson (SHMT.), Calcutta, 1961.

——: Hindi Trans. by Muni Lal Gupta, Gita Press, Gorakhpur.

Viṣṇudharmottara Mahâ-Purâṇa: Venkatesvara Press, Bombay, Saka 1834.

Other Literary Sources

Amarasiṁha, *Amarakoúa:* Ed. by P. Sivadatta, Bombay, 1889; ed. by T. Ganapati Sastri, 4 Pts. *TSS.* 1914-17; Hindi trans. by H. Sastri, Varanasi, VS. 2014 (= 1957).

Bâna, *Kâdambari,:* Kasinath Pandurang Parab edn. Bombay, 1896; Eng. trans. by C.M. Ridding, London, 1896; Ed. and trans. with commentary by M.R. Kale, 4th edn. Delhi, 1968; Hindi trans. by Mahesh Bharatiya, Gahaziabad, 1973-74.

Harsacarita: Ed. by J. Vidyasagara, Calcutta, 1892; also by Pandurang Pandit Parab, 3rd edn. Bombay, 1912; trans. by E.B. Cowell and F.W. Thomas, RAS; London, 1897; Hindi trans. by V.S. Agrawala, *Harsacarita; Ek Sâṁskṛtic Adhyayana,* Patna, 1964.

Bharatamuni, *Nâtyasastra:* Ed. with the commentary of Abhinaavagupta by Manavalli Ramakrishna Kavi, 3 Vols. *GOS;* Baroda, 1926-54.

Bhâravi, *Kirâtarjuniyam:* Trans. and annotated by P. Pandey, Cantos—1 & 2, Varanasi, 1983; Ed. and tr. with the Comm. of Mallinatha (Ghantapatha) by S.N. Sen, Canto—XIV, Calcutta, 1940; Canto—XIII, Calcutta, 1940: Canto XII by S. Ray and K. Ray, Calcutta.

Daṇdin, *Daśakumâracarita:* Ed. by P. Banerji, Calcutta, 1888; ed, with an Eng. tr. by M.R. Kale, 3rd edn. Bombay, 1951, 4th edn. Delhi, 1966.

Harṣa *Ratnâvali:* Nirnaya Sagara Press, Bombay, 1885; trans. with the commentary by R.C. Mishra, Varanasi, 1959.

Hemachandra, *Abhidhânacintâmani:* Pub. by Girdharlal Shah, Ahmedabad, Sam, 2013: Ed. by Von. O Bohtlingk and C. Rieu, St. Petersburg, 1847.

Kâlidâsa, Kumârasambhava: Ed. tr. and annot. with the commentary (Sanjivani) of Mallinatha by M.R. Kale, 1st edn. Bombay, Jan. 1923, 6th edn. Delhi, 1967

—*Raghuvaṁśa:* Ed. tr. and annot. with the comm. of Mallinatha by M.R. Kale, Delhi, 1972: ed. by N.R. Acharya with introd. by H.D. Velankar, 11th edn. Bombay, Saka 1870 (15 Octob. 1948); ed. and tr. with Mallinatha's comm. by Pt. Brahma Shankar Mishra, Varanasi, 1956.

—*Meghaduta:* Ed. and tr. with notes, map, etc. by M.R. Kale, Delhi, 1969.

—*Vikramorvasiyam:* Ed. by B.R. Arte with notes, Bombay Skt. Series (No. XVI), 3rd edn. May 1899.

Kalhana, Râjatarangini: Tr. by Aurel Stein, 2nd edn, Delhi, 1960; tr. by R.S. Pandit, 1st edn. Allahabad, 1935, Delhi, 1968.

Kautilya, Arthaúâstra: Ed. by R. Shamasastri, Mysore, 1909; tr. by the same, 3rd edn.. Mysore, 1929; ed. with Hindi tr. by Vachaspati Gairola, 3rd edn. Varanasi, 1984.

Pañcatantra: Ed. by Kielhorn & Buhler; trans. (Bombay Skt. Sen), 1887.

Panini, *Aṣṭâdhyâyi:* Ed, by Von Otto Bohtliugk (Panini's Grammatik), Leipzig, 1887; cd. with Eng. tr. by S.C. Vasu, 7 Vols. Allahabad, 1891-98, 1929; with Bhasya by Pt. Brahmadatta Jijnasu, Pt. 1, 1st edn. Amritsar, Samv. 2021; Pt. II, 2nd edn, Amritsar, VS. 2031.

Patañjali. *Mahâbhâṣya:* Ed. by F. Kielhorn, 3 Vols. (Bombay Skt. Series), Bombay, 1880-85, 1892-1909.

Râjasekhara, *Kâvyamima'sâ:* Ed. by C.D. Dalai and R.A.K. Sastri, *GOS.,* No. 1, 1916.

Sûdraka, *Mṛcchakatika:* Tr. by MR. Kale, 3rd edn. Delhi, 1972.

Vallabhadeva, *Subhâsitavali:* Ed. by Peterson, Bombay, 1886.

Varâhamihira. *Bṛhatsaṁhitâ:* Ed. by S. Dvived, Varanasi, 1895-97; ed. by H, Kern, *BIS,* Calcutta, 1865; Eng. tr. by him *JRAS.,* 1870, pp. 430-79; 1871, pp. 45-90, 231-88; 1873, pp. 36-91, 179-138; I875,.pp. 81-134; Hindi tr. by Baldeya Pd. Mishra, Bombay, Samv. 2009.

Vararuchi, *Prâkṛt Prakâsh:* Varanasi, (VS. 2016), 1959.

Vararuchi Saṁgraha: Ed. by T. Ganapati Sastri, *(TSS.),* No. 33.

Viúâkhadatta, Mudrârâkṣasa: Ed. Hillebrandt (Breslau, 1912); also ed. by Telang, Bombay, 1893; Eng. tr. by M.R, Kale, 6th edn., Delhi, 1976: ed. with Sanskrit & Hindi Commentaries by Satyavrata Singh, Varanasi, 1973.

Yâska, Nirukta: Ed. with Durgacharya's Comm. by V.K. Rajavade., Poona, 1921-26; ed. by R. Roth, Gottingen, 1852; ed. with Comras. by P.S. Samasrami, Calcutta, 1882; ed. with Hindi tr. by Uma Shankar Sharma, Varanasi, 1966.

Buddhist and Jain Works

Apadâna-I-II; PTS; London (not yet edited).

Ârya— Mañjusri— Mulâkalpa (Tibetan text): Ed. by Ganapati Sastri, TSS; 1925: ed. by. K.P. Jayaswal (on which his work "An Imperial History of India", Lahore, 1934 is based) in collaboration.with Rahula Sankrtyayana.

Gaudavaho of Vâkpatiraja Ed. by S.P. Pandit, Bombay, 1887.

Jambûdvipaprajñaptih with the commentary of Sânticandra: Bombay, 1920.

Jâtakas: Ed. by Fausboll, London, 1877-97; trans. from Pali by various hands under the editorship of E.B. Cowell, 7 Vols. Combridge, 1895-1913.

Lalita—Vistara: Ed. by R.L. Mitra, BIS; Calcutta, 1857.

——: Ed. by 5. Lefmann, Halle, 1902-8.

——: German trans. (I—V), S. Lefmann, Berlin, 1874.

——: Trans. by R.L. Mitra, Calcutta, 1881.

Milinda-Pañha Ed. by Trenckner, London, 1880.

——: Trans. by T.W. Rhys Davids, *SBE*; Vols. XXXV, XXXVI. Oxford, 1890-94.

——: R.D. Vadekar's edn. Bombay, 1940.

——: Trans. partly into French by M. Louis Finot in the Series—Les Classiques de L' Orient, 1923.

Sammoha-Vinodani: PTS. London.

Sumaṅgala-Vilâsini, Comm. ortithe Digha Nikdya,: Ed. Rhys Davids, Pts. I -II, PTS. London, 1886.

The Tantras

Bṛahan—Nilatantra (Patala—VI based on the Kâlikâ Purâna). Hevajra Tantra (of the Buddhist).

Jñânârnava Tantra Kubjika Tantra: MS. No. 3174, RASB; also in *JPASB* (LXYol. XIV, No. 1, Calcutta, 1948.

Kulârnava Tantra (DCSM ASB., *Calcutta VIII, pp. 110-111):* Ed. by Taranatha Vidyaratna, with an int. in Eng. by Arthur Avalon, *Tantrik Texts,* Vol. V. Calcutta & London, 1917.

Prânatosani Tantra Rudrayâmala Tantra Ùaktisaṅgama Tantra; MS. No. 323, ASB. Library, Calcutta. MS. *GOS.,* Baroda (BK. Ill, Patala, VH).

Ùatpañcâsaddeùavibhâga (Patala VII of BK. III of the Saktisan-gama Tantra, DCSM, ASB, Vol. IV, 1923: MS. No. 9660, ASB. Library, Calcutta, Also in Vol. III of the Saktisangama Tantra, Pub. in 1947, pp. 66ff.

Sammoha Tantra Yogini Tantra: Hindi trans. by Pt. Kanhaiya Lal Mishra, Bombay, Saka, 1878 (=1956 a.d.)

The Tantrasâra (a Tantric Encyclopaedia) by Krinananda Agama Vagia contains the important passages from the different Tantras.

Some South Indian Works

Narâsimâcârya's *Kavicarita:* Bangalore, 1924.

Nijagunayogi's *Vivekacintâmani:* Bangalore, 1893.

Pampâ Râmâyana of Abhinava Pampâ: B.L. Rice, Bangalore, 1892.

Vikramârjunavijaya or Pampâ—Bhârata by Abhinava Pampa: B.L. Rice, Bangalore, 1898.

The Chronicles and Vamúâvalis or Genealogical Records

Itihâsa Prakâúa (a chronicle of Nepal lying in Mrgasthali: Vol. I, 1955-56; Vol. II, 1956-57.

The Parbatiya Vamúâvali: By Munshi Shiva Shankar Singh and Pt. Shri Gunananda.

——: Daniel Wright's *History of Nepal with an introductory sketch of the country and people of Nepal.* (Ist Pub. Cambridge, 1877, reptd. Kathmandu (1972) is primarily based on the translation of this work.

Râjamâlâ (A verse Chronicle of Tripura in Bangali, preserved in ASB. Library, Calcutta): First compiled by Durlabhendra, Banesvara and Sukresvara in 1458; Pts. II—IV compiled between the 16th and 18th century.

—: Ed. by Kali Prasanna Sen, 3 Vols. Agartala, 1926, 1927 and 1931.

—: J. Long's Analysis, *JASB.*, Vol. XIX, Nos. I—VII, Calcutta, 1950.

Svayambhu Purâṇa (A Buddhist text: Composed in its present form in the 15th century.

Vamúâvali Texts (of Nepal): 2 Vols. in Sanskrit composed in c. 1350 A.D. and other—*Gopâlarâja Vamúâvali,* in three parts in Sanskrit and partly in old Newari. Pub. together inc. 1390 A.D. (discovered by C. Bendall during 1884-85, in Darbar Library, Kathmandu).

Foreign Sources: Texts and Translations

(a) Greek and Latin

Arrian, *Indika:* First Part, chapters, I—XVII, Leipzig, 1867.

Arrian, *Indika,:* Eng. trans. by J.W. McCrindle, *Ancient India as Described by Megasthenes and Arrian* (reptd. with additions from the *Ind.* Ant. 1876-77), London, 1877, Revd. 2nd edn. Calcutta, 1960.

——: *Arrian Scripta Minora,* pp. 1-55, ed. R. Hercher, Leipzig, 1885.

——: Eng. trans. by E.J. Chinnock, London, 1893.

Hecataeus, *Fragments, F.H.G., I, 1–31:* Ed. C. Muller, Paris, 1841.

Herodotus, *History:* Ed. O. Hude, 2nd. edn. Oxford, 1913-14.

——: Eng. trans. G. Rawlinson, London, 1858-60.

——: Eng. trans. G.C. Macaulay, London and New York, 1904.

——: Eng. trans. A.D. Godley, 4 Vols. Harvard, 1946.

Ktesias, *Fragments of the Indika:* Ed. C. Muller in Dindorf's Herodotus, Paris, 1844.

——: Eng. trans. ot the *Indika* by PHOTIOS, and of the Fragments of that work preserved in other writers by J.W. McCrindle, *Ancient India as Described by Ktesias the Knidian* (reptd. with additions from the Ind. Ant., 1881), London, 1882, reptd. Delhi, 1973.

Ktesias, *Fragments of the Indika:* Lassen's Review of Ktesias accounts concerning India, trans. from his *Ind. Alt.* (a German source) Vol. II, pp. 641 ff, 2nd edn. Leipzig 1874 by J.W. McCrindle, infra.

——: H.H. Wilson's *Notes on the Indika of Ktesias,* OUP. 1836.

Megasthenes, *Fragments of the Indika:* Ed. E.A. Schwanbeck, Bonn, 1846.

——: Eng. tr. J.W. McCrindle, *Ancient India as Described by Megasthenes and Arrian,* London 1877, New edn. Calcutta, 1926.

——: Eng. tr. J.W. McCrindle, *Ind.* Ant. (JOR) ed. JAS. Burgess, Vol. VI, Bombay; 1877.

——: Ed. R.C. Jain, McCrindle's *Ancient India as Described by Megasthenes and Arrian,* Delhi, 1972.

Nonnos, *The Dionysiaka or Bassarika:* Eng. tr. *J.ty.* McCrindle, *Ancient India as Described in Classical Literatare* (See. XIII, pp. 196-200), Westminster, 1901, reptd. Delhi, 1984.

Periplus Maris Erythraet or The Periplus of the Erythraean sea: Ed. B. Fabricius, Leipzig, 1883.

——: Tr. and annot. by W.H. Schoff (in English), London, 1912.

——: Trans. (text ascribed to Arrian) by W. Vincent, Oxford, 1809.

The Periplus: Trans, from the text as given in the *Geographi*

Groeci Minores (ed. C. Muller, Paris, 1855) by J.W/McCrindle, Ind; Ant; (JOR) ed. by J.A.S: Burgess, Vol. VIII, Bombay, 1879.

Pliny; *Naturalis Historia:* Ed. C. Mayhoff, leipzig, 1892-1909.

——: Loeb Classical Library (hereafter abbrev. as LCL.) edn., 10 Vols., reprint Ldndon and Cambridge, 1956-63.

——: Eug. tr. by B. Riley, *The Natural History of Phny, II,* London, MDCCCLV.

Ptolemy. *Geographike' Huphegesis:* Ed. C.F.A. Nobbe, 3 Vols., Leipzig, 1998, etc.

——: French tr. by L. Renou, *La Geographic de Ptolemee L' Inde.* (VII 1.4.), Paris, 1925.

——: Eng. tr. by E.L. Stevenson, Geography of Claudius Ptolemy, New York, 1932.

——: Eng. tr. J.W. McCrindle, *Ancient India as Described by Ptolemy,* (reptd.' from the Ind. Ant. 1814), London, 1885.

——: Ed. with notes by S.N. Majumdar Sastri, *McCrindle's Ancient India as Described by Ptolemy* edn., Calcutta, 1927.

—-: Ed. by R.C. Jain, McCrindle's *Ancient India as Described by Ptolemy* (being a tr. of the chaps. which describe India and central and Eastern Asia), Revd. edn. Delh., 1973-74.

Strabo, *Geographica:* Ed. A. Meineke, Leipzig, 1866-7.

——: LCL. edn., 8 Vols, London & Cambridge, 1917-58.

——: Eng.tr. H.L. Jones, *The Geography of Strabo,* 8 Vols., London, 1949.

——: Erfg. tr. H.C. Hamilton and W. Falconet London, 1854-7.

Some other Eng. Trans. of Classical Texts with notes, Remarks, etc. and Works based on them:

Genni G.E.: *Researches on Ptolemy's Geography of Eastern Asia* (Asiatic Society Monographs; No. 1 Pab. in conjunction with the RGS.), London, 1909, 2nd edn. Delhi, 1974.

Kennedy, J.: "Some Notes on the Periplus of the Erythraean Sea." *JRAS.* London, 1961.

Majumdar, R.C.: *The Classical Accounts of India* (being compitation of the Eng Trans of Classical accounts, which have bearing on ancient Indian History and civilization), Calcutta, 1960.

Mc Crindle, J.W.: *Ancient Indid as Described in Classical Literature* (being a collection of Greek and Latin texts Relating to India extracted from Herodotus (by Bohn, tr. by Cary), Strabo, Plinius, Aelian and others), Westminster 1901, rept. Delhi, 1984.

Mc Crindle, J.W. *The Cemmerce and Navigation of the Erythraean Sea* (being trans of the Periplus Maris Erythraei and partly from Arrian's Account of the Voyage of Nearkhos and Ktesias' account as given in his *Indika),* London, 1879, 1882, reptd, Calcutta, 1973.

—— *The Invasion of India by Alexander the Great as described by Arrian, Curtius. Diodorus, Plutarch and Justin,* 2nd end., 1896.

Schoff, W.H.: "The Name of the Erythraean Sea," *JAOS.* XXXIII 349-62, New Haven, 1913.

Taylor. J.: "Remarks on the Sequel to the Periplus of the Erythraean Sea and on the country of the seres as described by Ammianus Marcellinus, *JASB.,* Vol. XVI, Pt. 1, Calcutta, 1847.

(*b*) Chinese

Fa-Hien (or Fa-Hsien); Eng. tr. *Travels of Fa-Hien or a record of Buddhistic Kingdoms* (A.D. 399-414) by J. Legge, Oxford, 1886, reptd. 2nd edn. Delhi, 1972. retrans, by H.A. Giles, Cambridge, 1923, Varanasi, 1972.

Hiuen Tsang *(or Yuan Chwang): Si-Yu-Ki*, Eng. tr. by S. Beal, *Buddhist Records of the Western World*, 2 Vols. London, 1884, 1906, reptd; Delhi 1969; S. Beal, *The life of Hiuen* Tsiang, London, 1884, A A. Delhi, 1973, T. Watters, On Yuan Chwang's *Travels in India* (a.d. 629-45), ed. by T.W. Rhys Davids and S.W. Bushell, Vols. I-II, RAS London, 1904-5. 2nd Ind. edn. Delhi, 1973.

(*c*) Arabic

Al-Biruni, *Tahqiq-i-Hind:* Ed. by E.G. Sachau, London, 1887.

——: Eng. tr. Sachau, *Alberunis India, 2* Vols., London, 1888. 1910, reptd. Delhi, 1964.

Ibn-Battuta's *Reh-la:* Eng. tr., *Travel in Asia and Africa,* 1325-1354 by H.A.R. Gibb, London, 1929.

2. SECONDARY SOURCES

Agrawala, P.K. *(ed): Itihâsa—Darśana* (collection of papers of the late Prof. V.S. Agrawala), Varanasi, 1978.

Allay, Santosh: *Magar Jati Ko Itihasa Ani Sanskriti,* Sikkim ko Sandarbhama, in Nepali, Darjeeling, 2003.

Agrawala, V.S.: *Bhârata Sâvitri: A Study of the Mahâbhârata* Vols. I-II, 2nd edn. Delhi, 1977, Vol. 3, first edn. Delhi, 1968.

——: *India as Described by Manu* (ICS. No. XIV), Varanasi, 1970.

——: *India as known to Pâṇiṇi: A study of Aṣṭâdhyâyi,* 2nd edn. Banaras, 1963.

——: *"Geographical Data in Pâṇiṇi's Aṣṭâdhyâyi JUPHS";* Vol. XVI, Pt. 1, Lucknow, 1943.

Aiyangar, P.T.S.: *Life in Ancient India in the Age of the Mantras,* Madras, 1812.

Ali, S.M.: *The Geography of the Puranas,* 3rd. edn. Delhi, 1983.

Allan J.: Catalogue of the coins of Ancient India, London, 1936.

Allen, B.C., Gait, E.A., Allen, C.G.H. and Howard, H.F.: *The Gazetteer of Bengal and North-East India,* Delhi, 1979.

Ambedkar, B.R.: *Who were the Shudras? How they came to be the fourth varna in the Indo-Aryan society,* Bombay, 1946.

Anville, D.: *Recherches geographiques et historiques Surla-Serique des Anciens,* Paris, 1768.

Apte, V.S.: *Sanskrit—English Dictionary,* Delhi, 1968.

Atkinson, E.T.: *Notes on the History of the Himalaya of the N.W. Province India,* Calcutta, 1883.

——: *The Himalayan Gazetteer,* Vols. I-II, Delhi, 1973.

Bagchi. P.C. (tr.): *Pre-Aryan and Pre-Dravidian in India by Sylvain Levi,* J. Przyluski and J. Bloch (tr. from French), Calcutta, 1929.

——: *Studies in the Tantras,* Calcutta, 1937.

——: *India and China,* Calcutta, 1944, Bombay, 1950.

Banerjee, N.V.: *Studies in the Dharma Sastra of Manu,* Delhi, 1980.

Banerjee, S.C.; *Dharma Sutras: A Study in their origin and development,* Calcutta, 1962.

Barnett, L.D,: *Antiquities of India: An Account of the History and Culture of Ancient Hindustan,* London, 1913, Calcutta, 1964.

Barua. B.M.: *Asoka and His Inscriptions,* 2nd edn. Calcutta, 1955, 3rd edn. 1968.

Barua. K.L.: *Early History of Kamarupa,* Shillong, 1933, 2nd edn. Gauhati, 1966.

Basak. R.G.: *History of North-Eastern India* (c. a.d. 320—760), Calcutta, 1967.

Bell, Charles: *Tibet Past and Present,* Oxford, 1924.

Bendall, C: *A Journey of Literary and Archaeological Research in Nepal and Northern India* (1884-85) Cambridge, 1886.

——: "A History of Nepal and Surrounding Kingdoms (1000-1600)." *JASB:* LXXII, 1903, pp. 1-32.

——: *Catalogue of Palm-Leaf and selected paper Manuscripts belonging to the Durbar Library,* Nepal, 2 Vols. Calcutta, 1905 & 1906.

Benedict, P.K.: *Sino-Tibetan: A Conspectus,* Cambridge, 1972.

Bertrand, G.: *Secret Lands where Women Reign,* London, 1958.

Bettany, G.T.: *The Inhabitants of Asia: The History of Existing and Extinct Nations, their Ethnology, Manners and Customs,* Varanasi, 1973.

Bhandarkar, R.G.: *Vaisnavism, Saivism and minor Religious Systems,* Strassburg, 1913, Varanasi, 1965.

Bhandarkar, D.R.: *Asoka,* Calcutta, 1923, 3rd edn, Calcutta, 1955.

——: *Inscriptions of Asoka,* Calcutta, 1920.

Bhattacharya, N.N.: *Indian Mother Goddess,* Calcutta, 1971.

Bird: *The Political and Statistical History of Gujarat,* London, MDCCC XXXV.

Borooah, A.R.: *Ancient Geography of India,* Gauhati, 1971.

Bouquet, A.C.: *Comparative Religion: (A collection of Lectures),* The Univ. of Cambridge, 1932-55.

Briffautt, R.: *The Mother,* London, 1952.

Brown, J.C.: *Catalogue of Pre-historic Antiquities in the Indian Museum at Calcutta,* Simla, 1917.

Brown, Percy: *Picturesque Nepal,* Calcutta, 1912.

Buthler G.: *Indische Palaeographic,* Strassburg, 1896. Eng. version: *Indian Palaeography,* ed, J.F. Fleet. *Ind. Alt.* 1904, APP. 3rd edn, Varanasi, 1963.

Bunbury, E.H.: *A History of Ancient Geography among the Greeks and Romans,* 2 Vols. London, 1879, 1883, 2nd edn. New York, 1959.

Chemjong, Iman Singh,: *History and Culture of the Kirât People,* 1966.

Carnegy, P.: *Notes on the Races, Tribes and Castes Inhabiting the Province of Avadh,* Lucknow, 1868.

Chakladar, H C.: *The Geography of Kalidasa* (Indian Studies, Past and Present, hereafter *ISPP)* Calcutta, 1963.

——: The Aryan Occupation of Eastern India *(ISPP),* Calcutta, 1962.

——: Eastern India and Aryavarta, *IHQ.,* Vol. IV, pp. 84-101.

Chakraberti, C.: *Classical studies in Ancient Races and Myths,* Delhi, 1979.

Chanda, R.P.: *The Indo-Aryan Races, 1st pub.* Rajshahi, 1916, reptd. Delhi, 1978.

Chatterji, S.K.: *Kirata-Jana Krti* 2nd edn. The Asiatic Society, Calcutta, 1974.

Chatterji, S.K.: *Indo-Aryan and Hindi,* Calcutta, 1969.

——: *The place of Assam in the History and Civilization of India,* Gauhati Univ., 1955

——: "Race-Movements and Pre-historic Culture". *The Vedic Age,* pp. 143-71.

——: "Non-Aryan Elements in Indo-Aryan". *JGIS;* Vol. II, pp. 42ff.

——: *The Origin and Development of the Bengali Language,* London, 1970.

—— *(ed): The Cultural Heritage of India,* Vol. V (The Ramakrishna Mission Institute of Culture), Calcutta, 1978.

—— & others: *Indian Culture,* Delhi, 1966.

Chattopadhyaya, S.: *Racial Affinities of Early North Indian Tribes,* Delhi, 1973.

Chaturvedi, G.S.: *Purana Parisilana,* Patna, VS. 2027 (= A.D. 1970).

Chaudhari, S.B.: *Ethnic Settlements in Ancient India,* Calcutta, 1955.

Christian, J.L.: *Burma,* London, 1945.

Collins, M.: *Geographical Data of Raghwamsa and Dasakumarcarita,* Leipzig, 1907.

Coivell, E.B., Elphhinstone and others: *Ancient India,* Delhi, 1963.

Crooke, W.: *Races of Northern India,* Delhi, 1973.

Crooke, W, (ed.): *Tavels in India by J.B. Tavernier* (tr. by *V. Ball from original French edn. of* 1676), Vol. II, O.U.P. 1889, London, 1925.

Cunningham, A: *The Ancient Geography of India,* Varanasi, 1979.

——: *Coins of Ancient India from the earliest times down to the Seventh Century* a.d., London, 1891, Varanasi, 1971.

Daftari, K.L.: *The Astronomical method and its application to the Chronology of Ancient India,* Nagpur Univ. 1942.

Dalton, E.T.: *Tribal History of Eastern India,* Delhi, 1978.

Das, S.C.: *A Journey to Lhasa and Central Tibet*, 1904.

Dalton, E.T.: *Descriptive Ethnology of Bengal, Calcutta,* 1872, reptd. from *ISPP.* Calcutta, 1960; also *Tribal History of Eastern India,* Delhi, 1978.

Dani, A.H.: *Prehistory and Protohistory of Eastern India, Calcutta,* 1960.

Das, A.C.: *Rgvedic India, 2* Vols. Delhi, 1980.

Dasgupta, K.K..: *A Tribal History of Ancient India: A Numismatic Approach,* Calcutta, 1974.

De, S.C.: *Historicity oj Ramayana and the Indo-Aryan Society in India and Ceylon,* Delhi, 1976.

Dey, N.L.: *The Geographical Dictionary of Ancient and Medieval India* (2nd edn. London, 1927*),* 3rd edn. Delhi, 1971.

——: *Civilization in Ancient India,* Delhi, 1972.

Dikshitar, V.R.R.: "Aryanization of East India (Assam)", *IHQ.* Vol. XXI, 1945. pp. 29-33.

Dinkar, R.S.; *Samskrti Ke Car Adhyaya,* Delhi, 1956.

Dutt, N.K.: *Origin and Growth of Caste in India* c. b.c. 2000-300) Vol. I. (London, 1931), Calcutta, 1968.

——: *Aryanization of India,* Calcutta, 1915.

Dutt, S.C.: *The Wild tribes of India,* Delhi, 1st pub. 1884, reptd. 1984.

Edgar. J.W.: *Report on a visit to Sikkim and the Tibetan Frontier,* 1873. (ed. by H.K. Kuloy, *BHS.* I, Vol. 2), 1st. pub. 1874, Delhi, 1969.

Ehrenfels, O.R.: *Mother Right in India,* Hyderabad, 1941.

Eliot, Charles,: *Hinduism and Buddhism,* Vol. II, London, 1st pub. 1921, reptd. I957.

Farquthar, J.N.: *An outline of the Religions Literature of India* (Oxford, 1920), Delhi, 1967.

Fleet, J.F.: *Corpus Inscriptionum Indicarum,* Vol. III. Calcutta, 1888.

Foote, R.B.: *Notes on the Ages and Distrbution of the Indian Prehistoric and Protohistoric Antiquities,* Madras, 1916.

Gairola V.: *Sanskrit Sahitya Ka Itihasa,* Varanasi, I960.

Gait. E.: *A History of Assam,* Calcutta, 2nd. edn. 1926, 4th edn. 1964.

Giuseppe: "An Account of the kingdom of Nepal" *As. Res,* Vol. II, pp. 253f. Delhi, 1979.

Gordon. D.H.: *The Prehistoric Background of Indian Culture,* Bombay, 1958.

Grant, Charies (ed.): *The Gazette of the Central Province of India,* Delhi, 1984.

Grierson, G.A.: *Linguistic Survey of India,* Vols. 1-3, reptd. Delhi, 1967.

Gupia, P.: *Geographical Names in Ancient Indian Inscriptions* (up to 650 A.D.; Delhi, 1977.

Gupta, S P. and Ramachandran, K.S. (ed.): *Aspects of Indian History and Archaeology:* (A Collection of 43 Research papers by H.D. Sankalia), Delhi, 1977.

Hammerton, J.A. (ed.): *Tribes, Races and Cultures of India and Neighbouring countries,* Delhi, 1984.

Hooker, J.D.: *Himalayan Journals,* London, 1855, rept. Delhi, 1987.

Harvey, G.E.: *History of Burma from the Earliest times to 10th March 1824,* London, 1925.

——: *British Rule in Burma,* 1824-1942, London.

Hazra, R.C.: *Studies in the Puranic Records of Hindu Rites and Customs,* Dacca, 1940. reptd. 2nd. edn. Delhi, 1975.

——: *Studies in the Upapuranas I and II,* Calcutta, 1958, 1963.

Hedin, S.: *Trans-Himalaya: Discoveries and Adventures in* Tibet, 3 Vols. London 1913.

Heeren, A.H.L.: *Historical Researches into the Politics, Intercourse and Trade of the Principal Nations of Antiquity: Asiatic Nations,* 2 Vols. Oxford, 1833.

Held, G.J.: *The Mahabhdrata: An Ethnological Study,* London, 1935.

Hodgson, B.H.: "On the Aborigines of the Sub-Himalayas", *JASB.* Vol. XVI, pt. II, 1847, pp. 1235ff.

——: "On the Aborigines of the Eastern Frontier", *JASB.* Vol. XVIII, pt. II, 1849.

——: *Essays on the Language, Literature and Religion of Nepal and Tibet,* London, 1874.

——: "On the Kirantis Language of Nepal", *JASB.* Vol. XXVI, 1857, pp. 333ff, rept. in *Misce. Essays on Indian Subjects,* Vol. I, pp. 176ff, 320ff, London, 1880.

Hooker, J.D.: *Himalayan Journals,* London, 1855.

Hopkins. E.W.: *Transactions of the Connection of the Academy of Arts and Sciences,* XV, 21 sq. (on the Pancavimsa Brahmana).

Hult-Zsch, E.: *Corpus Inscriptionum Indicarum,* Vol. I. Oxford, 1925.

Hulton, J.H.: "The Mixed Culture of the Naga Tribes", *JRAL* Vol. 95. pts I & II, London, 1965.

——: "Some Megalithic Works in the Jaintia Hills", *JPASB.* (New Series), Vol. XXII, 1926, Calcutta, 1928.

Jain, J.C.: *Life in Ancient India as depicted in Jaina canons and commentaries,* Bombay, 1947, Delhi, 1984.

Jain, R.C.; *Ethnology of Ancienl Bharata,* Varanasi, 1970.

James, E.O.: *Prehistoric Religion,* New York, 1957.

Jayaswal, K.P.: *Hindu Polity,* 5th edn., Bangalore, 1981.

——: "Chronology and History of Nepal. 600 b.c. to 800 a.d." *JBORS,* Vol. XXII, Sept. 1936, pt. Ill, pp. 157-264.

Kakati, B.K.: *The Mother Goddess Kamakhya* (Studies in the fusion of Aryan and Primitive beliefs of Assam), 1st edn. Gauhati, 1948, 3rd edn. 1967.

——: *Assamese: Its Formation and Development,* Gauhati, 1941.

Kane, P.V.: *Dharamasdstra Ka Itihasa* (tr. in Hindi by Arjuna Chauve Kashyap), 1st edn. Lucknow, 1963. 3rd edn. 1980.

Keith, A.B.: *A History of Sanskrit Literature,* Oxford, 1928, repted., Delhi, 1973.

——: The Religion and Philosophy of the Veda and Upanishads, *HOS.* (ed. by C.R. Lanman) Vols. 31 & 32, 1st edn. Cambridge, Mass., 1925, 2nd Indian rept. Delhi, 1976.

Kirkpatrick: *An Account of the Kingdom of Nepal,* London, 1811.

Kosambi, D.D.: *The Culture, and Civilization of Ancient India in Historical outline,* Delhi, 1972.

——: *An Introduction to the Study of Indian History,* 2nd edn., Bombay, 1975.

Krishnamachariar, M.: *History of Classical Sanskrit Literature* 3rd edn. Delhi, 1974.

Lassen, Chr.: *Indische Alterthumskunde,* 4 Vols. Bonn and Leipzig, 1847-61 (Vols. I and II, 2nd edn.), Leipzig, 1858-1874.

Latham, R.G.: *Tribes and Races: A Descriptive Ethnology of Asia, Africa and Europe,* Vol. I, (1st pub. 1859), Delhi, 1983.

Lattimore, E. & Owen: *The Making of Modern China,* Washington, 1944.

Law, B.C.: *India as Described in Early Texts of Buddhism and Jainism,* Delhi, 1980.

——: *Geography of Early Buddhism,* Varanasi, 1973.

——: *Geographical Aspects of Kalidasa's Works,* Delhi, 1976.

——: *Historical Geography of Ancient India,* Paris, 1954 rept., Delhi, 1976.

——: *Geographical Essays,* London, 1937.

——: "Tribes in Ancient India", *BOS.* No. 4. Poona, 1943.

——: *Ancient Indian Tribes* (Law's Research Series, No. I), Vol. 2. London, 1934.

Law, B.C.: *Some Ksatriyas Tribes of Ancient India,* Calcutta, 1923, Delhi, 1979.

——: "Some Ancient Indian Tribes", *IC.* Vol. I, No. 3, pp. 381-82.

——: *Ancient Mid Indian Ksatriya Tribes,* Calcutta, 1924.

——: *Countries and Peoples of India",* (Epic and Pauranic Sources), *ABORI.* Vol. XVII. 1935-36; Vol. XXI, 1939-40.

——: *A History of Pali Literature,* 2 Vols. London, 1933.

——: *The Magadhas in Ancient India,* Varanasi, 1976.

Levi, Sylvain: *Le Nepal Etude Historique d'un Royau "me Hindou"* 3 Vols. Paris, 1905-8.

Lowic, R.H.: *Primitive Society,* 2nd edn. London, 1929, 3rd edn. California, 1979.

Luders, H.: A List of Brahmi Inscriptions from the earliest times to about a.d. 400. *Ep. Ind.* Vol. X, *APP.* Calcutta, 1910.

Mackay, E.: *Early Indus Civilization,* Delhi, 1976.

Martin, P.V. de St.: *Etude Sur La Geographie Grecque et Latin de L' Inde*, Patis, 1858.

——: *Further Excavations at Mohenjodaro,* Vol. I, Delhi, 1976.

Macdonell, A.A.: *A History of Sanskrit Literature,* 1st edn. Oxford, 1900, 3rd edn. Delhi, 1972.

Mocdonell, A.A. and Keith, A.B.: *Vedic Index of Names and Subjects,* 2 Vols. 1st edn. London, 1912, 3rd edn. Indian Texts Series, 1967.

Majumdar, A.K.: *Early Hindu India: A Dynastic Study,* 2 Vols. Dacca, 1917, 1920, Delhi, 1981.

Majumdar D.N.: *Races and Cultures of India,* Delhi, 1958.

Majumdar, R.C.: *Ancient India,* Delhi, 1977.

Majumdar, R.C.: Pusalker, A.D. (eds.) and Majumdar, A.K.: *The Vedic Age (HCIP.* Vol. I), Bombay, 4th impression, 1965.

Malalasekera, G.P.: *Dictionary of Pali Proper Names.* 2 Vols. London, 1937-38, Delhi, 1983.

Ma-Myasein : *Burma,* Oxford, 1943.

Mani, V.: *Puranic Encyclopaedia,* Delhi, 1979.

Marshall, Sir John: *Mohenjo-Daro and the Indus Civilization,* Vol. I, London, 1931, Delhi, 1973.

Martin, M.: "The History, Antiquities, Topography and Statistics of Eastern India", *Studies in Indian History,* No. 14, Vol. IV, 1st pub. 1831, Delhi, 1976.

Masson-Oursel, P. & C.: *Ancient India and Indian Civilization,* 1951.

Max Muller, F.: *A History of Ancient Sanskrit Literature,* Varanasi, 1968.

Mishra, B.P.: *Nepal Ka Itihdsa,* Bombay, Saka, 1826 (= a.d. 1904).

Mishra. D.P.: *Studies in the Proto-History of India,* Delhi, 1971.

Mitra, P.: *Prehistoric India,* Calcutta, 1927.

Monier-Williams, M.: *Religious Thought and Life in India, London,* 1891.

——: *Hinduism,* Delhi, 1971.

——: *Sanskrit-English Dictionary,* rept. Oxford, 1951, 1956.

Motichandra: Sarthavaha, Patna, VS. 2023 (= a.d. 1966).

——: *Geographical and Economic Studies in the Mahabharata* U.P. Hist. Soc. Lucknow, 1945.

Muir, J.: *Original Sanskrit Texts,* Vols. I-II, London, 1871-72.

Nath, R.M.: *The Background of Assamese Culture,* Shillong, 1948.

Nourse,: *A Short History of the Chinese,* London, 1938.

Oppert, Gustav.: *On the Original Inhabitants of Bharatavarsa* or India, Westminster, 1893, rept. Delhi, 1972.

Panchamukhi, R.S.: *Karnataka Inscriptions,* (KRS.), 1941.

Pradhan, Kumar: *The Gorkha Conquest,* Darjeeling, 1991.

Pandey, R.B.: *Bhartiya Itihasa Ka Parichaya,* Varanasi, 1963.

Pargiter, F.E.: *Ancient Indian Historical Tradition.* (1st edn. London, 1922), reptd. Delhi, 1972.

——, *(ed.): The Purana Text of the Dynasties of the Kali Age,* Oxford, 1913.

——: "Ancient Countries in Eastern India", *JASB,* Vol. LXVI, Pt. I, 1897.

Phayre, P.: *History of Burma* (1st pub. 1883) 2nd edn, London, 1967.

Piggott, S.: *Prehistoric India,* London, 1961.

Pillai, D.N.P.K.: *Pauranic Sandarbha Kosa,* Hyderabad, 1984.

Puri, B.N.: *India in the time of Patanjali,* Bombay, 1968.

——: *India as Described by Early Greek writers,* Varanasi, 1971.

Raghava, R.: *Prachin Bharatiya Parampara aur Itihasa,* Delhi, 1953.

Rai, S.K.: *Kirât Khambu Rais of Sikkim and Eastern Himalayas,* Gangtok, 2005.

Risley, H. *The Gazetteer of Sikkim*, Calcutta, 1894, rept. 1989.

Rai, R.K.: *Mahâbhârta Koúa,* Varanasi, 1982.

——: *Vâlmiki—Râmâyana Koúa,* Varanasi, 1965.

Rao, R.R.: *The Aryan Marriage with special reference to the Age-question: A Critical and Historical study,* Delhi, 1975.

Rapson, E.J. (ed): *The Cambridge History of India,* Vol. I, Cambridge, 1922, rept. Delhi. 1962.

——: *Ancient India,* Delhi, 1981.

Ray, H.C.: *The Dynastic History of Northern India,* 2 Vols. Calcutta, 1931 & 1936.

Ray Chaudhuri, H.C.: *Political History of Ancient India,* 6th edn. Calcutta, 1953.

——: *Studies in Indian Antiquities,* Calcutta, 1932, rept. 1958.

Regmi, D.R.: *Ancient Nepal,* 3rd edn. Calcutta, 1969.

——: *Inscriptions of Ancient Nepal,* 3 Vols. Delhi, 1983.

Rennell, J.: *The Geographical System of Herodotus,* 2nd edn. revised, London, 1830.

Reu, B.N.: *Rgveda Par Ek Aitihasik Drsti,* Delhi, 1967.

Rhys Davids, T.W.: *Buddhist India,* Delhi, 1971.

Rice, B.L.: *Mysore,* revised, edn. Westminster, 1897.

——: *Mysore and Coorg from the Inscriptions,* London, 1909, 1913.

Risley, H.: *Tribes and Castes of Bengal,* Calcutta, 1891-92.

——: *The People of India,* 2nd edn. London, 1915.

Robinson, W.: *A Descriptive Account of Assam,* 1st. Pub. 1841, reptd. Delhi, 1975.

Ronnow, K. "Kirata: A Study on Some Ancient Indian Tribe". (*Le Monde Oriental),* Vol. XXX, pp. 90-170, Uppsala, 1936.

Rote, H. A.: *Glossary of the Tribes and Castes of the Punjab and North-West Frontier Province,* 3 Vols. Lahore, 1911, 1914 and 1919.

Roy, J.: *History of Manipur,* 2nd edn. Calcutta, 1973.

Ruggeri, G.: *Outlines of Systematic Anthropology of Asia*, 1921.

Saletore, B.A.: *The Wild Tribes in Indian History,* Lahore, 1935

——: *Ancient Karnataka,* Poona, 1936.

Saletore, R.N.: *Encyclopaedia of Indian Culture,* Vol. II Delhi, 1983.

Sharma, J.L.: *Hamro Samaj: Ek Adhyayan, in* Nepali, Kathmandu, Samvat 2039, 1982.

Stein, O.: *The Jinist Studies*, ed. by J.V. Muni, Ahmedabad, 1948.

Sankalia, H.D.: *Prehistory of India,* Delhi, 1977.

——: *The Prehistory and Protohistory of India and Pakistan,* Poona, 1974.

Sankrtyayana, R.: *Puratattva Nibandhavali,* Allahabad, 1958.

——: *Pali Sahitya Ka Itihasa,* Lucknow, 1973.

Sarasvati, Dyananda: *Satyartha Prakasa,* Delhi, VS. 2019.

Sarkar, S.S.: *The Aboriginal Races of India,* Calcutta, 1954.

Sarma, D. (ed.): *Kamarupa Sasanavali* (tr. by P.D. Choudhury, R.K. Deva Sarma and D. Sarma, originally by P. Bhattacharyya

Vidyavinoda, 1868-1938), Gauhati, 1981.

Sastri, A.K.: *India as seen in the Brhatsamhita of Varahamihira,* Varanasi, 1969.

Sastri, M.: "Manu Smriti Ke Sambandha men Kucha Naye Anusandhan", *DAG.* pp. 308-11, Kashi, 1933.

Schmidt, I.J. (tr. & ed.) *"Geschichte der Ost-Mongolen"* (tr. from the text on the History of Mongols by Senangsatsen), St. Petersburg, 1829.

Schmidt, P.W.: *Die Mon-Khmer Volker,* Brunswick, 1906 (also in *JRAS.* 1907, pp. 187ff, 743ff).

Sewell, R. and Ajyangar, K.: *The Historical Inscriptions of Southern India,* Madras Univ. Hist. Series No. V, 1932.

Shafer, R.: *Ethnography of Ancient India,* Wiesbaden, 1954.

Shafer, R.: *Introduction to Sino-Tibetan,* Wiesbaden, 1974.

Shakabpa, T.W.D.: *Tibet: A Political History* (based on 57 original sources), 2nd edn. London, 1973.

Sharma, Atombapu.: *Rgveda,* Vol. I, Imphal, 1960.

Sharma, M.M.: *Inscriptions of Ancient Assam,* Gauhati Univ. Pub. 1978.

Sharma, M.M.: *Travels in the Central Himalayas,* Delhi 1978.

Sharma, P.P.: *Pauranic Kosa;* Varanasi, VS. 2028.

Sharma, R.S.: *Sudras in Ancient India* (A Survey of the position of the lower orders down to circa a.d. 500), Delhi, 1958.

——: *Social Changes in Early Medieval India* (c. a.d. 500-1200) Delhi, 1969.

——: *Light on Early Indian Society and Economy,* Bombay, 1966.

——: *Perspectives in Social and Economic History of Early India,* Delhi, 1983.

Sharma, R.V.: *Bharat Ke Prachin Bhasa Parivara aur Hindi,* Vol. 3, Delhi, 1981.

Sherring, M.A.: *Hindu Tribes and Castes,* Vol. I, Delhi, 1974.

Singh, L.I.: *Introduction to Manipur,* Imphal, 1963.

Singh, M.R.: *Geographical Data in the Early Puranas, Calcutta* 1972.

Singh, M.G.: *History of Himachal Pradesh,* Delhi, 1982.

Sircar, D.C.: *Studies in the Geography of Ancient and Medieval India,* Delhi, 1971.

——: *Indian Epigraphy,* Delhi, 1965.

——: *Select Inscriptions bearing on Indian History and Civilisation,* Vol. 1, 2nd edn. Calcutta, 1965; Vol. II Delhi, 1983.

——: *Studies in the Society and Administration of Ancient and Medieval India,* Vol. 1. Calcutta, 1967.

——: *Studies in the Religious Life of Ancient and Medieval India,* Delhi, 1971.

——: "Text of the Puranic List of Peoples", *IHQ.* (ed. N.N. Law), Vol. XXI, pp. 297-314, Calcutta, 1945.

——: *The Sakta Pithas,* Delhi, 1973.

——: "Some Aspects of the History of Assam and its Neighbourhood", *JARS.* Vol. XIV, pp. 1-22, Gauhati, 1978; *Research in Arunachal,* 1951-76, pp. 31-37. Shillong.

——, ed.: *The Sakti Cult and Tara,* Calcutta, 1967.

Smith, V.A.: *The Early History of India,* 4th edn. Oxford, 1924, revised edn. 1967.

——: *The Oxford History of India,* (revised by H.G. Rawlinson) 1st pub. Oxford, 1908, 3rd. Indian Impression, Delhi, 1981.

——: *Coins of Ancient India* (catalogue of the coins in the Indian Museum, Calcutta), Varanasi, 1972.

Sorensen, S: *Index to the Names in the Mahabharata,* London,1904.

Speir, Mrs. C.: *Phases of Indian Civilization,* Delhi, 1973.

Thapa, N.B.: *A Short History of Nepal,* Kathmandu, 1981.

Thapar, Romila; *Ancient Indian Social History,* (1st pub. 1978), reissued, Delhi, 1984.

——: *The Past and Prejudice,* Delhi, 1975.

Thurston. E. and Rangachari K.: *The Castes and Tribes of Southern India,* Vols. I-III (1st pub. Madras, 1909), Delhi, 1975.

Toynbee, A.J.: *A Study of History* (abridged edn, by D.C. Somervell, Vols. I-VI pub in 1946, VII-X in 1957). Complete in one volume, 1st. in 1960, 3rd. edn. London, 1970.

Tripathi, R.S.: *History of Ancient India,* Delhi, 1985.

Tylor, E.B.: *Primitive Culture,* 2 Vols. London, 1929.

——: *Religion in the Primitive Culture,* New York, 1958.

Upadhyaya, B.S.: *India in Kalidasa,* Delhi, 1968.

Upadhyaya, Vasudeva: *A Study of Ancient Indian Inscriptions,* Patna, 1970.

Vajracharya, Dh.: *Licchavi Kal Ka Abhilekha* (no. 91), Kathmandu, VS. 2030.

Vansittart, E.: *Gurkhas,* Calcutta, 1906, rept. 1997.

Vasu, N.N.: *The Social History of Kamarupa,* Vol. 1, Calcutta, 1922.

Vidyalankara, J.: *Bharatabhumi aur Uske Nivasi,* Bombay, 1952 (Punjab, VE. 1988).

Vidyalankara, S.: *Bharatiya Samskrti Ka Vikasa,* Delhi, 1979.

Warder, A.K.: *An Introduction to Indian Historiography,* Bombay, 1972.

Watt, Sir George,: *The Commercial Products of India,* (London, 1908), Delhi, 1966.

Weber, A.: *The History of Indian Literature* (Eng. tr. by J. Mann and Th. Zachariae. 2nd edn. London, 1882), Varanasi, 1961.

——: *Indische Studien,* Berlin, 1870-72.

Wheeler, J. Talboys.: India From the Earliest Ages, Vol. III, (of the History of India), Delhi, 1973.

Wheeler, M.: *Early India and Pakistan to Ashoka,* (Ancient peoples and places series), revd. 2 London, 1968.

——: *The Indus Civilization* (Supple. Vol. to *CHI)* 3rd edn. Cambridge, 1968.

Wilford, F.: "An Essay on the Sacred Isles in the West with other Essays...," *As. Res.* Vol. VIII, 1805.

——: "On the Ancient Geography of India" *As. Res.* Vol. XIV, Calcutta, 1822.

Wilson, H.H.: *Ariana Antiqua* (London, 1841), rept. Delhi, 1971.

Wilson, J.: *India Three Thousand Years Ago,* Bombay, 1858.

Winternitz, M: *A History of Indian Literature* (Eng. tr. from the original German by Mrs. S. Ketkar, Vol. I, 1st pub. by Calcutta Univ. 1927. reptd. Delhi, 1977).

Woodroffe, J.: *Principles of Tantra,* London, 1911.

——: *Shaktai-Shakta,* London, 1929.

Young, E.C.: "A Journey from Yunnan to Assam", *JRGS.* Vol. XXX, London. 1907.

Yule, H. (tr. & ed.): *Travels of Marco Polo,* 2 Vols. 3rd revd. edn. London, 1903.

Yule, H. and Cordier, H. (tr. & ed.): "Cathay and the Way Thither" Vols. I-IV, Hakluyt Society, London, 1915-16.

Zimmer, H.: *Altindisches Leben,* Berlin, 1879.

Index

N

O

P

V